DATA MODELS, DATABASE LANGUAGES AND DATABASE MANAGEMENT SYSTEMS

INTERNATIONAL COMPUTER SCIENCE SERIES

Consulting editors **A D McGettrick** University of Strathclyde
J van Leeuwen University of Utrecht

SELECTED TITLES IN THE SERIES

Clausal Form Logic: An Introduction to the Logic of Computer Reasoning *T Richards*
Numerical Methods with FORTRAN 77: A Practical Introduction *L V Atkinson, P J Harley and J D Hudson*
Software Engineering (3rd Edn) *I Sommerville*
High-Level Languages and their Compilers *D Watson*
Programming in Ada (3rd Edn) *J G P Barnes*
Elements of Functional Programming *C Reade*
Interactive Computer Graphics: Functional, Procedural and Device-Level Methods *P Burger and D Gillies*
Software Development with Modula-2 *D Budgen*
Common Lisp Programming for Artificial Intelligence *T Hasemer and J Domingue*
Program Derivation: The Development of Programs from Specifications *R G Dromey*
Program Design with Modula-2 *S Eisenbach and C Sadler*
Object-Oriented Programming with Simula *B Kirkerud*
Parallel Processing: Principles and Practice *E V Krishnamurthy*
Real Time Systems and Their Programming Languages *A Burns and A Wellings*
Programming for Artificial Intelligence: Methods, Tools and Applications *W Kreutzer and B J McKenzie*
FORTRAN 77 Programming: with an introduction to the Fortran 90 standard (2nd Edn) *T M R Ellis*
The Programming Process: an introduction using VDM and Pascal *J T Latham, V J Bush and I D Cottam*
Prolog Programming for Artificial Intelligence (2nd Edn) *I Bratko*
Principles of Expert Systems *P Lucas and L van der Gaag*
Logic for Computer Science *S Reeves and M Clarke*
Introduction to Expert Systems (2nd Edn) *P Jackson*
Computer Architecture *M De Blasi*

DATA MODELS, DATABASE LANGUAGES AND DATABASE MANAGEMENT SYSTEMS

Gottfried Vossen

Rheinisch-Westfalische Technische Hochschule Aachen

ADDISON-WESLEY
PUBLISHING
COMPANY

Wokingham, England · Reading, Massachusetts · Menlo Park, California
New York · Don Mills, Ontario · Amsterdam · Bonn
Sydney · Singapore · Tokyo · Madrid · San Juan

Cover design by Crayon Design of Henley-on-Thames and printed by
The Riverside Printing Co. (Reading) Ltd.
Typeset by the AMS from the author's LaTeX files.
Printed in Great Britain by T.J. Press (Padstow), Cornwall.

First printed 1990.

British Library Cataloguing in Publication Data
Vossen, G. (Gottfried)
Data models, database languages and database management systems
1. Database systems. 2. Database languages. 3. Database management systems.
I. Title II. Series
005.74

ISBN 0-201-41604-2

Library of Congress Cataloging in Publication Data
Vossen, Gottfried.
Data models, database languages and database management systems
p. cm — (International computer science series)
Includes bibliographical references
ISBN 0-201-41604-2
1. Database systems. 2. Database languages. 3. Database management systems.
QA81.87 1991
005.74

for my girls,

Martina and Laura

Preface

This is an introductory text on database management, an area of computer science that is roughly 30 years old. It is of great importance in practical applications, which can be seen from the large number of (software) systems that are now commercially available. There are an increasing number of areas of application that have either been based on such a system for some time already, or have more recently started to discover the database technology. In addition, there exists a considerable amount of interest in databases from the point of view of theoretical computer science.

The text provides an overview of data models that are in widespread use, together with an introduction to several database languages based on these models, and database management systems (DBMSs) based on these languages. Besides traditional topics in databases, more recent ones like semantic data models or non-standard applications for databases, extensions of the relational model and the use of object-oriented concepts are discussed as well. The material is divided into seven major parts. Emphasis is put on a formal precise presentation, which at the same time is intuitively understandable and oriented towards the various applications of DBMSs.

Part I is particularly meant for readers without prior knowledge in the area; its goal is to indicate why the area is important, and to outline some basic problems. Starting from a clear separation of time-varying and time-invariant aspects of databases, which is consequently adhered to, Parts II and III introduce *data models* for the conceptual level of a database, beginning with a discussion of the entity-relationship model for didactical reasons. Since the *relational* model is of particular importance, Part III is devoted to its exposition. First, the 'language' of this model is clarified; then various *query languages* for relational databases are introduced, which exhibit distinct degrees of expressive power. The theoretical foundations of this model will then be outlined by investigating certain *data dependencies* as particular integrity constraints. After that, this theoretical basis is applied to the *design of databases* in Part IV. One important aspect here is the fact that 'design' actually denotes a *process* which consists of a sequence of individual steps. At least for some of these steps, formal 'tools' are now available, under which the entity-relationship model together with its techniques for translation into other data models can already be classified. This model can also be considered as the first *semantic data model*, whose goal — broadly speaking — is to provide database designers with increased capabilities to model the semantics of a given application, going beyond the possibilities present within the language of a 'traditional' data model. Algorithmic tools for particular steps of the design process will be dealt with for the case of the relational model within the context of its *design theory*.

Another emphasis of the text is a comprehensive treatment of *database languages* in Part V, which presents primarily those that are representative for network and relational systems. As an example of a network system, *UDS* by Siemens is presented, which is characteristic for the class of network systems in the sense that it closely follows the standard for network databases and systems given by the CODASYL recommendations. For hierarchical systems, a rough description of *IMS* by IBM is given. A detailed description of the relational language *SQL* is given next, which forms the basis of the IBM's SQL/Data System (as well as many other relational systems), since it is now a standard. Finally, *higher languages* or language levels are discussed, which though currently still under development may be important in the future.

In Part VI, the *services* a user will expect from a database system are dealt with. Most important is the *management of transactions* as well as the problem of *recovery* from failures. In the final Part VII, traditional as well as more recent applications of database systems are discussed. *Object-orientation* is presented as a promising paradigm for coping with new applications, and the realization of the corresponding concepts in the *GemStone* database system are described. Finally, *extensibility* is described as a means to arrive at *open* database systems which can be customized towards the specific requirements of a given class of applications.

This text started out as a translation of my German book, *Datenmodelle, Datenbanksprachen und Datenbankmanagement-Systeme*, and ended up as what will probably be its second edition. I used the material for various undergraduate and graduate courses, seminars and labs on the subject I gave at the Technical University of Aachen, FRG, the University of California, San Diego, and the Universities of Kiel and Düsseldorf, FRG. All courses required some prerequisites on the student's part; in particular, the text assumes some familiarity with basic concepts of computer organization, programming, data structures, graph theory, complexity theory, and mathematical logic. While lectures were primarily based on Chapters 1–12, 16 and 18–23, material from other chapters formed the basis for the labs. All homework and examinations that accompanied the various events as well as many others have been included in the book, so that the reader is supported in assimilating the material. In addition, each part of the text contains a detailed survey of the relevant literature.

This book is intended for an undergraduate class on databases for senior-level students as well as for a first-year graduate class on the topic. It covers all topics recommended in the ACM 1978 Curriculum for CS11 'Database Management Systems Design', as well as more recent ones, since I consider these recommendations no longer completely up-to-date and I believe that what has been learned about database technology for non-standard applications in recent years is now in a stage that it can be communicated to students and hence included in course material. In addition, the text might be useful for students with computer science as their minor, or for readers who apply a database management system in their everyday practice. Although all chapters basically build upon each other, deviations from the given sequence may be appropriate, depending on prior knowledge or specific interests. For instance, the reader only interested in problems related to the design of databases may start with Chapter 10 and then read through Chapters 11, 4, 5, 7, 12 and 13. An introduction to relational database theory can be found in Chapters 7–9, 12, 17 and 21.

I would like to take this opportunity to thank all the people with whom I have been working in the area of databases over the years, and who have influenced me in various ways; in alphabetical order, these are Joachim Biskup, Volkert Brosda, Alois Peter Heinz, Walter Oberschelp, Yoav Raz, Marina Roesler, Victor Vianu and Kurt-Ulrich Witt. Major portions of the typesetting for this book were done by my wife Martina, whom I am also indebted to for her patience and support. Finally, thanks go to the people of Addison-Wesley for their professional handling of the project. In particular, I would like to mention my editor Sarah Mallen; in retrospect, I think that her being so tough on me has improved the output considerably.

Gottfried Vossen
Aachen
August 1990

Contents

III Foundations of the Relational Data Model 95

IV Database Design 189

Part I

Introduction

Chapter 1
A Historical Perspective

This chapter provides a brief description of the historical development of database systems over the last decades, beginning with file systems and their drawbacks, and ending up with database systems for non-standard applications.

Database systems are a widely accepted tool for the computer-aided management of large, formatted collections of data. Their historical development has been closely related to the development of computer hardware (and software), as is true for many other areas of computer science. With respect to hardware development, it is now common to talk about 'computer generations', and in a similar way several 'database system generations' can already be distinguished. In this chapter, a brief historical perspective of this evolution will be given, in which common agreement is blended with the personal perception of the author.

Several other disciplines have always influenced the area of databases and database management systems. Among these are hardware-oriented areas, such as the development of fast, 'secondary' memory, in particular magnetic disks, for storing large amounts of data. Closely related to this development are areas of computer science such as data structures and operating systems. Data structures are used to manage data in (secondary) memory in such a way that an efficient update and retrieval becomes possible. Operating systems nowadays provide, for example, multiprogramming or multiprocessing, which are important functions used by a database system. Other areas to be mentioned in this context, which are usually attributed to theoretical computer science or even mathematics, are graph theory, mathematical logic, the theory of language parsing and compiling or the theory of synchronizing parallel processes. The interactions of the database field with these other areas have not only resulted in *practical* experiences with database systems, which often stem from the requirement to cope with the everyday problems of certain users, but several branches of the database world have also seen the development of a major body of *theory* (such as the theory of the relational data model or the theory of database concurrency control). In the course of this text, points of contact between theoretical and practical aspects will often be encountered, and practical achievements will be evaluated from a theoretical point of view where possible.

The 'history' of database systems to date can be divided into five generations, which roughly follow the five decades of computing that start with the 1950s, the first two of which were concerned with predecessors of database systems. A central role in this development was played by the ongoing evolution of hardware and software on the one hand, and a continuous change (and increase) in user requirements for data processing on the other.

The *first generation* concerns the 1950s. In these early days the major task of any computer system was to *process* data under the control of a program, which primarily meant calculating, counting, and so on. Each individual program was either directly provided with the data set it operated upon, or it read its data from some secondary memory into the main memory of the computer, processed it, and finally wrote the

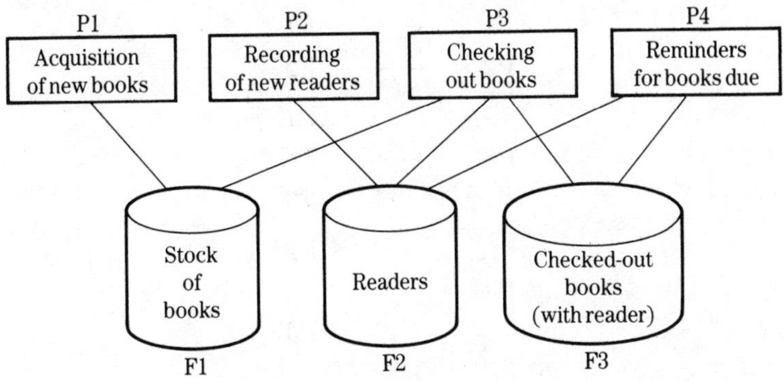

Figure 1.1 A library file system.

(eventually modified) set back to secondary memory. 'Secondary memory' then referred to punched cards or to magnetic tapes, both of which allowed *sequential* processing only. Thus, the first *file systems* exclusively allowed a sequential access to (the records of) a file.

The *second generation*, which will be taken here to mean the early 1960s, was different from the first one in several aspects. On the one hand, it became possible to use computers in dialogue mode as well as batch mode. On the other hand, the development of magnetic disks as 'fast' secondary memory led to the arrival of more sophisticated file systems, which now rendered *multiple access* possible. A *direct access file* allows access to a record in that file directly via its address (on the disk), without having to read or to browse through all the records which are physically located in front of it. Such an address can be located, for example, in a special index file or found by using a hash function.

Both generations were thus characterized by the availability of *file systems* only, which strictly speaking are the forerunners of database systems. Of central importance for the use of a file system is the *static* association of certain data sets (files) with individual programs which operate on these. As a concrete example, consider a library, which stores data on the books it owns, on the readers who may use the library, and on books which are currently checked out. A corresponding collection of programs and data is depicted in Figure 1.1. It is assumed that all possible events (recording of new acquisitions, etc.) are handled by particular programs, where each program is provided with a copy of the files it needs for the appropriate time period. Thus, individual files must exist in multiple copies, since in general all events occur overlapped in time and are hence processed in parallel. In addition, if the programs are written by distinct programmers, it might be difficult to enforce a uniform formatting when the individual files are being created. The reason is that the association between programs and files actually looks like Figure 1.2. (In Figure 1.2,

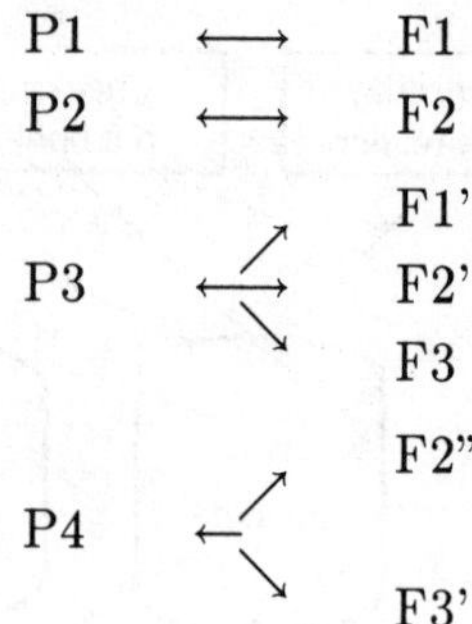

Figure 1.2 The library programs and their files.

single and double quotes are used to indicate that a program is statically associated with 'its' version of a certain file; file versions are distinguished physically, but might be closely related logically.)

It should be obvious that several problems result from this method of organization:

(1) There exists a high *redundancy* between files, which results from the fact that information is replicated in different places, and that these replications are not controlled by a central monitor.

(2) *Inconsistencies* might result from the possibility that a program makes changes on the files it uses without these changes being made (at the same time) by all other programs that use the same file. For example, the program for recording new readers could change the name of a reader — possibly after her marriage — in the readers-file, without this change being 'propagated' to the file which associates readers with the books they have currently checked out.

(3) There exists an *inflexibility* against changes in the application: if new actions or events arise in the course of time (such as, for example, the establishment of special catalogues for certain technical areas), these can be realized only at a substantial expense (of time). More concretely, a new program (with one or more new files) has to be written, which cannot necessarily be derived from an already existing one, even if there are minor differences only; the same applies to all the files it will operate upon.

(4) The work of many programmers involved is characterized by a *low productivity*, since *program maintenance is expensive*: if the structure of an existing file has to be modified during its lifetime (with

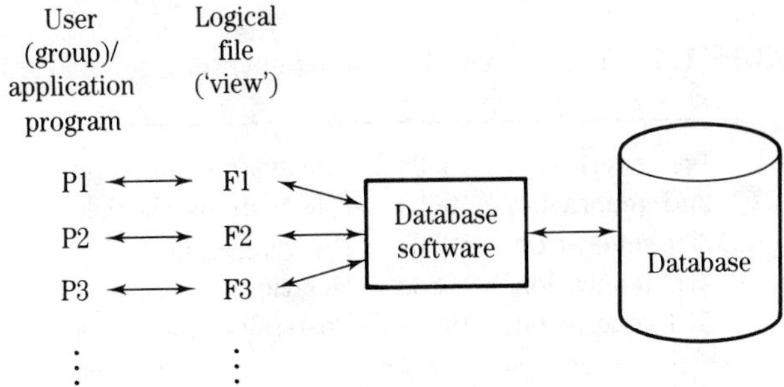

Figure 1.3 General scenario for a database system.

respect to field names or formats, for example), then all application programs have to be modified correspondingly.

(5) Finally, the problem of adopting and maintaining *standards* (with respect to coding, data formats, etc.) is to be mentioned, which is important for exchanging data (in the example between different libraries or distinct departments of the same library) or for a migration to a new operating-system release or even to a new computer system.

The *third generation*, which roughly coincides with the 1970s, but actually started in the late 1960s, is characterized by the introduction of a distinction between *logical* and *physical* information, which occurred parallel to an increasing need to *manage* large collections of data (as opposed to pure processing mentioned earlier). During that time, *data models* were used for the first time to describe physical structures from a logical point of view; however, the then emerging approaches such as the hierarchical or the network model have to be classified as 'implementation-oriented'.

Starting from this distinction between the (logical) meaning of data, that is, the syntax and the semantics of its description, and its current (physical) value, systems were developed which could *integrate* all the data of a given application into one collection (which was henceforth termed a *database*), and which provided individual users of this collection with a particular 'view' to it only. This (new) situation is illustrated in Figure 1.3.

The *fourth generation*, which generally reached the marketplace in the 1980s, saw systems, now generally called *database systems*, which in addition to storing data redundancy-free under a centralized control make a clear distinction between a physical and a logical data model, which is particularly true for the *relational* model of data. Systems based on this latter model are typically provided with a high degree of *physical data independence* and the availability of *powerful languages.* The former aspect means that any physical storing of data is transparent ('invisible') to the

Table 1.1 Timetable of database system generations.

1st generation	1950s	File systems on tape
2nd generation	1960s	File systems on disk
3rd generation	1970s	Pre-relational
4th generation	1980s	Relational
5th generation	1990s	Post-relational

users, and that in principle both the physical and the logical side may be changed without the other side being affected. The latter aspect primarily results from a transition from *record-oriented* to *set-oriented* management and processing of the data in a database. The language which users have at hand for working with a relational system considerably frees them from questions of 'how' to manage data; they may instead concentrate on the 'what'.

The fourth generation also saw an increasing penetration of the area of databases from a theoretical point of view, which in particular resulted in a now comprehensive theory of *relational* databases. Although this theory cannot be presented in its entirety in a text like this one (which is of more global character), certain of its aspects will be dealt with whenever it seems appropriate; in these cases, references are provided to enable the interested reader to find out more about this theory from the literature.

While the third generation might be termed 'pre-relational' and the fourth 'relational', it can be expected that the *fifth generation*, which is beginning to emerge for the 1990s, will be termed 'post-relational'. As the relational model in particular, and systems based on it, have produced nice tools and solutions for a large number of commercial applications, people have begun to understand that various other areas of application could benefit from database technology. This is resulting in the development of *extensible* systems, *logic-oriented* systems, and *object-oriented* systems, of which several aspects will be covered in Part VII. A summary of the historical perspective as given above is stated in Table 1.1.

Chapter 2
The Three-Level Architecture Concept

An architectural model for databases as perceived by their users is described; it distinguishes three levels of abstraction that carefully progress from physical storage to conceptual descriptions and to individual user views.

As a first conclusion from Chapter 1 some *advantages* can now be stated which are expected to result from the introduction of a database system (as opposed to the use of a traditional file system):

(1) *All* data arising in a particular, well-defined application is stored in an integrated stock termed a *database*; since individual data items are stored exactly once, this stock is basically *free of redundancies.*

(2) The entire management of the database (including all procedures and operations related to this) is performed by a central control authority, which in particular is able to execute changes ('updates') on physical data in such a way that *inconsistencies can be avoided.*

(3) All users, that is, both *ad hoc* or dialogue users and application programmers, work with the same stock of data on the *physical* level, so that a *unified* integrity control as well as security and safety mechanisms can be applied. (Note that the term 'security' refers, for example, to the exclusion of unauthorized access to the database, that is, the authorization control of the system. The term 'safety', on the other hand, refers, for instance, to the creation and management of ('log') copies of the entire database, which are needed for performing recovery from a system crash or from a head crash on a disk.)

(4) On the other hand, it is possible to provide individual users or user groups with a distinct *logical* view of the database, so that data can be *structured in an application-dependent way*, and that the *development of new applications* for a given database is *easy to realize.*

(5) Finally, the enforcement of *standards* is facilitated, since the redundancy-free storing can guarantee a unified formatting, among other things.

What these aspects should make evident is that the application or the introduction of a database system within or into a given enterprise is always connected to the goal of achieving **data independence**, that is, (considerable) independence of the data from the programs (or dialogues) that work on it. This term again has two different aspects which are discussed next.

On the one hand, users of a database are interested in *physical* data independence, which means that the physical organization of a database should be transparent to programs or dialogues operating on it. In particular, such a program or dialogue operation should not have to worry about the actual choice of data structures or its access paths. In the ideal case, it is therefore possible — as was mentioned in Chapter 1 — to change

row 1:	call number of the book
row 2:	ISBN
row 3:	author
row 4:	title
row 5:	Library of Congress classification
row 6:	publisher
row 7:	publication date and place
row 8:	edition number
row 9:	suggested retail price

Figure 2.1 Card organization of a card file for books.

the physical storing of the data partially or completely *without* having to change user programs or dialogues correspondingly.

On the other hand, it is desirable — in particular with respect to 'high' user interfaces —that a database system also supports *logical* data independence. This means that users want to be able to distinguish between a specific, application-oriented view of the database and its general logical structure; in addition, this global structure should be changeable without having to change (all) local structures as well, and vice versa.

In the remainder of this text, these two aspects of data independence will be returned to more than once; moreover, it will be possible — at least in specific contexts such as the context of the relational model — to make the distinction described above formally precise. However, it should have become obvious by now that, in order to achieve the 'advantages' of a database system listed above in general and data independence in particular, it is reasonable to view a database from *three* different *levels of abstraction*. In particular, the following sections will always distinguish between:

(1) the physical data organization,

(2) the logical general view of the data, and

(3) the individual, generally distinct user views.

These distinct ways of viewing a database will be illustrated by considering the 'stock of books' in the library application from Chapter 1. To this end, the reader is first reminded of the computerless, old-fashioned way of organizing data in a card file. If books in the library stock are recorded by means of cards, an entire card might be devoted to each book, whose contents look as shown in Figure 2.1. (In this example it is assumed that each book has exactly one author, and that there is a unique way of classifying a book.)

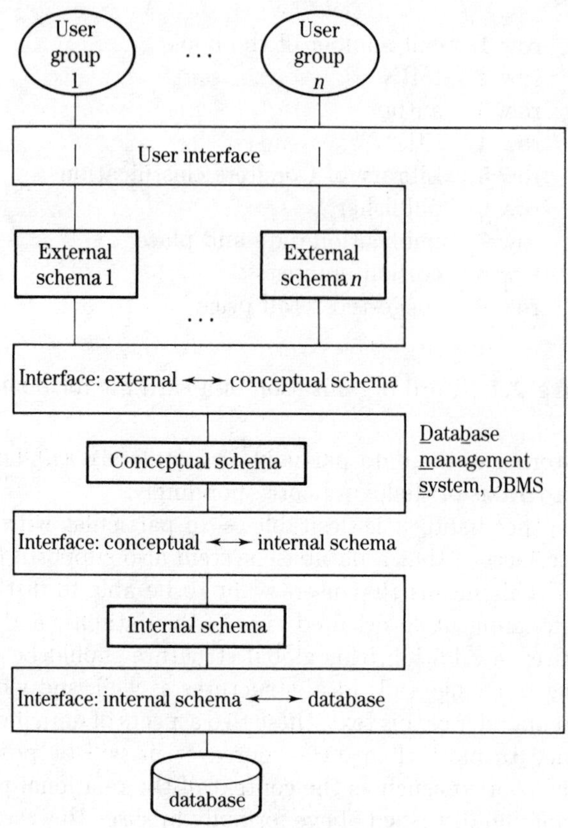

Figure 2.2 The three-level architecture of a database.

In this example, the *physical* data organization consists of the (card) file which contains the cards for all books, possibly sorted according to call numbers or authors. The *logical view* abstracts from particular books and describes features which are common to all cards and their rows; thus, for example, it will now talk about authors in general, but no longer about a particular author such as C.J. Date or J.D. Ullman. Finally, *one user view* could reflect, for instance, an interest in books of just one particular area, such as computer science or database management and, even more specific, within such an area just for the author and title of each book; another user view might be interested in prices only.

This division into three different levels of abstraction forms the basis of the **ANSI-X3-SPARC architecture concept** for databases, in which a separate **schema** is associated with each level as shown in Figure 2.2. The purpose of each of these levels and the corresponding schema is described next.

The **internal level** is the one which is closest to the physical memory. It is different from the latter since it treats *physically* stored data in terms of 'internal records' rather than pages or blocks. This view of the data is defined in the internal schema which contains information on which data structures are used (and thus in particular their definition), on what access mechanisms are available for these, and on how the records are distributed in the (logical) address space. The interface to the actual database thus, for example, has to implement the mapping of the logical to the physical address space, which is often performed by using functions provided by the underlying operating system.

On the **conceptual level**, the *logical general view* of all data in the database (and their relationships) is represented in a conceptual schema. To this end, a certain **data model** is used, which in particular renders an abstraction from the internal view possible; it will be seen later how well such an abstraction is actually achieved by particular data models. To ensure physical data independence, it is now important that the conceptual schema is free of data structure or access path definitions; instead, it consists purely of a definition of the information contents of the database in general. For the purposes of this definition, the 'language' of the data model chosen is available, which provides constructs such as 'table format' in the case of the relational model, or 'set type' in the case of the network model. This language appears to the defining user in the form of the 'data definition language' of the particular system at hand.

The **external level** comprises all *individual views* (sometimes called 'subschemata') of the users or user groups of the database, which include both application programmers and dialogue users. Each of these views is described in an individual external schema, which includes exactly that excerpt from the conceptual (general) view which the corresponding user wants to see or is allowed to see. Note that an external view is often defined for the reason that a user is only interested in a particular section of the conceptual schema; another reason can be to disallow a user to 'see' certain parts of that schema.

It should be mentioned that this third level of a (logical) view to a database is sometimes realized in the form of *exactly one* external schema, which is then available to *all* users. This might result from the fact that, in a particular system, no distinction is made between a particular user view and the conceptual general view of the database. In this case, the distinction between an external and a conceptual level has to be regarded as artificial; every user has unrestricted access to the conceptual schema. On the other hand, it is also possible that the external level provides a *different global* view of the database, so that both external and conceptual level consist of one schema only, each of which, however, is distinct. This is the case, for example, in the presence of a 'universal relation interface' on top of a relational database, which will be discussed in Chapter 17.

```
type t        = array[1..50] of char;
     b        = ↑book;
     book     = record
                    author :  alfa;
                    title :  t;
                    callno :  1..5000;
                    isbn :  alfa;
                    classification :  alfa;
                    publisher :  alfa;
                    place :  alfa;
                    year :  1..2000;
                    edition :  1..10;
                    price :  real;
                    next :  b
                end;
```

Figure 2.3 'Physical' definition of records in file 'books'.

As can be seen from Figure 2.2, and as was mentioned in the discussion of the internal level, all three levels communicate with each other or with their corresponding 'outside world' via interfaces, which are provided or realized by the software of the **database management system** (DBMS). These interfaces are *mappings* or transformations, in which the 'correspondence' between the external schemata and the conceptual schema, between the conceptual and the internal schema, and between the internal schema and the database is established. In addition, a DBMS always provides an interface to the user, which is 'located' between the external level and the users who work on this. This interface in particular comprises a *language* through which the users can communicate with the database or the DBMS; note that nowadays the user interface and its language are often based on menus or forms.

For the book example above, consider the following possibility to 'implement' the card file. A *linked list* is used as the data structure to physically store the file, into which books — lexicographically sorted on authors — can be inserted. Thus, each element in the list could be, say, a Pascal record with the structure shown in Figure 2.3. For processing the list, a variable `V` of type `b` pointing to the head of the list will (later) be needed, as will an auxiliary variable `H` of the same type for browsing through the list. Thus, our 'database' *physically* consists of a linked list of records, which can be processed sequentially.

At the *conceptual level*, the user is no longer interested in links and the details of how to manipulate them (for example, during an insert or

```
type bb = record
             callnumber :  integer (5000);
             isbn :  char (10);
             author :  varchar (20);
             title :  varchar (50);
             lib_of_congress_class :  varchar (30);
             publishing_co :  varchar (25);
             place_of_publ :  varchar (15);
             year_of_publ :  integer (2000);
             edition :  integer (10);
             price :  real
          end;
 stock_of_books = set of bb;
```

Figure 2.4 'Logical' definition of records in set 'books'.

delete operation applied to the list). Instead, all that is important now is what information on books can be found in this file. Hence, the file can *now* be considered as a *set*, whose declaration is shown in Figure 2.4.

The reader should note that it is supposed at this level that 'logical' data types are available, and that the DBMS is capable of identifying these with the actual 'physical' ones. For example, `integer (5000)` means that the callnumber field of any record of type `bb` can carry an integer whose value is less than or equal to 5000. Similarly, `char` (`varchar(n)`) is used to denote a data type for character strings of fixed (variable) length (up to) n, respectively. Any string of variable length n shall be stored with its rightmost character in position n of the field in the record, eventually filled with blanks in the front; however, this adjustment has to be done by the DBMS during the transformation from the conceptual to the internal level.

Also note that some fields in the set definition have 'new' names compared with the list definition, and that some of them even appear in a different location than before. Although it remains open at this point whether these aspects can indeed be realized, they indicate the essential possibilities which result from a distinction between a conceptual and an internal view of data.

Finally note that at the conceptual level the pointer is missing, which is used at the internal level to realize the linking of the list physically.

To conclude this example, a particular user might now be interested in the authors and titles of all books on computer science; assuming that the 'language' of the DBMS allows for this, a corresponding 'definition' for this view is shown in Figure 2.5.

```
type v1      = if bb.lib_of_congress_class =
                  'computer science'
                  then record
                          bb.author;
                          bb.title
                       end;
       view1 =  set of v1;
```

Figure 2.5 'External' definition of records in view 'computer science'.

Users of a database (which already exists) work with it either by posing *queries* or by making changes (that is, insertions, deletions, or modifications, which are collectively called *updates*) to it. To this end, the DBMS provides users with a **data manipulation language** (DML), which can have one of the following two outward manifestations (which are both realized in general).

The DML can be implemented as an *ad-hoc dialogue language*, that is, a user can work with a database directly via this language. Alternatively, the DML can be *embedded into a* so-called *host language*, where the host language is usually a high-level programming language such as C, Pascal or COBOL. In this latter case, programs written in the host language may contain DML statements so that the database will be accessed when the program is executed (in batch mode). Several approaches to such an embedding are in use today, which can broadly be classified as follows:

(1) There exists a *precompiler* that takes as input a program written in the host language which contains DML statements as well, and which translates this program into a 'pure' program of the host language; the latter can then be processed by an ordinary compiler for that language.

(2) For host-language programs with DML statements, an *extended compiler* is available, which directly translates the (extended) program into executable code.

(3) The DML itself contains elements of a high-level programming language (such as control structures), so that complete programs can be written in the DML directly; these programs are then processed by an independent *DML-compiler*. Note that this, strictly speaking, may no longer be termed an 'embedding'.

Some examples of queries and updates are listed next, where the stock of books of the library is used for illustration purposes; it is assumed that the underlying DBMS has a Pascal-like DML:

(1) **Ad-hoc queries**:

Q1: 'Show the titles of all books written by Date.'
Q2: 'Show a list of all publishers, of which books are in stock.'
Q3: 'Show the ISBN of each book which has been published in its first edition only.'

Possible ways to express these queries in a DML are the following:

Q1: SELECT title FROM stock_of_books WHERE author = 'Date';
Q2: SELECT publishing_co FROM stock_of_books;
Q3: SELECT isbn FROM stock_of_books WHERE edition = 1;

Let us take a closer look at the way query Q2 is processed. Since it was assumed at the conceptual level that query processing is *set-oriented*, all the user has to do is to enter the above statement. Internally, however, it was assumed that query processing is *record-oriented*; thus, the DBMS has to ensure that the following 'program' is actually executed in order to answer Q2 (where the variables `V` and `H` are defined as described above):

```
read(V);
H := V;
while H ≠ nil do
  begin
    writeln(H.publishing_co);
    H := H↑.next
  end;
```

(Note that an even more complex program might be required in order to avoid multiple listings of the same publisher.)
Thus, users have the impression that the whole database is contained in one card, from which all they want to see is the column named 'publishing_co'. The DBMS, on the other hand, has to process the file 'card by card', and to print the corresponding entry from each one.

(2) **Embedded queries**:

Q4: 'Compute the sum of the prices of all books in stock.'
Q5: 'Sort the stock lexicographically according to classifications, and within each classification according to authors.'

For Q4 a function 'SUM' might be available to the user, so that the (*ad hoc*) 'query' `SELECT SUM(stock_of_books.price);` is sufficient. Internally, however, the following 'program' would have to be executed (with a variable SUM of type real):

```
read(V);
H := V;
SUM := 0.0 ;
while H ≠ nil do
  begin
    SUM := SUM + H↑.price;
    H := H↑.next
  end;
writeln(SUM);
```

(3) **Updates**:

U1: 'Insert the book (473, '48337-0157', 'bradley, j.', 'database management', 'comp. science', 'holt-saunders', 'tokyo', 1983, 1, 45.60) into stock_of_books.'

U2: 'Delete all books published prior to 1930.'

Corresponding DML statements could now be the following:

U1: INSERT INTO stock_of_books (...);
U2: DELETE FROM stock_of_books WHERE year_of_publ < 1930;

When U1 is executed (internally), first the place in the list has to be located where the new entry has to be inserted; then the links to the neighbour-records have to be updated correspondingly.

Before users can actually work with a database, this database has to be created, which in particular means that all logical and physical database structures have to be defined. To this end, the DBMS has to provide a **data definition language** (DDL), as was mentioned earlier. The DDL allows us to define all details regarding the conceptual as well as the internal schema; once the conceptual schema has been established, it can be used as a basis for defining the external schemas.

The logical division of a database into three different layers sometimes has consequences for the DDL as well. Some systems separate a DDL (more or less strictly) into a *schema DDL* for the conceptual level, a *subschema DDL* for the external level, and a *data storage definition language* (DSDL) for the internal level.

With respect to the distinction between a DDL and a DML, different views can be adopted. In some existing systems, no clear distinction is made between the aspect of 'defining' and 'manipulating' a database, in the sense that it is generally possible to use DDL and DML commands in arbitrary order; in this case, the system has essentially just one 'language'. As a consequence, a user may define a conceptual schema in part only, and can then start working with this part immediately. At a later time, the conceptual schema may be extended, so that dynamic changes in the user's application can also be taken into consideration.

On the other hand, the following view might also be reasonable. Before a user can start working with a database, its conceptual schema should have been defined completely. Thus, the conceptual schema is considered as static, which implies that subsequent changes can either not be dealt with at all or can be dealt with only at high expenses.

It should be mentioned that the former approach can typically be found in implementations of relational database systems (such as the SQL/Data System by IBM, see Chapter 16), while the second approach is more often taken by network systems. As will be seen in later chapters, however, it might also be reasonable in the context of a relational system to consider the establishment of a conceptual schema as a non-recurring, static process, in particular where results from the 'design theory' for relational databases are to be applied.

One final aspect should be mentioned here. While the DML of a database system is in general available to *all* users of the system, the use of the DDL is sometimes reserved for *one* particular person, the **database administrator** (DBA). This 'authority', which may also be a group of people, is comparable to the operating group of a computer system, which takes care of the pure operating of the machine, but also, for instance, of advising users in its programming, of the installation and maintenance of program libraries, and so on. Similarly, the DBA is responsible for the (central) control of the entire database system. To this end, he or she must have a 'higher' database knowledge than the (ordinary) users, but also has higher competences. The latter might include, for example, that the DBA alone is allowed to create a (new) database, or to grant access rights to users stating who is allowed to work with which external schema.

In particular, with respect to the creation of a new database and to the definition of its conceptual schema, the DBA is expected to be able to recognize the 'image of the real world' that the database is intended to represent, to structure it appropriately, and finally to define it, on both the conceptual and the physical level; he or she should at least be able to provide guidance to the (potential) users in the accomplishment of these tasks. Other duties sometimes attributed to the DBA include:

(1) Definition of access and integrity controls.

(2) Definition of strategies for security and recovery.

(3) Monitoring of system load balance and performance.

(4) System tuning (within the scope of the possibilities of the DBMS at hand), in particular to ensure optimal adjustment to current and new or modified applications.

In later chapters, where some current systems will be discussed, special tasks which are or should be 'reserved' for the DBA will occasionally be mentioned. It will also be seen that more and more tools and interfaces are now under development which transfer 'higher' duties into the user's competence; design tools for relational databases are a typical example.

Chapter 3
Components of a DBMS

While the architecture of a *database* was discussed in the previous chapter, the attention will now be focussed on the organization (or architecture) of a database *management system*. Specifically, an overview is given of the various components included in such a system and how they interact.

From the descriptions in Chapters 1 and 2 it should have become apparent that a database system (DBS) is always considered to be a combination of a DBMS with one or more (distinct) databases (DB), which might 'mathematically' be captured by

$$\text{DBS} = n \times \text{DB} + \text{DBMS} \qquad n \geq 0$$

While an architectural concept for the first element on the right-hand side of this equation was dealt with in the previous chapter, something similar will be done for the second element in this chapter. In particular, the general organization of a DBMS will be sketched, and some of its major components identified, to give the reader an impression of the 'functionality' that can be expected from a DBMS, and to provide a framework for further discussions. (As an aside, it should be pointed out that the terms 'architecture' and 'organization' are used here in a similar way to their usual use in connection with a computer in general: while the *organization* of a computer (DBMS) refers to the logical arrangement of and relationship between its various components, the *architecture* of a machine (DB) refers to its appearance to the programmer (user), respectively.)

The organization and the components of a DBMS are considered next. The goal is not to establish an exact plan of what is going on in such a system. Instead, the emphasis will be to show which *functions* have to be provided by a DBMS internally, and how these functions cooperate logically or depend on each other. Thus, a *model* of a DBMS will be developed, which on the one hand was chosen with regard to the context of this text and therefore can serve (together with Figure 2.2 and its explanation, including the library example) as a 'guide' to what follows. On the other hand, the model is general enough to be applied easily to any 'reality'; in particular, the reader should have little trouble in identifying the components described here in a given real DBMS.

In analogy to and at the same time as an extension of Figure 2.2, it is possible to distinguish between the DBMS and *two* (actually three, as will be seen shortly) stocks of data upon which it operates. In the case of a realization or implementation in software, the DBMS resides in the main memory of the computer in question as an executable piece of code; today, parts of it might also be found to be realized in hardware ('database machines'). One of the data stocks is the database itself; the other consists of the schemas which are associated with the three distinct database abstraction levels. These schemas are handled similarly to the database in that they are stored in secondary memory (and in that appropriate safety mechanisms are applied to them); they are collectively termed the **data dictionary** (DD). This dictionary, sometimes also termed the 'meta-database' or 'database catalogue', contains 'data on the data' in the way explained in Chapter 2; thus, it has to be available to the DBMS permanently (like the database itself).

This distinction is reflected in Figure 3.1, which shows the major components of a DBMS together with their 'interconnections'. Note that just one database is considered here; where the DBMS manages several of them in parallel, each database would have its *own* stock of data, while the schema information for all databases would typically be kept in the *same* dictionary.

Directly associated with the user is an *I/O processor* which takes commands as input and reports either successful execution (more precisely: an 'answer' if the input was a query) or failure back to the user. This component is typically a (command- or menu-oriented) *monitor* (or supervisor) process, which activates other components or processes depending on the current user instruction. In particular, in the case of a batch processing of programs with embedded DML commands, the I/O processor may even be 'located' outside the DBMS at the operating-system level, or it may communicate with an associated batch processor on that level.

A user instruction directed to the database is first transferred to a *parser*, which performs a syntactical analysis. For *ad hoc* DDL or DML commands, the parser checks, for example, the correctness of keywords from the language used, or whether a command as a whole is built correctly (according to the syntax of the language). (It is thus similar in function to a parser for a high-level programming language.) To this end, information from the dictionary may be needed, or (as in the case of a DDL command) new dictionary entries may be prepared. Thus, the parser component of a DBMS has to 'communicate' with the dictionary manager. For embedded commands, a call to a *precompiler* (or, following the discussion in Chapter 2, to a DML compiler, or a transfer of the instruction as a whole to an external compiler) might be necessary. For both types of commands, however, an *authorization control* will have to be applied, which checks, for example, whether the user may work with the data requested at all or whether some action is intended that is either reserved for the DBA or at least requires DBA approval.

As a result of these initial steps, the original user instruction will have been transformed into some 'internal form' (similar to intermediate code passed by a compiler from one phase of compilation to the next). This form could be, for example, a tree representation in the case of a relational query, where leaves represent operands (relations) and interior nodes represent operations to be performed on these operands.

For the further processing of this intermediate form, it is assumed that the DBMS at least temporarily takes different actions depending on whether the original instruction was a query or a database update; note that further distinctions must be made for the correct processing of DDL instructions.

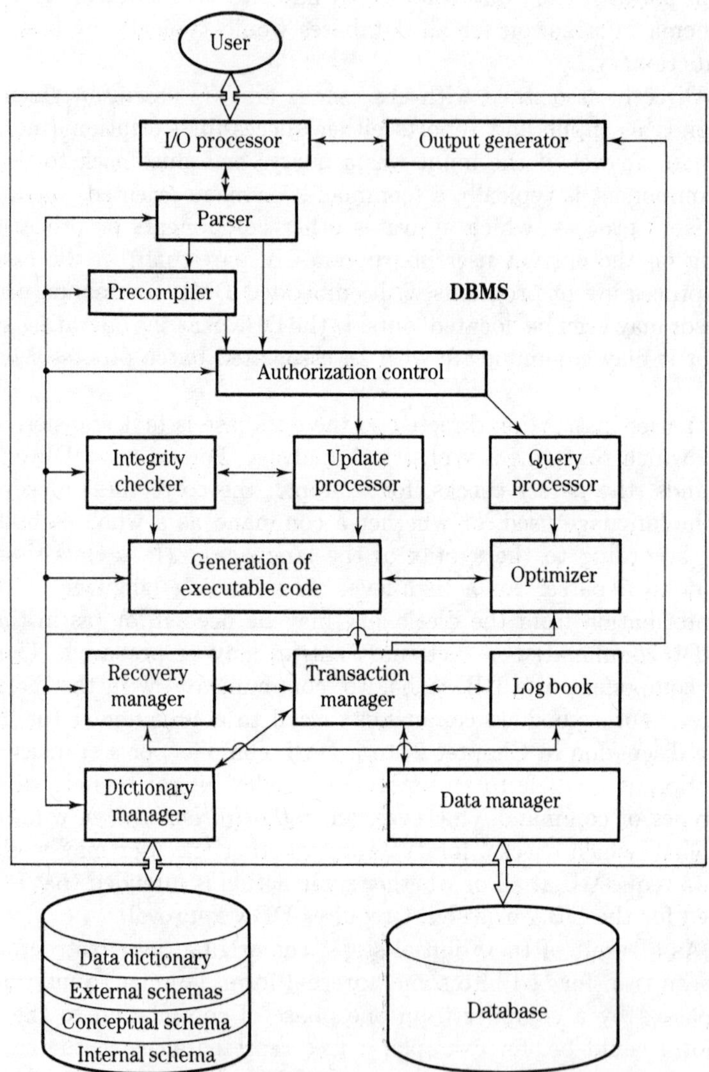

Figure 3.1 Organization/components of a DBMS.

In general, the execution of an update has to observe certain *integrity constraints* which control the *semantic* correctness ('consistency') of the underlying database. These are conditions (of a semantic nature) which can be observed in the 'outside world' or the application in question such as 'salaries are non-negative', 'salaries cannot decrease during a change', or 'a student's ID must be unique'; they are established during the definition of a conceptual schema and then have to be maintained by the DBMS automatically, that is, without any engagement from the user at run-time. Thus, the intermediate form of an update has to be augmented by the *update processor* correspondingly, by referring to the *integrity control.*

On the other hand, the execution of a query has certainly no need for checking integrity constraints, at least as long as this refers to 'conceptual' tests of the above mentioned kind only (since, intuitively, a query can in principle be posed to *any* state of a database, independent of whether it is consistent or not). However, if the integrity constraints refer to 'internal' tests as well, such as the requirement, for instance, that two user instructions issued to the system in parallel do not interfere with each other, then a corresponding 'test' has to be incorporated into a query execution also. Such problems can yet be associated with another level of processing, which will be discussed below.

If a query is directed to or formulated in terms of an external schema, then the *query-processor* has to 'translate' it into one directed to the conceptual schema, which means, for example, that user-defined abbreviations (such as the view 'v1' or 'view 1' used in Chapter 2) are expanded, that is, replaced by their corresponding definition. Finally, it could happen that a user's formulation of a query is 'unnecessarily complicated' (in a sense to be defined later), and that the system is able to recognize this, at least to a certain extent. In this case, the query would be passed to an *optimizer*, which manipulates the intermediate form in such a way that in the end it corresponds to a 'better', that is, more efficiently executable formulation, without any effect on the result.

The next task of a DBMS is to generate an *executable program*, that is, machine code for the original user instruction. To this end, it is important to note that any instruction, in whatever language it is initially written, finally results in a sequence of read and write commands for disk storage. This sequence is produced by the DBMS, eventually by once more applying certain steps of optimization.

In general, a single user does not have exclusive access to some database; instead, several users can access it simultaneously. The sequence of read and write commands, that is, the 'program' generated from an individual user instruction by the steps described above, is DBMS-internally considered as a *transaction.* The problem thus arising in a multi-user environment is that of synchronizing transactions which are issued or arriving in parallel. To this end, the DBMS is equipped with a *transaction manager* which ensures that the database appears to each user like an exclusively available resource. Internally, however, it does not make sense in general to run or process all transactions currently present within the system serially, that is, one after the other; this could result, for example, in the (undesirable) situation that a user with a 'short' program is blocked by someone else with a longer one and this happens although both users work with disjoint parts of the database. To avoid such situations, transactions are generally processed in a timely interleaved fashion ('concurrently'). Such an interleaving, however, has to face certain problems (as will be seen in Chapter 18), so that special regulations ('concurrency control') have to be provided.

From the point of view of an individual user, a transaction manager always operates according to an 'all or nothing' principle, that is, each transaction is either executed completely or not at all. During such an execution, however, the transaction manager could find out that some currently run transaction cannot be completed successfully. In this case, the transaction (or the control over it) will be passed to a *recovery manager*, which then has to bring the database back into the state it was in before the transaction was started. In particular, the recovery manager has to 'undo' all changes which the transaction has made to the database already; for doing so, it makes use of a *log book* in which (among other things) such changes are recorded. The recovery manager is also activated if the system encounters a hardware or software error (and this situation is recognized), or if the system 'crashes'. Examples include write or read errors on a disk, a hardware error in main memory, a crash of the operating systems, or some software error in the DBMS code. In all such cases, the recovery manager is responsible for a proper restart of the database system; in particular, a consistent state of the database has to be restored, typically by referring to some previously taken copy of the whole database, and all 'lost' transactions have to be started all over again ('redone').

Especially for being able to cope with crashes appropriately, it is necessary to keep the log book (as the data dictionary and the database itself) 'outside' the DBMS (such as on disk), and to apply similar safety mechanisms to it. Note that the log book therefore represents the third stock of data mentioned earlier, upon which a DBMS operates.

A final component to be mentioned at this point is the *device and storage manager*, often simply referred to as the 'data manager'. This component manages all hardware resources which are available to the DBMS, and it executes all physical accesses to the database under the control of the transaction or the recovery manager. For the sake of completeness it should be mentioned that the physical storage device(s) can be directly attached to the machine in question, that is, via channels or busses; especially in the case of a *distributed* database, the access may also have to go

Table 3.1 Database interfaces *versus* DBMS components.

Interface	*Associated DBMS component(s)*
To the user	I/O processor (monitor)
External $\leftrightarrow$ conceptual level	Parser, precompiler, update and query processor
Conceptual $\leftrightarrow$ internal level	Code generator, optimizer
Internal level $\leftrightarrow$ database	Transaction manager, device and storage manager

via some connection to a (local or wide area) network.

The dictionary manager has been described here only in connection with the parser so far, although this component — as can be seen from Figure 3.1 — actually communicates with several others as well. As the figure indicates, the data dictionary must be accessible for a number of distinct processes, and the information it contains is needed in several different contexts. However, one can distinguish between individual 'schema managers' (instead of just one dictionary manager), which are addressed by corresponding requests for information on specific schemas; note that this is not reflected in Figure 3.1.

In addition it should be noted that some DBMS components also make use of functions provided by the underlying operating system; thus, a DBMS will always have an 'interface' to that system, which is also not shown in Figure 3.1. A precise delimitation between DBMS and operating-system functions is possible only if the DBMS is independent of the hardware provided by a particular computer manufacturer (and hence portable).

As a conclusion, Figure 2.2 can now be returned to, and the different interfaces shown can be described somewhat more precisely; the association of components with interfaces is shown in Table 3.1.

Finally, it should also be mentioned, in particular with respect to the discussion that will follow in Part VII, that the collection of DBMS components as described above is not 'amorphous', but can be structured further into *layers*, each of which is responsible for a distinct set of functions and hence comprises the corresponding components. Layers are located on top of each other, so that again the level of abstraction increases from bottom to top, and each of them provides certain *services* to the next higher layer. One way of organizing the various DBMS components

Table 3.2 Layered organization of DBMS components.

Layer	*Associated components*
User interface layer	I/O processor, output generation
Language processing layer	Parser, precompiler, authorization control, update and query processors, optimizer
Access methods layer	Code generator, optimizer
Concurrency control layer	Transaction manager, recovery manager
Storage management layer	Data manager

from Figure 3.1 into layers is exhibited in Table 3.2; this aspect will be returned to in Chapter 23.

Bibliographic Notes

At the end of this introductory part, only some global hints to the literature are given; more detailed ones will be given later in the appropriate places. Introductions to the why and what of database systems (in particular as opposed to file systems) are given, for example, by Date (1986), Korth and Silberschatz (1986), Kroenke (1983), McFadden and Hoffer (1988), or Elmasri and Navathe (1989). The three-level architecture model for databases goes back to the ANSI (1975) document; further explanations are given by Tsichritzis and Klug (1978), Clemons (1985), Date (1986), or Elmasri and Navathe (1989). The tasks of a database administrator are discussed in detail by McFadden and Hoffer (1988).

The reader should also consult the bibliography on databases by Kambayashi (1981), which gives a complete survey of the database literature until 1980, for further references to distinct topics discussed in this and the following parts.

Exercises

(1) Give short and concise definitions for the following terms:

database	data independence
DBMS	embedded DML
DBA	host language
meta-data	recovery manager
conceptual schema	view
DDL	integrity constraint

(2) Discuss the advantages of a database system when compared with a file system. Are there also disadvantages and, if so, what are they?

(3) Informally describe examples of (semantic) integrity constraints for the library application from Chapter 1.

(4) Find out which simplifications apply to the DBMS model described in Chapter 3 for the case of a pure *information retrieval* system (which only allows queries, but no updates).

Part II

Traditional (Graphical) Data Models for the Conceptual Schema

Chapter 4
The Entity-Relationship Model

In this chapter a data model is presented which renders it possible to generate an abstract model of a section of the real world or a particular application. To this end, a couple of notions and notations are needed which are introduced first; these will serve to describe **entities** and their **relationships** formally. The resulting time-invariant specifications are then collected in an **entity-relationship schema**, which can be represented graphically as an **entity-relationship diagram**. Such schemas or diagrams emphasize the structure of a given application together with constraints on the states of those structures.

4.1 Entities

Well-distinguishable objects which exist in the real world are from now on called *entities*; examples are persons, cars, cities, companies, and so on. Individual entities which are similar or comparable are united in an *entity set*; examples are 'all employees of a company', 'all commercial vehicles of an enterprise', 'all persons living in San Diego', or 'all German cars taking unleaded gas'. In what follows, capital letters will be used to denote entity sets and small letters to denote single entities.

Entities have properties (such as the colour or the length of a car, a person's birthdate or address) which are called *values.* A 'restriction' is made here to consider *atomic* values only (this restriction will be called 'first normal form' in the context of the relational model in Chapter 7), that is, values are not allowed to be composed of other values (such as the elements of a Cartesian product, for example). (Later, in particular in Part VII, it will become clear why this can indeed be considered to be a restriction.) The set of all values which are possible or 'allowed' for a particular property of an entity is called the value set or *domain* of that property. For the time being at the level of an entity set, a property (applying to all entities in the set) is called an *attribute.* Thus, an attribute associates with each entity in an entity set a value from a particular domain (that of the attribute). 'dom(A)' will be used to denote the domain of an attribute named A.

As an example, consider the entity set named *Stock_of_Books* from Chapter 2; some attributes (previously called 'record fields') with possible domains are:

Attribute (-name)	*Domain*
Callnumber	4-digit integers
Author	character strings of length 20
Title	character strings of length 50
Publishing_Co	character strings of length 25

An important observation at this point is that the name of an entity set and its attributes are to be considered as *time-invariant.* In particular, attributes describe such (abstract) properties which *every* entity that belongs to the set in question at any time possesses; a particular entity is obtained by associating a value with each attribute. Therefore, the set of all attributes of an entity set is called an **entity format**.

On the other hand, the *contents* of an entity set (and hence the set itself) is *time-varying.* For example, at some time t_1 *Stock_of_Books* might consist of the two entities

e_1 = (0401, Date, Intro DBS, AW)

and

$$e_2 = (0405, \text{Ullman, Princ DBS, CSP})$$

only, whereas at time t_2 it also contains the entity

$$e_3 = (0408, \text{Kroenke, DB Proc, SRA})$$

This observation will now be formalized to make it possible to distinguish the time-varying aspects of an entity clearly from its time-invariant ones. To do so, however, one more 'component' is needed, which is described next.

To describe or 'identify' a particular entity, it is often not necessary to list values for all its attributes; instead, it can be sufficient to provide values for some attributes only which completely characterize the entity. (Think, for example, of the callnumber of a book.) Such attributes are called **key attributes**; correspondingly, their collection is called a **key** for the entity set in question.

Since it was assumed above that individual entities are 'well-distinguishable', it follows that the format of an entity set (that is, the set of *all* its attributes) is always a candidate for a key of this set. On the other hand, it is possible in general to distinguish certain attributes or combinations of attributes (but not all) as a (time-invariant) key. Thus, for example, the *callnumber* of a book is a key, provided it is unique for each book.

In addition, it is also possible that more than one key can be stated for an entity set, as in the following example:

entity set	*City*
attributes	*Zip-Code, State, Population, Area-Code*
key	*Zip-Code* or *Area-Code*

In such cases one key will always be marked as the **primary key** and added to the time-invariant description of the entity set. Before such a description is stated formally, the definition of a key is completed as follows. A key is required to be *free of redundancy*, that is, whenever two sets of attributes K_1 and K_2 have the identification property for an entity set in the sense described above and $K_1 \subseteq K_2$ holds, only K_1 is called a key, and K_2 is a **candidate key**. Thus, a *key* K is always a *minimal*, identifying combination of attributes; every (strict) superset of a key is a candidate key.

Definition 4.1

An **entity declaration** is a (named) pair $E = (X, K)$, where E is the name of the declaration, X is the format, and K is a primary key consisting of elements from X. The notation attr(E) is also used instead of X to denote the attributes associated with a declaration named E.

In principle an attribute is considered to be a pair of the form '(name : domain)' such as (*Author* : char (20)), for instance; however, if the domain of an attribute is clear from the context or currently unimportant, attributes will usually be identified with their respective names.

It should also be pointed out that this definition does not reflect the possibility of secondary keys (or, more generally, of 'integrity constraints' other than keys). This simplification is made here with regard to the capability of representing a declaration graphically in an entity-relationship diagram (see Section 4.4).

With respect to the format attr(E) of an entity declaration E, there are two possibilities to represent it, namely as a *set* or a *sequence*. The former expresses the fact that a particular sequencing of the attributes does not yet 'code' any information. This perspective is, as will be seen below, supported by entity-relationship *diagrams*, as well as by the relational data model. It implies the following formal definition of an entity: an *entity* e is an (injective) *mapping*

$$e : \{A_1, \ldots, A_n\} \rightarrow \bigcup_{i=1}^{m} \text{dom}(A_i)$$

for which the following holds:

$$(\forall i, 1 \leq i \leq m)\ e(A_i) \in \text{dom}(A_i)$$

Under this definition, an *entity set* E^t is an (arbitrary) subset of the set of all entities that (at least) satisfies the primary key K. (The 'timestamp' t is used to stress the variability of the set.) Here, 'satisfaction' can be written formally as follows:

(1) $(\forall\, e, e' \in E^t)\ e|_K = e'|_K \Rightarrow e = e'$

(2) K is minimal with respect to '$\subseteq$' with Property (1), that is, for no proper subset K' of K (1) is also true.

By '$e|_K$' the *restriction* ('projection') of entity e onto the attribute set K is denoted, that is, for $K = \{B_1, \ldots, B_r\}$ the 'subentity' ($e(B_1)$, …, $e(B_r)$).

In this and in the following two chapters the *sequence* notation will be used for formats, since it allows for simpler expositions appropriate for these contexts.

Definition 4.2

Let $E = (X, K)$ be an entity declaration, where X (= attr(E)) = $(A_1, \ldots, A_m)$. For A_i, $1 \leq i \leq m$, let dom(A_i) denote the domain of A_i, and let K denote a subsequence of X.

(i) An **entity** e (over E) is an element of the Cartesian product of all domains, that is, $e \in \text{dom}(A_1) \times \ldots \times \text{dom}(A_m)$.

(ii) An **entity set** E^t (over E, at time t) is a set of entities, that is, $E^t \subseteq \text{dom}(A_1) \times \ldots \times \text{dom}(A_m)$, that satisfies K (in the sense explained above). E^t is also called the **instance** or *current value* of declaration E at time t.

As an example, consider the library application with the following entity declarations:

B = ((Callnumber, Author, Title, Publ_Co), (Callnumber))
R = ((Reader_No, Name, Addr), (Reader_No))

Here, B is used as an abbreviation for *Stock_of_Books*, R for *Readers* (users of the library); each reader has a unique identifier *Reader_No*, a name and an address. At some time t, (valid) entity sets could be

$$B^t = \{(0401, \text{Date}, \text{Intro DBS}, \text{AW}), (0405, \text{Ullman}, \text{Princ DBS}, \text{CSP})\}$$
$$R^t = \{(500, \text{Joe}, \text{Los Angeles}), (502, \text{Nina}, \text{San Diego})\}$$

Note that, given R^t above, the entity (502, Linda, La Jolla) cannot occur in R^t (at this time), since the key *Reader_No* would be violated.

4.2 Relationships

Different entity sets of a given application generally do not exist in isolation; instead, they are usually associated with each other in some way. For example, in a library, books are 'checked out' by readers, which means that a certain book is (temporarily) associated with a particular reader. Such associations are called *relationships*; they involve entities or — more precisely — entity sets.

A relationship can also have attributes of its own, in order to capture special properties that have a meaning only for the relationship, but not for any of the entity sets involved (such as the 'return date' of a book that has been checked out by a reader). In addition, as was done for entities, the *time-invariant description* of a relationship will be distinguished from its *time-varying contents.* To this end, the following notions are introduced:

Definition 4.3

(i) *A* **relationship declaration** is a (named) pair R = (ent, attr); it consists of a name (R), which is sometimes simply termed the 'name of the relationship', a sequence ent of names of those entity declarations between which a relationship is to be established, and a (possibly empty) sequence attr of attributes. The notation ent(R) [attr(R)] is also used to refer to the names of the entity sets [attributes] belonging to declaration R, respectively.

(ii) Let ent(R) = $(E_1, \ldots, E_k)$, and for arbitrary, but fixed t let E_i^t be the instance of E_i (at time t), $1 \leq i \leq k$. Also, let attr(R) = $(B_1, \ldots, B_n)$. A **relationship** r (over R) is an element of the Cartesian product of all E_i^t and the domains of the B_j, that is,

$$r \in E_1^t \times \ldots \times E_k^t \times \text{dom}(B_1) \times \ldots \times \text{dom}(B_n)$$

or

$$r = (e_1, \ldots, e_k, b_1, \ldots, b_n)$$

where $e_i \in E_i^t$, $1 \leq i \leq k$, and $b_j \in \text{dom}(B_j)$, $1 \leq j \leq n$.

(iii) A **relationship set** R^t (over R, at time t) is a set of relationships, that is,

$$R^t \subseteq E_1^t \times \ldots \times E_k^t \times \text{dom}(B_1) \times \ldots \times \text{dom}(B_n)$$

Note that in this definition again both ent(R) and attr(R) are written as sequences. For the latter this is as before chosen at random, while for the former it is not. By writing the (names of) entity declarations participating in a relationship as a *sequence*, it becomes possible to express *role* information ('coded' into the sequence). This is particularly relevant to the case where an entity declaration appears in a relationship declaration more than once (which is permitted by the last definition), that is, $E_i = E_j$ for $i \neq j$ and two items E_i and E_j from some ent(R).

As a simple example, let E = *Person*, and let $R_1 = R_2 = ((E, E), \emptyset)$. If R_1 represents a 'parent-child' relationship, the first occurrence of E in R_1 may denote the parent, while the second denotes the child. Similarly, if R_2 represents an 'employee-manager' relationship, the first occurrence of E in R_2 may now represent an employee, while the second represents his or her manager.

When writing down concrete relationships or relationship sets, unnecessary parentheses will usually be omitted. For example, if O stands for the above mentioned relationship 'checked out' between entity declarations B (books) and R (readers), whose declaration is given by

$$O = ((B, R), (\textit{Return\_Date}))$$

the following relationship set can be formed from the entity sets B^t and R^t from Section 4.1 (with several parentheses already omitted):

O^t = {(0401, Date, Intro DBS, AW, 500, Joe, Los Angeles, 043087),
(405, Ullman, Princ DBS, CSP, 502, Nina, San Diego, 053187) }

Another simplification can be applied to the representation of relationships or relationship sets, which will primarily be used later (in the context of the relational model), and which will therefore not be formalized for relationship declarations. If a (primary) key has been defined for the entities participating in a relationship (in the corresponding entity declaration), then it is obviously sufficient to list the key values for each entity only when representing a relationship, since these identify each entity uniquely. In the library example, the representation of O^t above could thus be simplified to the following:

$$O^t = \{(0401, 500, 043087), (0405, 502, 053187)\}$$

Note that no information is lost in this simplified representation, since all non-key properties of a book or a reader (such as title or name, respectively) can easily be 'retrieved' from the underlying entity sets using the appropriate key-value.

Next let R = (ent, attr) be a relationship declaration, where ent(R) = $(E_1, \ldots, E_k)$. Then k is called the arity or the **degree** of R, denoted degree(R) (= k in this case).

It can be observed that the case $k = 2$ ('binary relationship') is by far the most frequent one in practical applications (see also 'O' in our library example). Therefore, it is common in this case (but also in the more general case $k \neq 2$) to assign a **complexity** to the relationship declaration in question, which makes a statement on how many entities of the second 'type' may or must be associated with an entity of the first one in a particular relationship.

For example, in a library it is possible that one reader has checked out several books at the same time; on the other hand, a book can only be given out to one reader at a time. For this reason, the relationship set O^t shown above is intuitively considered as 'correct'; the following one, however, has to be considered incorrect (one book is given out to two distinct readers):

$$O^{t'} = \{(0401, 500, 043087), (0401, 502, 053187)\}$$

To describe the complexity of a relationship, the following notation, which also covers the case degree$(R) > 2$, may be used: let R be a relationship declaration, where ent$(R) = (E_1, \ldots, E_k)$. If a particular entity $e_i \in E_i^t$, $1 \leq i \leq k$, can (at time t) appear in the relationship set R^t at least m times and at most n times, the notation

$$\text{comp}(R,\ E_i) = (m,\ n)$$

is used, which is formally defined as follows:

$$\text{comp}(R, E_i) = (m, n)$$

$$:\Longleftrightarrow (\forall t)(\forall e_i \in E_i^t) \mid \{r \in R^t \mid r[E_i] = e_i\}| \begin{cases} \geq m \\ \leq n \end{cases}$$

As an example, consider suppliers (S) who supply (*Supp*) parts (P) to a company (C) in some quantity (Q). This situation is modelled by the relationship declaration:

$$Supp = ((S, P, C), (Q))$$

to which the following complexities might be assigned:

comp(*Supp*, S) = $(0, \infty)$
comp(*Supp*, P) = $(0, 1)$
comp(*Supp*, C) = $(1, 3)$

Thus, if $Supp^t$ is a given relationship set (an instance of *Supp*), each S-entity may appear in $Supp^t$ arbitrarily often ($n = \infty$ implies that a supplier is allowed to supply several parts to different companies; $m = 0$ means that they are not necessarily supplying any part at time t). Similarly, a P-entity is not necessarily supplied at the moment ($m = 0$), but if it is supplied this may happen at most once ($n = 1$; note that this may restrict either the number of 'sources' or the number of 'destinations'). Finally, a company must be supplied (by someone or with something) at least once ($m = 1$), and may appear in at most ($n =$) 3 relationships simultaneously. Note that these assignments are completely arbitrary and not necessarily in correspondence with every 'reality'; however, for a particular situation they might be appropriate.

Attention is now restricted to the important binary relationships, for which the following specific types of complexity are introduced:

Definition 4.4

Let R = (ent, attr) be a relationship declaration, where ent(R) = (E_1, E_2), that is, degree(R) = 2.

R is of type	if comp$(R, E_1) \in$	and	comp$(R, E_2) \in$
$1 : 1$	$\{(0,1),(1,1)\}$		$\{(0,1),(1,1)\}$
$1 : n$	$\{(0,\infty),(1,\infty)\}$		$\{(0,1),(1,1)\}$
$m : n$	$\{(0,\infty),(1,\infty)\}$		$\{(0,\infty),(1,\infty)\}$

(Note that a certain inaccuracy of this definition results from the fact that the notion 'R is of type $1 : n$ or $m : n$' does not state exact bounds for m and n, as was the case for the comp notation above.)

A relationship R thus is of type $1 : 1$ (or, stated differently, E_1 and E_2 are in a **one-to-one** relationship) if in every relationship set over R

each entity over E_1 is associated with at most one entity over E_2 and vice versa. As an example, consider the relationship 'is manager of' between entity types *Employee* and *Department.* Each employee is manager of at most one department and, conversely, in each department there is at most one employee who acts as its manager.

A relationship R is of type $1 : n$ (**one to many**), if (in each R^t) an entity over E_1 is associated with $n \geq 0$ entities over E_2, but each entity over E_2 is related to at most one entity over E_1. Analogously, a relationship is of type $m : 1$ (**many-one**) if the roles of E_1 and E_2 are exchanged. For example, in the library application the relationship O (see above) between B and R is many-one; on the other hand, the (converse) relationship $O' = ((R, B), .)$ would be of type $1 : n$.

Finally, in case of an $m : n$ relationship (**many-many**) no restrictions are imposed on the pairing of entities in a relationship set. An example for this type is the relationship 'exports' between *Country* and *Product.*

$1 : 1$ or $1 : n$ relationships (between E_1 and E_2) can also be **hierarchical** in nature in the sense that the following dependency exists between the entities: a concrete entity e_2 ($\in E_2^t$) can exist only in conjunction with an entity e_1 from E_1^t, which in this case is uniquely determined. In other words, comp(R, E_1) is restricted to the case $(1\ ,\ 1)$. For example, if it is additionally required that the O relationship in the library example is hierarchical, this would imply that a book cannot appear in an entity set over B unless there exists a reader who checks it out.

Another important special case of a relationship is the following. In some cases, the entities in one entity set are not (only) distinguished via their attributes, but (also) through their relationship to entities in another entity set. As an example, consider the employees of an airline with the following entity declaration:

Emp = ((Emp#, Name, Addr, Profession, Salary), (Emp#))

For certain employees, additional attributes are relevant: a pilot's flight experience is measured in the number of hours spent in the air; also, every pilot's licence number is recorded. Technicians belong to distinct service teams. Thus, in both cases, there exist attributes that apply to some employees of the airline, but not to all. A reasonable way to model this is to introduce the following additional entity declarations:

Pilot = ((*Emp#*, *Hours*, *Lic#*), (*Emp#*))
Techn = ((*Emp#*, *Team#*), (*Emp#*))

Clearly, these declarations are closely related to *Emp* in that they actually represent *specializations* of this former declaration, which are associated with it through a so-called **IS-A relationship** (for example, 'every pilot IS An employee'). Thus, a particular pilot can be considered as an entity over *Emp* and as an entity over *Pilot*; however, as in the case of a hierarchical relationship, the occurrence of an entity in a set $Pilot^t$ should be bound to the occurrence of a corresponding ('generalized') entity in Emp^t (for each t).

If the attributes of *Pilot* are listed completely, it seems reasonable to include *all* attributes of the generalization in the corresponding declaration as well, which in this example results in:

$$Pilot = ((Emp\#, Name, Addr, Profession, Salary, Hours, Lic\#), (Emp\#))$$

Therefore, this type of relationship is formally defined as follows:

Definition 4.5

Let $E_1 = (\text{attr}(E_1), K_1)$ and $E_2 = (\text{attr}(E_2), K_2)$ be two entity declarations. There exists an **IS-A relationship** (of the form E_1 IS-A E_2) between E_1 and E_2, if the following hold:

(i) Every element of $\text{attr}(E_2)$ also appears in $\text{attr}(E_1)$;

(ii) at any time t, if $e_1 \in E_1^t$, then there exists an $e_2 \in E_2^t$ such that $e_1(A) = e_2(A)$ for every common attribute A.

Note that $E_1 \subseteq E_2$ will also be written in this case.

The explicit Condition (i) together with the implicit requirement that K_1 is a key for attr (E_1) (that is, for the sequence of *all* attributes) can have the following implications. In the most frequent case, $K_1 = K_2$ holds. K_2 may also be a subsequence of K_1; in this case there exist new attributes for (the 'specialization') E_1 which are needed to identify an entity. However, it can happen that K_1 and K_2 do not have attributes in common; in this case the key property of K_1 ensures that K_1 also identifies K_2 and hence entities over E_2. In Section 4.4, an example for each of these cases will be presented (see Figure 4.3). In the example above, the following can now be stated: $Pilot \subseteq Emp$ and $Techn \subseteq Emp$.

4.3 Entity-relationship schemas

The description of the **entity-relationship model** (abbreviated **ER model**) (or its particular version that will be used throughout this text, see the Bibliographic Notes for Part II) is now completed. A first formalism is available for describing particular applications. Such a description consists of *time-invariant* declarations which are collected in a *schema*:

Definition 4.6

An **entity-relationship** (ER) **schema** is a (named) pair $\mathcal{S} = (\mathcal{E}, \mathcal{R})$, where $\mathcal{E}$ contains entity declarations (each with a name, a sequence of attributes and their domains, and a key), and $\mathcal{R}$ contains relationship declarations (each with a name, a sequence of names of participating entity declarations, eventually new attributes and their domains, complexity or type declaration, and (eventually) a statement whether it is hierarchical or of type IS-A).

Thus, an ER schema $\mathcal{S}$ represents a collection of declarations that together describe the conceptual level of a 'database', and which can be considered as comparable to type declarations in high-level programming languages (see Part VII); in particular, $\mathcal{S}$ summarizes the *constraints* (such as keys or types of relationships) which *every* concrete set of data over this schema, that is, every instance of $\mathcal{S}$, has to satisfy. Clearly, all declarations can be made in an arbitrary way, as it is appropriate for the application the 'schema designer' has in mind. On the other hand, it should be noted that each conceptual declaration has implications for concrete, physically existing entities or relationships, so that the designer has to make sure that the resulting effect is indeed desirable from a point of view of the application modelled.

For example, the declaration of a key implies that *every* entity set that may exist in the database at any time has to observe this key. The key itself can (in principle) be modified only during the *design phase* of the database; once this phase is completed, it is considered as *static*. Similar remarks apply to all the other components of a conceptual database description by way of an ER schema.

4.4 Entity-relationship diagrams

To conclude this chapter, a common way of graphically representing the information that can be encoded in the 'language' of the ER model is presented. To this end, **entity-relationship diagrams** are used that consist of the following 'building blocks':

(1) An entity declaration is represented by a *rectangle* which carries the name of the declaration, and by *circles* for the attributes. Each circle is connected to the corresponding rectangle via an undirected edge. The attributes of the (primary) key are underlined; domains are not shown. (Clearly, ER diagrams can easily be augmented to show domains as well; one way to do so is to include the domains (instead of the attribute names) in the circles, and to use the attribute names as labels for the edges that connect the circles to the corresponding rectangle. This option is not used in Figures 4.1–4.3.)

(2) A relationship declaration is represented by a *rhombus* ('diamond') that carries the name of the declaration, and that is connected to the participating entity declarations (rectangles) by edges. These edges are again undirected, except for hierarchical or IS-A relationships (see below); if E_2 is hierarchically dependent on E_1, the corresponding edge is directed towards E_2. In the case of binary relationships, the edges can also be labelled with the type of the relationship.

    If an ordering among the entity declarations of a relationship is to be expressed, the edges can be numbered correspondingly.

    Finally, if a relationship declaration has separate attributes, these are again represented in circles and connected to the appropriate diamond by (undirected) edges.

(3) An IS-A relationship of the form $E_1 \subseteq E_2$ is also represented by a diamond, which is now labelled 'IS-A' and connected to E_1 and E_2. In this case, the edge to E_1 is undirected, while the other is directed. To simplify the graphical representation of an IS-A relationship, it is allowed that E_1 (the specialization) is only shown with the attributes that are either 'special' or members of its key.

Figure 4.1 shows an ER diagram for the library example from the previous sections; Figure 4.2 shows such a diagram for the (recursive and hierarchical) parent-child relationship mentioned in Section 4.2.

Figure 4.3 shows the (partial) ER diagram for an airline, which in particular exhibits the IS-A relationships mentioned previously (in different 'versions' with respect to the keys of the participating entity declarations). The following remarks on this figure are apt.

'Special' employees of the airline are the pilots and the technicians (see Section 4.2). Another distinction is made between data about particular planes owned by the airline (*Aircraft*, characterized by a serial number, a date of purchase, and so on) and data that applies to every plane of a particular type (collected in *Planes*); for example, it is assumed that every DC 10 travels at the same speed, but if the airline owns several of them these can be distinguished via their serial numbers. Similarly, a distinction is made between flights operating on a regular basis (such as 'LH451 from Los Angeles to Frankfurt', recorded in *Flight*), and particular 'instances' of a flight as they occur at specific dates (such as 'LH451 on 02/12/88 at 3:30 pm) which are carried out by a specific pilot on a particular aircraft, and which have certain passengers (*Departure*). The distinction between 'real' and 'virtual' planes and flights also makes it possible to differentiate between the concretely performed and the possible actions of a pilot: a pilot *can fly* not just a particular DC 10, but every plane of this type; on

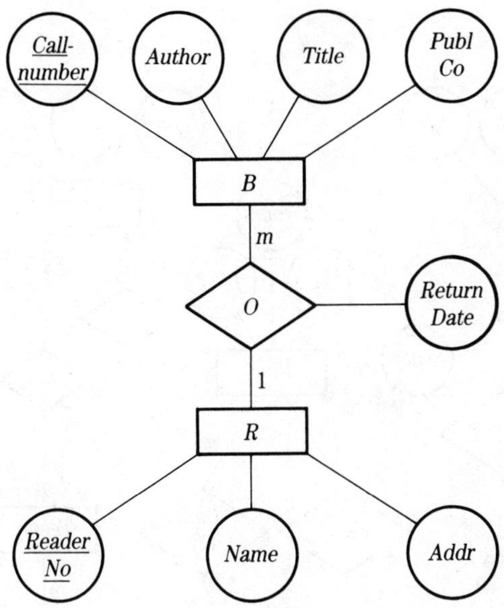

Figure 4.1 ER diagram for the library example.

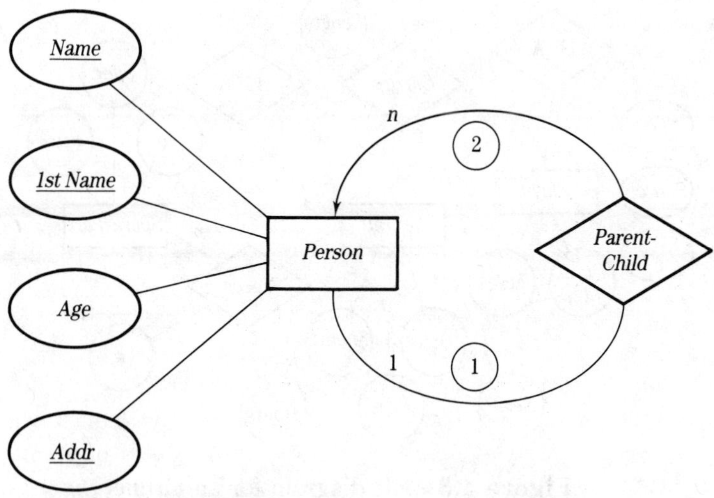

Figure 4.2 ER diagram for a parent-child relationship.

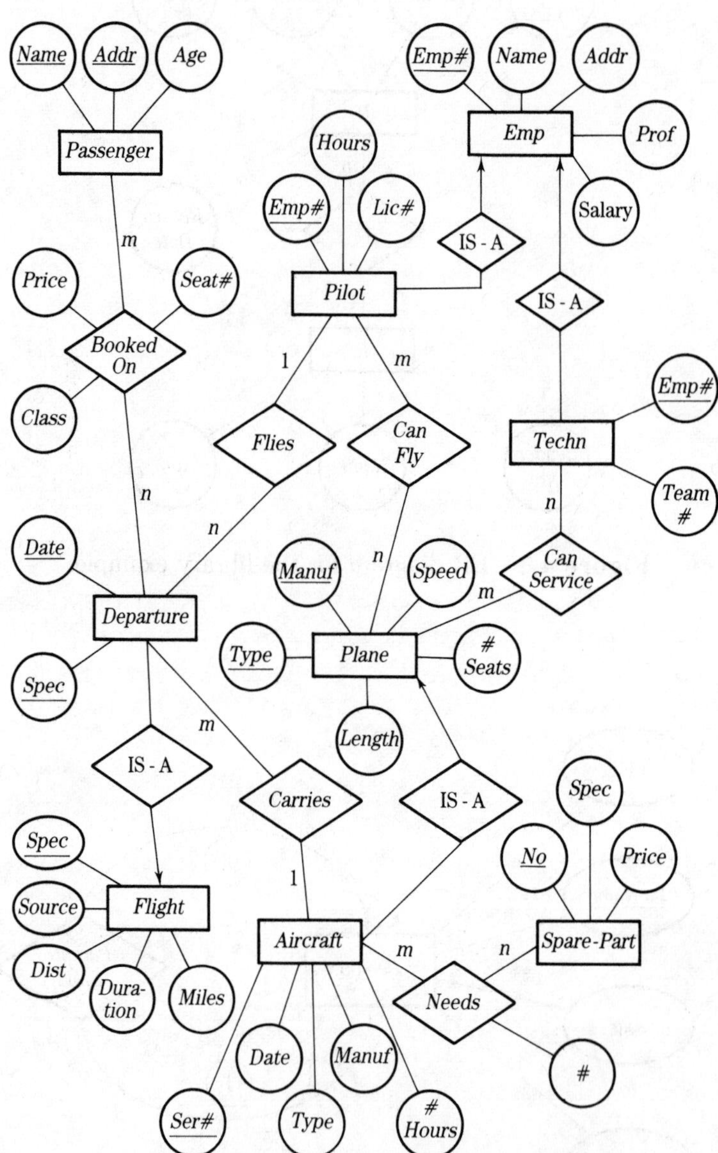

Figure 4.3 ER diagram for an airline.

the other hand, he is appointed to (*flies*) a particular departure, but not necessarily every flight with the same code.

In conclusion, it is now possible to perform an abstraction for a particular application at hand. In the following two chapters, 'concrete' data models will be considered, in the sense that these have been used as a foundation for various implementations of a database system over the past 20 years. One goal in these and Chapter 7 will be to introduce the 'language' of the model at hand and describe how a given ER schema or ER diagram can be 'translated' into one of these models.

It should be noted critically, however, that the language of the ER model as introduced in this chapter is of limited expressive power, which may force a database designer to model a given application in a way which is not the most natural. This can be seen from the following two examples, which again concern the library application.

In Section 4.1, every reader was said to have an address, and a corresponding attribute *Addr* was therefore included in the respective entity declaration. The underlying assumption was that an address can be represented as a string of characters, some of which denote a street, while others identify a city. However, it may be more appropriate (for example, for query purposes) to consider an address as a *tuple* or record with individually named components, thereby reflecting the fact that an address is *composed* of, say, a street, a city and a zip code. Clearly, attribute *Addr* could be replaced by the three attributes *Street*, *City* and *Zip* in the entity declaration for readers, which, however, has the consequence that it becomes more complicated to retrieve a reader's address as a whole (three values must be read instead of one).

While the problem that can be recognized in connection with addresses (or with names which are usually *composed* of a first and a last name) can still be solved in some way in terms of the ER model presented here, the following problem is more intricate. In Section 4.1, a book was said to have an 'author'. The problem here is that a value for attribute *Author* may actually be a *set* of names. Again this problem could be 'solved' by choosing character strings of variable length as the domain of *Author*; however, from the point of view of the 'structure' of this application, this solution is not the most appropriate.

Observations like these motivate the search for models with more 'flexibility' with respect to structure (and semantics), which will be discussed in Chapters 11, 21 and 22.

Chapter 5
The Network Model

The network data model is used as the conceptual data structure by a variety of commercially available DBMS products, one of which will be presented in detail in Chapter 14. Simply speaking, the network model can be considered as an ER model with only binary, many-one relationships allowed. This restriction makes it possible to represent logical structures in this model by ordinary **graphs**, which will be discussed first (in two steps). After the description of how to transform an ER diagram into the network model, this (graph) representation is extended from logical to physical structures. This will result in a particular **implementation** of a network structure, which turns out to be quite realistic from a user's point of view. On the other hand, it will lead to the difficulty of **navigation** through a network database, which is the key concept for working with databases that are managed by a DBMS from this category.

5.1 Bachman diagrams and logical networks

As discussed in the previous chapter, in an ER diagram entity declarations are represented by rectangles with connected circles. A representation of logical contexts that uses (ordinary) graphs is now needed. To this end, the representation of attributes appearing in an entity declaration will be neglected for the moment and the rectangles considered as **nodes** of a graph. **Edges** express binary relationships between nodes (entity declarations); an edge may be labelled with the name of the relationship in question. In addition, it will be assumed for the moment that a relationship does not have attributes of its own; a corresponding (and clearly necessary) 'integration' of these will be carried out later. Finally, the following restriction will be imposed.

If there exists a $1 : n$ relationship between 'nodes' E_1 and E_2, the corresponding edge will be directed from E_1 to E_2. (Note that a $1 : 1$ relationship can thus be represented as well, since it can be considered as a special case of a $1 : n$ relationship.) In the case of an $m : n$ relationship an undirected edge is used (as an 'abbreviation' for two directed edges in opposite directions labelled with the same name).

Definition 5.1

A data structure or **Bachman diagram** is a graph $B = (V, E)$ whose set V of vertices represents entity declarations, and whose set $E \subseteq V \times V$ of edges represents binary relationships between these (without attributes). Vertices and edges are labelled.

As a first example, consider the ER diagram from Figure 4.1; a corresponding representation as a Bachman diagram is given in Figure 5.1. Figure 5.2 shows an excerpt from the ER diagram for the airline from Figure 4.3, now shown as a Bachman diagram with undirected edges; Figure 5.3 shows a corresponding diagram with each undirected edge replaced by a pair of directed edges.

It is obvious that a Bachman diagram, when compared with an ER diagram, has the restriction that a k-ary relationship with $k > 2$ cannot be modelled directly, a property that is implied by the fact that edges 'are' binary. Before discussing ways of overcoming this problem, let us consider

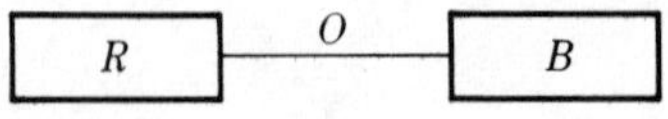

Figure 5.1 Bachman diagram corresponding to Figure 4.1.

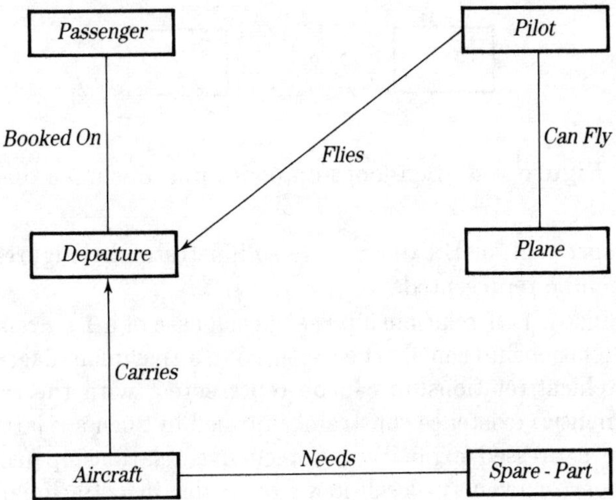

Figure 5.2 Bachman diagram for an airline with undirected edges.

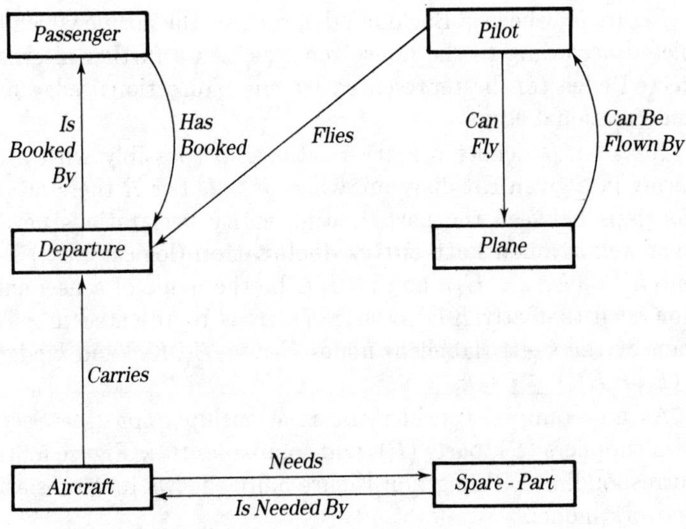

Figure 5.3 Bachman diagram from Figure 5.2 with directed edges only.

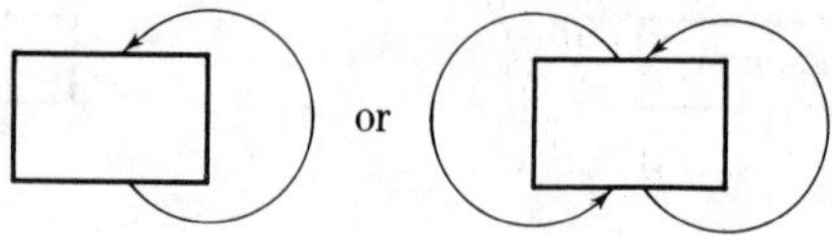

Figure 5.4 Self-loops on nodes in a Bachman diagram.

other aspects of an ER diagram (also illustrated by Figures 5.2 and 5.3) which *can* be represented.

Since a $1:1$ relationship is a special case of a $1:n$ relationship, this type of relationship can also be captured in a Bachman diagram. Similarly, a hierarchical relationship can be represented, with the restriction that the (semantic) existence constraint imposed by such a relationship cannot (yet) be expressed explicitly. A recursive relationship (see Figure 4.2) yields one (or even two) self-loops on nodes in a Bachman diagram, as shown in Figure 5.4. In this case, roles can easily be represented by using appropriate labels on edges. Finally, an IS-A relationship can be represented by an edge which is now directed towards the specialization; the reason for this reversion of the direction in comparison with an ER diagram will be given later, when the implementation of logical structures is discussed (see Section 5.2).

Figure 5.5 shows a Bachman diagram for the airline which has been completed according to the above remarks. As a further alternative, an undirected edge can be represented by *one* bidirectional edge instead of two unidirectional edges.

Next let R denote a k-ary relationship (possibly with attributes) appearing in a given ER diagram, where $k > 2$. For R there are k binary relationships between the participating entity declarations newly introduced as well as a new **kett-entity declaration** (logical 'link') as follows. Let $\text{ent}(R) = (E_1, \ldots, E_k)$, and let KE be the name of a new entity declaration such that $\text{attr}(KE) = \text{attr}(R)$. R is represented in a Bachman diagram by the $k+1$ (labelled) nodes $E_1, \ldots, E_k, KE$ and k edges of the form $(E_i, KE), 1 \leq i \leq k$.

As an example, consider the relationship *Supp* (see Section 4.2) between suppliers (S), parts (P), and companies (C). Figure 5.6(a) shows the corresponding ER diagram; Figure 5.6(b) shows its 'translation' into the network model.

It should be mentioned that the attributes of a given entity declaration can easily be represented in a Bachman diagram by using *composite* nodes. Instead of introducing this formally, it can be illustrated using the library example: Figure 5.7 shows a Bachman diagram that includes attributes. Using this way of representation, it is possible (as in an ER diagram, see Figure 4.1) to exhibit the (primary) key of each entity declaration by underlining its attributes. In addition, by 'placing' the edge

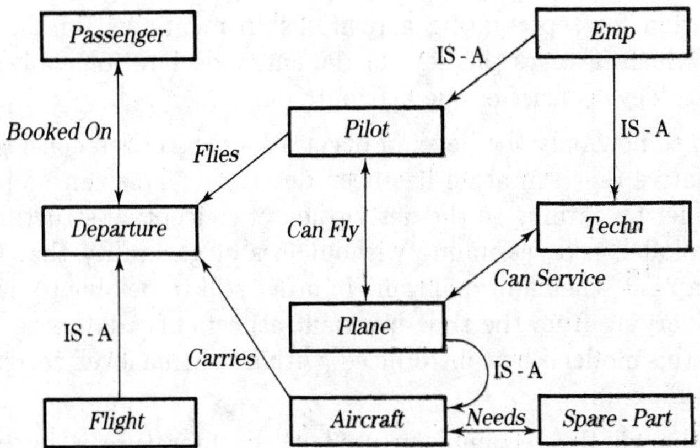

Figure 5.5 Completed Bachman diagram for the airline.

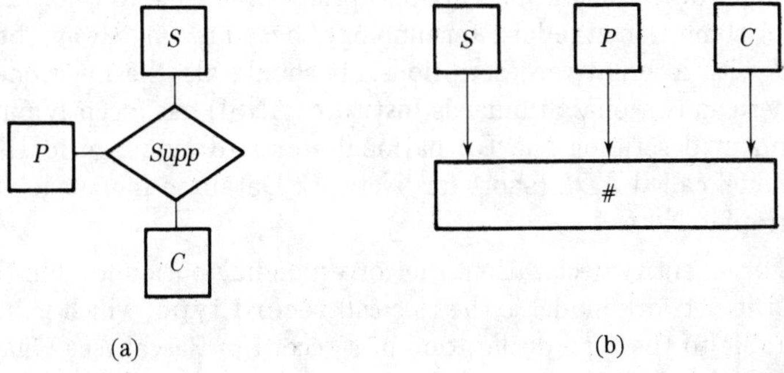

Figure 5.6 A ternary relationship and its translation.

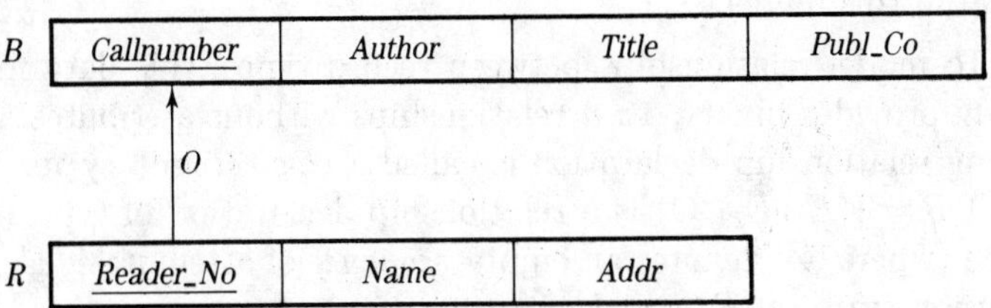

Figure 5.7 Bachman diagram for the library including attributes.

that expresses the relationship appropriately, it is possible to apply the simplification for representing a relationship mentioned in the previous chapter (which involves the keys of the entity declarations only) in cases where both keys consist of one attribute only.

Up to now only the 'level of declarations' has been considered, and an alternative representation has been described. This can be pursued a little further by turning to the description of conceptual structures in the network model next, assuming without loss of generality that these are given as an ER schema or diagram. In order still to be able to distinguish the time-varying from the time-invariant aspects of a database, the 'language' of this model is now introduced, with a 'schema level' corresponding to an ER diagram.

Although the terminology used in the literature is by no means uniform, a certain standardization has been achieved by the recommendations of the Data Base Task Group of the Conference on Data Systems Languages (better known under the acronym *CODASYL DBTG*), which will be mostly followed here. However, in order to illustrate certain concepts, slight deviations will seem appropriate from time to time. This will result in some non-standard terminology, but this will always be 'compatible' with alternative descriptions. It should also be mentioned that the American National Standards Institute (ANSI) has recently published a document describing the US national standard language for the network model called *NDL* (short for 'Network Database Language'; see the Bibliographic Notes).

For an entity declaration, the corresponding notion used in the context of the network model is the (*logical*) **record type**, which is basically comparable to the type declaration of a record in Pascal (see Chapter 2) or COBOL. A (concrete) **record** corresponds to an individual entity. A set of records (of the same type, in analogy to an entity set) is termed a **file** here; this is motivated by the idea of 'implementing' a set of records using a file as the (logical) data structure. A record type is described by a **name** and by **attributes**; the declaration of a (primary) key is considered optional in this model.

To model relationships between record types, this data model exclusively provides binary, $1:n$ relationships without attributes. A corresponding relationship declaration is called a (*logical*) **set type**. Furthermore, if $R = ((E_1, E_2), \emptyset)$ is a relationship declaration of type $1:n$ or a set type (where '$\emptyset$' denotes an empty *sequence* of attributes), E_1 is called the **owner type** (of R) and E_2 its **member type**.

Definition 5.2

A **logical network** is a Bachman diagram whose nodes represent record types, and whose edges represent set types.

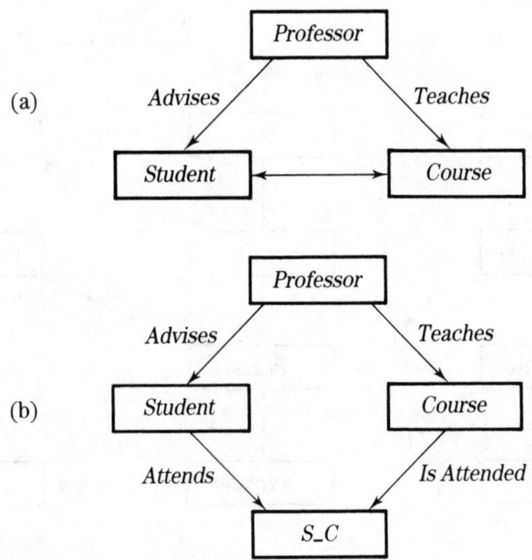

Figure 5.8 An $m : n$ relationship and its network representation.

While a Bachman diagram allows the use of undirected or bidirectional edges to represent $m : n$ relationships, the same is not valid in a logical network, because of the particular characteristics of a set type defined above. Thus, the next goal is to answer the question of how (if at all) such relationships can be modelled in a logical network. The same idea can be applied as that used earlier for representing k-ary relationships (where $k > 2$): introduce a new kett-record type *KE* and replace the $m : n$ relationship between E_1 and E_2 by a $1 : n$ relationship between E_1 and *KE* as well as an $m : 1$ relationship between *KE* and E_2.

As an example, consider the Bachman diagram for a university application shown in Figure 5.8(a). To represent the $m : n$ relationship between *Student* and *Course* in a logical network, it is broken down into two set types that involve the new kett-record type *S_C*. The result is shown in Figure 5.8(b); the record type *S_C* is a member type for the two owner types *Student* and *Course*, which in turn are member types for the same owner type *Professor*.

The transformation of a given ER diagram into a logical network can proceed in two steps:

(1) The ER diagram is transformed into a Bachman diagram; during this step, attributes of relationships are temporarily ignored, and k-ary relationships, where $k > 2$, are replaced by binary ones.

(2) From the resulting Bachman diagram, a logical network is derived

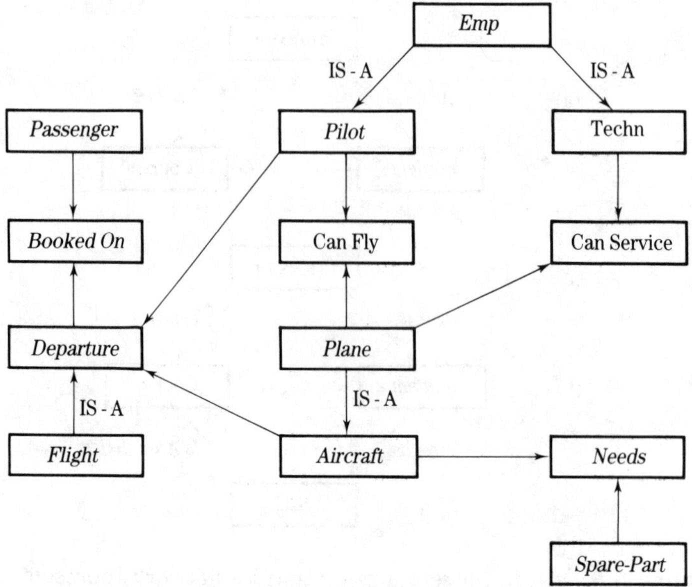

Figure 5.9 Logical network for the airline.

by 'reducing' $m : n$ relationships to $1 : n$ (or $m : 1$) relationships as described above.

If a given $m : n$ relationship originally had attributes, these can be associated with the (newly introduced) kett-record type; thus, the attributes are preserved, but set types remain free of attributes. Similarly, if a $1 : n$ relationship has attributes, another kett-record type can be created, which is used to 'carry' these attributes.

As an example, a logical network for the airline from Figure 5.5 is shown in Figure 5.9. Note that the (new) kett-record types, which replace the former $m : n$ relationships, are here equipped with the names previously used for the relationships, respectively; for purposes of simplification, distinct names for the existing *two* owner-member relationships in these cases are not introduced.

5.2 (Physical) network databases

The representation of a $1 : n$ relationship between two logical record types E_1 and E_2 in a network by an edge that is directed towards E_2 follows common practice. However, some descriptions of the network model represent such a relationship using an edge in the opposite direction, that is, directed from the member type towards its owner type. This is based on the (mathematical) interpretation that the arrow represents a (partial) *function* from E_2^t to E_1^t (for each t), which in some sense is a more correct 'mapping' of the underlying reality. More precisely, from a 'semantic' point of view a set type S with owner type E_1 and member type E_2 denotes a class of functions of the form $S^t : E_2^t \to E_1^t$, whose instances are the equivalence classes $(S^t)^{-1}(e_1) = \{e_2 \in E_2^t \mid S^t(e_2) = e_1 \in E_1^t\}$ with respect to the equivalence relation '$\approx$' defined by

$$e \approx e' \quad \text{if} \quad S^t(e) = S^t(e'),\ e, e' \in E_2^t$$

Nevertheless, the 'method' introduced in the previous section will be used here, since it can be extended straightforwardly to the level of concrete entities or relationships, as will be demonstrated next.

From now on, it will be assumed that a logical network $N = (V_N, E_N)$ is given, whose nodes represent record types, and whose edges represent set types. In order to be consistent with the previous chapter, the notations from Definitions 4.1 and 4.3 will be used for record and set types, respectively, that is:

$$E = (\text{attr}(E), .)$$

for a record type, and

$$R = ((E_1, E_2), \emptyset)$$

for a $(1 : n)$ set type (with owner type E_1 and member type E_2).

To complete the establishment of correspondences between the ER and the network model, a notion of a network **database** is introduced next, which will also be called a 'physical' network. This notion will serve as a model which from a user's point of view describes an (abstract) implementation of a logical network structure, and which at the same time is close to the actual realization of the internal level or a physical database accomplished by a network DBMS. Thus, it is possible to identify a physical network with the internal schema of a corresponding database.

If E_1 and E_2 constitute a set type (of the form $E_1 \to E_2$), the implicit assumption that this type is $1 : n$ implies that (at any time t) a record $e_1 \in E_1^t$ can be related to several records $e_2 \in E_2^t$; in this case, e_1 is called the **owner** (record), and each such e_2 a **member** (record) of a particular **set occurrence**. Clearly, it may happen that some owner record does not 'possess' member records at a particular time; conversely, a member record may currently belong to at most one (or even no) set occurrence. The collection of all set occurrences of the same set type (at time t) is simply called a **set** (over that type).

In conclusion, this gives the list of correspondences in terminology between the ER and the network model shown in Table 5.1.

Table 5.1 Correspondences between ER and network models.

ER model	*Network model*
Entity declaration	(Logical) record type
Entity set	'File' (of records)
Entity	Record
Relationship declaration (binary, $1 : n$)	(Logical) set type
Relationship set	Set
Relationship	Set occurrence

A given logical network, N, can be associated with a graph N^t (at time t), at the level of records and set occurrences, whose set of nodes consists of all records that are present in the 'database' at that time, and in which each edge represents a membership in a set occurrence.

Figure 5.10(a) shows an excerpt from the network shown in Figure 5.8(a); Figure 5.10(b) shows a corresponding graph (for some time t) at the record level.

For working with such a 'database' it will turn out to be helpful to assume that all members of a given set occurrence are (totally) *ordered*; this will make it possible to talk about the 'first', 'second', 'next', or 'last' member of a set occurrence. Figure 5.10(c) shows a correspondingly modified graph for the example from Figure 5.10(b).

In this way, the type declaration '$1 : n$' is now captured graphically as well. Next, if a member-record type is actually a kett-record type, this implies that it is simultaneously a member type of two (or more) owner types. Records over this member type now have to establish the $m : n$ relationship between the records over the owner types that has been observed in the underlying application. The modelling of this situation at the 'physical' level can be illustrated using the $m : n$ relationship between *Student* and *Course* from Figure 5.8; it is assumed that (at time t) the following relationship set is given:

{(U145, CS160), (U145, CS165), (U200, CS165),
(U321, CS165), (U343, CS160), (U343, CS176) }

(Thus, for instance, the student with 'key' U145 is attending the courses with keys CS160 and CS165; course CS165 is attended by students U145, U200 and U321, and so on.)

Following the representation shown in Figure 5.10(b), an 'imple-

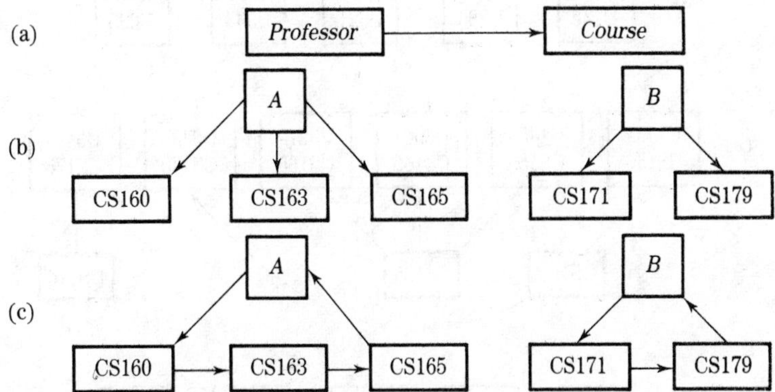

Figure 5.10 A set type with two unordered/ordered occurrences.

mentation' of this relationship in the network model could look as depicted in Figure 5.11(a). If additionally an ordering is imposed on each set occurrence, the representation shown in Figure 5.11(b) will result.

Note that it may also happen (and can be modelled) that a record of one owner type is currently not associated with any record of the second owner type through a set occurrence; this record then forms a *trivial* set occurrence (see, for example, the record denoted U386 in Figure 5.11(b)).

The representation of an IS-A relationship (and of a hierarchical one) at the physical level apparently still causes trouble; the problem is to express the existence constraint implicitly coded by such a relationship appropriately (see Definition 4.5 (ii)). For example, in the airline application, $Pilot \subseteq Emp$ expresses the fact that for each concrete pilot in $Pilot^t$ there exists an entity in Emp^t containing general data about this pilot as an employee. This constraint can be represented in the network model by (i) choosing *Emp* as the owner and *Pilot* as the member type of a corresponding set type (see Figures 5.5 and 5.9), *and* (ii) declaring a particular 'mode of membership' for members (that is, pilots) in a concrete set occurrence in the (yet to be described) definition of this set type.

In the example, a pilot may occur as a record of type *Pilot* in the database only if there already exists an employee (record) for the same person. Hence, a member record can only exist in conjunction with some owner record in this case; in other words, the owner-member relationship has to be *static*. Furthermore, a member record can only be deleted from some set occurrence if it is either inserted into another occurrence of the same type ('*MODIFY*'), or removed from the database completely ('*ERASE*'). For this case, the DBTG recommendations provide the possibility of declaring the member type of a set type as *MANDATORY*. Note that this (and the 'supplement' described next) will not occur in a logical

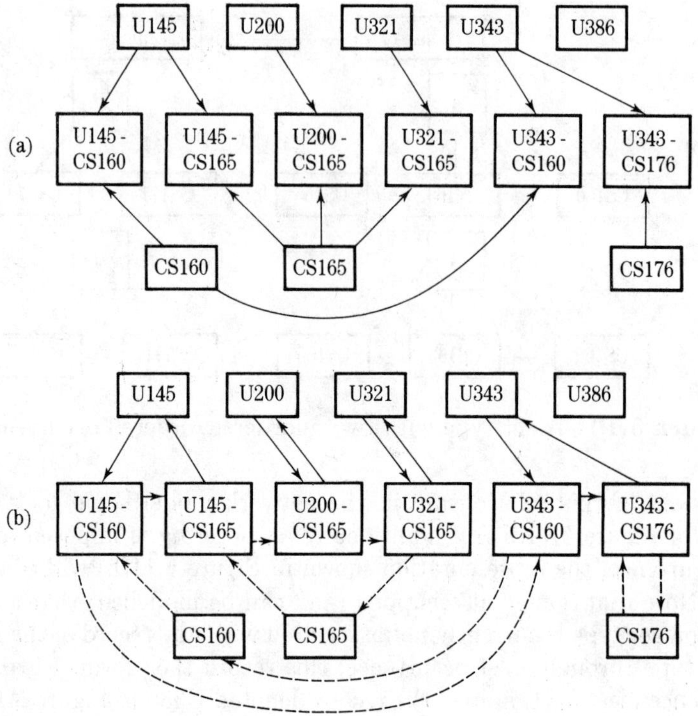

Figure 5.11 An 'implementation' of the *Student-Course* relationship.

network, but only in the corresponding definition of a conceptual schema using the DDL underlying a particular network DBMS.

If now a member record is inserted into a database, the corresponding owner record must exist already (in the case of an IS-A/MANDATORY relationship), or it must be inserted simultaneously. To ensure that the connection between owner and member is indeed established physically, the member type must additionally be declared as *AUTOMATIC*, which means that when inserting a member this will immediately be associated with 'its' owner, so that a new set occurrence is created 'automatically'.

Figure 5.12 shows a valid section of network database regarding pilots and employees of the airline. At this point the reason for choosing to reverse the direction of an arrow representing an IS-A relationship, made during the discussion of Bachman diagrams in Section 5.1, should become clear.

For the sake of completeness, the other 'modes' of set membership for member records which are available in the DBTG recommendations and supported by every network DBMS should be mentioned.

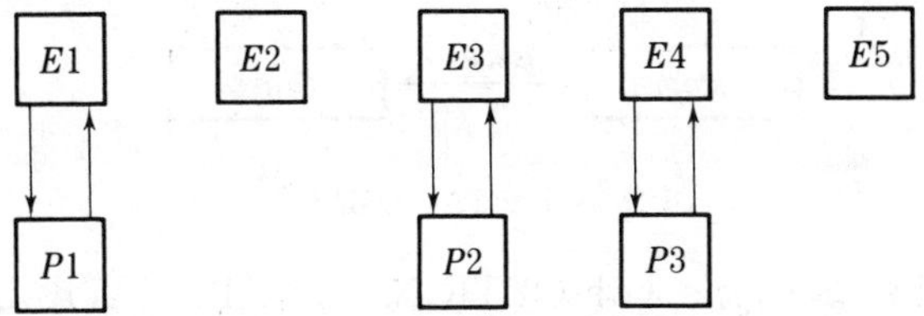

Figure 5.12 'Instance' of the IS-A relationship *Pilot* $\subseteq$ *Emp.*

The two alternatives to MANDATORY are called *OPTIONAL* and *FIXED*, respectively. When the former declaration is used, it is up to the user to establish ('*CONNECT*') or destroy ('*DISCONNECT*') the connection between a member and an owner record; in particular, a connection can be broken without the member record being deleted. When the declaration FIXED is used, a record may not be moved from a set occurrence once it has been placed (stored) there; thus, a record remains associated with the owner (until it is deleted from the database) with which it was connected first.

The 'opposite' of AUTOMATIC is termed *MANUAL*. Under this definition of a member type, a member record is not automatically injected into a set occurrence upon its insertion into the database, but membership in such an occurrence has to be enforced explicitly by a corresponding DML command ('*CONNECT*').

In addition to IS-A relationships, the following are examples of the usage of these options when defining the member type of a set type.

If a *Customer* issues an *Order* (say, to a *Company*), it seems reasonable to associate the corresponding order record with its customer record *automatically*, since an order 'exists' only after it has been issued. If in addition orders that have been settled remain in the database — for example, for statistical purposes — the member type should also be declared as *optional*. Figure 5.13 shows the corresponding logical network. Alternatively, the member type could also be declared as *fixed*, so that an order remains associated with its customer.

The MANUAL option can be used, for example, if a record type is a member type of several set types. Consider the logical network shown in Figure 5.14. Among the employees working on a particular project, one is chosen to be the head. However, not every employee working on a project is also its head; furthermore, the head of a project may change over time, so that it seems reasonable in this case to define the set type *Heading* as MANUAL and OPTIONAL.

This latter discussion of membership options shows that the conceptual description of a network database that can be given using the language of a DBMS (such as the system UDS described in Chapter 14) will often contain more information than a logical network *N* or a 'physi-

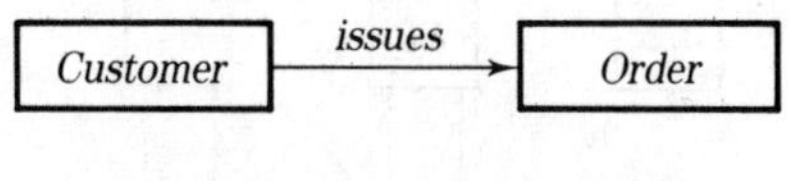

Figure 5.13 Set type with OPTIONAL/AUTOMATIC member type.

cal' one N^t, where N^t denotes the entirety of all records ('over N' at time t) together with their membership within (ordered) set occurrences. Thus, a physical network in particular is a graph (at the 'level of entities'), which in general will have many cycles, and which represents the current contents of a network database. Although this 'definition' does not yet yield a 'storage-mapping', the terms 'physical network' and 'network database' are used interchangeably in this book.

The following discussion of the basics of working with a network database will be based on this model of the physical level.

5.3 Recordwise navigation

This section discusses the principal issues regarding queries to and updates on a network database; as before, the DBTG recommendations will be followed for the most part. Once these issues have been clarified, it will be possible to concentrate on the description of an actual language in Chapter 14, where the network system UDS will be introduced. (In a sense, the 'DB part' of a network DBS is dealt with here, and its 'DBMS part' later.)

A physical network is perceived by the user as a graph, whose nodes invariably represent individual records. Two types of instructions can be applied to such a 'database graph': retrieval of information, and updates on data. The retrieval of data, that is, records (or parts thereof), will be dealt with first. 'Retrieval' essentially means to 'fetch' or to 'read' something from the database (in general according to given search conditions); in a network database, this takes place in two steps. In the first step, a certain record is *accessed*; in the second this record is *made available* (from the database) to the user. The access can be executed either *directly* or

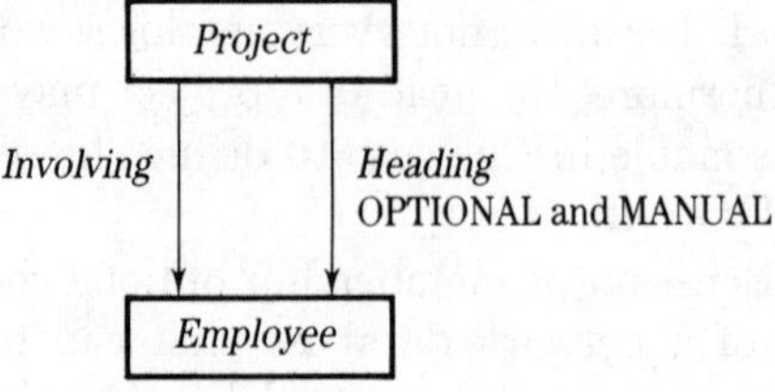

Figure 5.14 Set type with one OPTIONAL/MANUAL member type.

sequentially; in the former case, the desired record can be located instantaneously (via its physical address), while in the latter it is found on the basis of its position within a record ordering. In particular, in this second case the physical network has to be traversed node by node ('*recordwise*', via the edges) until the record in question is reached, a way of retrieval that is generally termed **navigation** through a network database.

The records in a network database must satisfy the following *implementation conditions*:

(1) Each record belongs to exactly one record type; each relationship between two records is of exactly one set type.

(2) Each record is **accessible**, that is, for the (according to (1)) uniquely determined record type to which a record belongs there exists a **key**. The record can either be identified through a given value for this key, or it can be reached via some sequence of set occurrences that starts from a key value for another record; such a starting record is consequently termed an **entry point** (into the database).

It follows that an entry point is always determined by a (value for a) key. However, it is no longer required that this key is defined explicitly (in the sense of the primary key of an entity declaration). As has been mentioned already, there is a file (of records) in the network model corresponding to an entity set of the ER model; this term has been chosen to emphasize its correspondence to the physical realization of a set of records over the same record type. A file can be organized in a variety of ways, which are called **location modes**; in particular, the following modes can be distinguished:

(1) **DIRECT** In this case records are exclusively identified via their (physical) address within the file (system). This implies that an explicit definition of a key (for the corresponding types) is not required; the address of a record is called its **database key**, which is uniquely assigned (by the system) when the record is inserted into the database. A database-key value is usually never changed during the 'lifetime' of a record. In more recent ANSI/NDL terminology, a database key is also called a **cursor**.

(2) **CALC** In this mode a record is located by computing its address from given values for the attributes of a (declared) primary key (often using a hash function). The resulting **CALC key** (value) can then be used to access a record directly like a database key.

(3) **VIA SET** If a record type E is defined with this location mode ('VIA setname SET', see below), it has to be the member type of the set type specified. Each record over E can then be located 'via' the set occurrence in which it appears.

If a record type is defined using the DBTG implementation option

LOCATION MODE IS DIRECT

a value for the database key of a record over this type is created when this record is stored. This value represents the physical address of the record in secondary memory and can therefore be used to access the record *directly* (as was mentioned above).

Alternatively, a user can choose to define a primary key explicitly by saying

LOCATION MODE IS CALC <hash routine>
USING <attribute list>

In this case, <attribute list> consists of the attributes of the key; when a record is stored and hence values for these attributes are supplied, its address can be *calc*ulated using the <hash routine>. In order to access the record, it is again sufficient to supply values for the CALC key; using these, the record can again be located directly.

While a network DBMS typically assigns values for a database key for each record type in a sequential manner and hence stores the records at consecutive addresses, the use of a CALC key generally results in a scattered way of storing according to the particular hash function applied.

Next let E_2 be the member type of a set type R with owner type E_1, then E_2 may be declared with the option

LOCATION MODE IS VIA R SET

This implies that records over E_2 can only be accessed via their occurrence in a set in conjunction with a record over E_1. Each record over E_2 is located via its associated owner record, but no longer directly via a key. Clearly, the use of this option is therefore advisable if access to all members of a particular owner is required frequently.

The association of a (unique) database-key value with every record which is (newly) stored into a network database has an interesting implication: It is possible that *distinct* records exist in a database which have *identical* values for their attributes. Consider, for example, a record type *Person* with attributes *Last_Name*, *First_Name* and *Child*. If *two* records of the form '(Miles, John, Mary)' occur in the corresponding file, the meaning is that two *distinct* persons share the *same* name and both have a child named 'Mary'. Both records can be *identified* via their associated database-key values. As will be seen in Chapter 7, this feature is not available in the relational model, where an 'instance' of a 'type' is a *set* and can therefore not have duplicate elements, even if they are not identical (an 'artificial' key like '*Person_No*' will be needed to distinguish them). In other words, each record stored in a network database has a unique *identity*, a feature that has recently gained new attention in the area of *object-oriented databases* which will be discussed in Chapter 22.

Before it is possible to explain how access to records and navigation through a network database actually take place, some more explanations are needed.

One important concept to be introduced is the (**storage**) **area** (also called **realm** in more recent CODASYL terminology). An area is a named, continuous section of secondary memory that contains a well defined part of a network database. An area is created at the definition time of the database and is also typically used physically to 'cluster' record or set types that are logically related. Note that areas are also a paradigm to implement certain requirements of data safety or security.

In the airline example, the physical realization could, for instance, consist of a partition into three distinct areas, which correspond to the three departments 'personnel', 'machinery' and 'air operations', respectively. Then, for each record type it has to be decided to which area(s) it belongs; records over this type will be stored only in the appropriate storage realm. Set types may be spread over more than one area, for example, with the owner type in one and the member type in another area.

Of central importance for working with a network database is the organization of the run-time environment for the underlying DBMS. First recall the components of a DBMS, which is a main-memory resident program, shown in Figure 3.1. The DBTG recommendations are primarily based on the assumption that a network database is accessed from an application program (with embedded database commands), although 'modern' implementations also provide access through a dialogue language. Such an application program 'uses' the DBMS for the execution of its embedded instructions; in particular, it activates the device and storage manager for physical accesses to the database. The program itself maintains a special workspace within main memory, the **user working area** (UWA), through which it communicates with the DBMS as follows.

DML instructions first 'operate' on the database ('FIND') and then copy records that have been located into the UWA ('GET'); only when this is completed can the program process these records, or modify them and finally initiate their 'return' ('STORE') into the database.

On the one hand this *two-phase process* corresponds to a partitioning of the available DML instructions into instructions that operate exclusively on the database, while others take care of all transfers from the database to the UWA or vice versa. On the other hand, the two phases are reflected in a particular decomposition of the UWA into distinct logical sections. The most important of these sections, the **currency table**, will now be described in more detail; this table among other things makes it possible to access certain records in the underlying database directly (via their database key).

The currency table is a collection of **currency pointers**, each of which contains the physical address (that is, the database key) of some most recently accessed record. All currency pointers are maintained automatically by a network DBMS, that is, initialized and updated appropriately. The values of these pointers, which are database-key values, are available to the application program in question; they are simply used by some commands, but affected by others, as will be discussed shortly.

In detail, for every record type whose name is used in a program (or dialogue) there exists a currency pointer, for every set type used and for each area accessed, as well as for the program itself. The records associated with these respective database-key values are named as follows:

(1) CRR: Current (Record) of Record (type)
For each record type E used, the 'current of E' points to the most recently accessed record over E.

(2) CRS: Current (Record) of Set (type)
For each set type R with owner type E_1 and member type E_2 used, the 'current of R' points to the most recently accessed record within a set occurrence over R; thus it points either to an owner record (over E_1) or to a member record (over E_2).

(3) CRA: Current (Record) of Area
For each area A used, the 'current of A' points to the most recently accessed record within this area.

(4) CRU: Current (Record) of Run Unit
The CRU, also termed the **session cursor** in ANSI's NDL proposal, contains the address of the most recently accessed record of all, where 'run unit' denotes the application program or the dialogue in question. It immediately follows that the CRU most often equals one or more of the other currency pointers maintained.

Figure 5.15 shows the general structure of the 'programming environment' underlying the interaction with a network database. A closer look at this environment, using the two fundamental instructions for the retrieval of data, follows.

When a **FIND** command is issued, some record will be located within the database (according to a condition that must be provided). Next, the (always existing) database-key value of this record is entered into the currency table; as a result, the record becomes the 'current record' of its record type, eventually of a set type, of its storage area, and of the run unit. As long as this address remains in the currency table, the record can be accessed directly.

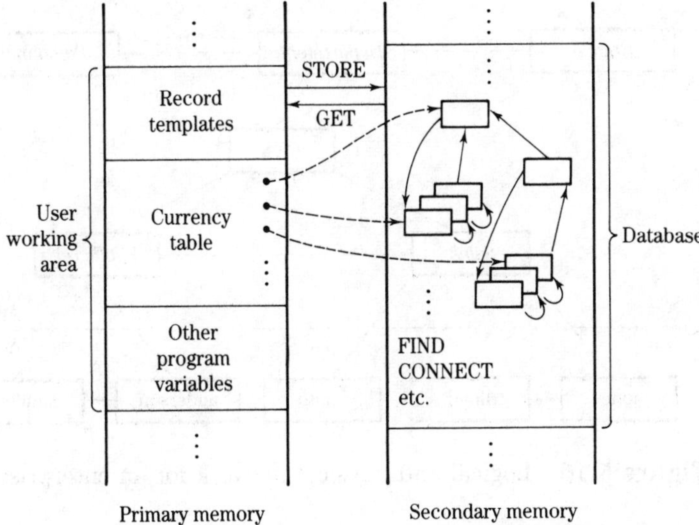

Figure 5.15 User working area vs. network database.

As an example, consider the logical network shown in Figure 5.16(a) for some enterprise; Figure 5.16(b) shows a current instance of the corresponding database. Here it is assumed that the record type *Department* [*Personnel*] has been assigned to area *A* [*B*]. Table 5.2 shows the contents of the currency table corresponding to this example, and how it changes depending on the different FIND commands shown; all pointers are assumed to be initialized to 'nil', and for simplicity database-key values and records are identified.

By a **GET** command a previously located record is made available in the UWA by copying it from the database, in order subsequently to display it onto a screen, to process it further within the application program, or to modify certain values of the record. This command is executed by the DBMS by first retrieving the current value of the CRU from the currency table, next accessing the record found under this address, and finally placing a copy of it in the UWA; thus, the value of the CRU must have been set appropriately by a preceding FIND command.

A further illustration of the use of FIND and GET is found in the section of the university application from Figure 5.8(b) shown in Figure 5.11(b); it is now assumed that record type *Student* has attributes *Id*, *Name* and *Addr*, and that record type *Course* has attributes *Course#* and *Title*. In addition, let a record type *S_C* be declared with attributes *Id* and *Course#* (establishing a relationship between students and courses), as well as the set types *Attends* with owner type *Student* and member type *S_C*, and *Is_Attended* with owner type *Course* and member type *S_C*. The

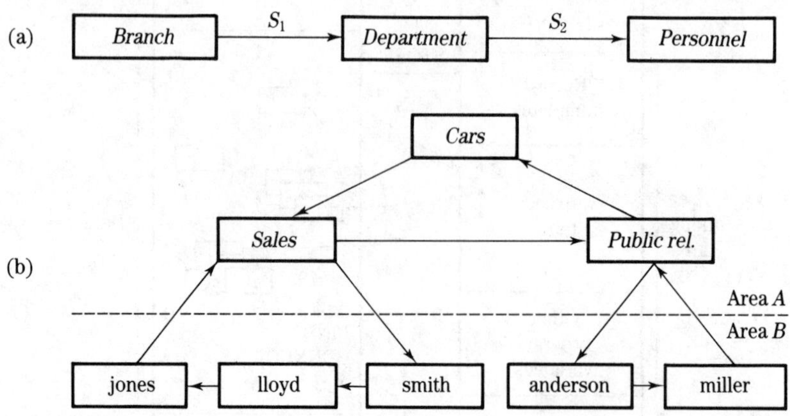

Figure 5.16 Logical and physical network for an enterprise.

possible modes of access can now be described.

5.3.1 Direct access at the level of record types

A direct access is performed by using either the database key or the CALC key. The values for this key must be provided by the user within that part of the UWA that is reserved for records (the 'record-template section'), that is, either a database key is specified explicitly, or values for the attributes of the CALC key are given. For example, if *S* denotes a template within the UWA that is reserved for storing records over *Students* temporarily (that is, an auxiliary record-variable of type *Student*), and if *Id* serves as the CALC key, the record describing the student whose id is U145 is located by the following sequence of instructions:

S.Id := 'U145';
FIND *Student* BY CALC KEY;

A subsequent

GET *Student*; *Name*

will copy the student's name into *S.Name.*

The next example illustrates the usage of the database key during direct access. The Current of *Student* is to be copied from the database into the UWA; let *X* be a variable in the UWA:

X := CRR-*Student*;
FIND *Student* BY DATABASE KEY *X*;
GET *Student*;

Table 5.2 A currency table and its relationship to FIND.

		Instruction				
		FIND smith	FIND jones	FIND sales	FIND public rel.	FIND anderson
CRU	nil	smith	jones	sales	public rel.	anderson
CRA						
Area A	nil	nil	nil	sales	public rel.	public rel.
Area B	nil	smith	jones	jones	jones	anderson
CRS						
S_1	nil	nil	nil	sales	public rel.	public rel.
S_2	nil	smith	jones	sales	public rel.	anderson
CRR						
Branch	nil	nil	nil	nil	nil	nil
Dept.	nil	nil	nil	sales	public rel.	public rel.
Personnel	nil	smith	jones	jones	jones	anderson

(The 'network language' used here, and in particular the syntax of FIND and GET as well as that of other commands used below, is primarily oriented on the DBTG recommendations; minor deviations may occur for concrete languages such as the UDS language introduced later.)

5.3.2 Sequential access at the level of record types

Since a CALC key is in general calculated by a hash routine, it may happen that distinct records possess the same CALC key value (which can be avoided by an option in the definition of a record type). In this case it is possible to retrieve all records with the same value for the CALC key by *scanning* the corresponding file; thus, a scan returns all records yielding a particular 'hash collision'. In the running example, let *Name* become the CALC key of *Student*; the following 'procedure' will retrieve all students named 'Miller':

```
S.Name := 'Miller';
FIND Student BY CALC KEY;
while not eof do
begin
    GET Student;
    FIND DUPLICATE WITHIN Student BY CALC KEY
end;
```

If an ordering has been declared among the records of type *Student*, a scan of the entire file can be performed as follows:

```
FIND FIRST Student;
while not eof do
begin
    GET Student; Name;
    FIND NEXT Student;
end;
```

5.3.3 Direct access at the level of set types

The next example determines the number of each course which the student whose id is U145 attends. To this end, the corresponding set occurrence for this student record has to be located first; after that, its members are scanned sequentially. The *S_C* template is initialized appropriately, and then it can be proceeded as follows:

```
S_C.Id := 'U145';
FIND S_C WITHIN Attends USING S_C.Id;
while not eof do
begin
    GET S_C; Course#;
    FIND DUPLICATE S_C WITHIN Attends USING S_C.Id;
end;
```

By the first command in this sequence, the value U145 is assigned to the *Id*-field of the UWA variable *S_C*; the first FIND command consequently locates a record whose *Id*-field matches this value. Next, the **while** loop covers the case that the student with id U145 attends several courses. If the record corresponding to this student has been accessed previously and the CRS-*Attends* has not been changed in the meantime, the sole issuing of the FIND command appearing in the **while** loop would locate a record which is different from the one pointed to by the CRS, but which shares the same *Id*-value.

5.3.4 Sequential access at the level of set types

This final way of access was mentioned in Section 5.3.3 in the form of a FIND DUPLICATE embedded into a **while** loop. In addition to this, it is possible to make use of an ordering imposed on the set occurrences of some set type (see also Section 5.3.2). The determination of the *Titles* of all courses which U145 attends provides a detailed example. The following is a 'program' that retrieves the desired records; the reader should verify that this is indeed correct, and that the currency pointers used do indeed have the contents given as comments:

```
S.Id := 'U145';
FIND Student BY CALC KEY;
(* CRU = U145, CRR-Student = U145, CRS-Attends = U145 *)
FIND NEXT S_C WITHIN CURRENT Attends;
(* CRU = U145-CS160, CRS-Attends = U145-CS160,
CRS-Is_Attended = U145-CS160 *)
FIND OWNER OF CURRENT Is_Attended;
(* CRS-Is_Attended = CS160, CRR-Course = CS160 *)
GET Course; Title;
FIND NEXT S_C WITHIN CURRENT Attends;
(* CRS-Attends = U145-CS165, CRS-Is_Attended = U145-CS165 *)
FIND OWNER OF CURRENT Is_Attended;
GET Course; Title;
```

Clearly, this program will only work exactly for the 'state' shown in Figure 5.11(b); more realistically, if it is not known in advance how many courses a given student attends, a **while** loop as shown below has to be used. In this case, the 'cycle' formed by a set occurrence is scanned sequentially; if the owner of this occurrence is reached for the second time (meaning that the cycle scan is completed), this is indicated by the system setting a *fail* flag:

```
S.Id := 'U145';
FIND Student BY CALC KEY;
while not fail do
begin
    FIND NEXT S_C WITHIN CURRENT Attends;
    FIND OWNER OF CURRENT Is_Attended;
    GET Course; Title;
end;
```

In conclusion, the FIND statement can be used to perform the following types of accesses:

(1) Find a record via its database key.

(2) Find a record, given a value for its CALC key.

(3) Scan a file of records, and find all records within that file with a given CALC key value.

(4) Scan all members of a set occurrence.

(5) Find certain members of a set occurrence.

(6) Find the owner of a record in a set occurrence.

(7) Find the 'current record' of a set type (using 'FIND CURRENT OF <set-type-name>' not explained above) or of a record type ('FIND CURRENT OF <record-type-name>'), thus making a CRS or a CRR the CRU.

The corresponding versions of the FIND statements are summarized below (in an abbreviated form):

(1) FIND ... BY DATABASE KEY

(2) FIND ... BY CALC KEY

(3) FIND NEXT [USING] / FIND DUPLICATE ... WITHIN ... BY ...

(4) FIND FIRST/NEXT ... WITHIN CURRENT ...

(5) FIND FIRST/NEXT ... WITHIN CURRENT ... USING .../ FIND DUPLICATE ... WITHIN CURRENT ... USING

(6) FIND OWNER ...

(7) FIND CURRENT ...

Finally, it should be mentioned that there also exists a fifth type of (sequential) access at the level of areas; here, the CRAs can be utilized in a completely similar way.

It should also be noted that concrete implementations of a network DBMS, in particular those following the ANSI document on NDL, will show deviations in syntax from the 'language' described above. In particular, the FIND command might be augmented by a *WHERE clause* (similar to the WHERE clause in a SELECT statement of the relational language SQL, see Chapter 16, and also similar to the IF clause in a FIND statement of the UDS language, see Chapter 14), which allows a search condition to be directly included in a FIND statement (as opposed to the preparation of record templates used above, which are then referred to by a FIND). An analogous simplification applies to several of the update instructions discussed in the next section.

5.4 Database updates

Besides queries, updates also play a fundamental role in everyday work with a database. This section introduces this kind of user instruction to a network database. The term 'update' collectively refers to an insertion, a modification, or a deletion of a record; in the case of a physical network, it further refers to updates at the level of a file, and, more generally, to updates at the level of a set occurrence.

Note that it is *always* assumed here that a user *is allowed* to perform all the updates (and in particular modifications or deletions) described below; the related problem of granting access rights will be dealt with later.

Using again the model of the programming environment described in the previous section, recordwise updates will be discussed next. Recall the 'set-insertion options' (or 'Connect options') AUTOMATIC and MANUAL, and the 'set-retention options' (or 'Disconnect options') MANDATORY, OPTIONAL and FIXED from Section 5.2; these are briefly summarized here, since it is now possible to fill in some previously missing details:

(1) AUTOMATIC: A new member record is automatically inserted into a set occurrence (the one determined by the corresponding CRS) when it is stored.

(2) MANUAL: A new member record has to be inserted to the desired set occurrence explicitly (by CONNECT).

(3) MANDATORY: A member record can only be removed from a set occurrence if it is either deleted from the database or (immediately) reinserted into another occurrence; thus, the record is always a member of some occurrence.

(4) OPTIONAL: A member record can be deleted from a set occurrence (DISCONNECT), but remain in the database; whether a record is connected to an occurrence or not is determined by the user.

(5) FIXED: A member record can only be removed from the set occurrence in which it has been stored if it is deleted from the database; thus, the record always remains a member of the same occurrence.

A record is inserted into a network database by using the **STORE** instruction. Before it can be stored, however, it has to be created within the UWA under the name of a corresponding variable (template); after this, it can be transferred into the database by

STORE <record-type-name>

(Thus, the STORE operation is in a sense complementary to the GET operation.) The record in question thereby becomes the CRR of its type, the CRU, and the CRS of each set type in which this record type appears either as owner or as member type; for example, if the record type is owner type of R_1, the new record becomes the owner of a (new, currently trivial) set occurrence. Similarly, if the record type is member type of R_2 and declared as AUTOMATIC with respect to insertions, the record is automatically inserted into a set occurrence over R_2; the selection of the appropriate occurrence is made according to a **set selection** clause, which has to be provided at definition time, and which can have one of the following forms:

(1) SET SELECTION IS THRU CURRENT OF SET

(2) SET SELECTION IS THRU LOCATION MODE OF OWNER

In case (1), the new record will be inserted into the set occurrence determined by the corresponding CRS. In case (2), it is necessary for the owner type to be declared of location mode DIRECT or CALC, where in the latter case the occurrence of duplicates must additionally be excluded.

If a record type has been defined as MANUAL member type of a set type, a record over this type can only be inserted into a set occurrence by an explicit use of the **CONNECT** command. As an example, consider the student database from Figure 5.11(b) (with the attributes that were used in Section 5.3) and the goal to store a new record over *S_C* carrying the information that student U386 attends course CS165; assume that *S_C* is MANUAL member type of *Attends*:

```
S_C.Course# := 'CS165';
S_C.Id := 'U386';
STORE S_C;
S.Id := 'U386';
FIND Student BY CALC KEY;
CONNECT S_C TO Attends;
```

Note that a CONNECT instruction simply connects the CRU to the set occurrence referenced by some CRS (maintaining the order of the occurrence if one is defined).

Similarly, the CRU is disconnected from a particular set occurrence by the **DISCONNECT** command; here it is required that the type of the CRU record is not declared as MANDATORY or FIXED and AUTOMATIC member type in the corresponding set type.

The **ERASE** command deletes the record determined by the CRU from a database; this record is simultaneously deleted from all set occurrences in which it appears.

Finally, the **MODIFY** command is available for changing the record referred to by the CRU. Here, 'change' can mean that some attribute values of the record are updated, or that the record is transferred from one set occurrence to another. As an example for the former case, let student U343 move from El Cajon to La Jolla; the corresponding update of attribute *Addr* is performed as follows:

```
S.Id := 'U343';
FIND Student BY CALC KEY;
```

Table 5.3 Types of set membership *versus* update commands.

		Type of set membership					
		MAND AUTO	MAND MAN	OPT AUTO	OPT MAN	FIX AUTO	FIX MAN
Membership is established by	STORE	yes	no	yes	no	yes	no
	CONNECT	no	yes	yes	yes	yes	yes
Membership is cancelled by	ERASE	yes	yes	yes	yes	yes	yes
	DISCONNECT	no	no	yes	yes	no	no
Alternation between set occurrences	MODIFY	yes	yes	yes	yes	no	no

S.Addr := 'La Jolla';
MODIFY *Student*; (or MODIFY *Student*; *Addr*;)

As an example for the latter case, let student U343 replace U145 in the kett-record (U145, CS165), that is, this record is modified to (U343, CS165):

C.Course# := 'CS165';
FIND *Course* BY CALC KEY;
FIND NEXT *S_C* WITHIN CURRENT *Is_Attended*;
S_C.Id := 'U343';
MODIFY *S_C*;

Again it is assumed that *C* is a UWA variable for *Course*, and that *Course#* is the CALC key of this record type. The corresponding set occurrences will then be modified appropriately.

Finally, the interdependencies between types of set membership and the update commands described above are summarized in Table 5.3.

Chapter 6
The Hierarchical Data Model

This chapter briefly introduces the hierarchical data model, which is historically the 'oldest' of the data models presented in this Part. A major motivation to develop this model was to devise a convenient way for processing data records of variable length.

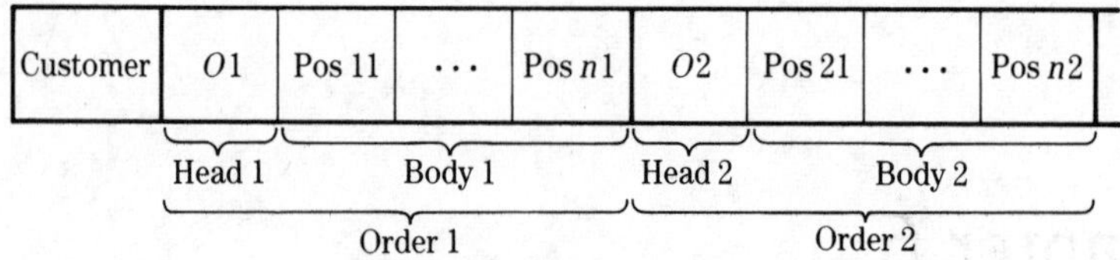

Figure 6.1 A (variable-length) customer record.

A record of variable length is characterized by the fact that the number of fields may vary from one record to another, as in the following example. The customer file of a company contains information about customers, the orders placed by them, and the invoices that have been mailed already. It is assumed that each order or invoice consists of a head and a body, respectively, where the body may contain one or more positions. Thus, an individual customer record might look as shown in Figure 6.1.

Observe that this situation cannot be modelled directly using the tools introduced so far, since, for example, in the network model every record type is required to have a *fixed* format. On the other hand, it can be stated that apparently there exists a $1:n$ relationship between customers and orders as well as between customers and invoices; in addition, for each individual order or invoice of a customer, there exists a $1:n$ relationship between its head and the positions in its body, respectively. Furthermore, all these relationships are hierarchical in nature (in the sense defined in Chapter 4); for example, the positions in the body of an order cannot exist without a concrete order.

These observations suggest the following representation of this situation: the hierarchical $1:n$ relationships are modelled explicitly by introducing a separate record type for each 'repeating group'; for the above example, the result of this step is shown in Figure 6.2. In this way, a *hierarchy* or a *tree* is obtained, whose nodes represent (in network model terminology) logical record types, and whose edges represent logical set

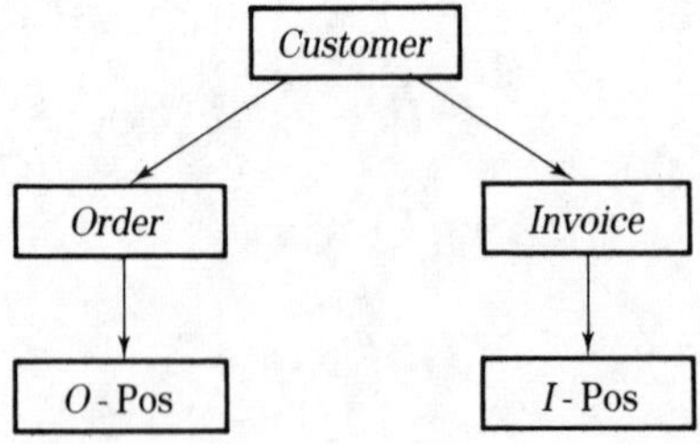

Figure 6.2 (Logical) representation of variable-length records as a hierarchy.

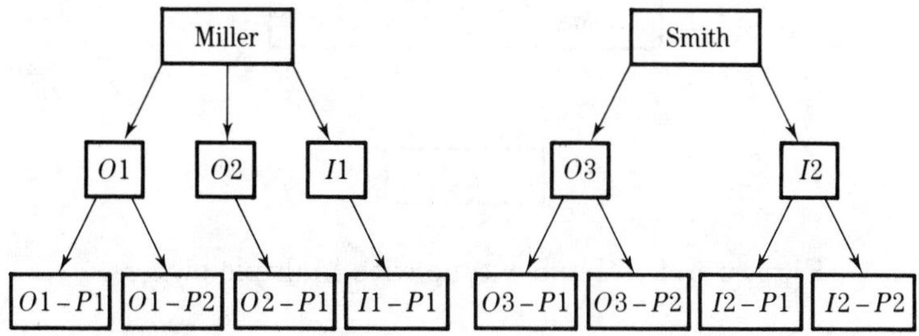

Figure 6.3 A forest representing a hierarchy at the physical level.

types, which are hierarchical in the direction from the 'father' to the 'son'. (In Chapter 21 a completely different way — the *nested* relational model — will be presented to represent records of variable-length format.)

At the physical level of records (in continuation of the analogy to the network model) a set of trees, that is, a *forest*, can be associated with such a hierarchy; an example is shown in Figure 6.3.

As was done for set occurrences in a physical network in the previous chapter, it is assumed that all sons of a father are *ordered*, for example, according to order or position numbers in the above example.

Clearly, only a root-record type or root record may exist 'independently' in a ('logical' or 'physical') tree; any 'set membership' hence is of type MANDATORY (in DBTG terminology).

This concludes the description of the basic characteristics of the **hierarchical data model**. At the logical level, an application is represented in this model exclusively by (a forest of) hierarchies; at the physical level, to each (logical) tree again corresponds a forest, for which the following holds: all relationships appearing in this forest are *total*, that is, if E_2 is a son of E_1, then (at any time t) a record $e_2 \in E_2^t$ belongs to some record $e_1 \in E_1^t$. In addition, logical relationships are unnamed and do not possess attributes. (This latter condition actually does not impose a restriction; since the tree property implies that there can exist at most one relationship between two record types, the attributes can always be associated with the son type.)

In order to establish a (logical) forest of hierarchies, we can in principle first generate an ER diagram for the application in question, and next transform this into a logical network. Thus, it is assumed in what follows that the application to be represented in the hierarchical model is given as a network, that is, a directed graph. In general, this graph, which already contains binary relationships only, will not yet be a tree; in particular it may include kett-record types (representing an $m : n$ relationship) which are member type (son) of two owner types (fathers).

As an example, consider the students database from Figure 5.8(b). In the logical network, the kett type *S_C* is member type of both *At-*

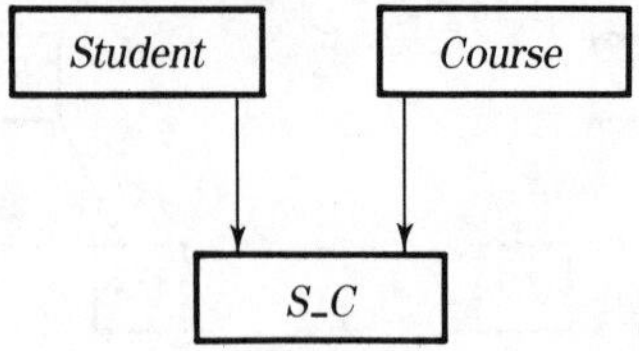

Figure 6.4 Member type with multiple owners.

tends and *Is_Attended*; hence it has *Student* and *Course* as its fathers (see Figure 6.4).

A first possibility to represent such a situation in the hierarchical model could be to transform this (sub-)network into hierarchy by duplicating record types, as shown in Figure 6.5. The problem with this approach is that the fundamental 'database principle' of avoiding redundancy among data (see Chapter 2) is violated.

The approach just described was originally used in the hierarchical model. Besides the problem of introducing redundancy, however, there exists another drawback that will be discussed in greater detail later when ways to query a hierarchical database are presented: a physical hierarchy can always be traversed starting from the root only. Here it is assumed that each record type is associated with exactly one hierarchy in a unique way. If — as in the example above — records over the same type(s) should now be processed in different contexts, the corresponding record type must be included in (at least two) distinct logical hierarchies and therefore be formally treated as a new record type each time it occurs.

For these reasons, a different approach is actually chosen for transforming a graph into a tree: if a situation like the one shown in Figure 6.4 occurs, the corresponding 'son type' will be duplicated (see Figure 6.5), but each copy will represent a **virtual record type**. At the physical level, 'son records' are only stored in the hierarchy in which the 'real' type appears at the logical level; all 'virtual occurrences' of this type will be realized only by pointers which contain the 'address' of an associated 'real' record.

Figure 6.6(a) shows the application from Figure 6.4 once again, now in a hierarchical model extended by virtual record types; Figure 6.6(b)

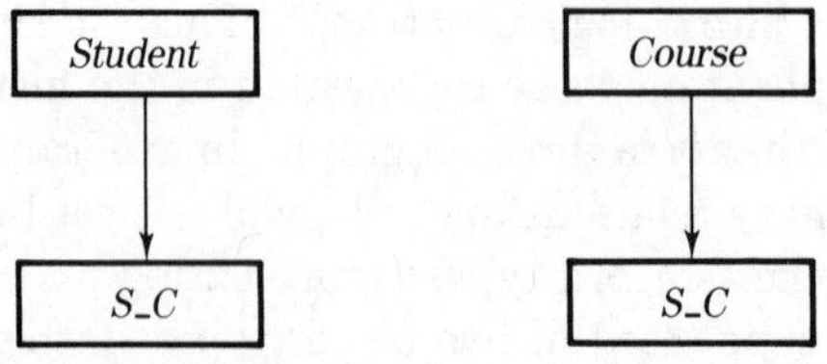

Figure 6.5 Duplicating sons to cope with multiple fathers/owners.

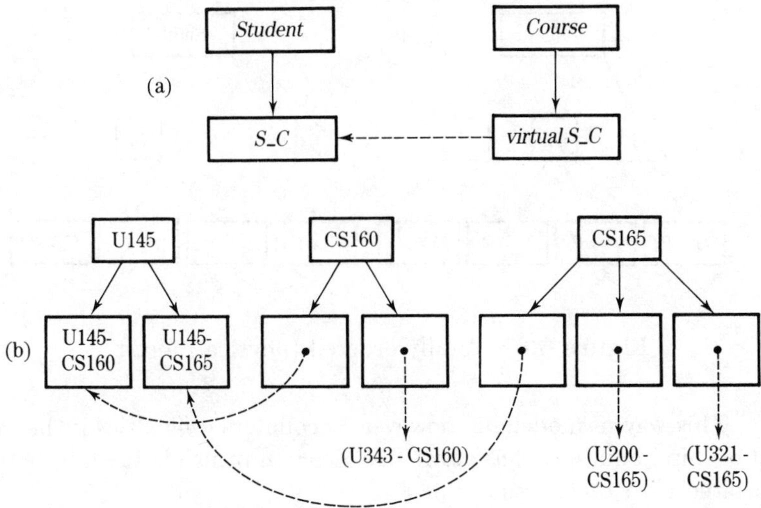

Figure 6.6 Use of virtual record types.

shows a section from Figure 5.11(b) in the corresponding representation at the physical level. Using virtual record types, it can be guaranteed that every record is stored at most once. In addition, distinct hierarchies can now be connected via pointers, so that in particular one hierarchy may appear as part of another (which, however, is transparent to the user).

The above mentioned 'traversal' of a hierarchy starting from the root only can — in particular for $m : n$ relationships — be circumvented in both directions using virtual record types. As an example, consider the fragment *Aircraft Needs Spare-Part* from the Bachman diagram shown in Figure 5.5. For each record type, an additional virtual type is introduced, as shown in Figure 6.7. This renders it possible to directly determine all spare parts needed by an aircraft as well as the aircrafts in need of every spare part.

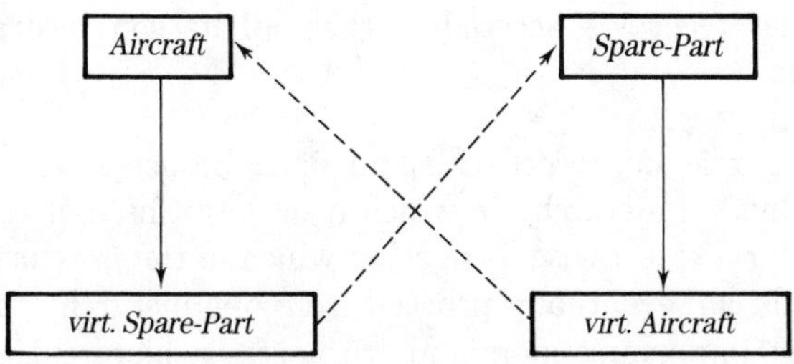

Figure 6.7 Two virtual record types modelling an $m : n$ relationship.

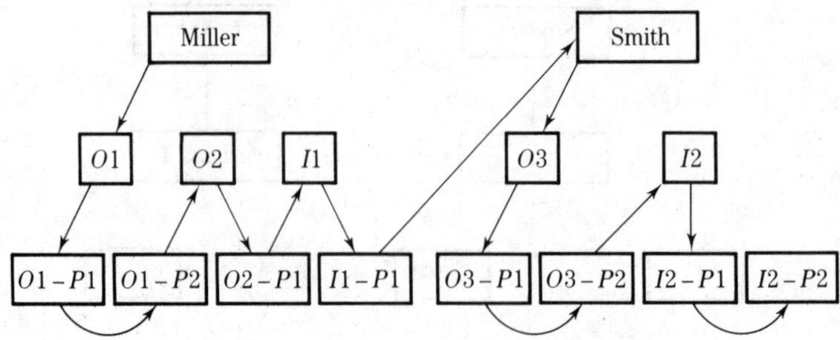

Figure 6.8 Totally ordered (physical) forest.

This way of modelling, however, encounters difficulties if the $m : n$ relationship in question has attributes, since in principle these have to be associated with *each* virtual type.

Besides the already mentioned ordering among the sons of the same father in a physical hierarchy, it is additionally assumed for working with a hierarchical database that an ordering exists for each record type, which implies that *all* records in the database can be (linearly) ordered. In this way it becomes possible to traverse each individual physical hierarchy, beginning at its root, in a standard order of succession, which corresponds to a 'root-left-right' traversal of binary trees (first visit the root, then the left subtree, then the right subtree, and repeat this recursively for all subtrees). Figure 6.8 shows a corresponding ordering for the forest from Figure 6.3.

In addition to these assumptions, it is required with regard to queries and updates that a primary key is defined for every root-record type of a logical hierarchy. Furthermore, as for network database records, every record in a hierarchical database must be *accessible* as follows:

(1) Every root record is accessible either via its primary key, or according to the sequencing given by the (overall) order (see the root of the second hierarchy in Figure 6.8).

(2) If a father record is accessible, then all its son records are also accessible.

Thus, a particular record can and must be accessed via the root record of the physical hierarchy in which it occurs; this root record forms an entry point for a recordwise navigation which in the presence of virtual (pointer) records can eventually proceed from one hierarchy to another.

The most important commands to access a hierarchical database can now be described. The language DL/I of the IMS system by IBM is used for this purpose and will be described in some more detail in Chapter

15. IMS is the best-known hierarchical DBMS, so that the use of DL/I is not really a specialization.

The strict distinction between a user working area and the database, described in the previous chapter, is basically unknown in the context of the hierarchical model; therefore, the GET commands introduced next correspond to a FIND/GET sequence of the DBTG recommendations.

As a running example, the students database (see Figure 6.6) is used once more. A particular record access always starts in a root; from there, a path can be traversed. The commands to do so are the following:

(1) **Get Unique** (GU)
accesses a particular record; the path from the corresponding root to this record must be specified exactly, as for example in:

GU *Student* (*Id* = 'U145') *S_C*

Using this instruction, the *first* son (U145-CS160) of U145 is retrieved. The *next* son of some father is retrieved as described next.

(2) **Get Next within Parent** (GNP)
access the next son for the same father; for example, all courses which U145 attends are retrieved by:

GU *Student* (*Id* = 'U145') *S_C*;
while not fail do GNP *S_C*;

(Here it is assumed that 'fail' serves a purpose similar to that served during navigation through a network.)

(3) **Get Next** (GN)
accesses the next record according to the total ordering described above; for example, all courses which U145 and U200 attend are retrieved by:

GU *Student* (*Id* = 'U145') *S_C*;
while not fail do GNP;
GN *S_C*; (* retrieves the next record over *S_C* and hence the next
 but one — see Figure 5.11(b) — in this case,
 according to the ordering *)
while not fail do GNP;

(4) Additional DL/I commands to be mentioned at this point are (see Chapter 15 for further details):

Get Hold Unique (GHU)

Get Hold Next (GHN)
Get Hold Next within Parent (GHNP)
The effects of these commands correspond to their versions without 'Hold'; the use of this option results in a 'holding' of the record in question for a subsequent deletion or modification.

(5) **Insert** (ISRT) : Insertion of a new record
Delete (DLET) : Deletion of a record
Replace (REPL) : Modification of a record
As an example, in order to delete record U145–CS160 from the database, the following commands can be issued:

GHU *Student* (*Id* = 'U145') *S_C*;
DLET;

Bibliographic Notes

The Entity-Relationship model was originally introduced by Chen (1976); other papers by Chen on this model include Chen (1980, 1985), and Dogac and Chen (1983). These and other references, like Chen (1983), Batini and Lenzerini (1984), Batini and Santucci (1980), and Elmasri and Navathe (1989), show that it is no longer appropriate to talk about 'the' ER model nowadays, since the original has undergone a variety of additions, extensions and modifications, each of which actually yields a new model. Approaches to deal with this model formally can be found, for instance, in Casanova and de Sa (1983) or Ng and Paul (1980).

Although the ER model has not yet been used as the foundation of a commercially available implementation, several authors discuss the design and features of high-level languages based on this model. Examples include Atzeni and Chen (1983), Campbell et al. (1985), Elmasri and Larson (1985), Lusk and Overbeek (1980), and Roesner (1985). Two particular examples of such languages that are available as experimental systems are *ERLANG*, see Malhotra et al. (1986), and *ERROL*, see Markowitz and Raz (1983) and Raz (1987a,b).

More important here is the use of the ER model as a basis for conceptual database design. The approach of first establishing an ERD and then translating this into another model is also proposed, for example, by Chen (1985), Korth and Silberschatz (1986), Ullman (1988), and Elmasri and Navathe (1989). Some authors already propose automated tools that are based on this 'design method'; the reader is referred to Atzeni et al. (1983), Batini et al. (1985), and Tamassia et al. (1983).

Bachman diagrams are named after Charles W. Bachman, who discussed the problem of 'database navigation' in Bachman (1973). For this logical data model, the reader is also referred to Clemons (1985) and Kroenke (1983).

The major basis of the network model are the reports by CODASYL (1971, 1978). The DBTG activities during the 1970s are surveyed by Kroenke (1983); ANSI (1984) describes a preliminary version of the NDL standard for network languages, which was finally approved in 1986; Grant (1987) gives a description of this language, including new features like the insertion option STRUCTURAL and the direct usage of a WHERE condition in a FIND statement. Further information on this data model is provided, for instance, by McFadden and Hoffer (1988), Date (1986), Hevner and Yao (1985), Taylor and Frank (1976), and Ullman (1988). These books also contain additional material on the hierarchical model, for which the reader is also referred to Clemons (1985) and Hubbard (1985).

Bibliographic Notes

Exercises

(1) A car dealer has a certain stock of cars as well as a body of regular customers. Cars have the following properties: type (model), variant of equipment ('SE', 'GTE', 'XI', etc.), id number of chassis and engine, engine type, cylinder capacity, horsepower, and price. Customers are characterized by name, address, phone number, and a period of time for which this dealer has served them. For both 'classes of entities', give a corresponding entity declaration and two entity sets each (for distinct times t_1 and t_2).

(2) For the application described in Exercise 1 define a relationship 'currently drives' between customers and cars by stating (i) a corresponding relationship declaration that includes the new attribute 'date of purchase', and (ii) two distinct relationship sets.

(3) For each of the following possible relationship types between entities, give two examples not mentioned in the text: $1:1$; $1:n$; $m:n$; $1:n$ and recursive; $m:n$ and recursive; $1:1$ and hierarchical; $1:n$ and hierarchical; $1:n$ and IS-A.

(4) The database of a supermarket can informally be described as follows:

(a) For each employee, his or her id number, name, address and department are stored.
(b) For each department, its name, employees, manager and the articles offered are accumulated.
(c) For each article offered, its name, supplier and sale price as well as two id numbers (one provided by the supplier, the other by the supermarket) are kept on file.
(d) For each supplier, a name, address and the items delivered to the supermarket (together with their prices) are stored.

Describe this application in the language of the ER model and draw an ER diagram.

(5) In a university database, information on the following is to be kept:

(a) faculty (name, department, title, office, extension, email address)
(b) staff (name, department, job, extension)

(c) graduate students (id, name, address, previous degree, program enrolled for)
(d) undergraduate students (id, name, address, year, major)
(e) teaching assistants (id, name, quarter, course)
(f) readers (id, name, quarter, course, hours)
(g) course (id, title, day, hour, room)
(h) review sections (course id, TA, day, hour, room)

The following constraints apply: professors have a teaching assistant (TA) for each course they teach. A TA (reader) must be a graduate (undergraduate) student. TAs hold review sections for some (currently given) courses. Several readers can be assigned to one course and/or review section. All students (and hence TAs and readers) attend courses.

Develop an ER diagram for this application.

(6) The ERD for the airline shown in Figure 4.3 is to be augmented according to the following specification:

(a) Further 'special' employees of the airline are *Flight Attendants* who can be assigned to a particular *Departure*. For each flight attendant, his or her overtime is recorded.
(b) Any *Trouble* that has occurred for some *Aircraft* is recorded. Keeping this additional information implies that *Spare-Parts* are no longer needed by an aircraft, except in relation to some trouble an aircraft got into. Any such case is characterized by some identification, a short description of the kind of trouble, the date of its (last) occurrence, and the total number of all occurrences in the past.
(c) Each case of *Trouble* is *Taken Care* of by some *Service Team*; any such team has an id (see *Technician*) and a certain number of members. Each team also *Services* certain *Aircraft*, where a particular service is characterized by a code, a date, and a number of working hours.

Complete the ERD for the airline accordingly.

(7) In Definition 4.1, the possibility that the primary key of an entity declaration is empty was not included. However, there are situations in which an entity declaration cannot be assigned 'sufficiently many' attributes to form a key. Such a declaration is called *weak*, and entities over it are correspondingly termed **weak entities** (as opposed to *strong* ones possessing a key). Clearly, a weak entity does not exist in isolation, but is always related to some strong entity via an existence constraint. Give an example of an application where the concept of weak entities makes sense; draw a corresponding ERD, using doubly lined rectangles to represent weak declarations.

(8) In some situations, there might even be a need to represent a relationship between relationships (not only between entities). As an example, consider *Students* who *Work* on certain *Assignments*, and who *Use* a lab

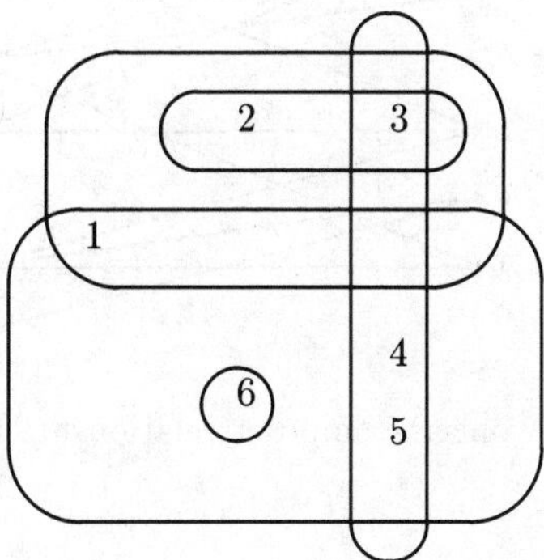

Figure E.1 Hypergraph for Exercise 10.

of *Computers* for this work. This can be represented by two relationship declarations: *Work* (involving *Students* and *Assignments*), and *Use* (involving *Students*, *Assignments* and *Computers*). In principle, it would be desirable to combine the two, in order to avoid the storing of redundant information. However, logically it might be desirable to keep the destinction. A solution to this problem is to use **aggregation**, a kind of abstraction that allows to treat relationship declarations together with 'their' entity declarations as a new entity declaration. In the example above, *Students*, *Works*, and *Assignments* could be aggregated into *WORK*, which remains related to *Computers* via *Use*.

Give two more examples where aggregation is useful, and develop a way to represent aggregated objects in an ERD such that their 'inner structure' remains visible.

(9) Extend the transformation of an ER diagram to the network model described in Chapter 5 to capture weak entity declarations and aggregated objects as well.

(10) In a Bachman diagram the use of 'composed' nodes can be avoided by using **hypergraphs** to represent logical structures. A hypergraph $H = (N, K)$ consists of a set N of nodes and a set K of **hyperedges**, which are *arbitrary* non-empty subsets of N. Here, 'arbitrary' in particular means that the edges need not necessarily connect exactly two nodes, as is the case for ordinary graphs. The hypergraph shown in Figure E.1 consists of 6 nodes and 5 hyperedges.

(a) Describe a way to represent the information contained in an ERD without IS-A relationships as a hypergraph.

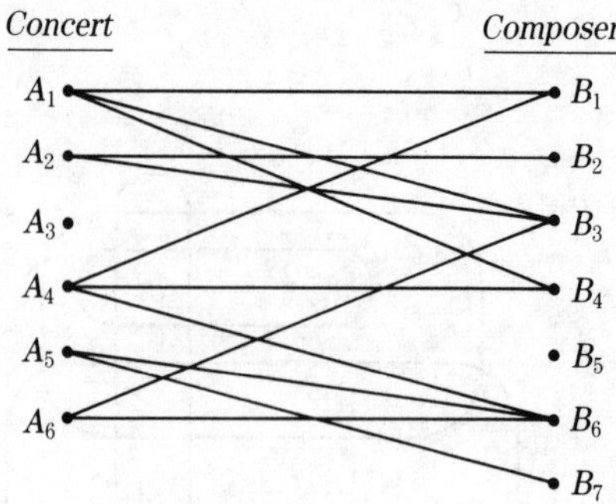

Figure E.2 Concert-composer relationship for Exercise 12.

(b) Give a hypergraph representation for the ERD from Figure 4.1.
(c) Extend the representation found under (b) to capture ERDs with IS-A relationships in a hypergraph, and 'test' it by devising a corresponding (extended) hypergraph for the airline-ERD shown in Figure 4.3.

(11) Derive a logical network for the ERD resulting from Exercise 5.

(12) During a *Concert*, usually works of different *Composers* are performed; the works of a *Composer* are generally performed in distinct *Concerts*. Consider the concrete $m : n$ relationship (at some time t) between (correspondingly defined entity declarations) *Concert* and *Composer* shown in Figure E.2. Make this relationship useful for a representation in the network model (by introducing a kett-record-type to be interpreted as the performed individual works), and describe the resulting 'database' (graphically) at the level of (physical) records.

(13) Let the three entity declarations *Project*, *Component* and *Supplier*, abbreviated by P, C and S, respectively, be given together with a ternary relationship between them, which is given at the level of relationship sets by $D \subseteq P^t \times C^t \times S^t =: E$.

The **transitive closure** $T(R_1, R_2, R_3)$ of three relations $R_1 \subseteq P^t \times C^t$, $R_2 \subseteq P^t \times S^t$, and $R_3 \subseteq C^t \times S^t$ is defined as the smallest set T of triples from E for which the following holds:

$$\begin{array}{ll} & ((p,c) \in R_1 \wedge (p,s) \in R_2 \implies (p,c,s) \in T) \\ \vee & ((p,c) \in R_1 \wedge (c,s) \in R_3 \implies (p,c,s) \in T) \\ \vee & ((p,s) \in R_2 \wedge (c,s) \in R_3 \implies (p,c,s) \in T) \end{array}$$

The **natural join** $N(R_1, R_2, R_3)$ is defined as follows:

$$N(R_1, R_2, R_3) := \{(p,c,s) \in E \mid (p,c) \in R_1 \wedge (p,s) \in R_2 \wedge (c,s) \in R_3\}$$

Show that for each relation D of the form given above the following holds:

$$D \subseteq N(D[P^t \times C^t], D[P^t \times S^t], D[C^t \times S^t])$$

$$\subseteq \; T(D[P^t \times C^t], D[P^t \times S^t], D[C^t \times S^t]) \subseteq E$$

Here, $D[P^t \times C^t]$, for example, denotes the restriction ('projection') of D onto P^t and C^t. Are there examples for which these inclusions are strict?

(14) Exhibit one (new) example each for a logical set-type (with owner- and member-type), where the following combinations of options are reasonable in the declaration of the member-type:

(a) MANDATORY AUTOMATIC
(b) MANDATORY MANUAL
(c) OPTIONAL AUTOMATIC
(d) OPTIONAL MANUAL
(e) FIXED AUTOMATIC
(f) FIXED MANUAL

(15) In Chapter 5 it was stated that an IS-A relationship should be modelled as part of a logical network by making the specialization the member type of a set type and to declare it as MANDATORY and AUTOMATIC. Discuss whether the combination FIXED and AUTOMATIC would be even more appropriate.

(16) Establish a currency-table for the concert database from Exercise 12, and record its contents according to the following sequence of (simplified) FIND-commands (which are to be executed in the sequence given):

FIND A_1; FIND $A_1 - B_3$; FIND $A_1 - B_4$; FIND B_4;
FIND $A_4 - B_4$; FIND A_4; FIND A_6; FIND $A_6 - B_3$;

Let each record-type be associated with an area of its own (A, B and C, respectively), and let the table be initialized with 'nil'.

(17) A network database with the following 'schema' is given:

record-type *Salesperson* with attributes *Sname, Age, Salary*;
record-type *Order* with attributes *No, Cname, Sname*;
record-type *Customer* with attributes *Cname, City, Branch*;
(Let the first attribute of each record-type be its CALC key, respectively.)
set-type *Shipping* with owner-type *Salesperson*, and member-type *Order*;
set-type *Receiving* with owner-type *Customer*, and member-type *Order*.

Express the following queries as FIND/GET sequences, and the updates in the CODASYL/DBTG language from Chapter 5:

(a) Find
— all customers named 'ABC Company';
— all orders by customer ABC Company;
— the corresponding salesperson.

(b) Modify the name of customer ABC Company to 'Computers, Inc.'. Change *Order* records correspondingly, assuming that *Receiving* has been defined as MANDATORY.
(c) Delete all orders that have been sold by salesperson Parker.

Part III

Foundations of the Relational Data Model

Chapter 7
Relations and Relation Schemas

This chapter presents the last of the three major data models which are currently used in commercially available DBMSs, the **relational model**, which goes back to the work of E. F. Codd. Following the pattern of the previous chapters, the 'language' of this model is described first, with the derivation of a relational database specification from an ER diagram. In the discussion of the basic concepts underlying this model, the use of a mathematically precise notation is emphasized (in some sense as an extension of what was done in Chapter 4), which will allow the concise presentation of the foundations of the theory of the relational model in this and the following chapters.

7.1 Relations

An idealized case of the file-card data model used in Chapter 2, in which it is assumed that *one* such card suffices to record the entire contents of a file, will be used here. Figure 7.1 shows the organization and partial contents of a file card for the library example. The card contains a *table* which consists of a collection of rows. Among these rows, the headline is special in that it contains the time-invariant 'properties' of each book. All other rows contain concrete data on one book each.

If it is further assumed that an (arbitrary, but fixed) ordering is defined among the attributes, the time-varying contents of such a card become describable by the mathematical concept of a **relation** known from set theory: if $(A_1, \ldots, A_m)$ is a sequence of attributes with domains $\text{dom}(A_i)$, $i = 1(1)m$, respectively, a relation r is a subset of the Cartesian product of these domains, that is:

$$r \subseteq \text{dom}(A_1) \times \ldots \times \text{dom}(A_m)$$

In the terminology of Chapter 4, a relation is thus a set of entities. In slight modification of the representation of a collection of attributes or of an entity format as a sequence used in that chapter, however, any such format specification will now be written as a *set*, since the choice of a particular sequencing is not supposed to carry any additional information.

So let X be a set of attributes, $X = \{A_1, \ldots, A_m\}$, and let each attribute $A \in X$ have a non-empty domain $\text{dom}(A)$ with at least two elements; thus, every domain permits at least assertions of the form 'true/false' or 'yes/no'. (On the one hand, this assumption is most often trivially satisfied in practical applications; on the other hand, it is relevant for certain results in the theory of the relational model; see, for example, the proof of Theorem 9.2. In addition, in reality domains are always finite, a prerequisite that is not yet needed here.) For the set $\cup_{A \in X}\text{dom}(A)$ of all values, the notation $\text{dom}(X)$ will be used as a shorthand.

A **tuple** over X is a (for the moment total and) injective mapping $\mu : X \rightarrow \text{dom}(X)$, for which the following holds:

Callnumber	...	*Author*	*Title*	...	*Publ_Co*	...
1	...	Date	Intro DBS	...	AW	...
2	...	Ullman	Princ DBS	...	CSP	...
3	...	Kroenke	DB Proc	...	SRA	...
⋮		⋮	⋮		⋮	

Figure 7.1 A sample table.

$(\forall A \in X)\ \mu(A) \in \text{dom}(A)$

For a given set X of attributes, let $\text{Tup}(X)$ denote the set of all tuples over X; the injectivity assumption assures that $\text{Tup}(X)$ is indeed a set (without duplicate elements). A **relation** r over X is a (finite) set of tuples over X, that is, $r \subseteq \text{Tup}(X)$; the set of all relations over X is denoted by $\text{Rel}(X)$.

As was illustrated by the analogy to file cards, a relation over a set X of attributes can be represented as a table, if an ordering is imposed on the elements of X. When representing a relation in this form, the attributes will always be included as a 'headline' (as in Figure 7.1); the tuples or elements of the relation form the remaining rows of the table.

It is now possible to state some first correspondences between the entity-relationship and the relational model. A single entity is a tuple in a relation; a relation corresponds to the notion of an entity set, where the use of 'timestamps' can now be avoided if it is assumed that the notation '$r \in \text{Rel}(X)$' always refers to some relation over X that exists at a not explicitly specified time (in a database).

At the level of time-invariant descriptions, the set of attributes of a relation corresponds to the format of an entity declaration; this is why the term **relation format** is also used in the present context. In addition, it will turn out to be important in this model to be able to refer to a relation by a *name*, which will serve here — as it did for the entity-relationship model — the purpose of 'identifying' a 'relation schema'. However, before what is meant by such a schema can be stated, further preparations are needed.

It should be pointed out that, because of the statements made above, it is so far only possible to talk about tuples or relations which are *total* in the sense that for *every* attribute an element from the underlying domain has to be provided. For modelling certain real-world situations, this view is insufficient, as can be seen from the following example.

The employee relation of some enterprise could have the format $X = \{$ *Name, Address, Phone, Hiring_Date, Salary, Emp_No* $\}$. It may happen that some employees do not possess a home phone, or that their phone number, for instance, for personal or security reasons, is not known to the company. Using the formalism introduced above, no such employee can be represented by a tuple μ in the employee relation, since $\mu(Phone) \notin \text{dom}(Phone)$ holds if it is assumed that $\text{dom}(Phone)$ consists, say, of 12-digit numbers (and an all-zero number is either not allowed or stands for some particular number).

To be able to cope with situations like these in the context of the relational model, it is necessary to introduce **null values**. For many applications, it might be sufficient to extend the domain of each attribute by a special symbol '?' and to treat this like a 'real' value, so that $\mu(A)$

may be assigned the value '?' if the (actual) value of μ at 'point' A is unknown. In particular, commercial database systems like SQL/DS (see Chapter 16) frequently follow such an approach. Formally, the domain $\text{dom}(X)$ of a relation format X is then extended by the single null value '?'; for each tuple in a relation over X, the following has to hold:

$$(\forall\, A \in X)\ \mu(A) \in \text{dom}(A) \vee \mu(A) = ?$$

From a theoretical point of view, this approach to dealing with incomplete information is insufficient. First, it is impossible to distinguish several interpretations that a null value may have (such as 'value exists, but is currently unknown', or 'value does not exist', see the *Phone* attribute in the above example). Second, one has to be careful when manipulating relations with null values and in particular when comparing attribute values, since, for example, the fact that $\nu(A) = \mu(A) = \mu(B) = ?$ in general neither implies that the entities μ and ν possess the same value at point A, nor means that the μ values for A and B agree.

For these reasons, a formal treatment of partial information first has to fix a certain *interpretation* for the null values used (or even to distinguish several classes of null values, each of which has its own interpretation); in addition, null values may eventually be indexed for identification purposes, and finally domains of attributes have to be augmented as appropriate.

This is explained in more detail for the case that all null values used are of type 'values exists, but is currently unknown'. All null values to be used are collected in a countable, possibly infinite **null-value domain** $\mathbf{N} = \{\delta_1, \delta_2, \delta_3, \ldots\}$, for which the following holds:

$$(\forall\, A \in X)\ \text{dom}(A) \cap \mathbf{N} = \emptyset$$

A **partial** tuple over X then is a mapping $\mu : X \to \text{dom}(A) \cup \mathbf{N}$ such that

$$(\forall\, A \in X)\ \mu(A) \in \text{dom}(A) \vee \mu(A) \in \mathbf{N}$$

A relation r over X is called *partial* if it contains partial tuples.

Null values will not be elaborated upon any further here; instead, the following text will refer to total relations (which will consequently not be mentioned explicitly).

7.2 Data dependencies and relation schemas

Relations over a given set X of attributes, that is, elements of $\text{Rel}(X)$, are considered next. In general, not *all* elements of this set are of interest, but only those which satisfy certain *semantic conditions* that can be observed

	Callnumber	*Author*	*Title*	*Publ_Co*
	1	Date	Intro DBS I	AW
r_1:	2	Date	Intro DBS II	AW
	3	Ullman	Princ DBS	CSP
	4	Kroenke	DB Proc.	SRA
	1	Date	Intro DBS I	AW
r_2:	2	Date	Intro DBS II	AW
	1	Ullman	Intro DBS I	CSP
	2	Kroenke	DB Proc.	SRA

Figure 7.2 Two relations over the library format.

in the underlying application, and which represent a current 'section of the real world' in this sense.

As an example, consider once more the stock of books in a library with format $X = \{Callnumber, Author, Title, Publ\_Co\}$ (see Figure 7.1). Figure 7.2 shows two distinct relations $r_1, r_2 \in \text{Rel}(X)$. While r_1 will intuitively be considered as a 'reasonable' relation over the given format, the same does not hold for r_2. First, because of the 'semantics' of a call number, it appears unreasonable to assign one such number to several books simultaneously. Secondly, it could be required, for example, that each author uses a title for his book(s) which is not yet used by another author, so that titles may agree (in two different tuples) only if the same holds for author and publisher (values of these tuples).

The former of these observations has been formalized in Chapter 4 through the notion of a key. The latter, however, shows that the key concept might not be sufficient for modelling observations made in a particular application, which are semantic in nature. In general, observations or conditions of this kind are called **data dependencies**; they make it possible to state precisely which relations from a given set $\text{Rel}(X)$ of all possible states are to be considered as 'reasonable' or 'valid' (and may therefore occur in a corresponding database), and which are not.

Essentially two classes of data dependencies can be distinguished. A *static* dependency ('over X') has to be satisfied by every 'current state' or relation $r \in \text{Rel}(X)$; examples are the dependencies stated above for the library example. A *dynamic* dependency, on the other hand, affects the *transition* from one (current) relation $r \in \text{Rel}(X)$ to another relation $r' \in \text{Rel}(X)$ as it takes place during an update operation; an example is the requirement that salaries of the employees of some company can only be increased or remain unchanged, but can never shrink.

Attention is restricted here to the treatment of static data dependencies as semantic conditions, which often refer exclusively to *one* set X of attributes or *one* 'state space' $\text{Rel}(X)$ only, and which are then termed

intrarelational constraints. Formally, such a constraint is a (possibly partial) mapping σ from Rel(X) into the set $\{0, 1\}$ of Boolean truth values (where 0 stands for 'false' and 1 for 'true'), which hence associates a truth value with (certain) elements of Rel(X):

$$\sigma : \text{Rel}(X) \rightarrow \{0, 1\}$$

If $\sigma(r) = 1$ holds for a relation $r \in \text{Rel}(X)$, then r **satisfies** the dependency σ, or σ is *valid* in r.

A set Σ_X of 'dependencies over X' can also be considered as such a mapping:

$$\Sigma_X : \text{Rel}(X) \rightarrow \{0, 1\}$$

such that

$$\Sigma_X(r) := \wedge_{\sigma \in \Sigma_X} \sigma(r)$$

where '$\wedge$' denotes Boolean conjunction. It follows immediately that a relation $r \in \text{Rel}(X)$ satisfies a set Σ_X of intrarelational constraints if r satisfies *every* dependency $\sigma \in \Sigma_X$.

As a very common example for an intrarelational constraint, (primary) *keys* are considered next which were introduced in Chapter 4:

Definition 7.1

Let X be a set of attributes, and let $K \subseteq X$.

(a) K is called a **key** for $r \in \text{Rel}(X)$ if:
(i) $(\forall\, \mu, \nu \in r)\ \mu[K] = \nu[K] \Longrightarrow\ \mu = \nu$ holds,
(ii) for no strict subset $K' \subset K$ (a) also holds.

(b) A **key dependency** $K \rightarrow X$ denotes the following semantic condition. Let $r \in \text{Rel}(X)$:

$$(K \rightarrow X)(r) := \begin{cases} 1 & \text{if } K \text{ is a key for } r \\ 0 & \text{otherwise} \end{cases}$$

As in Chapter 4, the **restriction** of μ to $K \subseteq X$ is here denoted by $\mu[K]$.

If a time-varying relation $r \in \text{Rel}(X)$ is considered, a set $K \subseteq X$ of attributes forms a key for r if any two tuples $\mu, \nu \in r$ differ on K ($\mu[K] \neq \nu[K]$), and K obeys the minimality requirement. (If the latter is not the case, then K is called a **candidate key**, see Chapter 4 and Exercise 1.)

On the other hand, if a time-invariant format X is considered, the specification of a key dependency of the form $K \rightarrow X$, or the declaration of a subset K of X as a key, means that a relation $r \in \text{Rel}(X)$ is considered a 'valid instance' of X only if it satisfies $K \rightarrow X$; that is, $(K \rightarrow X)(r) = 1$ holds (K is a key for r).

Since the 'full' format of the relation from Rel(X) in question always appears on the right-hand side of a key dependency σ of the form $K \rightarrow X$, a shorter notation for this type of dependency can be introduced: σ and K are identified, so that a set $\{K_1 \rightarrow X, \ldots, K_n \rightarrow X\}$ of key dependencies can be written as $\{K_1, \ldots, K_n\}$. If $n = 1$ the key can be marked by underlining (as in ERDs) when a relation is exhibited in table form. (If $n > 1$, at least the *primary key* can be identified in this way.)

Note that this particular instance of a data dependency (as a special case of a so-called **integrity constraint**) again demonstrates the distinction between time-invariant and time-varying aspects of a database. While a set $K \subseteq X$ of attributes may be a key in one relation, but not in others, the declaration of a key *dependency* requires a restriction of the 'world' to those relations that satisfy the key.

Next let X be a relation format, and let Σ_X be a set of dependencies over X. For the set of all relations $r \in \text{Rel}(X)$ that satisfy Σ_X the following notation is introduced:

$$\text{Sat}(X, \Sigma_X) := \{r \in \text{Rel}(X) \mid \Sigma_X(r) = 1\}$$

Definition 7.2

A **relation schema** has the form $R = (X, \Sigma_X)$; it consists of a name (R), a format (that is, a set of attributes) X and a set Σ_X of intrarelational data dependencies. If the set X is clear from the context, it is permissible to write Σ instead of Σ_X.

A relation schema $R = (X, \Sigma_X)$ is thus used as a time-invariant description of the set Sat(X, Σ_X) of all relations over X that satisfy Σ_X. Such relations are henceforth also called (valid) **instances** of R; in general, Sat(X, Σ_X) will be abbreviated as Sat(R) if it is obvious which schema R is under consideration.

As an example, the relation schema for the stock of books in the library example is described as follows:

$$B = (\{\mathit{Callnumber}, \mathit{Author}, \mathit{Title}, \mathit{Publ\_Co}\},\\ \{\mathit{Callnumber} \rightarrow \{\mathit{Callnumber}, \mathit{Author}, \mathit{Title}, \mathit{Publ\_Co}\}\})$$

or shorter

$$B = (\{\ \mathit{Callnumber},\ \mathit{Author},\ \mathit{Title},\ \mathit{Publ\_Co}\ \}, \{\ \mathit{Callnumber}\ \})$$

Here, it is always assumed that the domain of an attribute occurring in a relation format is *elementary* in the sense that all its values are atomic, but not itself sets or relations for example. If this requirement is met for some relation schema R, R is said to be in **first normal form** (1NF). Here and in what follows, relations whose schema is in 1NF will be considered; deviations from this approach will be described in Chapter 21.

7.3 Relational databases and database schemas

The next goal is to completely represent a given ER diagram or schema in the relational model. To this end, first consider *entity declarations* of the form $E = (\text{attr}(E), K)$. For each such declaration, a separate relation schema of the form $E = (X, \{\sigma\})$ is introduced, which has the same name as the entity declaration, and whose set X of attributes is obtained as follows. Let $\text{attr}(E) = (A_1, \ldots, A_m)$, then $X := \{A_1, \ldots, A_m\}$. If in addition $K = (A_{i_1}, \ldots, A_{i_n})$, the key dependency σ is defined as $\{A_{i_1}, \ldots, A_{i_n}\} \to X$ or simply $\{A_{i_1}, \ldots, A_{i_n}\}$, $\{i_1, \ldots, i_n\} \subseteq \{1, \ldots, m\}$.

Next, consider *relationship declarations* which are not necessarily binary; note that, for representing these in the relational model, again only the concept of a relation (schema) is available. Thus, with each such declaration a relation schema is associated in the following way.

Let $R = (\text{ent}(R), \text{attr}(R))$, where $\text{ent}(R) = (E_1, \ldots, E_k)$ and $\text{attr}(R) = (B_1, \ldots, B_n)$. In addition, let K_i denote the primary key of entity declaration E_i, $1 \le i \le k$, respectively, and without loss of generality let $K_i = (A_{i1}, \ldots, A_{in_i})$. The relation schema corresponding to R has the form $R = (X, \emptyset)$, where the name is again preserved, and X is defined as follows:

$$X := \{A_{11}, \ldots, A_{1n_1}, \ldots, A_{k1}, \ldots, A_{kn_k}, B_1, \ldots, B_n\}$$

(Here it is assumed that all attributes occurring in X have distinct names, which can easily be achieved by renaming (some of) them if necessary.)

As an example, consider the ER diagram for the library application from Figure 4.1. For the two entity declarations, the following two relation schemas are obtained in this case:

$$B = (\{\textit{Callnumber}, \textit{Author}, \textit{Title}, \textit{Publ\_Co}\}, \{\textit{Callnumber}\})$$

and

$$R = (\{\textit{Reader\_No}, \textit{Name}, \textit{Address}\}, \{\textit{Reader\_No}\})$$

For the relationship declaration named O, the following third relation schema is obtained:

$$O = (\{\textit{Callnumber}, \textit{Reader\_No}, \textit{Return\_Date}\}, \emptyset)$$

As is demonstrated by this example, relation schemas that are derived from a relationship declaration can also be equipped with a key de-

Table 7.1 Correspondences in terminology between ER and relational models.

ER model	*Relational model*
Entity declaration, relationship declaration	Relation schema
Entity set, relationship set	Relation (table)
Entity, relationship	Tuple (row of a table)

pendency in a natural fashion. If — as in the case of the library example — the relationship declaration has new attributes $B_1, \ldots, B_n$ expressing special properties of the relationship in question, it is near at hand to declare the key dependency $K \rightarrow X$, where $K = X - \{B_1, \ldots, B_n\}$. If the declaration has no new attributes (that is, $n = 0$), the same approach yields the *trivial* key dependency $X \rightarrow X$, which is satisfied by every relation over X.

This general approach can be refined by taking the type of a binary relationship declaration into account. If R represents an $m : n$ relationship between E_1 and E_2, and E_i has the key $K_i, i = 1, 2$, respectively, it is appropriate to choose $K_1 \cup K_2$ as the key for the corresponding relation schema R, since only the specification of values for *all* attributes in $K_1 \cup K_2$ identifies a 'relationship tuple'. However, if R represents a $1 : n$ relationship between E_1 and E_2, it is sufficient to choose K_2 as the key for R, since, according to the 'semantics' of this type of relationship, for every K_2 value in a relationship set (over R) there can exist at most one associated K_1 value. Since a $(K_1 \cup K_2)$ value describes a concrete relationship completely, it follows that a K_2 value is identifying (and redundancy-free).

Finally, in the case of a $1 : 1$ relationship, either K_1 or K_2 can be chosen as the key for R. These considerations can be applied to non-binary relationships in an analogous fashion.

As a result of the transformation of an ER diagram or schema into the relational model, a set $\mathbf{R} = \{R_1, \ldots, R_k\}$ of relation schemas is obtained, where a formal distinction can no longer be made between schemas that have been derived from entity declarations and schemas that represent relationships. Thus, the list of terminological correspondences between the ER model and the relational model shown in Table 7.1 is arrived at.

Definition 7.3

Let $\mathbf{R} = \{R_1, \ldots, R_k\}$ be a (finite) set of relation schemas (in 1NF), where $R_i = (X_i, \Sigma_i)$, $1 \leq i \leq k$, and $X_i \neq X_j$ for $i \neq j$.

(a) A (relational) **database** d (over $\mathbf{R}$) is a set of (base) relations, $d = \{r_1, \ldots, r_k\}$, such that $r_i \in \text{Rel}(X_i)$ for $i = 1(1)k$. Let $\text{Dat}(\mathbf{R})$ denote the set of all databases over $\mathbf{R}$.

b:

Callnumber	*Author*	*Title*	*Publ_Co*
1	Date	Intro DBS I	AW
2	Date	Intro DBS II	AW
3	Ullman	Princ. DBS	CSP
4	Kroenke	DB Proc.	SRA

r:

Reader_No	*Name*	*Address*
500	Joe	Los Angeles
550	Nina	San Diego
600	Peter	La Jolla

o:

Callnumber	*Reader_No*	*Return_Date*
1	550	043088
2	550	053188
3	600	053188

Figure 7.3 A sample relational database.

(b) A database $d \in \text{Dat}(\mathbf{R})$ is **pointwise consistent** if $r_i \in \text{Sat}\ (R_i)$ holds for each $r_i \in d$. Let $\text{Sat}(\mathbf{R})$ denote the set of all pointwise consistent databases over $\mathbf{R}$.

For a set $\mathbf{R}$ of relation schemas as used in Definition 7.3, the term **database format** will also be used (in analogy to relation formats). Note that this is a slight abuse of the intuition behind a format, which actually should be written as $\{X_1, \ldots, X_k\}$ (disregarding the 'local' dependencies).

Lower-case (greek or latin) letters are generally used for time-varying objects in the relational model (such as tuples, relations or databases). Upper-case letters are used to denote time-invariant objects (like individual attributes, sets of attributes, relation schemas, and so on), where sets of attributes of the form $X = \{A, B, C\ \ldots\}$ can also be written as a concatenation of their elements (that is, $X = ABC\ \ldots$). Exception to this notational convention are individual data dependencies, for which lower-case greek letters are also used in general.

An example for a relational database according to Definition 7.3 is shown in Figure 7.3; the database shown is over the format $\mathbf{R} = \{B, R, O\}$ and contains a current instance of the library application.

Two things should be noted at this point. First, the complexity or the type of a relationship declaration has been neglected in the transformation described above (besides using it to derive a key). Secondly, there is still no possibility of expressing the hierarchical dependency which is implicit in an IS-A or a hierarchical relationship. These issues will be discussed next.

Both types of 'restrictions' can be expressed in the relational model by using **interrelational dependencies** which render it possible to make statements on when a database, that is, a set of relations, is 'reasonable' or 'valid' in its entirety.

For example, in the library schema O models a $1 : n$ relationship between B and R; consequently, a database d should be considered 'valid' (with respect to the real world) only if the relations b and r (and eventually o) occurring in it obey their respective keys, meaning that d is pointwise consistent, *and* no book is given out to more than one reader at a time; that is, if $\mu \in o$ and $\mu(\mathit{Callnumber}) = i$, then there exists no $\nu \neq \mu$ in o such that $\nu(\mathit{Callnumber}) = i$.

It seems convenient to use the *comp-notation* from Chapter 4 to describe the complexity of relationships as interrelational constraints in the relational model. Let $R = (X, \Sigma)$ be a relation schema representing a relationship declaration, and let $X = K_1 \ \ldots \ K_k Y$, where K_i denotes the primary key of the relation schema R_i representing the ith entity declaration 'participating' in R, $1 \leq i \leq k$, and Y denotes the set of 'special' attributes of R. Finally, let $d \in \mathrm{Dat}(\mathbf{R})$ be such that $r_1, \ \ldots \ , r_k, \ r \in d$:

$$\mathrm{comp}(R, R_i) = (m, n)$$
$$:\Longleftrightarrow (\forall \mu \in r_i) \ \mid \{\nu \in r \ \mid \ \nu[K_i] = \mu[K_i]\} \mid \begin{cases} \geq m \\ \leq n \end{cases}$$

The complexity of a relationship will not be discussed in much further detail here, but it will be used as a first example for an interrelational dependency that allows a statement about the contents of more than just one relation.

Formally, such a dependency can again be considered as a mapping σ from $\mathrm{Dat}(\mathbf{R})$ to $\{0, 1\}$, for which — in analogy to intrarelational dependencies — $\sigma(d) = 1$ holds for $d \in \mathrm{Dat}(\mathbf{R})$ if the database d **satisfies** the dependency σ, or σ *holds* in d. A set $\Sigma_{\mathbf{R}}$ of interrelational dependencies over a set $\mathbf{R}$ of relation schemas also represents a mapping of this type:

$$\Sigma_{\mathbf{R}} : \mathrm{Dat}(\mathbf{R}) \rightarrow \{0, 1\}$$

such that

$$\Sigma_{\mathbf{R}}(d) := \wedge_{\sigma \in \Sigma_{\mathbf{R}}} \sigma(d)$$

It follows that a database d satisfies $\Sigma_{\mathbf{R}}$ if d satisfies *every* dependency in $\Sigma_{\mathbf{R}}$, that is, $\Sigma_{\mathbf{R}}(d) = 1$. Next let

$$\mathrm{Sat}(\Sigma_{\mathbf{R}}) := \{d \in \mathrm{Dat}(\mathbf{R}) \ \mid \ \Sigma_{\mathbf{R}}(d) = 1\}$$

The attention is restricted here to interrelational dependencies which cannot be represented as interrelational ones as well (which is not stated formally).

For the library example, the complexity of O with respect to B and R can now be stated precisely as follows. Let σ_1 and σ_2 be mappings from Dat($\mathbf{R}$) to $\{0, 1\}$ defined by:

$$\sigma_1(d) := \begin{cases} 1 & \text{if comp}(O,\ B) \in \{(0,1),(1,1)\} \\ 0 & \text{otherwise} \end{cases}$$

$$\sigma_2(d) := \begin{cases} 1 & \text{if comp}(O,\ R) \in \{(0,\infty),(1,\infty)\} \\ 0 & \text{otherwise} \end{cases}$$

(Here it is assumed that $\mathbf{R} = \{B, R, O\}$ and $d \in \text{Dat}(\mathbf{R})$.)

The requirement that a book cannot be given out to more than one reader simultaneously, which was stated informally above, can thus be formalized as a set $\Sigma_{\mathbf{R}} = \{\sigma_1, \sigma_2\}$ of interrelational dependencies.

As a second — and for our purposes more important — instance of interrelational dependencies **inclusion dependencies** are considered next, which among other things will make it possible to formalize the existence constraint inherent in an IS-A relationship.

As an introductory example, consider the following state of the library database. Let b and r be as shown in Figure 7.3, and let o' have the following contents:

	Callnumber	*Reader_No*	*Return_Date*
o':	1	550	043088
	6	550	053188

In this example, a book has been given out whose call number is not recorded in relation b that represents the entire stock of books. This contradicts the 'semantics' of a relationship in the ER model, since relationships should only exist between entities which are 'actually present'. In the 'language' of the relational model, this means that if R is a schema describing a relationship and if $\mu \in r$, then for each 'entity schema' E_i participating in the derivation of R there must exist a tuple ν in the corresponding relation e_i such that $\mu[K_i] = \nu[K_i]$ (for $i = 1(1)k$).

In the library example, database states like the one shown above can be prevented by requiring that only books which are actually present can be checked out (and, analogously, that only readers who are 'known' to the library may check out books).

Definition 7.4

Let $\mathbf{R}$ be a set of relation schemas, $R_i, R_j \in \mathbf{R}$, $R_i \neq R_j$, $R_i = (X_i, \Sigma_i)$, $R_j = (X_j, \Sigma_j)$. In addition, let V $[W]$ be a sequence of n distinct attributes from X_i $[X_j]$, respectively. An **inclusion dependency** (IND)

$R_i[V] \subseteq R_j[W]$ denotes the following semantic condition. Let $d \in \text{Dat}(\mathbf{R})$:

$$(R_i[V] \subseteq R_j[W])(d) := \begin{cases} 1 & \text{if } \{\mu[V] \mid \mu \in r_i\} \subseteq \{\mu[W] \mid \mu \in r_j\} \\ 0 & \text{otherwise} \end{cases}$$

Several remarks on this definition are apt. The assumption '$R_i \neq R_j$' can be omitted if 'intrarelational' inclusions should be representable as well. However, it is important to require that the 'comparison attributes' V and W are now considered as *sequences*, in order to be able to uniquely identify corresponding values of tuples or values to be compared via their positions.

In particular, it may happen that $V \neq W$ holds (as in the case of a general hierarchical relationship, see below). In this case, the relations mentioned in the defining condition have different formats, which makes them incomparable with respect to '$\subseteq$'; the condition must hence be modified as follows (for $V = (A_1, \ldots, A_n), W = (B_1, \ldots, B_n)$) :

$$(\forall \mu \in r_i)(\exists \nu \in r_j)(\forall i = 1(1)n)\ \mu(A_i) = \nu(B_i)$$

If no confusion can arise, the notation introduced in Definition 7.4 will always be used.

As a first application of inclusion dependencies, consider the description of a hierarchical relationship between employees and departments of an enterprise. A department has many employees $(1 : n)$, but each employee must always be associated with a particular department. It is assumed that the following relation schemas have been declared already:

Dept = ({ *Dept#, Name, Emp#* } , $\emptyset$)

Emp = ({ *Emp#, Name , ...* } , { *Emp#* })

The existence constraint mentioned above is then captured formally by the IND:

Emp[Emp#] $\subseteq$ *Dept[Emp#]*

As a second application, consider IS-A relationships and in particular the example *Pilot* $\subseteq$ *Emp* from Chapter 4 (airline). In slight modification of Definition 4.5, it shall not be required in the relational model that all *Emp* attributes also appear in the relation format for *Pilot*. Instead, it is now sufficient to list the key attributes together with the 'special' properties of the specialization (that is, the simplification which was used for ER diagrams, see Figure 4.3). In addition, it is required that the IND *Pilot[Emp#]* $\subseteq$ *Emp[Emp#]* holds; other INDs that can be derived from Figure 4.3 in a similar way are:

Departure[Spec] ⊆ *Flight[Spec]*
Aircraft[Manuf, Type] ⊆ *Plane[Manuf, Type]*
Technician[Emp#] ⊆ *Emp[Emp#]*

The example shows that IS-A relationships lead to inclusion dependencies in a natural fashion; it also demonstrates that it might be reasonable to include such a dependency even in the absence of an IS-A relationship.

In the library application so-called **foreign keys** occur. According to the above discussion, it is reasonable to require the INDs *O[Callnumber]* ⊆ *B[Callnumber]* and *O[Reader_No]* ⊆ *R[Reader_No]*. In this case, attribute *Callnumber* is the key for schema B, which implies that a value for this attribute can occur at most once in b, and a similar statement holds for attribute *Reader_No* of schemas O and R. Both *Callnumber* and *Reader_No* form a foreign key for O.

In general, $K \subseteq X$ is a foreign key in $R = (X, .)$ if K is a key in $R' \neq R$ and it is required that the K values of every relation over R agree with those of the relation over R' that belongs to the same state. It is therefore obvious that foreign keys can also be described by inclusion dependencies (of the form $R[K] \subseteq R'[K]$). INDs of this type are also called **key-based**.

The transformation of an ER diagram into the relational model described above can now be completed for the case of binary relationships as follows.

If a relation schema R represents an $m : n$ relationship between E_1 and E_2 in the underlying ERD, and if the relation schemas $E_i = (X_i, \{K_i\})$, $i = 1, 2$, correspond to these entity declarations, respectively, the following inclusion dependencies are also required to hold:

$$R[K_1] \subseteq E_1[K_1] \qquad \text{and} \qquad R[K_2] \subseteq E_2[K_2]$$

In particular, dependencies of this form are required for the special cases $m = 1$ or $n = 1$. Finally, it is obvious that the case of a non-binary relationship can be treated analogously; this will not be discussed in further detail here.

It is now possible to transform a given ER diagram or schema into a conceptual database description according to the relational model. On the other hand, the notion of a 'conceptual schema' can be defined formally in this model, which summarizes the above exposition.

Definition 7.5

Let $\mathbf{R}$ be a set of relation schemas, and $\Sigma_\mathbf{R}$ be a set of interrelational dependencies.

(i) A **database schema** (in the relational model) is a named pair $\mathbf{D} = (\mathbf{R}, \Sigma_\mathbf{R})$. It represents a time-invariant (conceptual) description of the set

$$\mathrm{Sat}(\mathbf{D}) := \mathrm{Sat}(\mathbf{R}, \Sigma_{\mathbf{R}}) := \mathrm{Sat}(\mathbf{R}) \cap \mathrm{Sat}(\Sigma_{\mathbf{R}})$$

of all those databases over **R** satisfying all intra- and interrelational dependencies.

(ii) A database $d \in \mathrm{Dat}(\mathbf{R})$ is called **consistent** if $d \in \mathrm{Sat}(\mathbf{D})$ holds. Each $d \in \mathrm{Sat}(\mathbf{D})$ is also termed an **instance** or **current state** of **D**.

The subsequent chapters will deal primarily with database schemas for which $\Sigma_{\mathbf{R}} = \emptyset$ holds. Note that in this case the notions of 'pointwise consistency' and 'consistency' coincide.

Chapter 8
Data Manipulation in the Relational Model

This chapter will first familiarize the reader with **relational algebra**, a query language for relational databases. Then **relational calculus**, a query language based on first-order logic, is discussed; some evidence is provided that this 'declarative' approach to querying relational databases has the same expressive power as the other 'procedural' approach. Next, it will be shown that some queries cannot be expressed in either of these languages, which motivates the search for extensions; to this end, the notion of a **computable query** is presented as the most general approach, and **Datalog** queries are introduced as an important special case. After that, **updates** on relations are discussed, which formally differ from queries in various ways.

Finally, updates on **views** of databases are investigated, which pose additional problems not present for updates on base relations.

8.1 Relational algebra; Setwise navigation

Operations on relations are presented next; these can be used to define the semantics of a data manipulation language called relational algebra.

To begin with, unary operations are introduced which can be used to 'shorten' a (two-dimensional) table in vertical ('projection') or horizontal ('selection') direction.

Definition 8.1

Let $R = (X, .)$ be a relation schema, $r \in \text{Rel}(X)$, and $Y \subseteq X$:

(i) $\pi_Y(r) := \{\mu[Y] \mid \mu \in r\}$ is called the **projection** of r onto Y, where $\mu[Y]$ again denotes the restriction of tuple μ onto Y ($\mu[Y] \in \text{Tup}(Y)$).

(ii) Let $A \in X, a \in \text{dom}(A)$, and let $\Theta \in \{<, \leq, >, \geq, =, \neq\}$:
$\sigma_{A\Theta a}(r) := \{\mu \in r \mid \mu(A)\Theta a\}$ is called the **selection** of r with respect to $A\Theta a$.
(In case $\Theta \in \{<, \leq, >, \geq\}$, it is assumed that $\text{dom}(A)$ is ordered.)

As an example, consider the following relation $r \in \text{Rel}(ABC)$:

r:

A	B	C
1	2	1
1	1	1
2	2	2

Then the following holds:

$\pi_{AC}(r)$:

A	C
1	1
2	2

(Note that the result of a projection — as a set — does not contain duplicate elements; thus, the computation of a projection involves a removal of certain columns, followed by an elimination of then duplicate tuples.)

$\sigma_{A=1}(r)$:

A	B	C
1	2	1
1	1	1

$\sigma_{C>1}(r)$:

A	B	C
2	2	2

'Atomic' selection conditions of the form '$A\Theta a$' may also be combined, using '$\wedge$', '$\vee$', '$-$' and parentheses as appropriate, into a more complex condition C. The attributes of such a condition will be denoted by attr(C). For example, '$\sigma_{A=a}(\sigma_{B=b}(r))$' is written shorter as '$\sigma_{A=a\wedge B=b}(r)$' or more generally:

$$\sigma_{C1}(\sigma_{C2}(r)) = \sigma_{C_1\wedge C_2}(r)$$

In the example above, $\sigma_{B=2\wedge(A=1\vee C=2)}(r)$ yields the following result:

A	B	C
1	2	1
2	2	2

Several basic laws are stated next that apply to selection and projection; the proof is left to the reader as an easy exercise:

Theorem 8.1

Let $r \in \mathrm{Rel}(X)$:

(1) $Z \subseteq Y \subseteq X \Longrightarrow \pi_Z(\pi_Y(r)) = \pi_Z(r)$

(2) $Z, Y \subseteq X \Longrightarrow \pi_Z(\pi_Y(r)) = \pi_{Z\cap Y}(r)$

(3) $\sigma_{C_1}(\sigma_{C_2}(r)) = \sigma_{C_2}(\sigma_{C_1}(r))$

(4) $A \in Y \subseteq X \Longrightarrow \pi_Y(\sigma_{A\Theta a}(r)) = \sigma_{A\Theta a}(\pi_Y(r))$
or more generally
$\mathrm{attr}(C) \subseteq Y \subseteq X \Longrightarrow \pi_Y(\sigma_C(r)) = \sigma_C(\pi_Y(r))$

For example, (3) follows from the commutativity of '$\wedge$':

$$\sigma_{C_1}(\sigma_{C_2}(r)) = \sigma_{C_1\wedge C_2}(r) = \sigma_{C_2\wedge C_1}(r) = \sigma_{C_2}(\sigma_{C_1}(r))$$

The first binary operations which will be defined are the well-known set operations intersection ($\cap$), union ($\cup$) and difference ($-$) :

Definition 8.2

Let $r, s \in \mathrm{Rel}(X)$:

(i) $r \cap s := \{\mu \in \mathrm{Tup}(X) \mid \mu \in r \wedge \mu \in s\}$
(ii) $r \cup s := \{\mu \in \mathrm{Tup}(X) \mid \mu \in r \vee \mu \in s\}$
(iii) $r - s := \{\mu \in r \mid \mu \notin s\}$

Note that for these operations it is important that both operands are relations over the same format.

The next operation is of central importance for working with relational databases. It is first defined for more than two operands; the important special case of two operands is then derived from the following definition.

Definition 8.3

Let $X_1, \ldots, X_n$ be sets of attributes, and let $r_i \in \text{Rel}(X_i)$ for $1 \leq i \leq n$:

$$\bowtie_{i=1}^{n} r_i := \{\mu \in \text{Tup}(\cup_{i=1}^{n} X_i) \mid (\forall\, i, 1 \leq i \leq n)\ \mu[X_i] \in r_i\}$$

is called the **natural join** of $r_1, \ldots, r_n$.

For the case $n = 2$, the following is directly implied by Definition 8.3:

$$r_1 \bowtie r_2 = \{\mu \in \text{Tup}(X_1 X_2) \mid \mu[X_1] \in r_1 \wedge \mu[X_2] \in r_2\}$$

As an example, consider the following three relations:

r_1:

A	B	C
1	1	1
1	2	2
2	0	2

r_2:

A	D
1	1
0	1
2	0

r_3:

C	D	E
1	1	0
0	1	1
2	1	0
2	2	1

Then the following holds:

$r_1 \bowtie r_2$:

A	B	C	D
1	1	1	1
1	2	2	1
2	0	2	0

$(r_1 \bowtie r_2) \bowtie r_3$:

A	B	C	D	E
1	1	1	1	0
1	2	2	1	0

Thus, the natural join computes a new relation from two or more given ones, whose set of attributes is the union of the sets of attributes of all its operands; a tuple in the result is derived from those tuples in the operands that have *equal* values on *common* attributes.

Some simple properties of the join operation are the following:

Theorem 8.2

Let $r_i \in \text{Rel}(X_i)$ for $1 \leq i \leq 3$:

(1) $r_i \bowtie r_i = r_i$

(2) $r_1 \bowtie r_2 = r_2 \bowtie r_1$

(3) $(r_1 \bowtie r_2) \bowtie r_3 = r_1 \bowtie (r_2 \bowtie r_3)$

(4) $X_1 \cap X_2 = \emptyset \Longrightarrow r_1 \bowtie r_2 = r_1 \times r_2$

(5) $X_1 = X_2 \Longrightarrow r_1 \bowtie r_2 = r_1 \cap r_2$

It follows that the join operation is commutative and associative; it 'degenerates' to a Cartesian product (intersection) if the sets of attributes of the operands are disjoint (identical), respectively. Note that a Cartesian product of two relations — strictly speaking — yields a set of ordered pairs and hence is formally 'incompatible' with the result of a join operation. However, this subtle point will be neglected here (see Chapter 16).

Theorem 8.3

Let $X = \cup_{i=1}^{n} X_i$, $r \in \text{Rel}(X)$, $r_i \in \text{Rel}(X_i)$ for $1 \leq i \leq n$. Then the following hold:

(1) $r \subseteq \bowtie_{i=1}^{n} (\pi_{X_i}(r))$

(2) $(\forall\, j, 1 \leq j \leq n)\ \pi_{X_j}(\bowtie_{i=1}^{n} r_i) \subseteq r_j$

(3) $(\forall\, j, 1 \leq j \leq n)\ \pi_{X_j}(\bowtie_{i=1}^{n} (\pi_{X_i}(r))) = \pi_{X_j}(r)$

Proof. For (1), let $\mu \in r$. Then

$$(\forall\, i, 1 \leq i \leq n)\ \mu[X_i] \in \pi_{X_i}(r)$$

by the definition of projection. Next, from the definition of join, it can be concluded that

$$\mu \in \bowtie_{i=1}^{n} (\pi_{X_i}(r))$$

For (2), let $\mu \in \pi_{X_j}(\bowtie_{i=1}^{n} r_i)$ for some $j \in \{1, \ldots n\}$. This implies

$$(\exists\, \nu \in \bowtie_{i=1}^{n} r_i)\ \nu[X_j] = \mu$$

which in turn implies

$$(\forall\, i, 1 \leq i \leq n)\ \nu[X_i] \in r_i$$

Thus, in particular, $\nu[X_j] = \mu \in r_j$ holds. Finally, for (3), two inclusions have to be shown: for '$\subseteq$', let

$$\mu \in \pi_{X_j}(\bowtie_{i=1}^{n} \pi_{X_i}(r))$$

Then it follows that

$$(\exists\, \nu \in \bowtie_{i=1}^{n} \pi_{X_i}(r))\ \nu[X_j] = \mu$$

which implies that

$$(\forall i, 1 \leq i \leq n)\ \nu[X_i] \in \pi_{X_i}(r)$$

and in particular $\nu[X_j] = \mu \in \pi_{X_j}(r)$. For '$\supseteq$', let $\mu \in \pi_{X_j}(r)$. This implies

$$(\exists\, \nu \in r)\ \nu[X_j] = \mu$$

from which by (1) it follows that

$$\nu \in \bowtie_{i=1}^{n} (\pi_{X_i}(r))$$

which finally implies

$$\nu[X_j] = \mu \in \pi_{X_j}(\bowtie_{i=1}^{n} (\pi_{X_i}(r)) \; \square$$

The next example shows that equality does not hold in general in parts (1) and (2) of Theorem 8.3. For (1), let r be the following relation:

A	B	C
0	0	0
1	0	1

Then $\pi_{AB}(r) \bowtie \pi_{BC}(r)$ is the relation

A	B	C
0	0	0
0	0	1
1	0	0
1	0	1

which is not equal to r.

For (2), consider the following two relations $r_1 \in \text{Rel}(AB)$ and $r_2 \in \text{Rel}(BC)$:

r_1:

A	B
0	0
0	1

r_2:

B	C
0	0
0	1

Then the following holds:

$r_1 \bowtie r_2$:

A	B	C
0	0	0
0	0	1

and hence

$\pi_{AB}(r_1 \bowtie r_2)$:

A	B
0	0

$\neq r_1$ $\square$

These examples show that join and projection are in general not the 'inverse' of each other. If equality holds in part (1) of Theorem 8.3, the 'decomposition' of $r \in \text{Rel}(X)$ onto the sets X_i of attributes is said to be **lossless**, since a join of all projections of r restores the original *exactly.* Otherwise, the join is called **lossy**, which basically means that the join yields *more* tuples (in the result) than were originally present in r (see the example above).

Additional rules for the operations introduced so far are presented next; again, the proof is left to the reader.

Theorem 8.4

Let $r \in \text{Rel}(X)$, $s \in \text{Rel}(Y)$ and $t \in \text{Rel}(Z)$.

(1) $\text{attr}(C) \subseteq X \implies \sigma_C(r \bowtie s) = \sigma_C(r) \bowtie s$

(2) $\text{attr}(C) \subseteq X \wedge X = Y \implies \sigma_C(r - s) = \sigma_C(r) - s$

(3) $\text{attr}(C) \subseteq X \cap Y \implies \sigma_C(r \bowtie s) = \sigma_C(r) \bowtie \sigma_C(s)$

(4) $\text{attr}(C) \subseteq X \cap Y \wedge X = Y \wedge \Theta \in \{\cup, -\}$
$\implies \sigma_C(r\Theta s) = \sigma_C(r)\Theta\sigma_C(s)$

(5) $V \subseteq XY \implies \pi_V(r \bowtie s) = \pi_V(\pi_W(r) \bowtie \pi_U(s))$,
where $W = X \cap VY$, $U = Y \cap VX$

(6) $Y = Z \implies r \bowtie (s\Theta t) = (r \bowtie s)\Theta(r \bowtie t)$,
where $\Theta \in \{\cup, -\}$

(7) $X = Y = Z \implies (r \cup s) - t = (r - t) \cup (s - t)$
$\wedge\ r - (s \cup t) = (r - s) \bowtie (r - t)$

At this point the definition of other relational operations (like division, total projection, equi-, theta-, or semi-join, renaming) is dispensed with, since a 'complete' set of operations (in a sense to be made precise later) is already at our disposal; however, additional operations will be defined when they are needed (see the Exercises and Chapter 16).

If it is assumed that a relational database is — at the internal level — a set of relations, whose contents are *a priori* unknown to a user, he or she needs a *language* in order to be able to work with that database. To this end, he can utilize certain schema information and in particular formulate queries as (abstract) expressions, in which names of relation schemas appear instead of concrete instances. The **syntax** of such a language is now introduced.

Definition 8.4

Let $\mathbf{D}$=($\mathbf{R}$, .) be a database schema, where $\mathbf{R}=\{R_1, \dots, R_k\}$. The set RA (more precisely: $\text{RA}_\mathbf{D}$) of **expressions from relational algebra** (over $\mathbf{D}$) is recursively defined as follows:

(i) $R_i \in \text{RA}$ for all $R_i \in \mathbf{R}$;

(ii) If $E_1 \in \text{RA}$, $E_2 \in \text{RA}$, C is a selection condition, and $X \subseteq \cup_{i=1}^{k} X_i$, then

$$\sigma_C(E_1) \in \text{RA}$$
$$\pi_X(E_1) \in \text{RA}$$
$$E_1 \bowtie E_2 \in \text{RA}$$
$$E_1 \cup E_2 \in \text{RA}$$

$$E_1 - E_2 \in \text{RA}$$

(iii) only those expressions that can be derived by a repeated application of (i) and (ii) belong to RA.

If the operators '∪' and '−' are done without in Definition 8.4 in order to build expressions, the special case of **SPJ expressions** results, which is of particular importance for practical applications. As the name suggests, SPJ expressions contain the operators 'σ', 'π' and '$\bowtie$' only. The set of all SPJ expressions is denoted by SPJ (more precisely $SPJ_{\mathbf{D}}$).

If a user issues an expression $E \in \text{RA}$ to a relational DBMS, it is the task of the query processor of the system (see Figure 3.1) to translate it to the level of the database; in particular, 'relation variables' or names have to be replaced by their current value, and then the operations have to be executed. This is formalized as a **semantics** for the language RA as follows.

Definition 8.5

Let $\mathbf{D} = (\mathbf{R}, .)$, $E \in \text{RA}$. The **evaluation** of E with respect to $d \in \text{Dat}(\mathbf{R})$ is defined as follows:

$$v_E(d) := \begin{cases} r_i & \text{if } E = R_i \\ \sigma_C(v_{E_1}(d)) & \text{if } E = \sigma_C(E_1) \\ \pi_X(v_{E_1}(d)) & \text{if } E = \pi_X(E_1) \\ v_{E_1}(d) \bowtie v_{E_2}(d) & \text{if } E = E_1 \bowtie E_2 \\ v_{E_1}(d) \cup v_{E_2}(d) & \text{if } E = E_1 \cup E_2 \\ v_{E_1}(d) - v_{E_2}(d) & \text{if } E = E_1 - E_2 \end{cases}$$

As an example, consider the library database shown in Figure 7.3, to which several queries are formulated next in the language of relational algebra:

(1) 'Show all books by author '*Date*'.'
$E_1 = \sigma_{Author='Date'}(B)$

(2) 'Show all publishers (from which books are available).'
$E_2 = \pi_{Publ\_Co}(B)$

(3) 'Show the return dates of the books that have call number 1 or 2.'
$E_3 = \pi_{Return\_Date}(\sigma_{Callnumber=1 \vee Callnumber=2}(C))$

(4) 'Show the address of each reader who has currently checked out a book.'
$E_4 = \pi_{Address}(R \bowtie C)$

(5) 'Show book title and reader name of every current checkout event.'
$E_5 = \pi_{Title,Name}(B \bowtie R \bowtie C)$

(6) 'Show the book relation.'
$E_6 = B$

Next let $d = \{b, r, c\}$ be the database shown in Figure 7.3; then an evaluation of these query expressions yields the following results:

(1) $v_{E_1}(d) = \sigma_{Author='Date'}(b)$:

Callnumber	*Author*	*Title*	*Publ_Co*
1	Date	Intro DBS I	AW
2	Date	Intro DBS II	AW

(2) $v_{E_2}(d)$:

Publ_Co
AW
CSP
SRA

(3) $v_{E_3}(d)$:

Return_Date
043088
053188

(4) $v_{E_4}(d) = \pi_{Address}(r \bowtie c)$:

Address
San Diego
La Jolla

(5) $v_{E_5}(d)$:

Title	*Name*
Intro DBS I	Nina
Intro DBS II	Nina
Princ. DBS	Peter

(6) $v_{E_6}(d)$:

Callnumber	*Author*	*Title*	*Publ_Co*
1	Date	Intro DBS I	AW
2	Date	Intro DBS II	AW
3	Ullman	Princ. DBS	CSP
4	Kroenke	DB Proc.	SRA

This example illustrates a central feature of the relational model that should be emphasized at this point. The user no longer perceives the database as an (ordered) collection of records which can be scanned sequentially via pointers. Instead, he now 'sees' a family of sets, individual members of which can always be addressed in their entirety; in particular, vertical or horizontal fractions of a (tuple-) set can be extracted, or new (tuple-) sets can be composed from already existing ones. Hence, in this data model it is appropriate to speak of **setwise navigation**, where the term 'navigation' primarily refers to the specification of 'join paths'.

The distinction made here between a (query) *expression* (at the conceptual level) and its *evaluation* (at the internal level) not only renders it possible to formally separate the two layers; in addition, it forms the basis for an *implementation-independent* **optimization** of relational expressions, for which the following notion is important.

Definition 8.6

Let $\mathbf{D} = (\mathbf{R}, .)$, and let E and E' be expressions from RA. E and E' are called **equivalent**, abbreviated $E \approx E'$, if the following holds:

$$(\forall\, d \in \text{Dat}(\mathbf{R}))\quad v_E(d) = v_{E'}(d)$$

Thus, two expressions E and E' are termed equivalent if they yield the same result when evaluated with respect to *any* current state over the given database schema **D**.

Based on the various theorems stated earlier regarding the laws that apply to the relational operations, examples for expressions that are pairwise equivalent can be provided immediately:

(1) Let $E = R_1 \bowtie R_2, E' = R_2 \bowtie R_1$. Then $E \approx E'$, since if $d \in \text{Dat}(\mathbf{R})$ is arbitrary, but fixed, it follows that $v_E(d) = r_1 \bowtie r_2 = r_2 \bowtie r_1 = v_{E'}(d)$.

(2) Let $E = R_1 \bowtie R_2, E' = R_1 \bowtie (R_1 \bowtie R_2)$. Then $E \approx E'$, since for every $d \in \text{Dat}(\mathbf{R})$ it is true that $v_E(d) = r_1 \bowtie r_2 = r_1 \bowtie r_1 \bowtie r_2 = r_1 \bowtie (r_1 \bowtie r_2) = v_{E'}(d)$.

(3) Let $R_1 = (AB, .)$, $R_2 = (BC, .)$, $E = \sigma_{A=1}(R_1 \bowtie R_2)$, $E' = \sigma_{A=1}(R_1) \bowtie R_2$. Again, $E \approx E'$, since for any $d \in \text{Dat}(\mathbf{R})$, $v_E(d) = \sigma_{A=1}(r_1 \bowtie r_2) = \sigma_{A=1}(r_1) \bowtie r_2 = v_{E'}(d)$ holds.

(4) Let $R_1 = (AB, .)$, $R_2 = (CD, .)$, then $E = \pi_{AB}(\sigma_{A=5}(R_1 \bowtie R_2)) \approx E' = \sigma_{A=5}(R_1)$.

In all four cases, one expression can be transformed into the other without changing the result of an evaluation, just by referring to the laws of relational algebra and to schema information. In cases (2) and (4), the number of join operations could be reduced; in example (3), when

E' is evaluated the selection will be performed *earlier* than during the evaluation of E.

The importance behind these observations lies in the fact that selections and projections generally 'reduce' (intermediate) results (with respect to the number of rows or the number of columns), which does not hold for a join. In this way it is often possible to cut the evaluation or *response time* down without even knowing the particular choice of the internal data structures for storing the relations involved. This can be graphically illustrated for a given expression from relational algebra by means of a **query tree**, whose leaves represent the operands, whose root represents the result and whose inner nodes represent the operations. Optimization of the original expression then means a transformation of the corresponding tree, during which projections and selections are pushed towards the leaves. Details are omitted.

It should also be mentioned that the language of relational algebra provides a tool for specifying (external) views over a conceptual schema **D**. A user view in the relational model can be defined by an expression $E \in \text{RA}$ (which will in general be *named*, that is, a view definition will have the form $V := E$, see Section 8.5). A query to such a view E is another expression E', for example, from RA in which E appears as a subexpression. The evaluation of E' is done in the same way as described in Definition 8.5.

8.2 Relational calculus

While relational algebra is a **procedural** language, in which an expression states *how*, that is, by applying which operations, the result can be obtained, a **declarative** language, relational tuple calculus, is now described, in which the tuples that shall appear in the result are described by their *properties*, but without also specifying a procedure for their computation.

In this section the approach originally described by Codd will be followed in that relational algebra is considered as a yardstick for the expressive power of query languages for relational databases. In detail, a relational query language L is called as **expressive** as a language L' if for each expression $E \in L$ there exists an expression $E' \in L'$ such that $E \approx E'$ holds, where it is assumed that equivalence has been defined by evaluations appropriately. Next, two languages are called **equivalent** if one is as expressive as the other and vice versa. Finally, a language is called **Codd-complete** if it is as expressive as RA.

As will be sketched below, RA is as expressive as the tuple calculus that will be introduced in this section. In addition, it can be shown, by additionally considering the relational *domain* calculus, that RA and both calculi are pairwise equivalent (under the prerequisite that a rename operation is included in RA), so that the tuple calculus is in particular Codd-complete.

Relational tuple calculus, abbreviated RTC, is closely related to the language of first-order predicate logic. Differences result from the fact that RTC uses variables for tuples (of a relation, 'tuple variables') instead of variables of individual domain elements. On the other hand, certain restrictions need to be applied in order to guarantee that the answer to a query is always a finite set (of tuples).

Before a formal definition of RTC is given, some intuition is provided about how expressions from relational algebra can be rewritten in a 'logical' manner. Let R be relation schema with attributes $ABCD$, and let $r \in \text{Rel}(ABCD)$.

(1) Consider $\pi_{AB}(r)$ which, by definition, is $\pi_{AB}(r) = \{ \nu[AB] \mid \nu \in r \}$. Any tuple μ that appears in the result relation generated by this projection can alternatively be described as follows:

$$\mu \text{ is in the result} \iff (\exists\, \nu)\ (\nu \in r \wedge \nu[AB] = \mu)$$

(2) Next consider $\sigma_{C=1}(r) = \{ \nu \in r \mid \nu[C] = 1 \}$. Again, an alternative description of the results is:

$$\mu \text{ is in the result} \iff \mu \in r \wedge \mu[C] = 1$$

(3) Now let $r, s \in \text{Rel}(ABCD)$. A union $r \cup s = \{ \nu \mid \nu \in r \wedge \nu \in s \}$ can be rewritten as:

$$\begin{aligned} &\mu \text{ is in the result} \\ &\iff (\exists\, \nu_1)(\exists\, \nu_2)[(\nu_1 \in r \wedge \nu_1 = \mu) \vee (\nu_2 \in s \wedge \nu_2 = \mu)] \end{aligned}$$

Similarly, the result of a join operation can be written in this way; for example, let $r \in \text{Rel}(AB)$ and $s \in \text{Rel}(BC)$, then

$$r \bowtie s = \{ \nu \in \text{ Tup}(ABC) \mid \nu[AB] \in r \wedge \nu[BC] \in s \}$$

and

$$\begin{aligned} &\mu \text{ is in the result} \\ &\iff (\exists\, \nu_1)(\exists\, \nu_2)(\nu_1 \in r \wedge \mu[AB] = \nu_1 \wedge \nu_2 \in s \wedge \mu[BC] = \nu_2) \end{aligned}$$

The important observation here is that the tuples which appear in the result of the evaluation of an RA expression can be described by a *formula* that becomes 'true' when evaluated on given relations. Thus, logical formulas will be the basic ingredients of the language introduced in this section, and the initial approach to answering a query written in this language is to take the operand relation(s) and determine the truth value of the defining formula with respect to all their tuples. However, since a query is meant to produce an output, that is, a result that can be returned to the user as in the case of RA, and since the truth value of a formula alone is certainly not sufficient as an output, the language to be introduced must actually allow for writing 'expressions' (involving formulas); the evaluation of such an expression intuitively consists of evaluating the formula and collecting all tuples for which it yields 'true' in the operand(s) in question.

This is now made precise by defining the 'building blocks' of RTC formulas, which is done in several steps and for which it is assumed that some database schema $\mathbf{D} = (\mathbf{R}, .)$ is given.

Definition 8.7

(i) The set of **symbols** of RTC contains the following elements:

(a) *relation names* R such that $R \in \mathbf{R}$;

(b) *constants* c such that $c \in \text{dom}(\cup_i X_i)$;

(c) *tuple variables*: for each $i \geq 0$, let T_i be an (infinite) set of tuple variables of arity i; let $T := \cup_{i \geq 0} T_i$ denote the set of all tuple variables, and for $t \in T$ let $\alpha(t)$ denote the *arity* of t;

(d) *comparison symbols*: $=, \neq, <, \leq, >, \geq$;

(e) *logical symbols* and *parentheses*: $(,), \wedge, \vee, \neg, \forall, \exists$.

(ii) A **term** of RTC is either a constant or the restriction of a tuple variable $t \in T$ to some position k, that is, a term has the form either c or $t[k]$ for $k \in \{1, \ldots, \alpha(t)\}$.

(iii) An **atomic formula** of RTC has the form either $R(t)$ with $\alpha(R) = \alpha(t)$ or $x \Theta y$, where x and y are terms and Θ is a comparison symbol.

(iv) The set of **formulas** of RTC is the smallest set F of expressions that contains the atomic formulas and for which the following holds: if γ and δ are in F, then so are $(\gamma \wedge \delta), (\gamma \vee \delta), (\neg\gamma), (\forall t)(\gamma), (\exists t)(\gamma)$.

If no confusion can arise, pairs of parentheses may be omitted from a given formula. As in mathematical logic, free and bounded (occurrences of) variables are declared as follows:

(1) Each occurrence of a tuple variable in an atomic formula is **free**.

(2) If t occurs free in γ, then t is **bounded** by $(\forall t)(\gamma)$ or $(\exists t)(\gamma)$.

(3) If t occurs free (bounded) in γ or δ, this occurrence is also free (bounded) in $(\neg\gamma), (\gamma \wedge \delta), (\gamma \vee \delta)$.

Clearly, there will be no interest in formulas that are *nonsensical*, as in the following example. Let $R_1 = (AB, .)$ and $R_2 = (BC, .)$. Then the formula '$R_1(t) \wedge R_2(t)$' is nonsensical, intuitively, because there exists a 'type conflict'; variable t can not be of 'type' R_1 *and* of 'type' R_2 simultaneously. This will not be defined formally here (by introducing the *type* as well as the *mention set* of a formula; see the references). Instead, the reader's intuition is relied upon with regard to this issue. Only *sensical* formulas will be considered in what follows.

Expressions of RTC can now be defined as expressions of the form

$$E = \{ t \mid \delta(t) \}$$

where δ is an RTC formula, and t is the only free tuple variable in δ that is considered to describe the 'output' of δ (see above).

As some first examples for the usage of RTC, expressions are exhibited for some simple RA expressions; while a way of evaluating RTC expressions has not been defined yet, these correspondences should be straightforward:

$E \in$ RA	$E \in$ RTC
$R \cup S$	$\{t \mid R(t) \vee S(t)\}$
$R \cap S$	$\{t \mid R(t) \wedge S(t)\}$
$R - S$	$\{t \mid R(t) \wedge \neg S(t)\}$

If in particular $R = (ABCD, .)$ (see above), the projection $\pi_{AB}(R)$, for instance, can now be written as an RTC expression as follows:

$$\{t \mid (\exists u)(R(u) \wedge t[1] = u[1] \wedge t[2] = u[2])\}$$

Here it is assumed that $\alpha(t) = 2$, and that 1 represents the 'position' A, and 2 the position B. Similarly, the following expression for $\sigma_{C=1}(R)$ is obtained:

$$\{t \mid R(t) \wedge t[3] = 1\} \text{ with } \alpha(t) = 4$$

Next, if both are combined into $\pi_{AB}(\sigma_{C=1}(R))$, the following results:

$$\{t \mid (\exists u)(R(u) \wedge t[1] = u[1] \wedge t[2] = u[2] \wedge u[3] = 1)\} \ (\alpha(t) = 2)$$

With respect to evaluation of RTC expressions, the basic idea — as was indicated earlier — is the following. Given an RTC expression of the form $\{ t \mid \delta(t) \}$, it is first necessary to fix a way in which the tuple variable t that occurs free in δ is associated with the actual tuples that appear in the underlying domain; this process is called **substitution** (or *tuple assignment*). It renders it possible to decide whether a given formula is true or false when 'applied' to a given tuple. Rather than introducing a formal notation for this, the idea can be illustrated by way of an example, where attention is restricted to tuples that occur in a given relation (which is a subset of the underlying domain). Consider the following books relation b from our library application:

Callnumber	*Author*	*Title*	*Publ_Co*
1	Date	Intro DBS I	AW
2	Date	Intro DBS II	AW
3	Ullman	Princ. DBS	CSP
4	Kroenke	DB Proc.	SRA

If $\delta(t) = (B(t) \wedge t[2] = Date)$, where $\alpha(t) = 4$, t can be sequentially substituted by each tuple $\mu \in b$ and the truth of δ with respect to this tuple can be checked. If μ denotes the first tuple occurring in b, the substitution yields

$$\delta(\mu/t) = B(\mu) \wedge Date = Date$$

which is a true statement. However, if μ denotes the third tuple listed above, the substitution yields

$$\delta(\mu/t) = B(\mu) \wedge Ullman = Date$$

which is false (the two constants occurring in the result of the substitution are not equal). In this way, the truth value of a given formula with respect to a state can be determined and in particular all tuples can be found for which the formula evaluates to *true*.

In other words, a given formula in which a tuple variable occurs free can be **interpreted** by substituting an arbitrary concrete tuple for the free variable and determining whether or not the result is true. Next, the **evaluation** $v_E(d)$ of a given RTC expression $E = \{ t \mid \delta(t) \}$ with respect to a given database state d can be defined as the set of all tuples μ from d for which $\delta(\mu/t) =$ 'true'.

The usage of the 'query language' RTC will be demonstrated primarily on an intuitive level here, again using the library database from Figure 7.3; for the RA expressions from the previous section, corresponding RTC expressions are now stated which have the same evaluations, respectively:

(1) $E_1 = \{t \mid B(t) \wedge t[2] = \text{'Date'}\}$ $(\alpha(t) = 4)$

(2) $E_2 = \{t \mid (\exists u)(B(u) \wedge t[1] = u[4])\}$
$\alpha(t) = 1$; $u[4]$ corresponds to the attribute *Publ_Co*)

(3) $E_3 = \{t \mid (\exists u)(C(u) \wedge t[1] = u[3] \wedge (u[1] = 1 \vee u[1] = 2))\}$
$(\alpha(t) = 1)$

(4) $E_4 = \{t \mid (\exists u)(\exists v)(R(u) \wedge C(v) \wedge u[1] = v[2] \wedge t[1] = u[3])\}$
$(\alpha(t) = 1)$

(5) $E_5 = \{t \mid (\exists u)(\exists v)(\exists w)(B(u) \wedge R(v) \wedge C(w) \wedge u[1] = w[1] \wedge w[2] = v[1] \wedge t[1] = u[3] \wedge t[2] = v[2])\}$ $(\alpha(t) = 2)$

(6) $E_6 = \{t \mid B(t)\}$

For example, in (4) the result is obtained by using a variable u $[v]$ to 'scan' the current instance of R $[C]$ and checking whether the first component of u (*Reader_No*) agrees with the second of v (*Reader_No*); if equality holds, t gets the value of the third component of u (*Address*).

A general problem with the language RTC as it now stands is that the interpretations of formulas are, in a sense, *unlimited*, since it was allowed that arbitrary tuples from the underlying domain are considered as candidates for variable substitution; as a consequence, expressions can be stated whose evaluation yields an *infinite* result. For example, if R is a relation name and t is a tuple variable such that $\alpha(R) = \alpha(t)$, the evaluation of $E = \{ t \mid \neg R(t) \}$ yields an infinite set of tuples if domains are infinite. Note that this is no longer a relation in the sense defined in Section 7.1, since relations were required to be finite. It follows immediately that E cannot be 'equivalent' to any expression from RA. In addition, it is not clear whether there is an effective evaluation for every expression.

For these reasons, a restriction is needed. Clearly, a first approach is to consider **limited** interpretations and evaluations only, where the set of candidates for substitution is limited (basically to tuples appearing in a given state or whose values are 'immediate' in a given formula), as was done for the example of the books relation above. Another approach, followed here, is to consider a restricted class of RTC expressions; in particular, the class will be chosen so that (1) for each expression in this class its evaluations under unlimited and limited interpretation are identical (which does not hold for the first approach), and (2) it can be shown that it is as expressive as RA and vice versa.

If $E = \{ t \mid \gamma(t) \} \in$ RTC, E will only be allowed as a query expression if its evaluation results in a *relation*, that is, a *finite* set of tuples; if this is the case, E will be called *safe*. In order to make this precise, the following definition is needed.

Definition 8.8

Let $\mathbf{D} = (\mathbf{R}, .)$, $d \in \text{Dat}(\mathbf{R})$, and $X = \cup_{R_i \in \mathbf{R}} X_i$.

(i) For $R_i \in \mathbf{R}$, $A \in X_i$, and $r_i \in d$,

$$\text{adom}(A, r_i) := \{a \in \text{dom}(A) \mid (\exists \mu \in r_i)\ \mu(A) = a\}$$

is called the **active domain** of A (with respect to r_i), and

$$\text{adom}(R_i, r_i) := \cup_{A \in X_i} \text{adom}(A, r_i)$$

is called the **active domain** of R_i (with respect to r_i).

(ii) If $E \in$ RTC with $E = \{ t \mid \gamma(t) \}$, then

$$\text{dom}(\gamma) := \{c \in \text{dom}(X) \mid c \text{ occurs (explicitly) in } \gamma\} \cup \bigcup_{R_i\text{"}\in\text{"}\gamma} \text{adom}(R_i, r_i)$$

is called the (extended active) **domain** of γ.

Hence, a constant c informally belongs to dom(γ) for an RTC formula γ if c either occurs explicitly in γ or is the value of a tuple in some relation from d whose name appears in γ. An expression E of the form above will in particular be called 'safe' if $t[i] \in \text{dom}(\gamma)$ holds for all $i, 1 \leq i \leq \alpha(t)$ and all t satisfying γ (see Definition 8.9).

It should be noted that dom(γ) is dependent on the current database instance d; since each relation $r_i \in d$ is finite, dom(γ) will always be finite.

As an example, let $R = (AB, .)$ and $\gamma(t)$ be the formula $t[1] = a_1 \vee t[1] = a_2 \vee R(t)$. Then dom($\gamma$) can be described by $\text{dom}(\gamma) = \{a_1, a_2\} \cup \pi_A(r) \cup \pi_B(r)$.

Definition 8.9

Let $E \in$ RTC with $E = \{t \mid \gamma(t)\}$. E is called **safe** if the following conditions are satisfied for every substitution applied to γ:

(1) If $\gamma(\mu/t)$ is true then $(\forall i, 1 \leq i \leq \alpha(t))\ \mu[i] \in \text{dom}(\gamma)$.

(2) For each subformula of γ of the form $(\exists u)\delta$, where u occurs in δ, the following holds. If $\delta(\mu/u)$ is true for any choice of the remaining free variables of δ, then $(\forall i, 1 \leq i \leq \alpha(u))\ \mu[i] \in \text{dom}(\delta)$.

(3) For each subformula of γ of the form $(\forall u)\delta$, where u occurs in δ, the following holds. If $\mu[i] \notin \text{dom}(\delta)$ for some $i \in \{1, \ldots, \alpha(u)\}$, then $\delta(\mu/u)$ is true for any choice of the remaining free variables in δ.

While the first of these conditions is intuitively clear (see the discussion above; it guarantees finite results), the other two are more technical in nature; informally, they require that the first condition also applies to the various sets of tuples being constructed during the generation of the evaluation result for an RTC formula. In particular, (2) and (3) guarantee that the 'safety' of a quantified (sub)formula of the form $(\exists u)\delta$ or $(\forall u)\delta$ can be tested 'locally'. Only those μ are allowed that have components in dom(δ). (For example, (2) is satisfied by $(\exists u)(R(u) \wedge \ldots)$ and (3) by $(\forall u)(\neg R(u) \vee \ldots)$.)

Next let SRTC denote the subset of RTC which consists of safe expressions only. As was mentioned earlier, it can be shown that SRTC is complete (with respect to RA); furthermore, their equivalence can be proved (relative to the inclusion of a rename operation in RA). Only the proof of one direction of this equivalence will be looked into here, and the reader is referred to the Bibliographic Notes for further information. Specifically, it will be shown that RA (without renaming) is as expressive as SRTC.

Theorem 8.5

For each expression $E \in$ RA there exists an expression $E' \in$ SRTC which is equivalent to E (in the sense that it describes the same set of tuples as results from an evaluation of E on some database state d).

Proof. The proof proceeds by induction on the structure of E according to Definition 8.4 or, more precisely, the number of operation symbols occurring in E.

(a) Let $E = R_i$, then E' has the form $\{t \mid R_i(t)\}$. Clearly, $E' \in$ SRTC, since

$$\text{dom}(R_i(t)) = \text{adom}(R_i, r_i)\ \forall d \in \text{Dat}(\mathbf{R}), r_i \in d$$

(b) Next the inductive assumption is made that E_1 and E_2 are elements of RA, and that corresponding expressions E_1' and E_2' from SRTC are known already. Now five cases have to be considered:

(1) Let $E = \sigma_C(E_1) \in$ RA, where C is a selection condition. If E_1' has the form $\{t \mid \gamma_1(t)\}$, then E' has the form $\{t \mid \gamma(t) \wedge C'\}$, where C' is obtained from C by replacing each attribute A occurring in C by the corresponding tuple-variable component $t[i]$. E' is safe since each component of t is restricted to those constants to which it is restricted by $\gamma_1(t)$.

(2) Let $E = \pi_X(E_1)$, where X represents the sequence $A_{i_1}, \ldots, A_{i_n}$ of attributes. If E_1' has the form $\{t \mid \gamma_1(t)\}$, then E' has the form $\{t \mid (\exists u)(\gamma_1(u) \wedge t[1] = u[i_1] \wedge \ldots \wedge t[n] = u[i_n])\}$, where $\alpha(t) = n$. Clearly, E' is safe, given that E_1' is safe.

(3) Let $E = E_1 \bowtie E_2$. Let attr(E_i) denote the format of the result relation generated by E_i, $i = 1, 2$, and let attr$(E_1) = \{A_1, \ldots, A_{n_1}\}$, attr$(E_2) = \{A_{n_1+1}, \ldots, A_{n_2}\}$, attr$(E_1) \cap$ attr$(E_2) = \{A_{i_1}, \ldots, A_{i_n}\}$. Next, let E_1' have the form $\{t \mid \gamma_1(t)\}$ with $\alpha(t) = n_1$, E_2' the form $\{s \mid \gamma_2(s)\}$ with $\alpha(s) = n_2 - n_1$: Then E' has the form

$$\{u \mid (\exists t)(\exists s)(\gamma_1(t) \wedge \gamma_2(s) \wedge t[1] = u[1] \wedge \ldots \wedge t[n_1] = u[n_1]$$

$$\wedge s[n_1 + 1] = u[n_1 + 1] \wedge \ldots \wedge s[n_2] = u[n_2]$$
$$\wedge t[i_1] = s[i_1] \wedge \ldots \wedge t[i_n] = s[i_n])\}$$

where $\alpha(u) = (n_1 + n_2) - n$. E' is safe since $u[j]$ is restricted to values which $t[j]$ can assume for $j, 1 \leq j \leq n_1$, and to those $s[j]$ can assume for $j, n_1 + 1 \leq j \leq n_2$.

(4) Let $E = E_1 \cup E_2$ and E_i' have the form $\{t \mid \gamma_i(t)\}$ for $i = 1, 2$. Then E' has the form $\{t \mid \gamma_1(t) \vee \gamma_2(t)\}$; E' is safe since for $i, 1 \leq i \leq \alpha(t)$ now $t[i] \in \text{dom}(\gamma_1) \cup \text{dom}(\gamma_2)$ holds if t satisfies the formula $\gamma_1(t) \vee \gamma_2(t)$.

(5) Let $E = E_1 - E_2$, and let E_1' be as in case (4), $i = 1, 2$. Then E' has the form $\{t \mid \gamma_1(t) \wedge \neg\gamma_2(t)\}$; since $\text{dom}(\gamma_1(t) \wedge \neg\gamma_2(t)) = \text{dom}(\gamma_1) \cup \text{dom}(\gamma_2)$, is E' safe.

This concludes the proof of Theorem 8.5. □

For proofs of additional 'reductions' between relational query languages, it is convenient to introduce another language, **Relational Domain Calculus** (RDC), which is distinct from RTC in that variables now represent single domain values instead of entire tuples, and to complete the 'chain' of reductions by first showing that [S]RTC is as expressive as [S]RDC, and finally proving that [S]RDC is as expressive as RA. Rather than presenting these steps in detail here, only an example of an RDC expression is given here; the reader is referred to the literature for further information.

Again, let a database schema $\mathbf{D} = (\mathbf{R}, .)$ be given. **Atomic formulas** of RDC have the form either $R(a_1, \ldots, a_n)$, where $R \in \mathbf{R}$, $R = (A_1 \ldots A_n, .)$, and the a_i symbols are variables or constants, or $x\Theta y$, where x and y are variables or constants, and Θ is a comparison symbol (as in Definition 8.7). **Formulas** are built in the same way as before, and an RDC **expression** has the form

$$\{ x_1 \ldots x_n \mid \delta(x_1, \ldots, x_n) \}$$

where δ is an RDC formula and $x_1, \ldots, x_n$ are the only free variables in δ.

Next, consider the books relation of our library example as well as the expressions $E_1 = \sigma_{Author='Date'}(B)$ and $E_2 = \pi_{Publ\_Co}(B)$ discussed above. Corresponding RDC expressions are the following, respectively:

for $E_1 : \{ catp \mid B(catp) \wedge a = Date \}$
for $E_2 : \{ p \mid (\exists c)(\exists a)(\exists t) B(catp) \}$

Here, it is assumed that c (a, t, p) is the variable corresponding to *Callnumber* (*Author*, *Title*, *Publ_Co*).

8.3 Beyond RA expressive power; Datalog

While it could be seen in the previous section that relational algebra is a 'robust' concept in the sense that a completely different approach to providing a query language yields the same expressive power (RTC is Codd-complete), a natural question to be asked is whether RA (or, equivalently, SRTC) allows the expression of all queries. Clearly, to answer this question in detail it will be necessary to state what 'all' refers to, but the fact that the answer will be 'no' can be seen from the following.

Definition 8.10

Let $X = AB$ and $r \in \text{Rel}(X)$. The **transitive closure** of r, denoted r^+, is defined as follows:

$$r^+ := \{\, \mu \in \text{Tup}(X) \mid (\exists\, \mu_1, \ldots, \mu_n \in r, n \geq 1)\ \mu(A) = \mu_1(A) \wedge (\forall\, i = 1(1)n-1)\ \mu_i(B) = \mu_{i+1}(A) \wedge \mu_n(B) = \mu(B)\}$$

Theorem 8.6

Let R^+ denote the query expression yielding r^+ when evaluated with respect to some state d such that $r \in d$. There exists no expression $E \in$ RA such that $E \approx R^+$, that is, $(\forall d)\ v_E(d) = r^+$.

Note that in what follows the distinction between the (pure) transitive closure r^+ of a relation r and its *reflexive and* transitive closure, often denoted r^*, is basically neglected; this distinction is unimportant here.

The proof of Theorem 8.6 is omitted here (see Exercise 9 on p. 185). However, the theorem shows that the expressive power of RA (and hence that of [S]RTC and [S]RDC) is not sufficient for computing the transitive closure of a (binary) relation. It is easily seen that the requirement to compute such a closure arises in many applications (think, for example, of a parent/child relationship and a query that asks for ancestors).

Since the transitive closure is an operation that goes beyond the expressive power of relational algebra, the question arises of how the language RA can be extended so that 'more' database queries can be formulated. One approach, which is often taken in practical DBMS implementations, is to 'interface' a given database language with a host language, that is, a general-purpose programming language. While this will obviously work, since programming languages allow us to compute everything that is 'computable', it is unsatisfactory from a theoretical point of view, since the level of abstraction provided by RA (to consider sets of tuples independent of their internal representation) is generally lost. Another, more appealing approach therefore is to extend the relational language itself with constructs (like one for computing transitive closures) that yield additional power. Clearly, the question that remains is whether some such constructs, and if so which, are sufficient to express *all* queries.

In order to answer questions like this, it makes sense to first figure out what 'all' means. To this end, the notion of a 'computable query' is presented next as a widely accepted standard for describing the class of 'all' queries. In what follows it will be assumed for simplicity that all attributes appearing in a database format have the same finite domain, which is denoted by 'dom'. Consequently, a database schema will for the moment be written as a triple:

$$\mathbf{D} = (\text{dom}, \mathbf{R}, .)$$

and a database $d \in \text{Dat}(\mathbf{R})$ consists of relations r_i such that

$$r_i \subseteq \text{Tup}(X_i) = \{\mu \mid \mu : X_i \rightarrow \text{dom}^{|X_i|}\}$$

where $R_i = (X_i, .) \in \mathbf{R}$.

Definition 8.11

Let $\mathbf{D} = (\text{dom}, \mathbf{R}, .)$ be as above, where $\mathbf{R} = \{R_1, \ldots, R_k\}, R_i = (X_i, .)$ for $i = 1(1)k$, and let $X \subseteq \cup_{i=1}^{k} X_i$. A **computable query** of type ($\mathbf{D}$, X) is a partial function

$$Q : \text{Dat}(\mathbf{R}) \rightarrow \text{Rel}(X) = 2^{\{\mu \mid \mu : X \rightarrow \text{dom}^{|X|}\}}$$

which satisfies the following conditions:

(i) If $d \in \text{Dat}(\mathbf{R})$ and $Q(d)$ is defined, then $Q(d) \subset \text{Tup}(X)$.

(ii) Under an appropriate encoding of values, tuples and relations, Q is partial recursive.

(iii) Q preserves database isomorphisms in the following sense. Let d [d'] be a database with k relations over dom [dom'], respectively, and let h : dom $\rightarrow$ dom' be an isomorphism such that $h(r_i) = r_i'$ under a canonical extension of h for each $i, 1 \leq i \leq k$, where $r_i \in d$ and $r_i' \in d'$, that is, d and d' are isomorphic under h. Then $Q(h(d)) = h(Q(d))$.

Conditions (i) and (ii) basically say that Q is a partial recursive (that is, computable) function which maps databases into relations over the domain of the given argument. Condition (iii), often referred to as the *consistency criterion*, says that the output of a query should be independent from the internal representation of the database. The following can now be proved.

Theorem 8.7

Let $E \in \text{RA}_{\mathbf{D}}$, where $\mathbf{D}$ is as in the previous definition. Then v_E, the evaluation of E, is a computable query.

The proof of this theorem is straightforward and therefore omitted. As a corollary, it can be concluded that CQ, the class of all computable queries, contains RAQ, by which the class of all queries from relational algebra is denoted, now considered as functions from database states to relations:

$$\text{RAQ} \subseteq \text{CQ}$$

By the results described in the previous section, [S]RTCQ, defined similarly, is also contained in CQ. It is also easy to see that r^+ as defined above denotes a computable query. Thus, by Theorem 8.6, the inclusion just described is strict, that is,

$$\text{RAQ} \subset \text{CQ}$$

This observation raises the question of how to provide a language L in such a way that the class LQ of all queries expressible in this language indeed equals CQ. (Note that such a language would be 'complete' in a generalized sense.) As it turns out, such a language can be devised in a variety of ways, all of which basically generalize relational algebra into a programming language by introducing variables (that take relations as values), assignment statements and control structures like if-then-else and while-do constructs.

A language for expressing computable queries will not be introduced formally; the interested reader is referred to the references cited below. A general problem that has to be faced when devising such a language is that the complexity of query evaluation may increase considerably. For obvious practical reasons, our interest is in languages whose queries can be computed 'efficiently', that is, in time polynomial in the size of the underlying database state. This requirement gives rise to the class PQ (also referred to as 'P-queries') of all queries from CQ that can be computed in *polynomial* time. The following can now be proved.

Theorem 8.8

PQ ⊂ CQ, that is, the class of all polynomial time queries is strictly contained in the class of all computable queries.

In addition, it is easily verified that relational algebra queries can be computed in polynomial time, so that the following relationship is arrived at:

$$\text{RAQ} \subset \text{PQ} \subset \text{CQ}$$

Note that the first containment is also strict since the transitive closure, outside RAQ, is polynomial-time computable.

Because of this result, it no longer makes sense to look for a language to express the elements of CQ here; instead, the remainder of this section will indicate how to come up with an 'intermediate' language whose expressive power lies between RAQ and PQ. In detail, the following will briefly be discussed: (1) How to augment RDC with a *least fixpoint operator* (or, equivalently, how to augment RA with an *iteration construct*), and (2) *Datalog*, the 'database adaption' of Prolog.

The former is discussed first, where RDC is used instead of RA for convenience. As an introductory example, consider a binary relation $r \in \text{Rel}(AB)$ with the following contents:

r:

A	B
1	2
2	3
3	4
4	1

Then the (reflexive and) transitive closure r^+ of r, according to Definition 8.10, is the relation

A	B
1	2
2	3
1	3
3	4
1	4
2	4
4	1
4	2
2	1
3	1
3	2
4	3
1	1
2	2
3	3
4	4

Note that r can be interpreted as a directed graph $G = (V, E)$, where $V = \pi_A(r) \cup \pi_B(r)$ (constants occurring in r are considered as nodes), and $E = r$ (two nodes x and y are connected if $(x, y) \in r$). It follows that computing the transitive closure of r is equivalent to computing the transitive closure G^+ of G; formally, $G^+ = (V, E^+)$, where E^+ is recursively defined as follows:

$$(x, y) \in E^+ :\Leftrightarrow (x, y) \in E \vee (\exists z)((x, z) \in E \wedge (z, y) \in E^+)$$

Next this equivalence can be 'translated' into the following *equation* involving query expressions from RDC:

$$T(x,y) \equiv R(x,y) \vee (\exists z)(R(x,z) \wedge T(z,y))$$

The right-hand side of this equation consists of a formula δ involving the free variables x and y as well as the (binary) relation symbol T, written $\delta(x,y;T)$.

Definition 8.12

Let $\delta(x_1,\ldots,x_n;S)$ be an (RDC) formula in which variables $x_1,\ldots,x_n$ occur free, and where S is a symbol for an n-ary relation.

(i) $\delta(x_1,\ldots,x_n;S)$ is **positive** in S if every occurrence of S in δ is under an even number of negations only.

(ii) $\delta(x_1,\ldots,x_n;S)$ is **monotone** in S if the following holds: if d is a database state over all relation symbols occurring in δ except S, then for all relations s, s' over S, $s \subseteq s'$ implies

$$\{(a_1\ldots a_n) \mid \delta(a_1,\ldots,a_n;s) \text{ is true}\} \subseteq \{(a_1\ldots a_n) \mid \delta(a_1,\ldots,a_n;s') \text{ is true}\}$$

where the a_i's are values from d, s, or s'.

(iii) For given d, let $\Delta_\delta^d(s)$ denote the set

$$\{(a_1,\ldots,a_n) \mid \delta(a_1,\ldots,a_n;s) \text{ true}\}$$

as used in part (ii), that is, Δ_δ^d denotes the mapping from n-ary relations derived from d to an n-ary relation that is induced by δ. An n-ary relation s is a **fixpoint** of $\delta(x_1,\ldots,x_n;S)$ if $\Delta_\delta^d(s) = s$.

(iv) A fixpoint s of δ is a **least** fixpoint (lfp) of δ if $s \subseteq s'$ holds for every other fixpoint s' of δ.

As an example, consider the formula $\delta(x,y;T)$ given above. Clearly, δ is positive in T. The fact that δ is also monotone is implied by the following theorem.

Theorem 8.9

Positivity implies monotonicity.

Next, another result from mathematical logic is used which assures the existence and efficient computability of least fixpoints.

Theorem 8.10

Let $\delta(x_1, \ldots, x_n; S)$ be a formula as in the previous definition. If δ is monotone in S, then δ has a least fixpoint s, which can be computed as follows:

$$\begin{aligned} s_0 &:= \emptyset \\ s_{i+1} &:= \{(a_1, \ldots, a_n) \mid \delta(a_1, \ldots, a_n; s_i) \text{ true}\} \\ s &:= \cup_{i \geq 0} s_i \end{aligned}$$

Returning to the above RDC equation for the transitive closure, it can now be concluded further that $\delta(x, y; T)$ has an lfp. Let $d = \{r\}$ be as shown above, then there exists a binary relation t such that

$$\Delta_\delta^d(t) = t$$

and t is minimal with respect to '$\subseteq$' with this property. To compute t, the method described in the last theorem is used, that is,

$$\begin{aligned} t_0 &= \emptyset; \\ t_1 &= \{(x, y) \mid [R(x, y) \vee (\exists z)(R(x, z) \wedge T_0(z, y))] \text{ true}\} \\ &= r \\ t_2 &= \{(x, y) \mid [R(x, y) \vee (\exists z)(R(x, z) \wedge T_1(z, y))] \text{ true}\} \\ &= r \cup \{(4, 2), (1, 3), (2, 4), (3, 1)\} \end{aligned}$$

and so on. Finally, t is obtained as the union of all t_i values, that is, the lfp of $\delta(x, y; T)$ is r^t, shown above.

Now it should be obvious that one way to extend RDC is to add expressions of the form 'lfp(δ)', where δ is an RDC formula of the form presented above involving an 'extra' relation symbol of the appropriate arity that occurs positively in δ, and where the semantics of lfp(δ) is defined along the lines of Definition 8.12. As a result, the class FPQ of **fixpoint queries** is obtained; queries in this class allow us to take the fixpoint of a first-order formula, apply other (first-order) operators to the result, take another fixpoint on a different relation symbol and so on.

Theorem 8.10 suggests a different way of including an lfp operator in a query language in order to augment its expressive power, which is particularly convenient if our discussion is rephrased in terms of RA instead of RDC. From the point of view of a procedural language, the computation of a fixpoint (under the assumptions above) can be considered as an *iterative* construction that is easily expressed in 'program form' if the use of assignment statements, sequencing of 'instructions' and some kind of control structure in combination with the relational operators is allowed. For example, it is easily seen that the transitive closure T of a relation R is 'computed' by the following program:

$T \leftarrow R$;
while $T \neq R'$ **do**
  begin
    $R' \leftarrow T$;
    $T \leftarrow T \cup \pi_{R.A,T.B}(\sigma_{R.B=T.A}(R \times T))$
  end;

(Here it is assumed that the RA operators used allow Cartesian products and selections as well as projections of the given form.)

Thus, it turns out that both the declarative and the procedural approach to query languages can be equipped with more expressive power in a variety of ways. Careful formal treatment (beyond the scope of this section) will reveal that

$$\text{RAQ} \subset \text{FPQ} \subset \text{PQ} \subset \text{CQ}$$

holds. The reader is again referred to the literature cited below for further details.

To conclude this introductory survey of how to query a relational database beyond the capabilities of Codd-complete languages, *logic programming* is briefly considered (as another important area where fixpoints arise) which can also be used to define a natural set of queries. To introduce the different notation used in this context, consider a first-order formula without existential quantifiers written in prenex conjunctive normal form, like

$$f \equiv (\forall x)(\forall y)(p(x,y) \vee \neg q(x,y)) \wedge (r(x,y) \vee \neg s(x,y))$$

Each term of the form $\neg A_1 \vee \neg A_2 \ldots \vee \neg A_n \vee B_1 \vee B_2 \ldots \vee B_m$ can be written as $A_1 \wedge A_2 \ldots \wedge A_n \rightarrow B_1 \vee B_2 \ldots \vee B_m$; for example,

$$f \equiv (\forall x)(\forall y)(q(x,y) \rightarrow p(x,y)) \wedge (s(x,y) \rightarrow r(x,y))$$

Next, quantification is suppressed (it is restricted to be a universal one for each variable), as are conjunction symbols, and the formula is written in a form that looks similar to (a sequence of) assignment statements in a programming language:

```
p(x, y) :- q(x, y).
r(x, y) :- s(x, y).
```

Thus, the original f has been rewritten in the form of a 'logic program'. In a similar way, more complex programs can be written, representing more complex formulas from first-order logic with the 'interpretation' indicated above. To be more precise, the basic ingredients of **Datalog** need to be introduced; this is the 'database adaption' of the logic-programming language Prolog, which has received wide attention recently.

The basic idea behind this language and its application of expressing queries to a relational database is to define a new (derived or *intensional*) relation in terms of the (*extensional*) relations in a given database *and* the new relation itself, and to do so by providing a set of (function-free) Horn clauses defined next.

An **atom** in Datalog is an expression of the form $P(x_1, \dots, x_n)$, where the predicate P denotes a (base or derived) relation, and the x_i symbols are variables or constants. A **literal** is either an atom ('positive literal') or a negated atom ('negative literal'); a **clause** is a disjunction of literals. A **Horn clause** (named after the German mathematician Alfred Horn) is a clause with at most one positive literal, and a Datalog **program** is a finite set C of Horn clauses.

As an example, consider predicates T and R denoting binary relations. Then the clauses

$$C_1 \equiv \neg R(x, y) \vee T(x, y)$$

and

$$C_2 \equiv \neg R(x, z) \vee \neg T(z, y) \vee T(x, y)$$

are Horn clauses which, by rewriting them as above, can also be written as the Datalog program $C = \{C_1, C_2\}$ in the notation

$T(x, y)$:- $R(x, y)$.
$T(x, y)$:- $R(x, z), T(z, y)$.

The argument now is that this program is to be interpreted as the query that computes (in T) the transitive closure (of R). To see this, the following informal semantics is given to each Horn clause of the form 'A :- $B_1, \dots B_n$.': 'For each assignment of each variable, if B_1 is true and B_2 is true and ... and B_n is true, then A is true.' Hence, the first clause informally says that 'for every choice of x and y, if (x, y) is a tuple in (the current instance of) R, then include it in (the result-relation over) T.' Similarly, the second clause can be interpreted as 'for every choice of x, y and z, if (x, z) is in R and (z, y) is in T, then (x, y) is also in T.' Note that the universal quantification of z used here is logically equivalent to the existential one used earlier in this section.

The following terms are commonly used in connection with logic programs: if B :- A_1, A_2, ..., A_n. is a clause occurring in a program, then B is called the **head** of the clause, and $A_1, \dots, A_n$ is called its **body**. According to the definition of a Horn clause (having at most one positive literal), three special cases can occur. (1) The clause consists of exactly one positive literal, and nothing else. In this case, the clause is written as

$P(x, y)$:-

```
program      ::=  clause [ clause ...]
clause       ::=  { rule | fact | int_constr }.
rule         ::=  head :- body
fact         ::=  head :-
int_constr   ::=  body
head         ::=  literal
body         ::=  literal [, literal ...]
literal      ::=  pred_symb ( term_list )
term_list    ::=  term [, term ...]
term         ::=  constant | variable
```

Figure 8.1 Datalog syntax.

and called a **fact**. Facts are a convenient way to describe the contents of a given database in a Datalog program. (2) The clause has no positive literal; in this case it is called an **integrity constraint**. This is not considered further. (3) The clause is a **rule**, that is, it consists of one positive literal and one or more negative ones. With these notions, the syntax of Datalog can concisely be defined as shown in Figure 8.1, where brackets delimit optional elements and vertical bars denote alternatives. Note that any program derived from this grammar must additionally satisfy the *safety condition* that each variable occurring in the head of a rule must also appear in the body of the same rule.

Syntactically, a Datalog program is a set C of Horn clauses, which needs to be given a semantics. A possible approach is to give such a program an interpretation like the following: if R is a predicate occurring in a given program C, a *relation* r for R is a set of **ground** atoms, that is, atoms without variables (but constants only). The *input* to C consists of a relation for each predicate that does not appear in the head of any rule. The *output* computed by C basically consists of a relation for each predicate that occurs in the head of some rule; this computation proceeds as follows. The contents of a database is considered to be given as ground atoms, which can be incorporated into C as facts. A rule states that, if certain facts are known, others can be deduced from them. Newly deduced facts become ground atoms in the output and are at the same time considered to become available as (further) input, so that the rules can be applied again to deduce additional new facts. More precisely, a rule is used to deduce a new fact by *instantiating* its variables with constants, that is, substituting a constant for each occurrence of a variable. If, under such an instantiation, each atom in the body of the rule in question becomes a ground atom, the instantiated head of the rule is added to the output.

It can be shown (see the references cited below) that the 'procedure' sketched above, which does not assume any ordering on the application of rules, describes a least fixpoint computation, whose result (for Datalog programs introduced so far, that is, without negation in rule bodies) alternatively is the (uniquely determined) minimal model of the program in a *model-theoretic* sense, or the set of all facts deducible from the given database in a *proof-theoretic* sense. Furthermore, there is a way to describe it as a (view-defining) *equation* of relational algebra (similar to the equation involving RDC expressions presented earlier), which for the example of the transitive closure has the form

$$T(x, y) = R(x, y) \cup \pi_{x,y}(R(x, z) \bowtie T(z, y))$$

Note that, owing to the recursion involved, the meaning of this expression, obtained by adding a while loop to RA (see the 'program' presented above), is not obtainable by an 'ordinary' RA expression.

It might be suspected that, since the transitive closure is expressible in Datalog, this language is again strictly more powerful than RA. However, it can be shown that Datalog programs are *monotone* in the sense that enlarging the input d to a Datalog program cannot yield a 'smaller' result than on d itself. Using this property, it can be shown that the (set) difference of two relations cannot be computed by any Datalog program, while this can easily be done by an RA or an RDC query. Thus, the set DQ of all queries expressible by Datalog programs and RAQ are incomparable with respect to '$\subseteq$'; in particular, the following can be proved:

(1) $\text{RAQ} \cap \text{DQ} \neq \emptyset$

(Non-recursive Datalog programs and *positive* relational algebra (without difference) are equivalent.)

(2) $\text{RAQ} - \text{DQ} \neq \emptyset$

(RA expressions involving '$-$' are not Datalog expressible.)

(3) $\text{DQ} - \text{RAQ} \neq \emptyset$

(Recursive queries are not RA expressible.)

In addition, it can be shown that $\text{DQ} \subset \text{FPQ}$ holds.

A final aspect to be pointed out here is the 'weakness' of Datalog of not allowing the use of negation in rule bodies. While this would again result in an increase of expressive power, simply allowing the use of negative literals seems inappropriate since rule evaluation becomes nondeterministic in general. One way around this problem is to control the use of negation by a **stratification** of Datalog programs. Informally, a Datalog query is *stratified* if the following holds: if a negative literal $\neg P$ is used in the body of a rule, then P must have been computed completely at this point. In other words, the corresponding program can be divided into **strata** or layers which are evaluated separately in a sequential manner.

As an example, consider the task of computing the *complement* of the transitive closure of a relation. This cannot be accomplished by an ordinary Datalog program; however, the following Datalog$^\neg$ program does it:

$T(x,y)$:- $R(x,y)$.
$T(x,y)$:- $R(x,z), T(z,y)$.
$C(x,y)$:- $\neg T(x,y)$.

The first two lines represent Layer 1 of the stratification and are used to compute the transitive closure (of R in T) as before. The third line, Layer 2, uses this result for computing the complement. The idea henceforth is to have Layer 1 processed completely before Layer 2 is entered (and to continue in the same way in the presence of more than two layers).

With this semantics of Datalog$^\neg$, the following inclusions hold between the various classes of queries that were mentioned in the course of this section. SDQ denotes the set of all queries from Stratified Datalog$^\neg$:

$$\begin{matrix} \text{RAQ} \subset & & \\ & \text{SDQ} \subset \text{FPQ} \subset \text{PQ} \subset \text{CQ} \\ \text{DQ} \subset & & \end{matrix}$$

In this section, Datalog has been described as a paradigm for defining intensional relations as a whole. Users of a database will often only be interested in a subset of such relations, which can be captured by introducing **goals** into Datalog programs. A goal might be written as '?–literal' and expresses an *ad hoc* query against a view defined in the program. For both the evaluation of goals and the computation of intensional relations a variety of methods are described in the literature which exhibit various degrees of efficiency. For further information, the reader is again referred to the Bibliographic Notes.

8.4 Database updates

While queries can be understood as mappings from the set of all databases over a format **R** to the set of all sets of base and derived relations over **R** (see Definition 8.11), an **update** can be understood as a mapping from the set of all databases to itself, that is, an update u has the general form

$$u : \text{Dat}(\mathbf{R}) \rightarrow \text{Dat}(\mathbf{R})$$

Update operations are DML operations which allow us to change the contents of a given database. Clearly, such operations need to be present in a database language (like SQL, see Chapter 16). In this section, a formalism is introduced which allows us to express a restricted but useful class of updates. The basic idea is to use three common types of basic operations, namely *insert, delete* and *modify*, and — in certain analogy to relational algebra — to allow their 'composition' into a straight-line program called an (IDM) *transaction*. As will be seen, these transactions come close to what can be done in languages like SQL, and interesting new questions need to be investigated for them.

To define the syntax of update operations and transactions, the notion of a 'condition' is needed.

Definition 8.13

Let $R = (X, .)$ be a relation schema.

(i) A **condition** over R is an expression of the form '$A = a$' or '$A \neq a$', where $A \in X$ and $a \in \text{dom}(A)$.

(ii) A tuple μ over X **safisfies** the condition $A = a$ $[A \neq a]$ if $\mu(A) = a$ $[\mu(A) \neq a]$. If C is a *set* of conditions, then μ satisfies the set C if μ satisfies every condition in C.

In what follows, only finite and *meaningful* sets of conditions are considered, which do not contain mutually exclusive conditions (for example, $C = \{A = a, A \neq a\}$ is not satisfiable for any $a \in \text{dom}(A)$). A set C of conditions over a given relation schema R specifies a set of tuples over R, namely the set of those tuples satisfying the conditions; for such a set, the intuitive term **hyperplane** will be used, which is denoted by $\text{H}(R, C)$. Thus,

$$\text{H}(R, C) = \{\mu \in \text{Tup}(X) \mid \mu \text{ satisfies } C\}$$

Note that $\text{H}(R, C) \neq \emptyset$ if C is satisfiable; in addition, $C_1 = C_2$ follows from $\text{H}(R, C_1) = \text{H}(R, C_2)$. If the relation schema in question is clear from the context or immaterial, the shorthand $\text{H}(C)$ will be used for $\text{H}(R, C)$.

The syntax of the basic instructions for describing updates can now be defined as follows.

Definition 8.14

Let $\mathbf{D} = (\mathbf{R}, .)$ be a database schema.

(i) An **insertion** over **D** is an expression of the form $i_R(C)$, where $R \in \mathbf{R}$ and the conditions in C describe exactly one (complete) tuple over R.

(ii) A **deletion** over **D** is an expression of the form $d_R(C)$, where C is a set of conditions over R, $R \in \mathbf{R}$.

(iii) A **modification** over **D** is an expression of the form $m_R(C_1; C_2)$, where $R \in \mathbf{R}$, C_1 and C_2 are sets of conditions over R, and for each attribute A of R either $C_1|_A = C_2|_A$ (the conditions from C_1 involving

A agree with those from C_2 involving A) or '$A = a$' $\in C_2$ for some $a \in \text{dom}(A)$ (the equalities present in C_2 but not in C_1 indicate how to modify the tuples from $\text{H}(C_1)$).

(iv) An **update instruction** over $\mathbf{D}$ is an insertion, a deletion or a modification over $\mathbf{D}$.

As an example, consider the library database for which a possible state was shown in Figure 7.3. The following are update instructions (or *updates* for short) over the corresponding schema together with their intended meanings:

(1) i_B(7, Paredaens, Rel. Model, Springer)

(Insert the new book by Paredaens into the current relation over B.)

(2) $d_O(\mathit{Reader\_No} = 550)$

(Delete all entries for Nina from the current relation over O, that is, record the fact that Nina has returned all her books.)

(3) $m_O(\mathit{Reader\_No} = 600;\ \mathit{Reader\_No} = 600,\ \mathit{Return\_Date} = 073188)$

(Extend the return date for Peter by two months.)

Next, the semantics of an update instruction over a database schema $\mathbf{D} = (\mathbf{R}, .)$ is described as a mapping from the set $\text{Dat}(\mathbf{R})$ of all instances of $\mathbf{D}$ into itself, which is called the *effect* of that instruction.

Definition 8.15

For $\mathbf{D} = (\mathbf{R}, .)$ let $d \in \text{Dat}(\mathbf{R})$, and let $d[R]$ denote the relation from d corresponding to relation schema $R = (X, .) \in \mathbf{R}$.

(i) The **effect** of $i_R(C)$ is the mapping

$$\text{eff}[i_R(C)]: \text{Dat}(\mathbf{R}) \rightarrow \text{Dat}(\mathbf{R})$$

defined by

$$\text{eff}\,[i_R(C)](d)(S) := \begin{cases} d[R] \cup \{C\} & \text{if } S = R \\ d[S] & \text{otherwise} \end{cases}$$

(ii) The **effect** of $d_R(C)$ is the mapping

$$\text{eff}[d_R(C)]: \text{Dat}(\mathbf{R}) \rightarrow \text{Dat}(\mathbf{R})$$

defined by

$$\text{eff}\,[d_R(C)](d)(S) := \begin{cases} d[R] - \text{H}(R, C) & \text{if } S = R \\ d[S] & \text{otherwise} \end{cases}$$

(iii) The **effect** of $m_R(C_1; C_2)$ is the mapping

$$\text{eff}[m_R(C_1; C_2)]\colon \text{Dat}(\mathbf{R}) \rightarrow \text{Dat}(\mathbf{R})$$

defined by

$$\text{eff}[m_R(C_1; C_2)](d)(S) := \begin{cases} (d[R] - \text{H}(R, C_1)) \\ \cup \{m_R(C_1; C_2)(\mu) \\ \quad \mid \mu \in \text{H}(R, C_1) \cap d[R]\} & \text{if } S = R \\ d[S] & \text{otherwise} \end{cases}$$

Here, the modified version $m_R(C_1; C_2)(\mu_1)$ of each tuple $\mu_1 \in \text{H}(R, C_1)$ under $m_R(C_1; C_2)$ is the tuple $\mu_2 \in \text{H}(R, C_2)$, where

$$\mu_2(A) = \begin{cases} \mu_1(A) & \text{if } C_1|_A = C_2|_A \\ a & \text{if `}A = a\text{' } \in C_2 \end{cases}$$

for each $A \in X$.

An almost trivial observation from the above exposition is that now a way is available to 'generate' some database state reflecting a real-world situation from an empty initial state which is 'produced' (by a DBMS) as the result of a format or schema declaration. In addition, it is possible to alter any such state by executing modifications, deletions or insertions. Also, it is easily verified that the set of update instructions introduced in Definition 8.14 is *non-redundant*; in particular, a modify operation can in general not be 'simulated' by deletions and (re)insertions alone, since the exact set of tuples to be modified is usually not known in advance (it is only described by some conditions).

The application of these update instructions is so far limited to individual operations only. On the one hand, this is inconvenient for practical applications, since, for example, a user may want to insert several tuples into a database in one operation. On the other hand, update operations will in reality often be executed relative to integrity constraints that the database state has to satisfy (see Section 9.5), that is, the result of an update operation will have to be consistent in the sense of Definition 7.5. For example, if relation schemas R_1 and R_2 are 'connected' via an IND of the form $R_1[V_1] \subseteq R_2[V_2]$, an insertion of something new into r_1 may need to be accompanied by an insertion into r_2, and both insertions have to be executed as one *atomic* step. These observations assist the introduction of the notion of a *transaction* (generally understood as a consistency-preserving unit), whose syntax and semantics can be defined as follows.

Definition 8.16

(i) An (IDM) **transaction** over a database schema **D** is a finite sequence of update instructions over **D**.

(ii) Let t be a transaction over **D**. The *semantics* of t, called its **effect** and denoted eff(t), is a mapping

$$\text{eff}(t) : \text{Dat}(\mathbf{R}) \rightarrow \text{Dat}(\mathbf{R})$$

defined as follows. Let $t = u_1 \ldots u_m$, then

$$\text{eff}(t) := \text{eff}[u_1] \circ \text{eff}[u_2] \circ \ldots \circ \text{eff}[u_m]$$

Hence, eff(t) is the composition of the effects of the updates that make up t.

As an example, the following transaction t (atomically) inserts John as a new reader into the corresponding relation of the library from Figure 7.3 and transfers Date's books from Nina to John:

$$\begin{aligned} t = {} & i_R(650, \text{John}, \text{Oceanside}) \\ & m_O(\mathit{Callnumber} = 1;\ \mathit{Callnumber} = 1,\ \mathit{Reader\_No} = 650) \\ & m_O(\mathit{Callnumber} = 2;\ \mathit{Callnumber} = 2,\ \mathit{Reader\_No} = 650) \end{aligned}$$

From Definition 8.16, a notion of equivalence for transactions can straightforwardly be derived as follows. Two transactions t and t' over **D** are **equivalent**, denoted $t \approx t'$, if eff(t) = eff(t'), that is, t and t' have the same effect on every state.

As was mentioned above for relational algebra, an immediate application of such a notion of equivalence is the issue of *optimization*, now meaning the replacement of a given transaction by another one that is in some sense 'simpler' to execute. For example, consider a relation schema R with attributes A and B; then

$$t_1 = i_R(A = 0, B = 0)\ d_R(A = 0) \quad \approx \quad t_2 = d_R(A = 0)$$

and clearly t_2 requires less effort than t_1 during execution.

To make that practical, it is first necessary to determine whether equivalence of transactions is decidable and even efficiently decidable. To this end, the following can be proved.

Theorem 8.11

Let t_1 and t_2 be two IDM transactions over the same database schema **D**. Then it can be decided in time polynomial in the lengths of the transactions (the respective number of update instructions) and the number of constants in them whether $t_1 \approx t_2$.

One approach to proving the decidability result of Theorem 8.11 is to provide a sound and complete axiomatization for the notion of equivalence. Following is an (incomplete) list of such axioms, in which C_1, C_2, C_3 and C_4 denote sets of conditions describing pairwise disjoint hyperplanes, all over the same relation schema R (so that R can be omitted as index):

(1) $i(C_1)i(C_2) \approx i(C_2)i(C_1)$

(2) $d(C_1)d(C_2) \approx d(C_2)d(C_1)$

(3) $d(C_1)i(C_2) \approx i(C_2)d(C_1)$ if $C_1 \neq C_2$

(4) $m(C_1; C_2)m(C_3; C_4) \approx m(C_3; C_4)m(C_1; C_2)$ if $C_3 \neq C_1, C_2$ and $C_1 \neq C_4$

(5) $m(C_1; C_2)i(C_3) \approx i(C_3)m(C_1; C_2)$ if $C_1 \neq C_3$

(6) $m(C_1; C_2)d(C_3) \approx d(C_3)m(C_1; C_2)$ if $C_3 \neq C_1, C_2$

(7) $i(C_1)d(C_1) \approx d(C_1)$

(8) $d(C_1)i(C_1) \approx i(C_1)$

(9) $m(C_1; C_1) \approx \epsilon$

(10) $m(C_1; C_2)i(C_2) \approx d(C_1)i(C_2)$

(11) $i(C_1)m(C_1; C_2) \approx i(C_2)m(C_1; C_2)$

(12) $m(C_1; C_2)d(C_1) \approx m(C_1; C_2)$

(13) $m(C_1; C_2)d(C_2) \approx d(C_1)d(C_2)$

(14) $d(C_1)m(C_1; C_2) \approx d(C_1)$

(15) $m(C_1; C_2)m(C_2; C_3) \approx m(C_1; C_3)m(C_2; C_3)$

The axioms, the first six of which are *commutativity rules*, assume that the transactions involved are *normalized* in the sense that all hyperplanes corresponding to distinct sets of conditions occurring in the transaction are disjoint. Thus, for applying the axioms in transforming a transaction t into another, equivalent one, it is first necessary to normalize t. For example, if

$$t = d_R(A = 0)\ m_R(A \neq 7; A = 5)$$

then obviously $\mathrm{H}(R, \{A = 0\}) \cap \mathrm{H}(R, \{A \neq 7\}) \neq \emptyset$. Normalization would transform t into the (equivalent) transaction

$$t' = d_R(A = 0)\ m_R(A = 0; A = 5)\ m_R(A \neq 0, A \neq 5, A \neq 7; A = 5)$$

and can also be described formally by 'split axioms' (see the references).

Since the axioms do not lead to an efficient 'procedure' for proving equivalence, the question arises of how such a procedure can be obtained. Also, criteria for transaction optimization need to be established, as do ways to meet them. Other questions, for which answers can be found in the references, regard the expressiveness of the IDM language introduced above as well as possible extensions, or the relationship of IDM transactions to integrity constraints.

8.5 Manipulation of views

In this section the case (which was sketched in Chapter 2) will be briefly considered that individual **views** are available at the external level for the users of a (relational) database, as is intended by the three-level architecture concept; such views generally result from the design phase of the database in question (see Chapter 10). In particular, this section will illustrate why commercially available *relational* systems often provide a two-level architecture of databases only (up to now), which in fact distinguishes a conceptual from an internal level, but does not support external schemas in its full generality (as a user might expect). Specifically, views as introduced at the end of Section 8.1 apparently do not pose problems with respect to querying a database, but are not as easily handled with respect to updates.

The discussion in this section assumes relational algebra as the underlying query language. Consider an employee relation named *EMP* of some enterprise with the attributes *EMP#* (employee number), *NAME*, *BRANCH*, where the enterprise is assumed to have two branches, one in San Diego and one in Los Angeles, that is, dom(*BRANCH*) = {SD, LA}; finally, the company has a football team, and attribute *FB* contains information on whether an employee is a member of the football team or not, that is, dom(*FB*) = $\{Y, N\}$. Next, let two views be declared over this relation, one for the manager of the LA branch, and one for the coach of the football team:

$$\begin{array}{ll} LA\_EMP & := \sigma_{BRANCH=LA}(EMP) \\ FOOTBALL & := \sigma_{FB=Y}\ (EMP) \end{array}$$

Any such expression can obviously be evaluated in the way that was introduced earlier, namely by replacing the name of each occurring relation by its current value and applying the operations as specified.

If a (relational) database system is to support a view of the data on *three* levels, it must be possible for a user first to declare certain views on the conceptual schema at the external level (as 'subschemas' thereof in the sense of UDS, see Chapter 14) and then to work with these as if they were stored relations. This latter aspect of 'working' with a view in particular means that a user must be allowed to both query and update the view as desired.

First note that *queries* to a view do not raise new basic problems. The corresponding DBMS must be capable of accepting view names (besides the names of base relations) in a query, and of deriving their contents from the base relations, since only the definition is generally stored (in the catalog) for any view. The evaluation of such an 'extended' query hence involves a preprocessing step, in which all view names are replaced by their respective definition; the result of this step can then be evaluated as before.

In the example above, the football coach might pose the query 'Show all players from LA', which is written in relation algebra as

$$\sigma_{BRANCH=LA}(FOOTBALL)$$

its 'translation' or 'expansion' into an (ordinary) expression of relational algebra would then yield

$$\sigma_{BRANCH=LA}(\sigma_{FB=Y}(EMP))$$

The execution of database *updates* via views, on the other hand, is a problem of completely different quality. Consider the following examples, which are written using the update instructions from the previous section:

(1) Let the manager of the LA branch issue the following command to his view:

$$d_{LA\_EMP}(EMP\# = 25)$$

A reasonable evaluation of this command with respect to the current contents of relation *EMP* obviously consists of a deletion of the employee with employee number 25, that is, this employee gets fired.

(2) Let the coach of the football team issue the following command to his view:

$$d_{FOOTBALL}(EMP\# = 18)$$

Now it is unrealistic to delete the employee with employee number 18 from relation *EMP* as well, unless the coach is allowed to fire employees. Instead, it seems reasonable in this case to modify the *FB* value of the tuple with $EMP\# = 18$ in relation *EMP* to 'N'.

Thus, while the view deletion was evaluated as a deletion from the

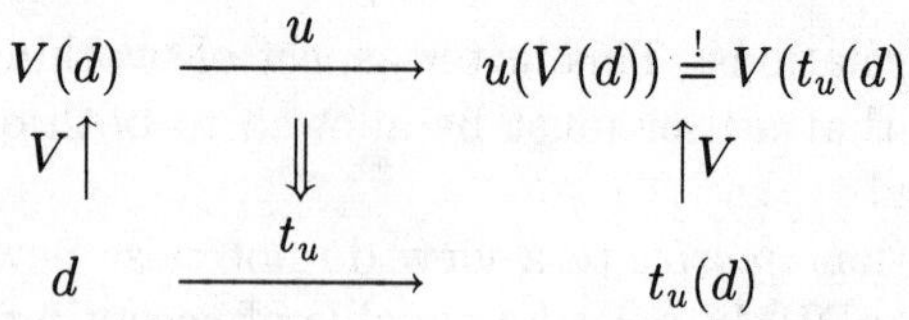

$$\begin{array}{ccc} V(d) & \xrightarrow{\quad u \quad} & u(V(d)) \stackrel{!}{=} V(t_u(d)) \\ V\uparrow & \Downarrow & \uparrow V \\ d & \xrightarrow{\quad t_u \quad} & t_u(d) \end{array}$$

Figure 8.2 Formalization of the view update problem.

underlying base relation in the first example, the view deletion in the second results in a replacement or modification of some tuple from *EMP*.

This problem of evaluation or 'translation' of view updates into database updates is solved in a very rudimentary way by commercially available systems so far. In the remainder of this section, a brief introduction to the problem of updating relational views will be given. First, an intuitively appealing formalization of the problem will be presented; next, some of the criteria will be summarized which an evaluation mechanism for update commands that involve views should satisfy. Finally, it will be indicated how such a mechanism can be realized, where the discussion will stick to the 'selection views' introduced above.

In what follows, let V denote a view definition, which is given in the form of an expression from relational algebra over some database schema **D**. In particular, the view specified by V will be termed an S- (P-, J-, SPJ-) view if its definition is an S- (P-, J-, SPJ-) view, respectively, where 'S' means selection, 'P' projection and 'J' join (see Section 8.1).

A view state, that is, the result of an evaluation of V with respect to a (consistent) database state $d \in \text{Sat}(\mathbf{D})$ is denoted $V(d)$. A **database update** can be written as a mapping of the form $t : \text{Sat}(\mathbf{D}) \rightarrow \text{Sat}(\mathbf{D})$, and let d' denote the 'sucessor state' of d generated by t, that is, $t(d) = d'$. A **view update** u is specified by the user with respect to $V(d)$; it has to be 'translated' into some database update t_u such that the new view state $V(d')$, which the user has specified by $u(V(d))$, can be derived from the new database state $d' = t_u(d)$. The attention here is restricted to so-called 'elementary' view updates by which exactly one tuple (at a time) is to be inserted or deleted (or modified).

More formally, the diagram shown in Figure 8.2 shall commute; in other words, a database update t_u is called a **translation** of the view update u if the following holds:

$$u(V(d)) = V(t_u(d))$$

(Note that other authors call the translations as defined above 'exact' or 'valid' translations since they maintain the consistency constraints required for **D**.)

As the examples given above indicate, in general there exist *several* translations for a given view update. In this case, a so-called **translator** associates a particular translation t_u with the given view update u. The **view update problem** can hence be considered as the task of finding a translator for a given set of view updates.

As should no longer be surprising, a translator for view updates or the translations it produces have to meet certain requirements; the 'design' of a translator that really satisfies such criteria is in fact the core of the view update problem.

Some requirements to the translations of a view update will be listed next; these are intuitively clear, but not always easy to satisfy formally.

(1) The integrity constraints of the underlying database schema **D** have to be maintained, that is, each translation t_u of u actually has to represent a mapping from Sat(**D**) to itself (see above).

(2) Only those database tuples should be affected by the changes that are made in the current state d which (partially or completely) occur in $V(d)$, that is, a translation should be free of 'side effects' on d.

(3) If a view update u is without effect on $V(d)$ (like in the case where an insertion of some tuple follows the deletion of that very tuple), then t_u does not change d at all. In this case, t_u is also called *acceptable*; using the above formalism, the condition can be written as

$$u(V(d)) = V(d) \Longrightarrow t_u(d) = d$$

(4) For each view update u there exists an 'inverse' (mapping) w which satisfies

$$w(u(V(d))) = V(d)$$

Next, let a *selection view* of the form $V = \sigma_C(R)$ be given (see the introductory example above). Also, let $R = (X, \{K\})$ (see Chapter 7: K is declared as a key for R), and let $\mu \in \text{Tup}(X)$ be a (user-defined) tuple which is to be *inserted* into $V(d) = \sigma_C(r)$. It is also assumed that $\mu \notin \sigma_C(r)$ holds. With respect to the conditions listed above, the following requirements have to be met by a realization of this view update:

(1) $(\forall\, \nu \in \sigma_C(r))\ \nu[K] \neq \mu[K]$
(note that K is also a key for the view in this case);

(2) μ satisfies the selection condition C.

As a consequence, the following two translations can immediately be stated:

I1: If $\nu[K] \neq \mu[K]$ holds for all $\nu \in r$, then insert μ into r ($r := r \cup \{\mu\}$).

I2: If there exists a tuple $\nu \in r$ such that $\nu[K] = \mu[K]$, then replace ν by μ ($r := r - \{\nu\} \cup \{\mu\}$).

It is easy to see that these translations satisfy the conditions listed above.

In the employee example, let *EMP#* be the key for relation *EMP*. If the tuple μ =(30, MAIER, LA, N) is to be inserted into view *LA_EMP*, the following applies: under the assumption that $\mu(EMP\#) \notin \pi_{EMP\#}(emp)$, μ is inserted into relation *emp* over schema *EMP* in this case according to **I1**. Since μ satisfies the selection condition of the view, the tuple becomes visible in the new view state.

However, if $\mu(EMP\#) \in \pi_{EMP\#}(emp)$ holds, that is, there exists a tuple $\nu \in emp$ such that $\mu(EMP\#) = \nu(EMP\#)$, it follows from condition (1) above that

$$\nu \notin \sigma_{BRANCH=LA}(emp)$$

and hence $\nu(BRANCH)$ = SD. The view update described by

$$i_{LA\_EMP}(30, \text{MAIER, LA, N})$$

hence essentially describes the moving of the employee with employee number 30 from San Diego to Los Angeles in this case; acoding to **I2**, tuple ν will consequently be replaced by μ in *emp*.

Next let $\mu \in \sigma_C(r)$ be a view tuple that is to be deleted from $V(d)$; as is known from the introductory examples, (at least) two translations are possible:

D1: Delete μ from r ($r := r - \{\mu\}$).

D2: Let $A \in X - K$ and $a \in \text{dom}(A)$ be an A value which does not satisfy the selection condition C. Next let μ' be defined by

$$(\forall B \in X)\ \mu'(B) := \begin{cases} a & \text{if } B = A \\ \mu(B) & \text{otherwise} \end{cases}$$

Then μ is replaced by μ' ($r := r - \{\mu\} \cup \{\mu'\}$).

Again it is easily verified that these translations of a deletion meet the above conditions.

In the example of the view *FOOTBALL*, the tuple μ =(30, MAIER, SD, Y) is to be deleted. μ satisfies the selection condition '$FB = Y$'; the non-key attribute *FB* can alternatively assume the value 'N', so that the deletion of μ from the current state of *FOOTBALL* can be translated according to **D2** as a replacement of $\mu \in emp$ by μ' =(30, MAIER, SD, N).

For view *LA_EMP*, on the other hand, it is not clear at first glance whether the deletion of tuple μ =(30, MAIER, SD, Y) (assumed to exist in the view state) should be translated as a deletion from *emp* or as a replacement by μ' =(30, MAIER, SD, Y).

It should be apparent from these elementary examples of updating a view by inserting or deleting *single* tuples that a corresponding translator will in general not be able to function without certain additional information.

While in the case of the insertion above it could be decided on the basis of the new tuple alone whether translation **I1** or **I2** should be applied (under the given assumptions), a similar criterion does not exist for a deletion. In this situation, a possible solution is to conduct a *dialogue with the user* to clarify which translation is desired. It should be mentioned that similar observations with respect to the ambiguity of translations also apply to tuple modifications or to other kinds of views (like projection or join views or combinations thereof). A corresponding dialogue could be initiated by the DBMS at the definition time of the view in question; the DBA or the view creator should be asked certain questions, answers to which make it possible to choose a translator uniquely. For further information on this approach, the reader is referred to the references cited at the end of this Part.

Chapter 9
Functional Dependencies

In this chapter a particular kind of intrarelational constraints, **functional dependencies**, is considered and studied in detail. It will turn out that these constraints generalize the concept of 'key dependencies', and that there exist close connections to methods and paradigms used in logic.

9.1 Definition of functional dependencies; Implication

The reader is first reminded of the (intrarelational) key dependencies introduced in Definition 7.1; a different way to interpret such a dependency of the form $K \to X$ is to say that (in each valid relation) given values for K 'functionally' determine the values for X. This is now generalized as follows.

Definition 9.1

Let V be a set of attributes, and let $X, Y \subseteq V$. A **functional dependency** (FD) $X \to Y$ denotes the following semantic constraint. Let $r \in \text{Rel}(V)$:

$$(X \to Y)(r) := \begin{cases} 1 & \text{if } (\forall \mu, \nu \in r)\ (\mu[X] = \nu[X] \Longrightarrow \mu[Y] = \nu[Y]) \\ 0 & \text{otherwise} \end{cases}$$

Thus, r *satisfies* $X \to Y$, or $X \to Y$ is *valid* in r, if any two tuples from r which agree on X also agree on Y.

It immediately follows that a key dependency is a *special* FD. Let $r \in \text{Rel}(V)$ and $K \subseteq V$, then the following holds:

$$\begin{aligned} &(K \to V)(r) = 1 \\ &\quad \Longrightarrow (\forall \mu, \nu \in r)(\mu[K] = \nu[K] \Longrightarrow \mu[V] = \mu = \nu[V] = \nu) \end{aligned}$$

For this reason, the notation usually reserved for FDs was used for key dependencies in Chapter 7. The generalization consists of allowing *subsets* of the entire attribute set on the right-hand side of the arrow.

As a first example, let $V = ABCDE$, and let $r \in \text{Rel}(V)$ be as follows:

	A	B	C	D	E
	1	1	1	1	1
r:	1	0	1	1	1
	2	2	0	0	1
	2	3	2	0	1

It is easily verified that r satisfies the FD $AB \to C$, since any two tuples from r are distinct on AB. In addition, r satisfies the FDs $A \to D$ and $D \to E$ and hence the following *set* of FDs:

$$F = \{AB \to C, A \to D, D \to E\}$$

Based on the close relationship between key dependencies and FDs, a first procedure can be stated to test whether a given relation $r \in \text{Rel}(V)$ satisfies an FD $X \to Y$.

First, r is sorted according to the values of the attributes in X in such a way that tuples with equal X-entries are grouped together. Next, r is scanned sequentially, and for each 'new' set of tuples with equal X-values it is tested whether these tuples also agree on Y. If this is always the case, then r is valid, otherwise it is not.

In this 'procedure' the following equivalence is used, whose proof is left to the reader as an exercise:

$$(X \to Y)(r) = 1 \iff (\forall\ X\text{–values } x) \mid \pi_Y(\sigma_{X=x}(r)) \mid \leq 1$$

(Here it is assumed that the shorthand '$X = x$' is allowed as a selection condition.)

The following notations are introduced for FDs. Individual FDs of the form $X \to Y$ are often equipped with a 'name' and then written as $f : X \to Y$ or simply f (the notation $f : X \to Y$ is used to emphasize the functionality of this type of constraint). The left-hand (right-hand) side of an FD f is generally denoted by L_f (R_f) and the set $L_f \cup R_f$ of all attributes appearing in f is denoted by attr(f); for example, if $f : AB \to C$, then $L_f = AB, R_f = C$, and attr$(f) = ABC$.

Following Chapter 7, a set F of functional dependencies can be considered as a 'semantic constraint' for a relation. In particular, if $R = (X, F)$ is a relation schema with attribute set X and FD set F (where $(\forall f \in F)$ attr$(f) \subseteq X$ is always assumed), then we are interested only in those elements r of Rel(X) which satisfy F. Since only *individual* relation schemas are being considered for the moment, one can also write Sat(F) instead of Sat(R) if the underlying set of attributes is understood.

With respect to update operations, FDs represent special consistency or integrity constraints. If it is assumed that these are checked by a DBMS at run-time, it is clearly desirable to have efficient algorithms available for performing these checks. With this goal in mind, the following notions are introduced.

Definition 9.2

Let F and G be two sets of FDs over an attribute set V, that is, $(\forall f \in F)$ attr$(f) \subseteq V$ and $(\forall g \in G)$ attr$(g) \subseteq V$.

(i) F and G are called **equivalent**, abbreviated $F \approx G$, if Sat$(F) =$ Sat(G) holds.

(ii) F is called **redundant** if there exists a set $F' \subset F$ of FDs such that $F' \approx F$.

Under the interpretation that a set of FDs represents a semantic specification for a given relation format (according to the application at hand), these two notions have a natural meaning: two sets F and G

are termed 'equivalent' if they are identical as semantic specifications, that is, if they yield the same restriction with respect to the entire 'state space'. Similarly, redundancy means that a given specification F contains 'more constraints than necessary'; some of these can be omitted without changing the space of 'valid' states.

It turns out that both notions can be reduced to a more basic one.

Definition 9.3

Let F be as above, and let f be an FD with $\text{attr}(f) \subseteq V$. F **implies** f, abbreviated $F \models f$, if $\text{Sat}(F) \subseteq \text{Sat}(\{f\})$ holds, that is, every relation (over V) which satisfies F also satisfies f.

With this notion, the following can immediately be concluded.

Theorem 9.1

Let F and G be as in Definition 9.2. Then the following hold:

(1) $F \approx G \iff (\forall f \in F)\ G \models f \wedge (\forall g \in G)\ F \models g$

(2) F is redundant $\iff (\exists f \in F)\ F - \{f\} \models f$

The proof of this theorem is straightforward and therefore omitted. The result demonstrates that the notion of implication can replace the two notions introduced before, so that it can be considered as the most important one among the three notions presented so far. In this chapter the question of how implication can be tested will be dealt with in particular; from an answer to this question it is then easy to derive tests for equivalence and redundancy using Theorem 9.1.

To illustrate these notions, consider the set $V = ABC$ of attributes, and the two sets of FDs

$$F = \{A \to B, B \to C, A \to C, AB \to C\}$$

and

$$G = \{A \to B, B \to C, AB \to C\}$$

Next let $r \in \text{Rel}(ABC)$ be the following relation:

	A	B	C
	1	1	1
r:	2	0	1
	0	0	1

It is easily verified that r satisfies both F and G. More generally, it is even possible to prove, using Definition 9.1, that *every* relation from $\text{Rel}(ABC)$

which satisfies F also satisfies G and vice versa. For example, if s is a relation that satisfies G, let $f : A \to C$. Then the following holds:

$$\begin{aligned}(\forall \mu, \nu \in s)\ \mu[A] = \nu[A] & \\ \Longrightarrow \mu[B] = \nu[B], & \text{ since } s \text{ satisfies } A \to B \in G \\ \Longrightarrow \mu[C] = \nu[C], & \text{ since } s \text{ satisfies } B \to C \in G\end{aligned}$$

It follows that $A \to C$ is also satisfied by s. Hence it can be concluded that $F \approx G$ holds, and that F is redundant.

9.2 Derivation; The membership problem

The notion of implication is investigated in more detail next and appropriate tools are derived to test it. This will in particular lead to 'calculations' involving FDs in the sense of logical derivations. First, another notion is introduced.

Definition 9.4

Let F be as in Definition 9.2.

$$F^+ := \{f \mid \text{attr}(f) \subseteq \cup_{g \in F} \text{attr}(g) \wedge F \models f\}$$

is called the **closure** of F.

It follows immediately that $F \subseteq F^+$ holds for every set F of FDs. With this notion, 'testing implication' means to determine whether a given FD f is a member of the closure of a set F of FDs. This question of deciding, for given F and f, whether $f \in F^+$ holds is called the **membership problem** for functional dependencies.

In the last example of the previous section, the following can be observed: $A \to C \in G^+$ (since $G \models A \to C$). In addition, for example, $AC \to C \in G^+$ can be stated, since for every relation r satisfying G the following holds:

$$(\forall \mu, \nu \in r)\ \mu[AC] = \nu[AC] \Longrightarrow \mu[C] = \nu[C]$$

These observations are now generalized in the following way. *Rules* will be established that allow us to determine (certain) members of a closure in an easy way; as before, it is assumed that all sets of attributes used are subsets of a 'universe' V:

(A1) $Y \subseteq X \implies X \to Y$
(A2) $X \to Y \wedge Y \to Z \implies X \to Z$ ('transitivity')

These rules are to be read as follows.

Rule (A1): If $Y \subseteq X \subseteq V$ holds (for some set V of attributes), then *every* relation $r \in \text{Rel}(V)$ satisfies the FD $X \to Y$. Since in this case the right-hand side is contained in the left-hand side, such an FD is called **trivial**.

Rule (A2): If a relation satisfies the two FDs $X \to Y$ and $Y \to Z$, then it also satisfies $X \to Z$; a proof of this can be given immediately by generalizing the example discussed above.

While (A1) and (A2) might not be particularly surprising as rules by which new FDs can be derived (eventually from already existing ones), the next rule is not as straightforward:

$$\text{(A3)} \quad X \to Y \wedge Z \subseteq W \implies XW \to YZ \quad \text{('augmentation')}$$

In order to prove the 'correctness' of this rule, let r be a member of Sat$(X \to Y)$. Then the following holds for r: $(\forall \mu, \nu \in r)\ \mu[X] = \nu[X] \implies \mu[Y] = \nu[Y]$. It has to be shown that r also satisfies the FD $XW \to YZ$. So let $\mu, \nu \in r$ such that $\mu[XW] = \nu[XW]$. It follows that $\mu[Y] = \nu[Y]$, since $X \to Y$ is valid in r, and $\mu[Z] = \nu[Z]$, since $Z \subseteq W$ and $\mu[W] = \nu[W]$. Thus, it can be concluded that $\mu[YZ] = \nu[YZ]$, which was to be shown.

If these rules are applied to the problem of computing a closure, the following are obtained:

(1) $Y \subseteq X \implies X \to Y \in F^+$ (even if $F = \emptyset$)

(2) $\{X \to Y, Y \to Z\} \subseteq F \implies X \to Z \in F^+$

(3) $X \to Y \in F \wedge Z \subseteq W \implies XW \to YZ \in F^+$

This derivation of new FDs from given ones is now formalized.

Definition 9.5

Let F be a set of FDs (over V), and let $X \to Y$ be an FD such that $XY \subseteq V$. $X \to Y$ is called **derivable** from F, denoted $F \vdash f$, if there exists a sequence $f_1, \dots, f_n$ of FDs with the following properties:

(1) f_n is of the form $X \to Y$;

(2) for each $i, 1 \leq i \leq n$, either $f_i \in F$ holds, or f_i can be generated from $\{f_1, \dots, f_{i-1}\}$ by using rules (A1), (A2) and (A3).

It follows immediately that every FD f which is derivable from some set F by using the three rules given above is also implied by F. Therefore (following common practice in mathematical logic) the system of rules consisting of (A1), (A2) and (A3) is called **sound** (or *correct*), since any derivation based on it yields FDs which are implied (valid). The next theorem shows that this rule system is also **complete** in the sense that every (valid) FD, which is implied by some set F, is also derivable from F using these rules.

Theorem 9.2

Let F be a set of FDs and f be a single FD. Then

$$F \models f \quad \text{iff} \quad F \vdash f$$

Proof. The 'if' part is obvious by what was said above. For the 'only if' part, its contraposition is shown. If f is not derivable from F, then f is also not implied by F.

Let F be given with $\cup_{f \in F} \text{attr}(f) \subseteq V$, and let $X \to Y$ be not derivable from F $(X, Y \subseteq V)$. The following set of attributes is defined:

$$X^+ := \{A \in V \mid F \vdash X \to A\}$$

By Rule (A1) it follows that $X \to A$ holds for all $A \in X$ and hence $X \subseteq X^+$. Furthermore, $X \to X^+$ is derivable from F, since, for example, if both $X \to A$ and $X \to B$ are derivable from F, then so are $X \to XA$ and $XA \to AB$ (by Rule (A3)) and thus $X \to AB$ (by Rule (A2)).

It is argued next that $Y \not\subseteq X^+$ holds. Assume, on the contrary, that Y is a subset of X^+. Then $X^+ \to Y$ can be derived using (A1). Since it is already known that $F \vdash X \to X^+$ holds, (A2) implies $F \vdash X \to Y$, a contradiction. Hence, there exists some $B \in Y$ such that $B \notin X^+$.

A relation $r \in \text{Rel}(V)$ is now exhibited which satisfies F, but which does not satisfy $f : X \to Y$. r has the following form:

		X^+	$V - X^+$
$r:$	μ	1 1 ... 1 1	1 ... 1
	ν	1 1 ... 1 1	0 ... 0

Relation r is a so-called **two-tuple relation**, that is, r contains exactly two tuples, which agree on X^+ and disagree everywhere else. (Note that it is assumed as a simplification that all attributes from V share the same domain, which in particular contains 0 and 1. The reader is also reminded that, according to the general assumption made in Section 7.1, $|\text{dom}(A)| \geq 2$ always holds.) It follows immediately that r does not satisfy the FD $X \to Y$, since $\mu[X] = \nu[X]$ $(X \subseteq X^+)$, but $\mu(B) \neq \nu(B)$ $(B \in Y)$.

It remains to be shown that r satisfies F. To this end, let $S \to T \in F$, and let $\mu[S] = \nu[S]$. It follows that $S \subseteq X^+$, by construction of r, and hence $F \vdash X^+ \to T$ by (A3). Using (A1), $T \to A$ can additionally be derived for every $A \in T$, so that $X^+ \to A$ can also be derived, using (A2). From this, $X \to A$ follows by (A2) for all $A \in T$, and hence $T \subseteq X^+$ as well as $\mu[T] = \nu[T]$.

Therefore, it can finally be concluded that $F \not\models X \to Y$. □

The derivation rules (A1)–(A3) are called **Armstrong's axioms** (after W.W. Armstrong, see the Bibliographic Notes); now Theorem 9.2 states that the Armstrong axioms are sound and complete, that is, the notions of implication and derivation *coincide* for functional dependencies.

A relation such as the one used in the proof of Theorem 9.2, which satisfies *exactly* the dependencies in F^+ (and nothing else), is also called an **Armstrong relation** (for the set F in question). Given some set F of FDs and an FD $f \notin F^+$, an Armstrong relation for F can also be considered as a *counterexample relation* for $F \models f$.

Let us call a relation **trivial** if it contains (at most) one tuple. Clearly, a trivial relation satisfies any FD. Next, call a set F of FDs **inconsistent** if $r \in \text{Sat}(F)$ implies that r is trivial. (If F is inconsistent, then F does not represent a meaningful semantic specification.) Call F **complete** if $F \cup \{f\}$ is inconsistent for every $f \notin F^+$. (If F is complete, there is no good reason to enlarge F, since any augmentation results in an inconsistent specification.) Now the following holds for every set F of FDs.

Theorem 9.3

Inconsistency of F implies that F is complete, which in turn implies that F has an Armstrong relation.

Proof. Let F be inconsistent, that is, $(\forall\, r \in \text{Sat}(F)) \;\; |\, r \,| = 1$. Since any such r satisfies all members of F^+, F is trivially complete. If F is complete, two cases have to be considered: if F is inconsistent, every trivial relation is also an Armstrong relation for F; otherwise, that is if F is consistent, there exists a non-trivial relation r satisfying F. The claim is that r is an Armstrong relation. Suppose, on the contrary, that r satisfies f, but $f \notin F^+$; since r is non-trivial and $r \in \text{Sat}(F \cup \{f\})$ holds, it follows that $F \cup \{f\}$ is consistent, a contradiction to the assumption that F is complete. □

It should be mentioned that the previous theorem is easy to prove for functional dependencies; it can be extended to other types of dependencies as well.

The implication problem for FDs is now returned to, using the knowledge that $F \models f$ holds if and only if $F \vdash f$ holds. Thus, to show an implication it is sufficient to state a derivation. The next goal is to show that derivations can be performed in some 'normalized' manner. To this end, some additional derivation rules are listed:

(A4) $X \rightarrow Y \;\wedge\; X \rightarrow Z \Longrightarrow X \rightarrow YZ$ ('additivity')
(A5) $X \rightarrow Y \;\wedge\; Z \subseteq Y \Longrightarrow X \rightarrow Z$ ('projectivity')

The correctness of (A4) follows from the proof of Theorem 9.2; for (A5) this is obvious.

(A6) $X \rightarrow X$ ('reflexivity')

(A7) $X \rightarrow YZ \ \wedge \ Z \rightarrow AW \implies X \rightarrow YZA$ ('accumulation')

Theorem 9.4

The rule system { A5, A6, A7 } is sound and complete.

Proof. Correctness (soundness) is trivial; completeness is shown by deriving the Armstrong axioms from these three rules, so that the assertion is implied by the completeness of the Armstrong axioms.

(A1): $X \rightarrow X$ and $Y \subseteq X$ implies $X \rightarrow Y$ by (A5).

(A2): Let $X \rightarrow Y$ and $Y \rightarrow Z$ hold. By (A6), $X \rightarrow X$ also holds. By a repeated application of (A7), $X \rightarrow XY$ is derived first and then $X \rightarrow XYZ$. Using (A5), $X \rightarrow Z$ follows.

(A3): Let $Z \subseteq W$, and let $X \rightarrow Y$ hold. From (A6), it follows that $XW \rightarrow XW$ is valid, so that a repeated application of (A7) yields $XW \rightarrow XWY$, and finally (A5) implies $XW \rightarrow ZY$. □

The rule system { A5, A6, A7 } will be called the **RAP rules** (as an acronym for **R**eflexivity, **A**ccumulation, and **P**rojectivity). This system is used to state derivations in the following form, which is consequently called a **RAP derivation**.

An FD $X \rightarrow Y$ is an element of F^+ if and only if there exists a derivation sequence $f_1, \ldots, f_n$ for which the following holds:

(1) f_1 is of the form $X \rightarrow X$,

(2) f_n is of the form $X \rightarrow Y$,

(3) $(\forall i, 2 \leq i \leq n-1)\ f_i \in F \vee f_i : X \rightarrow Z$ is derivable using (A7).

Thus, in a RAP derivation rule R ≡ (A6) is used first, rule P ≡ (A5) is used last, and in between only rule A ≡ (A7) is applied (so that such a derivation could also be termed a 'RA*P derivation').

Consider the following example. Let $F = \{AB \rightarrow E, BE \rightarrow I, E \rightarrow G, GI \rightarrow H\}$. In order to solve the membership problem 'does $AB \rightarrow GH \in F$ hold?' the following RAP derivation is used:

$f_1:$	$AB \rightarrow AB$	(A6)	R
$f_2:$	$AB \rightarrow E$	$\in F$	
$f_3:$	$AB \rightarrow ABE$	(A7)	A
$f_4:$	$BE \rightarrow I$	$\in F$	
$f_5:$	$AB \rightarrow ABEI$	(A7)	A
$f_6:$	$E \rightarrow G$	$\in F$	
$f_7:$	$AB \rightarrow ABEIG$	(A7)	A
$f_8:$	$GI \rightarrow H$	$\in F$	
$f_9:$	$AB \rightarrow ABEIGH$	(A7)	A
$f_{10}:$	$AB \rightarrow GH$	(A5)	P

Since it is possible to derive $AB \rightarrow GH$ from F, it can be concluded that $AB \rightarrow GH \in F^+$ holds.

The particular way of proceeding during a RAP derivation bears some resemblance to the proof of Theorem 9.2, where the set X^+ of all those attributes A for which $F \vdash X \rightarrow A$ was true was considered. On the basis of this theorem, the following notation for this set can now be introduced.

Definition 9.6

For $X \subseteq V$ and a set F of FDs (over V)

$$cl_F(X) := \{A \in V \mid X \rightarrow A \in F^+\}$$

is called the **closure** of X (under F). (Instead of $cl_F(X)$ the reader will often find the notation X^+ in the literature; see the proof of Theorem 9.2.)

Observe that a RAP derivation for $X \rightarrow Y$ does nothing else but to *enlarge* X until either Y is contained in the resulting set or it has been shown that Y is not functionally implied by X entirely. In this latter case, the RAP derivation actually computes $cl_F(X)$ and concludes from $Y \not\subseteq cl_F(X)$ that $X \rightarrow Y \notin F^+$ holds. The next theorem shows that the converse is also valid.

Theorem 9.5

Let F be a set of FDs (over V), and let $X, Y \subseteq V$:

$$X \rightarrow Y \in F^+ \iff Y \subseteq cl_F(X)$$

Proof. '$\Longrightarrow$': Let $X \rightarrow Y \in F^+$. It follows that $X \rightarrow A \in F^+$ for every $A \in Y$ by Rule (A5) and hence $Y \subseteq cl_F(X)$.

'$\Longleftarrow$': Let $Y \subseteq cl_F(X)$. Now it follows that $cl_F(X) \rightarrow Y \in F^+$ by Rule (A1); because of $X \rightarrow cl_F(X) \in F$ it may then be concluded, using

(A2), that $X \to Y \in F^+$. □

A useful paradigm is now available for solving the membership problem for functional dependencies. Basically, this problem can be solved by first computing F^+ for given $X \to Y$ and F and then testing whether $X \to Y$ is a member of this set. However, in general $|F^+|$ is exponential in $|F|$; for example, if $F = \{A \to B_1, \dots, A \to B_n\}$, then $A \to Y \in F^+$ for each $Y \subseteq \{B_1, \dots, B_n\}$; hence, F^+ has at least 2^n elements.

On the other hand, Theorem 9.5 renders it possible to state an algorithm to compute X^+ in time polynomial in the length of the representation of F:

Algorithm CLOSURE
Input: A set F of FDs and a set X of attributes.
Output: $cl_F(X)$
Method:

```
begin
    Y := X;
    while (∃ S → T ∈ F) S ⊆ Y ∧ T ⊈ Y
    do Y := YT
end;
```

Theorem 9.6

Algorithm *CLOSURE* terminates and computes $cl_F(X)$.

Proof. Clearly, the algorithm terminates as soon as no more element of F satisfies the while condition. Let Z be the set of attributes that is computed by *CLOSURE* on input F and X.

It is first shown that $Z \subseteq cl_F(X)$ holds, by an induction on the individual steps. In the beginning, $Y = X$ holds, that is, the assertion holds because of $X \subseteq cl_F(X)$. Next let the assertion be valid for some intermediate result Y (that is, $Y \subseteq cl_F(X)$), and let $S \to T \in F$, where $S \subseteq Y$. From $\{X \to Y, Y \to S, S \to T\} \subseteq F^+$ it follows that $X \to YT \in F^+$, and hence $X \to A \in F^+$ for all $A \in YT$ (according to the rules stated earlier). Thus, $YT \subseteq cl_F(X)$.

It remains to be shown that Z is not a *strict* subset of $cl_F(X)$: Suppose there exists an attribute A such that $A \in cl_F(X) - Z$. Then $X \to A \in F^+$ holds, since $A \in cl_F(X)$. Next let $r = \{\mu, \nu\}$ be a relation (over the underlying set V of all attributes) such that

$$\mu(B) = \nu(B) \iff B \in Z$$

Clearly, $r \notin \text{Sat}(\{X \to A\})$, since $A \notin Z$. On the other hand, $r \in \text{Sat}(F)$ holds, since otherwise, that is if $r \notin \text{Sat}(F)$, there exists an FD $S \to T \in F$ such that $S \subseteq Z$, but $T \not\subseteq Z$. In this case, Z cannot be the final output of the algorithm, a contradiction to our initial assumption. It follows that $r \in \text{Sat}(F)$ and hence $X \to A \notin F^+$, a contradiction. Hence, $Z = cl_F(X)$ as desired. □

It is now evident that Algorithm *CLOSURE* can be extended into a membership test by appending a test of whether the desired right-hand side is a subset of the final result. The complete algorithm can thus be stated as follows:

Algorithm FD-MEMBERSHIP
Input: F, X and Z
Output: $\begin{cases} \text{'true' if } X \to Z \in F^+ \\ \text{'false' otherwise} \end{cases}$
Method:

```
begin
    membership := false;
    Y := CLOSURE(F, X);
    if Z ⊆ Y then membership := true
end;
```

The following theorem, which is stated without proof, states that the membership problem for FDs is efficiently solvable in a complexity-theoretic sense.

Theorem 9.7

The membership problem for functional dependencies can be solved in time linear in the length of the representation of the input for Algorithm *CLOSURE*.

As a first application of Algorithm *FD-MEMBERSHIP*, the problem of testing equivalence, discussed in the previous section, can now be clarified:

Algorithm EQUIVALENCE
Input: Two sets F and G of FDs (over the same set of attributes)
Output: $\begin{cases} \text{'true' if } F \approx G \\ \text{'false' otherwise} \end{cases}$
Method:

```
begin
    equivalence := false;
    if (∀ X → Y ∈ F) FD-MEMBERSHIP(G, X, Y)
        and (∀ Z → W ∈ G) FD-MEMBERSHIP(F, Z, W)
        then equivalence := true
end;
```

Similarly, Algorithm *FD-MEMBERSHIP* can be used to test whether a given set F of FDs is redundant; however, stating a corresponding procedure is postponed (see the next section), since the interest is not only in an answer to the question whether some F is redundant, but in deriving a *redundancy-free* F' such that $F \approx F'$.

As another application of the membership algorithm, the computation of a key for a given relation format V, for which a set F of FDs has been stated as integrity constraints, is considered next. Using Algorithm *FD-MEMBERSHIP*, the following algorithm apparently has the desired effect:

Algorithm KEY
Input: A set $V = A_1 \ldots A_m$ of attributes
and a set F of FDs over V.
Output: A key $K \subseteq V$ (for $R = (V, F)$).
Method:

```
begin
    K := V;
    for i := 1 to m do
        if FD-MEMBERSHIP(F, K − {A_i}, V)
            then K := K − {A_i} ;
end;
```

Algorithm *KEY* sucessively removes attributes from the initialization $K = V$ and tests whether the resulting set still functionally implies the entire set V of attributes. The result of the algorithm is a set K with $K \rightarrow V \in F^+$ and $K' \rightarrow V \notin F^+$ for all $K' \subset K$.

For example, let $V = ABCDE$, and $F = \{AB \rightarrow C, A \rightarrow D, D \rightarrow E\}$. In this case $(BCDE)^+ = BCDE$, that is, A cannot be removed from V without violating the identification property. Furthermore, $(ACDE)^+ = ACDE$, $(ABDE)^+ = (ABE)^+ = (AB)^+ = ABCDE$, so that the result is $K = AB$.

Clearly, Algorithm *KEY* also runs in polynomial time. On the other hand, it computes an *arbitrary* key for $R = (V, F)$, which only depends on the input sequence of the attributes (which has to be fixed for implementation purposes). It may happen that several keys exist for a given relation schema, and that it is desirable to determine the one that has the smallest cardinality, for example in order to be able to test the key condition as efficiently as possible during updates.

For example, let $F = \{AB \rightarrow E, BE \rightarrow I, E \rightarrow G, GI \rightarrow HB\}$. If Algorithm *KEY* is applied to the input sequence *ABEIGH*, the output will be the key *AIG*; however, for the input *AEIGHB*, it will be *AB*.

The next theorem shows that the problem of determining a key of minimal cardinality is probably not efficiently solvable.

Theorem 9.8

Let F be a set of FDs over V, and let k be a positive integer. The problem to decide whether there exists a key $K \subseteq V$ such that $\mid K \mid \leq k$ is NP-complete.

Proof. (For the purposes of this proof the reader is assumed to be familiar with the basics of the theory of NP-complete problems; see the Bibliographic Notes.) The proof proceeds in two steps.

(i) It is easy to see that the problem at hand belongs to the class NP of problems solvable in non-deterministic polynomial time: simply 'guess' a subset K of V with k elements and verify (in polynomial time) that K is a key.

(ii) To show that the problem is complete for NP, the *set covering problem* will be reduced to it, which can be stated as follows. Given a family $M = \{M_1, \ldots, M_p\}$ of finite sets and a positive integer $k \leq p$, decide whether there is exists a subfamily $\{M_{i_1}, \ldots, M_{i_k}\}$ such that $\cup_{i=1}^{p} M_i = \cup_{j=1}^{k} M_{i_j}$.

Let $\{M_1, \ldots, M_p\}$ and k be given, and let $M = \cup_{i=1}^{p} M_i$. Also, let $N = \{A_1, \ldots, A_p\}$ be a set of p (new) elements not occurring in M. From this, an instance of the key-determination problem is constructed as follows: let $V := M \cup N$ be the set of attributes, and let

$$F := \{M \rightarrow N\} \cup \{A_i \rightarrow M_i \mid 1 \leq i \leq p\}$$

be the set of FDs. The following will be proved: there exists a cover for M with k elements if and only if there exists a key $K \subseteq V$ for (V, F) such that $\mid K \mid \leq k$.

(only if) Let $M' = \{M_{i_1} \ldots, M_{i_k}\}$ be a cover of M. Then for $K := \{A_{i_1} \ldots, A_{i_k}\}$ the following holds: $\mid K \mid = k$, and $K \rightarrow V \in F^+$ since $V \subseteq K^+$ (note that $A_{i_1} \ldots A_{i_k} \rightarrow M_{i_1} \ldots M_{i_k} \in F^+$, and, by $M_{i_1} \cup \ldots \cup M_{i_k} = M$, $K \rightarrow M \in F^+$; hence $M \rightarrow N \in F$ implies $K \rightarrow V \in F^+$). In addition, K is minimal with respect to $K \rightarrow V$; thus, K is the desired key.

(if) Next let K be a key with $\mid K \mid \leq k$. Without loss of generality, it may be assumed that $K \subseteq N$ holds, since if $B \in K \cap M$ it follows that $B \in M_j$ for some $j \in \{1, ..., p\}$; in this case, B can be replaced by A_j. In particular, let $K \subseteq \{A_{i_1} \ldots, A_{i_k}\}$. If there exists some $B \in M - (\cup_{j=1}^{k} M_{i_j})$, consider the following relation $r \in \text{Rel}(V)$:

	B	$N - \{A_{i_1} \ldots, A_{i_k}\}$	remaining attributes ($\supseteq K$)
μ	1	1 … 1	1 … 1
ν	0	0 … 0	1 … 1

It is now easy to see that $r \in \text{Sat}(F)$ and $r \notin \text{Sat}(\{K \rightarrow V\})$ hold, a contradiction to the assumption that K is a key. It follows that $M - \cup_{j=1}^{k} M_{i_j} = \emptyset$, which means that $\cup_{j=1}^{k} M_{i_j}$ covers M.

Finally, it should be noted that F can be constructed in polynomial time, so that the above reduction is indeed polynomial. The NP-completeness of the key-determination problem thus follows from the NP-completeness of the set covering problem. □

9.3 Alternative characterizations of FD implication

Our next goal is to state additional characterizations of the notion of implication for FDs. The first of these intuitively says that a test of whether $F \models f$ holds based on Definition 9.3 can be restricted to certain relations.

Theorem 9.9

Let F and f be as in Theorem 9.2. Then the following holds:

$$F \models f \iff \text{every 2-tuple relation satisfying } F \text{ also satisfies } f.$$

Proof. '$\Longrightarrow$': Trivial, since if $F \models f$ every relation that satisfies F also satisfies f by Definition 9.3; this in particular holds for all relations containing two tuples only.

'$\Longleftarrow$': Suppose that f is not implied by F, that is, $f \notin F^+$. Let f have the form $X \to Y$. Consider the following relation r over V:

	$cl_F(X)$	$V - cl_F(X)$
μ	$1 \ldots 1$	$1 \ldots 1$
ν	$1 \ldots 1$	$0 \ldots 0$

As in the proof of Theorem 9.2 it can now be shown that $r \in \text{Sat}(F)$, but $r \notin \text{Sat}(\{X \to Y\})$. Hence there exists a relation with two elements which satisfies F, but not f, a contradiction. □

Theorem 9.9 shows that the relation used in the proof of Theorem 9.2 has not been chosen at random.

Next, a relation $r = \{\mu, \nu\} \in \text{Rel}(V)$ is encoded as a **Boolean expression** as follows. Each attribute $A \in V$ is interpreted as a Boolean variable which can only be assigned the ('truth') values 0 or 1. A valuation of A by r is defined by

$$A := \begin{cases} 1 & \mu(A) = \nu(A) \\ 0 & \text{otherwise} \end{cases}$$

By A' the complement of A is denoted ($A' = 1 \iff A = 0$), and — in analogy to the theory of switching functions — the symbol '$\cdot$' ['+'] is used for Boolean *And* [*Or*], respectively; a product $A \cdot B$ of Boolean variables is abbreviated AB.

If r is a relation as above ($|\, r \,| = 2$) and $r \in \text{Sat}(\{A \to B\})$ holds, it follows that

$$\mu(A) = \nu(A) \implies \mu(B) = \nu(B)$$

or with respect to truth values that

$$A = 1 \implies B = 1$$

On the other hand, if $\mu(A) \neq \nu(A)$, then either '=' or '≠' may hold with respect to B ($A = 0 \implies B = 0 \vee B = 1$). Therefore, the FD $A \to B$ can be interpreted as Boolean implication ('⇒') of the corresponding variables and represented as in the following table:

A	B	$A \Rightarrow B$
0	0	1
0	1	1
1	0	0
1	1	1

It is easily seen that this representation can be extended to general FDs: if $X \to Y$ is given, where $X = A_1 \ldots A_n$, $Y = B_1 \ldots B_m$, the following holds:

$$\begin{aligned}
& r \text{ satisfies } X \to Y \\
& \quad \iff (\mu[X] = \nu[X] \;\Rightarrow\; \mu[Y] = \nu[Y]) \\
& \quad \iff [(\mu(A_1) = \nu(A_1) \wedge \ldots \wedge \mu(A_n) = \nu(A_n)) \\
& \qquad\quad \Rightarrow (\mu(B_1) = \nu(B_1) \wedge \ldots \wedge \mu(B_m) = \nu(B_m))] \\
& \quad \iff [(A_1 = 1 \wedge \ldots \wedge A_n = 1) \Rightarrow (B_1 = 1 \wedge \ldots \wedge B_m = 1)] \\
& \quad \iff (A_1 \ldots A_n \Rightarrow B_1 \ldots B_m)
\end{aligned}$$

For this last expression it is shorter to write $X \Rightarrow Y$. Next, the identity

$$(X \Rightarrow Y) = 1 \iff X' + Y = 1$$

known from propositional calculus is used, so that the following can be stated.

Theorem 9.10

Let $r = \{\mu, \nu\}$. Then $(X \to Y)(r) = 1$ iff $X' + Y = 1$.

(Note that, if no confusion can arise, the same symbol is used for an attribute and for its corresponding Boolean variable.)

It should be noted that the consideration of two-element relations is not mandatory in this context; however, this proceeding is also intuitively appealing since the validity of an FD $X \rightarrow Y$ in some relation r requires that *any two* tuples agree on Y if they agree on X.

If $F = \{X_1 \rightarrow Y_1, \ldots, X_n \rightarrow Y_n\}$ is a set of FDs, a relation r satisfies F if r satisfies *every* FD from F. In Boolean terminology this means that the *conjunction* of $X_1' + Y_1, \ldots, X_n' + Y_n$ evaluates to 1. Hence, the set F can be written as a Boolean function as follows:

$$F = (X_1' + Y_1) \cdot (X_2' + Y_2) \cdot \ldots \cdot (X_n' + Y_n)$$

Next, the following result from the theory of Boolean functions is made use of: every Boolean function F (in several variables) can be uniquely represented as the sum of those minterms encoding an argument for which F evaluates to 1 (such minterms are sometimes called 'positive'). This representation is called the **disjunctive normal form** (DNF) of F. This is illustrated using the following example. Let $F_1 = \{AB \rightarrow C, A \rightarrow B, B \rightarrow C, A \rightarrow C\}$ be a set of FDs over $V = ABC$. The representation of F_1 as a Boolean function is given by

$$F_1 = ((AB)' + C)(A' + B)(B' + C)(A' + C)$$

To determine the minterm-representation of F_1, the following truth table is considered:

A	B	C	$(AB)'+C$	$A'+B$	$B'+C$	$A'+C$	F_1
0	0	0	1	1	1	1	1
0	0	1	1	1	1	1	1
0	1	0	1	1	0	1	0
0	1	1	1	1	1	1	1
1	0	0	1	0	1	0	0
1	0	1	1	0	1	1	0
1	1	0	0	1	0	0	0
1	1	1	1	1	1	1	1

The equivalent DNF representation for F_1 is consequently

$$F_1 = A'B'C' + A'B'C + A'BC + ABC$$

Note that every minterm contains *all* 'variables' from V. Any such term M can be decomposed into a 'positive' and a 'negative' part as follows. A variable $A \in V$ belongs to the positive (negative) part of M if A occurs non-negated (negated) in M.

For the previous example, the set $P_1 = \{C, BC, ABC\}$ contains the positive portions of all minterms from the DNF shown above.

As a second example, consider the set $F_2 = \{AB \rightarrow C, A \rightarrow D, D \rightarrow E\}$ with the Boolean representation

$$F_2 = ((AB)' + C)(A' + D)(D' + E)$$

and the DNF

$$\begin{aligned}F_2 = & A'B'C'D'E' + A'B'C'D'E + A'B'C'DE + A'B'CD'E' \\ & +A'B'CD'E + A'B'CDE + A'BC'D'E' + A'BCDE' \\ & +A'BC'DE + A'BCD'E' + A'BCD'E + A'BCDE \\ & +AB'C'DE + AB'CDE + ABCDE\end{aligned}$$

The set P_2 of positive portions of all minterms occurring in this representation is:

$$\begin{aligned}P_2 = \{ & E, DE, C, CE, CDE, B, BCD, BDE, \\ & BC, BCE, BCDE, ADE, ACDE, ABCDE\}\end{aligned}$$

With respect to the second alternative characterization of the notion of implication announced earlier, the following can now be stated.

Definition 9.7

Let V be a set of attributes, $S \subseteq V$.

(i) S is called **closed** with respect to the FD $X \to Y$ if $X \subseteq S$ implies $Y \subseteq S$.

(ii) S is called **closed** with respect to the set F of FDs if S is closed with respect to every $f \in F$.

Theorem 9.11

Let F denote the representation of a set of FDs over V as a Boolean function in DNF. Then the following holds for every $S \subseteq V$: S is closed with respect to the set F of FDs iff S is the positive portion of a minterm occurring in the DNF of F.

Theorem 9.12

Let F be a set of FDs, and f an FD. Then the following holds:

$$F \models f \iff (\forall S \subseteq V)\ (S \text{ closed w.r.t. } F \ \Rightarrow\ S \text{ closed w.r.t. } f)$$

These last two theorems will not be proved here; instead, their usage is illustrated on the following example.

Let F_2 be as above, and let $f_1 : AB \to DE$. It is easy to verify that any set $Z \in P_2$ is closed with respect to f_1, that is, $F_2 \models f_1$ (note that in this case only for $Z = ABCDE$ it is true that $AB \subseteq Z$, which implies $DE \subseteq Z$). Next consider $f_2 : B \to C$. For $B \in P_2$ now $B \subseteq B$, but $C \not\subseteq B$ holds. Hence there exists a set, namely $\{B\}$, which is closed with respect to F, but not closed with respect to $B \to C$. It follows that $B \to C \notin F_2^+$.

For proofs of these last theorems, the reader is referred to the literature listed in the Bibliographic Notes. It seems interesting to emphasize, however, that the intuitively simple notion of a functional dependency can be investigated from a mathematical point of view in a variety of ways. In particular, FDs can be identified with Boolean functions, which make methods and results from propositional calculus applicable. (For example, the correctness of derivation rules can now be verified using a truth table.) What was also pointed out in this section is that a change in the level of reflection can be fruitful from time to time. Theorem 9.11 indicates a possibility to 'compute' closed sets; Theorem 9.12 uses the result of such a computation to further characterize the notion of implication.

9.4 Dependency bases

The problem of redundancy of a given set F of FDs is now reconsidered. As was mentioned already, redundancy intuitively means that F is more comprehensive than necessary when considered as a semantic specification. A redundancy-free specification will now be asked for to accomplish the same as F with respect to the set of admissible relations. To this end, the following notion is introduced.

Definition 9.8

Let F and G be sets of FDs such that $F \approx G$. Then F is called a **cover** of G (and correspondingly G is a cover of F).

It follows that a given set F of FDs is redundant if there exists a subset $F' \subset F$ that covers F. With respect to questions related to database design to be discussed in a later chapter, the interest is in covers which are not only redundancy-free, but also 'clearly arranged' in the following sense.

Definition 9.9

Let F be a set of FDs, $f : X \rightarrow Y \in F$:

(1) f is called **l(eft)-minimal** (or 'full') if there exists no $X' \subset X$ such that $F - \{f\} \cup \{X' \rightarrow Y\} \approx F$.

(2) f is called **r(ight)-minimal** if $\mid Y \mid = 1$ holds.

(3) F is called **minimal** if every element of F is l- and r-minimal.

(4) A cover G of F is called a (dependency) **basis** of F if G is non-redundant and minimal.

As an example, consider $F = \{A \rightarrow BC, B \rightarrow C, AB \rightarrow D\}$. Then $F' = \{A \rightarrow B, A \rightarrow C, B \rightarrow C, AB \rightarrow D\}$ is an r-minimal cover of F,

	10	11	01	00 = AB
$C = 1$	0	1	1	1
$C = 0$	0	0	0	1

Figure 9.1 Karnaugh diagram for a Boolean function in three variables.

$F'' = \{A \rightarrow B, A \rightarrow C, B \rightarrow C, A \rightarrow D\}$ is a minimal cover of F, and $G = \{A \rightarrow B, B \rightarrow C, A \rightarrow D\}$ is a basis of F.

It should be noted that the term 'basis' can be understood here in analogy to the basis of a vector space in linear algebra. While each element of a vector space can be represented as a linear combination of the elements of a basis for that space, in the case of FDs every member of the closure of a given set F can be derived from the elements of a basis of F.

Clearly, the notion of a basis goes beyond redundancy-freedom. Intuitively, the derivation of a basis means, for instance, with respect to update operations that as few dependencies as possible should have to be checked (in order to make sure that all implied ones are maintained); at the same time, the individual checking of an FD should be as efficient as possible.

The next question to be addressed is how to compute a basis algorithmically. The theory of Boolean functions can be used: for each Boolean function F, there exists a simplified representation as a disjunction of prime implicants, which can be derived either from the Karnaugh diagram of F, or by using the Quine/McCluskey algorithm. As an example, consider the set $F = \{AB \rightarrow C, A \rightarrow B, B \rightarrow C, A \rightarrow C\}$ once more, whose DNF was shown in the previous section. The Karnaugh diagram of F has the form shown in Figure 9.1. From this the equivalent simplified form

$$F = BC + A'B'$$

can be derived. This form is modified further by 'adding' 0 $(= BB')$ as well as the third prime implicant $A'C$; using the rules from Boolean algebra, the following is thus obtained:

$$F = BC + A'B' + BB' + A'C = (A' + B)(B' + C)$$

Finally, this representation is translated back into FD notation, which yields $\{A \rightarrow B, B \rightarrow C\}$ as a basis of F.

Instead of doing basis-computations via Boolean algebra, the membership algorithm from Section 9.2 will generally be used.

Theorem 9.13
For every set F of FDs there exists a basis G.

Proof. Consider the following algorithm:

```
Algorithm BASIS
Input: F = {f1, ..., fn}
Output: A basis G of F.
Method:
    begin
        (* make F r-minimal *)
        G := ∅;
        for i := 1 to n do
            if fi : X → Y and Y = A1 ... Am
                then G := G ∪ {X → A1, ..., X → Am};
        (* w.l.o.g. let G = {f1, ..., fk} *)

        (* make G l-minimal *)
        for i := 1 to k do
            if fi: X → A and X = B1 ... Bs
                then for j := 1 to s do
                    if FD-MEMBERSHIP(G, X − Bj, A)
                        then X := X − {Bj};

        (* remove redundant FDs *)
        for i := 1 to k do
            if FD-MEMBERSHIP(G − {fi}, L_fi, R_fi)
                then G := G − {fi};
    end;
```

It is easily verified that G = *BASIS*(F) is indeed a basis of F: l-minimality can be achieved using the membership test above for the following reason. Let

$$H := G - \{X \to A\} \cup \{(X - B_j) \to A\}$$

Then the following holds:

$$G \approx H \iff \text{Sat}(G) = \text{Sat}(H) \iff G^+ = H^+$$

In addition, $G^+ \subseteq H^+$, since $X \to A$ can be derived from H using Rule (A3). It remains to be tested whether $H^+ \subseteq G^+$ holds and hence $(X - B_j) \to A \in G^+$. This, however, is true iff $A \in cl_G(X - B_j)$ holds, so that the membership test within the second for loop can even be replaced by

'$A \in CLOSURE\ (G, X - B_j)$'. □

As an example, consider $F = \{AB \rightarrow C, C \rightarrow A, BC \rightarrow D, ACD \rightarrow B, D \rightarrow EG, BE \rightarrow C, CG \rightarrow BD, CE \rightarrow AG\}$. The splitting of right-hand sides yields

$$G = \{ AB \rightarrow C, C \rightarrow A, BC \rightarrow D, ACD \rightarrow B, D \rightarrow E, D \rightarrow G, BE \rightarrow C, CG \rightarrow B, CG \rightarrow D, CE \rightarrow A, CE \rightarrow G\}$$

The reduction of left-hand sides to achieve l-minimality can only be applied to $ACD \rightarrow B$ in this case; this FD is replaced by $CD \rightarrow B$. If finally redundancy is checked for according to the sequencing of G shown above, the following basis of F results:

$$G = \{AB \rightarrow C, C \rightarrow A, BC \rightarrow D, D \rightarrow E, D \rightarrow G, BE \rightarrow C, CG \rightarrow B, CE \rightarrow G\}$$

This example also shows that there might exist more than one basis for a given set of FDs; another basis for F is

$$G' = \{ AB \rightarrow C, C \rightarrow A, BC \rightarrow D, CD \rightarrow B, D \rightarrow E, D \rightarrow G, BE \rightarrow C, CG \rightarrow D, CE \rightarrow G\}$$

Similarly to the problem of determining a key, the following holds for bases. It is computationally easy to find an *arbitrary* basis for a given set of FDs; however, the problem of determining a basis with the smallest number of occurring attributes, for example, is NP-complete. In light of the practical usability of bases (for consistency checks during updates or for design purposes), the next theorem shows that the particular choice of a basis is irrelevant, in the sense that any two bases for some set F of FDs have a 'similar' structure.

Definition 9.10

Two sets X and Y of attributes are **equivalent** with respect to a set F of FDs, denoted $X \leftrightarrow Y$, if $\{X \rightarrow Y, Y \rightarrow X\} \subseteq F^+$ holds.

Theorem 9.14

Let G and H be two non-redundant covers of F, $G \neq H$. Then the following holds:

$$(\forall\, X \rightarrow W \in G)(\exists\, Y \rightarrow Z \in H)\ \ X \leftrightarrow Y \ \ (\text{w.r.t. } F)$$

In other words, for every FD in a basis G of F with left-hand side X there exists an FD in the basis H with left-hand side Y such that $cl_F(X) = cl_F(Y)$ holds.

For example, let $G = \{A \to B, A \to C, B \to A, AD \to E\}$, and $H = \{A \to B, B \to A, A \to C, BD \to E\}$, then $AD \leftrightarrow BD$ holds.

9.5 FDs and updates

As was mentioned in Section 8.4, integrity constraints like FDs are particularly relevant in the presence of database updates, since the latter have to preserve them. Thus, a DBMS in principle has to make sure that the database state resulting from an update operation or transaction is again consistent. This can be achieved by performing an explicit test on the new state prior to 'committing' an update transaction. In this section, an alternative approach is briefly described, in which only 'update transactions' which maintain all required integrity constraints 'automatically' are made available to the user. To illustrate this approach, consider the following example.

Let $R_1 = (AB, \{A\}), R_2 = (AC, \{A\})$, and $\mathbf{D} = (\{R_1, R_2\}, \{R_2[A] \subseteq R_1[A]\})$. As basic update instructions, the following *parameterized* insertions and deletions with respect to R_1 and R_2 are allowed:

Insertion: $i_{R_1}(A = a, B = b),\ i_{R_2}(A = a, B = b)$
Deletion: $d_{R_1}(A = a),\ d_{R_2}(A = a)$

Such an instruction is 'used' by replacing the (formal) parameters by constants from the corresponding domain; it can then be evaluated according to Definition 8.15. Next, the user will only be allowed to use the following two *parameterized* transactions:

$$
\begin{aligned}
t_1(a, b, c) &:= d_{R_1}(A = a)\ d_{R_2}(A = a) \\
&\qquad i_{R_1}(A = a, B = b)\ i_{R_2}(A = a, C = c) \\
t_2(a) &:= d_{R_2}(A = a)
\end{aligned}
$$

The evaluation (semantics) of an *instantiation* of such a transaction (obtained by replacing each parameter by a constant) is declared as in Definition 8.16.

It is then intuitively clear that *any* evaluation of t_1 or t_2 with respect to $d \in \text{Sat}(\mathbf{D})$ maintains all dependencies defined: t_1 assures that the key A is not violated (by the two deletions executed first), and that the inclusion dependency is obeyed (by the two insertions performed next). t_2 makes it possible to generate a state $d = \{r_1, r_2\}$ such that $\pi_A(r_2) \subset \pi_A(r_1)$ holds.

Next, if d is the empty state, that is, $r_1 = r_2 = \emptyset$ for $d = \{r_1, r_2\}$, it can be shown in this particular example that *every* state $d' \in \text{Sat}(\mathbf{D})$ can be generated from d via a sequence of t_1 or t_2 transactions; conversely, every state generated by $\{t_1, t_2\}$ is a member of $\text{Sat}(\mathbf{D})$. Thus, the 'specification' $\mathbf{D}$ (see above) can be replaced by a specification of the form

$$\mathbf{D}' = (\{AB, AC\}, \{t_1, t_2\})$$

that consists of the two relation formats only, together with the two 'parameterized' transactions (clearly, $\mathbf{D}'$ is not a 'database schema' in the sense defined in Chapter 7).

This approach indicates that the 'state space' derivable from a *static* database specification (that is, a database schema as introduced in Chapter 7) is sometimes alternatively obtainable from a *dynamic* one, which consists of a format together with a set of allowed (parameterized) transactions, and which henceforth can be termed a **transactional schema**. Clearly, the question arises for which types of dependencies or dependency schemas transactional schemas with the same set of 'legal' database states exist. The following theorem is a first answer:

Theorem 9.15

Let $\mathbf{R}$ be a database format. For each set F of FDs over $\mathbf{R}$ there exists a finite set T of parameterized transactions (involving insertions and deletions only) such that Sat($\mathbf{R}$) equals the set of all states which can be generated from the empty state by a sequence of instantiations of transactions from T.

The proof of this theorem can be found in the references. Its idea is indicated in the following example: let $\mathbf{R} = \{R\}$, $R = (ABCD, \{A \to B, A \to C, C \to D, BD \to A\})$, and consider the following parameterized transaction:

$$\begin{aligned} t_R(a,b,c,d) = {} & d_R(A = a, B \neq b)\ d_R(A = a, C \neq c) \\ & d_R(C = c, D \neq d)\ d_R(B = b, D = d, A \neq a) \\ & i_R(A = a, B = b, C = c, D = d) \end{aligned}$$

It can be verified that $T = \{t_R\}$ can be used to generate the entire set Sat($\mathbf{R}$) from $r = \emptyset$.

Bibliographic Notes

The relational model of data was originally introduced by Codd (1970). It soon became the subject of intensive investigations and practical implementations. Areas of investigation that are important from a theoretical point of view include data dependencies, query languages, maintenance of integrity constraints and consistency during update operations, design problems such as the translation of another data model into the relational model (see Chapter 7), query optimization, or realization of updates on views; a comprehensive description is given by Paredaens et al. (1989). These areas also include the problem of dealing with null values in database relations, which was only sketched here. Further details on this can be found, for instance, in Codd (1975, 1979), ANSI (1975), Biskup (1981, 1983), Date (1983), Lipski (1981), Vassiliou (1980), and in the corresponding references given by Maier (1983).

Inclusion dependencies were first described by Fagin (1981); additional information can be found in Casanova et al. (1984, 1989), Laver (1985), Mitchell (1983), and Sciore (1983). In particular, a derivation calculus can be established for this type of dependency, and their interactions with functional dependencies can be investigated.

In the exposition of relational algebra, a practice which is now common is followed in this text; see, for example, Maier (1983), Paredaens et al. (1989), Ullman (1988) or Yang (1986). The translations of SRTC into the domain calculus RDC and (from there) back to RA, which were only mentioned in Chapter 8, but which are essential for proving that SRTC and RDC are Codd-complete, can be found in Maier (1983), Paredaens et al. (1989), Ullman (1988) or Yang (1986). Relational tuple calculus is used as a query language for example by the INGRES system; see Stonebraker (1986c). In this text an emphasis is put on relational algebra; concrete 'RA languages' will be dealt with in greater detail in Part V.

Surveys of the theory of relational queries and languages to express them are provided by Chandra (1988) and Kanellakis (1988). Theorem 9.6, the fact that transitive closure cannot be expressed in relational algebra, was first proved by Aho and Ullman (1979). Subsequently, several authors investigated possibilities of going beyond the expressive power of Codd-complete languages; in particular, Chandra and Harel (1980, 1982) introduced the notion of a computable query and presented a language for the fixpoint queries. The complexity of relational queries is discussed in detail by Chandra and Harel (1982), Immermann (1986) and Vardi (1982); these papers exhibit various classes of queries according to the complexity of their evaluation, where different measures can be applied (like 'data complexity' or 'expression complexity' discussed by Vardi). For a general background on results from complexity theory and its relationship to mathematical logic as they are useful in this context, see Gurevich (1988).

An introduction to the area of logic programming and deductive databases is given by Lloyd (1984); a collection of important papers on these topics was edited by Minker (1988). An in-depth presentation of Datalog can be found in Maier and Warren (1988), Ceri et al. (1989, 1990), and Ullman (1988, 1989). Ceri et al. (1986) and Ullman (1988) describe the translation from Datalog to relational algebra. Bancilhon and Ramakrishnan (1986) survey evaluation strategies for logic programs. A formal treatment of the semantics of logic programs can be found in van Emden and Kowalski (1976); this paper laid the foundations for much subsequent work in this area, like the one reported by Apt and van Emden (1982) or Apt et al. (1988). This latter reference in particular discusses stratification of Datalog programs as a way to handle negation; see also Apt and Pugin (1987) or Chandra and Harel (1985). A different kind of semantics, not mentioned in Chapter 8, is obtained by considering **inflationary** fixpoints and, consequently, an inflationary semantics for Datalog$^{\neg}$ programs; to this end, the reader should consult Abiteboul and Vianu (1988b) as well as Kolaitis and Papadimitriou (1988). Abiteboul and Vianu (1988b) in particular establish interesting relationships between query languages for relational databases and **update languages** for specifying changes. Sagiv (1988) considers the optimization of Datalog programs. An extension of Datalog called *LDL* is described by Naqvi and Tsur (1989) and Chimenti et al. (1990).

A general introduction to the topic of database updates is given by Abiteboul (1988). The exposition in Section 8.4 is based on Abiteboul and Vianu (1988a) as well as on Karabeg and Vianu (1988). Theorem 8.11 is from the former reference, while the latter contains a complete axiomatization for transaction equivalence.

An introduction to the issues involved in the updating of relational views as well as a survey of work in this area is given by Furtado and Casanova (1985). One central problem in this context is the characterization of those database updates which correctly translate a given view update. To this end, a general approach is proposed by Bancilhon and Spyratos (1981). The notion crucial in this work is that of a *view complement*: informally, a view V' is a complement of view V if the specification of states for V and V' is sufficient for a reconstruction of the entire database state. Since every view possesses a complement, a requirement to a translator for V updates could then be to produce translations only for which the complement of V remains *constant*. In an extension of the results on view updating under constant complement, Cosmadakis and Papadimitriou (1984) show (among other things) that the problem of determining a *minimal* complement for a given view is NP-complete.

An alternative formalization of correct translations which in particular avoids 'side effects' on the view state is given by Dayal and Bernstein (1982). Furtado et al. (1979) allow the union operation in view definitions. The exposition in Section 8.5 partially follows the work of Keller (1985); other work on this topic includes Masunaga (1984), Medeiros and Tompa (1985) and Shmueli and Itai (1984).

The exposition of the theory of functional dependencies, which were first investigated by Codd (1970), and in particular the proof of Theorem 9.2 substantially follows Vardi (1988). The completeness of Armstrong's axioms was first proved by Armstrong (1974); the concept of RAP derivations is from Maier (1983). The latter reference also proves the following theorem: if there exists an 'Armstrong derivation' for an FD f from F, there also exists a RAP derivation for f from F. Theorem 9.7 is proved by Beeri and Bernstein (1979); Theorem 9.8 is from Lipski (1977). For the theory of NP-completeness, the reader is referred to Garey and Johnson (1979).

Theorem 9.9 is shown in more detail by Sagiv et al. (1981). The relationship between functional dependencies and Boolean functions is investigated further by Delobel and Casey (1973) or Fagin (1977c); it is extended to multivalued dependencies ('MVDs', see Chapter 12) by Parker and Delobel (1979), Sagiv (1980) or Sagiv et al. (1981). An introduction to the theory of Boolean functions and their representation through normal forms such as DNF and by prime implicants is given by Oberschelp and Vossen (1989).

The notion of a closed set of attributes goes back to Beeri et al. (1984); in this paper a proof for Theorem 9.11 can be found as well. Further details on this notion can be found in Jou and Fischer (1982); this concept will be returned to in Section 12.2 in connection with Boyce-Codd normal form. Theorem 9.12 is from Hanatani and Fagin (1985). Another characterization of functional dependency implication is given by Vossen (1988).

The problem of computing an FD dependency basis is also treated by Maier (1980, 1983), and Ullman (1988); a proof that the problem of determining an 'optimal' cover is NP-complete is given by Mannila and Räihä (1983). Theorem 9.14 is from Bernstein (1976). Several of the theorems stated here for functional dependencies remain valid for multivalued dependencies and even for 'mixed' sets (consisting of FDs and MVDs) such as Theorems 9.3, 9.9, 9.11 and 9.12.

Parameterized transactions in the form presented here were originally proposed by Abiteboul and Vianu (1985); in this paper as well as in Abiteboul and Vianu (1986), several fundamental results are obtained regarding the questions mentioned in Chapter 9; in addition, a variety of issues is shown to be undecidable. Theorem 9.15 is from Abiteboul and Vianu (1985).

Exercises

(1) (a) Let X be a set of attributes, and let $r \in \text{Rel}(X)$ be a relation over X. Describe a simple procedure to determine a key for r.

(b) Next let $K \subseteq X$. K is called **candidate key** for r if K only has the identification property with respect to r, that is, $(\forall\, \mu, \nu \in r)\ \mu[K] = \nu[K] \implies \mu = \nu)$, but is not necessarily minimal with this property with respect to '$\subseteq$'. Prove or disprove:

(i) If K_1 and K_2 are both keys for r, the same is true for $K_1 \cup K_2$.

(ii) If K_1 and K_2 are both candidate keys for r, then $K_1 \cap K_2$ is a key for r.

(c) Let $R = (X, \{K\})$ be a relation schema with the key dependency $K \to X$. Show that:

$$(\forall\, r \in \text{Rel}(X))\ (K \to X)(r) = 1 \implies (\forall\, K\text{–values } k)\ \mid \sigma_{K=k}(r) \mid \leq 1$$

(A 'K value' is a (partial) tuple from Tup(K).) Does the converse also hold? How can the validity of an FD be characterized in a similar way?

(2) Prove Theorem 8.4.

(3) Let the Supplier-Parts database shown in Figure E.1 be given, which describes an application consisting of suppliers (S), parts (P), and a binary relationship between them (*SUPPlies*). For each of the following queries, provide a corresponding expression from relational algebra and show the result of its evaluation on the given database state:
(a) Show the number and the distance values for each supplier from Paris.
(b) Show the *Parts* table.
(c) Show the number and colour of every part whose weight is ≥ 15 and ≤ 20.
(d) For each part supplied, show its number and where it is stored.
(e) For each part supplied by a London supplier, show its number and quantity.
(f) Show the colour of each part supplied by a Paris supplier.

(4) For each RA expression found in Exercise 3, give a corresponding SRTC expression.

(5) Give an RA expression for

S:	S#	Sname	City	Dist
	S1	Smith	London	20
	S2	Jones	Paris	10
	S3	Blake	Paris	30
	S4	Clark	London	20
	S5	Adams	Athens	30

P:	P#	Pname	Colour	Weight	Stored_In
	P1	Nut	Red	12	London
	P2	Bolt	Green	17	Paris
	P3	Screw	Blue	17	Rome
	P4	Screw	Red	14	London
	P5	Cam	Blue	12	Paris
	P6	Cog	Red	19	London

SUPP:	S#	P#	Qty
	S1	P1	200
	S1	P2	200
	S2	P3	400
	S3	P3	200
	S3	P4	500
	S4	P6	300
	S5	P2	200

Figure E.1 Sample database for Exercise 3.

$$r_1 := \begin{cases} r & \text{if } |r| \geq 2 \\ \emptyset & \text{otherwise} \end{cases}$$

You may use selections of the form $\sigma_{A\Theta B}(r) := \{\mu \in r \mid \mu(A)\Theta\mu(B)\}$ for $\Theta \in \{=, \neq\}$, $\text{dom}(A) = \text{dom}(B)$.

(6) Let $r \in \text{Rel}(X), s \in \text{Rel}(Y)$. $r \ltimes s := \pi_X(r \bowtie s)$ is called the **semijoin** of r with s. Prove the following:
(a) $r \ltimes s = r \bowtie \pi_{X \cap Y}(s)$
(b) $r \bowtie s = (r \ltimes s) \bowtie s$
(c) Let $r' := r \ltimes s, s' := s \ltimes r'$, then $r \bowtie s = r' \bowtie s'$.

(7) Let the following relational database schema be given:

Lives = ({ *Pname, City, Street* } , .)
Works = ({ *Pname, Cname, Salary* } , .)
Located_At = ({ *Cname, City* } , .)
Reports_To = ({ *Pname, Mname* } , .)

(For the name attributes, P stands for person, C for company, and M for manager.) Give an RA expression for each of the following queries:

(a) Show name and city for each person working for Wells Fargo.
(b) Show all persons working and living in the same city.
(c) Show the name of each person who does not work for Wells Fargo.
(d) Show all managers of each company which is not located at Munich or Vienna.
(e) Show the names of all companies which are located at every city at which Wells Fargo is located. (Assume that a company resides at several locations; use the division operation from the next exercise.)

(8) Let $Y \subseteq X, r \in \text{Rel}(X), s \in \text{Rel}(Y)$, and $Z := X - Y$.

$$r/s := \{\rho \in \text{Tup}(Z) \mid (\forall \nu \in s)(\exists \mu \in r)\ \mu[Z] = \rho \wedge \mu[Y] = \nu\}$$

is called the **division** of r by s.

(a) Let r, s, and t be given as follows:

r:

A	B
a	1
a	2
a	3
b	1
b	2
c	1
c	2
c	3
c	4
d	2

s:

B
1
2
3

t:

B
1

Compute r/s as well as r/t.

(b) Let r and s be as above, but with X and Y such that $X \cap Y = \emptyset$. Show that $(r \bowtie s)/s = r$.

(c) Show that $r/s = \pi_Z(r) - \pi_Z((\pi_Z(r) \bowtie s) - r)$

(9) Prove Theorem 8.6.

(10) Prove Theorem 8.7.

(11) Suppose an operator for computing the transitive closure of relations has been added to RA; call the result RA*. Next consider the ternary relation $R = (ASD, .)$, where A is the name of an airline, and S $[D]$ is the source [destination] of a flight offered by this airline, that is, a tuple (a, s, d) is in a relation over R iff a has a flight from s to d. Show the following:

(a) The query 'show all tuples (a, s, d) from R such that s and d are connected by a *positive* number of flights, all by the same airline a' cannot be expressed in RA*.

(b) The above query *can* be expressed if a fixpoint (or iteration) construct is added to RA.

(12) For each of the operators of relational algebra besides difference, write a corresponding Datalog program.

(13) With every Datalog program C a directed graph G_C, called the **dependence graph** of C, can be associated in the following way: G_C has a node for each distinct predicate occurring in C, and an edge from P to Q if P appears in the body of some rule and Q is in the head of the same rule. A program C is **recursive** if G_C is cyclic. This representation can be extended to programs involving negative literals in rule bodies as follows: if $\neg P$ appears in a rule body and Q is in the head of the same rule, the edge from P to Q is labelled by '$\neg$'. Show that a Datalog$^\neg$ program C is stratified iff G_C does not contain a cycle on which the label '$\neg$' appears.

(14) Show that '$\cup$' is independent of the operations $-$, σ, π and $\bowtie$ in the following sense: for $R \cup S$, there is no expression $E \in$ RA which contains R and S as operands only, in which only $-$, σ, π and $\bowtie$ are used, and for which $(\forall\, d \in \text{Dat}(\mathbf{R}))\ v_E(d) = r \cup s$ holds.

(15) Describe a database schema as well as an update over it which cannot be the effect of an IDM transaction as introduced in Definition 8.16.

(16) Show that the following two transactions over the same schema $R = (AB, .)$ are equivalent:

$$t_1 = i(A = 0, B = 3)\ m(A = 0; A = 1, B = 1)$$
$$t_2 = m(A = 0; A = 1, B = 1)\ i(A = 1, B = 1)$$

(17) Show that for the following two transactions over $R = (A, .)$, their equivalence cannot be proved using the axioms stated in Section 8.4:

$$\begin{aligned} t_1 = {} & d(A = 4)\ m(A = 1; A = 4)\ m(A = 2; A = 1) \\ & m(A = 4; A = 2)\ m(A = 3; A = 4) \\ t_2 = {} & d(A = 4)\ m(A = 3; A = 4)\ m(A = 2; A = 3) \\ & m(A = 1; A = 2)\ m(A = 3; A = 1) \end{aligned}$$

(18) Determine which translations are possible for a *modification* of tuples in a selection view, and design a (reasonably short) dialogue (between DBA and DBMS) through which the semantics of possible replacements can be established uniquely at view definition time.

(19) Describe possible translations for view updates with respect to a projection view, making the same assumptions as in Section 8.5 for selection views.

(20) Prove Theorem 9.1.

(21) Prove or disprove the correctness of the following derivation rules:
(a) $X \to Y \wedge YZ \to W \implies XZ \to W$
(b) $X \to Y \wedge W \to Z \wedge Y \supseteq W \implies X \to Z$
(c) $XY \to Z \wedge Z \to X \implies Z \to Y$

(22) For the university application described in Exercise 5 of Part II, find at least seven non-trivial functional dependencies and identify the redundant ones among them.

(23) Prove:
(a) $F^+ = (F^+)^+$ for any set F of FDs
(b) $F \subseteq G \implies F^+ \subseteq G^+$

(24) Let $F = \{AB \to C, B \to D, CD \to E, CE \to GH, G \to A\}$. Using a RAP derivation, show that $BG \to DH \in F^+$.

(25) Let V =*ABCDE*, and $F = \{A \to BC, CD \to E, AC \to E, B \to D, E \to AB\}$.
(a) Determine *all* keys for $R = (V, F)$.
(b) Find two non-trivial elements of $F^+ - F$.
(c) For the FDs found under (b), show their membership in F^+ by a RAP proof.
(d) Exhibit a relation $r \in \text{Sat}(F)$ such that $r \neq \pi_{ABC}(r) \bowtie \pi_{CDE}(r)$, that is, the 'decomposition' of $R = (V, F)$ onto $V_1 = ABC$ and $V_2 = CDE$ is not lossless.

(26) (a) For $V = ABC$ and $F = \emptyset$, compute F^+.
(b) Using the result from (a), find all members of F^+ for $F = \{AB \to C, C \to B\}$.

(27) Let $G = \{A \to C, AB \to C, C \to DI, CD \to I, EC \to AB, EI \to C\}$. Compute a basis for G:
(a) by applying Algorithm *BASIS*,
(b) by computing the prime implicants of the Boolean function representing F.

(28) Let V =*ABCDEI*, and $F = \{AB \to C, B \to A, AD \to E, BD \to I\}, G = \{AB \to C, B \to A, AD \to EI\}$. Show that:
(a) $F^+ = G^+$,
(b) Neither F nor G is redundant.

(29) Complete the proof of Theorem 9.9.

(30) Complete the proof of Theorem 9.13, and determine the time complexity of algorithm *BASIS* under realistic assumptions on the machine-internal encoding of the input.

(31) Prove Theorem 9.14.

(32) With a relational database schema $\mathbf{D} = (\mathbf{R}, .)$, where $\mathbf{R} = \{R_1, \ldots, R_k\}$, a hypergraph $H(\mathbf{D})$ (see Exercise II.10) can be associated in the following

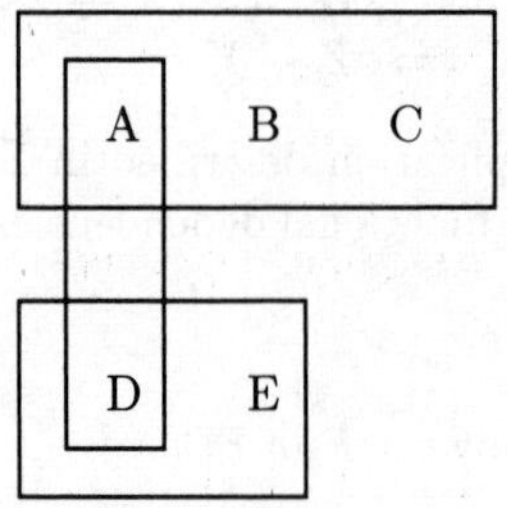

Figure E.2 Hypergraph for Exercise 28.

way: $H(\mathbf{D}) := (N, K)$, where $N := \cup_{i=1}^{k} X_i$, and $K := \{X_1, \dots, X_k\}$. Figure E.2 shows a hypergraph for the example $X_1 = ABC, X_2 = AD, X_3 = DE$. Next, the following 'algorithm' is to be applied to a given hypergraph $H(\mathbf{D})$ as long as possible: (i) if there exists edges k_1 and k_2 in K such that $k_1 \subset k_2$, remove k_1 from K; (ii) if $A \in N$ occurs in exactly one $k \in K$, remove A from N (and k). $H(\mathbf{D})$ is called **acyclic** if this algorithm stops with the empty set (of nodes and edges) when applied to N and K.

(a) For the sample hypergraph given, show a corresponding sequence of steps that transforms $H(\mathbf{D})$ into $\emptyset$.
(b) Is the hypergraph for the database schema from Exercise 7 acyclic?
(c) Decide whether the result produced by the algorithm is uniquely determined, or whether different sequences of steps can yield different results.
(d) For a given schema $\mathbf{D}$ let $H(\mathbf{D})$ be cyclic. By a simple extension $H(\mathbf{D})$ can be transformed into an acyclic hypergraph. Find out which one.

Part IV
Database Design

Chapter 10
The Design Process

This chapter surveys the database design process, which refers to the task of 'mapping' a given real-world application onto a database management system. This process consists of several distinct steps, whose central portion is to model the given application using the language of some data model.

In Parts II and III, a detailed look was taken into the modelling of real-world situations using a particular data model. In each case, the goal was to come up with a (formal) 'image' of a certain application which could subsequently be used as a conceptual foundation of a database for this application. This modelling is one step within the process generally called **database design**. This process bears some resemblance to the design of a large program system in software engineering in that it is actually part of the *life cycle* of a database. In this chapter, a brief look is taken into this process in its entirety; a top-down division into *seven* steps is followed:

(1) requirements analysis and specification,

(2) conceptual design,

(3) logical design,

(4) implementation design,

(5) physical design,

(6) distribution design,

(7) prototyping.

Each of these steps will be described in more detail in this chapter. In Chapter 11, alternatives for the conceptual and the logical design will be discussed that go beyond the capabilities of the entity-relationship model. In Chapter 12, a closer look will be taken at logical design in the context of the relational model.

In the first phase of the design process, the phase of **requirements analysis and specification**, the requirements that all potential users of the database may have are specified. These requirements have to be recorded and documented, so that they can subsequently be analysed.

The requirements to a database can be classified in a variety of ways, such as from which group of users (application programmers, technical staff, management) they originate. The important aspect is that they include statements on *what* data is to be stored, and *how* this data is to be processed. This makes it reasonable to distinguish at least two kinds of requirements:

(1) **Information requirements**: This refers to all *static* information to be used by the database system later, when the database is in operation. They include, for example, statements about entities (database 'objects') and their types, attributes and their domains, relationships between individual entities, entity types or groups of entities, and identifiers (keys) for entities and relationships.

(2) **Processing requirements**: This refers to the specification of *dynamic* processes that later should run upon or use the database. These include information on *which* processes are to run on the database, such as DML operations like queries or updates, evaluations, report generation, and the like. In addition, information is to be gathered on how *often* an individual process will be executed, whether processes can execute in a certain sequence only or, more generally, what kinds of *dependencies* (such as priorities) exist between them, what *data volume* will be required by each process, and so on. These requirements in particular include statements on the availability or the safety of data in the database, or the specification of access rights regarding data security.

In order to accomplish this initial phase, a designer of a database up to now has basically no formal tools at his disposal. Generally, he or she would try to interview representatives of each user group, thereby figuring the facts and statements needed; especially predesigned forms or questionnaires might be of help.

In the second phase, the phase of **conceptual design**, a database designer's goal is to transform the descriptions received from individual users or user groups into **views** on an individual basis, where an abstract, 'conceptual' data model will be employed. Each such view represents a preliminary, yet formal description of information structures as they are required by the corresponding group. For this **view modelling** step, a data model is used which is in general distinct from the model underlying the 'target-DBMS', for reasons that will be discussed in Chapter 11. In particular, the entity-relationship model can be used to model individual views, independent of whether the DBMS available for finally managing the database is based on the network, the relational or another data model.

Alternatively, the data model to which the application in question has to be mapped (later) can be used in this phase; for example, if a relational DBMS will be employed, the result of view modelling could be a set of ('initial') database schemas $\mathbf{D}_1, \ldots, \mathbf{D}_n$.

The second step in a conceptual design consists of an *integration* of all individual views designed previously (**view integration**), that is, of the derivation of a global conceptual view of the database from these. More precisely, this may imply the construction of a 'global ERD' from a set of ERDs or the derivation of *one* relational schema $\mathbf{D}$ from initial schemas $\mathbf{D}_1, \ldots, \mathbf{D}_n$.

The integration step in turn consists of two substeps. First, an *analysis* of the given individual views has to uncover inconsistencies, redundancies and conflicts between these; for example, there can exist unintended indentities of or differences between names, or views might be partially or completely identical. After these issues have been resolved, the global view is established through a process of *schema merging*, where the eventually existing dependencies or relationships between views have to be taken into consideration.

In the third phase, called the **logical design**, a translation or transformation of the global schema resulting from the second phase into the data model underlying the target-DBMS takes place. In Parts II and III, this step has been dealt with for the special case that the global schema is given as an entity-relationship schema or diagram, and that the DBMS in question is based on the network, the hierarchical or the relational data model. Hence, the result of this phase is, for instance, a logical network with certain additional information (like MANDATORY/OPTIONAL selections or set-selection clauses), or it is a relational database schema consisting of a database format together with intra- and interrelational constraints.

For the particular case of the relational model, some 'postprocessing' or 'optimization' of the resulting database schema may finally be performed; by this it is referred here to the process of *normalization* that will be described in detail in Chapter 12.

In the fourth phase, the **implementation design**, the goal is to 'implement' the conceptual schema as well as the external ones using the DDL of the system that is to be used. In the case of a network system, for example, record and set types have to be declared in this phase, CALC keys need to be established, subschemas have to be generated, and so on. In the case of a relational system, relation schemas will be declared, each one consisting of attributes and their associated domains, keys, and so forth; in addition, views have to be defined that are built according to the requirements of certain users or user groups, and that therefore reflect the results of earlier design phases. Finally, access rights have to be granted, thereby establishing at least some 'processing relationships' at the conceptual level.

The **physical design** consists of a definition of the internal schema and of the system parameters associated with this. In light of the processing requirements collected earlier (see above), appropriate storage structures for the individual elements of the conceptual schema together with their access mechanisms need to be determined; this might be, for example, an *inverted file* ('index', see Chapter 13) to support an efficient access to the values of some attribute. In addition, the physical design may include the definition of parameters for hash methods provided by the system (or supported by the underlying operating system), of the size of pages for communication between primary and secondary memory, or of the size of the database buffer that is maintained in the main memory of the host machine (see Chapter 19).

The sixth step, the phase of **distribution design**, is obviously applicable only if the database under design is not managed centrally by one machine, but is instead distributed over several hosts that can communicate via a network. For this situation, which for example applies to (nationwide) banking through teller machines or to airline reservation systems, it has to be clarified which data is to be stored at what location according to which criteria. An important aspect underlying such decisions may be the goal to keep the entire database *transparent* to the individual user, that is, a distributed database should appear to the user as if it was centralized. Depending on the application, the opposite of this might also be desirable. For example, in a fileserver/workstation environment the distinction between private 'local' and public 'global' parts of the database could be relevant and should therefore be 'visible' to its users. A distribution design in general will not be performed until after the physical design has been concluded. If a distributed environment is to be set up, this goal has to be taken into consideration from the requirements analysis onwards.

The final step in the design process will consist of a **prototyping** of the result obtained. This term refers to the computer-aided generation and loading of a sample database in order to 'verify' the entire design. By incorporating a 'random-data generator', a data set can be produced in this phase that will aid in measuring the system performance based on the decisions that were made during the design process. Clearly, the goal here is to obtain statements on whether the efficiency requirements to the database are met by the current design *before* the data that actually has to be managed will be loaded, so that changes and modifications can be made in time. The reader should be aware that this step today is seldom an 'official' step of the design process; corresponding methods are in their development stage.

Prototyping can also be understood in a different way. Similarly to a (rapid) prototyping that is well known in software engineering, this might refer to the (early) provision of a 'prototype' that accompanies *all* design phases, in order to be able to validate the result of each step in this process as early as possible. Note that commercial DBMSs usually provide a reasonable prerequisite for supporting rapid prototyping, since, for example, a schema might be implemented in part only, so that sample data can be loaded by utilities, and initial performance tests can be conducted before the implementation design is completed.

In summary, the design process can be illustrated as shown in Figure 10.1; Steps 2 and in particular 3 will be investigated in greater detail in the following chapters.

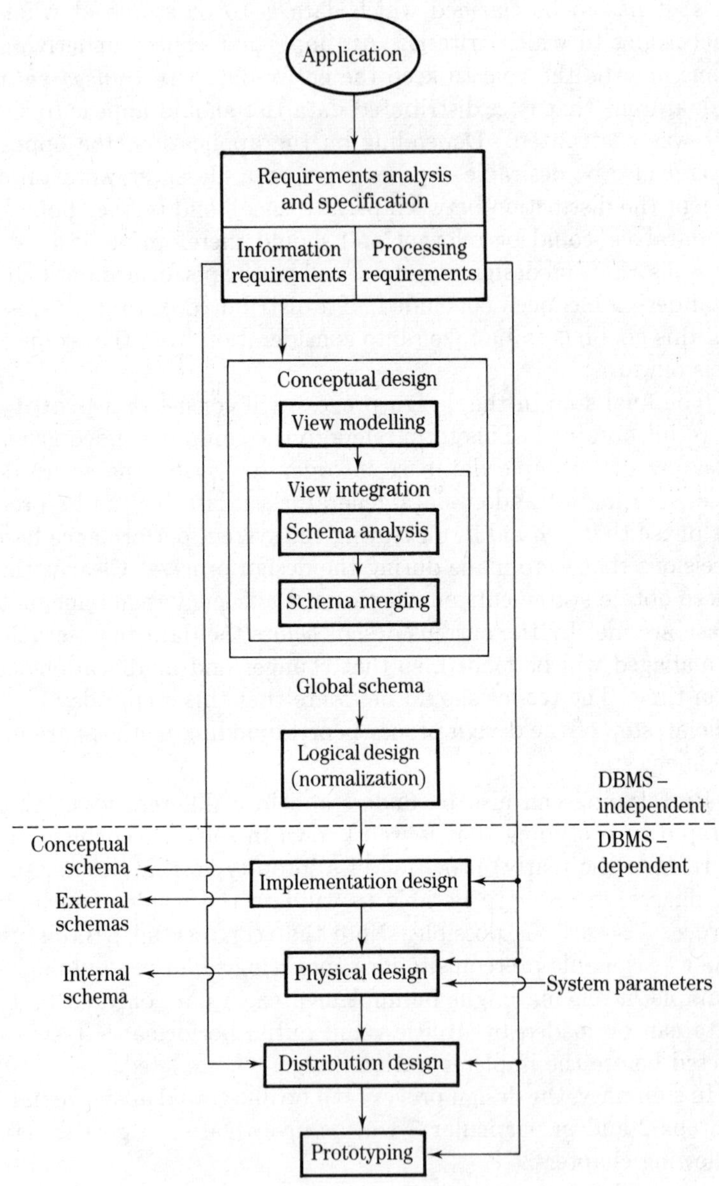

Figure 10.1 The database design process.

Chapter 11
Semantic Data Models

The conceptual design of a database has so far been based on the entity-relationship model. This chapter considers possibilities to generalize from that model, based on the goal of capturing as much semantic information from an application as possible. This idea underlying **semantic data models** is illustrated using the IFO model as a running example.

To design a database conceptually the user can — following the strategy described in Parts II and III — first model the application in question using the ER approach and then transform the result into the desired 'target' data model. As has been seen already, it is basically possible to represent all concepts that can be modelled in an ERD in any of the three 'classical' data models, so that these can be considered 'complete' or 'universal' with respect to the entity-relationship model. However, the ER model presented in Chapter 4 was chosen so that such a transformation into one of the other three models presented became possible; as the remarks at the end of Chapter 4 suggested, there exist extensions to this model which do not necessarily preserve this transformability.

The aspect of this way of proceeding when designing a database that is of central importance to us is that the use of the ER model renders it possible for a designer to organize his or her 'knowledge' or findings about the given application *without* taking the particular restrictions or characteristics of a 'concrete' model into account at this stage (like the exclusive usage of binary $1:n$ relationships in the network model). This distinction between various ways of viewing or representing an application becomes even more striking under the observation that the network and the hierarchical, but also the relational model are in a sense more *machine-oriented* than user-oriented. Note that in the former models the primary physical data structure is the record or the file that is composed of records; the conceptual level allows for a direct description of this structure, which 'just' abstracts from actual values.

In the relational model, this situation is not fundamentally different, since a table from a physical point of view also consists of records of *fixed format*, with the only difference that their internal organization (like a concatenation via pointers) is no longer visible. This results in an improved user-friendliness as compared with the other two models; however, this is the reason why even the relational model actually has to be considered (like network and hierarchical model) as a *syntactical* data model.

The concept of fixed formatting, which is central in all three models, has been used in Chapter 4 to represent entities and relationships; this rendered a vastly *uniform* description of this and the other models possible, which was originally considered essential for this model by its author Chen. On the other hand, it needs to be pointed out critically that it has only been possible to represent *certain* (static) aspects of a given application in either of these models. The following example, which continues the discussion from the end of Chapter 4, again illustrates the inherent limitations of this approach.

Let an entity-type *EMP*loyee of a company be given. Employees have attributes, like *Name, Dept* (Department) or *Sal*ary. In addition, let each employee speak zero or more foreign languages *FLang*, and have an

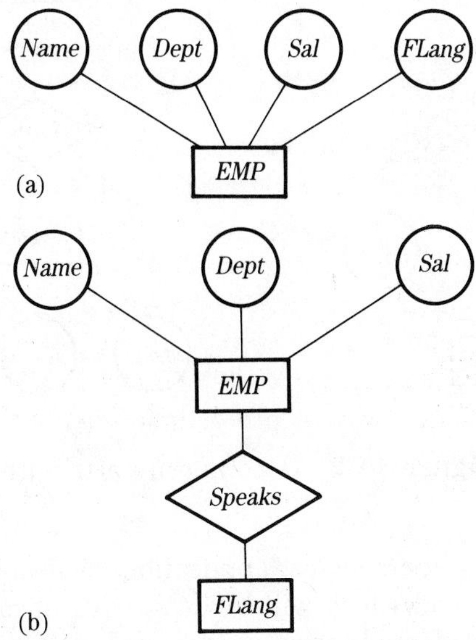

Figure 11.1 Set-valued attributes versus relationships.

Address. In order to model this situation in an ERD, several possibilities occur. In Figure 11.1(a) it is assumed that *FLang* represents a *set-valued* attribute; in a relational representation, this would result in redundancies that are not desirable. Figure 11.1(b) shows an alternative representation, where *EMP* is related to *FLang* through the relationship-type *Speaks*; here it is necessary to distinguish whether *Speaks* is a unary relationship having *FLang* as an attribute, or whether it is indeed binary as shown.

Attribute *Addr* is considered next. In Figure 11.2(a) this is represented as a single attribute. However, from a point of view of the application it could be more appropriate to specify the information that constitutes an address more precisely, for example by breaking it down into *Street, City* and *Zip*, so that queries for complete addresses as well as for parts of it become possible. A corresponding representation is shown in Figure 11.2(b); note that it is necessary to introduce a new relationship that associates employees with their addresses, respectively.

These examples indicate that sometimes decisions have to be made when the modelling tools introduced so far are used, since it may happen that not all aspects of the application in question can be expressed simultaneously or equally well in the language of the model chosen. In addition, the languages introduced in Parts II and III hardly provide possibilities to express dynamic aspects of an application (like *operations* on entities or relationships or even *relationships* between operations) as well.

This lack of 'expressiveness' of the data models discussed so far is

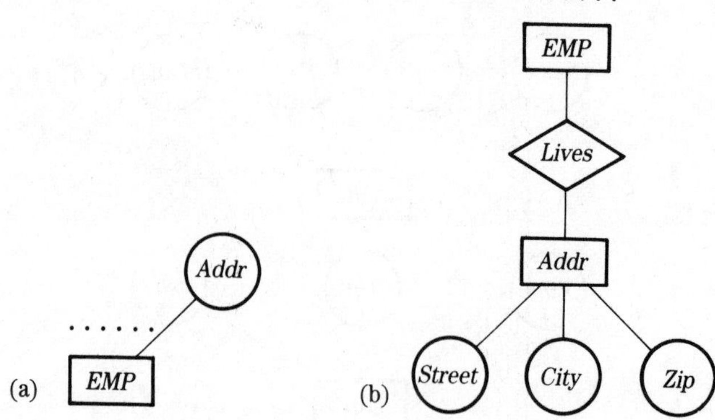

Figure 11.2 A composite attribute.

even more evident in *non-standard* applications that now increasingly ask for DBMS support, and which will be dealt with in more detail in Part VII. In these areas of application, which include artificial intelligence, computer-aided design (CAD), office automation and software engineering, but also in more traditional ones there exists an increasing demand for special data models (at least) for the phase of conceptual design. In this phase it should be possible for a designer to generate an abstraction of an application using a data model that besides syntax also allows for a representation of the *semantics* of the 'mini-world'; only in subsequent design phases should it be attempted to transform this representation into one of the classical data models (if this is still required because of the fact, for example, that a DBMS directly supporting a semantic model is not yet available).

It is this desire for a 'better' support of conceptual database design than that currently known, but also the need of advanced modelling capabilities arising in applications like the ones mentioned, that has led to the development of **semantic data models** that provide the user with augmented and more 'natural' possibilities for expressing and modelling conceptual (logical) aspects. Clearly, in such a 'higher' model (as opposed to a syntactical one) it should be possible to represent the statics *and* the dynamics of an application, that is, in addition to specifying 'data objects' it should be possible to express operations or processes that act on these. As will primarily be discussed in Part VII, this has led to an extension of known data models as well as to an integration of concepts that have previously been 'reserved' for other areas of computer science. Most notable among recent developments is the area of *object-oriented* database management, in which concepts from object-oriented programming are brought together with some of the 'established' concepts from database management (see Chapter 22). As will also be discussed later, database design or the lack of expressiveness in current data models is only one of the aspects that have triggered the pursuit of new approaches; another, for example, is concerned with data manipulation languages, which to date are among the few possibilities (if any) available to bridge the gap between the semantics of an application as it is represented in a database or its schema and the actual semantics of the application proper (see the discussion in Section 8.3).

The entity-relationship model in the form it was originally proposed, which is not exactly identical to the one used in Chapter 4, can be considered as the 'prototype' of a semantic data model. With other, more recent such models it has in common that it allows for a *graphical* representation of the conceptual view of a given application. This feature is of particular importance with respect to the development of advanced user interfaces which make the result of a conceptual design, that is, the 'graphical schema', available for working with the database as well; the idea is to let a user, for instance, pose queries by 'navigating' through this schema (in a way that will be sketched below).

Semantic data models were originally developed to provide for higher levels of abstraction as with 'record-oriented' data models when describing the logics behind an application; the designer should be able to represent data directly as it is observed in the outside world. For this reason, the language of a semantic model often supports a modular, top-down oriented view of an application or its 'schema', thereby simplifying the task of database design and (hopefully) making the result easier to use.

In this chapter, some fundamental 'language elements' that are available or supported in this or a similar form in every semantic data model will be introduced as examples, thereby introducing the reader to this alternative approach to database design. In passing, it will be discussed whether and how a conceptual description of an application given in terms of such a model can be transformed, for 'implementation purposes', say, into the relational model; this question will be returned to in Part VII in connection with extensions of the relational model. In the Bibliographic Notes for this part some well-known semantic models will briefly be surveyed.

It should be mentioned that the reader who is familiar with the (historical) development of high-level programming languages will recognize a series of similarities; in particular, the distinction between a 'syntactical' and a 'semantic' data model can be compared with the transition from imperative programming as performed, for instance, when using languages like Pascal or C, to functional, object-oriented or even logic programming, based on languages like LISP, Smalltalk, or Prolog, respectively.

The central notion present in any semantic data model is that of a (data) **object**, which primarily replaces the familiar term 'entity' (tuple, record). Concrete objects can be collected to form *sets* of objects, and objects are always of a predefined (object) **type**. What is essential is that a set of objects can be directly represented and manipulated without forcing the user to think in terms of records. (For this reason, semantic data models are sometimes also termed ('structurally') *object-oriented* data models, although object-orientation in a programming-language sense requires additional characteristics, see Chapter 22.) In addition, it is possible to compose or derive **complex** objects or types from more basic or **atomic** ('indivisible') ones using certain constructs provided by the model.

As a running example, this chapter will consider a travel agency that is recording information on people taking business trips as well as on people going on vacations. The (atomic) object types allowed are *PERSON* (abstracting from the different kinds of people whose data is recorded) and *COMPANY* (telling for whom a business traveller is working).

Intuitively, some objects existing in the world are **abstract** in the sense that they cannot be 'printed' or represented on a screen, while others are **printable**; for example, it is impossible to print a *PERSON*, whereas a person's name or address can be printed. Therefore, (atomic) abstract object types are also distinguished from (atomic) printable types.

In the example, *PERSON* and *COMPANY* are considered as abstract types, whereas, for instance, *Pname* and *Cname* are allowed as printable ones, respectively. In order to capture this distinction graphically, *diamonds* will be used to depict abstract types, and *rectangles* to represent printable ones.

From atomic objects complex ones can be derived through two constructs that introduce *structure* into the model; these are *aggregation* and *grouping*. Roughly, the former corresponds to forming Cartesian products (tuple construction), while the latter refers to the construction of sets, both in a recursive manner.

Aggregation refers to a particular form of abstraction that formally composes a new object type from already defined ones by forming a Cartesian product. As an example, consider the object type *Addr*ess described above, which can be composed of the atomic (printable) object types *Street*, *City* and *Zip*. Formally, this can be described as

$$Addr : \times(Street,\ City,\ Zip)$$

capturing the meaning that a concrete ('physical') address always consists of three distinct parts. Consequently, an object set of type *Addr* is a set of triples, each of which represents an object of type *Addr*. To represent this graphically, the symbolism shown in Figure 11.3 is used. In this way it becomes possible for a user either to refer to an abstract address without regard to its components, or to refer to an individual statement that is part of an address.

Grouping, on the other hand, denotes the collecting of elements of an already existing (atomic) type to form a set; thus, formally this is a

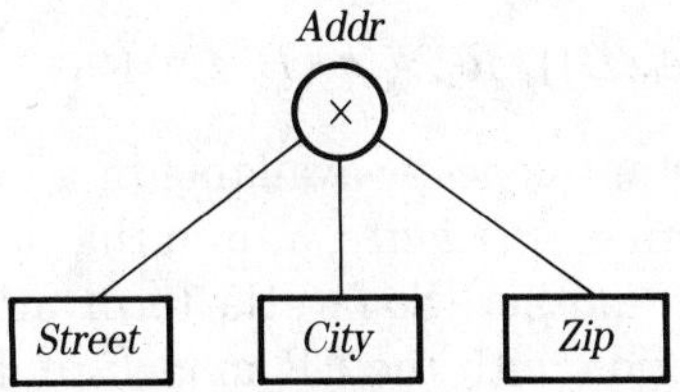

Figure 11.3 Example of an aggregation.

construction of (finite) *power sets.* In our running example, consider the atomic type *FLang* as well as the type *Dest*ination: both 'properties' of a traveller or a *PERSON* will in general be set-valued and can therefore be used to derive two new types, *FLangs* and *Dest*ination*s*, formally described as follows:

$$FLangs : *(FLang)$$
$$Dests : *(Dest)$$

This notation is used to express that a (concrete) object, say, of type *FLangs* consists of zero or more (but at most finitely many) objects of type *FLang*; if this type is (later) associated with the type *PERSON*, it will become possible to record the (possibly unary set of) languages a person speaks. For the purpose of graphically representing grouping, the symbolism shown in Figure 11.4 is used.

Aggregation and grouping can in general be used to construct *recursive* object types of arbitrary complexity, such as

$$Addresses : *(Addr\text{: } \times(Street,\ City,\ Zip))$$

for people with several addresses, and the 'data-model language' currently being introduced now offers the possibility to express certain phenomena, for which 'external statements' were needed previously (like dependencies 'over' schemas in the relational model), directly through structure. In particular, it is easily seen that the structural portion of the relational model ('formats') is subsumed by this 'type model'; for example, a database schema $\mathbf{D} = (\mathbf{R}, .)$, where $\mathbf{R} = \{R_1, R_2\}$, $R_1 = (AB, .)$, and $R_2 = (BC, .)$, can be represented as a *single* type

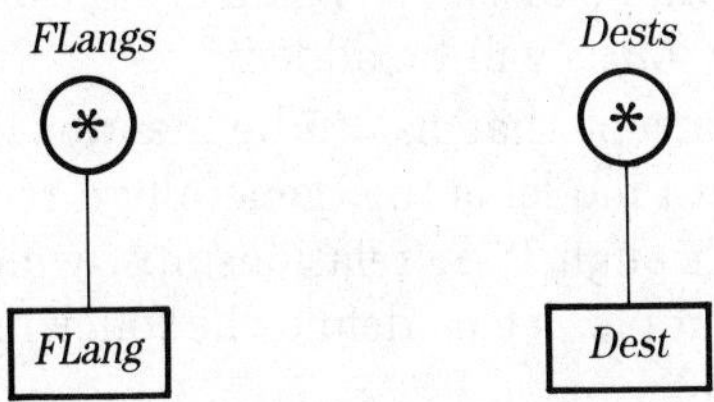

Figure 11.4 Example of grouping.

$\mathbf{D}$: $\times(R_1{:}\ *(\times(A, B)), R_2{:}\ *(\times(B, C)))$

A second important concept available in a semantic data model is the direct representation of *attributes*, a term that now refers to a *mapping* from one object type to another. So far, the term 'attribute' has been used, in particular in connection with the ER model, to denote the 'association of a property with an entity or a relationship'. Using the terminology of semantic models already available, an attribute may now be termed to be the 'association of a property with a printable object type', that is, an attribute (as a function) has an object type as its *domain.* In the special case of the ER model, the domain of an attribute is restricted to be a printable type.

This latter restriction is typically dropped in a semantic model; in addition, an atomic or even a complex object type is also allowed as the *range* of an attribute (thereby giving up the restriction that the range is a set of 'elementary' values).

In our running example, these new possibilities will be illustrated using four attributes for object type *PERSON*, which are 'functionally' defined as follows:

$Named : PERSON \rightarrow Pname$
$Lives : PERSON \rightarrow Addr$
$Speaks : PERSON \rightarrow FLangs$
$Travels : PERSON \rightarrow Dests$

In addition, *Named* is assumed to be a bijective and total mapping, which can be expressed graphically, for instance, by using a double arrow ($\Longleftrightarrow$) within the directed edge representing the attribute (see Figures 11.5 and 11.6). From a user's point of view, it is then possible to refer to persons via the printable type *Pname.* (Clearly, *Company* and *Cname* in this example can be handled in a similar way.) Attributes *Speaks* and *Travels* are both set-valued, since they associate a *set* of languages or destinations with each person, respectively; they are represented graphically using directed edges (without labels) that connect the attributes with the type *PERSON.*

Figure 11.5 summarizes the representation of our example obtained so far; the attributes will be discussed again later, especially when a graphical representation for *Lives* will be added.

A final basic concept that has to be mentioned as being characteristic for a semantic data model is the (generally direct) representability of *sub-* and *supertypes* through IS-A relationships, which was introduced in Chapter 4. In our example, let us define the following two subtypes:

TOURIST IS-A *PERSON*
BUSINESStraveler IS-A *PERSON*

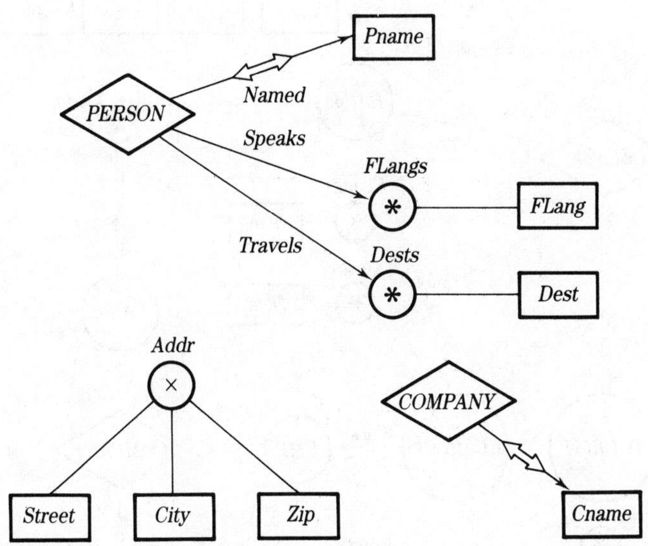

Figure 11.5 Intermediate representation of the running example.

Contrary to the graphical representation used earlier, IS-A relationships will now be drawn as follows. A *circle* is used to represent a subtype; this circle is then connected to the corresponding general type by a double-arrow ($\Longrightarrow$). In general a distinction can be made between 'user-defined' subtypes, which are declared at the design-time of a schema, and *derived* subtypes, which are constructed at run-time; most semantic models allow for such a distinction.

Subtypes may also have attributes of their own (as in the ER model); in our example, the following might be used:

$$\begin{array}{lll} Practices & : & BUSINESS \rightarrow Profession \\ Has & : & TOURIST \rightarrow Hobbies \end{array}$$

where

$$Hobbies : *(Hobby)$$

However, as was seen in connection with the ER model, a supertype *inherits* all its attributes to each of its subtypes; hence, each attribute associated with the generalization is also an attribute of the specialization. While these latter terms have been used interchangeably in Chapter 4, in general a clear distinction has to be made between an IS-A relationship expressing a 'specialization' and one expressing a 'generalization'.

Intuitively, a **specialization** can be used to establish possible *roles* for objects of a given type ('a person can be a tourist'). A **generalization**,

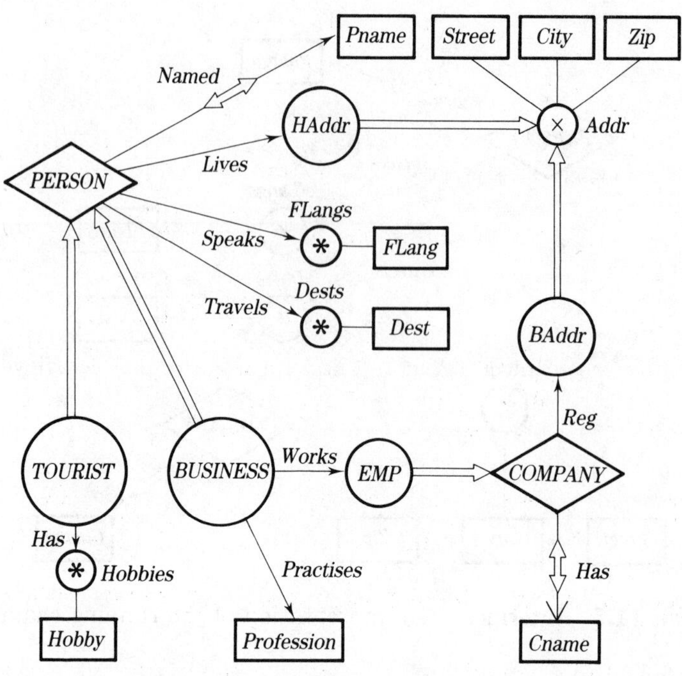

Figure 11.6 Complete representation of the sample application.

on the other hand, describes a situation in which distinct, already existing object types are composed to form a new ('virtual') type, such as the combination *VEHICLE* of the types *Train, Bus* and *Car*. At the level of concrete objects, a requirement to a generalization is that the supertype is 'covered' by its subtypes ('the set of all vehicles is the union of trains, buses and cars'), which in general is not requested for a specialization. In addition, the role of a subtype within a specialization may change over time, which is not allowed for a generalization.

Returning to our running example, *TOURIST* and *BUSINESS* are thus considered to be specializations of *PERSON*; conversely, *PERSON* is *not* considered to be a generalization of these subtypes.

When representing the attribute *Lives* of *PERSON* defined above, it makes sense to take into consideration that a *COMPANY* has an *Addr*ess of the same 'structure', so that *Addr* can be referenced by two distinct object types. A particular address can thus play the role of a *H*ome*Addr*ess of a person or that of the *B*usiness*Addr*ess of a company. The attributes *Lives* of *PERSON* and *Reg*istered, defined by

$$Reg : COMPANY \rightarrow Addr$$

will therefore be expressed graphically by introducing an intermediate node in each case that represents a specialization and hence a subtype of *Addr*, and that is connected to *Addr* via an IS-A edge. In this way, the 'range' of *Lives* and *Reg* is restricted to the different roles of an address.

A final attribute to be considered is '*Works* for' associated with the (sub)type *BUSINESS*; this type represents a specialization of *PERSON* which will be distinguished from other specializations of this type by this particular attribute. (In a similar way special attributes were used in Chapter 4 to separate pilots from employees in the airline example.)

Finally, a business traveller *Works* for a particular *EMP*loyer, who in turn is a *COMPANY*. In this case, one specialization (*BUSINESS*) can be used to state a domain for an attribute, another (*EMP*) to yield its range. The example application is summarized in Figure 11.6, which uses a redundant edge for representing the attribute

$$Works : BUSINESS \rightarrow EMP$$

just introduced. This provides a natural kind of 'clustering' of certain sections of the overall information contained in this schema.

Figure 11.7 shows one possible relational database schema that corresponds closely to the conceptual schema shown in Figure 11.6, with key as well as inclusion dependencies that capture at least parts of the semantics of this application. It should be noted that this schema is in 4NF (see Section 12.4).

The semantic data model that has been used in this chapter for purposes of illustration is known in the literature as the **IFO model**. This model has been chosen as a concrete example of the approach to conceptual database design provided by a semantic model, which uses a high level of abstraction. The IFO model seems reasonably representative of the large number of semantic models that have been proposed recently; in addition, it has several special properties (like the possibility of formally describing database updates) that make it an appropriate basis for studying further questions.

The advantages of using such a model for conceptual database design can be summarized as follows:

(1) Semantic models are *object-oriented* as opposed to record-oriented and hence allow a user to proceed in a more 'direct' fashion when defining (and in principle also when manipulating) data than is made possible by the constraint to translate observations from the real world into a record-formatted representation. Although it will later be seen that 'object-orientation' strictly speaking (and from a point of view of programming languages) refers to additional characteristics, 'modelling' as an initial task in developing computerized

$$\mathbf{D} = (\mathbf{R}, \mathrm{I}), \text{ where}$$
$$\mathbf{R} = \{ \mathit{PERSON, SPEAKS, TRAVELS, COMPANY, TOURIST, BUSINESS} \}$$

$$\begin{aligned}
\mathit{PERSON} &= (\{\mathit{Pname, Street, City, Zip}\}, \{\mathit{Pname}\}) \\
\mathit{SPEAKS} &= (\{\mathit{Pname, FLang}\}, \emptyset) \\
\mathit{TRAVELS} &= (\{\mathit{Pname, Dest}\}, \emptyset) \\
\mathit{COMPANY} &= (\{\mathit{Fname, Street, City, Zip}\}, \{\mathit{Fname}\}) \\
\mathit{TOURIST} &= (\{\mathit{Pname, Hobbies}\}, \emptyset) \\
\mathit{BUSINESS} &= (\{\mathit{Pname, Profession, EMP}\}, \{\mathit{Pname}\})
\end{aligned}$$

$$\begin{aligned}
I = \{ \; & \mathit{SPEAKS[Pname]} \subseteq \mathit{PERSON[Pname]}, \\
& \mathit{TRAVELS[Pname]} \subseteq \mathit{PERSON[Pname]}, \\
& \mathit{TOURIST[Pname]} \subseteq \mathit{PERSON[Pname]}, \\
& \mathit{BUSINESS[Pname]} \subseteq \mathit{PERSON[Pname]}, \\
& \mathit{BUSINESS[EMP]} \subseteq \mathit{COMPANY[Fname]} \, \}
\end{aligned}$$

Figure 11.7 Relational database schema corresponding to Figure 11.6.

support for some application should not be restricted from the very beginning by the limited expressive power of the language of the system at hand.

(2) Closely related is the fact that a semantic model typically provides a much larger repertoire for expressing relationships between data objects or object types than does a record model. Thus, a semantic model serves to bridge the gap between the semantics of an application as its arises in reality and the way this semantics can be represented in a database, its model or its language, respectively. Traditional models, on the other hand, often have representational features which are semantically overloaded in the sense that semantically distinct types of relationships can only be modelled by one particular construct, or that semantically equal or identical types have to be modelled by different constructs.

(3) Semantic models usually provide a variety of mechanisms to view and to manipulate the information contained in a conceptual schema at different levels in a top-down fashion. For example, the (inner) structure of an object can be hidden or made visible, or may even evolve in a sequence of steps; similarly, attributes of object types can be ignored or viewed 'explicitly', or the 'quality' of an IS-A relationship can be enhanced in the course of (design-) time.

Another aspect of the high level of abstraction present in a semantic model is the *modularity* of such a model; for example, information regarding a particular object type only can easily be extracted, or semantic connections between types (of a graphically representable schema) that are closely related can easily be found.

The IFO model has not been presented in detail here; the description has concentrated on certain structural aspects. What should be emphasized are the basic possibilities available in semantic data modelling, of which the following have been discussed in the context of this model:

(1) Three kinds of *object-types* (abstract, printable, and derived (sub) types).

(2) Two *constructs* for structuring, that is, for defining complex objects (aggregation and grouping), to be called 'tuple-' and 'set-constructors' in Chapter 21, respectively.

(3) Attributes for defining *functional* relationships between object types.

(4) *IS-A relationships* for the declaration of sub- and supertypes.

These modelling capabilities can be considered as typical for a semantic data model; they can be augmented, for instance, by 'nested' or 'aggregate-valued' attributes, for example, of type *Sum* or *Average*, or by facilities to represent hierarchical relationships that are not necessarily of type IS-A. (Some of these extensions are also present in the IFO model.)

There are several implications of the advantages of semantic modelling mentioned above, which result from the use of such a model, that was originally intended for design purposes only, regarding working with a database in general.

The direct approach to modelling in an object-oriented model carries over to the formulation of queries as well. An as example, consider the following query to a database over the schema shown in Figures 11.6 and 11.7, respectively:

'Show the location of the employer of business traveller Miller.'

Using the relational schema from Figure 11.7 and relational algebra as a query language, this can formally be written as follows:

$$\pi_{City}(\pi_{EMP}(\sigma_{Pname='Miller'}(BUSINESS)) \\ \bowtie rename_{Fname:=EMP}(COMPANY))$$

Informally, *BUSINESS* is first searched for Miller's employer and then *COMPANY* for the corresponding value of *City*; before a (natural) join of the given projection of *BUSINESS* and *COMPANY* can be formed, it is necessary to (temporarily) *rename* attribute *Fname* of *COMPANY* to

EMP. (Alternatively, a selection can be used instead of 'rename', in which a condition of the form '*COMPANY* = *EMP*' is allowed.)

The same query can be formulated with respect to the 'IFO schema' from Figure 11.6 in a purely functional way as follows:

$$(Reg(Works('Miller'))).City$$

Here, the employer of business traveller Miller is determined by *Works('Miller')* (see the definition of attribute *Works* as a function above). As a result, an employer is obtained who in particular is a company, whose location is in turn obtained by 'applying' attribute *Reg*. Finally, this location is an address, whose first component is extracted by '.*City*'. Note that here the user, in some sense, is 'navigating' through the schema directly by applying given functions to a (concrete) object of a given type; in particular, the use of types that are external to the query (such as *Fname* in the RA expression shown above) can be avoided.

The improved possibilities for modelling relationships of different qualities when using a semantic approach are also exhibited in Figures 11.6 and 11.7. For example, the *one* relation schema *PERSON* represents both the functional relationship to attribute *Pname* and the relationship of a person to his or her address as well as the aggregation of *Street*, *City* and *Zip* into an address. On the other hand, *PERSON*, *SPEAKS* and *TRAVELS* all describe the *same* set of objects, which can only be expressed by an appropriate use of foreign keys (see Section 7.3) as well as renaming of schemas. The IFO schema is therefore capable of providing a clear separation of 'concepts' as well as a unified representation.

In the relational model it is possible to express certain semantic aspects of an application by specifying intra- and interrelational constraints appropriately. A semantic model like IFO goes beyond this in that it tries to model schema-information of type 'integrity constraint' structurally as well. Unfortunately, it seems impossible to represent every relationship or property of a relationship directly in a structural way. For this reason, even a semantic model often includes possibilities to specify integrity constraints, where *dynamic* ones (see Section 7.2) are seldom covered.

Another area of application for semantic models, which is of increasing interest today, goes beyond the aspect of pure *modelling* of a given world (and the subsequent transformation of the result into one of the 'traditional' models). As has been seen in the discussion of the network model, the description of an application at a logical level by a graph ('logical network', see Definition 5.2) can in principle be considered as a basis for an 'implementation of the schema' and hence for working with a network database. In a semantic model that includes graphical representation facilities as well this is similar; an *IFO schema*, for example, is formally a directed graph $G = (V, E)$, whose set V of nodes and set E of edges consist of elements of various types; for example, V can be described by

$$V = V_p \cup V_a \cup V_s \cup V_x \cup V_*$$

where p stands for 'printable' (object), a for 'abstract', s for 'subtype', x for 'aggregation', and $*$ for 'grouping', respectively. An *IFO database* can hence be considered as an instantiation of this graph, to which queries can be directed in the form of paths through the graph, as indicated above. Independent of which physical realization is chosen for the database, this graph can be used as the basis of some (graphical) *user interface*; this is one of the aspects currently under investigation in connection with semantic models. This aspects leads, for example, to the question of how to formalize a semantic model appropriately, and in particular to the integration of dynamic aspects like the specification (and 'implementation') of (update) transactions or so-called *events* that drive certain *triggers*.

Chapter 12
Design Theory for Relational Database Schemas

In this chapter, the logical design of database schemas in the relational model is considered; specifically, formal methods — **decomposition** and **synthesis** — are presented for deriving schemas with 'desirable' properties, among which are various **normal forms**.

12.1 Update anomalies

Consider the following example. An enterprise is going to store information on its suppliers, in particular their names (N), the name of the city where a supplier is located (C) and the distance (D) to this city (from the location of the enterprise); in addition, for each part supplied an identifier (I) and the number of how many parts are in stock (S) are recorded. If the attention is restricted to these five attributes, the application can be modelled in an ERD as shown in Figure 12.1. A transformation of this diagram into the relational model yields two relation schemas:

$$R_1 = (NIS, \{NI \rightarrow S\})$$
$$R_2 = (NCD, \{N \rightarrow CD\})$$

Note that attributes N, I, and C, as shown in Figure 12.1, actually represent entity types which have one or two attributes only, so that in addition to the above 'relationship schemas' the following is obtained:

$$R_3 = (N, \{N \rightarrow N\})$$
$$R_4 = (I, \{I \rightarrow I\})$$
$$R_5 = (CD, \{C \rightarrow D\})$$

Finally, inclusion dependencies between various schemas are obtained, which are not listed. It is obvious that this result carries redundancies and is therefore not satisfactory. The example serves to introduce the following alternative way of designing relational database schemas.

The starting point is the particularly simple case of a global database schema **D** — resulting from the conceptual design phase of a database — which consists of a *single* relation schema only. During the phase of logical design, the goal is to determine whether this schema is 'well-suited' for being stored in a data dictionary. (The methods described in this chapter will also be applicable where the input to a logical design consists of *several* relation schemas; in principle, each such schema can then be dealt with individually in the way described in what follows.)

For the single relation schema given it is assumed that it contains *all* attributes arising in the underlying application, together with func-

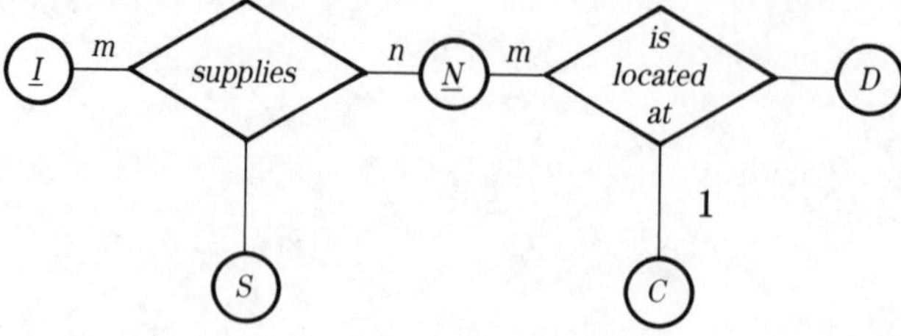

Figure 12.1 A sample application.

tional dependencies between them. In addition, it is required that for each attribute its meaning is completely expressed by its name; thus, each attribute has exactly one globally unique meaning, and attributes with distinct meanings are distinguished by their names. (For example, in the employee database of a company the names of employees are distinguished from the names of managers, or the birthdate of an employee from his hiring date.)

This requirement is known as the **universal relation schema assumption** (URSA); a set of attributes obeying this assumption is also termed the *universe* ('of discourse') U underlying the given application, and functional dependencies 'by default' refer to U (that is, for each FD f it is true that $\text{attr}(f) \subseteq U$). The reasoning usually associated with this assumption is that the application in question basically *can* be represented using just one relation schema of the form $R = (U, F)$. In this chapter, 'evaluation criteria' for such an initial schema will be established, and formal *design* methods for database schemas will then be presented that (try to) achieve them. In Chapter 17, this assumption and its interpretation will be reconsidered, and possible implications for the *manipulation* of a (relational) database and for the design of a user interface will be discussed.

Now consider the above example once more and assume that the application is described by a 'universal schema' as follows:

$$R = (U, F)$$

where

$$U = NISCD,\ F = \{NI \to S, N \to C, C \to D\}.$$

Next consider the relation $r \in \text{Rel}(U)$ shown in Figure 12.2. Clearly, $r \in \text{Sat}(R)$ holds, but r is not a 'good' candidate for being stored in a database since it exhibits certain problems called *anomalies*.

(1) **Insertion anomaly**: A (new) tuple can be inserted only if complete information (on all attributes) is available, although partial tuples like (L5, T2, 100, δ_1, δ_2) may also contain 'facts' from the real world that a user might want to store in the database. (Even if null values were allowed, a supplier could be recorded only if supplying at least one part, since otherwise the key NI would contain a null value.)

(2) **Deletion anomaly**: If the 'last' entry of a supplier is deleted, that is, if this supplier is currently not supplying any part, the location information is also lost, so that it has to be re-recorded if the supplier starts supplying again.

(3) **Update anomaly**: If a supplier moves from one location to

N	I	S	C	D
S1	P1	300	London	600
S1	P2	200	London	600
S1	P3	400	London	600
S1	P4	200	London	600
S1	P5	100	London	600
S1	P6	100	London	600
S2	P1	300	Paris	450
S2	P2	400	Paris	450
S3	P2	200	Paris	450
S4	P2	200	Brussels	150
S4	P4	300	Brussels	150
S4	P5	400	Brussels	150

Figure 12.2 A sample 'universal relation'.

another, in general *several* tuples need to be updated, and this needs to be done in an uninterruptible fashion (through a transaction in the sense of Section 8.4), since otherwise consistency problems may arise if the system allows for multiple simultaneous users.

In addition, *redundancies* can be observed in this example, like the fact that for every supplier supplying several parts the information regarding the C and D attributes is repeated for each entry; this redundancy obviously implies the update anomaly mentioned above.

It could be suspected at this point that (1) and (2) above can be resolved simply by allowing null values in relations, so that it becomes possible to store partial tuples, and to replace real values by null values during a deletion. This approach, however, is problematic for two reasons. First, the DBMS eventually has to manage a huge amount of null values, which may lead to efficiency problems for relations containing many tuples (for example, when checking integrity constraints). Secondly, the third anomaly, above as well as redundancies, is not necessarily removed.

For these reasons, a different approach will be pursued here; specifically, these problems, which are generally known as **update anomalies**, will be analysed by looking at the 'structure' of the dependencies required, which for the time being are exclusively the FDs. This primarily intuitive analysis will uncover certain 'undesirable' properties of functional dependencies; **normal forms** for relational schemas will then be defined which try to avoid these. After this, the question of how to design database schemas with 'normalized' components *algorithmically* will be discussed. Finally, *multivalued dependencies* will be briefly presented, and it will be shown that even in the absence of a specification of FDs certain anomalies may remain.

12.2 Normal forms for FD schemas

In this section and the next, relation schemas that are constrained by FDs as intrarelational dependencies ('FD schemas') are exclusively considered; furthermore, the reader should keep in mind that it is always assumed that the relation schemas in question are in 1NF (see Section 7.2).

The sample schema $R = (U, F)$, where $U = NISCD$, $F = \{NI \rightarrow S, N \rightarrow C, C \rightarrow D\}$, introduced in the previous section is now analysed in more detail; first observe that NI is the only key. More generally, the following is defined.

Definition 12.1

Let $R = (U, F)$. $A \in U$ is called **key attribute** (or **prime**) if there exists a key K for R such that $A \in K$. (Otherwise, A is called a **non-key attribute**, abbreviated NKA, or **non-prime**.)

It follows that in our example N and I are prime, whereas S, C, and D are non-prime or NKAs. Since NI is a key, the new FDs $NI \rightarrow S$, $NI \rightarrow C$, and $NI \rightarrow D$ can be derived from F. These FDs are non-trivial and r-minimal (see Definition 9.9); on the other hand, $NI \rightarrow C$ is not l-minimal because of the existence of $N \rightarrow C$ in F.

If the reader is willing to accept the intuitive interpretation of the semantics of a (non-trivial and r-minimal) FD that its left-hand side (implicitly) determines an 'entity' or a 'relationship', of which the right-hand side attribute is a 'property', then the situation above can be described as follows. There exists an NKA (attribute C) which is a 'property' of a subset of some key.

In this example even more can be observed. There also exists some NKA (attribute D) which is a property of some other non-key attribute (C). This statement results from the two FDs $N \rightarrow C$ and $C \rightarrow D$, which make the 'transitive' FD $N \rightarrow D$ derivable.

Definition 12.2

Let $R = (U, F)$. $A \in U$ is called **transitively dependent** on $X \subseteq U$ (or the FD $X \rightarrow A$ is called **transitive**) if the following hold:

(1) $X \rightarrow A \in F^+$

(2) $A \notin X$

(3) $(\exists\, Y \subseteq U)\ [X \rightarrow Y \in F^+ \wedge Y \rightarrow X \notin F^+ \wedge Y \rightarrow A \in F^+ \wedge A \notin Y]$

If A is not transitively dependent on X and $X \rightarrow A \in F^+$, A is called **directly dependent** on X (or $X \rightarrow A$ is called a **direct** FD).

Condition (1) of Definition 12.2 says that A is functionally dependent on X at all, while Condition (2) requires that this dependency is non-trivial. Condition (3) finally excludes the possibility that X and Y are equivalent (in the sense of Definition 9.10) and that $Y \rightarrow A$ is trivial.

After these preparations, 'normal forms' can now be defined which are intended to avoid the semantic 'problems' related to FDs described above.

Definition 12.3

Let $R = (U, F)$ be a relation schema in 1NF.

(1) R is in **second normal form** (2NF) if for every NKA $A \in U$ and every key K for R the FD $K \rightarrow A$ is l-minimal.

(2) R is in **third normal form** (3NF) if for every NKA $A \in U$ and every key K for R the FD $K \rightarrow A$ is direct.

(3) R is in **Boyce-Codd normal form** (BCNF) if every attribute $A \in U$ is directly dependent on every key for R.

It is easy to see that 2NF excludes the former situation described above, while 3NF excludes the latter. BCNF is motivated by the fact that even in case *every* $A \in U$ is prime certain 'FD anomalies' can be observed.

For the supplier example, the following can be concluded. R is not in 2NF, since $NI \rightarrow C$ is not full. R is not in 3NF, since D is transitively dependent on N; in detail, the following holds: $N \rightarrow D \in F^+ \wedge D \notin N \wedge [N \rightarrow C \in F^+ \wedge C \rightarrow N \notin F^+ \wedge C \rightarrow D \in F^+ \wedge D \notin C]$. R is not in BCNF, since this normal form is based on a condition which is even more strict than 3NF.

In general, the following can be shown regarding the relationships between these normal forms.

Theorem 12.1

Let $R = (U, F)$ be in 1NF.

(1) R is in BCNF $\Longrightarrow$ R is in 3NF

(2) R is in 3NF $\Longrightarrow$ R is in 2NF

Proof. (1) is trivial, since the BCNF condition in particular captures all non-key attributes. In order to prove (2), the contraposition is shown. Assume that R is not in 2NF. This implies that there exists a non-prime attribute $A \in U$ and a key K for R such that the FD $K \rightarrow A$ is not l-minimal ('partial'), which means the following:

$$(\exists Z \subset K)\ Z \rightarrow A \in F^+$$

In addition, it follows that $Z \rightarrow K \notin F^+$, because K (as a key) is minimal. Finally, since A is not prime, it follows that $A \notin K$. In conclusion, $K \rightarrow A \in F^+, A \notin K, [K \rightarrow Z \in F^+ \wedge Z \rightarrow K \notin F^+ \wedge Z \rightarrow A \in F^+ \wedge A \notin Z]$, which shows that A is transitively dependent on K. Thus, R is not in 3NF. □

The following examples show that, for both statements of Theorem 12.1, the converse does not hold in general, that is, each normal form mentioned is a strict aggravation of the previous one:

(1) Let $R = (ABC, \{A \rightarrow B, B \rightarrow C\})$. Clearly, R is in 2NF, but not in 3NF.

(2) Let $R = (ABC, \{AB \rightarrow C, C \rightarrow B\})$. R is in 3NF, since AB and AC are the only keys. Thus, all attributes of R are prime, which implies that the 3NF condition is trivially satisfied. On the other hand, the FD $AC \rightarrow B$ is transitive, since $AC \rightarrow B \in F^+ \wedge B \notin AC \wedge [AC \rightarrow C \in F^+ \wedge C \rightarrow AC \notin F^+ \wedge C \rightarrow B \in F^+ \wedge B \notin C]$. It follows that R is not in BCNF.

It turns out that 3NF and BCNF can alternatively be characterized as follows.

Theorem 12.2

Let $R = (U, F)$. Then the following hold:

(i) R is in 3NF $\Longleftrightarrow$
$(\forall X \subseteq U)(\forall A \in U, A \text{ NKA})\ [X \rightarrow A \in F^+ \wedge A \notin X \Longrightarrow X \rightarrow U \in F^+]$

(ii) R is in BCNF $\Longleftrightarrow$
$(\forall X \subseteq U)(\forall A \in U)\ [X \rightarrow A \in F^+ \wedge A \notin X \Longrightarrow X \rightarrow U \in F^+]$

Proof. (i) '$\Longrightarrow$': Let R be in 3NF. Also, let $X \subseteq U$, and $A \in U$ be an NKA such that $X \rightarrow A \in F^+$ and $A \notin X$ hold. Suppose that X is not a candidate key for R, that is, $X \rightarrow U \notin F^+$. Next consider an arbitrary key K for R; then the following holds: $K \rightarrow X \in F^+ \wedge X \rightarrow K \notin F^+$ (otherwise $X \rightarrow U \in F^+$ would follow, a contradiction to our indirect assumption) $\wedge$ $A \notin K$ (since A is an NKA). Hence, A is transitively dependent on K, which contradicts the assumption that R is in 3NF.

'$\Longleftarrow$': Let $K \subseteq U$ be a key for R, and let $A \in U$ be an NKA. It follows immediately that $K \rightarrow A \in F^+$ and $A \notin K$. Suppose the FD $K \rightarrow A$ was transitive, that is, $(\exists\, Y \subseteq U)[K \rightarrow Y \in F^+ \wedge Y \rightarrow K \notin F^+ \wedge Y \rightarrow A \in F^+ \wedge A \notin Y]$. Because of our assumption it follows that $Y \rightarrow U \in F^+$ and, since $K \subseteq U$, also $Y \rightarrow K \in F^+$, a contradiction.

(ii) The proof is analogous to (i) and therefore omitted. □

As another example, consider $R = (U, F)$, where $U = ABCDEG$, $\{AB \rightarrow E,\ AC \rightarrow G,\ AD \rightarrow B,\ B \rightarrow C,\ C \rightarrow D\}$. It is easily verified that AB, AC, and AD are keys for R. E and C are the only non-key attributes; hence, by Theorem 12.2 (i), R is in 3NF. However, R is not in BCNF, since neither B nor C is a key.

Intuitively, Theorem 12.2 (ii) says that a relation schema R is in BCNF if and only if the left-hand side of every non-trivial FD 'over' R is a candidate key. Using the notion of closure of a set of attributes from Definition 9.7, this normal form can now be characterized as follows.

Theorem 12.3

Let $R = (U, F)$.

$$R \text{ is in BCNF} \iff (\forall\, X \subseteq U)\ X \text{ closed (w.r.t. } F) \vee X \rightarrow U \in F^+$$

In order to prove this theorem, some preparations are needed.

Lemma 12.1

Let $R = (U, F)$, $X, Y \subseteq U$. Then the following hold:

(1) $cl_F(X)$ is closed (w.r.t. F)

(2) X is closed (w.r.t. F) $\iff X = cl_F(X)$

The proof of Lemma 12.1 is left to the reader (see Exercise 2).

Definition 12.4

Let $R = (U, F)$. $A \in U$ is called **abnormal** if the following condition is satisfied:

$$(\exists\, X \subseteq U)\ X \rightarrow U \notin F^+ \wedge A \in cl_F(X) - X$$

A is called **normal** if A is not abnormal.

For example, let $R = (ABC, \{AB \rightarrow C, C \rightarrow B\})$. Then B is abnormal, since B is an element of the closure of C without C, and C is not a candidate key.

Lemma 12.2

$R = (U, F)$ is in BCNF iff every $A \in U$ is normal.

Proof. '$\Longrightarrow$': Let R be in BCNF. Suppose $A \in U$ is abnormal, that is, $(\exists\, X \subseteq U)\ X \rightarrow U \notin F^+ \wedge A \in cl_F(X) - X$. Hence, $X \rightarrow A \in F^+$ and

$A \notin X$, that is, $X \to A$ is a valid, non-trivial FD. By Theorem 12.2 (ii), it follows that $X \to U$ is valid, a contradiction.

'$\Longleftarrow$': Suppose R is not in BCNF. Then there exists a non-trivial FD $X \to A$ in F^+ such that $cl_F(X) \neq U$. Since $A \notin X$, it follows that $A \in cl_F(X) - X$; hence, A is abnormal, a contradiction. □

Proof of Theorem 12.3: '$\Longrightarrow$': Two cases are distinguished:

(i) Suppose that for $X \subseteq U$ it is true that $X \to U \notin F^+$. Since, by Lemma 12.2, every $A \in U$ is normal, it follows that $cl_F(X) - X = \emptyset$, that is, $cl_F(X) = X$. Thus, by Lemma 12.1 (2), X is closed.

(ii) Suppose now that $X \subseteq U$ is not closed. This implies $cl_F(X) \neq X$, that is, $(\exists A \in U)\ A \in cl_F(X) - X$. Since A is normal according to our assumption, it follows that $X \to U \in F^+$.

'$\Longleftarrow$': Assume that R is not in BCNF. By Lemma 12.2, there exists an abnormal attribute $A \in U$, that is, $(\exists X \subseteq U)\ X \to U \notin F \wedge A \in cl_F(X) - X$. The latter condition implies $cl_F(X) \neq X$. By Lemma 12.1 (2), X is thus neither a key candidate nor closed, a contradiction. □

The next question discussed is whether it is possible, on the basis of the above characterizations of 3NF and BCNF, to devise efficient tests for checking whether a given relation schema obeys one of these normal forms. The following theorem shows that in such a test it is *not* necessary to check whether *every* NKA is directly dependent on *every* key; instead, it is sufficient to consider one arbitrarily chosen key only.

Theorem 12.4

Let $R = (U, F)$. R is in 3NF iff every NKA is directly dependent on any key.

Theorem 12.4 follows from the next result as a corollary.

Lemma 12.3

Let $R = (U, F)$, $A \in U$. If there exists a key K for R such that:

(i) $A \notin K$ and $K \to A$ is not l-minimal, or

(ii) $K \to A$ is transitive,

then A is transitively dependent on every key for R.

Proof. Let $K \to A$ be not l-minimal, and let $A \notin K$. Then there exists some $X \subset K$ such that $X \to A \in F^+$; in addition, $A \notin X$ holds. As in the proof of Theorem 12.1 (2) it can now be concluded that $K \to X \in F^+$ and $X \to K \notin F^+$. Thus, the FD $K \to A$ is transitive. Next let K' be another key for $R, K' \neq K$. It follows that $K' \rightarrow A \in F^+$ and $K' \rightarrow X \in F^+$. In addition, $X \rightarrow K' \notin F^+$, since otherwise $X \rightarrow K \in F^+$ would also hold, a contradiction. Thus, A is transitively dependent on K' as well. □

Based on Theorem 12.4, the following algorithm can be stated which tests a given relation schema $R = (U, F)$ for 3NF:

(1) Determine an arbitrary key K for R.

(2) Determine all non-key attributes from U.

(3) Test whether every attribute found under (2) is directly dependent on K.

While Step 1 can be executed in time polynomial in the length of the representation of the input R (according to results from Section 9.2), the same may not be true for Step 2, since the following holds.

Theorem 12.5

Let $R = (U, F)$. The problem to decide whether an attribute $A \in U$ is prime is NP-complete.

When testing for 3NF, the search for prime attributes may even be restricted to abnormal ones, owing to the following statement on 3NF, which is analogous to Lemma 12.2: a relation schema is in 3NF iff every NKA is normal (see Exercise 3). Unfortunately, this observation does not improve the running time of the algorithm sketched above significantly. Furthermore, the 'prime-attribute problem' described in Theorem 12.5 can be polynomially reduced to the '3NF problem', which means:

Theorem 12.6

Let $R = (U, F)$. The problem to decide whether R is in 3NF is NP-complete.

On the other hand, with respect to testing a relation schema $R = (U, F)$ for BCNF the following statement holds (as an 'aggravation' of Theorem 12.2 (ii)).

Theorem 12.7

$R = (U, F)$ is in BCNF $\Longleftrightarrow$ $(\forall f \in F, f$ non-trivial$)$ $L_f \rightarrow U \in F^+$

Proof. '$\Longrightarrow$': Let $f \in F$ be non-trivial. Since L_f is not closed, $L_f \rightarrow U \in F^+$, by Theorem 12.3.

'$\Longleftarrow$': Let $L_f \to U \in F^+$ hold for every FD $f \in F$. It will be shown that in this case U does not contain abnormal attributes, so that the assertion follows from Lemma 12.2. Suppose some attribute $A \in U$ is abnormal, that is,

$$(\exists X \subseteq U)\ X \to U \notin F^+ \wedge A \in cl_F(X) - X$$

Clearly, X is not closed. The computation of $cl_F(X)$ from F can be performed using a RAP derivation, which without loss of generality yields the following representation:

$$cl_F(X) = X \cup R_{f_1} \cup R_{f_2} \cup \ \dots \ \cup R_{f_n}$$

where $f_i \in F$ for $1 \le i \le n$. Since $A \in cl_F(X) - X$, it follows that $A \in R_{f_i}$ for some $i \in \{1, \ \dots \ , n\}$. Now it is easily seen that for this FD f_i it is true that $cl_F(L_{f_i}) \subseteq cl_F(X)$. From $X \to U \notin F^+$ it can then be concluded that $L_{f_i} \to U \notin F^+$, a contradiction. □

It follows from this theorem (in connection with Theorem 9.7) that one can determine in polynomial time whether a given relation schema is in BCNF.

The next section returns to these complexity results and considers with what complexity database schemas with normalized components can be designed algorithmically.

12.3 Decomposition and synthesis

The first example given in this chapter, $R = (NISCD, \{NI \to S, N \to C, C \to D\})$, is now reconsidered. As could be seen above, this schema exhibits anomalies and redundancies, which was analysed above by taking a look at the 'FD structure'. As a result, it turned out that R is not in 2NF (and therefore neither in 3NF nor in BCNF). The idea to remedy this situation, which will also be presented formally, is to replace R by a database schema that (1) models the same application as R, but which (2) is 'better' suited for this modelling than R itself.

For example, if the database format $\mathbf{R} = \{R_1, R_2, R_3\}$ is considered, where $R_1 = (NIS, \{NI \to S\}), R_2 = (NC, \{N \to C\}), R_3 = (CD, \{C \to C\})$, first observe that R and $\mathbf{R}$ are 'closely' related: both representations carry the same attributes as well as the same dependencies. In addition, each relation schema occurring in $\mathbf{R}$ is in BCNF. The 'decomposition' (projections) of the relation from Figure 12.2 shown in Figure 12.3 is finally free of the anomalies and redundancies observed above.

This approach of **design by normalization**, whose general goal is to replace a 'problematic' database schema by a less problematic one, will now be discussed in more detail, where the attention is restricted to the

r_1:	N	I	S
	S1	P1	300
	S1	P2	200
	S1	P3	400
	S1	P4	200
	S1	P5	100
	S1	P6	100
	S2	P1	300
	S2	P2	400
	S3	P2	200
	S4	P2	200
	S4	P4	300
	S4	P5	400

r_2:	N	C
	L1	London
	L2	Paris
	L3	Paris

r_3:	C	D
	London	600
	Paris	450
	Brussels	150

Figure 12.3 A decomposition of the relation from Figure 12.2.

case that the 'problematic' schema consists of a single universal schema of the form $R = (U, F)$. If R is to be replaced by some database schema **D**, a notion of 'representation' is apparently needed stating criteria under which R and **D** describe the 'same' application. In addition, **D** should represent the application in a 'better' way; according to the results from the previous section, the normal forms will be used as a yardstick in this respect. Therefore, the following is defined first.

Definition 12.5

A database schema $\mathbf{D} = (\mathbf{R}, .)$ is in 2NF [3NF, BCNF] if every $R_i \in \mathbf{R}$ is in 2NF [3NF, BCNF], respectively.

With regard to representing the 'same' application, it is first required that schemas R and **D** which are comparable in this (still intuitive) sense have *exactly* the same overall set of attributes; that is, if $R = (U, .)$ and $\mathbf{D} = (\mathbf{R}, .)$, where $\mathbf{R} = \{R_1, \ldots, R_k\}$, then $\cup_{i=1}^k X_i = U$ holds.

A similar requirement holds for the dependencies as well; this property of 'inheriting' or 'preserving' a semantic specification during the transition from $R = (U, F)$ to $\mathbf{D} = (\mathbf{R}, .)$, where $R_i = (X_i, F_i)$ for $1 \leq i \leq k$, can formally be written as

$$(\cup_{i=1}^k F_i)^+ = F^+$$

and is motivated by the following example.

Let $U = CAZ$, where C stands for 'City', A for 'Address', and Z for 'Zip Code'. Also, let $F = \{CA \rightarrow Z, Z \rightarrow C\}$. Note that this example with different names for the attributes was discussed above; hence it is known already that R is not in BCNF. R could be replaced with the BCNF database schema $\mathbf{D} = (\{R_1, R_2\}, \emptyset)$, where

$$R_1 = (ZC, \{Z \rightarrow C\}), \;\; R_2 = (ZA, \emptyset)$$

Now consider the following sample database; it will turn out that this decomposition is unreasonable. Let r_1 and r_2 denote the following relations:

r_1:	Z	C
	92037	SD
	92093	SD

r_2:	Z	A
μ	92037	3745 Miramar
ν	92093	3745 Miramar

The tuples in r_2 are meaningful only if C values can be associated with each of them. Now let c_1 (c_2) be the C value associated with μ (ν), respectively. By $Z \rightarrow C$, that is, the zip code determines the city, and since no other zip codes are currently stored in r_1, it follows that $c_1 = c_2$ = 'SD'. Thus, identical CA pairs are obtained for distinct Z values, which contradicts the FD $CA \rightarrow Z$. In this example, $\mathbf{D}$ represents the functional relationship $Z \rightarrow C$ only, but not $CA \rightarrow Z$ as well.

As a final condition, a decomposition is required to be free of loss of information. Intuitively, this means that if an application can in principle be represented by a single relation (over the universal schema), this relation can be reconstructed *exactly* from a 'corresponding' state of the corresponding database schema.

As an example, consider the universe U, consisting of the attributes C (customer), $A\#$ (account number), A_B (account balance), and B (bank branch), and the FDs $C \rightarrow A\_B$ and $A\# \rightarrow \{B, A\_B\}$. Figure 12.4(a) shows a universal relation r for this schema. Now consider the query 'show all branches where Peter has an account'. From r, the answer is 'La Jolla'; a corresponding RA expression is $\pi_B(\sigma_{C='Peter'}(R))$. Next consider the decomposition of R (r) into r_1 and r_2 shown in Figure 12.4(b). To answer the same query, a join has to be formed: $\pi_B(\sigma_{C='Peter'}(R_1 \bowtie R_2))$. The result of an evaluation of this expression can be seen from Figure 12.4(c); apparently, the answer is { La Jolla, Mira Mesa }. It follows that the join of R_1 and R_2 (or of r_1 and r_2, respectively) in this case is lossy; although the answer contains *more* tuples, it carries *less* information.

Based on these observation, the following is defined.

Definition 12.6

Let $R = (U, F)$ and $\mathbf{D} = (\mathbf{R}, .)$, where $R_i = (X_i, F_i)$ for each $R_i \in \mathbf{R}, 1 \leq i \leq k$.

(i) $\mathbf{D}$ is called a **decomposition** of R if the following conditions are satisfied:

(a) $(\forall i = 1(1)k) \; X_i \subseteq U$

(b) $\cup_{i=1}^{k} X_i = U$

(c) $(\forall i, 1 \leq i \leq k) \; F_i^+ \subseteq F^+ \mid_{X_i} := \{f \in F^+ \mid \text{attr}(f) \subseteq X_i\}$

r:

C	$A\#$	A_B	B
Peter	5000	100	La Jolla
Paul	7000	100	Mira Mesa

(a)

r_1:

$A\#$	A_B	B
5000	100	La Jolla
7000	100	Mira Mesa

r_2:

C	A_B
Peter	100
Paul	100

(b)

$r_1 \bowtie r_2$:

C	$A\#$	A_B	B
Peter	5000	100	La Jolla
Peter	7000	100	Mira Mesa
Paul	5000	100	La Jolla
Paul	7000	100	Mira Mesa

(c)

Figure 12.4 Example of a lossy decomposition.

(ii) A decomposition **D** of R is called
 (a) **lossless** (w.r.t. R) if $(\forall r \in \text{Sat}(R)) \;\; r = \bowtie_{i=1}^{k} \pi_{X_i}(r)$
 (b) **independent** (w.r.t. R) if $(\cup_{i=1}^{k} F_i)^+ = F^+$

The latter notion of 'independence' of a decomposition implies (as could also be seen from the *CAZ* example above) that it is possible to restrict one's attention to checking the correctness of individual relations occurring in a database state d when performing updates in order to ensure that the relation over U that results from a join of all elements in d satisfies F. More precisely, if $d = \{r_1, \ldots, r_k\}$ and $r_i \in \text{Sat}(R_i)$ for $i, 1 \leq i \leq k$, the following holds for an independent decomposition: $\cup_{i=1}^{k} F_i \models f$ for every $f \in F$ (and obviously $F \models f$ for every $f \in \cup_{i=1}^{k} F_i$). Next, if all component relations are correct, then $\bowtie_{i=1}^{k} r_i \in \text{Sat}(F)$ holds; to see this, it suffices to show that the join relation satisfies every FD $f \in \cup_{i=1}^{k} F_i$, which can be concluded from the correctness of the r_i values.

Independence can be tested with the methods known from Chapter 9, in particular the membership algorithm. A method for testing losslessness is described next.

Definition 12.7

Let $\mathbf{D} = (\mathbf{R}, .)$ be a given database schema, where $\mathbf{R} = \{R_1, \ldots, R_k\}$, and $|\cup_{i=1}^{k} X_i| = m$. The **schema tableau** $T_{\mathbf{D}}$ for **D** is a table with m

w_0:	N	I	S	C	D
w_1:	a_1	a_2	a_3	b_{14}	b_{15}
w_2:	a_1	b_{22}	b_{23}	a_4	b_{25}
w_3:	b_{31}	b_{32}	b_{33}	a_4	a_5

Figure 12.5 Schema tableau for supplier example.

columns and $k+1$ rows, whose first row w_0 contains the attributes from $\cup_{i=1}^{k} X_i$, and whose other columns w_i correspond to the relation schemas R_i as follows:

$$w_i = (x_{i1}, \ldots, x_{im})$$

where

$$x_{ij} := \begin{cases} a_j & \text{if } A_j \in X_i \\ b_{ij} & \text{otherwise} \end{cases}$$

Here it is assumed that $a_1, \ldots, a_m, b_{11}, \ldots, b_{km}$ are pairwise distinct symbols.

As a first example, consider the decomposition **D** of $R = (NISCD, .)$ from Figure 12.3; Figure 12.5 shows the corresponding schema tableau for **D**. As a second example, consider the decomposition $A\# \; A\_B \; B$ and $C \; A\_B$ of the banking application described above; the corresponding schema tableau is shown in Figure 12.6.

Next, consider the following algorithm:

Algorithm LJP ('lossless join property')
Input: A universal schema $R = (U, F)$ and a decomposition **D** of R.
Output: 'true' if **D** is lossless (w.r.t. R) and 'false' otherwise.
Method:

```
begin
    ljp := false;
    construct T_D;
    while T_D can be changed do
    begin
```

w_0:	C	$A\#$	A_B	B
w_1:	a_1	b_{12}	a_3	b_{14}
w_2:	b_{21}	a_2	a_3	a_4

Figure 12.6 Schema tableau for banking example.

	N	I	S	C	D
w_1:	a_1	a_2	a_3	a_4	a_5
w_2:	a_1	b_{22}	b_{23}	a_4	a_5
w_3:	b_{31}	b_{32}	b_{33}	a_4	a_5

(Header row: w_0: N I S C D)

Figure 12.7 Result of applying *LJP* to the tableau from Figure 12.5.

choose some FD $X \rightarrow Y \in F$;
if $(\exists\ w_i, w_j \text{ in } T_{\mathbf{D}},\ i \neq j \wedge i, j \neq 0)$
    w_i and w_j agree in the columns of X
then
    identify w_i and w_j in the columns of Y
    as follows: Let $A_l \in Y$: if $x_{il} = a_l$, then
    set $x_{jl} := a_l$; if $x_{jl} = a_l$, then set
    $x_{il} := a_l$; otherwise, set (w.l.o.g.)
    $x_{jl} := b_{il}$;
end;
if $(\exists$ row w_i in $T_{\mathbf{D}},\ i \neq 0)(\forall j = 1(1)|U|)$
    $x_{ij} = a_j$
then ljp := true;
end;

Figures 12.7 and 12.8 show the result of applying Algorithm *LJP* to the schema tableau from Figures 12.5 and 12.6, respectively. For the former tableau the result is 'ljp = true', while for the latter it is 'ljp = false'.

Theorem 12.8

Algorithm *LJP* is correct, that is, a decomposition $\mathbf{D}$ is lossless w.r.t. R iff $LJP(R, \mathbf{D})$ = true.

For a proof of this theorem, the reader is referred to literature cited in the Bibliographic Notes below. Using this theorem, it is easy to verify

w_0:	C	$A\#$	A_B	B
w_1:	a_1	b_{12}	a_3	b_{14}
w_2:	b_{21}	a_2	a_3	a_4

Figure 12.8 Result of applying *LJP* to the tableau from Figure 12.6.

the following.

Theorem 12.9

Let $R = (U, F), U = XYZ$. If $X \to Y \in F^+$ holds, then the decomposition $\mathbf{D} = (\{R_1, R_2\}, .)$, where $R_1 = (XY, \{S \to T \in F \mid S, T \subseteq XY\})$ and $R_2 = (XZ, \{S \to T \in F \mid S, T \subseteq XZ\})$, is lossless.

Proof. Under the given prerequisites, the schema tableau $T_{\mathbf{D}}$ contains two rows w_1 and w_2 that agree on X. In addition, w_1 (w_2) contains a-values in the columns of Y (Z), respectively. Thus, by applying the FDs from F to $T_{\mathbf{D}}$ according to *LJP*, a-values in all X^+ columns of w_2 can be generated; after the algorithm has terminated, w_2 will consist of a-values only since $Y \subseteq X^+$. □

This theorem motivates a first formal **design algorithm** for database schemas with normalized components. In order to be able to give a concise description of this method, the following notation for the 'projection' of a set of dependencies is introduced, which was used in Theorem 12.9.

Definition 12.8

For a set X of attributes and a set F of FDs, the **restriction** of F to X is defined as $\pi_X(F) := \{f \in F \mid \text{attr}(f) \subseteq X\}$.

For example, if $F = \{AB \to C, C \to A\}$, then $\pi_{ABC}(F) = F$, $\pi_{AC}(F) = \{C \to A\}$, and $\pi_{BC}(F) = \emptyset$.

Note that Condition (c) in the definition of a decomposition (see Definition 12.6 (i)) can now alternatively be written:

$(\forall i, 1 \le i \le k)\ F_i^+ \subseteq \pi_{X_i}(F^+)$

The design algorithm which will be presented next is called **decomposition**; it is able to generate a lossless decomposition from a given universal schema $R = (U, F)$ whose components are in BCNF:

Algorithm DECOMPOSITION
Input: A universal schema $R = (U, F)$.
Output: A lossless BCNF decomposition $\mathbf{D} = (\mathbf{R}, .)$ of R.
Method:

```
begin
    R := {R};
    done := false;
    while not done do
        if (∃ R_i ∈ R) R_i not in BCNF,
            that is, (∃ Y → Z ∈ F_i^+, Z ⊈ Y)
```

```
                    Y → X_i ∉ F_i^+
              then
                    begin
                          X_i1 := YZ;
                          X_i2 := X_i − Z;
                          R_i1 := (X_i1, π_{X_i1}(F_i^+));
                          R_i2 := (X_i2, π_{X_i2}(F_i^+));
                          R := (R − {R_i}) ∪ {R_i1, R_i2} ;
                    end;
              else done := true
        end;
```

The correctness of this algorithm will not be shown formally here; just note that this method forces all components to be in BCNF, and that the losslessness of the result is easily verified by Theorem 12.9. The next example shows that it can happen that dependencies are 'lost' during the decomposition process, so that the result is not independent in general.

Consider $R = (NISCD, \{NI \rightarrow S, N \rightarrow C, C \rightarrow D\})$. As is known already, R is not in BCNF. Without loss of generality, let $N \rightarrow C \in F^+$ be chosen for the first decomposition step ($N \rightarrow NISCD \notin F^+$). Then the following is obtained:

$$R_1 = (NC, \{N \rightarrow C\})$$
$$R_2 = (NISD, \{NI \rightarrow S, N \rightarrow D\})$$

R_1 is in BCNF, but R_2 is not, since $N \rightarrow NISD \notin F_2^+$. As a consequence, R_2 is decomposed further in a second step into:

$$R_{21} = (ND, \{N \rightarrow D\})$$
$$R_{22} = (NIS, \{NI \rightarrow S\})$$

Now $\mathbf{D} = (\{R_1, R_{21}, R_{22}\}, .)$ is in BCNF, but one of the original FDs is no longer represented: $C \rightarrow D \notin (F_1 \cup F_{21} \cup F_{22})^+$.

It is easy to see that the following decomposition is also a possible result of the above algorithm:

$$R_1 = (NIS, \{NI \rightarrow S\})$$
$$R_2 = (NC, \{N \rightarrow C\})$$
$$R_3 = (CD, \{C \rightarrow D\})$$

In addition to being lossless, this decomposition is also independent. It follows that the result the algorithm generates is not uniquely determined, since during the execution of the **if** statement an FD on which the next decomposition step is based is chosen *non-deterministically.*

There are cases in which BCNF and independence cannot be achieved simultaneously. For example, consider $R = (CAZ, \{CA \rightarrow Z, Z \rightarrow C\})$ once more, which is in 3NF but not in BCNF. If R is decomposed according to $Z \to C$, the components shown previously are obtained with formats ZC and ZA, respectively, from which $CA \to Z$ can no longer be derived. In this case, no independent BCNF decomposition exists. It can even be proved that the problem to decide whether a lossless and independent BCNF decomposition exists for a given schema $R = (U, F)$ is NP-hard.

Another problem is that the algorithm exclusively proceeds over F^+ (or F_i^+), so that in principle closure computations (which have exponential time complexity in general) are required. In addition, it can be shown that every attribute which is normal in the input schema $R = (U, F)$ is also normal in each decomposition component in which it appears (see Exercise 9 on p. 261); the converse, however, is not true in general. Thus, if the **if** statement for testing BCNF is executed by searching for abnormal attributes, it is not guaranteed that these become normal in a component. It can be proved that testing whether some $A \in U$ is abnormal with respect to $X \subseteq U$ is NP-complete. From this, it can further be concluded that testing whether the components generated in a single step are in BCNF is NP-hard; the complementary problem of deciding whether a schema $\mathbf{D}$ generated via decomposition is *not* in BCNF is NP-complete.

Because of these problems in connection with BCNF, it seems reasonable to 'reduce' the normal-form requirement to 3NF. The design approach presented below is able to achieve 3NF decompositions which are both independent and lossless. This approach is known as **synthesis**; its basic idea is to generate a separate schema for each (distinct) left-hand side of an FD occurring in a basis for the given FD set. In this way, the 'implicit semantics' of an FD, which intuitively says that a (minimal) left-hand side represents an 'entity' or a 'relationship' with 'properties' given on the right-hand side, is used to 'separate concepts' included in the underlying universe. This way of separating is also termed the '**one fact in one place**' principle of database design.

To describe this idea informally, the following steps are sufficient, which show the essence of the approach; let $R = (U, F)$ be given:

```
begin
    G := BASIS(F);
    R := ∅;
    for each Y → A ∈ G do
        R := R ∪ {(YA, π_YA(G))}
end;
```

The synthesis approach is introduced in more detail next; therefore a complete algorithm is described as follows:

Algorithm SYNTHESIS
Input: A universal schema $R = (U, F)$.

Output: A lossless and independent 3NF decomposition $\mathbf{D}$ of R.
Method:

```
begin
    G := BASIS(F);
    R := ∅; i := 0;
    for each Y ⊆ U such that (∃A ∈ U) Y → A ∈ G do
        begin
            i := i + 1;
            X_i := Y ∪ {A ∈ U | Y → A ∈ G};
            R_i := (X_i, π_{X_i}(G));
            R := R ∪ {R_i};
        end;
    if (∀R_i ∈ R) X_i → U ∉ G⁺ then
        begin
            i := i + 1;
            X_i := KEY(U, G);
            R_i := (X_i, ∅);
            R := R ∪ {R_i}
        end;
    D := ( R, ∅ );
end;
```

Theorem 12.10

Let $R = (U, F)$. Then *SYNTHESIS(R)* is a lossless and independent 3NF decomposition of R.

Proof. Clearly, $\mathbf{D}$ = *SYNTHESIS(R)* is a decomposition of R in the sense of Definition 12.6. Let $\mathbf{D} = (\ \mathbf{R}, \emptyset\ )$, where $\mathbf{R} = \{R_1, \ldots, R_k\}$. By construction, all FDs contained in G are 'inherited' to the components. Thus, $F^+ = G^+ = (\cup_{i=1}^k F_i)^+$, that is, $\mathbf{D}$ is independent.

To show losslessness, we can proceed as follows. Let $X = X_i$ for $R_i \in \mathbf{R}$ be such that $X_i \rightarrow U \in F^+$ (note that such an R_i always exists). Algorithm *LJP* is applied to R and $\mathbf{D}$, where in particular changes are watched for that occur in the row of X. Since $X \rightarrow U \in F^+$, it follows that $CLOSURE(F, X) = U$. Now let $A_1, \ldots, A_n$ denote the sequence in which the elements of $U - X$ are added to X or $cl_F(X)$, respectively. Using induction on $i, 1 \leq i \leq n$, it can easily be shown that the A_i column of the schema tableau $T_{\mathbf{D}}$ gets value a_i in the row of X during the execution of *LJP*. Since $X \cup A_1 \ldots A_n = U$, the X row will finally consist of a-values only; thus, $\mathbf{D}$ is lossless.

In order to show that all components are in 3NF, first consider $R_k = (X_k, \emptyset)$, that is, X_k was explicitly included in $\mathbf{D}$ as a key for $R = (U, F)$. R_k is trivially in 3NF. Next let $R_i = (X_i, F_i)$ be a schema which was generated by an element of G, and suppose R_i is not in 3NF. This means

$$(\exists Z \subseteq X_i)(\exists A \in X_i, A \text{ NKA})\ Z \rightarrow A \in F_i^+ \wedge A \notin Z \wedge Z \rightarrow X_i \notin F_i^+$$

(see Theorem 12.2 (i)). Let R_i have been generated because of $Y \rightarrow B \in G$, and let X_i have the form $YB_1 \ldots B_n$. It follows that $ZA \subseteq YB_1 \ldots B_n$. Now two cases have to be considered.

(i) $A = B_j$ for some $j \in \{1, \ldots, n\}$. In this case, $Z \subseteq Y$ and even $Z \subset Y$ since $Z \rightarrow X_i \in F_i^+$. Hence $Y \rightarrow B_j$ is not l-minimal, since this FD can be shortened to $Z \rightarrow B_j$; this contradicts the construction underlying G.

(ii) $A \neq B_j$ for all $j \in \{1, \ldots, n\}$. Now it follows that $A \in Y$. Since A is an NKA and Y is a candidate key for R_i, there exists a key $V \subset Y$ (such that $A \notin V$). Now $V \rightarrow B_j$ for $1 \leq j \leq n$ holds, that is, $Y \rightarrow B_j$ is not l-minimal, a contradiction. □

As an example for the application of *SYNTHESIS*, consider the supplier schema first: $F = \{NI \rightarrow S, N \rightarrow C, C \rightarrow D\}$ is a basis already. The **for** loop yields the three relation schemas:

$$R_1 = (NIS,\ \{NI \rightarrow S\})$$
$$R_2 = (NC,\ \{N \rightarrow C\})$$
$$R_3 = (CD,\ \{C \rightarrow D\})$$

(see above). Since R_1 already contains a candidate key for $U = NISCD$, this decomposition represents the result.

Next consider the address example, where $U = CAZ$ and $F = \{CA \rightarrow Z, Z \rightarrow C\}$: $R = (U, F)$ is in 3NF already. In this case, the synthesis algorithm yields the (obviously redundant) decomposition:

$$R_1 = (CAZ,\ \{CA \rightarrow Z, Z \rightarrow C\})$$
$$R_2 = (ZC,\ \{Z \rightarrow C\})$$

Finally, consider the universal schema $R = (U, F)$ for the banking example, where $U = \{C,\ A\#,\ A\_B,\ B\}$, and $F = \{C \rightarrow A\_B, A\# \rightarrow BA\_B\}$; the synthesis algorithm now yields the following result:

$$R_1 = (CA\_B,\ \{C \rightarrow A\_B\})$$
$$R_2 = (A\#A\_BB,\ \{A\# \rightarrow B, A\# \rightarrow A\_B\})$$
$$R_3 = (CA\#,\ \emptyset)$$

In this case, a 'database key' (schema R_3) is added explicitly in order to guarantee losslessness. The schema tableau consequently gets the form shown in Figure 12.9(a) (compare this with the one shown in Figure 12.6); the result of applying *LJP* to this tableau is shown in Figure 12.9(b).

The synthesis algorithm is similar to the decomposition method in that it is a *non-deterministic* design procedure. The version presented above is efficiently implementable with respect to time complexity; it can

C	$A\#$	A_B	B
a_1	b_{12}	a_3	b_{14}
b_{21}	a_2	a_3	a_4
a_1	a_2	b_{33}	b_{34}

(a)

C	$A\#$	A_B	B
a_1	b_{12}	a_3	b_{14}
b_{21}	a_2	a_3	a_4
a_1	a_2	a_3	a_4

(b)

Figure 12.9 Schema tableau for the banking example after synthesis.

be shown that it takes time quadratic in the length of the machine-internal representation of its input. However, it should be noted that for guaranteeing this polynomial complexity, it is crucial that it was not required in Definition 12.6 (1) that $F_i^+ = F^+|_{X_i}$ holds for all components of a decomposition. If this stricter condition is imposed on the notion of decomposition, then $\pi_{X_i}(G^+)$ has to be determined during the generation of R_i within the **for** loop of *SYNTHESIS*, which in general takes exponential time. The algorithm can be further improved with respect to the goal to find a decomposition with as few components as possible. If G contains FDs f and g whose left-hand sides are equivalent in the sense of Definition 9.10, that is, $L_f \rightarrow L_g \in F^+$ and $L_g \rightarrow L_f \in F^+$, the components 'induced' by f and g can be combined into one. Since this may, however, result in a loss of the 3NF property for the new schema (because transitive dependencies may now occur), further modifications of the algorithm become necessary.

12.4 Multivalued dependencies

In this section, another type of (intrarelational) dependencies will briefly be studied. To introduce the new type, consider the relation r shown in Figure 12.10. As is easily verified, r does not satisfy any FDs besides the trivial ones; thus, the schema of r is in BCNF. On the other hand, there exists the following dependency between data values: each employee determines a *set* of children as well as a *set* of (working) areas; r also contains certain redundancies. This observation is formalized as follows.

Employee	*Child*	*Area*
Hilbert	Hilda	Mathematics
Hilbert	Hilda	Physics
Pythagoras	Peter	Mathematics
Pythagoras	Paul	Mathematics
Pythagoras	Peter	Philosophy
Pythagoras	Paul	Philosophy
Turing	Peter	Computer Science

Figure 12.10 A relation satisfying a multivalued dependency.

Definition 12.9

Let V be a set of attributes, $X, Y \subseteq V$. A **multivalued dependency** (MVD) $X \rightarrow\rightarrow Y$ denotes the following semantic constraint. Let $r \in \text{Rel}(V)$:

$$(X \rightarrow\rightarrow Y)(r) := \begin{cases} 1 & \text{if } (\forall \mu, \nu \in r) \\ & (\mu[X] = \nu[X] \Longrightarrow (\exists \rho \in r)(\rho[X] = \\ & \mu[X] = \nu[X] \wedge \rho[Y] = \mu[Y] \wedge \\ & \rho[V - XY] = \nu[V - XY])) \\ 0 & \text{otherwise} \end{cases}$$

For symmetry reasons it follows immediately that if r satisfies the MVD $X \rightarrow\rightarrow Y$, there exists another tuple ρ' such that $\rho'[X] = \mu[X] = \nu[X] \wedge \rho'[Y] = \nu[Y] \wedge \rho'[V - XY] = \mu[V - XY]$. Intuitively, an MVD $X \rightarrow\rightarrow Y$ therefore says that every X value (in a valid relation) determines a set of Y values, but there exists no relationship between these Y values and the values the tuples in question have on the (remaining) attributes from $V - XY$. In other words, the attributes in Y are 'independent' of those in $V - XY =: Z$; consequently, the more suggestive notation $X \rightarrow\rightarrow Y|Z$ is frequently used.

In the example given above, the following MVDs are satisfied:

Employee $\rightarrow\rightarrow$ *Child*
Employee $\rightarrow\rightarrow$ *Area*

Intuitively, every employee has a set of (zero or more) children and works in one or more areas; obviously, there is no direct connection between these two sets (there is only the indirect connection via an employee who is the father of a child and works in a certain area).

The validity of an MVD can alternatively be characterized as follows.

Theorem 12.11

Let $X, Y \subseteq V, Z := V - Y$. Then

$$(\forall\, r \in \mathrm{Rel}(V))\ ((X \rightarrow\rightarrow Y)(r) = 1 \Longleftrightarrow r = \pi_{XY}(r) \bowtie \pi_{XZ}(r))$$

Proof. '$\Longrightarrow$': Suppose r satisfies $X \rightarrow\rightarrow Y$. By Theorem 8.3 (1), it suffices to show that

$$r \supseteq \pi_{XY}(r) \bowtie \pi_{XW}(r)$$

where $W := V - XY$ ($XZ = XW$ implies $\pi_{XZ}(r) = \pi_{XW}(r)$). Hence let $\mu \in \pi_{XY}(r) \bowtie \pi_{XW}(r)$. Then there exists a tuple $\mu_1 \in \pi_{XY}(r)$ and a tuple $\mu_2 \in \pi_{XW}(r)$ such that

$$\mu[XY] = \mu_1 \qquad \mu[XW] = \mu_2$$

It follows that $\mu[X] = \mu_1[X] = \mu_2[X], \mu[Y] = \mu_1[Y]$ and $\mu[W] = \mu_2[W]$. Then there also exist tuples ν_1 and ν_2 in r such that

$$\mu_1 = \nu_1[XY] \qquad \mu_2 = \nu_2[XW]$$

and hence

$$\mu[X] = \nu_1[X] = \nu_2[X] \qquad \mu[Y] = \nu_1[Y] \qquad \mu[W] = \nu_2[W]$$

The validity of $X \rightarrow\rightarrow Y$ in r now implies $\mu \in r$ by Definition 12.9.

'$\Longleftarrow$': Let $\mu, \nu \in r$ such that $\mu[X] = \nu[X]$. Then there exists some $\mu_1 \in \pi_{XY}(r)$ such that $\mu_1 = \mu[XY]$, as well as some $\mu_2 \in \pi_{XW}(r)$ such that $\mu_2 = \nu[XW]$. Since $r = \pi_{XY}(r) \bowtie \pi_{XW}(r)$, there now exists a tuple $\rho \in r$ such that $\rho[XY] = \mu[XY], \rho[XW] = \nu[XW]$. Thus it follows that $\rho[X] = \mu[X] = \nu[X], \rho[Y] = \mu[Y], \rho[W] = \nu[W]$, which implies that $X \rightarrow\rightarrow Y$ is valid in r. □

This theorem motivates the question for a decomposition method for universal relation schemas based on MVDs that guarantees losslessness of the components. An answer to this question, which is closely related to the question for 'higher' normal forms than BCNF, will be sketched in the remainder of this section.

First note that for MVDs a notion of implication and one of derivation can be defined in a similar way as was done for FDs earlier (that is, $M \models m$ if every relation over the given set of attributes satisfies m if it satisfies every MVD in M); both notions can again be proved to be equivalent. In particular, it can be shown that the following system of axioms for MVDs is sound and complete. Let X, Y, Z, and W be subsets of a given set V:

(A0) $X \rightarrow\rightarrow Y \Longrightarrow X \rightarrow\rightarrow V - Y$ ('complementation')
(A1) $Y \subseteq X \Longrightarrow X \rightarrow\rightarrow Y$ ('reflexivity')

(A2) $Z \subseteq W \wedge X \rightarrow\rightarrow Y \Longrightarrow XW \rightarrow\rightarrow YZ$ ('augmentation')
(A3) $X \rightarrow\rightarrow Y \wedge Y \rightarrow\rightarrow Z \Longrightarrow X \rightarrow\rightarrow Z - Y$

For example, the correctness of (A0) is shown here; the rest is left to the reader (see Exercise 14 on p. 262).

Theorem 12.12

Axiom (A0) is correct.

Proof. Let $X, Y \subseteq V$ and $Z := V - Y$. By Theorem 12.11, the following holds for every relation $r \in \text{Rel}(V)$:

$$(X \rightarrow\rightarrow Y)(r) = 1 \Longleftrightarrow r = \pi_{XY}(r) \bowtie \pi_{XZ}(r)$$

This implies:

$$\begin{aligned} &(X \rightarrow\rightarrow Y)(r) = 1 \\ &\Longleftrightarrow r = \pi_{XZ}(r) \bowtie \pi_{XY}(r) \\ &\Longleftrightarrow r = \pi_{XZ}(r) \bowtie \pi_{X\cup(V-Z)}(r) \\ &\Longleftrightarrow (X \rightarrow\rightarrow Z)(r) = 1 \ \square \end{aligned}$$

Finally, implication and derivation can be considered for 'mixed' sets of dependencies, consisting of FDs *and* MVDs, and the interactions between these two types can be investigated. Derivation rules for this context are the following, for example:

(FM1) $X \rightarrow Y \Longrightarrow X \rightarrow\rightarrow Y$
(FM2) $X \rightarrow\rightarrow Y \wedge S \rightarrow T \wedge S \cap Y = \emptyset \Longrightarrow X \rightarrow Y \cap T$

Thus, every FD can in particular be considered as an MVD; an MVD together with an FD eventually implies a new FD.

With respect to database design based on MVDs (and FDs), the following normal form, which is a direct generalization of BCNF, is relevant.

Definition 12.10

Let $R = (U, F \cup M)$. R is in **fourth normal form** (4NF), if for every MVD of the from $X \rightarrow\rightarrow Y$ implied by $F \cup M$, where $Y \not\subseteq X$ and $XY \subset U$, the FD $X \rightarrow U$ is also implied by $F \cup M$.

In other words, a relation schema is in 4NF if the left-hand side of every non-trivial MVD (that is derivable) is a superkey for the given set of attributes. It can be shown that 4NF implies BCNF; the converse does not hold in general.

For example, let $R = (ECA, \{E \rightarrow\rightarrow C, E \rightarrow\rightarrow A\})$ be the schema for the relation given above. R is not in 4NF, since $E \rightarrow CA$ is not a valid FD. Using the MVD $E \rightarrow\rightarrow C$, R can be decomposed into the two relation schemas

$$R_1 = (EC, \{E \rightarrow\rightarrow C\})$$
$$R_2 = (EA, \{E \rightarrow\rightarrow A\})$$

in which both MVDs now have become trivial (they are satisfied by *every* relation over the respective schema) since they 'cover' the entire set of attributes of their schema. Thus, R_1 and R_2 are in 4NF, and, by Theorem 12.11, this decomposition is also lossless.

Chapter 13
Notes on Data Structures

This chapter rounds off the discussion of database design with a brief description of data structures that are used for storing data in secondary memory. The choice of such structures is — from the user's point of view — an aspect of the physical design stage; it has consequences, for instance, for the efficiency of query processing. From the point of view of the system developer, the question of which data structures should be provided by a particular system is important. A brief, general introduction to this topic will be given, and important representatives of classes of data structures will be presented primarily by way of examples.

13.1 Sequential files and indexes

In this chapter it is assumed that the data belonging to a database will be physically stored in *files* which cannot be kept in main memory, because of their size and number; instead, data and the files which contain the data are stored in secondary memory like a magnetic disk. More concretely, for a network database one can think of a file as a set of *records*; in particular, for every (logical) record type there exists a particular file, and individual elements of this file (that is, records of this type) consist of *fields* for storing the corresponding attribute values. In the case of a relational database, one can correspondingly think of each relation as a file whose records represent the tuples of this relation.

The operations a user performs on a database are transformed by the DBMS into operations on physical files; in particular, queries to a database result in search or selection operations, and updates yield insertions, deletions or modifications of records. The only aspect the user is interested in is that the operations are executed quickly; consequently, it is of central importance for the DBMS that all existing files are organized in such a way that the operations mentioned can be performed *efficiently*.

As was mentioned already, it is assumed here that the files are physically stored on magnetic disks, which in particular are characterized by *random access*. Typically, such a disk is subdivided into into *blocks* (or pages) of fixed size which are individually addressable and which form the 'unit' of any data transfer taking place between secondary and primary memory. As a consequence, one file is often spread over several blocks, and each block contains one or more records from the file.

As a concrete example, the relation shown in Figure 13.1 will be considered. Assuming that each tuple in this relation is stored as a record in a file, the resulting file contains $n = 8$ records.

The most basic storage structure for a file is the **sequential** organ-

S#	*Sname*	*City*	*Dist*
L1	Smith	London	20
L2	Jones	Paris	10
L3	Blake	Paris	30
L4	Clark	London	20
L5	Adams	Athens	30
L6	Hart	Chicago	80
L7	Parker	New York	70
L8	James	Athens	25

Figure 13.1 A sample relation.

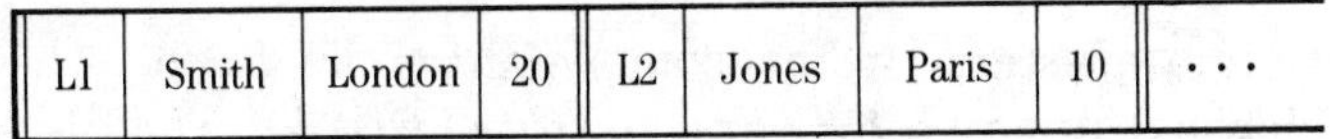

Figure 13.2 A sequential file.

ization, in which all records of a file are stored in a physically connected manner, and which requires that a processing takes places according to this ordering ('one after the other'). Figure 13.2 shows a corresponding organization under the assumption that secondary memory can in principle be represented as an (endless) 'tape' (of memory cells).

If $b > 1$ records can be stored in one block (and the address of a block is available, say, in a pointer), the situation shown in Figure 13.3 may result. While a file organized as shown in Figure 13.2 can be read sequentially only, it is possible in general (that is, in case $b > 1$) to jump 'block-wise'. In both cases, the operations mentioned above can be realized as follows.

In order to *search* for a particular tuple (in particular during a selection), the entire file has to be scanned sequentially, that is, in approximately n/b accesses to secondary memory the file has to be loaded into main memory so that the desired tuple can be identified. An *insertion* of a new tuple can always be performed at the end of the file; if the last block belonging to the file does not contain any more free space, the file has to be extended by one (or more) blocks. The *deletion* of a tuple creates free space within the file; in order to avoid large gaps within blocks, a reorganization of the file (called *garbage collection*) might be required as a result. The *modification* of a tuple can in principle be performed in place (provided the updated tuple remains within its previous space bounds).

The amount of work required for searching can be reduced if a file is stored in *sorted* order, typically according to the values of a key for

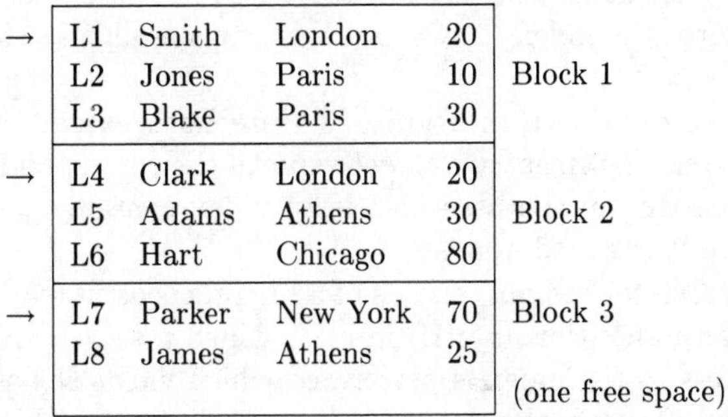

→	L1	Smith	London	20	
	L2	Jones	Paris	10	Block 1
	L3	Blake	Paris	30	
→	L4	Clark	London	20	
	L5	Adams	Athens	30	Block 2
	L6	Hart	Chicago	80	
→	L7	Parker	New York	70	Block 3
	L8	James	Athens	25	
					(one free space)

Figure 13.3 A sequential file with $b = 3$.

the relation in question. In the example above, let *S#* be a key for the relation having format { *S#, Sname, City, Dist* }. The file shown in Figure 13.3 is sorted according to ascending values for this attribute. As a consequence, a tuple with a given *S#* value can be found by **binary search** (if it exists). This means that the 'middle' block of the file is read first; if this block does not contain the desired record, the search continues within the middle block of the remaining 'upper' or 'lower' half of the file depending on whether the target value is 'smaller' or 'larger' than the values occurring in the last block read. The process is iterated as long as necessary; the order of magnitude of the resulting number of accesses is proportional to $\log_2(n/b)$.

For the insertion of new records into a sorted file, at least two strategies are available. A new tuple can be stored in an arbitrary free place (for example, at the end of the file); subsequently, the file has to be sorted again. Alternatively, the position of the new record within the sorted order can be determined first; after this, all subsequent records are relocated accordingly (eventually crossing block boundaries), so that a place for the new record becomes available. Updates can still be executed as described above. For deletions it is relevant whether or not gaps (free places) are allowed within the sorted order.

The access to individual records of a given file and in particular the search for certain records can be made even more efficient if for the values of distinct fields an additional 'dictionary' is maintained, which is called an **index**. An index for a file is comparable to the index of a book which tells, in alphabetical order, for every keyword appearing in the text the page number(s) on which this keyword occurs. An index is an additional file, typically containing the values of some attribute occurring in the database file in question together with the address of the corresponding record.

In our running example, assume that the tuples shown in Figure 13.1 are sequentially numbered (from 1 to 8, top-down). Then Figure 13.4(a) shows an index for attribute *Sname*. Figure 13.4(b) shows an index for *City*; for cases where several tuples in the base relation share the same *City* value, the index — without loss of generality — shows the first of these.

The indexes shown in Figure 13.4 are both examples of a **dense** index which contains an entry for *each* value of the corresponding attribute currently occurring in the base file. If an index contains entries only for some of them, it is called **sparse**.

The search for certain records of a file proceeds in two phases in the presence of an index (for an attribute for which a search value is given). First, an access to the index is performed which yields the address of the desired record(s); next, this record is located directly within the file and read. If the index is kept in sorted order, binary search can be employed during the first phase. If the 'indexed' attribute does not have the key

Sname	'Address'
Adams	5
Blake	3
Clark	4
Hart	6
James	8
Jones	2
Parker	7
Smith	1

(a)

City	'Address'
Athens	5
Chicago	6
London	1
New York	7
Paris	2

(b)

Figure 13.4 Informal example of an index.

property with respect to the file in question (see Figure 13.4(b)), a search through the index yields the address of the first tuple having the desired value only; the file has then to be scanned sequentially from this address on. The same applies in the case of a sparse index. As a consequence, the use of a dense index (in particular for key attributes) generally allows for a more efficient processing than the use of a sparse one. On the other hand, storing a sparse index obviously requires less space.

For example, let a file contain $n = 100,000$ records, and let there exist a dense index for some key attribute. Clearly, this index also contains 100,000 records. Furthermore, let a block contain 10 records of the file or 100 records of the index (which in general are 'smaller' than data records). For storing the index, 1000 blocks are then needed in addition to the 10,000 blocks required for the file. However, if a sparse index for the same key attribute contains one record per block only, this index contains 10,000 entries or 100 blocks only. A binary search in the dense (sparse) index consequently requires approximately 11 (7) accesses, respectively.

Such considerations, which reveal a certain 'trade-off' between the time and space requirements (for accessing a file or for storing an index, respectively), are also relevant for the execution of update operations. Independent of which kind of index is used, the index in principle has to be updated every time a tuple is inserted into or deleted from the underlying file. The insertion of a new record into a dense index is carried out in the same way as the insertion of a record into a sorted file, while a sparse index does not necessarily require an insertion at all. Corresponding remarks apply to deletions of records from a file. Finally, the insertion or deletion into or from a sorted file can also result in a change of index entries.

If an index exists for some file which is stored in sorted order (say, according to increasing values of the [primary] key), and if this index provides the addresses of the tuples corresponding to key values, this form

City	'Address(es)'
Athens	5,8
Chicago	6
London	1,4
New York	7
Paris	2,3

Figure 13.5 Example of an inverted file.

of organization is called an **index sequential** file. If in particular the index is a sparse one which is 'block oriented', any file access involves a search through the index followed by an (eventually sequential) access to the records proper; this method is generally know as the **indexed-sequential access method** (ISAM, see also Chapter 15).

An index for the primary key of a file is often called a **primary index**; analogously, an index for a secondary key or an arbitrary other attribute (or combination of attributes) is called a **secondary index**. A special case of a secondary index is the **inverted file** or **inverted list**. In this case, for each distinct value of the underlying (non-key) attribute the address of *every* record having this value (not just one) is recorded. Figure 13.5 shows a completion of the index from Figure 13.4(b) for the *City* attribute so that an inverted list results.

If an index contains sufficiently few blocks, it may even be possible to keep it in main memory. As a result, the time required for searching within the indexed file will in general drop considerably. If the index has to be transferred to secondary memory, such a search requires, as was mentioned above, that index blocks are first brought into main memory. In order to shorten this (additional) transfer time, it might be useful to treat the index itself like an ordinary file by providing it with an(other) index, which, for example, contains an entry for each individual block of the first index. Figure 13.6 illustrates the idea behind this organization for sparse, block-oriented indexes. More generally, a hierarchical or **multi-stage** index (for some fixed attribute of a file) is a *sequence* of indexes, whose first element indexes the attribute directly, and in which every other element indexes the preceding index.

13.2 Tree structures

An index-sequential file organization has the disadvantage that the performance of query and update operations will deteriorate as the file grows. The only way to cope with this situation is to reorganize the file from

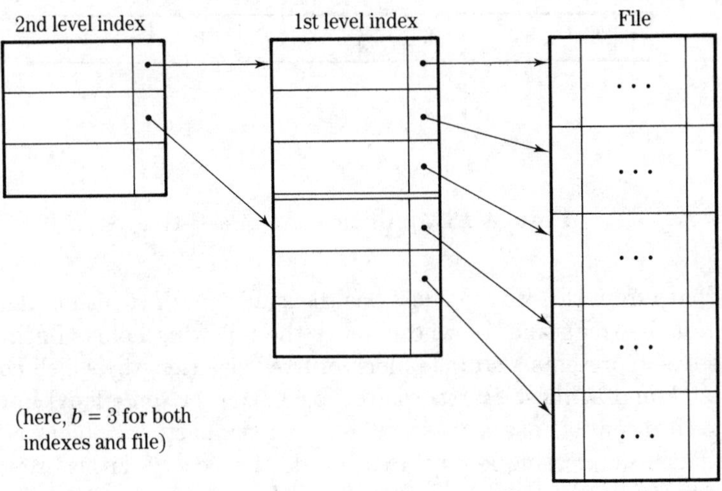

Figure 13.6 Hierarchical organization of indexes.

time to time, for example by doing garbage collection after a substantial number of deletions; however, a reorganization itself can be expensive, in particular if the file has a large number of records. In this section, data structures will be presented which allow for an efficient execution primarily of search operations; in addition, a reorganization especially following update operations will in general require 'local' modifications only, which in exceptional cases affect the entire structure, and which are henceforth also efficiently executable.

A multi-stage index (see Figure 13.6) basically has the form of a **tree**, whose leaves contain the data records of the (indexed) file, and whose other vertices contain address references (like pointers), for example, to certain blocks on a disk. This form of organization will now be generalized, assuming that the index itself is so large that it cannot be kept in main memory. A multi-stage index stored in secondary memory often contains some redundancy, since at least values for the (key) attribute according to which the entire index is formed are repeated at various levels of the hierarchy. Such redundancies can be avoided, for instance, if *complete* records of the file to be indexed are allowed to occur in the index itself (that is, on higher levels than just the bottom one). Besides such data records, 'nodes' in the index hierarchy can contain references to other records, which carry a smaller or larger value of the underlying key.

This idea forms the basis of the **B-tree** (a shorthand for 'balanced tree' or 'Bayer-tree' after its author). A B-tree is a directed tree in which

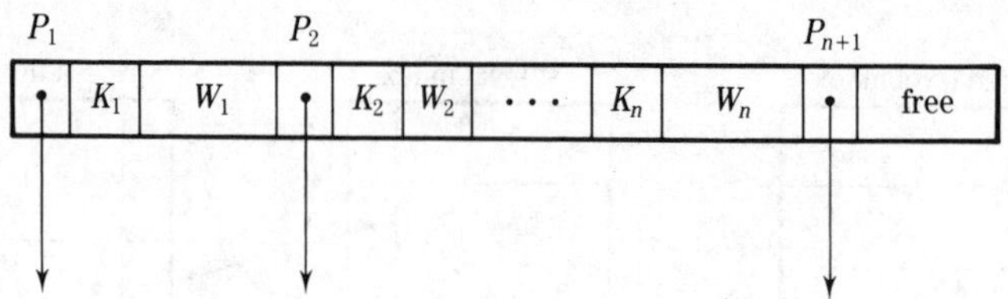

Figure 13.7 Inner node of a B-tree.

every path from the root to a leaf has the same length (which is called the *height* of the tree), and for whose nodes the following holds. Each vertex of the tree represents a storage block of fixed size (length) which contains at least k and at most $2k$ records (of fixed size) for some fixed integer k; each record consists of a key as well as a non-key part; each block is sorted according to increasing key values. In addition, every 'father' represents an index for all of its 'sons'; the root has either no son or at least two sons, and each 'inner' vertex (which is neither root nor leaf) has the maximally possible number of sons, that is, it has $n + 1$ sons if n key values are present.

Figure 13.7 shows the structure of a B-tree node which is neither leaf nor root. In this figure, $K_1, \ldots, K_n$ represent the values for the key attribute for which this tree is generated as an index, that are stored in this node; $W_1, \ldots, W_n$ stand for the remaining values of a record of the file in question. Thus, an individual record has the form (K_i, W_i), $i \in \{1, \ldots, n\}$.

As a first example of a B-tree, Figure 13.8 shows such a tree with parameter $k = 1$. As a simplification it is here assumed that each record exclusively consists of a key value; each block provides space for at most two records (as well as three pointers). Inner nodes with $k = 1$ record have two, nodes with $2k = 2$ records have three sucessors.

An important feature of this structure is that a B-tree is always **balanced**; every path starting at the root and ending in a leaf has the same constant length. On the other hand, a B-tree is a **sorted key tree**

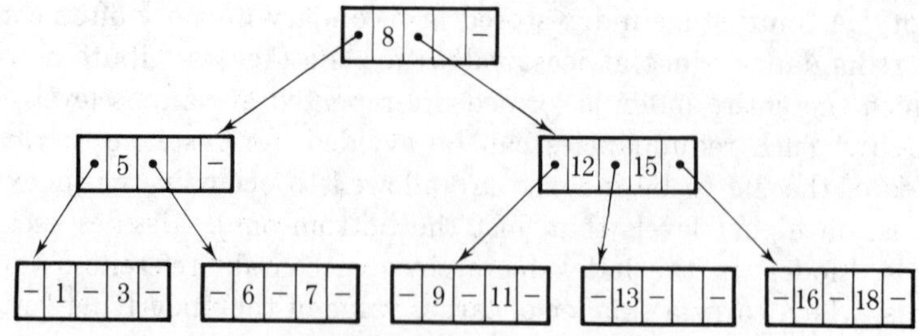

Figure 13.8 B-tree of height 2 for $k = 1$.

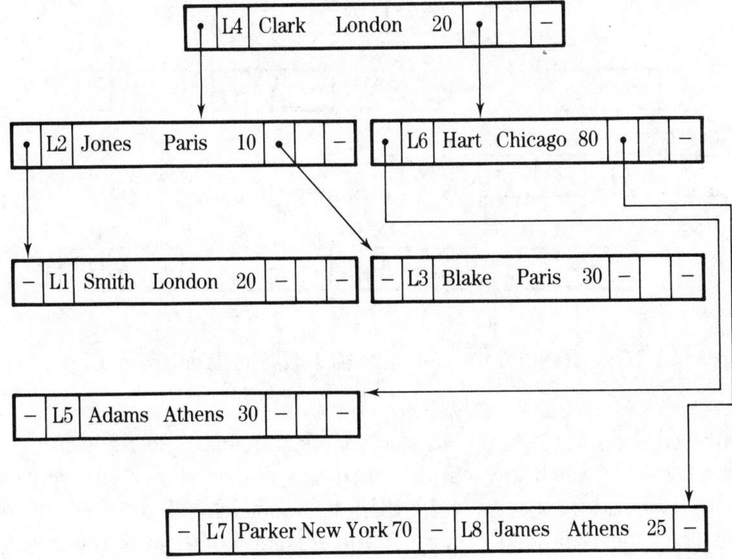

Figure 13.9 B-tree for the relation from Figure 13.1.

in which for every triple of the form (P_i, K_i, P_{i+1}) (see Figure 13.7) of a non-leaf node the following holds: all key values contained in the node referenced by P_i are smaller than K_i, while all those from P_{i+1} are larger than K_i.

As a second example, Figure 13.9 shows a B-tree for the sample relation from Figure 13.1, where it is again assumed that $S\#$ is the key.

In order to *search* for a record whose key value is given in a B-tree, the following method can be applied. First, the root is accessed, and a path from there in the direction of the leaves is scanned. Each current node (which is the root in the first step) is tested to determine whether the given key value is present. If this is the case, the search ends and the record found is returned. Otherwise, if $K_1, \ldots, K_n$ are the key values of the current node, and K is the value searched for, then

(1) if $K_i < K < K_{i+1}$ holds for some i, $1 \leq i < n$, the search is continued in the node referenced by P_{i+1},

(2) if $K < K_1$ $[K_n < K]$, the search continues in the node referenced by P_1 $[P_{n+1}]$, respectively.

It can be shown that for searching for a record in a B-tree (in the average as well as in the worst case) approximately $\log_2 n$ nodes have to be accessed if the underlying file contains n records in total.

The *insertion* of a new record into a given B-tree is more complicated, since the resulting tree now has to be balanced again (which was

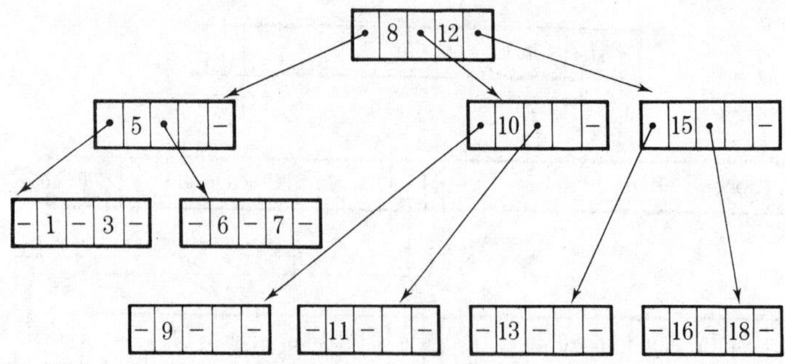

Figure 13.10 Result of inserting 10 into the tree from Figure 13.8.

not required for multi-stage indexes); thus, for example, it is impossible to insert a record with key value 2 into the B-tree shown in Figure 13.8 simply by appending a new leaf to the leftmost leaf of the tree. In order to keep the tree balanced and to maintain the conditions regarding the degree of filling as well as the structure of a node, it is necessary to proceed in a different way. Given a record to be inserted with the (new) key value K, first a 'search for K' is performed; since — as was assumed — no record having this key value already exists in the given tree, this search ends in the leaf in which the record would be stored if it existed. If this leaf contains less than $2k$ elements, the new record is inserted into this leaf (in the 'correct' position according to the ordering). (As an example, the reader may consider the insertion of value 14 into the B-tree from Figure 13.8.) However, if the leaf contains the maximal number of $2k$ records already, $2k+1$ records now occur at this place; the next step is to *decompose* this leaf into three distinct parts. The first part is assigned the records with the k smallest key values and stored in the place of the 'old' leaf. The second part contains the records with the k largest key values and is stored in a new leaf. The third part consists of only that record with the middle one of the $2k+1$ key values and is stored in the father node of the old leaf; its left (right) pointer is set to point to the leaf corresponding to the first (second) part of this decomposition, respectively. These steps have to be iterated if the father node contains the maximal number of records allowed already, so that in the worst case a new root for the tree will be created; as a result, the height of the tree then grows by 1.

As an example, consider the insertion of key value 10 into the B-tree shown in Figure 13.8; the result is shown in Figure 13.10. In a first step the leaf containing key values 9 and 11 is decomposed. The new value 10 is assigned to the father node, which now is over-full. Thus, in a second step this father node is decomposed, and its middle value of 12 is stored in the root.

During the *deletion* of a record from a B-tree, again the balancing

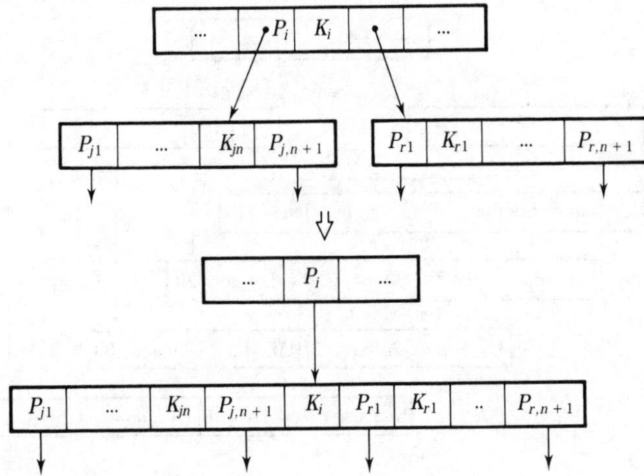

Figure 13.11 Joining nodes after a deletion in a B-tree.

condition has to be maintained, and no node may become 'under-full'. In detail, a deletion proceeds as follows. As during an insertion, the first step consists of a search for the record containing the value that is to be deleted (which is now successful). If the node found during this search is a leaf, the record in question is deleted. If, as a result, this leaf now contains less than k elements, a local reorganization is performed as follows. If there exists, within the same subtree, a right-hand brother of this leaf with more than k elements, the leaf in question can be refilled by a rotation of records, a step that involves the father as well. (For example, if 13 is deleted from the tree shown in Figure 13.10, the then empty leaf gets the value 15 via such a rotation, while 15 in the father node is replaced by 16 from the right-hand brother.) Clearly, the left-hand brother can be considered in the same way if necessary.

Alternatively, the leaf in question can also be joined with one of its brothers to form a new leaf; again, this brother must have the same father and needs to be referenced by an adjacent pointer within the father node; it also needs to have exactly k elements. Note that, although one key now gets transferred from the father node to the new leaf, the resulting node still has at most $2k$ elements. Figure 13.11 shows what happens during a join of two leaves. If, as a result, the father 'underflows', that is, contains less than k elements, this reorganization has to be repeated on the next higher level.

If the record to be deleted is currently not stored in a leaf, this record is replaced by a record from a leaf. According to the requirement that the entire tree is a sorted key tree, it is, for instance, possible to choose the record in this case which has the largest key value in the rightmost leaf of the left-hand subtree. For example, if key value 8 is deleted from

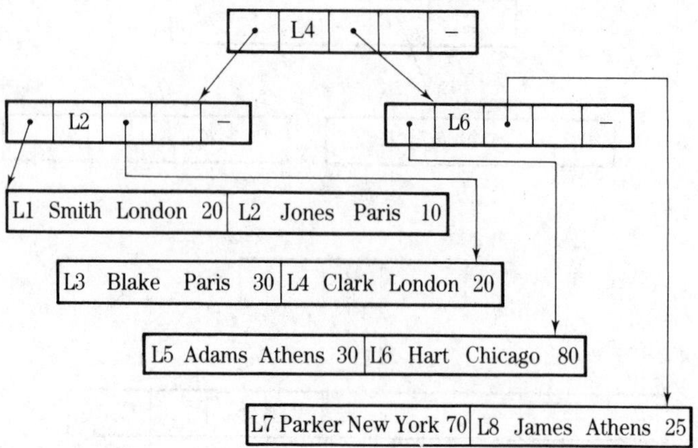

Figure 13.12 B*-tree for the relation from Figure 13.1.

the tree shown in Figure 13.10, its place is filled by value 7, which was previously stored in a leaf. If a leaf contains less than k elements after such a deletion, the reorganization has to be repeated as described above.

These update operations on B-trees can be implemented efficiently (as was the case for searching), since approximately $\log_2 n$ blocks, that is, nodes of the tree, have to be accessed or modified.

If the individual records stored in a given file are 'long', it may be useful to store key values together with a pointer to the corresponding record in the node of a B-tree only. 'Mixed forms' are also possible, in which records are stored partially within tree nodes and partially outside the tree. Another variant is to store all records of the file — independent of their lengths — in leaves, and to organize the remaining nodes of the tree as an index for these (with 'short' records), which can eventually be kept in main memory. This idea underlies **B*-trees**, which are B-trees that require a certain degree of filling for leaf nodes only. Figure 13.12 shows a B*-tree for the relation from Figure 13.1, whose B-tree organization was shown in Figure 13.9. The operations of searching, insertion and deletion are realized in a way similar to B-trees, with the exception that deletions are less expensive.

For the tree structures presented so far, it has always been assumed that an index is primarily created for a particular key of some file, and that this key consists of one attribute only. This assumption, which is frequently satisfied in real-world applications, in general captures only those situations in which a key-oriented processing is performed. On the other hand, a B-tree like the one shown in Figure 13.9 is not suited for efficiently answering a query like 'show the name of every supplier from London or Paris', since the selection condition given in this query is 'orthogonal' to the key according to which the tree is sorted. Choosing the appropriate data structures for a database is in reality frequently dependent on the kind of queries which can be expected and is therefore a design problem. Data structures like the ones described so far in this section, which support *exactly one* attribute with respect to selection, insertion and deletion, are often classified as **one-dimensional** data structures. As the example just mentioned indicates, the selection condition of a query to a database often specifies values for more than one attribute; the answer should contain all records having these 'properties'. Queries of this kind are called **partial-match queries**; consequently, data structures supporting them are termed **multidimensional**. This notion is based on the geometrical interpretation that the attributes of a given 'record format' span a *space* in which individual records represent *points.* Thus, a partial-match query specifies a *hyper-rectangle* within this space; an answer to it contains all points that lie in this rectangle. Even more general are **partial-range queries**, which ask for those records in a file whose values for certain attributes fall into some specified interval. In terms of the geometrical model range queries specify *unions* of hyper-rectangles.

One example of a multidimensional data structure which in particular supports partial-match queries in an efficient manner is the **k-d-tree**. This type of tree generalizes (one-dimensional) *binary* search trees, in which the nodes of a tree are sorted according to exactly one attribute ($k = 1$), and in which for each node the number of its successors is bounded above by 2. Opposed to this, it will now be assumed that each record of a given file has $k \geq 1$ 'key' fields. Every node in a k-d-tree contains exactly one such record as well as space for two pointers (to the eventually existing left/right-hand son, respectively). Without loss of generality, let $A_1, \ldots, A_k$ be the key attributes of a given file, where this sequence is considered as fixed. On the first (root) level of a k-d-tree, it is now branched left or right depending on the value given for A_1; in particular, during the insertion of a new record it is branched left (right) if the A_1 value of the record to be inserted is smaller (larger) than the A_1 value of the current (root) record, respectively. Additional branching on subsequent levels is performed in the same way, but with A_1 replaced by A_2 at level 2, by A_3 at level 3, and so on; at level $k+1$ branching is again based on A_1.

Figure 13.13 shows a sample 3-d-tree for storing the relation from Figure 13.1. At the highest level, a selection is based on $A_1 = S\#$; at the second (third) level, it is based on $A_2 = \mathit{Sname}$ ($A_3 = \mathit{City}$), respectively.

If at least for some of the attributes $A_1, \ldots, A_k$, on which a corresponding k-d-tree is based, values are given in a partial-match query, the set of all records having these values in the appropriate places can be determined as follows. A path starting at the root is scanned; each node

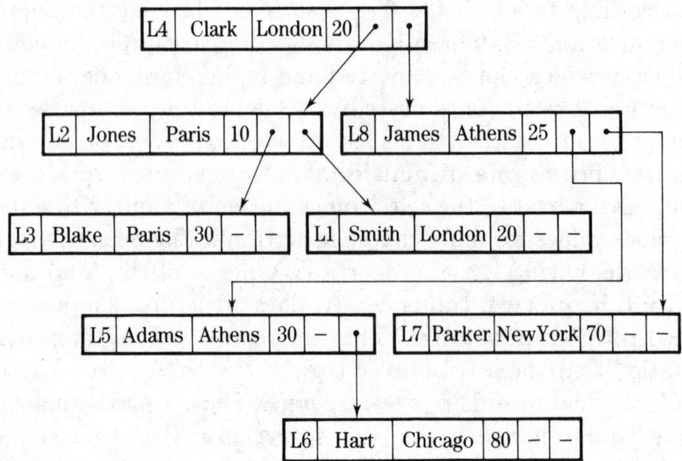

Figure 13.13 3-d-tree for the relation from Figure 13.1.

reached, at which branching is based, say, on A_j, is checked to determine whether a value for A_j was specified in the query. If so, it is branched to a son of this node according to this value; otherwise the search continues in both sons. It can be shown that for n records approximately $t \cdot n^{1-t/k}$ steps are sufficient for answering a partial-match query, if t out of k key values are specified. (For example, if $n = 10^6$, $t = 4$ and $k = 6$, then approximately 400 records have to be checked in order to answer such a query.)

Update operations on k-d-trees again require (local) reorganizations in general (like a splitting of nodes during an insertion). Further details on this type of tree as well as on additional multidimensional data structures can be found in the Bibliographic Notes.

13.3 Hash organization

One drawback of the organization schemes for indexes presented so far is that every access requires the scanning of a certain path, that is, a traversal of the index. The **hash technique** discussed in this chapter avoids this; instead, the address of a record is now *computed* directly from given values for a key.

The underlying situation is the following. Let a logical record type or a relation format be given, consisting of attributes; in addition, let a key be known which without loss of generality consists of exactly one attribute that may assume numerical values, that is, let key A have the domain, say, $\text{dom}(A) = \{1, \ldots, 10^5\}$. Then there potentially exist 10^5 distinct records, which in general will not be stored simultaneously in the database, however. (In the terminology used in Section 8.2, in the case of a relation r_i only the active domain of A, $\text{adom}(A, r_i)$, is stored in memory at any moment, and in general $|\text{adom}(A, r_i)| << |\text{dom}(A)|$ holds.) Therefore, it is not necessary (and in reality it is seldom possible) to reserve storage space for the *entire* set of records possible. Instead, there exists a limited number of storage 'cells' only, which are assumed to be capable of storing one record each, and which are 'described' by an address. If S denotes the set of all available memory addresses, the task is to associate some cell with address $s \in S$ with every record identified by key value $a \in \text{dom}(A)$. If possible, $|S|$ should be chosen such that at least for some *expected* number of records enough space is available; however, $|S| << |\text{dom}(A)|$ will hold in general.

Next, a **hash function** is a mapping from $\text{dom}(A)$ to S:

$$h : \text{dom}(A) \rightarrow S$$

Owing to the above assumption on the cardinalities of $\text{dom}(A)$ and S, it is impossible in general to choose h as an injective function, that is, $h(a) = h(b)$ does not necessarily imply $a = b$.

The storing of records using a hash function is performed by applying this function to the key value of a given record and storing this record under the resulting address. As a first example of a hash function, the **division-remainder method** is considered. For $|S| = n$ and $a \in \text{dom}(A)$, $h(a)$ is defined as the (integer) remainder of dividing a by n:

$$h(a) := a \bmod n$$

For example, if $n = 10^3$ the following holds:

$$\begin{aligned} &\text{h}(5) &&= 5 \\ &\text{h}(233) &&= 233 \\ &\text{h}(27685) &&= 685 \\ &\text{h}(43005) &&= 5 \end{aligned}$$

hence, the records with key values $A = 5$ and $A = 43005$ are assigned the same address.

A situation like this is called a **collision**; it can be avoided only by choosing a hash function that is injective with respect to the set of keys to be maintained. Since this is impossible in general, the use of hash functions requires certain provisions for dealing with collisions. A method common in practical applications consists of associating a separate **overflow area** with each distinct address, which can be reached from such an address via a pointer, and which is organized as a simply linked list. This principle is illustrated in Figure 13.14. Clearly, additional space is needed; also, searching for a particular record can become inefficient. The worst case occurs if *all* records to be stored are mapped to the *same* address

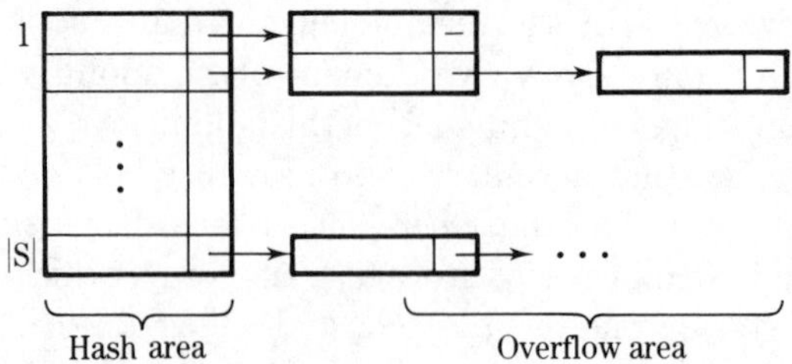

Figure 13.14 Hashing with separate overflow area per address.

and therefore have to be placed in the overflow area (besides the first record). Thus, a linear list results, which can only be searched sequentially. As a consequence, it seems appropriate to assure that a hash function distributes the records to be stored evenly over the available address space.

A variant of organizing overflows in a *separate* storage area outside the area which is subject to hashing is to reserve free space immediately following the largest address the hash function can compute, and to allocate this space in the order in which collisions occur. This method is illustrated in Figure 13.15. A number of alternative strategies for organizing an overflow area exist. In order to choose a particular one in a given application, the issues to be taken into consideration include the expense of reorganizations, which can become necessary, for example, if records for which overflow records exist already are deleted.

Another way of handling collisions is to use an **open hash** method. If a collision occurs, a second address is computed by applying a second hash function. If this alternative address is also in use already, a third address is computed via a third hash function, and so on. Clearly, any such method stops after at most $|S|$ steps (if all addresses are in use); it consists of providing a 'primary address' $h_o(a)$ for $a \in \text{dom}(A)$ *and* a sequence of $|S| - 1$ (pairwise distinct) alternative addresses $h_1(a), \ldots, h_{n-1}(a)$ with

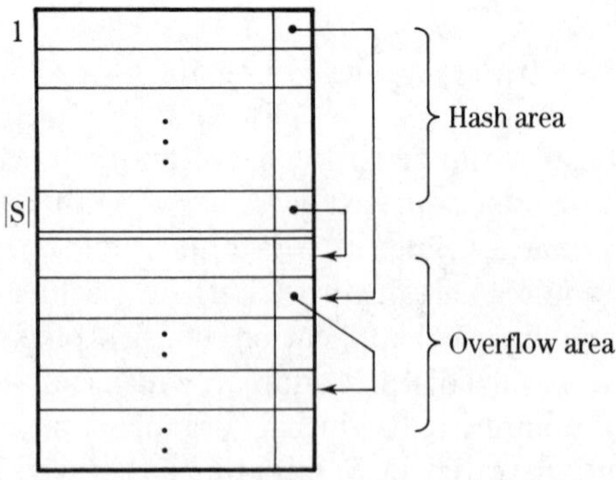

Figure 13.15 Hashing with separate but continuous overflow area.

$n = |S|$ (where $h_i(a)$ denotes the alternative address for h_{i-1}, $1 \leq i \leq n-1$).

When an open hash method is used, the computation of $h_o(a)$ itself is often called **hashing**, while the computation of alternative addresses is called **probing**. An example of such a method is the division-remainder method with **linear probing**, which is defined as follows:

$$h_i(a) := \begin{cases} a \bmod n & \text{if } i = 0 \\ (h_o(a) + i) \bmod n & \text{otherwise} \end{cases}$$

$$0 \leq i \leq n-1 \qquad |S| = n \qquad a \in \text{dom}(A)$$

With this method, consecutive addresses are checked for availability, so that actually not the entire hashing area is being used. As a consequence, collisions can occur frequently. A solution to this problem is to use **quadratic probing**, which computes alternative addresses as follows:

$$h_i(a) := (h_o(a) + i^2) \bmod n$$

Depending on the size of the hash area (which is *a priori* determined and fixed), this method also allows for frequent collisions, since the domain $\{1, \ldots, n\}$ for alternative addresses is eventually not fully used. However, simple modifications (see Exercise 24 on p. 261) of quadratic probing render a full use of the entire hash area possible.

The simplifying assumption made here that the individual cells of a hash area can carry exactly one record is often not valid in reality; instead, a 'cell' is typically a block of fixed size (which is often termed a 'bucket' in this context). Such a block can contain either the records themselves or corresponding pointers; a collision occurs only if all cells in a block are filled.

The operation implicitly favoured in this chapter was the *insertion* or the storing of new records. As has been pointed out during the discussion of tree structures, storing can, in a sense, be considered as an 'unsuccessful search'. Therefore, it is easy to see that a selection or search proceeds similarly in the presence of a hash function. An address is calculated for one (or several) given key value(s); if the record searched for is stored under this address the search terminates, otherwise it continues within the overflow area or under an alternative address. After deletions, a reorganization may become necessary, which typically includes the recalculation of addresses for many records. Precise cost estimates for the execution for these operations can be found in the references cited below.

The basic approach to searching as described above reveals that a hash organization is appropriate for files only if a major portion of the expected queries are partial-match queries (see Section 13.2). Since in queries of this type generally values for *several* attributes are given, in reality **multidimensional** hash functions are often required, for which the reader is also referred to the literature.

The hash functions discussed in this chapter are all **static** functions in the sense that the size n of the storage area available for hashing is *fixed.* If it turns out over time that n was chosen too small and hence must be enlarged, the address of each record already stored has to be recomputed (for example, for the division-remainder method the modulus n changes in this case). This drawback can be avoided by using a **dynamic** hash function; here the idea is that if a collision occurs, that is, some bucket overflows, a new hash function is chosen for this bucket, which is then employed for reorganizing the bucket as well as a 'local' overflow area. Once again, details can be found in the references.

Bibliographic Notes

Surveys of the design process of a database (partially including detailed descriptions of individual phases) are given by Ceri (1983), Elmasri and Navathe (1989), Kroenke (1983), Reiner (1984), Teorey and Fry (1982), Yao et al. (1982) and Yao (1985). Proposals for performing a requirements analysis are made by Dubois et al. (1986) and Kahn (1985), as well as by McFadden and Hoffer (1988). During a conceptual design, the integration of user views into a global schema is a central and difficult problem; the reader is referred to Casanova and Vidal (1983) or Batini and Lenzerini (1984). Biskup and Convent (1986) present a formal method for view integration; Convent (1986) indicates the limits of computer-aided integration methods. The special case of merging relationships during an integration of views is considered by Navathe et al. (1984). Teorey et al. (1986) present a comprehensive methodology for designing relational database schemas using an extension of the ER model; see also Yang et al. (1985). Schkolnick (1982) surveys techniques for physical database design; methods for prototyping a design are described by Barzilai and Barzilai (1985), Bitton et al. (1983), and Boral and DeWitt (1984).

Of increasing interest nowadays are computer-aided tools for database design; approaches in this direction are reported in Reiner (1984), Brägger et al. (1985), Chan and Lochovsky (1980), Cobb et al. (1984) and De Antonellis and Di Leva (1985a,b). A tool to support the physical design of an SQL/DS database is presented by Finkelstein et al. (1986).

The introduction to semantic modelling given in Chapter 11 closely follows Hull and King (1987); other surveys of this topic include Bic and Gilbert (1986), Brodie (1984), Hull (1987), King and McLeod (1985), Lochovsky (1985), Peckham and Maryanski (1988) and Urban and Delcambre (1986). An overview of recent research activities in the area of (structurally) object-oriented data models and DBMSs is provided by Dittrich and Dayal (1986); see also the Bibliographic Notes for Part VII. All different 'types' of data models discussed so far are also dealt with in the book by Tsichritzis and Lochovsky (1982). The limited modelling capabilities of record-oriented data models is also explained by Kent (1979).

The IFO model that was used for illustration purposes in Chapter 12 is from Abiteboul and Hull (1985, 1987); its basics are also discussed in the papers by Hull (1987) and Hull and King (1987). A graphics facility to manage IFO schemas is described by Bryce and Hull (1986). Other semantic models are the entity-relationship model, for which references were given in Part II, the *Event Model* by King and McLeod (1984, 1985), the *Functional Data Model* (FDM) by Shipman (1981), the *Semantic Data Model* (SDM) by Hammer and McLeod

(1981), the *Semantic Hierarchy Model* (SHM) by Smith und Smith (1977a,b) with the extension into SHM+ by Brodie and Ridjanovic (1984), the *Relational Model/Tasmania* (RM/T) by Codd (1979), and the *Taxis* model by Mylopoulos et al. (1980); RM/T is also described by Date (1983, 1986). Lyngbaek and Vianu (1987) show how to translate a semantic model into the relational model using the *IRIS* model (see also the references on object-oriented systems in Part VII).

There exists an extensive literature on the (logical) design of relational database schemas. Surveys are provided, for instance, by Korth and Silberschatz (1986), Lien (1985), Maier (1983), Paredaens et al. (1989), Ullman (1988) and Yang (1986). Anomalies in relations were already observed by Codd (1971), which motivated him to define 2NF, 3NF and later BCNF. Good introductions to this subject are given by Beeri et al. (1978) and Kent (1983). A certain problem with the work on normal forms is that generally the *formal* notion of normal form is contrasted with the *intuitively* described concept of anomalies, without being able to prove that 'freedom from anomalies' is characterized by a certain normal form. A formal approach to define anomalies, with renders such an equivalence proof possible, is presented by Vossen (1986, 1988); the reader is also referred to Bernstein and Goodman (1980a) or LeDoux and Parker (1982).

Theorem 12.3 is from Jou and Fischer (1980, 1982); in the latter paper Theorem 12.6 is proved as well. Theorem 12.4 is from Ling et al. (1981); see also Yang (1986). The result that testing primeness of attributes is NP-complete was obtained by Lucchesi and Osborn (1978). Our presentation of the design theory again partially follows Vardi (1988). 'Desirable' properties of a decomposition were first investigated by Rissanen (1977, 1978). Algorithm *LJP* is from Aho et al. (1979), who also prove Theorem 12.8. Theorem 12.9 is from Heath (1971); its converse was shown by Rissanen (1977). NP-completeness results in connection with BCNF decompositions are presented by Jou and Fischer (1980) as well as Beeri and Bernstein (1979). The synthesis algorithm was first proposed by Bernstein (1976); the importance of including a 'database key' in a decomposition (see the proof of Theorem 12.10) was discovered by Biskup et al. (1979). For this design approach, the reader is also referred to Beeri et al. (1978); a comparison between synthesis and decomposition is given by Fagin (1977a). Meanwhile, many variants and extensions of this method have been proposed; notable ones include those of Beeri and Kifer (1986), Biskup and Meyer (1987), Maier (1983), Vossen (1986) and Yang (1986).

MVDs were independently introduced by Fagin (1977b), Delobel (1978) and Zaniolo (1976). In particular, Theorem 12.11 is from Fagin (1977b). The axiomatization of multivalued dependencies is investigated by Beeri et al. (1977), Biskup (1978, 1980) and Mendelzon (1979). An algorithmic solution for the membership problem for MVDs is presented by Beeri (1980) or Beeri et al. (1977); for 'bases' and how to compute them, see Galil (1982) or Ozsoyoglu and Yuan (1985).

Alternative design methods, which partially take interrelational constraints into account as well, are proposed, for example, by Goodman and Tay (1983), Lien (1985) and Mannila and Räihä (1986a). Mannila and Räihä (1986b) question the traditional approach to relational database design and argue that a reasonable 'design tool' based on an algorithm like synthesis or decomposition should also output sample (Armstrong) relations that might be stored under the schemas produced; based on an analysis of the size of such 'prototype relations', they propose ways to generate them. In certain applications (such as distribution design), 'horizontal' decompositions instead of the 'vertical' ones discussed here are desired; for more on this, see de Bra (1985), Fischer and van Gucht (1984), Paredaens et al. (1989) or Yang (1986).

The normal forms presented here form the basis for the 'classical' normalization theory; however, many other normal forms have been proposed in the past. Zaniolo (1982) describes the *Elementary Key Normal Form* (EKNF), which lies between 3NF and BCNF; see also Yang (1986). An *Improved 3NF* was proposed by Ling et al. (1981). Fagin (1979) presents the *Project-Join Normal Form* (PJNF), which is termed *5NF* by Date (1986); additional information on Fifth Normal Form is provided by Korth and Silberschatz (1986), Maier (1983) and Yang (1986). Fagin (1981) introduces the *Domain-Key Normal Form* (DKNF). This listing is far from complete.

Functional and multivalued dependencies only form the foundation of the theory of data dependencies. More complete expositions of this theory can be found in Fagin (1982), Fagin and Vardi (1984), Thalheim (1986), Vardi (1987) and Yannakakis and Papadimitriou (1982).

The reader interested in basic introductions to the areas of data structures and efficient algorithms (such as for searching and sorting) is referred to the textbooks by Aho et al. (1983), Horowitz and Sahni (1976), Knuth (1973) and Mehlhorn (1984). The implementation of database systems is discussed by Wiederhold (1987); this text in particular describes and analyses a variety of schemes for organizing and accessing files.

More detailed descriptions of index structures as well as of index-sequential files or inverted lists can be found in Korth and Silberschatz (1986), Teorey and Fry (1982), Ullman (1988), Wiederhold (1987) and Cardenas (1985). Introductions to the definition and application of tree structures to organize indexes are provided by Korth and Silberschatz (1986) and Ullman (1988). B-trees were first introduced by Bayer and McCreight (1972); see also Held and Stonebraker (1978). The parallel execution of query and update operations on B-trees is investigated, for example, by Bayer and Schkolnick (1977), Lausen (1984) and Sagiv (1985). The results of performance investigations on these and other classes of trees are reported by Arnow and Tenenbaum (1984) as well as Kriegel (1984). For further details on B*-trees, the reader should consult Teorey and Fry (1982). A generalization of B-trees are **multidimensional B-trees** ('*kB-trees*'), which are described by Güting and Kriegel (1980), Kriegel (1982), Ouksel and Scheuermann (1981) or Scheuermann and Ouksel (1982). The k-d-tree structure was originally proposed by Bentley (1975); other work on this structure includes Chang and Fu (1981) or Flajolet and Puech (1983). Multidimensional variants of this structure are, among others, the '**extended k-d-tree**' by Bentley (1979), the **KDB-tree** by Robinson (1981), or the 'mixed version' of both, the **kdB-tree**, by Kuchen (1984); see also Chang and Fu (1981). An introduction to the theoretical foundations of (static) hash functions is given by Knuth (1973). The use of hash organizations in database systems is described, for example, by Korth and Silberschatz (1986), Teorey and Fry (1982) and Wiederhold (1987); additional information is provided by Burkhard (1976, 1979).

A survey of multidimensional as well as of dynamic hash functions is given by Kuchen (1984). A particular multidimensional method is described by Bolour (1979). In general, there exist two classes of dynamic methods. Methods in the first class use a particular operation for extending the storage area when a bucket overflows. Examples include the methods **extendible hashing**, see Fagin et al. (1979), Mendelson (1982), Tamminen (1982), Kelley and Rusinkiewicz (1986), Otoo (1988); **virtual hashing**, see Litwin (1978) and **dynamic hashing**, see Larson (1978). For maintaining the relationships between already extended (decomposed) and original buckets, these approaches use either tree structures or tables, whose size always depends on the number of stored records. For methods in the second class, the size of such auxiliary structures is approximately constant (and in particular independent of the number of records); a particular method in this class is **linear hashing**, see Litwin (1980), Larson (1980), Mullin (1981), Burkhard (1983), Otoo (1985), Schlatter-Ellis (1985), Yuen and Du (1986) or Hutflesz et al. (1988a). Other dynamic hash methods are reported, for instance, in Scholl (1981) and Ramamohanarao and Lloyd (1982).

In the context of database applications which require 'higher' data models than the record-oriented ones, there is an increasing interest nowadays in data structures suited for storing 'space objects' besides 'point objects'. Examples of such structures are the **R-tree** by Guttman (1984), the **R$^+$-tree** by Sellis et al. (1987) and in particular the multidimensional dynamic hashing scheme called **grid file**, described, for instance, by Hinrichs (1985), Nievergelt et al. (1984) or Ouksel (1985). This latter organization scheme has attracted many researchers' attention recently, as can be seen from the number of variations that have been proposed; among them are the **multilevel grid** file by Whang and Krishnamurthy (1985), the **balanced and nested grid** (BANG) file by Freeston (1987), the **twin grid** file by Hutflesz et al. (1988b), and the directory-less version by Kriegel and Seeger (1986, 1988).

To deepen the understanding of the material discussed in Chapter 13, the reader is also referred to Solomon and Bickel (1986).

Exercises

(1) Let $F = \{AB \to E, AC \to G, AD \to B, B \to C, C \to D\}$.
(a) Show that C and D are prime.
(b) Show that C is transitively dependent on AB and AD as well as directly dependent on AC. How is D dependent on these keys?

(2) Prove Lemma 12.1.

(3) Prove: $R = (U, F)$ is in 3NF $\iff$ every NKA $A \in U$ is normal.

(4) Consider $R = (ABCDEFGHI, \{A \to BDE, B \to ACDE, DE \to A, C \to DF, D \to I, I \to G, F \to G, FD \to H, D \to G\})$. Determine whether the decomposition of R into components that have formats *ABCDE*, *CDF*, *DIG*, *FDHG*, respectively, is lossless. (Use Algorithm LJP.)

(5) Show that the converse of Theorem 12.9 holds.

(6) Complete the proof of Theorem 12.10.

(7) Consider the following 'universe' U of attributes: C (Course), T (Teacher), H (Hour), R (Room), S (Student), G (Grade). Let the following FDs be required: $C \to T, HR \to C, HT \to R, CS \to G, HS \to R, HR \to T$.
(a) Use *SYNTHESIS* to derive a relational database schema from this input.
(b) Apply *DECOMPOSITION* to the same input.

(8) Find a relation r over a suitably chosen set X of attributes such that the natural join of *three* projections of r is lossless, while every join of two projections is lossy. (Let the format of every projection be different from X in both cases.)

(9) Let $R = (U, F)$ and $A \in U$ be normal (with respect to R); in addition, let $R' = (V, \pi_V(F^+))$ for $V \subseteq U$ such that $A \in V$. Show that A is normal in V (that is, with respect to R') as well.

(10) Using the counterexample $R = (ABCD, \{A \to B, BD \to AC\})$, show that an attribute which is prime with respect to R is not necessarily also prime in a projection of R in which it occurs. (Hint: Consider B and $V = ABC$.)

(11) Consider $R = (ABCDEG, \{E \rightarrow D, C \rightarrow B, CE \rightarrow G, B \rightarrow A\})$.
(a) In which normal form is R?
(b) Find a lossless and independent 3NF decomposition of R.
(c) Find a lossless BCNF decomposition of R.
(d) Determine whether the decomposition with formats DE, BC, CEG, AB is lossless.

(12) Consider the schema $R = (ABCDE, \{A \rightarrow BC, CD \rightarrow E, B \rightarrow D, E \rightarrow A\})$. Apply *SYNTHESIS* to R and explain the 'problem' from Exercise 25 (d) in Part III.

(13) For the basis found in Exercise 27 in Part III, compute the decomposition generated by the synthesis algorithm.

(14) Prove the *correctness* of the MVD axioms (A1), (A2) and (A3); also, show that the following axioms are correct:
(A4) $X \rightarrow\rightarrow Y \wedge X \rightarrow\rightarrow Z \Longrightarrow X \rightarrow\rightarrow YZ$
(A5) $X \rightarrow\rightarrow Y \wedge X \rightarrow\rightarrow Z \Longrightarrow X \rightarrow\rightarrow Y \cap Z \wedge X \rightarrow\rightarrow Y - Z$
(A6) $X \rightarrow\rightarrow Y \wedge YW \rightarrow\rightarrow Z \Longrightarrow XW \rightarrow\rightarrow Z - (YW)$

(15) Show that every relation schema in 4NF is also in BCNF; provide a counterexample for the converse direction.

(16) Describe preliminaries under which a dense index is preferable over a sparse one; do so assuming that the records to be stored belong to (a) a relational database, (b) a (physical) network database.

(17) Let two relations $r \in \text{Rel}(X)$ and $s \in \text{Rel}(Y)$ be given. Write a 'procedure' for computing $r \bowtie s$, assuming that an index exists for each of the common attributes $X \cap Y = \{A, B\}$ and that the relations are stored in sequential files with block length 1 according to increasing pairs of AB values.

(18) Represent the key values 2, 3, 5, 7, 11, 13, 17, 19, 23, 29, 31, 45, 57 in a B-tree with parameters $k = 1$ and $k = 2$, respectively.

(19) For the B-trees resulting from Exercise 18, describe the steps required to solve the following tasks:
(a) Select the record with key value 17.
(b) Select all records having key values greater than 20.
(c) Insert value 9.
(d) Insert value 60.
(e) Delete all values between 20 and 25.

(20) Let relation format $X = \{A_1, \ldots, A_7\}$ with $\text{dom}(A_i) = \{1, \ldots, 100\}$ for $1 \leq i \leq 7$ be given. Let each of the attributes $A_1, \ldots, A_4$ be a key for X. For this format, program a file organization that is based on a 3-d-tree structure and that allows for selections, insertions and deletions of individual tuples.

(21) For the key values from Exercise 18 and a storage size of $n = 22$, determine the hash addresses resulting from the division-remainder method.

(22) Determine a lower bound for the space requirement for determining alternative addresses using quadratic probing. In particular, describe a recursive scheme for computing squares (using the binomial formula $(i+1)^2 = i^2 + 2i + 1$).

(23) Prove that for every natural number the following holds:

$$i^2 \equiv (n-i)^2 \bmod n$$

Use this to show that even for quadratic probing collisions may occur frequently.

(24) Prove that a given storage area consisting of n addresses is used in its entirety when computing alternative addresses if the latter are determined by

$$h_i(a) := (h_o(a) + (-1)^{i+1} \cdot i^2) \bmod n$$

and $n \equiv 3 \bmod 4$ is a prime number. (Examples of such n are 3, 7, 11, 31, 59, 1019, 2027.)

Part V

Selected Database Languages and Systems

Chapter 14
The Network System UDS (Siemens)

UDS (*U*niversal *D*atabase *S*ystem) is a network database system based on the CODASYL recommendations, which is marketed by Siemens for mainframes running the BS2000 operating system. In this chapter, first a summary of the major system components is given, as well as of the steps that have to be gone through for creating a new database. Then its schema and subschema DDL for defining conceptual and external network schemas are described. Finally, parts of the embedded and the stand-alone query languages are presented, and the FIND and GET commands are emphasized in each case.

14.1 UDS components; Utilities for database creation

The components of UDS can be classified into four different groups corresponding to the four distinct tasks that are relevant in the context of a network database. These groups are first surveyed together with those parts of the entire program system which are associated with them. Notice that the groups are not completely disjoint.

14.1.1 Creating the dictionary of a database

A data dictionary contains the schema information associated with the three levels of a database (see Figure 2.1) and can be created by the DBA or a user. UDS distinguishes the following languages:

(1) A **Schema DDL** for defining a conceptual global schema, that is, to formally describe a logical network as well as additional information like ordering of members, mandatory-optional, automatic-manual, location modes, in particular CALC keys and set selection clauses.

(2) A **Subschema DDL** for describing external (sub)schemas derived from the conceptual schema, which provide a view ('window') to the database for certain users.

(3) A **Storage Structure Language** (SSL) to determine and influence the way data is physically stored.

The four utilities *BCREATE, BGSIA, BFORMAT* and *BGSSIA* are provided for dictionary creation; in general, the approach taken is that any description is written into a file first, which is then processed by a corresponding compiler. As a consequence, the respective description (of schema, subschemas or storage structures) should be *complete*, since later additions and/or changes can be accomplished to a certain extent only and are difficult to convey to the system.

14.1.2 Database generation

Before Schema and Subschema DDL are described in more detail, a brief look is taken into the process of generating a new database, which uses various other components and utilities. This process, to be performed by the DBA, can be considered as consisting of nine steps altogether, which are gone through sequentially, and which are as follows:

(1) Use *BCREATE* to format the **compiler database** consisting of *DBDIR* (Data Base Directory) and *DBCOM* (Data Base Compiler

Realm). Both areas (of files) are needed for storing information resulting from the compilation of Schema DDL and SSL, which is later used by the DBH (see below) and by the DDL compiler for compiling the subschemas.

(2) Compile the schema description that was produced using the Schema DDL; the output is stored in DBCOM and is later used by the SSL compiler and the *BGSIA* utility.

(3) (optional) Compile the SSL file provided (if any), which contains user or DBA supplied specifications on the physical database structure.

(4) Use *BGSIA* to create the **schema information area** (SIA), using information already available in DBCOM, and store it in DBDIR. The SIA is primarily used by the DBH for storing data in a user working area, or for the retrieval and update of data.

(5) In Step 4, BGSIA has also created the **standard hash module**, which is now entered into a library named *dbname.HASHLIB* (by the operating-system utility LMR), where *dbname* is the name of the database under generation.

(6) Use *BFORMAT* to format the user areas of the database currently created. The information needed in this step is taken from DBDIR; information on the areas formatted is added to the SIA.

(7) Generate one or more subschemas (even if no views are needed, *one* subschema consisting of the entire schema itself must be created, since an application program cannot access a conceptual schema directly). To this end, compile the subschema description produced using the Subschema DDL; the output is stored in DBCOM.

(8) Generate the **subschema information area** (SSIA), using the *BGSSIA* utility and information from DBCOM. The SSIA generated is also stored in DBDIR.

(9) Use *BPRIVACY* to introduce three-part userids (see Section 14.3, consisting of user name, user group and password) and to define access rights. This utility can be called at any time after *BFORMAT* has successfully terminated and hence in particular before subschema descriptions are compiled (unless subschemas are referenced within the definitions supplied to *BPRIVACY*).

The utility program *BINILOAD* can finally be used to load already existing sets of data into an empty or partially filled database. The information contained in DBDIR can at run-time be used by the *CHECK* utility to perform a variety of consistency and correctness tests on the physical structure of a database, which for example enables a user to determine whether a transaction that was started on a consistent state has indeed preserved the consistency property.

14.1.3 Using a database in applications

For writing application programs, two languages are provided: The **COBOL DML** is an extension of ANS-COBOL by 16 different DML statements for working with UDS databases. Programs written in assembly language, FORTRAN or Pascal can access such a database using the **CALL DML**. (While the COBOL DML is hence based on an appropriate compiler extension, corresponding precompilers are used in connection with the CALL DML; see also Chapter 2.)

In addition, there exist the program generator *PROGEN* for the online (dialogue) creation of COBOL read-programs which can run in batch mode, as well as the *compatible database interface KDBS* to support a transfer of application programs written for another DBMS to the UDS system, or to access a UDS database from a different host or DBMS. For working with a database in a dialogue mode, the system IQS is available, whose language IQL (*I*nteractive *Q*uery *L*anguage) renders it possible to access a UDS database directly from a terminal using German, English or Italian keywords. IQS is also used by the report generator *ADILOS*.

14.1.4 Database administration

Under UDS, it is the responsibility of the DBA to create and maintain the individual databases, to start and finish individual sessions, and to control the execution of sessions. Especially for this latter task, the *DAL* (*D*B*AL*anguage) is at the DBA's disposal. In addition, there exists a variety of utility programs, such as for the dynamic modification of certain parameters (like *BREORG* for changing the sizes of areas or hash spaces or, more generally, for optimizing the organization of an internal level), for the implementation of schema modifications (like *BCHANGE, BALTER* for deleting or adding record- or set-types and areas), for maintaining system security (*BSECURE*) or for acquiring information on a schema or a subschema (*BPSIA*) or on the current contents of an area (*BPRECORD*).

Finally, a central component is the **DBH** (*D*ata*b*ase *H*andler), which takes care of any data transfer between the database and the user working area (UWA) of an application program, thereby, for instance, checking access rights. For the simultaneous execution of several programs with database access, for which individual accesses may therefore concur, the program system **Independent DBH** is available, which synchronizes a (quasi) parallel access. A primary responsibility of the DBH is to make the system robust against various kinds of errors that may occur during normal operation.

14.2 The Schema DDL

When describing the syntax of DDL and DML commands in this and subsequent sections, common practice will be followed by the use of the following conventions. Those parts of a word occurring in a command written in capital letters represent the shortest possible abbreviation of this word; words written in small letters also represent keywords of the command in question, but may be omitted. Everything put in square brackets is optional and may also be omitted. Words put in curly brackets represent alternatives, one of which has to be specified; those put in '< ... >' either stand for identifiers that are chosen by the user or are explained elsewhere. When representing (parts of) the syntax of the language graphically, items in boxes are always specified in detail elsewhere, while items in circles or ovals are terminal symbols of the UDS grammar. The description of the UDS language given in this chapter is by no means complete; therefore, reading through this chapter cannot be considered a substitute for reading the appropriate manuals.

Working with a database under UDS is based on a network schema, which is described using the Schema DDL, and which has to be defined completely before the database can be used for the first time. The definition of a UDS database schema consists of a declaration of the name of this schema, the definition of areas and logical record- and set-types. In general, the following restrictions apply for the language elements occurring in one of the subsequent syntax diagrams. Names (like *schemaname, subschemaname, recordname, setname, areaname*) consist of at most 30 symbols (letters, digits, hyphens) and must begin with a letter; integers (like *integer, integer1, integer2*) consist of at most 15 digits.

The definition of a database schema for UDS has the general form shown in Figure 14.1. Thus, a definition begins with a *schema definition*, followed by at least one *area definition*. For the sequencing of all subsequent area, record or set definitions, the following holds:

(1) Before a record (type) can be defined, all areas have to be declared which are referenced in the within-definition (see below) of this type definition.

(2) Before a set (type) can be defined, the record declarations for its owner and its member-type must have been provided.

As a consequence, it seems reasonable to follow the diagram shown in Figure 14.2 when defining a UDS schema, which automatically maintains these restrictions.

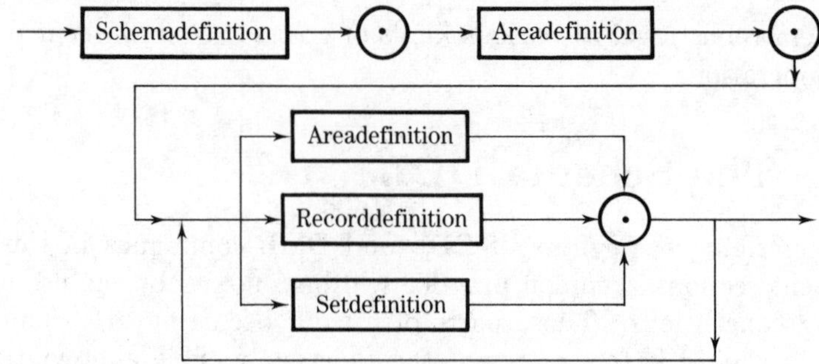

Figure 14.1 General form of a UDS database schema definition.

In a **schema definition**, a new UDS schema is given a name by

SCHEMA name is <schemaname>

(In addition, it is possible to protect the schema by giving it a password, using the PRIVACY LOCK clause not described here.)

The **area definition**

AREA name is <areaname> [area is TEMPorary]

declares a named (storage) area. Up to 240 areas may be defined, but at most one temporary one, where the latter is only used in connection with dynamic sets (described below).

A **record-type** is declared using the *record definition*, which has the general form shown in Figure 14.3. The structure of the individual definitions occurring in a record definition is as follows:

record name definition

RECORD name is <record-type-name>

location mode definition

LOCation mode is
{ DIRECT <attr-1 > OF <record-type-name> |

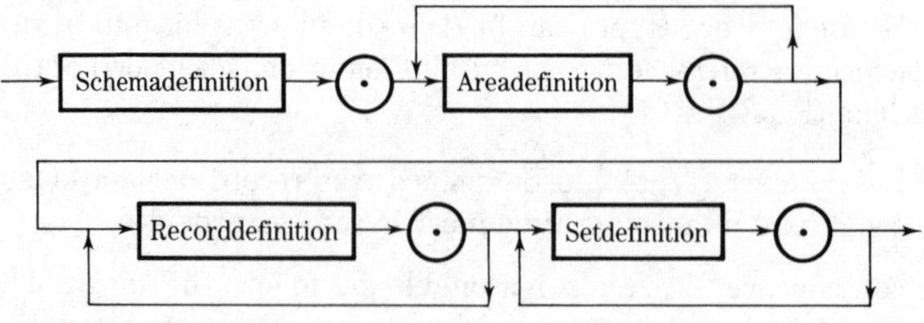

Figure 14.2 Proposed form of a UDS database schema definition.

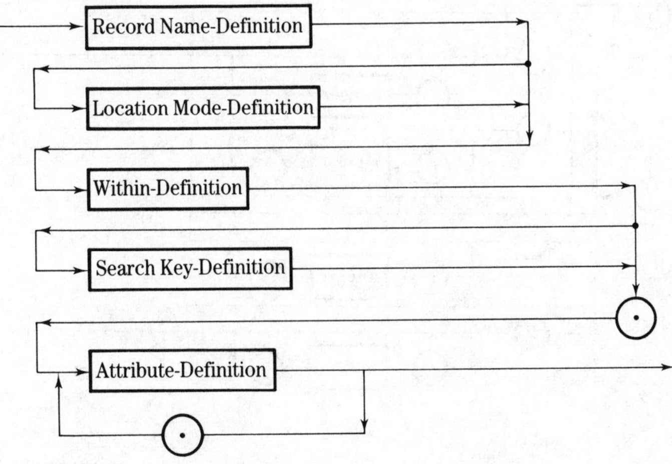

Figure 14.3 General form of a record definition.

CALC USING <attr-2 > [, <attr-3 > . . .]
DUPlicates are [NOT] allowed }

Here, <attr-1 > denotes an attribute from the record-type being defined which is (later) declared as being of type DATABASE KEY, while <attr-2 > . . . denotes (eventually several) attributes of this record-type which will be used for computing CALC keys.

within definition

WITHIN <areaname-1> [, <areaname-2> . . .]

search key definition

SEARCH key is <attr-1> [, <attr-2 > . . .]
USING { CALC | INDEX } DUPlicates are [NOT] allowed

In this way, a **secondary key** for the record-type in question, consisting of <attr-1> . . ., is declared; given values for these attributes, either a relative record address can be computed via some hash routine (CALC), or an index table can be created through which records over this type can be accessed directly.

The **attributes** of the record-type currently being defined are described in an *attribute definition.* The following syntax description presents only those language elements needed for the definition of 'elementary' attributes; the definition of so-called *vectors* or *repeating groups* with different levels of nesting (similar to COBOL or PL/I) will not be considered.

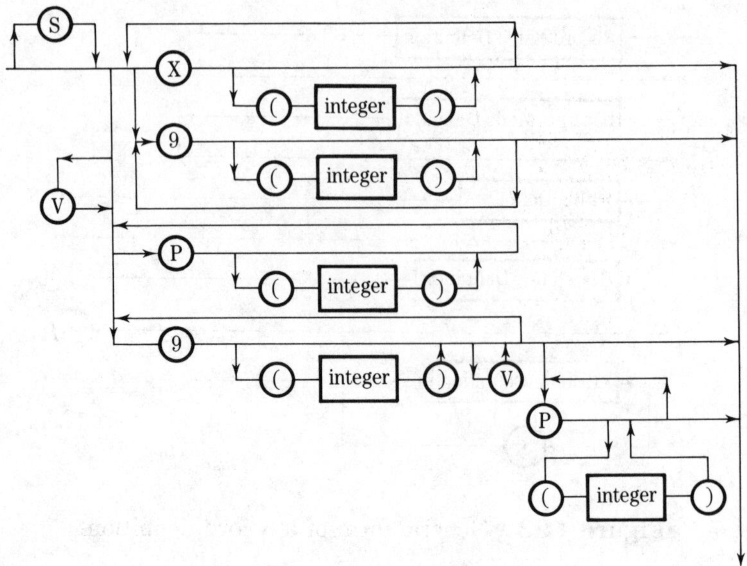

Figure 14.4 Syntax for defining a mask string in a picture clause.

attribute definition

<attributename> { PICture is <mask string> |
TYPE is { fixed real { BINary [{15|31}] |
DECimal <integer-1 > [, <integer-2 >]} |
CHARaracter <integer> | DataBase-KEY } }

Here, the following restrictions apply:

(1) Attribute names have to be unique within one record format only.

(2) For decimal numbers, at most 18 digits are allowed (for example, 'DEC 7,2' stands for a total of 7 digits with two of them following the decimal point); predefined are *integer-1* = 18 and *integer-2* = 0.

(3) $1 \leq integer \leq 255$.

The PICture clause is similar to what can be used in COBOL; it can be employed to declare unpacked numerical attributes or alphanumerical attributes of fixed or variable length, where <mask string> defines a domain by symbolically representing the field values allowed as shown in Figure 14.4. In this figure, 'S' is a placeholder for a sign, 'X' stands for an arbitrary symbol, '9' for a digit, 'V' for a decimal point, 'P' for a (thought-of) null if the decimal point is more than one position outside the mask. '(integer)' specifies how often the placeholder in front of it is to be repeated. Thus, for example,

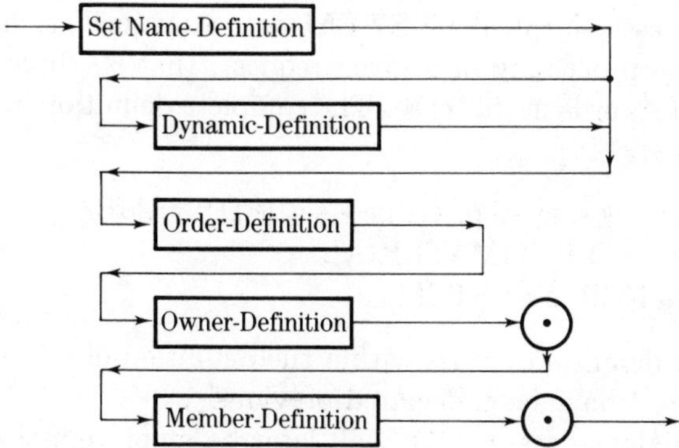

Figure 14.5 General form of a set definition.

`PIC 9(6)`	declares a 6-digit natural number
`PIC S9(7)`	declares a 7-digit integer
`PIC 99`	declares a 2-digit natural number
`PIC X`	declares an arbitrary symbol (string of length 1)
`PIC X(3)`	declares an arbitrary string of length 3
`PIC 9(6)V9(6)`	declares a 12-digit decimal number with a decimal point in the middle

Also, for example, the strings `PIC XXXXXX`, `PIC XX(4)X` and `PIC X(6)` are equivalent, since the repetition factor determines how often the symbol immediately preceding it is to be repeated. A mask string may generally consist of at most 30 symbols only, and it may define a field of at most 255 symbols, where the number of positions that can exclusively carry digits is limited to 18.

A **set-type** is declared using the *set definition*, which has the general form shown in Figure 14.5. The individual definitions appearing in this figure are as follows:

set name definition

SET NAME is <set-type-name>

dynamic definition

set is DYNAMIC

A dynamic set can (during the processing of some user request) be assigned records of different types (for example, as the intermediate result of a query); thus, membership in a dynamic set is of type OPTIONAL MANUAL, and there exists no concrete member-type. To assign records to a dynamic set, the existence of *one* set occurrence is sufficient, since members are not distinguished by owners; as a consequence, a dynamic set is declared as a so-called **SYSTEM set**. Any such set has members only during the processing of a given request, that is, there is no static membership of records in this case. The complete definition of a **dynamic set** is as follows:

SET name is <set-type-name> set is DYNAMIC
    ORDER is IMMATERIAL
    OWNER is SYSTEM

In case such a definition occurs within the definition of a schema, a temporary area must have been declared previously.

If the dialogue system IQS will later be employed, the subschema which is to be processed must contain eight dynamic sets named IQL-DYN1 through IQL-DYN8 (as well as exactly one temporary area).

order definition

ORDER is { LAST | FIRST | NEXT | PRIOR | IMMATERIAL |
    SORTED by { DataBase-KEY |
        DEFINED keys DUPlicates are [NOT] allowed } }

In this way, the sequencing of members within a set occurrence is specified. Here, LAST corresponds to the timely sequence of insertions of member records, that is, a newly stored record becomes the logically last one in 'its' occurrence (analogously for FIRST); NEXT and PRIOR are both meant relative to the current CRS contents.

The so-called **primary key** of a set-type is declared through the SORTED clause (see the member definition below); if this clause is used, member records will always be sorted according to the values of this key.

owner definition

OWNER is {<record-type-name> | SYSTEM }

Even if a record type does not have a relationship to a 'higher' record type in a logical network, this type may still occur as a member type of a SYSTEM set-type. This renders it possible, for instance, to order the records of this type according to some criterion which is different from the (ascending) order of database key values. In this case, the system will create *one* owner which gets assigned these records in the desired order (or in some desired selection) as members (in *one* set occurrence).

member definition

MEMBER is <record-type-name>
    { MANDatory | OPTional }{ AUTOmatic | MANUAL }
    [{ ASCending | DESCending } key is <attr-1> [, ...]]
    [<search-key definition>]

[set occurrence SELECTION is thru
{ CURRENT of set | LOCation mode of owner }

MANDatory or OPTional and AUTOmatic or MANUAL determine the kind of set membership, respectively, as explained in Chapter 5. Through the key clause (line 3 of the member definition) a primary key (see above) is defined, which determines the sequencing of member records within the individual set occurrences over this type; in particular, this key determines the attributes of the member by which the records are sorted in ascending or descending order within a set occurrence.

The SEARCH-key definition for set-types has the same structure and function (declaration of a secondary key) as for record-types and therefore needs no further explanation.

For sets of type 'OWNER is SYSTEM', the set SELECTION clause is not applicable; it needs to be specified in all other cases. 'thru LOCation mode of owner' can only be used if a unique CALC key ('DUP NOT') is defined for the owner-type. If the user subsequently specifies a key value, the corresponding owner record automatically becomes the CURRENT OF SET.

As an example for a schema definition under UDS, consider the student database from Figure 5.8(b) once more, for which the complete declaration is as follows:

```
SCHEMA NAME IS UNIVERSITY.
AREA NAME IS PERSONS.
AREA NAME IS OTHERS.
AREA NAME IS FORIQS AREA IS TEMPORARY.

RECORD NAME IS PROFESSOR
     LOCATION MODE IS CALC USING PNO
     DUPLICATES ARE NOT ALLOWED WITHIN PERSONS.
     PNO TYPE IS CHARACTER 7.
     PNAME TYPE IS CHARACTER 20.
     P-LOC TYPE IS CHARACTER 15.

RECORD STUDENT LOC CALC USING STUDID DUP NOT
     WITHIN PERSONS
     SEARCH KEY IS SNAME, S-LOC USING CALC DUP NOT.
     STUDID PIC 9(6).
     SNAME TYPE CHAR 20.
     S-LOC TYPE CHAR 15.

RECORD COURSE LOC CALC USING CNO DUP NOT
     WITHIN OTHERS
     SEARCH CNAME USING CALC DUP.
```

```
        CNO PIC 9(6).
        CNAME TYPE CHAR 30.

    RECORD S-C LOC DIRECT S-C-NO OF S-C
        WITHIN OTHERS.
        CNO PIC 9(6).
        STUDID PIC 9(6).
        S-C-NO TYPE DB-KEY.

    SET NAME IS ADVISES
        ORDER IS SORTED BY DEFINED KEYS DUP NOT
        OWNER PROFESSOR.
    MEMBER IS STUDENT OPTIONAL MANUAL
        ASCENDING KEY IS STUDID
        SET OCCURRENCE SELECTION IS THRU
        LOCATION MODE OF OWNER.

    SET NAME IS TEACHES
        ORDER SORTED BY DB-KEY
        OWNER PROFESSOR.
    MEMBER IS COURSE OPTIONAL MANUAL
        SEARCH CNO USING INDEX
        SELECTION IS THRU LOCATION MODE OF OWNER.

    SET NAME IS ATTENDS
        ORDER LAST
        OWNER STUDENT.
    MEMBER S-C MAND AUTO SELECTION IS THRU CURRENT OF SET.

    SET NAME IS-ATTENDED
        ORDER IMMATERIAL
        OWNER COURSE.
    MEMBER S-C MAND AUTO SELECTION CURRENT.

    SET NAME IS IQL-DYN1
        SET IS DYNAMIC
        ORDER IS IMMATERIAL
        OWNER IS SYSTEM.
    ...
    SET NAME IS IQL-DYN8
        SET IS DYNAMIC
        ORDER IS IMMATERIAL
        OWNER IS SYSTEM.
```

14.3 View definition using the Subschema DDL; Access rights

Using the Subschema DDL, a section from a network schema that has already been declared with the Schema DDL can be extracted. In particular, areas, record- and set-types as well as attributes can be excluded, or special selection conditions can be declared that filter out certain records of a given type.

The corresponding language elements will not be presented in detail here, but a representative excerpt from the syntax of the Subschema DDL is described. First, the declaration of a subschema has the following general structure:

```
IDENTIFICATION DIVISION.
      SUB-SCHEMA name is <subschemaname>
      of SCHEMA name <schemaname>.
   DATA DIVISION.
      AREA SECTION.
         { COPY ALL AREAS | COPY <areaname> [,...] }.
      RECORD SECTION.
         { COPY ALL RECORDS | COPY <record-type-name>
         [,...] }.
      SET SECTION.
         { COPY ALL SETS | COPY <set-type-name> [,...] }.
```

Here, selection conditions can only be used within the RECORD SECTION. Also, the <schemaname> must be identical with the one specified in the Schema DDL.

In order to grant access rights, the DBA has to create a file (using the ultility program *BPRIVACY* mentioned above) whose contents looks as follows:

PASSWORD
*NEW
*USERGROUP

group_1	names of the user groups
...	to be declared
group_n	(at most 8 symbols long)
*END	
*USER	
username_1 $group\_i_1$	
password_1	user names (up to 24 symbols long)
...	are associated with their groups;
...	each user is associated with a distinct password
username_m $group\_i_m$	(up to 10 symbols long)

```
password_m
*END
*END
:                          <declaration of access rights for the
                           individual user groups as described
$END                       below>
```

The declaration of rights to access the individual items in a database, for an already established user group, has the following form:

```
$USERGROUP = group e       where e ∈ { A , R }, see below
*dbitem                    where dbitem ∈ { AREA, RECORD,
                           SET, SUBSCHEMA }

<types of access,          (optional)
see below>

dbitem-name_1              names of those database items
...                        of type *dbitem for which the
...                        above access rights are to be
dbitem-name_n              declared
*END
```

The following table shows the implications of e = A(LLOW) and e = R(EFUSE), respectively:

e	Types of access	Without access type
R	*The types of access mentioned are forbidden* on the database item; all those not mentioned are allowed	All access-types to the database item are allowed
A	*The types of access mentioned are allowed* on the database item; all others are forbidden	All access-types to the database item are forbidden

As before, only the most important access-types are listed here:

(1) For database item *SET or *SUBSCHEMA:

Access-type	Meaning
+INSERT	Insertion of a member (CONNECT)
+REMOVE	Deletion of a member (DISCONNECT)
+IF-EMPTY	Testing whether the set occurrence of a particular set-type is empty
+FIND-OWNER	Finding of an owner record
+FIND-7A	Finding of several records using a condition (FIND, DISPLAY)

(2) For database item ∗RECORD or ∗SUBSCHEMA:

Access-type	Meaning
+MODIFY-RECORD	Modification of a record
+MODIFY-ITEM	Modification of individual attribute values of a record

It is allowed to specify rights to access distinct database items for the same user group; each new specification modifies the access rights of this group on 'their' database item. If the same database-item name is repeated for one user group, only the last definition is put into effect. (In a similar way, user groups can be granted access to individual programs.) Granted access rights can be modified after a database has been created.

14.4 Database queries using the COBOL DML

As was mentioned in Section 14.1, for using a network database from application programs the COBOL DML of the UDS system is available. This language is an extension of ANS-COBOL by the 16 data manipulation statements ACCEPT, CONNECT, DISCONNECT, ERASE, FETCH, FIND, FINISH, FREE, GET, IF, KEEP, MODIFY, READY, SET, STORE and USE. More detailed discussion will be limited here to the four of these which are relevant to querying a database, in order to emphasize the similarities or differences compared with the DBTG language described in Chapter 5.

FIND and GET both have the meaning and effect described in Chapter 5. FETCH combines the functionality of these two; hence, the effect of this command is to locate a record within a database, to enter its database key value into the currency table and to transfer this record to the UWA of the program in question. For a record listed in the currency table, ACCEPT delivers its database key value or the name of the area in which this record is stored to the application program.

The syntax of **ACCEPT** is as follows:

ACCEPT <fieldname> FROM
{ [<record-type-name> | <set-type-name> |
<area-name>] CURRENCY |
[<record-typ-name> | <set-typ-name> | <fieldname-1>]
REALM-NAME}

Concluding this command by CURRENCY results in a transfer of a database key value to the field <fieldname> within the UWA, where this value represents the corresponding CRR [, CRS, CRA] where <record-type-name> [, <set-type-name>, <area-name>] is specified, respectively. If none of these names is specified, <fieldname> gets the value of the CRU.

If the command is concluded by REALM-NAME, the name of that area is assigned to <fieldname>, in which the <record-type-name>, the <set-type-name> or the record whose database key value appears in <fieldname-1> is stored. Again, the default value is the area of the record referenced by the CRU.

The following sections will not distinguish between FIND and FETCH; therefore, the syntax is presented only for FIND. FIND can always be replaced by FETCH, which implies that the effect changes as described above. The general syntax of **FIND** is as follows:

FIND <expression> [RETAINING currency for
{ MULTIPLE | [REALM][RECORD]
[{ SETS | <set-type-name>, ... }] }]

Through the RETAINING clause, the user can suppress an update of the currency table apart from the CRU in general or on purpose. (A subsequent update is possible using FIND CURRENT ..., see <expression> Format 5 below).

The central portion of the FIND command is the (selection) **expression**, whose seven possible formats are described next (where the keyword FIND is always added for clarity):

Format 1:

FIND <record-type-name> DATABASE-KEY is <fieldname>

In this way, a *direct* access to a record is performed, via the database key value given in the UWA variable <fieldname>.

Format 2:

FIND { ANY | DUPLICATE } <record-type-name>

Here it is assumed that the corresponding record type has a CALC key; a *direct* access to a record is performed via this key, where the attributes belonging to the key have to be assigned values first (in a corresponding UWA variable) so that a hash address can be calculated.

Format 3:

FIND DUPLICATE WITHIN { <record-type-name> |
<set-type-name>} [USING <attribute-name>, ...]

In this way, a record, which agrees with the corresponding CRR or CRS in the eventually specified attributes, is accessed *sequentially.* As an alternative to this search for duplicates, an access to a record satisfying an <expression> that was processed immediately before (see Format 7) can be performed.

Format 4:

FIND { LAST | FIRST | NEXT | PRIOR | <integer>}
{ <record-type-name> | RECORD }
[WITHIN { <set-type-name> | <area-name> }]

With this format, the last/first record, the next/previous record relative to CRR, CRS, or CRA, or the record with the position specified as an <integer> is accessed in a *sequential* manner.

Format 5:

FIND CURRENT [<record-type-name>]
[WITHIN { <set-type-name> | <area-name>}]

In this way a *direct* access to the CRU or to the corresponding CRR, CRS, or CRA is performed.

Format 6:

FIND OWNER WITHIN <set-type-name>

This form of the FIND command can be used to locate the owner record of the set occurrence specified through the CRS of the corresponding set type.

Format 7:

FIND <record-typ-name>
[WITHIN <set-type-name-1> [CURRENT]]
{ USING <attribute-name>, ... |
[USING <condition>]
[RESULT in <set-type-name-2>]
[LIMITED by <set-type-name-3>]
[TALLYING <fieldname>] }

With this command, *all* records of type <record-type-name> are selected which either belong to an occurrence of the set-type <set-type-name-1> (determined by the CRS if the option CURRENT is used) or satisfy a

<condition> whose syntax is described below. (At this point, a deviation from the principle of recordwise navigation towards a setwise navigation can be recognized.) The records found are inserted into the occurrence of the dynamic set-type <set-type-name-2> as member records if the RESULT clause is used; only the first of these is recorded in the currency table. Using the LIMITED clause, the search can be restricted to those records which are members of the dynamic set-type <set-type-name-3> already. By specifying TALLYING, a counting of the records found is achieved; their number is stored in <fieldname>.

A **condition** has the following form:

condition:

{<condterm-1> [AND <condterm-2>]| <condterm-2>}

condterm-1:

[NOT] <condfac-1> [{ AND | OR } [NOT] <condfac-1>] ...

condfac-1:

<attribute-name-1> is [NOT] {= | > | <}
{<attribute-name-2 > | <literal>}

condterm-2: <condfac-2> [AND <condfac-2>]

condfac-2:

<attribute-name-3> is NEXT [NOT] {> | <}
{<attribute-name-4> | <literal>}

This syntax is basically self-explaining. <condfac-2> goes beyond <condfac-1> by specifying NEXT; while <condfac-1> yields *all* records satisfying an inequality, <condfac-2> returns only that record which satisfies it most precisely ('is next to it'). The dropping of attribute values through the use of masks will not be discussed here; the symbols =, <, and > can also be replaced by the corresponding keywords.

Finally, the examples from the university application presented in Section 5.3 will be described for illustrating the various access modes in UDS notation; the assumptions regarding the structure of the record-types are the same as given earlier (see Section 5.3 before the description of the access modes); however, all names are taken from the schema definition presented in Section 14.2.

(a) Direct access at the level of record types:

```
S.STUDID := 'U145';
FETCH ANY STUDENT;
```

or

```
X := CRR-STUDENT;
FETCH STUDENT DATABASE-KEY X;
```

(b) Sequential access at the level of record types:

```
S.SNAME := 'Miller';
FIND ANY STUDENT;
while not eof do
begin
    GET SNAME;
    FIND DUPLICATE WITHIN STUDENT USING SNAME;
end;
```

or

```
FIND FIRST STUDENT;
while not eof do
begin
    GET SNAME;
    FIND NEXT STUDENT;
end;
```

(c) Direct access at the level of set types:

```
S-C.STUDID := 'U145';
FIND S-C WITHIN ATTENDS USING STUDID;
while not eof do
begin
    GET CNO;
    FIND DUPLICATE WITHIN ATTENDS USING STUDID;
end;
```

(d) Sequential access at the level of set types:

```
S.STUDID := 'U145';
FIND ANY STUDENT;
while not fail do
begin
    FIND NEXT S-C WITHIN ATTENDS;
    FIND OWNER WITHIN IS_ATTENDED;
    GET CNAME;
end;
```

The **GET** command already used above has the following syntax:

GET [{<record-type-name> | <attribute-name>, ...}]

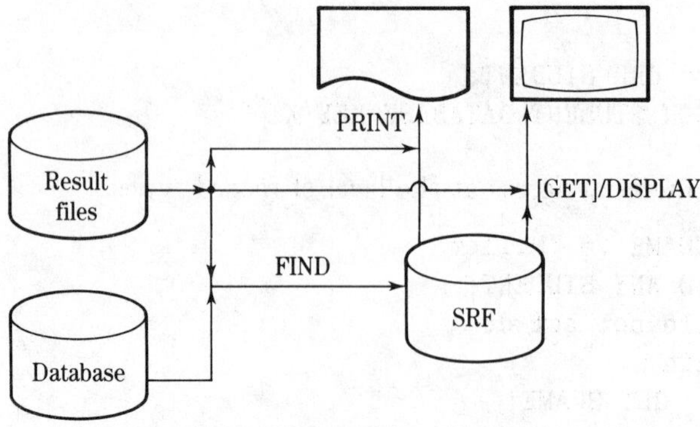

Figure 14.6 Run-time environment for IQS.

14.5 The dialogue query system IQS

With the Interactive Query System **IQS**, UDS users also have a tool available for manipulating a database directly within a dialogue. Of central importance for this form of working with a network database is a modified organization of the run-time environment. In particular, it is impossible to employ a UWA within a dialogue which, among other things, contains the currency table as well as record variables for the corresponding run unit. Since an 'embedding' application program is no longer present, record variables in their original sense are now obsolete; even more important is the fact that working under IQS is basically 'set oriented', so that 'cursors' for individual files or occurrences become obsolete too. The role of the UWA is now played by **result files**, which are used, for instance, as follows:

(1) For a FIND command, the result of the corresponding search is recorded in the **standard result file** (SRF); the number of records found is shown on the screen.

(2) For GET, the result of a selection or the contents of a result file is shown on the terminal.

(3) For PRINT, a selection result or result file is sent to a printer.

The modified environment is illustrated in Figure 14.6. The SRF is created automatically by IQS for the duration of a (terminal) session; it can also be addressed using the name STANDARD. IQS uses the SRF exclusively for storing one result of a search, which will be overwritten by the next FIND command. However, it is also possible to save a current SRF contents beyond the next FIND command, or even beyond the end of the current session.

The roles record variables play in a UWA are taken over by **user-variables** and **user records** in dialogue mode only to the extent that they can carry input values for FIND commands (like a CALC-key value); outputs of FIND commands, however, always go to the SRF. On the other hand, these variables and records can be used to realize new functions, like the modification of the structure of some record-type or its temporary renaming.

When dialogue mode is chosen, the DBH is replaced by the Independent DBH, which is able to manage several databases simultaneously, and which supervises all database activities. It also 'talks' to the DBA regarding error messages, receiving of instructions, and the like.

Before a user can start working, the DBA has to initiate a **session** (denoting the time from the first starting of the DBH with a particular database configuration until a normal termination of the session) using the utility *C.SYSINT*, thereby determining the load parameters for the DBH. During a session, the DBA can use DAL commands to instruct the DBH in various ways and can thus control the proceedings of a session. In particular, the DAL command 'INTR CLOSe RUN-units' terminates a currently ongoing session in a normal way. If a session is not terminated normally, such as when the system crashes, an extensive saving is performed, which depends on the choice of load parameters, so that a consistent database state can be restored for a restart of the session.

If the DBA has started the session for a particular database configuration, users can access their subschemas via IQS. The general form of an IQS session is as follows:

Calling of the procedure to start IQS,
IQS initiation dialogue;
IQS transactions (arbitrarily many);
END

Each such session is restricted to work with exactly one schema of the database, whose name <subschema-name> is requested in the initiation dialogue. In addition, IQS checks the exact combination of user name, user group, password and subschema name during this dialogue, based on the access rights granted by the DBA. A user without the appropriate access right is rejected. After termination of an IQS session through 'END', all temporary result files and declarations are deleted.

Basically, two kinds of IQS 'transactions' are distinguished, those with and those without the option to perform updates. A *transaction*, a term that will be explained in more detail in Chapter 18, denotes a sequence of instructions that leaves the database in a consistent state if applied to a state that is consistent and that is considered as a (semantic) unit, which means that a transaction is either executed completely or not at all. The concept of a transaction also applies to database accesses from an application program. So, for both dialogue and batch mode, provisions have to be made to ensure that distinct users do not interfere with each other. To this end, a transaction is 'encapsulated' by commands marking its beginning and end, respectively (and it is processed in a specific way).

A transaction *without* modify option is initiated by START, followed by arbitrarily many IQL commands, but excluding those which imply data modifications (that is, MODIFY, CANCEL, DELETE, STORE, DISCONNECT and CONNECT, see below). The transaction is terminated by STOP. All declarations entered during this transaction are then preserved; they are deleted at the end of the IQL session.

Transactions *with* modify option begin with START UPDATE, followed by arbitrarily many IQL commands without exceptions. Any such transaction can be terminated either by STOP UPDATE or by CANCEL UPDATE, where for the latter version all modifications made by this transaction on database items are reset (undone). For both ways of termination, all records that are protected against an access by another user after the execution of a modifying command are made available again.

The protection just mentioned is achieved through the use of the command

READY <areaname> ... USAGE MODE is
    [{ PROTECTED | EXCLUSIVE }]
    { RETRIEVAL | UPDATE }

which (logically) opens an area for a particular transaction and simultaneously locks it for all other users whose types of access are 'incompatible'. The following table shows for each of the six possible protection modes which usage modes of other users *are* compatible:

USAGE MODE	USAGE MODEs allowed for others
RETRIEVAL	all but EXCLUSIVE
UPDATE	all but EXCLUSIVE or PROTECTED
PROTECTED RETRIEVAL	RETRIEVAL, PROTECTED RETRIEVAL
PROTECTED UPDATE	RETRIEVAL
EXCLUSIVE RETRIEVAL	none
EXCLUSIVE UPDATE	none

14.5.1 The FIND command of IQS

The FIND command basically has the function that has been discussed previously in this text, where navigation under IQS proceeds 'file-wise' (see also COBOL DML FIND, Format 7 above); the same applies to the GET command discussed in the next subsection, which is now called DISPLAY. A combination of FIND and GET functions is once more provided by the

FETCH command, so that it is not necessary to distinguish FIND from FETCH. Three different formats are available for the **FIND** command, which will be discussed next:

FIND Format 1: (FIND from the database)

FIND { <record-type-name> | <userrecord> }
[IF <condition>] ...

Here, a user record can be composed in the following way:

userrecord:

{ <attribute-name> | <user-variable> | <statement> }, ...

In general, the attributes used can be denoted either by <attribute-name> or by <record-type-name.attribute-name> (for example, if equal names are used in different declarations to achieve uniqueness).

<user-variable> denotes a user variable that was previously declared using the LET command; as with all names used under IQS, no 'reserved words' may be employed.

statement:

<name> = { <expression> | <literal> | <attribute-name> |
<user-variable> }

With this assignment a new name can be introduced in a user record.

literal: { <string> |[+|−] <number> }

A string consists of up to 253 arbitrary symbols which must be included in quotes (and where the quote itself is disallowed within the string).

number: { <integer> [.[<integer>]]|. <integer> }

A number may be up to 15 digits long, where a sign is counted as a digit.

expression: [{+|−}] <subexpr> [[{+|−}] <subexpr>] ...

subexpr: <factor> [[{*|/}] <factor>] ...

factor:

{(<expression>)| <number> | [<record-type-name> .]
<attribute-name> | <user-variable> }

In this letter declaration, the attribute name or the user variable has to denote a numerical attribute.

By using a <condition>, certain records of a record type can be selected; again attention is restricted here to those language elements that refer to elementary attributes. All attributes occurring in a <condition>

must belong to a record-type; they are processed from left to right, and the use of parentheses is allowed.

condition: <condterm> [OR <condterm>]

condterm: <condfac> [AND <condfac>]

condfac: [NOT] { <condition> | <comparecond> }

comparecond:

{ <unknown> <compop> <known>
| <known> <compop> <unknown> }

unknown:

{ [<record-type-name>.] <attribute-name> | <user-variable> }

known: { <literal> | <user-variable> }

compop: {< | LT | LE | = | EQ | GE | GT | > | NE }

For the values to be compared all values have to be of the same type. In addition, the comparison value must not be longer than the value searched for (but it may contain the standard mask symbol '#' which prevents a particular position from being compared).

The following IQS examples refer to the university database whose schema was declared in Section 14.2.

Example 14.1

(a) Locate all course records: `FIND COURSE`

(b) Locate all courses on calculus:

```
FIND COURSE IF CNAME = 'CALCULUS'
```

(c) Locate all students' names with corresponding cities:

```
FIND SNAME, S-CITY
```

FIND Format 2: (FIND from a result file)

FIND {*| <userrecord>}[{ OF | FROM }] FILE
[<filename>][IF<condition> ...]

If <filename> is missing, this FIND command will refer to the SRF. '*' means that all records of the 'target type' are output.

Example 14.2

(a) Locate all students living in Aachen:

```
FIND STUDENT
FIND * FILE IF S-CITY = 'AACHEN'
```

(b) Store all student from Aachen in an auxiliary file and locate their IDs:

```
FIND STUDENT IF S-CITY = 'AACHEN'
KEEP S-FILE
FIND STUDID FROM FILE S-FILE
```

FIND Format 3: (FIND from a fixname)

FIND {*| <userrecord>} [{ OF | FROM }] Fix-Names <fixname>

Here, <fixname> is the name for a record selected using the FIX command (<userrecord> must be contained in this record).

Example 14.3

Select a <fixname> for course no. CS176 and locate the corresponding course name:

```
FIX F176 OF COURSE IF CNO = CS176
FIND CNAME FN F176
```

14.5.2 The DISPLAY command

For the **DISPLAY** command ('GET'), again three formats are distinguished for displaying results on a terminal:

DISPLAY Format 1: (DISPLAY from the database)

DISplay {<record-type-name> | <userrecord>}
[IF <condition>] ...

Example 14.4

Print the number of each calculus course:

```
DISPLAY COURSE.CNO IF CNAME = 'CALCULUS'
```

DISPLAY Format 2: (DISPLAY from a result file)

DISplay {*| <userrecord>}[, <aggregate> ...]
[{OF | FROM }] FILE [<filename>][IF <condition> ...]
[SORTED BY <sortexpr> [NO-DUPlicates]]
[GROUPED BY <groupexpr>]

(NO-DUP is allowed only if the command begins with DISPLAY ∗.)

aggregate:

[<name-1 >=]{ SUM | MINimum | MAXimum | AVeraGe }
({<name-2 > | <attribute-name> | <user-variable>})

The result produced by the aggregate function chosen is shown under the name <name-1>; all names occurring in parentheses must refer to attributes with numerical values, where <name-2> has to be a name declared in the previous statement of <userrecord>.

sortexpr:

{<attribute-name> | <user-variable>}, ...
[{ ASCending | DESCending }]

It is first sorted according to the first attribute specified; if these values are equal, it is then sorted according to the second, and so on (a repetition of attributes is not allowed); a sorting in ascending order is the default.

groupexpr: <sortfield> [, <sortfield> [, <sortfield>]]

sortfield: {<attribute-name> | <user-variable>}

First, groups are formed according to the first attribute specified; then subgroups are formed within these groups according to the second attribute specified, and so on.

Example 14.5

Print the smallest student ID:

```
FIND STUDENT
DISPLAY MIN(STUDID) FROM FILE
```

DISPLAY Format 3: (DISPLAY from a fixname)

DISplay {∗| <userrecord>}[{ OF | FROM }] Fix-Names <fixname>

Example 14.6

Choose a fixname for course CS176 and print the corresponding record:

```
FIX F176 OF COURSE IF CNO = CS176
DIS FN F176
```

14.5.3 Preparatory commands for FIND and DISPLAY

The **LET** command

LET <user-variable>=
{<expression> | <literal> | <areaname> | <name> |
<set-type-name> | <record-type-name> |
<attribute-name>}

is used for declaring user variables, where <name> must have already been defined in a previous LET command. A user variable defined in this way is reserved until the end of the current IQS session, unless it is deleted by a DROP command (see below).

If it is desired to address records of distinct types in one command, the user can (first) specify in a **selection structure** command which relationships have to exist between these types. Hence, the current selection structure influences the execution of the FIND, DISPLAY, STORE, MODIFY and DELETE commands.

selection structure:

Selection-Structure= {<record-type-name-1 > |
<set-type-name>, <record-type-name-1 >}
[, [{<joinexpr> | <set-type-name>},]
<record-type-name-2 >] ...

'<set-type-name>, <record-type-name-1 >' may follow the equality sign only if <record-type-name-1 > is member-type of the set-type <set-type-name> and SYSTEM is the owner-type. In general, <record-type-name-2> must stand in a set relationship to the preceding <record-type-name-1> (if several such relationships exist, one of them must be chosen by the preceding <set-type-name>), unless the connection is established through a <joinexpr>. In addition, at most eight record-type names may occur, where each distinct record- or set-type name may appear at most once, and 'SYSTEM' is not allowed. The various record type names should be ordered in such a way that types for which the expected number of records determined by a subsequent command is small appear close to the beginning.

joinexpr:

{<attribute-name-1 > | <user-variable-1 >}
= {<attribute-name-2 > | <user-variable-2 >}

In a join expression,

<attribute-name-1> [<user-variable-1>]

always refers to the preceding record-type name, while

<attribute-name-2> [<uservariable-2>]

refers to the succeeding one, respectively.

Example 14.7

(a) Print all courses given by professors (in the ordering in which *PROFESSOR* records occur):

```
SS = PROFESSOR, COURSE
DISPLAY COURSE
```

('*PROFESSOR*' is chosen as an entry point into the database; therefore, the set occurrence corresponding to the first entry in *PROFESSOR* is listed first, followed by the one corresponding to the second entry, and so on.)

(b) Print all professors giving courses:

```
SS = PROFESSOR, COURSE
DIS PROFESSOR
```

(the selection structure selects only those professors who give a course); similarly:

```
SS = COURSE, PROFESSOR
DIS PROFESSOR
```

(now, however, professors giving several courses will be listed many times, and their ordering is dependent on that for the entries in record type *COURSE*).

(c) Print the name of each course which student Miller attends:

```
SS = COURSE, S-C, STUDENT
DISPLAY CNAME IF SNAME = 'Miller'
```

(the selection structure selects those courses which are attended by students).

(d) Print the name of each course which at least one student attends, in alphabetical order:

```
SS = COURSE, S-C, STUDENT
FIND CNAME
DISPLAY * FILE SORTED BY CNAME NO-DUP
```

(without 'NO-DUP' each course name is listed several times depending on the number of attendants).

(e) Print the name of each student who takes a course from Professor Miller:

```
SS = STUDENT, S-C, COURSE, PROFESSOR
FIND SNAME IF PNAME = 'MILLER'
DIS * FILE SORTED BY SNAME NO-DUP
```

(the selection structure establishes the desired connection between *PROFESSOR* and *STUDENT*).

A selection structure will remain in effect until the end of the current IQS session, unless it is modified by another such command, or it is deleted by a DROP command.

The **DROP** command erases the declarations made by a LET or a Selection-Structure command:

DROP {<user-variable> | Selection-Structure }

The **FIX** command identifies a single selected record with a so-called FIX name:

FIX <fixname> { OF | FROM } <record-type-name>
    [WITH <selection-structure>]
    [IF <condition> ...]

<fixname> may be up to eight symbols long. The FIX command can only be used if exactly one record gets selected (fixnames are particularly useful in connection with STORE, CONNECT, or DISCONNECT commands). Up to 10 fixnames may be used simultaneously, which all remain in effect until the end of the current transaction.

14.5.4 Processing commands for result files

Using the **SORT** command, result files can be sorted and/or duplicates can be removed:

SORT FILE [<filename>] [BY <sortexpr>][NO-DUPlicates]

Results of a FIND or a DISPLAY command can be saved in a temporary or permanent result file using the **KEEP** command, which also serves to retain an appropriate area lock; permanent result files can be processed further outside an IQS session:

KEEP [{ STANDARD | <filename>} WITHIN] <name>
    [{ TEMPorary | PERManent }]

Under '<name>' the name of the SRF or of an already existing temporary result file <filename> is saved, where STANDARD is the default value (indicated above by the underlining), that is, 'KEEP <name>' is equivalent to 'KEEP STANDARD WITHIN <name>'.

If this name is the name of an already existing file, its contents are overwritten without comment (both for permanent as well as for temporary result files). In addition, the following apply:

(1) TEMP is the default type of the new result file.

(2) If the SRF is saved, it will afterwards be empty.

(3) STANDARD is not allowed as the name of the new result file. Apart from this, temporary [permanent] names are up to 8 [41] symbols long (excluding special characters), respectively, where the operating-system conventions for file names have to be observed and the name may not be qualified with a user identification.

In total, up to eight temporary result files may exist simultaneously. Any such file can be deleted using the **FREE** command:

FREE <filename>

14.5.5 Update commands

As was mentioned already, update commands are only allowed within transactions with update option. In order to store a record in a database, the **STORE** command is available, which can have one of two formats:

STORE Format 1:

STORE <record-type-name> [IN <areaname>]
WITH <modifyexpr> [IF <condition> ...]

Example 14.8

'Store professor Miller's data':

```
STORE PROFESSOR WITH PNO = 'P1', PNAME = 'MILLER'
P-ORT = 'SAN DIEGO'
```

STORE Format 2:

STORE <record-type-name> [IN <areaname>]
WITH <modifyexpr>
WITH <set-type-name> { OF | FROM } <fixname> [, ...]

Here, <set-type-name> denotes the set-type into which the corresponding record is to be inserted (this type must be declared as AUTOMATIC), and <fixname> denotes the owner record into whose set occurrence it is inserted. In general, the following hold:

(1) If the record type <record-type-name> is not AUTOMATIC member in any set-type, only Format 1 may be used, but no <condition> may be specified, and only literals may be assigned within the <modifyexpr>; in addition, no multi-stage selection structure may exist.

(2) If the record-type <record-type-name> is AUTOMATIC member in exactly one set-type, both formats can be used. If Format 1 is used, however, a SELECTION STRUCTURE without <joinexpr> must exist, in which <record-type-name> is the last and the name of the owner-type is the last but one entry. In addition, the selection structure together with the <condition>s must determine the owner record uniquely in this case.

(3) If the record type <record-type-name> is AUTOMATIC member in several set types, Format 2 has to be used, and for each of these set types the <set-type-name> and a <fixname> must be specified, so that the record to be stored can be inserted into all applicable set occurrences.

Example 14.9

Use of fixnames:

```
FIX C1 FROM COURSE IF COURSE.CNO = CS176
FIX S2 FROM STUDENT IF STUDENT.STUDID = U145
STORE S-C WITH CNO = CS176, STUDID = U145
WITH ATTENDS OF S2, WITH IS_ATTENDED OF C1
```

All records newly inserted into a database with a STORE command are available for other users after the end of the current transaction only (after the corresponding locks have been released).

If individual attribute values of a record are to be updated, the **MODIFY** command can be used:

MODify <record-type-name> WITH <modifyexpr>
[IF <condition> ...]

modifyexpr:

{<attribute-name> | <user-variable>} =
{<expression> | <literal> |[<record-type-name> .]
<attribute-name> | <user-variable>}[, ...]

The records of type <record-type-name>, which are selected through the selection structure, and the <condition>s are updated according to <modifyexpr>. Upon completion of this command, the SRF will be empty.

Records without members can be erased using the **DELETE** command:

DELete <record-type-name> [IF <condition> ...]

(Again, the SRF will be empty after this command has been executed.)

If a member record is to be connected to its corresponding owner record, the **CONNECT** command is used; once again, two formats are distinguished:

CONNECT Format 1:

COnnect <record-type-name> WITH <set-type-name>
[IF <condition> ...]

Record type <record-type-name> must be member-type in the set-type <set-type-name>, where this set-type is not allowed to be declared as MANDATORY AUTOMATIC. The two records to be connected must be determined uniquely by the <condition>.

Example 14.10

Use of CONNECT:

```
CONNECT COURSE WITH TEACHES IF PNO = 'P1'
IF COURSE.CNO = CS176
```

CONNECT Format 2:

COnnect <fixname-1 > WITH <set-type-name> { OF | FROM }
<fixname-2 > [, ...]

<fixname-1> must denote a member record which is to be connected with the owner record <fixname-2> of the set-type <set-type-name> (or with several owners). A selection structure has no effect on a CONNECT command.

For separating a member record from its owner record the **DISCONNECT** command is available:

DISCONNECT Format 1:

DisConnect <record-type-name> { OF | FROM } <set-type-name>
[IF <condition> ...]

The <condition>s must uniquely determine the member record to be disconnected; the set-type <set-type-name> must not be declared as MANDATORY.

DISCONNECT Format 2:

DisConnect <fixname> { OF | FROM } <set-type-name> [, ...]

Now <fixname> determines the member record to be separated. Again, a selection structure will be without effect.

14.5.6 Further IQL commands

Of the IQL commands SET, DEFINE, SHOW, PRINT, TARGET, CONTINUE and ABORT which have not yet been described, only the **SHOW** command is presented below. This can be used to query the system for various information. This command is known in the following five different formats:

Format 1:

SHOW CoMmanDS	shows a list of all IQL commands

Format 2:

SHOW CoMmanD <iql-command>	explains the syntax of the IQL command specified, and illustrates its use by way of an example

Format 3:

SHOW Selection-Structure	shows which selection structure is declared
SHOW VARIABLES	shows the user variables defined
SHOW <user-variable>	shows the assignment for this user variable
SHOW FILES	shows the temporary result files
SHOW FILE [<filename>]	shows type and structure of the result file <filename> or of the SRF, respectively
SHOW CommanDnames	indicates under what names certain commands are stored (see Section 14.5.7)
SHOW Fix-Names	shows the <fixname>s in use

Format 4:

SHOW RECORDTYPES	shows all record-types defined
SHOW SETS	shows all set-types defined
SHOW SETS {OF | FROM} <record-type-name>	shows all set-types in which the record-type <record-type-name> is owner- or member-type

Format 5:

SHOW {<record-type-name>	shows the definition
| <set-type-name>	of the database item specified
| <attribute-name>}	

14.5.7 Storing IQL commands

IQL automatically stores the last command that has been issued, upon completion of its execution, as the 'current' command. Any such command can be stored permanently using

WRIte-Command <command-name>

under an arbitrary name (consisting of up to eight symbols). A stored command is displayed using

REAd-Command [<command-name>]

and displayed and executed using

RUN-Command [<command-name>]

(if <command-name> is missing, these instructions will refer to the current command). Using

REMove-Command <command-name>

the command saved under <command-name> is deleted; otherwise, it will remain saved until the IQL session ends.

If commands are to be stored beyond the end of an IQS session, they have to be collected in command sequences and then stored as operating-system files. Such sequences can be created using either IQL commands or an editor.

From IQS, in particular the BS2000 editor EDT can be invoked using '$ EDT' (for example, for writing or modifying a command sequence), without interrupting the currently running transaction; a return to the IQS dialogue is achieved by HALT. Within a command sequence each individual command must be ended by a semicolon. The execution of a sequence stored in a file named <filename> is initiated by the command

RUN-Command-Sequence <filename>

Chapter 15
The Hierarchical System IMS (IBM)

This chapter returns to the hierarchical data model and briefly discusses the **IMS** database management system based on it, which was developed by IBM in the 1960s. **IMS** (Information Management System) was one of the first database systems that reached the market and is still in wide use today. But because its overall importance in the field is decreasing nowadays, only the basic steps for working with an IMS database will be given in this chapter.

In the following it is assumed that a given application is described as a logical hierarchy or a logical forest; also, for each record-type involved, it is assumed that its attributes are known. As an example, consider a slight modification of the university application known from Part II or Chapter 14, which is shown in Figure 15.1.

Logical record types are called **segments** under IMS, and sometimes also **segment types**; correspondingly, the physical records or segments that exist for a given type form a **segment occurrence**.

In order to define the conceptual schema of a hierarchical database, a **Data Base Description** (DBD) has to be written first, using macros from the IBM/370 assembler (hence, this latter language represents, in a sense, the 'DDL' of IMS). Next, this DBD is compiled, and corresponding entries are made in a system library ('dictionary').

For the above example, a corresponding DBD could look as follows:

```
1  DBD   NAME = UNIVDBD
2  SEGM  NAME = COURSE, BYTES = 35
3  FIELD NAME = (CNO, SEQ), BYTES = 6, START = 1
4  FIELD NAME = CTITLE, BYTES = 20, START = 7
5  FIELD NAME = PLACE, BYTES = 3, START = 27
6  FIELD NAME = TIME, BYTES = 6, START = 30
7  SEGM  NAME = PROF, PARENT = COURSE, BYTES = 46
8  FIELD NAME = (PNO, SEQ), BYTES = 6, START = 1
9  FIELD NAME = PNAME, BYTES = 40, START = 7
10 SEGM  NAME = STUDENT, PARENT = COURSE, BYTES = 106
11 FIELD NAME = (STUDID, SEQ), BYTES = 6, START = 1
12 FIELD NAME = SNAME, BYTES = 40, START = 7
13 FIELD NAME = ADDR, BYTES = 60, START = 47
```

In Line 1, the description is given a name (of up to eight characters). Line 2 declares the root segment type, which is given the name *COURSE* and for which an overall length of 35 bytes is specified; this

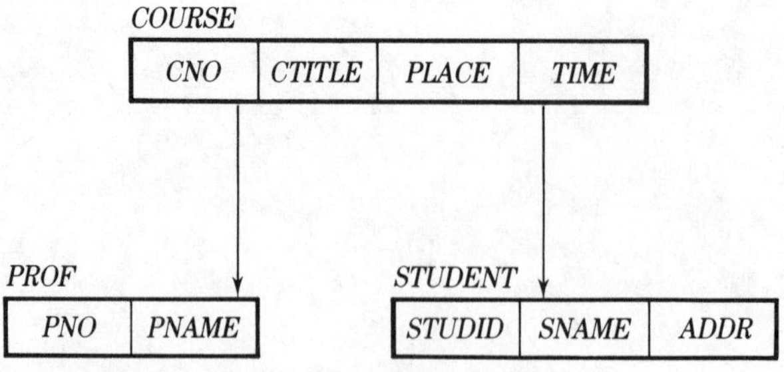

Figure 15.1 A university application.

length represents the sum of the lengths of its attributes (similarly for *PROF* and *STUDENT*). In Lines 3-6 these attributes are introduced; each one consists of a name, a length (in bytes) and a starting position (byte number) within the segment. Attribute *CNO* additionally has the *SEQ option*, which means that each *COURSE* occurrence will be stored sorted according to increasing *CNO* values (similarly for *PNO* and *STUDID*). In Line 7 the segment type *PROF* is declared as a (first) son of *COURSE*. All further lines have similar contents and therefore need no additional explanation.

For implementing such a 'logical database' (LDB) in a 'physical database' (PDB), IMS can internally utilize four different 'data structures', which are the standard file organization and access methods provided by the OS/VS operating system:

SAM: Sequential Access Method
ISAM: Indexed SAM
VSAM: Virtual Storage Access Method
OSAM: Overflow SAM

The routines or 'access methods' provided by IMS from a user's point of view for these structures, which are

HSAM: Hierarchical Sequential Access Method (for SAM)
HISAM: Hierarchical Indexed SAM (for I/O/V SAM)
HDAM: Hierarchical Direct Access Method (for O/V SAM)
HIDAM: Hierarchical Indexed DAM (for O/V SAM)

are first chosen at design time, and are then internally mapped to the corresponding VS file-organization form.

The IMS DML **DL/I** (Data Language/One) can be used from various host languages, like PL/I, COBOL or /370 assembly language. In any case, the corresponding application program operates on 'its' LDB, which is a section (view) from the global LDB. For purposes of communication with IMS, it must contain one or more **program communication blocks** (PCBs), which are combined into a **program specification block** (PSB) for a user. Each PCB describes a segment type needed by the application program or a section from a logical hierarchy. When an application program is executed, the PSB as well as the corresponding DBD must be in main memory, which is required for DL/I being able to correctly perform all database accesses requested by the program.

The DML statements of DL/I mentioned in Chapter 6 in general consist of a keyword followed by one or more search conditions, the 'Segment Search Arguments' (SSAs). The basic possibilities of data manipulation with DL/I are described next, where the university example is used again:

(1) *Direct access to records:*
'Fetch the first student named Joel':

```
GU COURSE
STUDENT (SNAME = 'Joel')
```

This GU command contains two SSAs; the first is without an additional condition, while the second is equipped with one.

(2) *Sequential access to records with unconditional SSA*:
'Fetch all students currently attending a course':

```
   GU COURSE STUDENT
1  GN STUDENT
   goto 1
```

with conditional SSA:
'Fetch all students living in San Diego currently attending a course':

```
   GU COURSE STUDENT (ADDR = 'San Diego')
1  GN STUDENT (ADDR = 'San Diego')
   goto 1
```

with multi-conditional SSA:
'Fetch all students living in San Diego currently attending a course in room PH110':

```
   GU COURSE (PLACE = 'PH110')
   STUDENT (ADDR = 'San Diego')
1  GN COURSE (PLACE = 'PH110')
   STUDENT (ADDR = 'San Diego')
   goto 1
```

without SSA:
'Fetch all segments of the database':

```
   GU COURSE
1  GN
   goto 1
```

within the father with SSA:
'Fetch all students of course CS176':

```
   GU COURSE (CNO = 'CS176')
1  GNP STUDENT
   goto 1
```

within the father without SSA:
'Fetch all son records (eventually over a different type) of course CS176':

```
   GU COURSE (CNO = 'CS176')
1  GNP
   goto 1
```

(3) *Insertion of a new segment:*
Before a new record can be inserted, the corresponding father must exist already, unless the new record is a root. Next, the insert command must contain a complete path to this father together with the type of the segment to be inserted. IMS will then insert the record into the correct position according to the SEQ information specified in the DBD.
'Insert a new student into the occurrence of course CS176':

```
(* Assembly of the STUDENT segment in the I/O area *)
ISRT COURSE (CNO = 'CS176') STUDENT
```

(4) *Deletion of a segment:*
'Delete course PS103':

```
GHU COURSE (CNO = 'PS103')
DLET
```

Note that DLET does not have an SSA (the same applies to REPL). If the segment to be deleted has sons, these will be deleted as well.

(5) *Update of a segment:*
'For student Joel attending CS176, modify his address to Kearny Mesa':

```
GHU COURSE (CNO = 'CS176')
STUDENT (SNAME = 'Joel')
(* Update of ADDR to 'Kearny Mesa' in the I/O area *)
REPL
```

Here it is important to note that an SEQ attribute cannot be modified by REPL, but only by DLET followed by ISRT; the modification of an SEQ attribute corresponds to the modification of a CALC key in the network model, which can also be accomplished by a deletion followed by a re-insertion (in a different place) only.

Chapter 14 touched briefly on transactions, an issue important to any DBMS. This chapter will be concluded with a brief introduction to another DBMS-internal issue — *recovery from failures* — which will be returned to in Chapter 19.

As with any complex software or hardware system, occasional error situations cannot be ruled out entirely. These can arise from a variety of sources, and it is among the responsibilities of a DBMS to be prepared for them. In particular, a DBMS must always keep enough information so that a recovery from an error situation can easily be performed. To this end, it is first necessary to make *backup copies* of the entire database under consideration from time to time. In IMS, this function is provided by the **image copy utility** (ICU), where an **image copy** is simply a block-for-block copy of a set of segments that is written to 'safe' secondary storage, that is, a tape. It should be noted that this utility does not perform any integrity checking; a successful termination only indicates that no I/O errors occurred during its execution.

Once a backup copy has been made, application programs can access the database. If these change the contents of the database, a record is kept of these updates in the form of *before* and *after images* of the corresponding segment, that is, if a segment is updated, its old and new values are entered into a set of **log segments**. Log information also includes changes in free-space information as insertions and deletions are performed, or information on how pointers used for segment addressing have changed. Clearly, it makes sense to keep log data on tape too, since a disk might, for example, be destroyed by a bad read/write head.

IMS applies the principle of 'log-tape write-ahead', which can be characterized as follows. If a database is changed by an application program, these changes are first made to a copy of the segments in question that is kept in a *system buffer*, that is, an area in main memory reserved for portions of the database; a separate buffer is additionally available for log information. Next, before updated segments are transferred from the buffer into the database (that is, back to disk), log information is written to the log buffer, so that this buffer is generally more up-to-date than the database itself. If an error occurs while a program accesses a database, a *recovery utility* is employed for restoring the state recorded in the last backup, which uses the ICU for copying database images. Next, the changes that had been made after the backup was taken can be reinstated using the log segments, so that a re-execution of the corresponding application programs is not necessary. Clearly, this approach might require a large number of log segments to be kept. In order to reduce these efforts, the **change accumulation utility** can be used. This utility reads the log segments created by application program updates and produces a 'summary' of these on a block-for-block basis. As a result, only the very latest changes to a particular segment need to be retained. Also, the recovery utility can 'merge' the image copy and the change accumulation records and then apply the information found in the latest log tape.

Chapter 16
The Relational SQL/Data System (IBM)

This chapter introduces **SQL/DS**, a prototypical realization of a database system based on the relational model, which features a version of the standard relational language **SQL**. SQL/DS is a relational system for mainframes running under DOS/VSE, VM/SP or VM/XA. It became commercially available in 1981 and Version 2 has been available since 1987.

16.1 Data definition

In this section, the central aspects regarding the declaration of relation schemas under SQL/DS are discussed; these include attributes and their data types, the allowance of null values, primary and foreign keys, indexes, aliases and access rights. Every such declaration is stored in the data dictionary of the system, which is briefly described at the end of the section.

When describing the SQL syntax, basically the same conventions are used as in Chapter 14, with the following simplification. Identifiers which can be chosen by the user, or parts of the language that are explained in a different place, are no longer included in '<, >', since a confusion with SQL keywords is impossible. As before, an underlined keyword represents a default value and hence goes into effect if an explicit specification is omitted.

16.1.1 Creating base tables

Under SQL/DS, the notion of a database schema as introduced in Chapter 7 and used in the subsequent chapters does not exist. Thus, there is no way to refer to a collection of relation schemas under a common name; instead, a set of relation schemas representing a particular application can only be 'tied together' implicitly (via the names of users who created or are allowed to use them, or by associating them with the same logical storage unit called a 'dbspace'). A relation schema consists of a name, a set of attributes with domains, an optional primary key and one or more optional foreign keys expressing key-based inclusion dependencies. A corresponding relation is called a **base table** or simply a **table**. SQL/DS does not distinguish a separate 'data definition phase'; instead, DDL and DML can be used in arbitrary sequencing. The following command creates a schema as well as an empty relation over it:

```
CREATE TABLE table-name
    ( column-name-1 type-1 [ NOT NULL [ WITH DEFAULT ] ]
    [, column-name-2 type-2 [ NOT NULL [ WITH DEFAULT ] ]
    ... ]
    [, PRIMARY KEY ( column-name-list ) ]
    [, FOREIGN KEY [ fk-name ] ( column-name-list )
        REFERENCES other-table-name
        [ON DELETE { RESTRICT | CASCADE | SET NULL }]
    [, FOREIGN KEY ... ]] )
[IN dbspace-name]
```

Here, table-name is the name under which the table can later be used; it has to begin with a letter, $, # or @ and can be up to 18 symbols long. Each column-name denotes an attribute of this table, each type the corresponding domain. For attribute names, the same convention as for table names applies.

16.1.2 Data types

The following data types are available as domains:

INTeger	for integers between −2 147 483 647 and +2 147 483 647
SMALLINT	for integers between −32 767 and +32 767
DECimal(m, n)	for m-digit floating-point numbers ($m \leq 15$) with n digits following the decimal point, $0 \leq n \leq m$
FLOAT(n)	for single ($n < 21$) or double-precision ($n < 54$) floating-point numbers in the interval 5.4E−79 to 7.2E+75
CHARacter(n)	for strings of fixed length $n \leq 254$
VARCHARacter(n)	for strings of variable length $n \leq 32\ 767$
LONG VARCHARacter	for strings of variable length with up to 32 767 symbols
DATE	for defining a date column
TIME	for defining a time column
TIMESTAMP	for defining a timestamp column

For decimal data types, default values go into effect if either n or both m and n are omitted; for example, DEC(3) and DEC(3,0) or DEC and DEC(5,0) are equivalent. For CHAR types, if n is omitted the default $n = 1$ is assumed.

The difference between VARCHAR and LONG VARCHAR is that for the former a variable number of bytes is reserved for storing a value, which depends on the number n specified, while for the latter 32 767 bytes will be reserved for each value independent of how long it actually is.

The date and time data types, which collectively refer to DATE, TIME and TIMESTAMP, come with corresponding operations and ('scalar') functions and allow users to define, manipulate and operate on data of any of these types. These types will first be described in more detail; the major functions that can be applied to them are discussed in Section 16.4 in connection with the SELECT statement.

A **date** is a value of the form '*yyyymmdd*' (year followed by month and day), where years range from 0001 to 9999, months from 1 to 12, and days from 1 to a number between 28 and 31 (depending on the month and, for February, also on the year). A **time** is a value of the form '*hhmmss*' (hour followed by minutes and seconds), where hours range from 0 to 24 (a range from 0 to 12 for US standard time can also be used), and minutes and seconds from 0 to 59. As a combination and extension of date and time, a **timestamp** is a value of the form '*yyyymmddhhmmssnnnnnn*' (year followed by month, day, hour, minutes, seconds and microseconds), where the ranges are as above.

In addition to the types listed above, graphical symbols can be stored using one of the three GRAPHIC data types, which are not discussed here.

SQL/DS supports *null values* in database relations; a null value ('?') is used, for example, if a value for some attribute is missing in a tuple, or if no value is applicable. Each column of a table can carry null values, unless the corresponding attributes have been declared as NOT NULL. This option is particularly useful for the attributes of a primary key. If a column is defined using the NOT NULL WITH DEFAULT option, which goes into effect whenever a new tuple is inserted into the corresponding table, a numeric attribute is set to 0, a fixed-length string is set to blank, and a varying-length string is set to be a string of length 0.

16.1.3 Schema modifications

A relation schema which has already been defined can be extended at any time. The command

```
ALTER TABLE [creator.] table-name
    ADD column-name data-type
```

will append *one* new attribute to an already existing table; this column is initialized with null values. There also exist several other versions of the ALTER TABLE command which will be explained below in the appropriate places. Only users whose names have been made known to the system by the database administrator can create, modify or delete tables. Internally, each table name is stored with a prefix showing its creator's name; the table itself is logically stored in a 'private' storage area called **dbspace**, which resembles the function of an area in a network system. If a user operates on tables that he or she has created, it is not necessary to specify the creator's name. However, if the user works with tables created by someone else, this extension is required. The command

```
DROP TABLE table-name
```

will delete both the contents and the schema of a table.

The converse process of dropping attributes from an existing table is slightly more complicated since no separate command is available. The idea is to create an auxiliary table first which no longer contains the attributes to be deleted, but apart from this is identical to the original table; the name of the intermediate table must be unique, since a table name may be used at most once. Next, the data is copied from the old to the auxiliary table by

```
INSERT INTO auxiliary-table SELECT select-list FROM original
```

(see Section 16.2). In the *select-list* of this statement, all attributes to be retained have to be listed; that is, here is where the actual deletion is performed (by specifying an appropriate projection). Next, the original table is deleted by DROP TABLE, and a new one is created that has the old name and whose format is identical to that of the auxiliary table. Finally, another command of the form 'INSERT ... SELECT' is used to transfer the (remaining) data back to this new table, and the intermediate one can be deleted.

16.1.4 Integrity constraints

Through the PRIMARY KEY clause, a (primary) key in the sense of Chapter 7 can be declared, which consists of one or more attributes that are declared in this table definition as NOT NULL. The system will then automatically create an index over the key attributes, no two entries of which will ever be equal (an index having this property is said to be *unique*). Alternatively, the definition of a primary key can later be added to a table declaration using

```
ALTER TABLE table-name
      ADD PRIMARY KEY ( column-name-list )
```

It can also be dropped dynamically using

```
ALTER TABLE table-name DROP PRIMARY KEY
```

In addition to key dependencies, SQL/DS supports key-based inclusion dependencies (in the sense of Section 7.3) or *foreign keys*, which reference the primary key of an already declared relation schema other than the one in which the declaration occurs (self-references are not allowed), and which may be named. Clearly, the cardinality of a foreign key must equal that of the referenced key, and the attributes of both must be pairwise type-compatible. Foreign keys can alternatively be added to an already existing table declaration via

```
ALTER TABLE table-name
   ADD FOREIGN KEY [ fk-name ] ( column-name )
      REFERENCES other-table-name
      [ON DELETE { RESTRICT | CASCADE | SET NULL }]
```

They can also be dropped using

ALTER TABLE table-name DROP fkname

The ON DELETE clause of a foreign-key declaration defines a *delete rule* for the referenced table with respect to that foreign key. The three possible options have the following meaning:

(1) RESTRICT: A deletion of tuples from the referenced table is executed only if no tuples exist in the referencing table which correspond to those to be deleted.

(2) CASCADE: A deletion of tuples from the referenced table implies a deletion of all corresponding tuples from the referencing table.

(3) SET NULL: A deletion of tuples from the referenced table does not imply a deletion of the corresponding tuples from the referencing table, but the attributes in question are set to null (if allowed).

These rules have several implications for the construction of 'chains' of foreign keys. If two or more tables are connected through foreign keys in a cyclic fashion, the corresponding sequence of delete rules must be interrupted at least once by RESTRICT. Also, if a table is connected to another via several 'foreign-key paths', the final edge on every path must have the same delete option, which must not be SET NULL.

With respect to insertions, foreign keys have the following effect. If table R has a foreign key referencing the primary key of table S, that is, $R[FK] \subseteq S[PK]$, an insertion into R is rejected if the new values for the attributes in question are not already present in S.

16.1.5 Indexes

Keys can also be declared implicitly. To this end and primarily for the purpose of speeding up accesses to frequently referenced attributes, indexes are available, which can be created or deleted at any time using the following commands:

```
CREATE [UNIQUE] INDEX index-name
    ON table-name (column-name-1 [ ASC | DESC]
        [, column-name-2 [ ASC | DESC]] ... )
    [PCTFREE = integer]
```

DROP INDEX index-name

The former command will generate an index for at least one column of the base table specified; the index is stored in an additional file containing pointers to the values occurring in the column or those columns for which the index is created. The index is kept sorted in ascending (descending)

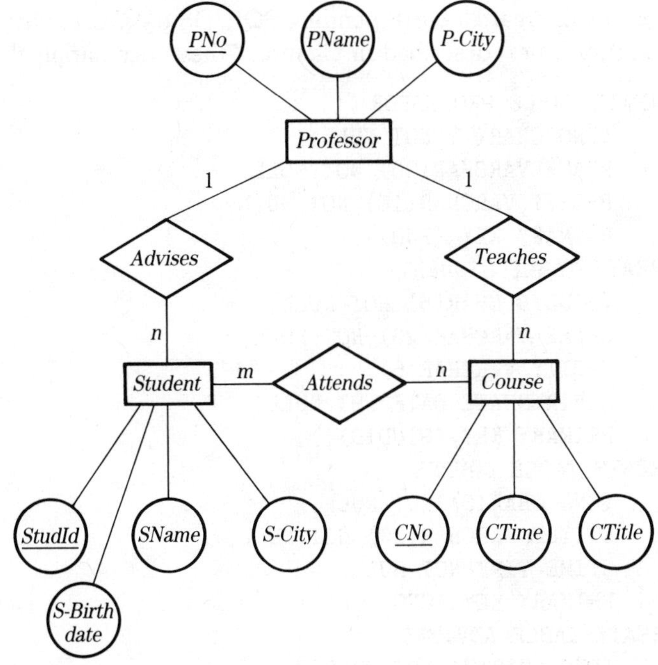

Figure 16.1 An ERD for the university application.

order if ASC (DESC) was specified in its declaration (where ASC is the default value), and will be modified accordingly by the system for each update that is performed on the underlying table. The creation of an index is not possible for views or for attributes with a 'LONG' domain.

If an index is created for a relation which is no longer empty, the current values are stored in the index in sorted order. If the index is defined with the option UNIQUE, no two tuples may have equal values in the columns to be indexed; if this is the case, the attempt to create a unique index will end in an error message.

The PCTFREE option refers to the percentage of space which is reserved within each page of the index file for later updates. Here, an integer between 0 and 99 can be specified; for system-internal reasons, however, the actual value should not be larger than 50; the default value is 10(%).

16.1.6 An example

As an example of a schema definition with SQL, let us again return to the university application (see also Chapter 14), now starting directly from the ER diagram shown in Figure 16.1. The sequence of DDL commands shown below will create a corresponding SQL/DS database; note that the 'transformation rules' described in Chapter 7 have been applied here:

```
CREATE TABLE PROFESSOR
     (PNO CHAR(7) NOT NULL,
     PNAME VARCHAR(20) NOT NULL,
     P-CITY VARCHAR(15) NOT NULL,
     PRIMARY KEY (PNO) )
CREATE TABLE STUDENT
     (STUDID CHAR(6) NOT NULL,
     SNAME VARCHAR(20) NOT NULL,
     S-CITY VARCHAR(5),
     S-BIRTHDATE DATE NOT NULL,
     PRIMARY KEY (STUDID) )
CREATE TABLE COURSE
     (CNO CHAR(6) NOT NULL,
     CTITLE VARCHAR(30) NOT NULL,
     CTIME TIME NOT NULL,
     PRIMARY KEY (CNO) )
CREATE TABLE ADVISES
     (PNO CHAR(7) NOT NULL,
     STUDID CHAR(6) NOT NULL,
     PRIMARY KEY (STUDID),
     FOREIGN KEY ADVFK1 (PNO)
       REFERENCES PROFESSOR
       ON DELETE RESTRICT,
     FOREIGN KEY ADVFK2 (STUDID)
       REFERENCES STUDENT
       ON DELETE CASCADE )
CREATE TABLE TEACHES
     (PNO CHAR(7) NOT NULL,
     CNO CHAR(6) NOT NULL,
     PRIMARY KEY (CNO),
     FOREIGN KEY TEACHFK1 (PNO)
       REFERENCES PROFESSOR
       ON DELETE RESTRICT,
     FOREIGN KEY TEACHFK2 (CNO)
       REFERENCES COURSE
       ON DELETE CASCADE )
CREATE TABLE ATTENDS
     (STUDID CHAR(6) NOT NULL,
     CNO CHAR(6) NOT NULL,
     PRIMARY KEY (STUDID, CNO),
     FOREIGN KEY ATTFK1 (CNO)
```

```
        REFERENCES COURSE
        ON DELETE CASCADE,
      FOREIGN KEY ATTFK2 (STUDID)
        REFERENCES STUDENT
        ON DELETE CASCADE )
```

16.1.7 Aliases and access rights

Several SQL commands pertaining to the definition of a database are listed next; the definition of views will be dealt with later. However, such views are also reflected already in some of the commands that follow.

Alternative names ('aliases') for base tables or views can be generated or deleted by the following commands:

CREATE SYNONYM identifier
FOR creator.{table-name | view-name}

DROP SYNONYM identifier

A user who is allowed to access tables created by another user must do so using 'creator.table-name'. By employing an alias, this can be abbreviated arbitrarily. An access right is granted or revoked as follows:

GRANT { list-of-privileges | ALL}
ON [creator.] { table-name | view-name}
TO { list-of-users | PUBLIC}
[WITH GRANT OPTION]

REVOKE { list-of-privileges | ALL}
ON [creator.] { table-name | view-name}
FROM { list-of-users | PUBLIC}

With the GRANT command, users can pass certain privileges on their own tables on to another user, or pass privileges that were granted to them on to third parties if WITH GRANT OPTION was specified. The creator of a table automatically possesses all privileges on this table together with the right to pass them on to others; the same holds for views. The following privileges can be specified (separated by commas if several are listed):

Privilege	*Base table*	*View*
SELECT	X	X
INSERT	X	X
DELETE	X	X
UPDATE [(column-name-list)]	X	X
INDEX	X	
ALTER	X	

There also exist three other formats of the GRANT and the REVOKE commands (such as for granting the right to start an application program 'owned' by another user) not discussed here. REVOKE can be used to withdraw privileges totally or in part, but only those which have previously been granted by oneself; if a privilege has meanwhile been passed on to a third party, the latter will lose it too.

16.1.8 Dictionary entries

As was mentioned in Chapter 2, the time-invariant description of a database is kept in a *data dictionary.* Correspondingly, all data definition commands affect the contents of the dictionary, that is, create new entries or modify existing ones. The dictionary of SQL/DS is itself organized in table form, where all tables are predefined and maintained automatically by the system (except for a few attributes only). All (row-wise) entries into these tables are also created automatically and can be queried like base tables. *Every* user can query the catalogue, where queries for passwords will remain unanswered. A user having DBA authority can additionally modify the contents of the catalogue. Hence, every user has the 'SELECT privilege' for each table of the catalogue, while only the DBA has the INSERT, DELETE, ALTER, and UPDATE privileges too.

Some tables of the SQL/DS dictionary are the following: *SYSCATALOG* contains one tuple for each table (base table or view) that is currently declared, including this table itself as well as all other catalogue tables. A row in this table contains values for the attributes *TNAME* (name of the table), *CREATOR* (userid of the creator), *TABLETYPE* ('R' for real, 'V' for virtual table), *NCOLS* (number of attributes), or *ROWCOUNT* (the current number of tuples in the table), among others.

SYSCOLUMNS contains a more detailed description of a database than SYSCATALOG; for each attribute of every base table or view, including the attributes of the catalogue tables, it has one corresponding tuple. The attributes include *TNAME, CREATOR, CNAME* (name of an attribute), *COLNO* (number of this attribute), *COLTYPE* (domain of the attribute), *LENGTH,* and *NULLS* ('Y' if null values are allowed and 'N' otherwise).

SYSINDEXES contains one row for each index that currently exists, including indexes automatically created for primary keys and indexes on catalogue tables. *SYSVIEWS* contains the definition of each view which currently exists. *SYSTABAUTH* contains information on privileges that individual users hold on the database tables; it records who granted each such privilege. *SYSUSERAUTH* serves a similar purpose, namely the description of rights of individual users; in addition, it is used to distinguish users with DBA authority from 'ordinary' users. *SYSUSERLIST* is a view derived from SYSUSERAUTH in which the column PASSWORD is missing.

Further catalogue tables are *SYSDROP*, which is used, for example, in connection with the deletion of (contents and format of) tables, *SYSSYNONYMS* for storing all table synonyms currently in use, *SYSDBSPACES* for describing the DBSPACEs available to the system, *SYSPROGAUTH* for describing the user privileges related to application programs and *SYSACCESS* as well as *SYSUSAGE* for internal usage in connection with access modules generated by a preprocessor.

The information SQL/DS keeps in its catalogue is partially static and partially dynamic in nature. Static information refers to the structure of a database (table names, number of attributes, domain types, etc.) and seldom changes over time. Dynamic information, on the other hand, includes, for instance, the number of tuples currently contained in a relation and hence is time-varying, where actualizations are caused by the use of the UPDATE STATISTICS command (see Section 16.8.1).

16.2 Updates on tables

After base tables have been created, a first operation will be to insert data into these; to this end, two commands are available:

```
INSERT INTO { table-name | view-name}
      [(column-names)]
      { VALUES ( data-items ) | select-command }

INPut [creator.] { table-name | view-name}
      [(column-names)]
      data items
      END
```

Through the INSERT command, a (new) tuple is inserted into a base table (or a view) directly, or several are inserted through a selection from another table. In the former case, the values of this tuple ('data items') are enclosed in parentheses and separated by commas; values of type 'character' have to be put in quotes, and date, time and timestamp values are considered to be character strings in this context. The following five different formats are supported for date and/or time strings:

ISO	International Standards Organization
USA	IBM Standard for the USA
EUR	IBM Standard for Europe
JIS	Japanese Industrial Standard for Christian Era
LOCAL	Any installation-defined format

For update operations, the following formats are used:

Format	Date	Time
ISO	yyyy-mm-dd	hh.mm[.ss]
USA	mm/dd/yyyy	hh:mm { AM | PM }
EUR	dd.mm.yyyy	hh.mm[.ss]
JIS	yyyy-mm-dd	hh:mm[:ss]

For dates, the yyyy part must always be specified as four digits, while the mm and dd parts may have leading zeros omitted; the latter also applies to the hh part of a time. For timestamp values, only the following format is valid:

yyyy-[m]m-[d]d-[h]h.mm.ss[.nnnnnnnn]

If values are provided (in an INSERT command) only for some of the attributes, but not for all, the columns that get values have to be listed explicitly; the system will assign a null value to all remaining columns of the tuple in question (unless this is prohibited by a NOT NULL declaration).

The INPut command renders a row-wise insertion of several tuples possible. Upon entering this command, the system will respond by listing the attributes of the desired relation together with their domains and a statement whether or not null values are allowed; after this, tuples can be inserted one at a time, following the same conventions that apply to the VALUES part of the INSERT command. An insertion of a sequence of tuples is concluded with END.

As an example, the data on two students for the database from the last section can be inserted into *STUDENT* as follows:

(1)
```
INSERT INTO STUDENT ('U126126', 'MILLER', 'SAN DIEGO',
    '1961-12-02')
INSERT INTO STUDENT ('U130248', 'MAIER', 'MIRA MESA',
    '1965-08-28')
```

(2)
```
INP STUDENT
'U126126','MILLER','SAN DIEGO','1961-12-02'
'U130248','MAIER','MIRA MESA','1965-08-28'
END
```

Date and time values are supplied to the system as character strings, and if they are supplied as values for an attribute of date or time type the system will interpret them correspondingly. Also, they can be entered in a variety of other forms.

The next commands, which are available for deleting or modifying (all those) tuples (satisfying a certain condition), are mostly self-explanatory; the forms a condition may have will be described below in connection with database queries.

DELETE FROM [creator.] table-name [WHERE condition]

(If the WHERE clause is omitted, all tuples in the relation will be deleted. The same effect can be achieved by the DROP command described above; however, a DROP command deletes the corresponding schema as well.)

```
UPDATE [creator.] table-name
    SET column-name-1 = expression-1
        [, column-name-2 = expression-2] ...
    [WHERE condition]
```

Here, each 'expression' has to yield exactly one (new) value for the corresponding attribute; it may contain constants, null and column-names as well as the arithmetic operations $+, -, *$ and $/$.

16.3 Theta-joins

Before the syntax and semantics of SQL queries are described, additional operations on the relations contained in a database are introduced (which will make it easier to talk about SQL semantics later). The first new operation will be used to formally distinguish Cartesian products from joins.

Definition 16.1

Let $r \in \text{Rel}(X)$, $s \in \text{Rel}(Y)$. Then

$$r * s := \{\mu\nu \mid \mu \in r \land \nu \in s\}$$

is called the **concatenation** of r and s. (Note that '$\mu\nu$' does *not* stand for a combination of μ and ν as functions, but simply for writing the two tuples one after the other.)

The concatenation — in analogy to a concatenation of strings in the theory of formal languages — forms a new tuple from two given ones simply by putting all their values in a sequence. As a first example, consider the two relations $r \in \text{Rel}(AB)$ and $s \in \text{Rel}(CD)$:

r:

A	B
0	0
1	1

s:

C	D
1	0
0	1

Then the following holds:

$r * s$:

A	B	C	D
0	0	1	0
0	0	0	1
1	1	1	0
1	1	0	1

Hence, the concatenation result contains tuples over the *disjoint* union of the attribute sets of the operands. Note that a concatenation *formally* does not produce the same result as a Cartesian product, since the latter yields a set of ordered pairs, where the first component is from one operand and the second is from the other:

$$r \times s := \{(\mu, \nu) \mid \mu \in r \wedge \nu \in s\}$$

It follows immediately that a concatenation does not necessarily yield a relation (in the sense of Chapter 7), since the attribute set of the result may contain duplicate elements and is henceforth formally a *multiset.* As a second example, consider two relations $r \in \text{Rel}(AB)$ and $s \in \text{Rel}(BC)$ as follows:

r:

A	B
0	0
1	1

s:

B	C
1	0
0	1

Then the following holds:

$r * s$:

A	B	B	C
0	0	1	0
0	0	0	1
1	1	1	0
1	1	0	1

Only if $X \cap Y = \emptyset$ holds for $r \in \text{Rel}(X)$ and $s \in \text{Rel}(Y)$ is it true that $r * s$ is a relation in the sense used here ($r * s \in \text{Rel}(XY)$); for these reasons this and the following operation were not introduced in Chapter 8 when relational algebra was discussed.

Using concatenation, another operation can now be defined which under certain prerequisites (guaranteeing that the result is a relation) generalizes the natural join introduced earlier. It will be employed below to make the semantics of the SELECT command precise.

Definition 16.2

Let $r \in \text{Rel}(X)$, $s \in \text{Rel}(Y)$, $A \in X$, $B \in Y$, $\Theta \in \{<, \leq, >, \geq, =, \neq\}$.

$$r[A\Theta B]s := \{\mu\nu \in r * s \mid \mu(A)\Theta\nu(B)\}$$

is called **Θ-join** (pronounced **theta-join**) of r and s. (In this definition, $\mu \in r$ and $\nu \in s$ as in Definition 16.1.) If Θ in particular is the symbol '=', the join is called an **equijoin** of r and s.

As an example, first reconsider the relations $r \in \text{Rel}(AB)$ and $s \in \text{Rel}(CD)$ shown above. The following holds:

$$r[B = C]s : \begin{array}{cccc} A & B & C & D \\ \hline 0 & 0 & 0 & 1 \\ 1 & 1 & 1 & 0 \end{array}$$

For $r \in \text{Rel}(AB)$, $s \in \text{Rel}(BC)$ as shown above, the following holds:

$$r[B < B]s : \begin{array}{cccc} A & B & B & C \\ \hline 0 & 0 & 1 & 0 \end{array}$$

Obviously, the following holds for any $r \in \text{Rel}(X)$ and $s \in \text{Rel}(Y)$. If $X \cap Y = \emptyset$, then $r * s$ is a relation (over XY). This implies that $r[A\Theta B]s$ is also a relation (over XY, where $A \in X, B \in Y$), so that the theta-join of r and s can be written as follows:

$$r[A\Theta B]s = \sigma_{A\Theta B}(r * s)$$

Note that a new kind of selection condition is used in the last formula, which is often included in relational algebra as well; the corresponding definition is as follows:

$$\sigma_{A\Theta B}(r) := \{\mu \in r \mid \mu(A)\Theta\mu(B)\}$$

In particular, this operation is undefined if the format of r (or that of $r * s$) contains duplicate attributes.

The definition of the theta-join operation can also be extended to more complex selection conditions (which are composed of simple ones).

16.4 The SELECT command

Queries of any kind are posed to an SQL database with the help of the **SELECT command**, which has the following simple basic structure:

SELECT	attributes	('output')
FROM	relation(s)	('input')
WHERE	condition	

In terms of relational algebra, a SELECT command basically specifies an SPJ expression (see Section 8.1), where 'J' no longer stands for 'natural join', but for 'theta-join'. The association can be made as follows. The

SELECT clause states onto which attributes a projection is desired (so that a more precise keyword here would be 'PROJECT'). The FROM clause specifies from which relations these attributes are to be taken (if a join is requested, at least two table names have to appear in this clause). Finally, the WHERE clause contains an (optional) selection condition and, in the case of a join, a condition that states how to form this join.

16.4.1 The syntax of SELECT

The syntax of the SELECT command is actually much more flexible and complex. Therefore, it will be presented completely in the form of diagrams first (see Figures 16.2–25 and 16.27); after this, its use will be illustrated by way of examples. In these diagrams, all items shown in rectangular boxes are explained further in another (usually subsequent) diagram (for example, the 'select-list' mentioned in Figure 16.2 is explained in Figure 16.3 or the 'column-name' in Figure 16.7), while ovals and circles carry keywords or terminals of the SELECT grammar; keywords written in capital letters can be used immediately, those written in small letters have to be filled in according to their respective meaning. Eventually, abbreviations are used within the diagrams; for example, 'creator.' means that the creator's name can or must be specified and is followed by a dot as delimiter.

Figure 16.2 shows the general structure of a SELECT command. It is important to note that DISTINCT may occur only once in a SELECT command (unless a 'subquery' as explained below is used as a *column-select*); if DISTINCT is used, the number of *items* occurring in the *select-list* is limited to 16.

For a join operation up to 15 tables may be specified in the FROM clause. If an attribute name occurs several times in a corresponding expression, it must be made unique by prefixing it with its table name. A join condition is *never* satisfied by a null value; corresponding tuples do not participate in the computation of the result. A table may also be joined with itself, by using an alias name ('range variable') in the FROM clause; if multiple joins of one table with itself are desired, the original name must appear sufficiently often, each time followed by a distinct alias.

The arithmetic operations (see Figure 16.5) can be used within a *select-list* (see Figure 16.3) only in connection with numerical data (of type INTeger, SMALLINT, DECimal or FLOAT), although an exception regarding addition and subtraction applies to date and time values (see below).

The possibilities for formulating *terms* are shown in Figure 16.6 and discussed next. It should be noted that some obvious restrictions apply to this figure, which will also be mentioned below.

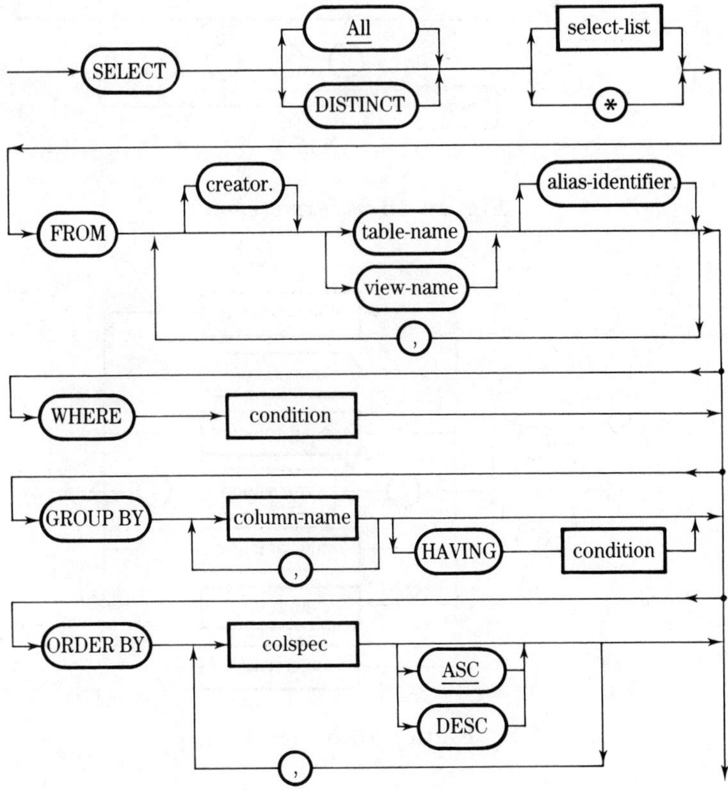

Figure 16.2 *SELECT command.*

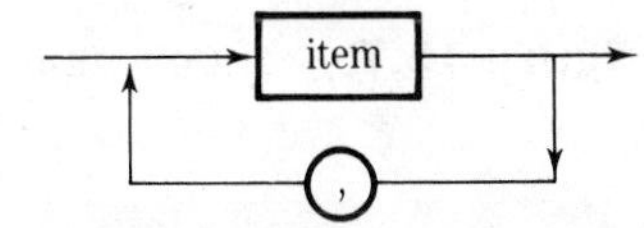

Figure 16.3 *select-list.*

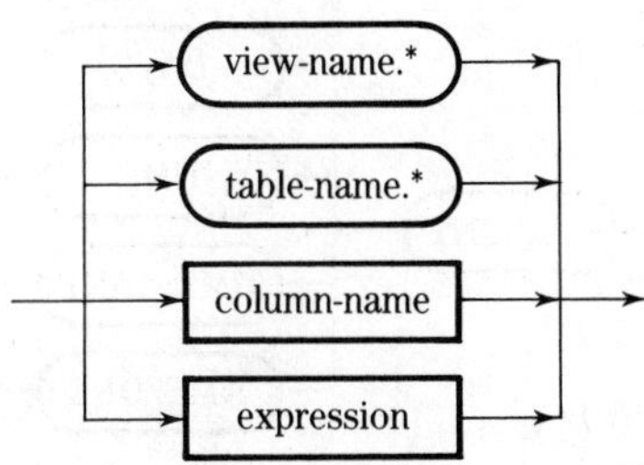

Figure 16.4 *item.*

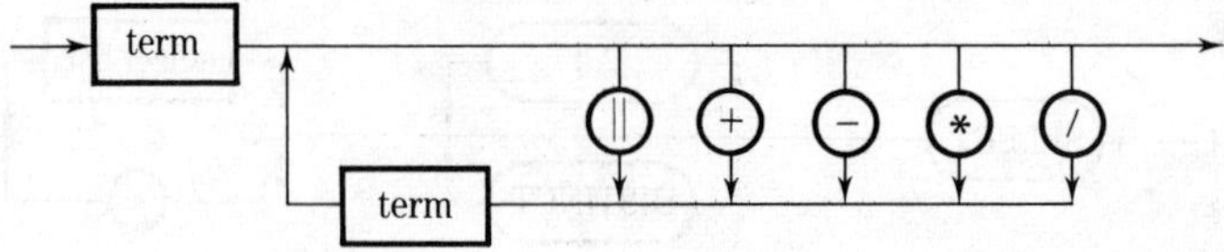

Figure 16.5 *expression.*

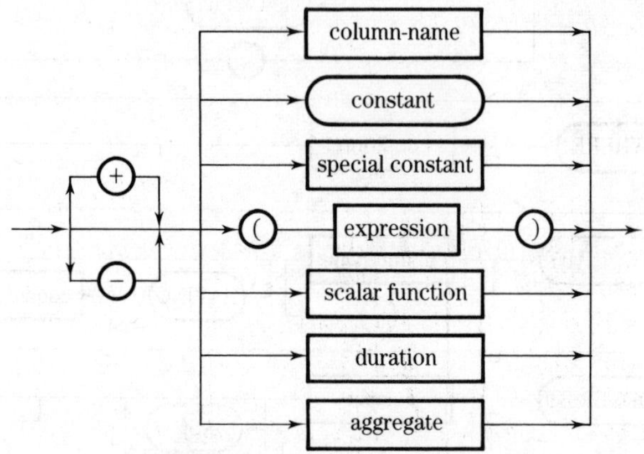

Figure 16.6 *term.*

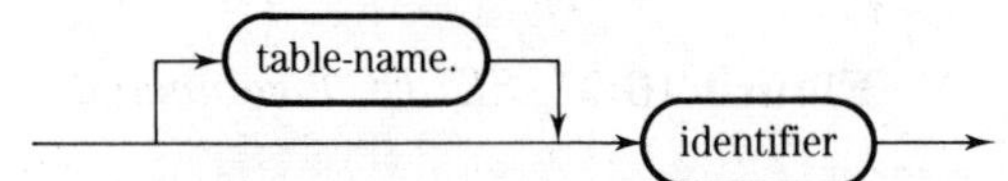

Figure 16.7 *column-name.*

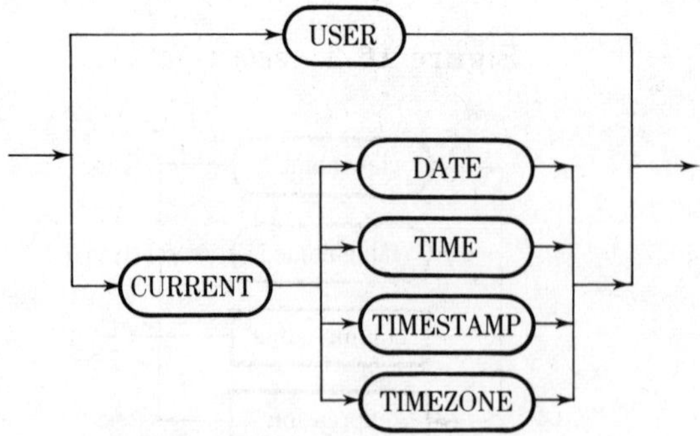

Figure 16.8 *special constant.*

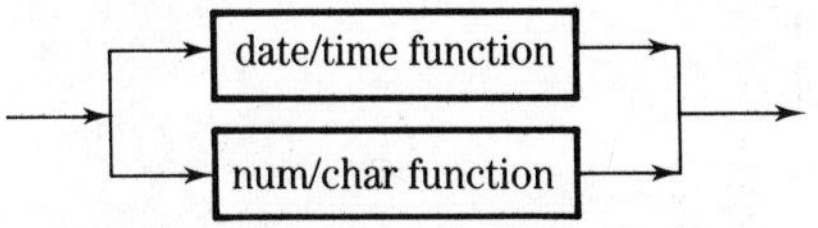

Figure 16.9 *scalar function.*

The first three of the CURRENT constants listed in Figure 16.8 return values of the respective type; these values are based on the time-of-day clock reading performed during the execution of the command containing the constant. However, it should be kept in mind that these constants are evaluated *at the beginning* of the execution of the command, so that in the answer to a query like

```
SELECT STUDID, CURRENT DATE FROM STUDENT
```

(referring to the example from Section 16.1) the *same* date will be shown for every distinct id.

The value of CURRENT TIMEZONE is a (signed) time duration containing the local time zone, where a positive (negative) value represents differentials east (west) of GMT, respectively (and the local time zone needs to be specified during the installation of the system). The CURRENT TIMEZONE can also be subtracted from a time or timestamp data type; the following rules apply: (1) In a subtraction from a time type, modular arithmetic based on a modulus of 24 is used; (2) in a subtraction from a timestamp type, the hours, days, months and years portions are adjusted as necessary.

The scalar functions fall into two categrories as shown in Figure 16.9: functions applicable to date and time values, and functions applicable to numerical values or character strings. The former are shown in Figure 16.10 and can be used to convert a character string into a date or time value or vice versa, to access some part of a date or time value, to calculate a date from an expression which represents a number of days, or to calculate the number of days which corresponds to a date or a timestamp value. Note that, in connection with these functions, a date or time value can also be a value returned by the DATE, the TIME or the TIMESTAMP function, or a value returned by a CURRENT special constant.

The 12 date/time functions can actually have a greater variety of inputs than is shown in Figure 16.10; a complete survey of their input and output data types in shown in Table 16.1. Some examples of how to use them are the following:

(1) The DATE function is used to get the date part of an expression. If TSTMP is an attribute of type TIMESTAMP with current value '1988-08-11-18.34.35.001253', then `DATE(TSTMP)` yields

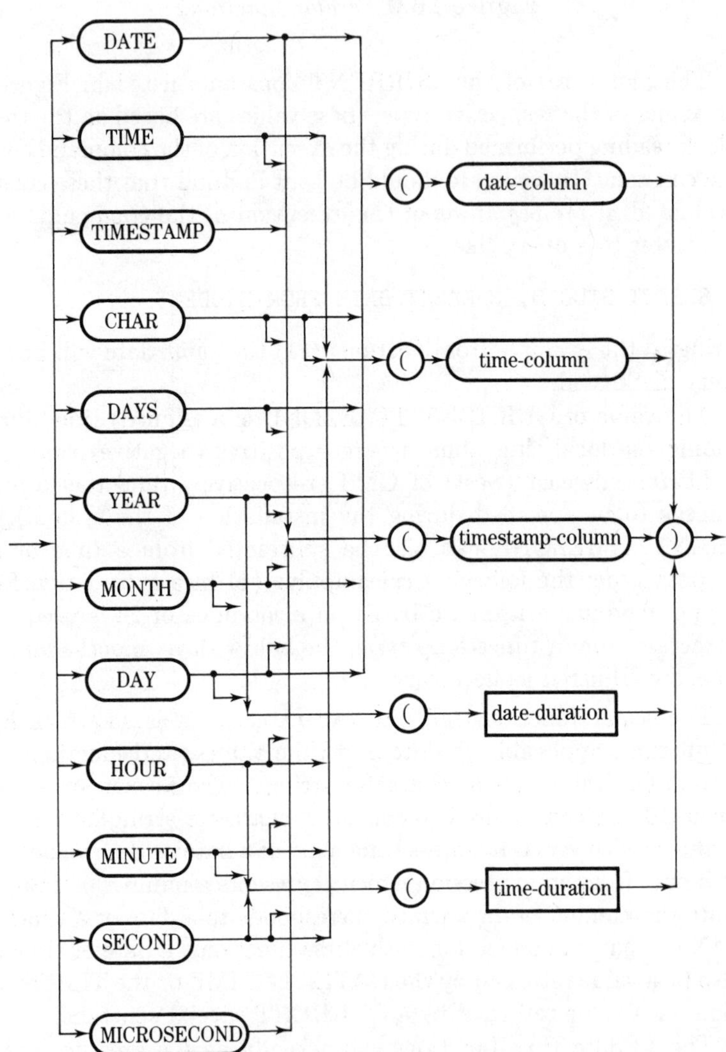

Figure 16.10 *date/time function.*

Table 16.1 Summary of SQL/DS date/time functions I/O.

Function	Input: DateCol	TimeCol	TstmCol	DateCha	TimeCha	TstmCha	DateDur	TimeDur	Output is of type
DATE	A		A	V					DATE
TIME		A	A		V				TIME
TIMESTAMP	F	S	A	F	S	V			TIMESTAMP
CHAR	A	A	A	V	V	V			CHARacter
DAYS	A		A	V		V			INTeger
YEAR	A		A	V		V	A		INTeger
MONTH	A		A	V		V	A		INTeger
DAY	A		A	V		V	A		INTeger
HOUR		A	A		V	V		A	INTeger
MINUTE		A	A		V	V		A	INTeger
SECOND		A	A		V	V		A	INTeger
MICROSECOND			A			V			INTeger

Col	means	Column
Cha		Character-string representation
Dur		Duration
A		Always allowed as input type
F		allowed as First parameter only
S		allowed as Second parameter only
V		allowed as Valid string only

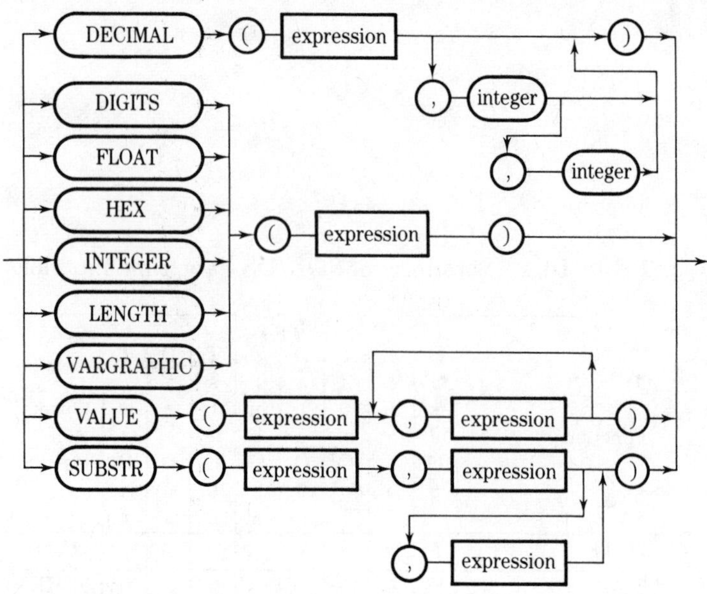

Figure 16.11 *num/char function.*

the value '1988-08-11'.
If DATE is applied to a character string of length 7 representing a Julian date, the result is the same date according to the Gregorian calendar:

`DATE('1987131')` yields 1987-05-11
`DATE('1985365')` yields 1985-12-31

The DATE function is the only scalar function which can also be applied to numerical expressions representing an integer n between 1 and 3 652 059; the result is a date representing n days starting from January 1st of year 1:

`DATE(1+2+3)` yields 0001-01-06
`DATE(3652057)` yields 9999-12-29

Similar remarks apply to the TIME function; it can be used to extract the time from a time value itself, from a timestamp value or from a character string with a length of at least 4 bytes; in the latter case, the result is the time represented by this string. For example, `TIME('9:30 AM')` yields 09.30.00.

(2) A call of the TIMESTAMP function has the form

TIMESTAMP(ex1[,ex2])

where ex2 is a time value that is used only if ex1 is a date value. Thus, a date and a time can be combined into a timestamp; also a character string of at least 16 bytes in length can be turned into a valid timestamp. For example,

```
TIMESTAMP('1988-08-11.18:51:09')
```

yields 1988-08-11-18.51.09.000000.

(3) The CHAR function can be used to obtain the character-string representation of a date or time value; the general format is

CHAR(exp [, { USA | EUR | ISO | JIS | LOCAL }])

For example, if MYDATE is an attribute having value '1988-10-05', then `CHAR(MYDATE,EUR)` yields '5.10.1988'; if MYTIME is an attribute having value '18.57.32', then `CHAR(MYTIME,USA)` yields '06:57 PM'.

(4) The DAYS function is used to calculate the number of days from December 31st of year 0 to a given date; the result is an integer. For example,

`DAYS('0001-01-31')`	yields 000000031
`DAYS('1987-05-11')`	yields 000725502

(5) The YEAR, MONTH and DAY functions are used to obtain the respective part of a date, while the HOUR, MINUTE and SECOND functions serve the corresponding purpose for a time. Unlike the functions discussed so far, the parameter passed to any of these functions can also be a date or time *duration*, respectively (see Figures 16.10 and 16.11). For example, if MYDATE1 [MYDATE2] has value '1988-05-15' ['1988-05-11'], respectively, then

`DAY(MYDATE1-MYDATE2)`	yields +4
`DAY(MYDATE2-MYDATE1)`	yields −4

Similarly, if MYTIME1 [MYTIME2] has value '15.45.00' ['09.30.10'], respectively, then

`SECOND(MYTIME1-MYTIME2)`	yields +50

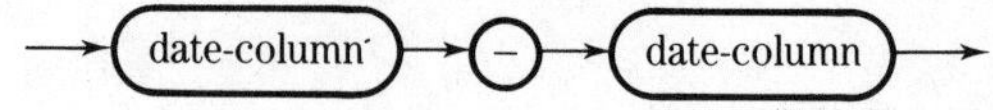

Figure 16.12 *date-duration.*

`SECOND(MYTIME2-MYTIME1)` yields −50

(6) Finally, the MICROSECOND function can be used to retrieve the microseconds part from a timestamp value (or its character-string representation).

In contrast to the date/time functions, the num/char functions as shown in Figure 16.11 are applicable to a variety of data types other than date or time. The following are some examples of their usage:

(1) DECIMAL can be used for obtaining the decimal representation of a numerical value. The general form is

DECIMAL (expression [, int-1 [, int-2]])

The result is a number with 'int-1' digits in total and 'int-2' digits following the decimal point.

(2) DIGITS converts a number into a character string; FLOAT, HEX and INTEGER have a corresponding effect.

(3) LENGTH determines the length of the given operand in bytes.

(4) VALUE can be used to replace a null value by a real one.

(5) SUBSTR can be used to extract a substring from a given character string; its general form is

SUBSTR (string, start [, length])

where 'start' denotes the beginning of the substring and 'length' its length.

In general, a duration as shown in Figure 16.14 denotes a time interval, like '2 years' or '3 days 5 hours'. Besides the date and time

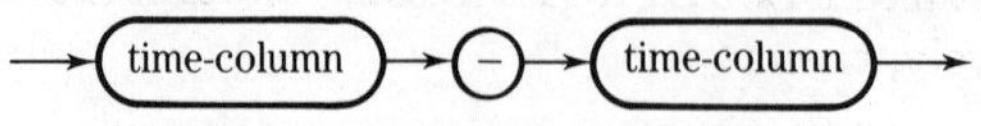

Figure 16.13 *time-duration.*

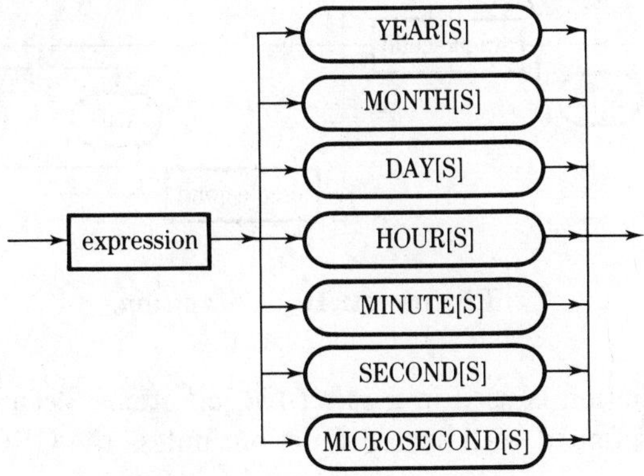

Figure 16.14 *duration.*

durations described above, SQL/DS has a third type of duration which is a (scalar) expression whose value is an integer representing a duration. This type is used in the format 'expression unit[s]', where the expression is of type numeric, like `1 MONTH` or `7 YEARS`. Durations of this form can be used further in (other) expressions, as in the following examples:

```
SELECT S-BIRTHDATE + 2 YEARS FROM STUDENT ...
SELECT CURRENT TIME + 3 HOURS + 12 MINUTES FROM ...
```

The following restrictions apply to the aggregate functions (see Figure 16.15). AVG and SUM can be used only on numerical data; when a value is computed for these functions, null values are ignored, so that both yield 0 if the column in question contains null values only. MIN and MAX can be applied to data of any type; again, null values are ignored. If all corresponding values equal 0, no return value will be computed. If an

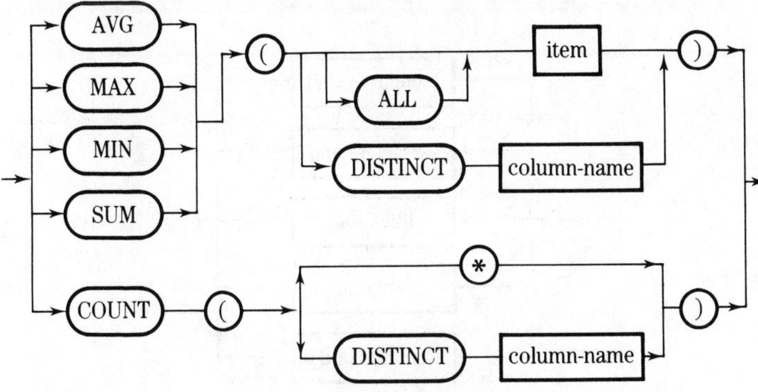

Figure 16.15 *aggregate.*

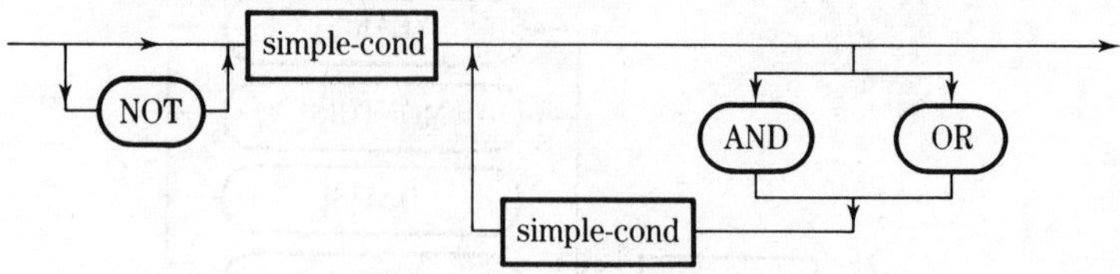

Figure 16.16 *condition.*

aggregate function is used in a *select-list*, *all* 'items' occurring in this list have to be equipped with such a function, unless the GROUP BY clause is used.

A search *condition* (see Figure 16.16) is built according to the same rules for all of SELECT, UPDATE and DELETE. Basically, such a condition is conjunction or disjunction of comparisons between pairs of *items*, where an *item* can be a constant, a column name or an expression. Constants can be numerical values, hexadecimal data or character strings, where the latter need to be enclosed in quotes (if a quote occurs within a string, it has to be replaced by two quotes). Conditions may be grouped using parentheses.

Finally, the special constants shown in Figure 16.8 (like USER) may be used in a search condition. In particular, when a query in which USER occurs is processed, the system replaces this keyword by the corresponding userid. As an example, the query for a professor's own address can be expressed using the condition '`WHERE PNAME = USER`'.

Comparisons (as shown in Figure 16.18) between arithmetic operands with different types are evaluated in the 'larger' of the two according to the following ordering: FLOAT > DECimal > INTeger > SMALLINT; a comparison of SMALLINT values will yield an INTeger result. When character strings are compared, the alphanumerical ordering is used, that is, $9 > 8 > \ldots 0 > Z > \ldots X \ldots > A > z \ldots > a >$

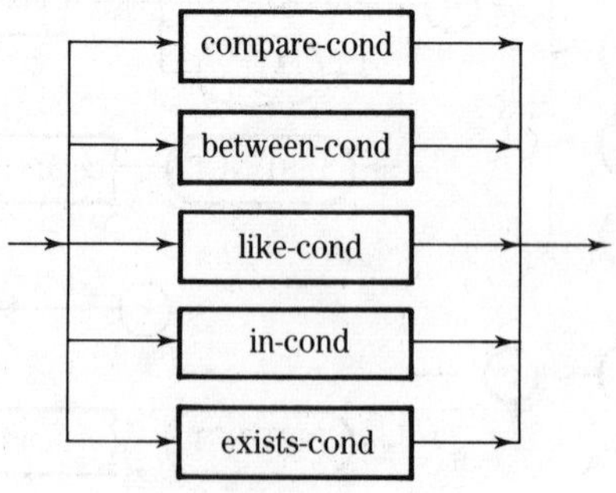

Figure 16.17 *simple-cond.*

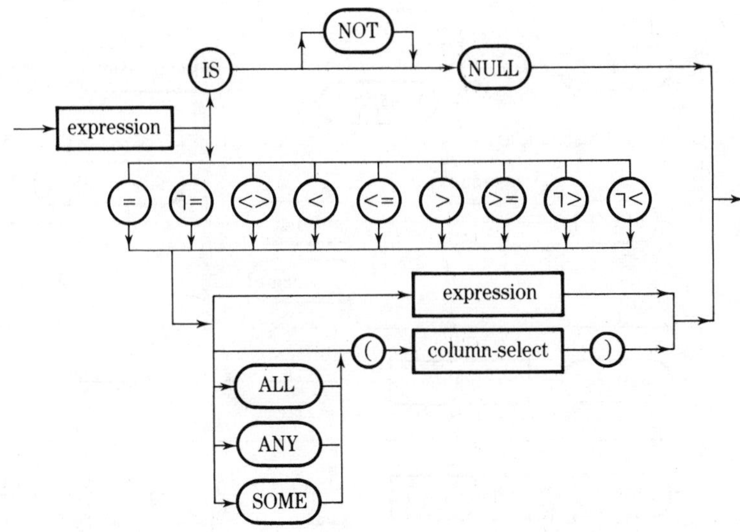

Figure 16.18 *compare-cond.*

<special characters>. If a string of fixed length is compared to one of variable length, the shorter one will be filled with blanks at the right end until the two lengths are equal. Two strings of variable length are considered equal only if they have exactly the same length and contents (for example, 'AA' ≠ 'AA ').

Conditions used in SELECT, DELETE or UPDATE commands and HAVING clauses may contain *subqueries* (see Figure 16.19), in our 'grammar' referred to as *column-selects*. In this case, a value or a set of values is computed as a result of the subquery and then used directly to evaluate the condition; however, this result is not stored for later usage. A subquery may only have a single attribute or a single *expression* in its SELECT clause; the use of ORDER BY is not allowed. The (intermediate) result produced by a subquery may contain several values only if an IN clause is used in the next 'higher' part of the entire query.

If a subquery is used in an UPDATE or DELETE command, it may not refer to the same table referenced by this command. The comparison operators of a *compare-cond*ition can be modified by ALL, ANY or SOME (a synonym for ANY) in the presence of a subquery.

Finally, a query can contain several subqueries and subqueries may be nested. In addition, a subquery can be 'correlated' with its superior query; in this case the search condition of the subquery depends on values of a table accessed by the outer query.

The *colspec* (see Figure 16.24) of an ORDER BY clause can be a name or a number. If a number is specified, it refers to an *item* from the

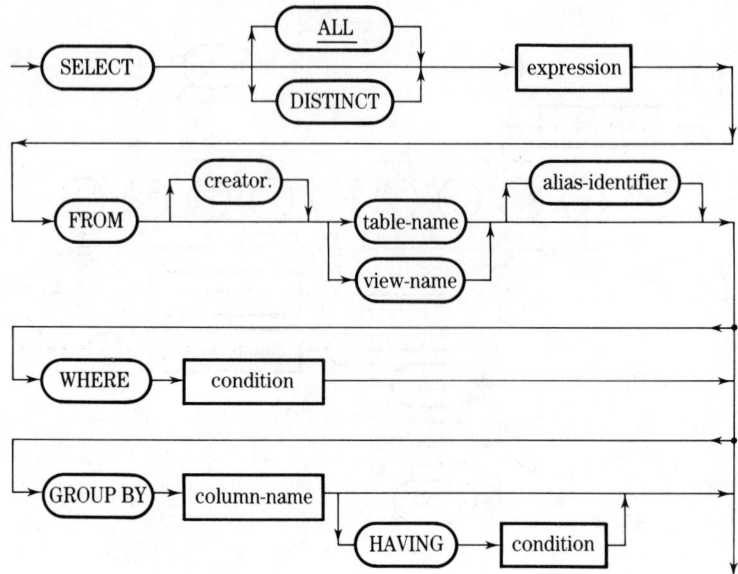

Figure 16.19 *column-select.*

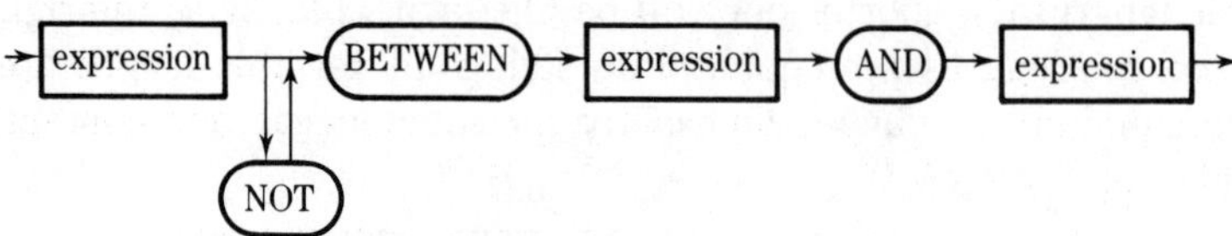

Figure 16.20 *between-cond.*

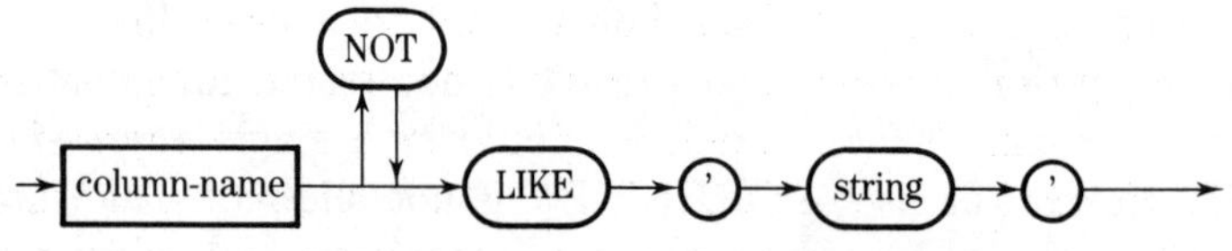

Figure 16.21 *like-cond.*

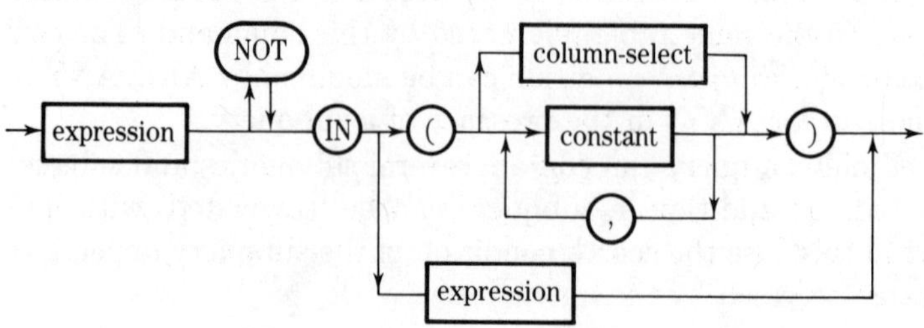

Figure 16.22 *in-cond.*

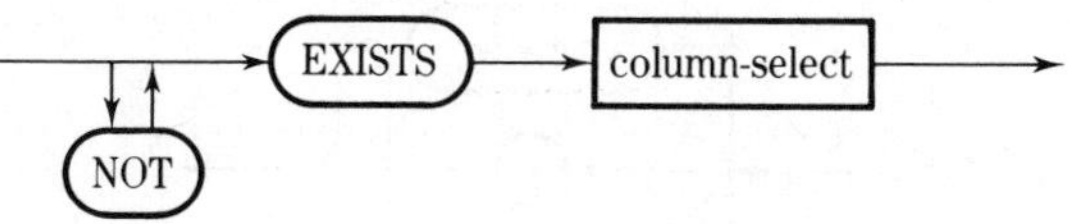

Figure 16.23 *exists-cond.*

select-list; for example, 'ORDER BY 3' means that the result is to be sorted (in ascending order) according to the third *item*.

16.4.2 On the semantics of SELECT

Before the use of the SELECT command when formulating queries is illustrated on a concrete example, several peculiarities of its semantics should be pointed out in terms of relational algebra given in Chapter 8. As a modification of the projection π as introduced in Definition 8.1 (i), the symbol π^+ is now used for a 'projection operation' that only removes certain columns of the operand without eliminating duplicate tuples that may exist as a consequence. Thus, the result of π^+ will in general not be a relation, but a multiset of tuples. For example, if $r \in \text{Rel}(ABC)$ denotes the relation

r:

A	B	C
1	2	1
1	1	1
2	2	2

then the following holds:

$\pi^+_{AC}(r)$:

A	C
1	1
1	1
2	2

$\neq \pi_{AC}(r)$

With this and the preparations from Section 16.3, the following general correspondences can now be stated:

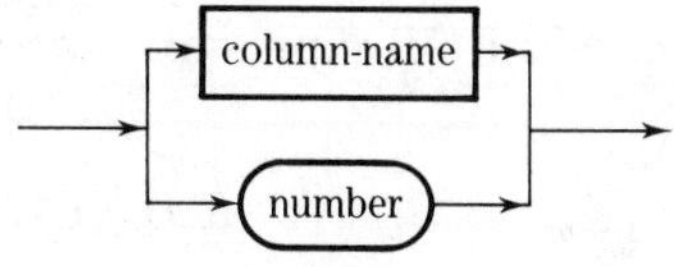

Figure 16.24 *colspec.*

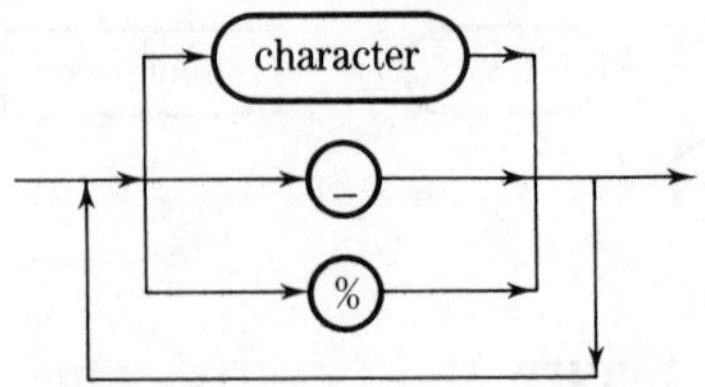

Figure 16.25 *string.*

Syntax	*Semantics*
SELECT Y FROM R	$\pi^+_Y(R)$
SELECT DISTINCT Y FROM R	$\pi_Y(R)$
SELECT $*$ FROM R WHERE C	$\sigma_C(R)$
SELECT Y FROM R WHERE C	$\pi^+_Y(\sigma_C(R))$
SELECT $*$ FROM R, S	$R * S$ (concatenation)
SELECT Y FROM R, S WHERE C	$\pi^+_Y(R[C]S)$

In this table it is assumed that Y denotes a sequence of attributes from the format of the corresponding operand, respectively (thus, Y denotes a *select-list* consisting of *column-names* in the left half of this table). Also, C denotes a *condition* containing only *compare-conditions* as *simple-conditions*, whose *expressions* in turn consist of *column-names* or *constants* (since selection was defined in Chapter 8 for this type of conditions only); a corresponding formal extension of the select operation is not defined here. (Obviously, such an extension comprising all *conditions* allowed in SQL can easily be stated.) Finally, some expressions in the right half of the above table contain the 'operation symbols' concatenation and theta-join, for which an evaluation has not been defined formally (along the lines of Definition 8.5); the intention behind these expressions should also be obvious.

For the last case listed in this table the condition C has to satisfy the 'conventions' of a theta-join (for example, if C has the form $A = B$, A $[B]$ must be an attribute of R $[S]$). In case attributes from distinct relation schemas share the same name, these attributes must have their corresponding schema name as a prefix ('$R.A$') for the purpose of uniquely specifying which attribute occurrence is meant. This is of particular importance for stating a SELECT expression that computes a *natural* join.

If R has attributes $A_1 \ldots A_n$ $B_1 \ldots B_m$, and S has attributes $B_1 \ldots B_m$ $C_1 \ldots C_l$, the SELECT expression corresponding to $R \bowtie S$ is as follows:

SELECT $A_1, \ldots, A_m$, $R.B_1, \ldots, R.B_m, C_1, \ldots, C_l$
FROM R, S
WHERE $R.B_1 = S.B_1$ AND ... AND $R.B_m = S.B_m$

In the *select-list* the union of the attribute sets has to be described explicitly (as a *set*), where it is irrelevant whether the common attributes are taken from R or from S, since an equijoin will be computed in this case. In the WHERE clause a test for equal values on these common attributes has to be stated completely and explicitly.

16.4.3 Examples

To illustrate the usage of SELECT, a *Weird-Animals Database* (adapted from an example proposed by Marina Roesler) will be employed which is used in a molecular biology lab doing research on transgenic mice. (Transgenic animals are animals born from eggs which have been successfully injected with foreign DNA.) The format and current contents of this database are as shown in Figure 16.26.

(Note that weights are shown in grams in the latter relation.) A sequence of examples of increasing difficulty will now be presented, which gives single-table queries first and then proceeds to multi-table ones.

Example 16.1

Show the contents of relation Animals: `SELECT * FROM ANIMALS`
The result is a copy of the first relation above.

Example 16.2

Show the animal number of each female mouse:

```
SELECT ANIMAL# FROM ANIMALS WHERE SEX = 'F'
```

The result is the following table:

ANIMAL#
15
18
23
92

Example 16.3

Show all room numbers: `SELECT ROOM# FROM CAGE`
The result is a table with one (*ROOM#*-) column containing each room number as often as it appears in *CAGE*; to avoid duplicates appearing in the result, the following must be used:

```
SELECT DISTINCT ROOM# FROM CAGE
```

ANIMALS:

ANIMAL#	SEX	COLOUR	BIRTHDATE
SMALLINT NOT NULL	CHAR	CHAR(5) NOT NULL	DATE NOT NULL
12	m	brown	1986-02-15
15	f	black	1986-02-22
18	f	red	1986-10-10
22	?	grey	1987-03-10
23	f	grey	1987-03-10
27	m	black	1987-04-01
35	m	brown	1987-08-22
43	m	brown	1987-11-30
52	?	green	1988-01-28
88	?	blue	1988-04-20
92	f	brown	1988-05-22

CAGES:

ANIMAL#	ROOM#	BOX#
SMALLINT NOT NULL	CHAR(4) NOT NULL	CHAR(3) NOT NULL
12	1140	120
15	1140	125
18	1140	120
22	1142	150
23	1142	155
27	2210	212
35	2210	212
43	2315	240
52	2315	240
88	2315	255
92	2315	240

TRANSGENICS:

ANIMAL#	INJ_DATE	INJ_TIME	WEIGHT
SMALLINT NOT NULL	DATE NOT NULL	TIME NOT NULL	DEC(5,2)
18	1986-04-04	15.30.09	50.25
22	1986-10-02	14.22.31	53.36
35	1987-01-05	20.14.22	48.00
88	1987-10-02	08.48.00	60.05
92	1987-12-12	10.12.30	72.18

Figure 16.26 The Weird-Animals Database.

Example 16.4

For each transgenic animal, show the animal number and weight in milligrams:

```
SELECT ANIMAL#, WEIGHT * 1000 FROM TRANSGENICS
```

Since the weight no longer has the original unit, it is reasonable to include the new one as a comment (that is, an *item* of type [*string*] *constant*):

```
SELECT ANIMAL#, 'WEIGHT IN MILLIGRAMS =',
        WEIGHT * 1000 FROM TRANSGENICS
```

The result looks as follows:

ANIMAL#		
18	weight in milligrams =	50250
22	weight in milligrams =	53360
35	weight in milligrams =	48000
88	weight in milligrams =	60050
92	weight in milligrams =	72180

Example 16.5

Show box number and animal number for mice in Room 2315:

```
SELECT ANIMAL#, BOX# FROM CAGE WHERE ROOM# = '2315'
```

Example 16.6

Show the animal number for mice in Room 2315, Box 240:

```
SELECT ANIMAL# FROM CAGE WHERE ROOM# = '2315'
        AND BOX# = '240'
```

Example 16.7

Show the animal number for all animals in Rooms 1140 and 2315:

```
SELECT ANIMAL# FROM CAGE WHERE ROOM# = '2315'
        OR ROOM# = '1140'
```

or

```
SELECT ANIMAL# FROM CAGE
        WHERE ROOM# IN ('2315','1140')
```

Example 16.8

Show the animal number for animals weighing more than 51 and less than 80 grams:

```
SELECT ANIMAL# FROM TRANSGENICS
     WHERE WEIGHT > 51 AND WEIGHT < 80
```

or

```
SELECT ANIMAL# FROM TRANSGENICS
     WHERE WEIGHT BETWEEN 51.01 AND 79.99
```

For *string*s occurring in a *like-condition*, the symbols '_' and '% ' have a special meaning: '_' is a placeholder for an arbitrary single symbol, while '% ' stands for a sequence of zero or more symbols.

Example 16.9

Show the animal number of each mouse whose colour begins with a 'b':

```
SELECT ANIMAL# FROM ANIMALS WHERE COLOR LIKE 'b%'
```

Example 16.10

Show the animal number for each mouse living on the second floor:

```
SELECT ANIMAL# FROM CAGES WHERE ROOM# LIKE '2___'
```

Example 16.11

Show animal number and injection time for all transgenics weighing less than 60 grams, in descending order of injection time:

```
SELECT ANIMAL#, INJ_TIME
     FROM TRANSGENICS
     WHERE WEIGHT < 60
     ORDER BY INJ_TIME DESC
```

The result is:

ANIMAL#	*INJ_TIME*
35	20.14.22
18	15.30.09
22	14.22.31

Example 16.12

Show the number of every room housing more than two mice:

```
SELECT DISTINCT ROOM# FROM CAGE
     GROUP BY ROOM# HAVING COUNT(*) > 2
```

The GROUP BY operator will rearrange the table specified in the FROM clause into groups such that all rows within a group have the same value for the GROUP BY attribute. The SELECT clause is then applied to each group, and groups not satisfying the HAVING condition are eliminated. Thus, grouping table *CAGE* in a first step to answer this query yields:

CAGES:	*ANIMAL#*	*ROOM#*	*BOX#*
	12	1140	120
	15	1140	125
	18	1140	120
	22	1142	150
	23	1142	155
	27	2210	212
	35	2210	212
	43	2315	240
	52	2315	240
	88	2315	255
	92	2315	240

Applying SELECT and HAVING finally results in:

ROOM#
1140
2315

Note that HAVING does to groups what WHERE does to tuples. If grouping is applied to a column containing nulls, the corresponding tuples will all be put in one group.

Example 16.13

Show the animal number for every mouse in a room housing more than two mice, in descending order of box numbers:

```
SELECT ANIMAL#
       FROM CAGE
       GROUP BY ROOM# HAVING COUNT(*) > 2
       ORDER BY BOX# DESC
```

The result is as follows:

ANIMAL#
15
12
18
88
43
52
92

Example 16.14

Show the animal number of all mice that were born in 1987:

```
SELECT ANIMAL# FROM ANIMALS
       WHERE BIRTHDATE BETWEEN '1987-01-01'
          AND '1987-12-31'
```

The following is simpler:

```
SELECT ANIMAL# FROM ANIMALS
       WHERE YEAR(BIRTHDATE) = 1987
```

Example 16.15

Show the animal number of all transgenics that were injected during afternoon or evening:

```
SELECT ANIMAL# FROM TRANSGENICS
       WHERE HOUR(INJ_TIME) >= 12
       AND HOUR(INJ_TIME) <= 24
```

Example 16.16

Show the number of transgenic mice:

```
SELECT COUNT(*) FROM TRANSGENICS
```

Example 16.17

Show the number of boxes currently in use:

```
SELECT COUNT(DISTINCT BOX#) FROM CAGES
```

Example 16.18

Show the number of animals in each room:

```
SELECT ROOM#, COUNT(ANIMAL#)
       FROM CAGES
       GROUP BY ROOM#
```

The result is:

ROOM#	
1140	3
1142	2
2210	2
2315	4

CAGES is divided into groups of equal room numbers, and for each group its members are counted.

Example 16.19

Show the animal number for each transgenic mouse weighing less than the average:

```
SELECT ANIMAL#
     FROM TRANSGENICS
     WHERE WEIGHT <
          (SELECT AVG(WEIGHT)
           FROM TRANSGENICS)
```

Example 16.20

Show all transgenics with animal number, sex, colour and weight only:

```
SELECT TRANSGENICS.ANIMAL#, SEX, COLOR, WEIGHT
     FROM TRANSGENICS, ANIMALS
     WHERE TRANSGENICS.ANIMAL# = ANIMALS.ANIMAL#
```

This expression corresponds to a (natural) join of *ANIMALS* and *TRANSGENICS*, whose result is projected onto the desired columns; the result is as follows:

ANIMAL#	*SEX*	*COLOR*	*WEIGHT*
18	f	red	50.25
22	?	grey	53.36
35	m	brown	48.00
88	?	blue	60.05
92	f	brown	72.18

Note that this is a case in which attribute names occurring in distinct formats (here: *ANIMAL#*) need to be denoted uniquely, by prefixing them with the corresponding table name.

Example 16.21

Show the room number and box number for boxes housing brown mice:

```
SELECT ROOM#, BOX#
     FROM ANIMALS, CAGES
     WHERE CAGES.ANIMAL# = ANIMALS.ANIMAL#
     AND COLOR = 'BROWN'
```

Again a natural join is performed. Therefore, both operands must be listed in the FROM clause, even though attributes from only one of them appear in the result. The same result can be obtained using a subquery as follows:

```
SELECT ROOM#, BOX#
      FROM CAGES
      WHERE ANIMAL# IN
            (SELECT ANIMAL#
              FROM ANIMALS
              WHERE COLOR = 'BROWN')
```

The subquery is evaluated first; its result is used to evaluate the WHERE clause of the outer query. Note that attributes whose names occur in several tables need no longer be qualified by a table name, since subqueries maintain an appropriate 'scoping'.

Example 16.22

Show room number and box number for boxes containing brown transgenic mice:

```
SELECT ROOM#, BOX#
      FROM ANIMALS, CAGES, TRANSGENICS
      WHERE ANIMALS.ANIMAL# = CAGES.ANIMAL#
      AND CAGES.ANIMAL# = TRANSGENICS.ANIMAL#
      AND COLOR = 'BROWN'
```

This will compute a join of all three tables, which can alternatively be obtained using two levels of subquery nesting:

```
SELECT ROOM#, BOX#
      FROM CAGES
      WHERE ANIMAL# IN
            (SELECT ANIMAL#
              FROM ANIMALS
              WHERE COLOR = 'BROWN'
              AND ANIMAL# IN
                   (SELECT ANIMAL#
                     FROM TRANSGENICS))
```

Example 16.23

Show the weight of brown transgenic mice living in room 2315:

```
SELECT WEIGHT FROM CAGES, TRANSGENICS, ANIMALS
      WHERE CAGES.ANIMAL# = TRANSGENICS.ANIMAL#
      AND CAGES.ANIMAL# = ANIMALS.ANIMAL#
      AND COLOR = 'BROWN' AND ROOM# = '2315'
```

Again, an alternative formulation using subqueries can easily be stated:

```
SELECT WEIGHT FROM TRANSGENICS
     WHERE ANIMAL# IN
        (SELECT ANIMAL# FROM CAGES
          WHERE ROOM# = '2315' AND ANIMAL# IN
             (SELECT ANIMAL# FROM ANIMALS
               WHERE COLOR = 'BROWN'))
```

Notice that the subqueries can be nested here in other orders too; while the result will be the same, the execution times might be different, depending, for example, on the size of intermediate results or on the availability of indexes for accessing the operands.

Example 16.24

Show the animal number and birthdate for all transgenic mice, in descending order of birthdates:

```
SELECT ANIMALS.ANIMAL#, BIRTHDATE
     FROM ANIMALS, TRANSGENICS
     WHERE ANIMALS.ANIMAL# = TRANSGENICS.ANIMAL#
     ORDER BY BIRTHDATE DESC
```

Example 16.25

Show all transgenics for which the time between injection date and birthdate was more than 200 days:

```
SELECT TRANSGENICS.ANIMAL#
     FROM ANIMALS, TRANSGENICS
     WHERE DAY(BIRTHDATE − INJ_DATE) > 200
     AND TRANSGENICS.ANIMAL# = ANIMALS.ANIMAL#
```

Example 16.26

A table can also be joined with itself. Show all pairs of animals living in the same box:

```
SELECT FIRST.ANIMAL#, SECOND.ANIMAL#
     FROM CAGES FIRST, CAGES SECOND
     WHERE FIRST.BOX# = SECOND.BOX#
     AND FIRST.ANIMAL# < SECOND.ANIMAL#
```

The result

ANIMAL#	*ANIMAL#*
12	18
27	35
43	52
52	92
43	92

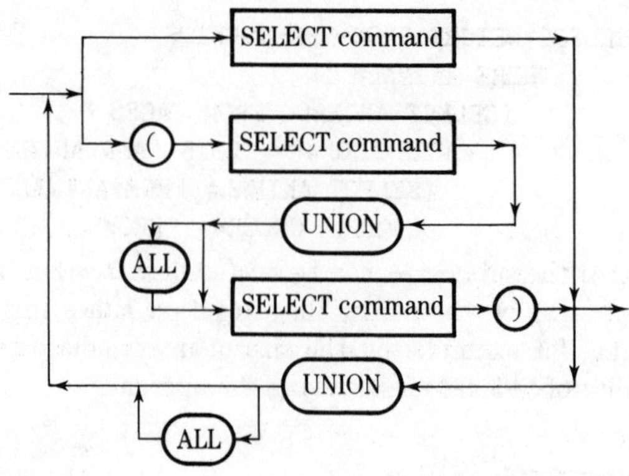

Figure 16.27 *union query.*

is obtained as follows. First, two copies of *CAGES* are created under the aliases *FIRST* and *SECOND*, respectively. These are then theta-joined according to equal box numbers, and finally all 'symmetric' tuples are removed by the second join condition.

Example 16.27

Show the total weight of all brown transgenics:

```
SELECT SUM(WEIGHT) FROM TRANSGENICS WHERE ANIMAL# IN
   (SELECT ANIMAL# FROM ANIMALS WHERE COLOR = 'BROWN')
```

16.4.4 Union queries

Several SQL queries can be combined into one to form a union query; the corresponding syntax is shown in Figure 16.27. A union query is evaluated by first evaluating the individual queries and then computing a global result, whose column names are those from the very first query and which does not contain duplicate tuples.

Example 16.28

Show the animal number for mice which were either born or injected in 1987:

```
SELECT ANIMAL# FROM ANIMALS
     WHERE YEAR(BIRTHDATE) = 1987
UNION
SELECT ANIMAL# FROM TRANSGENICS
     WHERE YEAR(INJ_DATE) = 1987
```

In a union query, an ORDER BY clause may only appear *after* the last query; it will then be applied to the overall result. In addition, a union query has to obey the following rules:

(1) The domains of corresponding *items* from the SELECT clauses of all queries must be identical. For example, if the first *item* in the SELECT clause of the first query is of type INTeger and may assume null values, the same must hold for the first *item* of *every* other query of the union.

(2) If the result of a union query shall be shown in a particular ordering, the corresponding ORDER list has to specify the *position* of an item, but not its name; for example, '`ORDER BY 1`' would be allowed in the above example, while '`ORDER BY ANIMAL#`' would not.

(3) The use of UNION is allowed neither in a subquery nor in a view definition.

The result produced by a query can be made to contain comments, which are *expressions* in the *select-list* of type 'constant'.

If SQL/DS is used interactively ('ISQL', see below), it is possible to save commands together with their formatting information for reuse. In addition, several SQL commands can be stored as a *routine*. The commands that are combined into a routine are stored by SQL/DS in table form like an ordinary relation, and this table can contain several distinct routines. A table for storing routines has to be created before a routine can be programmed.

16.5 Formatting query results

So far it has been tacitly assumed that the SQL statements described are used interactively. (Possibilities for working in batch mode will be briefly discussed later.) Thus, the result of a query will be shown on the screen. Now if it contains more tuples than can be put on one screen, the following commands are available for jumping n rows (tuples) in forward or backward direction, or to the beginning or the end of the entire output, in a similar way this can be done with a screen-oriented editor:

BACKWard [n | MAX]

or

FORWard [n | MAX]

If the result of a query shall be shown on the screen only from attribute n on (where counting proceeds from left to right), the following can be used:

COLumn [n]

A similar effect is achieved by LEFT [n] or RIGHT [n]; it is possible to jump 'attribute-wise' left or right.

If a SELECT command is used in an application program, its result can be brought to the screen using DISPLay. If a row of a result is more than 80 symbols long and therefore does not fit on the screen completely, the command TAB [n] will achieve a movement in a horizontal direction.

The central command for controlling the format of a result is called **FORMat** and will be described next; it begins with this keyword, optionally followed by one of the specifications listed below.

BTITle [string | ERASE]

specifies a footline for an output on a printer, where an old one is overwritten by ERASE, and a new one can be specified as a string of up to 100 characters.

COLumn colspec [DPLACes n | NAME string | WIDth n |
ZEROs { ON | OFF}]

formats a particular column with the following options: 'DPLACes n' specifies the desired number of digits for a numerical attribute (no rounding is performed). 'NAME string' introduces a column header (of up to 30 characters). 'WIDth n' results in displaying the leftmost n positions of the values of the attribute. 'ZEROs' controls a suppressing (OFF) or displaying (ON) of leading zeros for numerical attributes.

EXCLude [ALL BUT] { colspec | (colspec colspec ...)}

has the effect of suppressing certain columns when the result is shown on a screen. The complementary effect is achieved by 'INCLude [ONLY]'.

NULL string

specifies a string of length up to 20 characters replacing the '?' in fields that contain null values.

SEParator { n BLANKs | string}

specifies the number of blanks or a string (like '|') that will separate adjacent columns.

TTITle [string | ERASE]

achieves the printing of a headline ('top title', in analogy to BTITle).

VARChar n

specifies the width with which character strings of variable length are to be printed ($n \leq 254$).

Finally, it is possible to have sums and partial sums computed and displayed (or printed) for numerical attributes. To do so, the two options

TOTal { [EXEPT] { colspec | (colspec colspec ...)} | ERASE}

SUBTotal (same format)

are available. In both cases, the option should be preceded by a

FORMat GROUP { [EXCEPT]
{ colspec | (colspec colspec ...)}| ERASE }

For computing partial sums (subtotals) of a numerical attribute, it is even necessary to begin with a 'SELECT ... ORDER BY ... ', followed by a 'FORM GROUP ... ' applied to the same attribute as in the SELECT statement, and concluded by a 'FORM SUBT ... '.

16.6 Views

A (particular user) view is distinct from a base table in that it is a 'virtual' table which is derived from one or more base tables. This facility renders it possible to make data visible at the external level of a database according to certain criteria ('all brown mice'), or to keep data invisible. For each view that is created over a set of relations, SQL/DS (as do most other systems) will only store its definition in the data dictionary; whenever the view name occurs in a DML statement, its current value will be computed on the basis of the current contents of the database, and the corresponding operations or query will be applied to this value. Once the command has been executed, the view value is no longer stored.

Views can be created under unique names from base relations, or deleted at any time, using the following two commands:

CREATE VIEW view-name [(column-name-list)]
AS select-statement

DROP VIEW view-name

As an example, consider a relation *EMP* of employees of a company with the attributes (employee) number, name, address and a statement of whether or not the employee is a member of the company's football team (see Section 8.5). A view definition for all employees living in Los Angeles would then be:

```
CREATE VIEW LA_EMP AS
     SELECT * FROM EMP WHERE ADDR = 'L.A.'
```

Similarly, a view for the coach of the football team is created by

```
CREATE VIEW FOOTBALL AS
    SELECT * FROM EMP WHERE FB = 'yes'
```

Note that neither UNION nor ORDER BY may be used in a SELECT statement that defines a view.

The name of a defined view may be used in queries right away (as in `SELECT NAME FROM FOOTBALL`); the corresponding definition will then be evaluated. The following two restrictions apply, however: (1) If a column of a view was defined via an aggregate function, the name of this column may appear neither in the WHERE clause nor in another aggregate function occurring in the SELECT clause of a view query. (2) If a GROUP BY clause is used in a view definition, this view cannot participate in a join operation.

SQL views may also undergo update operations. An INSERT, DELETE or UPDATE command applied to a view is transformed into a corresponding command over the underlying base relation; updates on join views are not possible. The result of an update is eventually visible in the view itself (depending on the view definition); it is always visible in the underlying base relation, and eventually in some or all other views over this relation as well.

From a system's point of view, the creator of a view gets the privileges mentioned in Section 16.1 on this view, but will get the SELECT privilege only if the view contains a join (see above) or was defined using GROUP BY, DISTINCT or an aggregate function.

View columns which are computed via an expression from the underlying base relation also cannot be manipulated via UPDATE; an INSERT with respect to such columns is forbidden too, but a DELETE is not. When an INSERT on a view is executed, the attributes of the base relation which are missing in the view definition will be filled with null values. Finally, the following should be mentioned:

(1) It is possible to insert a tuple into a view (or to update it within a view) which violates a defining condition (like `ADDR = L.A.` above). Such an operation will be executed on the underlying table, and its result will not be visible in the view.

(2) Views may contain duplicate elements whose 'extensions' in the base relation are distinct. If this is the case, it is advisable to be careful in using UPDATE and DELETE, since undesired side-effects may occur.

16.7 Interfaces to SQL/DS

So far it has been assumed that a user is working with the SQL/Data System interactively, that is, from a terminal on a command-by-command basis; the commands which have been described (and all that will be described later) can all be used in this way. In this section, other interactive as well as the major batch interfaces available for this DBMS will briefly be described.

16.7.1 Interactive interfaces

The major interactive interfaces to SQL/DS are:

ISQL	Interactive SQL
QMF	Query Management Facility with
QBE	Query-By-Example
DBEDIT	Data Base EDIT Facility

ISQL is the standard interactive SQL/DS interface, which besides all 'ordinary' SQL commands provides several additional ones for controlling ISQL sessions as well as for communicating with the system. The interface is invoked by typing 'ISQL' and exited by 'EXIT'; between these two commands, all the commands described above can be used.

QMF is an operational SQL/DS interface providing the user with the two languages SQL and QBE for working with databases; these languages can be used in an alternating fashion within one QMF session. Query results generated in either language are returned in some standard format and can be used as input for the *report generator* available under QMF. In addition, QMF allows the storing of (parameterized) command sequences and their execution upon request, and the storing of query results for later processing. A QMF *report* is formatted according to a set of specifications called a *form*, which is stored in a (temporary) working area named FORM, and which can be displayed by switching to the *form panel* ('DISPLAY FORM'). Other working areas maintained by QMF are QUERY for SQL or QBE commands, DATA for storing a query result, PROC for QMF procedures, and PROFILE for specifying general parameters. Each area has associated with it a corresponding panel that can be displayed individually.

The details of report generation will not be discussed here, since this goes beyond the scope of this text. The major commands associated with the various working areas are SAVE, RUN, DISPLAY and PRINT, whose meanings are straightforward. For example,

RUN QUERY

executes the query currently stored in QUERY; the result is placed in DATA.

SAVE DATA AS dname

stores the current contents of DATA permanently under the name 'dname'.

DISPLAY FORM

shows the default format for the current contents of DATA.

PRINT QUERY

sends the contents of QUERY to a printer.

Some of the panels simply prompt the user for (additional) information; also, QMF assigns the function keys of the terminal with specific commands, so that in most situations either one of these keys can be pressed or commands can be typed alternatively. A complete report generation typically goes through steps such as the following:

(1) build a query in QUERY;

(2) execute (RUN) this query;

(3) inspect the default format and edit it as desired;

(4) generate a report by saying '{ PRINT | DISPLAY } REPORT';

(5) repeat Steps 3 and 4 as long as necessary.

As was mentioned above, the language **QBE** is available under QMF (and not outside this facility) as an alternative to SQL. QBE is a 'two-dimensional' screen-oriented query language, which initially provides the user with an empty *table skeleton* in a default format. The user then specifies a query by marking columns as desired, thereby eventually entering an 'example' (a sample table or part thereof).

Example 16.29

Consider the query

```
SELECT ANIMAL# FROM ANIMALS WHERE SEX = 'F'
```

from Section 16.4 once more. Under QMF, the result of this query can alternatively be obtained using QBE as follows.

(1) The command '`DRAW ANIMALS`' will generate the following empty table:

ANIMAL	*ANIMAL#*	*SEX*	*COLOUR*	*BIRTHDATE*

(2) In this table the columns to be shown are marked by 'P.' (PRESENT); in addition, the selection conditions are entered. The above query results in the following:

ANIMAL	ANIMAL#	SEX	COLOUR	BIRTHDATE
	P.	F		

Another interactive interface to SQL/DS is **DBEDIT**, by which a user can communicate with the system and the databases managed by it via masks that support a simple data entry and retrieval. New masks are generated, designed or modified using PFORM, and 'applied' using PQUERY. A notable feature of DBEDIT is the possibility to restrict the domain of an attribute in an application-specific manner, that is, to operate on (new or existing) tuples that have particular values only. For example, an attribute of type SMALLINT can be restricted to assume the values of an enumeration (sub)type in masks only.

16.7.2 Batch interfaces

Clearly, SQL/DS databases can also be accessed from application programs by **embedding** SQL commands appropriately. The available host languages currently include FORTRAN, PL/I, COBOL, System/370 Assembler, APL2 and VM/Prolog. While for the first four programs comprising SQL statements are first processed by a precompiler, the latter two interact with SQL/DS through a *communication interface*. In the remainder of this section, attention is restricted to the former approach.

A precompiler recognizes SQL statements by the prefix 'EXEC SQL' as in

```
EXEC SQL SELECT ANIMAL# FROM ANIMALS
```

Since SQL/DS always operates set-oriented as seen from outside and since conventional programming languages are typically unable to process data of type 'table' directly, a communication *area* is used to store query results; a program accesses such an area sequentially using a **cursor** similar in a way to the use of a currency pointer in a network system. A cursor acts like a tuple-variable; for each attribute of the relation on which an application program works, a *host variable* needs to be declared.

Example 16.30

The following excerpt from a PL/I program returns the weight of transgenic mouse number 35:

```
    :
EXEC SQL BEGIN DECLARE SECTION;
    DCL :ANIMAL# FIXED(5) DECIMAL;
    DCL :WEIGHT FIXED(5,2) DECIMAL;
EXEC SQL END DECLARE SECTION;
:
```

```
:ANIMAL# = 35;
:
EXEC SQL SELECT WEIGHT
     INTO :WEIGHT
     FROM TRANSGENICS
     WHERE ANIMAL# = :ANIMAL#;
:
```

Notice that (1) host variables are prefixed with a colon to distinguish them from attribute names, and that (2) the SELECT command now has an INTO clause for assigning a database value to a host variable.

The above example does not make use of a cursor yet, since the value retrieved is unique. However, if a table is returned instead of a single value or tuple, the user needs to proceed as in the following example:

Example 16.31

Consider the query

```
SELECT ANIMAL#, COLOR FROM ANIMALS WHERE SEX = 'M'
```

In order to process the resulting table in a tuple-by-tuple fashion, a cursor needs to be declared, opened, assigned (next) values and finally closed:

```
     :
EXEC SQL DECLARE ANIMALCURSOR CURSOR FOR
     SELECT ANIMAL#, COLOR
     FROM ANIMALS
     WHERE SEX = 'M';
:
EXEC SQL OPEN ANIMALCURSOR;
:
EXEC SQL FETCH ANIMALCURSOR INTO :ANIMAL#, :COLOR;
:
EXEC SQL CLOSE ANIMALCURSOR;
:
```

Here it is assumed that `:ANIMAL#` and `:COLOR` have also been declared properly; the FETCH will typically be executed in a loop.

Two further interfaces to SQL/DS are **SQLDBSU** (SQL Data Base Services Utility) and **REXX** (Restructured Extended Executor), an IBM command language. The former makes it possible to transfer data managed by SQL/DS into CMS files or vice versa (for example, for making safety copies); in particular, the following functions are provided:

(1) DATALOAD for loading data from a CMS file into SQL/DS tables,

(2) DATAUNLOAD for doing the converse of 1,

(3) UNLOAD for loading data from a table or a DBSPACE into a CMS file,

(4) RELOAD for reloading a CMS file previously created by UNLOAD into the database.

16.8 SQL/DS architecture

In this section a brief look will be taken at the architecture of the database system discussed in this chapter; details of the IBM operating-system environment are not discussed, but a few basic terms related to this context are mentioned.

The VM operating system provides each user with a *virtual machine* (VM), that is, the illusion that an entire computer is at his or her exclusive disposal. The operation of SQL/DS is based on another, specific VM called the *database machine* (DBM), which is responsible for all command processing and database accesses; a user's VM communicates with the DBM through a set-oriented interface provided by the CMS and CP subsystems of VM. Underneath this interface, the DBM comprises the **Relational Data System** (RDS), which communicates with the **Data Base Storage System** (DBSS) through a tuple-oriented interface. The RDS performs tasks like the parsing of commands, the checking of user authorizations, query optimization or code generation. The DBSS ('data manager') manages the system buffer maintained in main memory and is the only component that physically accesses a database (via an operating-system interface).

16.8.1 On the organization of the internal level

As was briefly mentioned in Section 16.1, tables are associated with **DBSPACEs**, where a DBSPACE is basically a logical storage segment that is subdivided into pages. These pages are mapped to (physical) *STORAGE POOLs*, which in turn consist of *DBEXTENTs*, that is, CMS 'minidisks' defined under VM/SP.

A user can influence the organization of the internal level, for example, by choosing a certain number and type of DBSPACEs, by associating tables with specific DBSPACEs (see the CREATE TABLE command in Section 16.1) or by doing the same for STORAGE POOLs.

If a table has been assigned to a particular DBSPACE, all indexes for this table will automatically be 'stored' in the same DBSPACE. To establish a new DBSPACE for usage, a command 'ACQUIRE ... DBSPACE ...' is available, which will not be explained here. A tuple of a table represents the smallest addressable unit, which is internally equipped with a unique **tuple identifier** (TID). A TID consists of a page number (for a STORAGE POOL) and a slot number (in the form of an offset from the *end* of the page); the slot in turn contains a pointer to the tuple (in the form of an offset from the *beginning* of the page). This scheme is used to facilitate database reorganizations.

As with the SSL of the UDS system, a user of SQL/DS has several possibilities to influence the systems's response time. For example, it is reasonable either to assign each table to a separate DBSPACE, or to create an index for each table if several are stored in the same DBSPACE. The reason for this is that, in the absence of an index, no information is maintained by the system regarding which DBSPACE pages the tuples of a given relation are stored in. As a result, the entire DBSPACE must be scanned whenever this relation is accessed. On the other hand, when an index is present the latter will be scanned first when a table-access is required; since an index is always implemented as a B*-tree whose leaves consist of value/TID pairs, the pages to be accessed can be determined uniquely.

```
EXPLAIN { explain-spec | ALL} [SET QUERYNO = n]
    FOR sql-command
```

provides information on the structure and the performance of an SQL command. This renders it possible, for example, to analyse a given database design ('prototyping', see Chapter 10). The system will put the corresponding information in one or more tables which can be listed (separated by commas) in the explain-spec: *REFERENCE, STRUCTURE, COST, PLAN.* By specifying a QUERYNO, the information in these tables can be uniquely identified. The following commands can be analysed: INSERT, DELETE, UPDATE, SELECT.

In particular, the EXPLAIN command is useful for analysing the 'query cost estimate', which is computed and displayed by the system for each query and which is stored in the *COST* table. In this context, another system component, the **query optimizer**, should be mentioned. This is employed by the RDS to generate an **access plan**, that is, procedures to compute a query result. SQL/DS maintains various information pertaining to the efficiency of query execution, like the number of tuples in a table, the number of pages occupied by a table, the percentage of pages occupied by a table within a DBSPACE, the number of distinct values in an index, the number of pages occupied by an index, the number of leaves and the height of an index (as a tree). These 'table statistics' are kept in particular dictionary tables; they are *not* updated by the system on a regular basis, but only if the user requests an update by

```
UPDATE [ALL] STATISTICS FOR
    { TABLE [creator.] table-name |
          DBSPACE [creator.] dbspace-name }
```

This command should be issued especially after a new table has been filled with data for the first time and after major modifications have been performed on its contents.

Based on the current statistics, the query optimizer makes decisions on how to translate a given query into an executable procedure ('access module'). In order to understand the result, the EXPLAIN command can be employed. After its execution, the *PLAN* table contains statements about the sequencing of table accesses for executing the query in question, the indexes used and the join-method employed (if applicable). The *REFERENCE* table contains a row for each attribute referenced by the command in question, while the *STRUCTURE* table contains a row for each query in the 'query block' of EXPLAIN. Thus, to get a query EXPLAINed is particularly useful for a frequently repeated one.

16.8.2 Transactions

In this subsection the concept of a *transaction*, mentioned in Chapter 14 and available in SQL/DS, will briefly be returned to. Recall that, in an application environment, a database is typically not accessed by one user only, but by several users simultaneously, and that it is important that these users do not interfere with each other, and that the activities executed by one user run independent of everybody else's. The way this is accomplished is to employ a *transaction management* which controls the (quasi-)parallel access to a database.

Each 'order' issued by a user is generally perceived by the DBMS at the (internal) system level as a sequence of read or write accesses to the database (see Chapter 18). For example, the request 'increase every *WEIGHT* value in relation *TRANSGENICS* by 5' could internally consist of first reading every tuple in that relation (from secondary) into main memory (where 'computations' of any kind can then be performed), adding 5 to the corresponding value in the *WEIGHT* field, and finally writing a new tuple (the updated one) back into secondary memory. As was discussed above, it is of central importance that the request is processed completely (not on a subset of the relation in question only, for whatever reasons); if this cannot be guaranteed, the user expects the system to interrupt the execution and to respond with an appropriate error message, since any partial execution is undesirable.

To this end, the concept of a **transaction** is also available in SQL/DS, which represents the 'logical unit' in which each user request is internally processed. In general, a single transaction consists of a sequence of (internal) steps; however, from a user's point of view it is *atomic* in the sense that it will be executed either completely or not at all (see also Section 8.4 on this issue).

For every SQL command transmitted to the system, a transaction in this sense is internally created. The successful (and complete) execution of such a command is signalled by the transaction management in a **COMMIT operation** which makes the modifications that the command or transaction may have performed on the database permanent (and thereby available for other users). However, if a logical unit cannot be processed completely (for instance because of the discovery that a key or index violation has occurred), a **ROLLBACK operation** will be executed, which will undo all modifications that have been done to the database so far, thus bringing the database into the state it was in before the transaction started (see also Part VI).

SQL/DS provides the user with a few possibilities to influence its transaction management. Under normal circumstances, the system will consider every user request (that is, each single command, every routine or every application program) as a transaction whose effect on the current database state will indeed be committed (made permanent) before a subsequent request (from this user) is processed; to this end, the *AUTOCOMMIT flag* will always be set (AUTOCOMMIT ON) after logging on, indicating that an 'automatic commit (attempt)' at the end of each transaction is intended. During an INSERT, a DELETE or an UPDATE, however, it may happen that the command refers to more than one tuple of a given relation; in this case the user can either trigger the execution of the commit operation by issuing the next command, or prevent its execution, thereby abandoning the entire command. The latter is achieved by using CANCEL or ROLLBACK WORK. The former immediately interrupts the execution of a transaction; the effect of the transaction will be undone, while the latter terminates a transaction normally, but without making its effect permanent. The AUTOCOMMIT flag can be reset by

SET AUTOCOMMIT OFF

In this way a user can make sure that modifications are made permanent in the database only if explicitly requested. As a result, all DML commands (and in particular INSERT, DELETE and UPDATE) will be executed temporarily only; all effects are temporary and visible for this particular user only. In order to make the effect permanent, the user must intentionally issue COMMIT WORK. A **synchronization point** to which subsequent COMMIT, CANCEL or ROLLBACK operations will refer is thereby set; for example, a later CANCEL will undo all modification from the last synchronization point on.

If the AUTOCOMMIT flag is set (to ON), the 'SAVE' command can be used *during* an INPut command, with the effect that all modifications (new tuples) created after the last SAVE are now saved (if there was no previous SAVE, all modifications since the beginning of the INPut command are saved). Analogously, all most recent changes (since the last SAVE or since the beginning of INPut) can be nullified by 'BACKOUT'.

If a transaction is executed by the transaction manager, all tables which need to be accessed during the transaction are **locked**, that is, temporarily withdrawn from public access; a table is locked in *SHARE mode* [*EXCLUSIVE mode*] if it will be accessed for reading [and/or writing], respectively. The user can also lock a table on his own using the following command:

```
LOCK {TABLE table-name | DBSPACE dbspace-name}
     IN {SHARE | EXCLUSIVE} MODE
```

The use of this command is only necessary, however, if a complete and uninterrupted processing of data from a 'public dbspace' is required. The lock set is kept until the next SQL command terminates when AUTOCOMMIT is ON; otherwise, it will be in effect until the next 'COMMIT' or 'ROLLBACK WORK' is issued.

16.9 The world of SQL

SQL/DS was developed between 1971 and 1981 as a relational prototype under the name 'System/R' at the IBM Research Center in San Jose, California. During that time, SQL was an acronym for SEQUEL (*Structured English Query Language*). The system became commercially available in 1981; in relationship with the product, SQL now stands for 'Structured Query Language'. Meanwhile, the SQL language is also used for other database management products by IBM, among them DB2 for machines with an MVS/370 or MVS/XA operating system and QMF ('Query Management Facility'), SQL/400 and the OS/2 EE Database Manager.

In 1982 the American National Standards Institute (ANSI) became involved in the process of standardizing SQL as a language for relational database systems; the standard came into effect in 1986. In this context, SQL finally became an acronym for 'Standard Query Language'. As a result of the ANSI and also ISO efforts, the language SQL is now employed by many other vendors of database systems as a user interface, among them Ingres (Relational Technology), Oracle (Oracle Corp.), Unify, Informix, Empress (Rhodnius), dBase IV (Ashton-Tate), NonStop-SQL (Tandem), Sybase (Sybase Inc.), Rdb (DEC) and many others.

To conclude this chapter, a brief 'comparison' will be made of the relational model of data as it was introduced in Chapter 7 and its implementation under SQL/DS, and of IBM-SQL and ANS-SQL.

The *model* is in general based on sets, at both the conceptual and the internal level. A relation schema comprises a *set* of attributes; a relation is a *set* of tuples. On the other hand, under SQL/DS a table format is a *sequence* of attributes, and a relation is a *sequence* of tuples in which duplicate elements may occur. For database queries, this view leads to operations (like concatenation and theta-join) whose result is formally not necessarily a relation, so that SQL and the language RA introduced in Chapter 8 must *formally* be classified as incomparable. Another distinction between the relational model in general and SQL/DS in particular must be seen in the fact that the notion of a 'database schema' in the sense of Definition 7.5 is unknown in this system. SQL/DS treats each relation schema as a separate 'unit'. As a result, a certain discrepancy can be recognized between the relational model from a theoretical point of view, and a practical 'realization' of it. It should be mentioned, however, that the same or similar 'restrictions' also apply to other 'relational' systems.

A similar discrepancy can be discovered between the IBM implementation of SQL and the language SQL as proposed in the ANSI standard. To this end, it should be mentioned first that IBM's SQL goes beyond the language standard in various ways (like the inclusion of data and time support); on the other hand, some features of the standard are not yet included (like a NUMERIC or REAL data type or an ESCAPE clause in a like-condition). IBM-SQL and ANS-SQL are incomparable in other issues too, one of which is as follows.

The possibility to declare database schemas in the sense explained above *is* included in the Standard, which actually distinguishes the following three types of SQL 'sublanguages':

(1) A **schema definition language** for defining the time-invariant structure of a database.

(2) A **module language** for declaring cursors and procedures associated with an application program written in one of the host languages COBOL, FORTRAN, Pascal or PL/I.

(3) A **data manipulation language** in the usual sense.

A **schema definition** in ANS-SQL has the following general syntax:

```
CREATE SCHEMA
      AUTHORIZATION user-name
      [ { table-definition | view-definition | privilege-definition }
      { ... } ]
```

A *table-definition* has the following form:

```
CREATE TABLE table-name-1
      ( column-name-1 type-1 [ NOT NULL [ UNIQUE ]]
            [ DEFAULT { literal-1 | USER | NULL } ]
```

```
[, column-name-2 ... ]
     ⋮
[, UNIQUE ( column-name-list ) [, UNIQUE ... ]]
[, PRIMARY KEY ( column-name-list )
[, FOREIGN KEY ( column-name-list )
     REFERENCES table-name-2 [( column-name-list )]
[, FOREIGN KEY ... ]]
[, CHECK ( condition ) [, CHECK ... ]] )
```

The features not supported by SQL/DS are the UNIQUE and CHECK clauses; the latter can be used to define checks on domains. The declaration of a one-attribute candidate key of the form `UNIQUE (A)` is equivalent to the attribute definition `A ... NOT NULL UNIQUE`.

Chapter 17
Implementation of Single-Relational Query Languages

This chapter deviates from the strategy so far employed in this part, which consists of the presentation of 'representative' database management systems that are commercially available, in that a particular branch of current research in databases will be described. On the one hand, this continues the exposition of the theory of the relational model that was begun in Chapters 8, 9 and 12; on the other hand, the purpose is to indicate *that* and *how* results obtained in this theory can be relevant for the practical implementation of user interfaces for database systems.

17.1 Window functions: databasewise navigation

In Chapter 12 a special aspect of the design problem for relational database schemas was considered; the aspect was 'special' in the sense that it is actually just one step of the design process as presented in Chapter 10. Of central importance for this chapter is the assumption made in Chapter 12 that a given application can *also* be decribed by one 'universal schema' $R = (U, F)$, provided that all attribute names are globally unique, which was captured by the Universal Relation Schema Assumption (URSA). This single relation schema never gets stored in a database, however, but is only used as a basis for the generation of a decomposition that (hopefully) is lossless and independent and that describes the *same* application as R itself. In this chapter another consequence from this assumption on the naming of attributes is considered, which has to do with *data manipulation* or the usage of a universal relation or a UR schema as a *manipulation aid.*

If **D** is a database schema whose attributes satisfy URSA, that is, each attribute name completely expresses the meaning of that attribute already, a query language like relational algebra can be simplified considerably for a user, by freeing him or her from certain 'navigations through the schema' that occur in connection with joins.

Example 17.1

Let the following excerpt from the university database (see Chapter 16) be given, which consists of three relation schemas:

$$\begin{aligned} STUDENT &= (\{\ STUDID,\ SNAME,\ S\text{-}CITY\ \}, \\ &\quad\ \{\ STUDID \rightarrow SNAME,\ S\text{-}CITY\ \}) \\ COURSE &= (\{\ CNO,\ CTITLE\ \},\ \{\ CNO \rightarrow CTITLE\ \}) \\ ATTENDS &= (\{\ STUDID,\ CNO\ \},\ \emptyset) \end{aligned}$$

If a user asks for the title of each course student Miller attends, this query can be expressed as follows using the language RA:

$$\pi_{CTITLE}(\sigma_{SNAME='Miller'}(STUDENT) \\ \bowtie ATTENDS \bowtie COURSE)$$

Informally, the database is first searched for the ID of student Miller in relation *STUDENT*; next, the corresponding course numbers are determined using relation *ATTENDS*; and finally the desired titles are found in relation *COURSE.* A formulation of the same query in SQL is as follows:

```
SELECT CTITLE FROM STUDENT, COURSE, ATTENDS
       WHERE SNAME = 'Miller'
             AND STUDENT.STUDID = ATTENDS.STUDID
```

```
AND ATTENDS.CNO = COURSE.CNO
```

The 'problem' a user has to solve is that a (setwise) 'navigation' through the given database is required as soon as more than one relation is addressed in a query; in particular, all join conditions must eventually be specified explicitly. To this end, knowledge on the conceptual schema of the database in question (or on an excerpt thereof) is needed; on the other hand, it is possible to work with physical data independence (see Chapter 1) since no knowledge is needed on the internal structure of the database. However, it is still impossible to talk of *logical* data independence as well, which would mean, for instance, that the formulation of a query is also independent of the particular form of the conceptual schema.

Under the assumption of global uniqueness of attribute names, the SQL query shown in the previous example (and also the corresponding RA expression) can in principle be simplified to

```
SELECT CNAME WHERE SNAME = 'Miller'
```

In this case, the user leaves all navigation to the DBMS; in particular, no statement of *which* occurrence of a certain attribute is meant is necessary.

In other words, under URSA it is (often) possible to simplify SPJ expressions to 'SP expressions', if the schema of the universal relation, which, for instance, was 'generated' for design purposes, is provided for the purposes of data manipulation as well and hence kept at the external level of the corresponding database. As a consequence, the user can make use of a '**single-relational**' language in which a specification of relation-schema names is no longer required, since an implicit reference is made to the schema of the universal relation. (A few exceptions in which it is still necessary to go beyond the capabilities of such a language will be discussed later.)

Figure 17.1 illustrates this new situation. Notice that now the case occurs in which the external level represents a *global view* of the database that *differs* from the one described in the conceptual schema; this was mentioned in Chapter 2 in connection with the three-level architecture model. This particular form of the external level is also termed a **universal-relation [schema] interface**, which is abbreviated **USI**.

In the presence of a USI, that is, if an external level is 'explicitly available', the corresponding DBMS gets the additional task of translating a ('database-wise') user query that is formulated with respect to R into an SQL expression or, more generally, into an RA expression, which can then be evaluated in the way described in Chapter 8. Such a translation is also called the **implementation** of the single-relational language. In this chapter, several strategies for obtaining such an implementation will be presented. Before that, a formal description of what an implementation

$$
\begin{array}{lll}
\text{external level:} & (U, F) & = R \\
& \Updownarrow & \\
\text{conceptual level:} & \{R_1, \ldots, R_k\} & = \mathbf{R} \\
& \Updownarrow & \\
\text{internal level:} & \{r_1, \ldots, r_k\} & = d
\end{array}
$$

Figure 17.1 The three database levels in the presence of a USI.

needs to accomplish will be given.

If selection conditions that might occur in a query are neglected for a moment, a query to R can be represented simply as a set $X \subseteq U$ of attributes; the 'query for X' has consequently to be answered by the DBMS by returning a relation r over X (to which selections as well as other operations can finally be applied). Thus, the central new task of a DBMS with USI can be described as follows. For given $X \subseteq U$ and $d \in \text{Sat}(\mathbf{D})$, compute a relation r over X. In other words, a USI formally provides a mapping W with range $2^U \times \text{Sat}(\mathbf{D})$. For X and D, $W(X, d) \in \text{Rel}(X)$. Any such mapping W is called a **window function** since it releases a certain section of a database (like a part seen through a window); the common notation is $[X, d]$ or simply $[X]$ if the application of $[.]$ to X (for fixed d) is meant.

Two classes of strategies for computing or 'implementing' such 'X-windows' or window functions will be presented next, which are referred to as 'bottom-up' and 'top-down', respectively. To unify the exposition, it is always assumed that relational algebra is available as the 'ordinary' query language, so that the goal of implementing an X-window is to derive an expression $E_X \in \text{RA}$; this latter expression can then be processed further by the DBMS as usual.

17.2 Bottom-up strategies

In the **bottom-up approach**, also known as **computational window functions**, a relation over the desired set X of attributes is computed directly ('bottom-up') from the current database state d. According to the philosophy of this approach, the hypothetical universal relation, which is never stored as part of the database, or an excerpt thereof is only a particular 'view' to the database.

A first idea for computing a window over some given X in this sense could consist of computing a (natural) join over the entire database $d = \{r_1, \ldots, r_k\}$ and projecting the result onto X, that is,

$$[X] := \pi_X(\bowtie_{i=1}^{k} R_i)$$

In practice, this approach is not used, for the obvious reason that such a join might be lossy, so that either the result could contain 'too many' tuples (and hence 'too little' information, see Chapter 12) or certain ('dangling') tuples which do not have 'join partners' could be lost during the evaluation of the window. In addition, the computation involved might be overly expensive, for example if the user asks for one attribute only.

A second idea for computing an X window consists of joining only 'as far as necessary'. A problem with this approach is that it may happen that certain join-connections cannot be formed at all or cannot be formed in a unique fashion. For example, consider the three relation schemas above as well as the query that asks for the IDs of all students; a decision has to be made whether the resulting RA expression involves relation *STUDENT* or relation *ATTENDS* only or whether it should comprise a join of the two.

The approach more commonly used in a bottom-up strategy is to generate and to evaluate certain *unions* of join expressions. The first two examples of experimental realizations which will be presented use particular 'navigation aids', which have to be fixed at the design-time of the conceptual schema and which predetermine certain (partial) join paths.

System/U is an experimental DBMS that was developed at Stanford University. A database schema **D** consists of relation schemas of the form $R = (X, F)$ with embedded 'objects', which are minimal set of attributes that have a collective meaning, and eventually FDs, where **D** is assumed to be lossless with respect to the objects. If the join-dependency thus specified is 'cyclic' (see Exercise 32 in Part III), the system computes an acyclic set **M** of so-called *maximal objects* at design-time; the latter are unions of objects from the relation schemas. For a given set X, the window $[X]_S$ is then computed as follows:

$$[X]_S := \bigcup_{M \in \mathbf{M}, X \subseteq M} \text{opt}(\pi_X(\bowtie_{R \in M} R))$$

For each maximal object M containing X a relational expression is constructed, which consists of the join of all relation schemas participating in M; this expression is optimized (indicated by 'opt' in the expression above) in a special way.

One problem with this approach could be seen in the fact that it is not possible in all cases to derive an answer for a given $X \subseteq U$; if X is not contained in any maximal object, it follows that $[X]_S = \emptyset$. In addition, it may happen that the user is forced to navigate through the set **M** of maximal objects, which is a certain contradiction to the general idea behind a USI. Finally, even in the absence of maximal objects it can be problematic to make the expression generated for answering the query $[X]_S$ plausible.

The system **PITS** (Pie In the Sky) was developed at the State University of New York at Stony Brook. The window function underlying its query language **PIQUE** is based on a set **A** of *associations* (an analogue to the objects of System/U), where a subset-relationship between associations is allowed. In addition, *objects* are used, which are unions of associations that describe (not necessarily elementary) relationships between sets of attributes. Objects can in some sense be compared with the maximal objects of System/U since they 'trigger' the computation of X-windows:

$$[X]_P := \bigcup_{Z \in \mathbf{O}, X \subseteq Z} (\pi_X (\bowtie_{R \in A, R \subseteq Z} R))$$

One drawback of this approach could be seen in the fact that the user needs to know the object-association structure of the underlying database in order to be able to formulate queries so that meaningful or the desired results can be obtained. Thus, knowledge is again required on a section of the conceptual level that corresponds to the conceptual schema.

Another system to be mentioned in this context uses the strategy to compute and evaluate *all* possible non-trivial partial joins which can be formed in the underlying database schema in order to compute a window: **DURST** is an experimental USI that was originally developed at the University of Dortmund, FRG. The window function implemented is as follows:

$$[X]_D := \tau_X (\otimes\ d)$$

where

$$\otimes\ d := \text{sub}(\bigcup_{E \in JP} \text{pad}_U (\bowtie_{R \in E} r))$$

and

$$JP := \{E \mid \emptyset \neq E \subseteq \mathbf{R}, E \text{ connected as a hypergraph}\}$$

Here, '$\otimes$' is called **complete join**; an evaluation of this operator with respect to the current state d first evaluates all (non-Cartesian) partial joins of the elements of d and extends the resulting tuples to tuples over U by padding them with a placeholder-null ('pad_U', see Section 17.3). Finally, the result is freed from redundancies ('sub', see also the next section) which arise if some tuples contain 'more information' than ('subsume') others. τ_X means 'total projection' (see Definition 17.4).

A certain problem with this approach is the fact that *all possible*

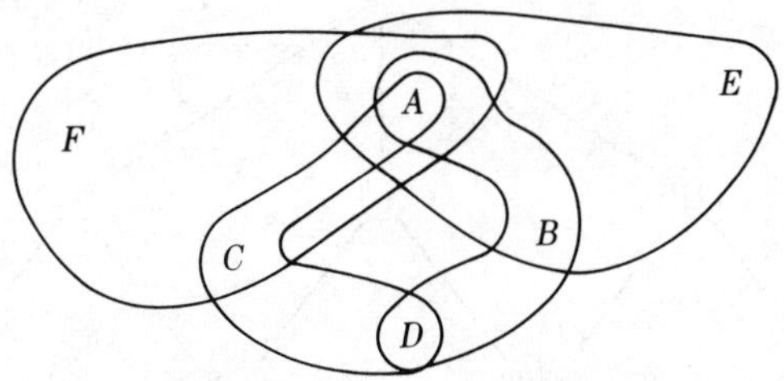

Figure 17.2 Hypergraph for Example 17.2.

join-paths are respected, since this is eventually neither desired by the user nor efficiently executable. So-called 'characteristic' attributes might provide a solution to this (see the references cited below); however, navigation aids of this kind should be avoidable according to the USI philosophy.

The approach just described can alternatively be characterized as follows (a proof of this statement is left to the reader). For a given X, the (largest) relation over X is constructed which is made possible by (connected) joins of base relations. Let $JP(X)$ denote the set of all (unshortable) join-paths through the given schema $\mathbf{D}$ that 'cover' X (in the sense that the union of all occurring attributes contains X); then this can be formally described as follows:

$$[X]_D = \bigcup_{E \in JP(X)} \pi_X(\bowtie_{R \in E} R)$$

The hypergraph interpretation of a database schema that was introduced in Exercise 32 in Part III is now applied and therefore is briefly repeated next. Let $\mathbf{D} = (\mathbf{R}, .)$, where $\mathbf{R} = \{R_1, \ldots, R_k\}$. A hypergraph $H(\mathbf{D})$ can be defined by $H(\mathbf{D}) := (N, K)$, where $N := \cup_{i=1}^{k} X_i$, and $K := \{X_1, \ldots, X_k\}$.

Example 17.2

Let $\mathbf{D}$ consist of four relation schemas with attribute sets ABE, ABD, ACD and ACF, respectively. The hypergraph $H(\mathbf{D})$ is shown in Figure 17.2. Next consider $X = BC$; the following set of join-paths covering X is obtained:

$$JP(BC) = \{\{ABE, ACD\}, \{ABD, ACD\}, \{ABE, ACF\}, \\ \{ABD, ACF\}\}$$

In slight abuse of our notation (identifying relation schemas and formats), the following SPJU (short for 'SPJ' plus Union) expression is obtained for the window on X:

$$[BC]_D = \pi_{BC}(ABE \bowtie ACD) \cup \pi_{BC}(ABD \bowtie ACD)$$

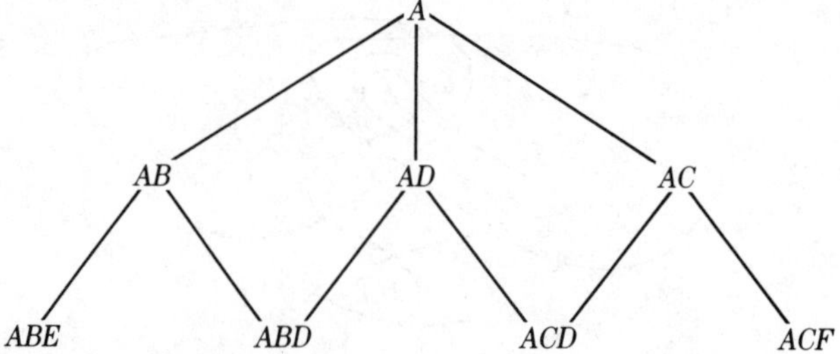

Figure 17.3 Intersection-tree for the hypergraph from Figure 17.2.

$$\cup\ \pi_{BC}(ABE \bowtie ACF) \cup \pi_{BC}(ABD \bowtie ACF)$$

The window strategies of System/U and PITS can also be rephrased in terms of hypergraphs, but this will not be demonstrated here. Instead, two other approaches will briefly be mentioned that are based on certain manipulations of the hypergraph representation of a database schema; although both differ from the DURST approach in general, it can be shown that all three agree if the condition of *γ-acyclicity* (see Definition 17.1 below) is imposed on the hypergraph (see Theorem 17.3).

For a given hypergraph $H(\mathbf{D})$, a tree can be constructed that represents all *non-empty intersections* which can be formed in a given database schema; obviously, such information is relevant to forming non-trivial joins in a database. Figure 17.3 shows the **intersection-tree** for the hypergraph from Figure 17.2. Next, the formats occurring in such a tree can formally be added to the underlying schema, thereby obtaining the **intersection-schema**, denoted $\mathbf{D}^{\cap}$. In this schema, the formats which stem from non-leaf nodes of the intersection-tree will in general not correspond to formats of base relations that were present before; therefore, relations over these formats need to be computed whenever such a format occurs in a join-expression. One way to do so is the following. Let V be a set of attributes, and let

$$\text{Cover}_{\mathbf{D}}(V) := \{Y \mid R = (Y, .) \in \mathbf{D} \text{ and } Y \supseteq V\}$$

Next, a 'view' with format V can be defined as follows (in further abuse of the notation used here, a format Y is identified with 'its' relation schema R):

$$R_V := \cup_{R \in \text{Cover}_{\mathbf{D}}(V)}\ \pi_V(R)$$

For example, let $H(\mathbf{D})$ be as in the previous example, and consider $V = AB$. Then

$$\text{Cover}_{\mathbf{D}}(AB) = \{\ ABE,\ ABD\ \}$$

and hence

$$R_{AB} = \pi_{AB}(ABE) \cup \pi_{AB}(ABD)$$

Views of this type will be used in the window functions described next. First recall from Exercise 32 in Part III the method for (eventually) reducing a given hypergraph $H(\mathbf{D}) = (N, K)$ to the empty set:

(1) If there exists edges k_1 and k_2 in K such that $k_1 \subset k_2$, remove k_1 from K.

(2) If $A \in N$ occurs in exactly one $k \in K$, remove A from N (and k).

This procedure is now modified slightly by allowing certain attributes to be *sacred* in the reduction. If a set X is sacred, a member of X will never be erased from the hypergraph (during the second step above). Clearly, a reduction to the empty set is no longer possible in the presence of a non-empty set of sacred nodes. For a given set X of nodes to be considered sacred, let $\text{red}(H, X)$ denote the result of a reduction of H. Now the fourth bottom-up strategy can be stated as follows. In order to compute the window on some set X of attributes, include R_V in a join expression, for each edge V in $\text{red}(H, X)$, and project the result onto X, that is:

$$[X]_1 := \pi_X(\bowtie_{V \in \text{red}(H,X)} R_V)$$

As an example, consider once more the hypergraph from Figure 17.2. It is easy to see that $\text{red}(H, BC) = \{ ACD, ABD \}$ and that $V = R_V$ for each V in $\text{red}(H, X)$ in this case. Thus,

$$[BC]_1 = \pi_{BC}(ACD \bowtie ABD)$$

The last bottom-up strategy that will be presented is a bit more involved. The idea is to construct the (largest) relation over a given set X which is made possible by (connected) joins of database relations *projected* onto non-empty intersections of their schemas.

In order to make this precise, some more terminology is needed. Let $H = (N, K)$ be a given hypergraph. A subset E of K which is connected and covers a given set X is called a **$\mathbf{D}^{\cap}$-connection** of X; such a connection E is **minimal** if it cannot be shortened, and no element in E can be replaced by a strict subset of itself. Let $\text{MC}(X)$ denote the set of all minimal $\mathbf{D}^{\cap}$-connections of X. The following can now be proved.

Theorem 17.1

(1) If $H(\mathbf{D})$ is connected, then $\text{MC}(X)$ exists for each set X of attributes, that is, $\text{MC}(X) \neq \emptyset$.

(2) In general, however, $\text{MC}(X)$ has one or more elements, that is, the minimal connection of some set X is not unique.

Another window function can now be defined as follows:

$$[X]_2 := \bigcup_{Y \in \text{MC}(X)} \pi_X(\bowtie_{V \in Y} R_V)$$

In the hypergraph of Figure 17.2, let X again be BC. Then MC(BC) = $\{AB, AC\}$. Furthermore,

$$R_{AB} = \pi_{AB}(ABE) \cup \pi_{AB}(ABD)$$
$$R_{AC} = \pi_{AC}(ACD) \cup \pi_{AC}(ACF)$$

and hence

$$[BC]_2 = \pi_{BC}(R_{AB} \bowtie R_{AC})$$

The important point now is that, although the last three window functions presented look significantly different at first glance (and indeed are in general), these differences disappear if the underlying hypergraph has the following property.

Definition 17.1

Let $H = (N, K)$ be a hypergraph.

(a) A sequence $(e_1, A_1, e_2, A_2, \ldots, e_m, A_m, e_{m+1})$ is called a **γ-cycle** (of length m) if the following hold:

(1) $A_1, \ldots, A_m$ are distinct vertices from N.

(2) $e_1 = e_{m+1}$, and $e_1, \ldots, e_m$ are distinct edges from K.

(3) $m \geq 3$.

(4) $(\forall\, i \in \{1, \ldots, m\})\ A_i \in e_i \cap e_{i+1}$.

(5) $(\forall\, i \in \{1, \ldots, m-1\})\ A_i \notin \bigcup_{j \in \{1 \ldots m\} - \{i, i+1\}} e_j$.

(b) H is **γ-acyclic** if H does not contain a γ-cycle.

Figure 17.4 shows an example of a hypergraph which is not γ-acyclic, while Figure 17.5 shows a hypergraph having this property. Each γ-acyclic hypergraph is acyclic in the sense defined in Exercise 32 in Part III; the converse, however, does not hold in general. The following results on γ-acyclic hypergraphs pertain to window functions.

Theorem 17.2

If H is a connected, γ-acyclic hypergraph, then the minimal connection of X is uniquely determined for every X.

As a result, the following theorem can be shown, the proof of which goes beyond the scope of this text.

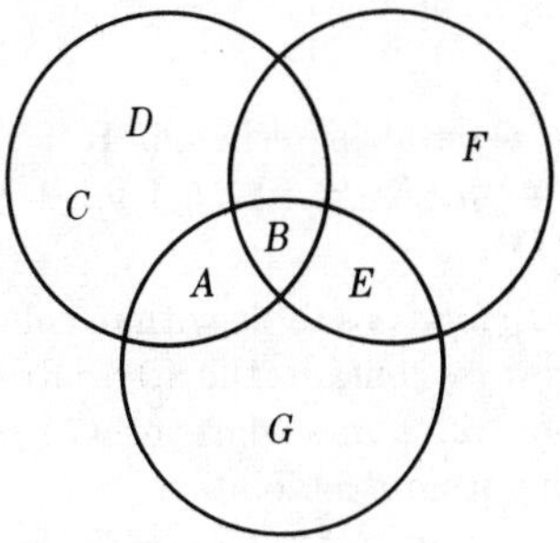

Figure 17.4 A γ-cyclic hypergraph.

Theorem 17.3

Let H be a γ-acyclic hypergraph, and let X be a subset of the vertices of H. Then $[X]_D \approx [X]_1 \approx [X]_2$ (where '$\approx$' means equivalence in the sense of Definition 8.6).

It follows from this theorem that the condition of γ-acyclicity is of particular relevance to the bottom-up approach to stating window functions. The (casual) user will in general not have any idea of the semantics of the underlying window function. If the hypergraph of the database schema in question is γ-acyclic, such knowledge, on the other hand, is *not required*, since this semantics is in some sense unique.

17.3 The representative instance of a database

The **top-down approach**, in which so-called **weak-instance windows** or *semantic* window functions are dealt with, is based on the assumption that for each database state d a certain universal relation, that is, a relation over the universe U, exists; basically, a (top-down) projection of this relation onto the desired attributes is computed. However, not the entire universal relation is actually constructed, but only the portion of it which is relevant to X.

In order to describe this approach in more detail, some further notions are needed which are introduced next.

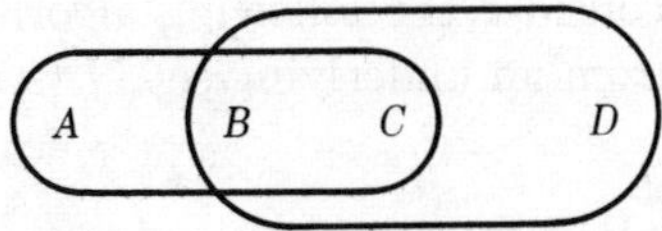

Figure 17.5 A γ-acyclic hypergraph.

Definition 17.2

Let $\mathbf{D} = (\mathbf{R}, \emptyset)$ be a database schema, $\mathbf{R} = \{R_1, \ldots, R_k\}$, where $\bigcup_{i=1}^{k} X_i = U$, $|U| = m$, $R_i = (X_i, F_i)$ for $1 \leq i \leq k$, and let $d = \{r_1, \ldots, r_k\} \in \text{Sat}(\mathbf{D})$.

The **state-tableau** T_d for d is a table with m columns and $n = \sum_{i=1}^{k} |r_i| + 1$ rows, whose first row w_0 contains the attributes from U (like a schema-tableau, see Definition 12.7), and whose other rows w_j correspond to the tuples in the relations from d as follows.

Let $r_i = \{\mu_{i1}, \ldots, \mu_{in_i}\}$ for $1 \leq i \leq k$. For $1 \leq p \leq k, 1 \leq q \leq n_p$ and $j = \sum_{i=1}^{p-1} n_i + q$, let $\mu_j = (x_{j1}, \ldots, x_{jm})$, where

$$x_{jl} = \begin{cases} \mu_{pq}(A_l) & \text{if } A_l \in X_p \\ \delta_{jl} & \text{otherwise} \end{cases}$$

Here, δ_{jl} denotes a null value of type '(real) value exists, but is currently unknown' (see also the discussion at the end of Section 7.1).

Informally, a state-tableau unites all tuples occurring in d to a table over U, where missing values for attributes are filled in by (unique) nulls.

As a first example, consider the state d of the supplier database from Chapter 12 shown in Figure 17.6(a): Figure 17.6(b) shows the corresponding tableau T_d. As a second example, consider the state d shown in Figure 17.7 (a), which is over the database format $\mathbf{R} = \{R_1, R_2, R_3\}$, where $R_1 = (ABC, \{A \rightarrow BC\})$, $R_2 = (BD, \{B \rightarrow D\})$, and $R_3 = (CD, \{C \rightarrow D\})$; the corresponding state-tableau is shown in Figure 17.7(b).

The strategy on which the construction of a state-tableau T_d is based is basically identical to the one applied in the window function of the DURST system mentioned in the previous section; there, it was denoted by 'pad_U'.

To a state-tableau, an algorithm similar to the procedure *LJP* for schema-tableaux (see Section 12.3) can be applied. The validity of FDs of the form $Y \rightarrow A$ from the components is 'enforced' in the relation over U described by T_d simply by equating any two tuples μ and ν, which are free of null values on Y and which agree on Y, on A. However, this unification is carried out only such that $\mu(A)$ is replaced by $\nu(A)$ if $\mu(A)$ is a null value (or vice versa, that is, $\nu(A)$ is replaced by $\mu(A)$ if $\nu(A)$ is a null value). Thus, either a null value is replaced by a 'real' one, or two null values are identified, where it is irrelevant in the latter case which of the two null values disappears.

More formally, consider the following algorithm, in which all null values used are taken from an underlying set $\mathbf{N}$ (see Section 7.1):

Algorithm CHASE
Input: A state-tableau T_d
Output: A modified state-tableau T_d^*.

N	I	S
S1	P1	300
S1	P4	200
S2	P2	400
S4	P5	400
S5	P3	100

N	C
S1	London
S2	Paris
S3	Paris
S4	Brussels

C	D
London	600
Paris	450
Brussels	150

(a)

	N	I	S	C	D
μ_1	S1	P1	300	δ_{14}	δ_{15}
μ_2	S1	P4	200	δ_{24}	δ_{25}
μ_3	S2	P2	400	δ_{34}	δ_{35}
μ_4	S4	P5	400	δ_{44}	δ_{45}
μ_5	S5	P3	100	δ_{54}	δ_{55}
μ_6	S1	δ_{62}	δ_{63}	London	δ_{65}
μ_7	S2	δ_{72}	δ_{73}	Paris	δ_{75}
μ_8	S3	δ_{82}	δ_{83}	Paris	δ_{85}
μ_9	S4	δ_{92}	δ_{93}	Brussels	δ_{95}
μ_{10}	$\delta_{10,1}$	$\delta_{10,2}$	$\delta_{10,3}$	London	600
μ_{11}	$\delta_{11,1}$	$\delta_{11,2}$	$\delta_{11,3}$	Paris	450
μ_{12}	$\delta_{12,1}$	$\delta_{12,2}$	$\delta_{12,3}$	Brussels	150

(b)

Figure 17.6 A state of the Supplier-Parts database and its tableau.

A	B	C
1	1	1

B	D
1	1

C	D
1	2

(a)

	A	B	C	D
μ_1	1	1	1	δ_{14}
μ_2	δ_{21}	1	δ_{23}	1
μ_3	δ_{31}	δ_{32}	1	2

(b)

Figure 17.7 Another database state and its tableau.

Method:

```
begin
    T*_d := T_d;
    while T*_d can be modified do
        begin
            choose an FD Y → A ∈ ∪_{i=1}^k F_i;
            if (∃ μ, ν in T*_d, μ ≠ ν) μ[Y] = ν[Y]
                    ∧ (∀ B ∈ Y)(μ(B) ∉ N ∧ ν(B) ∉ N)
            then if μ(A) ∈ N
                    then μ(A) := ν(A)
                    else if ν(A) ∈ N
                            then ν(A) := μ(A)
        end;
    if (∃ μ, ν ∈ T*_d, μ ≠ ν)(∀A ∈ U)
        ν(A) ∉ N ⟹ μ(A) = ν(A)
        then remove ν from T*_d;
    if (∃ Y → A ∈ ∪_{i=1}^k F_i)(∃ μ, ν in T*_d, μ ≠ ν)
            μ[Y] = ν[Y] ∧ μ(A) ∉ N ∧ ν(A) ∉ N ∧ μ(A) ≠ ν(A)
    then T*_d := ∅
end;
```

This procedure is illustrated using the state-tableaux shown above in Figures 17.6(b) and 17.7(b), respectively.

In Figure 17.6(b), it is found, for example, that $\mu_6[C] = \mu_{10}[C]$, and both tuples are 'real' on C. Furthermore, $\mu_6[D] = \delta_{65}, \mu_{10}[D] = 600$; hence, δ_{65} is replaced by 600. Analogously, $C \rightarrow D$ can be applied to μ_7 and μ_{11}, or to μ_8 and μ_{11}, or $N \rightarrow C$ can be applied to μ_1 und μ_6. Figure 17.8 shows the result of *CHASE*(T_d) in this case; notice that the tuples $\mu_6, \mu_7, \mu_9, \mu_{10}, \mu_{11}$ and μ_{12} no longer occur in T_d^*, since the following holds, for example, after the FDs have been applied to the initial tableau:

$$\mu_1 = (\text{S1, P1, 300, London, 600})$$

and

$$\mu_{10} = (\delta_{10,1}, \delta_{10,2}, \delta_{10,3}, \text{London}, 600)$$

In this case, μ_1 contains 'more information' than μ_{10} (μ_{10} is said to be **subsumed** by μ_1); therefore, μ_{10} is removed from T_d^* in the last but one if-statement of Algorithm *CHASE*. (This removal of subsumed tuples was meant by 'sub' in the description of the DURST window function.)

For the application of *CHASE* to the state-tableau from Figure 17.7(b) it is assumed that $\bigcup_{i=1}^{3} F_i = \{A \rightarrow B, A \rightarrow C, B \rightarrow D, C \rightarrow D\}$ holds. As a consequence, for instance, δ_{14} can be replaced by 2, since $\mu_1[C] = \mu_3[C]$. The 'candidate-tableau' T_d^* thereby produced cannot be modified further by applying the FDs. In the last but one if-statement

T_d^* :

N	I	S	C	D
S1	P1	300	London	600
S1	P4	200	London	600
S2	P2	400	Paris	450
S4	P5	400	Brussels	150
S5	P3	100	δ_{54}	δ_{55}
S3	δ_{82}	δ_{83}	Paris	450

Figure 17.8 Result of chasing the tableau from Figure 17.6(b).

of *CHASE*, tuple μ_3 is removed; in the last it is discovered that the FD $B \to D$ is violated, since the following holds:

$$\mu_1(B) = \mu_2(B) = 1, \text{ but } \mu_1(D) = 2 \neq \mu_2(D) = 1$$

Thus, the algorithm terminates with output $T_d^* = \emptyset$ in this example.

Definition 17.3

Let d be a database with associated state-tableau T_d. Then $T_d^* = CHASE(T_d)$ is called the **representative instance** of d and is denoted rep(d). (It is also common to say that 'rep(d) exists' if $T_d^* \neq \emptyset$.)

Without proof the following result is stated, which characterizes the existence of a representative instance.

Theorem 17.4

Let $\mathbf{D} = (\mathbf{R}, \emptyset)$ be a decomposition of $R = (U, F)$, and let $d \in \text{Sat}(\mathbf{D})$. Then the following holds:

$$\text{rep}(d) \text{ exists} \iff (\exists\, r \in \text{Sat}(R))\ (\forall\, r_i \in d)\ r_i \subseteq \pi_{X_i}(r)$$

Any relation $r \in \text{Sat}(R)$ for d, in whose projection onto format X_i of a component R_i the corresponding base relation r_i is contained (for each i), is called a **weak instance** for d. In the top-down approach for window functions it is generally assumed that a 'universal relation' of this type exists for each current database state, which can tested effectively by the last theorem.

A formal difference between a weak instance and a representative instance for some database d is that the former is a total relation (without null values), while the latter in general is a partial relation. An important point here is that all null values occurring in a relation rep(d) have the interpretation 'value exists, but is unknown'. Thus, it is in principle possible to replace all null values in rep(d) by real ones, thereby 'extending' rep(d)

to some weak instance; since the latter can obviously be done in various ways, there exist several weak instances for a given state d in general.

For the purpose of making the representative instance the basis of a top-down window function, the following theorem is important, which informally states that the 'real' information contained in a representative instance, that is, the 'total parts' of all tuples occurring in it, appears in this form also in *every* weak instance of the database state in question. In order to formulate the theorem, the following operation on relations with null values is needed.

Definition 17.4

Let r be a relation over the set X of attributes, in which null values of the type described above are allowed, that is, for every tuple $\mu \in r$ it is true that either $\mu(A) \in \text{dom}(A)$ or $\mu(A) \in \mathbf{N}, A \in X$. Also, let $Z \subseteq X$. Then

$$\tau_Z(r) := \{\mu \in \pi_Z(r) \mid (\forall A \in Z)\ \mu(A) \notin \mathbf{N}\}$$

is called the **total projection** of r onto Z.

Theorem 17.5

Let $R = (U, F)$, and let $\mathbf{D} = (\mathbf{R}, \emptyset)$ be a decomposition of R. In addition, let $X \subseteq U$, and for each database $d \in \text{Sat}(\mathbf{D})$, for which rep($d$) exists, let $W(d)$ denote the set of *all* weak instances of d. Then the following holds:

$$\tau_X(\text{rep}(d)) = \bigcap_{r \in W(d)} \pi_X(r)$$

For example, consider the representative instance shown in Figure 17.8 (for the database state from Figure 17.6(a)); then

$\tau_{NC}(\text{rep}(d))$:

N	C
S1	London
S2	Paris
S4	Brussels
S3	Paris

According to the last theorem, this relation is identical to the intersection of the projections of all weak instances onto NC.

These results, for which proofs can be found in the literature cited in the Bibliographic Notes, now allow us to define a window function in the top-down approach as follows:

$$[X] := \tau_X(\text{rep}(d))$$

For a practical implementation of this function, it seems reasonable not to construct rep(d) explicitly by applying algorithm *CHASE* to T_d;

instead, a 'simulation' of the *CHASE* through certain join operations on the elements of d seems more efficient. Additional requirements to the database in question and to its schema, which will not be discussed here, are needed, however, to make such a simulation possible in all cases (that is, for any given state). To this end, the reader is referred to the references listed in the Bibliographic Notes.

Bibliographic Notes

Further details on UDS can be found in the various manuals of the manufacturer, like Siemens (1982a-d, 1984, 1985, 1986). In some of the textbooks already mentioned, other network systems are described, such as IMAGE by Hewlett-Packard in McFadden and Hoffer (1988), IDMS by Cullinet Software Inc. in Date (1986) and Kroenke (1983), and TOTAL by Cincom Systems in Cardenas (1985) and Kroenke (1983). The reader is also referred to the survey by Taylor und Frank (1976).

The hierarchical data model and the system IMS are described in great detail by Cardenas (1985), Date (1981) and McGee (1977). An introduction to DL/I is given by Kroenke (1983). Further information on hierarchical systems can also be found in Tsichritzis and Lochovsky (1976).

The relational system SQL/DS evolved as a commercial product from the prototype System/R which was developed at the IBM Research Laboratory in San Jose, California; this prototype is decribed in the work by Astrahan et al. (1976) and Blasgen et al. (1981). Chamberlin et al. (1981) give a retrospective evaluation of System/R. A brief description of R^*, a distributed version of System/R, is given by Yost and Haas (1985).

A short characterization of SQL/DS as well as a number of other relational systems can be found in the books by Schmidt and Brodie (1983) and Valduriez and Gardarin (1989). Details of the standard language SQL can be found in ANSI (1985) and Date (1989). Vossen and Yacabucci (1988) describe an extension of SQL to capture certain intra- and interrelational constraints, some of which have also been included in the standard. The language SQL is also used by IBM itself for the database-system product DB2 (a 'reimplementation' of SQL/DS); hence the books by Larson (1988), Date and White (1989b), or Vossen and Witt (1990) can be used as references for SQL. For further details regarding the language and the usage of SQL/DS in practical applications, the reader is referred to the original literature by IBM (1983a-c, 1987), to Date and White (1989a) or to Vossen and Witt (1988). Performance investigations for this system are described by Reisner (1984); aspects of the optimization of queries are investigated by Lohman (1986). More or less detailed descriptions of the SQL language can also be found in the books by Cardenas (1985), Date (1981, 1986), Kroenke (1983) and Ullman (1988). Ceri and Gottlob (1985) describe the translation of SQL to relational algebra, as do Paredaens et al. (1989).

Other relational systems or languages, which are not presented in this text, include Ingres, see Stonebraker (1986c) and Date (1986, 1987), or Query-by-Example, see Cardenas (1985), Maier (1983) and Ullman (1988). The reader is also referred to the survey by Jarke and Vassiliou (1985) on query languages for databases. The current importance of relational systems from the point of view of its 'intellectual father' is discussed in the Turing-Award lecture of Codd (1982). The frequently posed question for 'criteria' that make a database system 'relational' is investigated by Codd (1986).

An introduction to the theory of the universal-relation data model is given by Maier et al. (1984) or Vardi (1987); the foundations of interfaces based on this model are described by Maier et al. (1986a) and Ullman (1983). Further details on PITS can be found in the papers by Maier et al. (1982, 1986) and Maier (1983); System/U is described by Ullman (1989) and Korth et al. (1984). The theoretical foundations of the DURST system are presented by Biskup and Brüggemann (1983) and Brüggemann (1986). Further details on the window function $[.]_1$ presented in Section 17.2, whose hypertree reduction technique is generally known as the **GYO reduction**, can be found in Goodman et al. (1984) or Maier and Ullman (1984); the technique itself goes back to Graham (1979) and Yu and Özsoyoglu (1979). The window function $[.]_2$ is from Yannakakis (1981) and Fagin (1983). This latter reference also gives an introduction to the various notions of acyclicity for hypergraphs as used in database theory; other work on this topic and on hypergraphs in general includes Berge (1976) or Biskup et al. (1986). For proofs of Theorems 17.1–17.3, the reader is referred to Brüggemann (1986).

Further details on the *CHASE* procedure can be found in the books by Maier (1983) or Ullman (1988), and on the representative instance of a given database state as well as on the corresponding window function from Section 17.3 in Sagiv (1981, 1983). Theorem 17.4 is by Honeyman (1980); see also Honeyman (1982). A complete proof of Theorem 17.5 is given by Vossen (1986); see also Maier et al. (1984).

An experimental system not described in the text is *MEMODAX*, which was developed at the Technical University of Aachen under the supervision of the author, and which is based on the representative instance approach. The theory underlying this implementation can be found in Vossen (1986) as well as Brosda and Vossen (1988), who also describe the foundations of the *MEMODAX* window function; see also Vossen and Brosda (1985b). The implementation of the universal-relation user interface is treated in Brosda (1984); an introduction to the usage of the USIL language is given by Vossen and Brosda (1985a).

Exercises

(1) Consider the ER diagram for an airline shown in Figure 4.3. Derive a logical network from it and give a schema definition for UDS. After this, formulate the following queries and updates in IQL:

(a) Show manufacturer and type of all planes which can seat more than 300 people.

(b) Which types of planes can be serviced by at least one technician?

(c) What is the smallest number of technicians who can service the same plane?

(d) List all 'service teams' with more than 10 members together with the manufacterer of each plane serviced by that team, excluding manufacturer 'Boeing', according to decreasing number of seats of the corresponding planes.

(e) Show the names of all employees earning more than $ 60,000.

(f) Which employees can fly at least one plane?

(g) What are the name and salary of each pilot who can fly a DC-10?

(h) Show the licence number and name for each pilot.

(i) Increase all salaries by 5%.

(j) Which passengers are more than 18 years old?

(k) Show the name of every passenger who has booked at least one flight.

(l) Determine the longest flight-time of a booked flight.

(2) Declare a relational database schema for the airline using SQL, taking into account the extensions and modifications from Exercise 6 in Part II, and formulate the following queries:

(a) Show the technical specification of the oldest and the youngest aircraft of the company.

(b) Which technicians can service an Airbus?

(c) Which teams have serviced an Airbus?

(d) Which spare parts have never been used in a case of trouble?

(e) Record the following update: On 10/01/85, the oldest aircraft owned by the company as well as all aircraft having more flight hours than the average have been serviced.

(f) How many employees are neither pilot nor steward?

(g) What is the average salary and average flight experience (in number of hours) of each pilot?

(h) Show the names of all pilots who can fly more than one plane, sorted according to increasing salaries.

(i) Which pilots make more money than any technician?

(j) Which technicians can service all aircraft owned by the company?

(k) Determine the sum of all salaries that are paid to technicians who can service a Boeing.

(l) For all booked flights, list the name and age of every passenger in alphabetical ordering of names, and in decreasing order of time (of the flights).

(3) Determine whether the attributes used in Exercise 2 satisfy the universal-relation schema assumption and apply appropriate corrections if this is not the case.

(4) Consider the set $\{ABE, ABD, ACD\}$ of relation formats. Derive the corresponding intersection-tree and determine MC(BD).

(5) Determine whether the hypergraph shown in Figure 17.2 is γ-acyclic.

(6) Show that the hypergraph shown in Figure 17.5 is γ-acyclic, and that the one in Figure 17.4 is not.

(7) Give a counterexample which shows that an acyclic hypergraph (in the sense of Exercise 32 in Part III) is not necessarily also γ-acyclic.

(8) Show that a hypergraph H is γ-acyclic iff H has neither a pure cycle nor a γ-circle, where

(a) a **pure cycle** is a sequence $(e_1, \ldots, e_{m+1})$ of (hyper-) edges such that

- (i) $e_1 = e_{m+1}$, and $e_1, \ldots, e_m$ are distinct edges
- (ii) $m \geq 3$
- (iii) $(\forall\, i \in \{1, \ldots, m\})\ e_i \cap e_{i+1} \neq \emptyset$
- (iv) $(\forall\, i, j, k \in \{1, \ldots, m\})$ $i \neq j \wedge j \neq k \wedge i \neq k \Rightarrow e_i \cap e_j \cap e_k = \emptyset$

and

(b) a **γ-circle** is a sequence of the form $(e_1, A_1, e_2, A_2, e_3, A_3, e_1)$ such that

- (i) A_1, A_2, A_3 are distinct vertices of H
- (ii) e_1, e_2, e_3 are distinct edges of H
- (iii) $A_1 \in e_1 \cap e_2 \setminus e_3 \wedge A_2 \in e_2 \cap e_3 \setminus e_1 \wedge A_3 \in e_1 \cap e_2 \cap e_3$

(9) Prove Theorem 17.2. Show that the reverse direction also holds.

(10) Consider the database state shown in Exercise 3 of Part III:

(a) Compute the representative instance of this state, if it exists.

(b) For the relation rep(d) found under (a), compute the total projection onto *City* and *Weight* as well as onto *Stored_In* and *Dist.*

(11) Prove that the *CHASE* algorithm has the **finite Church-Rosser property**, that is, it terminates after finitely many steps and the result is independent of the order in which FDs are applied to the input.

(12) Give an informal argument why the database state shown in Figure 17.7(a) does not possess a representative instance. Show that *every* state in which the (key) FDs stated in the text are satisfied also has a representative instance, if the relation format CD is replaced by CE (and $C \rightarrow D$ correspondingly by $C \rightarrow E$).

Part VI

Concurrency Control and Recovery

Chapter 18
Transaction Processing and Concurrency Control

Database systems generally allow multiple users to operate on the same data. To render **data sharing** possible, a DBMS has to support the notion of a **transaction** as a paradigm for parallelism and fault-tolerance. This chapter introduces the area of **concurrency control**, a central part of transaction processing.

18.1 Transactions

Transaction processing can be considered as a 'service' provided by a DBMS which is vastly invisible for the (outside) user. The term 'transaction' has occurred twice in this text already.

In Chapters 8 and 9, it was discussed how updates on a relational database can be described by operations like 'insert' and 'delete'. One goal was to specify transactional schemas so that checking integrity constraints becomes obsolete. In comparison to this approach, a basic assumption in the present chapter will be that the underlying DBMS is capable of checking integrity to some extent, so that a 'transaction', independent of its structure, leaves behind a consistent state if it was started on a state having this property.

In Chapter 16, transaction processing was mentioned in connection with SQL/DS at a different level. The internal processing of an update command (or command sequence) by the system (and in particular at the internal level) leads to a 'program' executing this 'application' on the database. The SQL/DS user can 'protect' this execution against commands or programs issued simultaneously by other users, for example to make sure that updates on some relation in a 'public dbspace' are performed completely and without interference from outside.

From both sections, certain concepts will be reconsidered here, in order to develop them further and to provide additional insight. However, the relational model is no longer emphasized in this chapter, since the concepts that will be introduced do not depend on the choice of a particular data model.

If a DBMS allows for a multi-user mode of operation, a database managed by the system appears to each individual user as an *exclusive resource*, that is, it seems that the database is at his or her sole disposal. On the other hand, the DBMS has to process the various requests coming in from its users more or less simultaneously, in order to achieve a 'good' throughput. This requires the synchronization of (quasi) parallel programs, which is the job of the **transaction manager**. Under the assumption that all orders submitted to the DBMS from outside are (application) programs (which obviously includes the simpler case that *ad hoc* commands written in the available DML are issued as well), each program occurs to the transaction manager as an 'object program' that was previously created by the code generator. A central objective of this program is to **preserve** the **consistency** of the database upon which it operates, which in general goes beyond the preservation of integrity constraints specified at the conceptual level. However, it may not be possible to guarantee a consistent state of the database after each individual instruction of the program (or its execution).

For example, in a banking application a (not exactly realistic) consistency constraint might require that the sum over all account balances at any time equals a constant number p. Now consider the transfer of money from one account to another. It is certainly necessary to do this in two steps, the first of which subtracts a certain amount from one account, while the second adds the same amount to the other. Even if the database is consistent before this 'program' starts execution, after the first step this will no longer be the case, since the overall sum is now less than p. However, after the second step, that is, after the program has finished, consistenty has been restored as intended.

This intuition that the execution of a 'program' (or a 'process') should always leave the database it operates on in a consistent state if it was started on a consistent one, but that temporary inconsistencies can be tolerated while the program is running, is logically captured by the notion of a **transaction**, a concept that is no longer confined to the area of database management (indeed, it is similar to the process concept in an operating system). A transaction manager therefore manages the user programs it receives in the form of transactions. It follows immediately that an important property of a transaction, which has to be guaranteed by the transaction manager in particular in the presence of 'concurrent' programs, is what is generally called **atomicity**. To the issuing user, the transaction that internally represents his program is executed *either completely or not at all*, since this is generally the only way in which database consistency can be assured. This 'all-or-nothing' principle alone, however, is not sufficient for making sure that distinct transactions do not interfere with each other, as will be seen from examples shortly.

In the presence of multiple transactions which are to be executed simultaneously, further issues arise. Even if several 'programs' are executed in a (quasi) parallel fashion, they should not interfere with each other; also, they should be robust against certain failures the DBMS may face during operation. The former aspect is generally termed the **concurrency control problem** for database systems and is discussed in this chapter, while the latter is known as as the **recovery problem** and is dealt with in the next chapter. Both aspects result in additional requirements to a transaction manager. First, each individual transaction should — as seen from outside — run in **isolation**; if this is the case, interference with other transactions is avoided. Second, each transaction should have **persistence** with respect to failures, that is, if a transaction has accomplished what it should do on a database and no failures have occurred so far, the 'results' it has produced in the database should survive every failure which occurs at a later time.

Although it remains unclear at this point how these various requirements, which are collectively called the **ACID principle** (**A**tomicity, **C**onsistency, **I**solation and **D**uration), can actually be achieved, some implications are straightforward. First, if some failure (like a head-crash on a disk) occurs while a transaction is running with the effect that this transaction cannot be completed successfully, the transaction does not leave 'garbage' behind in the database, due to its atomicity. Second, the database state that has to be restored after some failure is well defined, owing to persistence and atomicity. Finally, isolation avoids 'anomalies' in a multi-user environment which may occur even if each individual transaction runs (atomically) without problems and the system guarantees persistence.

In what follows it is assumed that the DBMS in question is 'smart' enough to inform a user whether or not a transaction could be completed successfully. In the positive case, the corresponding 'message' could consist of a request to issue another transaction (or of the 'answer' if the transaction was a query), while in the negative case an error message will be returned in general.

Internally, the 'logical unit' of a transaction is composed of a number of individual steps called *actions*. Actions are the 'physical units' that operate on the individual parts of the underlying database, where it depends on the internal structure of the database whether such a part or '*database object*' is a relation, a file, a record, a page or something else. For what follows it is basically irrelevant which 'view' the transaction manager has of a given database, so that database objects will generally remain unspecified, and will be denoted by lower-case letters (x, y, z ...); eventually, more precise information will be provided on what an object is.

Since physical database objects in general reside on secondary memory, they need to be transferred to main memory before they can be processed, and they need to be written back to secondary memory if this 'processing' has changed their value. To this end, a transaction (as the *execution* of a given application program) contains (at least) **read** and **write** actions, which will be written here as '$r(x)$' (meaning 'read object x') and '$w(x)$' ('write object x'). In addition, a transaction may contain other operations or actions which are 'local' in the sense that they operate on main memory only, but not on the database directly. On the other hand, read and write actions are the ones that 'affect' the database and must pass through the 'bottleneck' of the interface between primary and secondary memory. They may therefore interfere with the reads and writes of other transactions, which is why they need special attention. As a consequence, a *transaction* will here be considered as a 'read/write program'; note, however, that this view is a particular *abstraction* from the actual situation, which on the one hand conveniently captures how an application program is perceived at the internal level of the DBMS and on the other hand neglects certain interesting aspects of a transaction, in particular because it sees a transaction as a purely *syntactical* object.

It is assumed in what follows that a transaction comprises (at least)

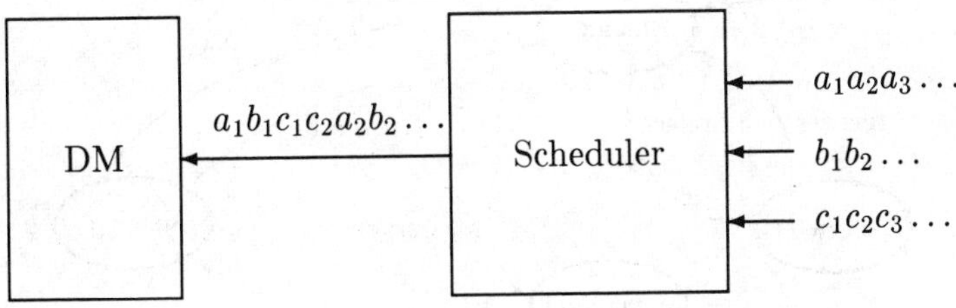

Figure 18.1 Situation when scheduling transactions.

read and write actions, which are generated by the code generator of the system (see Chapter 3) from an application program written in a high-level language. In the next subsection, certain problems are described which typically arise in a multi-user environment. These problems gave rise to the search for suitable 'correctness criteria' (serializability) for modelling parallelism in transaction processing (by *schedules*) or for synchronization. After such a criterion has been introduced, it remains to develop particular algorithms ('protocols') which produce execution sequences that satisfy it. The most popular protocol as well as alternatives will be described in Sections 18.4 and 18.5. Finally, a brief look will be taken at how to depart from the purely syntactical view of a transaction and how to make use of semantic information (on transactions) during the process of scheduling.

18.2 Problems with concurrent database operations

The central component of every tansaction manager, as will be discussed in more detail below, is a *scheduler*, which accepts as input the individual actions from distinct transactions, and which produces as output an execution sequence (which is processed further by the data manager) in which the actions from different transactions may be 'mixed'. This scenario is illustrated in Figure 18.1. Basically, the scheduler could simply proceed by outputting each submitted transaction completely before starting another. The resulting execution sequence would be a **serial** schedule, which is correct (integrity preserving) if this is the case for each individual transaction. On the other hand, a serial execution has serious drawbacks with respect to performance since 'long' transactions may hinder 'short' ones; in addition, the assumptions that a transaction is available completely when a scheduler starts operation is seldom satisfied in reality. Thus, it seems reasonable to start the 'execution' (scheduling) of a new transaction

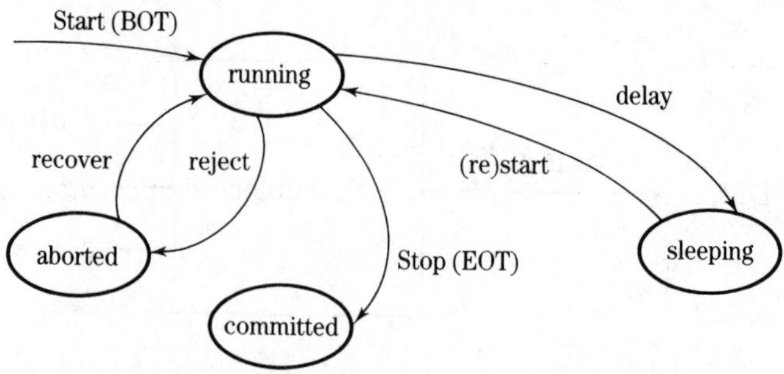

Figure 18.2 Possible states of a transaction.

before all transactions currently running have ended. As a result, several transactions will be under execution ('running') at the same time. If the DBMS is running on a single-processor machine — which is generally assumed here — only one of these, however, will be 'active' at any time (in the sense that it uses the processor).

This consideration leads to a distinction of the various **states** a transaction currently in the system can be in; these states (as well as the possible transitions between them) are shown in Figure 18.2. After a start by the transaction manager, a transaction t is first in state 'running', where it is assumed that the actions of a transaction are delimited by **BOT** ('begin of transaction') and **EOT** ('end of transaction'), so that the 'logical unit of work' in the sense described above can be recognized by the transaction manager. The 'resource' database is then made available for a certain time (explained in more detail in the next section). If the program could be completed successfully during this time, no conflict with another transaction has occurred and the consistency of the database is not violated, the transaction reaches the state 'committed', that is, the results it computed in the database become (permanently) available to other transactions. If t is not yet completed, but none of the other two problems has occurred, t reaches the state 'sleeping'; its execution is resumed at some later time. Otherwise, t is 'aborted', that is, interrupted and at least for the moment excluded from further processing; its effect on the database has to be 'undone' (because of atomicity), and t will eventually be restarted at a later time (depending on what caused the abort).

In the following description of problems that might occur in a multi-user (or multi-transaction) environment it is (temporarily) assumed that the following actions can also occur in a transaction (besides read and write): elementary assignments (in main memory), $u(x)$ ('update object x', also in main memory), commit(t) and abort(t). A commit action, as explained above, has the effect that all changes made by a transaction on a given database state are now made permanent in the database, while an abort action has the opposite effect of making everything the transaction did to the database undone.

The first problem is known as the **lost update problem**. Two transactions t_1 and t_2 are executed in (quasi) parallel fashion according to the following plan:

t_1	*Time*	t_2
BOT(t_1)	1	
$r(x)$	2	
	3	BOT(t_2)
	4	$r(x)$
$u(x)$	5	
	6	$u(x)$
$w(x)$	7	
EOT(t_1)	8	
	9	$w(x)$
	10	EOT(t_2)

At each point in time, exactly one of the two transactions is in state 'running'; both t_1 and t_2 operate on object x only. This object is first read, then modified, and finally written back. However, since t_2 reads the same initial value of x as t_1, but writes *after* t_1, the update made by t_1 on x is not 'visible' in the database; it is *lost*, since the new x value is immediately overwritten by t_2.

The second problem is known as the **dirty read problem**. Consider two transactions t_1 and t_2 which both operate on object x according to the following plan:

t_1	*Time*	t_2
BOT(t_1)	1	
$r(x)$	2	
$u(x)$	3	
$w(x)$	4	
	5	BOT(t_2)
	6	$r(x)$
	7	$u(x)$
abort	8	
	9	$w(x)$
⋮		⋮

In this case, t_2 reads an x value which has already been modified by t_1. After this read step of t_2, t_1 sends (or receives, say, from the transaction manager) an abort signal indicating abnormal termination of t_1, so that the x value read and processed by t_2 has never actually been in the database. Hence, the x value finally written by t_2 (at time 9) must be considered inconsistent.

The last problem is known as the **phantom problem**, or as the *unrepeatable-read problem*. Assume that x, y and z are numerical objects (like account balances in a banking application) currently having values $x = 40$, $y = 50$ and $z = 30$; hence, their sum equals 120. Next consider the following two transactions t_1 and t_2:

t_1	*Time*	t_2
BOT(t_1)	1	
$sum := 0$	2	
$r(x)$	3	
$r(y)$	4	
$sum := sum + x$	5	
$sum := sum + y$	6	
	7	BOT(t_2)
	8	$r(z)$
	9	$z := z - 10$
	10	$w(z)$
	11	$r(x)$
	12	$x := x + 10$
	13	$w(x)$
	14	commit
	15	EOT(t_2)
$r(z)$	16	
$sum := sum + z$	17	
EOT(t_1)	18	

Apparently, t_1 computes the sum of (account balance) objects x, y and z, while t_2 transfers 10 from z to x (so that the overall sum remains constant). Since this transfer happens before t_1 has read z, t_1 already 'sees' the updated version of z and hence computes a 'wrong' sum (110), and it does so in spite of the fact that both transactions, when considered in isolation, are consistency preserving.

What these examples show is that the desire or requirement *not* to process multiple transactions *sequentially* (serially) can lead to problems. If the goal is to process them in a (quasi) parallel fashion and the actions from distinct transactions are therefore merged, '*merge rules*' are needed which, for example, say how reads and writes from different transactions that access the same object have to be treated. In addition, '*merge procedures*' are needed which are able to generate sequences of actions for a given set of transactions that observe such rules. Both issues will be discussed in the next two sections.

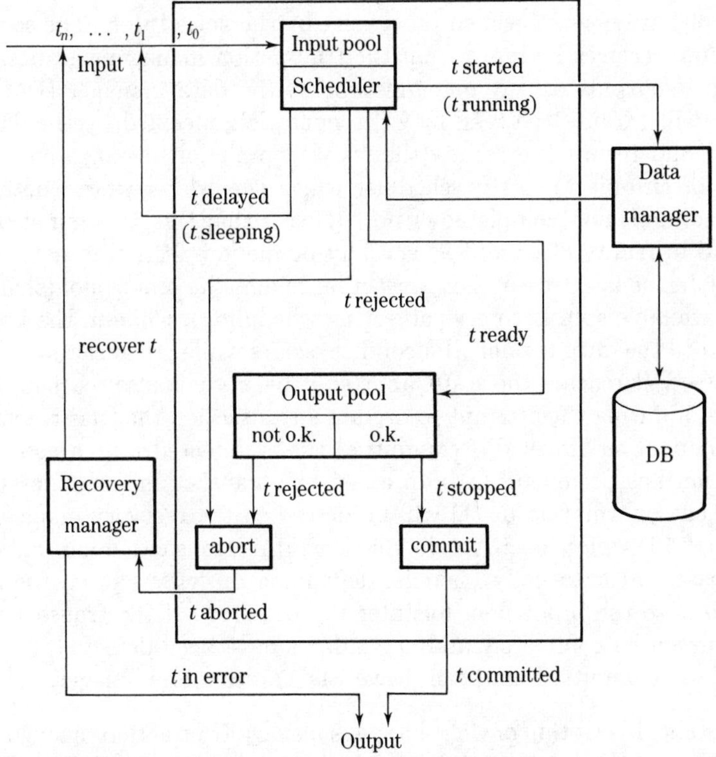

Figure 18.3 A model of a transaction manager.

18.3 Serializability

The assumptions on the states a transaction can be in will now be made more precise; at the same time, a model of a transaction manager is presented which continues the discussion from Chapter 3. Figure 18.3, in a sense, shows the 'magnification' of an excerpt from Figure 3.1. Basically, the situation is similar to the one frequently arising in a computer system, where an operating system has to grant access to (exclusively usable) resources. User requests are collected in a waiting pool, and access to the resource in question is granted according to a *scheduling strategy*, typically for the duration of a time slice. Requests that cannot be completed during this time return to the waiting pool for later rescheduling, while all others can leave the 'system'.

In the case of a transaction management this means that transactions (which have been produced in their internal form by the code generator) arrive at and wait in an *input pool* of the transaction manager until they are started, where starting a transaction t implies that the actions of t are now subject to processing by the **scheduler**. The scheduler therefore receives its input from the transaction manager and passes the action it outputs at any point in time to the data manager (DM). The latter will execute the read or write operation specified by the 'current' action and return the result (that is, a completion message and/or the value of an object) to the scheduler which then determines whether the transaction is now completed or not. (Notice that this determination may — and in reality often will — actually be made by the transaction manager.) In the latter case, the transaction rejoins the input pool (that is, its next available step becomes subject to scheduling), while in the first it is passed to the output pool. If a conflict occurs while a transaction is being processed, it reaches the state 'aborted'; this state is also reached, for example, if during the attempt to declare a transaction that has reached the output pool as 'finished' ('committed') it is detected that a consistency violation has occurred. In both cases, the transaction (or at least some pertinent information on it) will be passed to the recovery manager (see Chapter 19) which has to 'undo' all effects this transaction has had on the database and eventually (that is, depending on what caused the abort) return it to the input pool for later reprocessing. If the transaction has been executed completely and no conflicts have been detected, it reaches the state 'committed' and can 'leave' the transaction manager.

The description of what happens inside a transaction manager given here has model character only; in particular, it is assumed that the only task of a scheduler is to produce an **execution sequence** for the individual actions from distinct transactions which is correct (in a sense to be made precise shortly) and interleaves the actions over time. On the other hand, consistency checks are eventually made by other components of the transaction manager (or by other DBMS components with which it communicates).

The goal of this section is to come up with a 'correctness criterion' for schedules. To this end, some notions and notations will be needed, which are introduced next. It is assumed that the read and write actions occurring in a transaction are the only 'critical' ones (as opposed, for instance, to assignment statements, see the examples above); for these, an 'execution model' is introduced which captures the ordering in which these actions have to be transmitted from a scheduler to the data manager.

Definition 18.1

A **transaction** is a (finite) sequence $t = a_1 \ldots a_n$ of steps, where each step a_i, $1 \leq i \leq n$, is a read or write action of the form $r(x)$ or $w(x)$, and x denotes an object from the underlying database. A transaction is assumed to read or write every database object it operates upon at most once.

In the presence of several transactions, indices will be used to distinguish to which transaction a particular action belongs. As a first example of a transaction, consider

$$t_1 = r_1(x)r_1(z)w_1(x)$$

Transaction t_1 reads objects x and z and writes x (the new value of x may depend on the old values of x and z). The ordering of the steps is assumed to be established by the code generator, on the basis of the steps in the original application program. Note that the local (additional) operations a transaction contains (besides reads and writes) as a program can be inserted into such a sequence when needed.

What is important to note at this point is that a transaction as defined so far is a *purely syntactic* object. In particular, the perception that, from a *semantic* point of view, a transaction maps a consistent database state to another consistent state is by no means captured yet. In order to do so, it would be necessary to formally define an *interpretation* for a transaction which in particular takes into account what other steps are contained in the transaction and hence what its intended overall meaning is; a corresponding definition would then have to make precise *how* the transaction computes a new state from a given initial one. Following common practice in work on concurrency control, this issue will not be elaborated on further here, since an assumption generally made in this context is that the particular interpretation of a given transaction (as the implementation of an application program) is *unknown*. A *positive* implication of this assumption is that the results presented in what follows will be valid *independent* of a particular interpretation, while a *negative* one will be that the meaning of a transaction, which could be used to improve concurrency even further, is not taken into account. This issue will briefly be discussed in Section 18.6.

For the time being, the best that can be done is to assume a *pseudo-semantics* for a given transaction as follows. It is assumed that the (new) value of an object x written by some step $w(x)$ of a given transaction t depends on *all* values of objects that were previously read by t. The value of x read by some step $r(x)$ of t depends on the last $w(x)$ that occurred before $r(x)$ in t, or on the 'initial' value of x if no such $w(x)$ exists. This pseudo-semantics will implicitly be used frequently in what follows, and it will also implicitly be generalized to 'schedules' if actions from distinct transactions are interleaved.

When a *set* of transactions is to execute concurrently, their operations should be interleaved. Such an execution is modelled by a *schedule* for this set, which is introduced next.

Definition 18.2

Let $T = \{t_0, \ldots, t_n\}$ be a (finite) set of transactions. A **schedule** s for T is a sequence of steps consisting of all steps from the given transactions, possibly interleaved, and no other steps, such that for each transaction the ordering of steps in it is preserved in the schedule, that is, each $t \in T$ occurs in s as a subsequence.

Thus, a schedule for a set T of transactions informally is an execution sequence for the transactions from T which contains all individual actions and at the same time 'embeds' the individual orderings.

As an example, consider the set $T = \{t_0, t_1, t_2, t_3\}$, where t_1 is as above and

$$t_0 = w_0(x)w_0(z)w_0(y)$$
$$t_2 = r_2(x)w_2(y)$$
$$t_3 = r_3(z)w_3(z)w_3(y)$$

Then the following is a schedule for T:

$$s_1 = w_0(x)r_1(x)w_0(z)r_1(z)r_2(x)w_0(y)r_3(z)w_3(z)w_2(y)w_1(x)w_3(y)$$

Obviously, there exist many schedules for a given set T of transactions. In particular, there are the ones in which the elements of T occur strictly consecutively, which are called **serial**. For the above example, the following schedule is serial:

$$s_2 = w_0(x)w_0(z)w_0(y)r_2(x)w_2(y)r_1(x)r_1(z)w_1(x)r_3(z)w_3(z)w_3(y)$$

It can be written more briefly as $s_2 = t_0t_2t_1t_3$. Clearly, there always exist $n!$ serial schedules for a given set of n transactions.

Since a serial schedule is always 'correct' in the sense that it preserves the consistency of the underlying database (assuming that the transactions it contains are consistency preserving), it makes sense to establish a correctness criterion for non-serial schedules on the basis of a relationship to serial ones. The common way to achieve this is by first introducing an appropriate notion of *equivalence* for schedules and then defining *serializability* (the actual correct criterion) via equivalence to a serial schedule. All notions of serializability described in the literature are obtained in this way; clearly, the various notions proposed sometimes differ significantly with respect to the notion of equivalence used.

The first equivalence relation that will be discussed here is based on the intuition that only those schedules which have the same 'effect' on any given database state should be considered 'equivalent'. In other words, 'equivalent' schedules should represent the same 'computation' on every given (initial) state. Since this is difficult to capture in the absence of concrete interpretations for the various transactions, the best that can be done is to employ the pseudo-semantics described above in the following way.

Definition 18.3

Let T be a set of transactions, and let s be a schedule for T. Also, let $w_i(x), r_j(x)$ be two actions occurring in s.

(i) $r_j(x)$ **reads from** $w_i(x)$ (in s) if $r_j(x)$ occurs *after* $w_i(x)$ in s, and no action $w_k(x)$ occurring in s $(k \neq i, j)$ lies between them.
(ii) $w_i(x)$ is a **final write** (in s), if no $w_k(x)$, $k \neq i$, comes 'after' $w_i(x)$ in s.

As an example, consider the schedule s_1 shown above. The following holds:

$r_1(x)$ reads from $w_0(x), r_2(x)$ reads from $w_0(x)$
$r_1(z)$ reads from $w_0(z), r_3(z)$ reads from $w_0(z)$

The same obviously holds for s_2 shown above. In addition, the steps $w_1(x)$, $w_3(y)$ and $w_3(z)$ are the final writes in both schedules.

As another example, consider the following schedules:

$s = w_0(x)r_1(x)w_2(x)r_3(x)r_4(x)$
$s' = w_0(x)w_1(x)w_2(y)r_2(y)$

In s, $r_1(x)$ reads from $w_0(x)$, while $r_3(x)$ and $r_4(x)$ read from $w_2(x)$; in s', $w_1(x)$ and $w_2(y)$ are final.

The first notion of equivalence for schedules can now be stated.

Definition 18.4

Let s and s' be two schedules for the same set T of transactions. s and s' are **view-equivalent**, abbreviated $s \approx_v s'$, if the following holds:

(i) Every read action of the form $r_j(x)$ reads from the same write action $w_i(x)$ in both s and s' (that is, $r_j(x)$ reads from $w_i(x)$ in s iff $r_j(x)$ reads from $w_i(x)$ in s').

(ii) Both s and s' have the same final write steps (that is, $w_i(x)$ is final in s iff $w_i(x)$ is final in s').

It follows immediately that the schedules s_1 and s_2 shown above, which are over the same set $T = \{t_0, t_1, t_2, t_3\}$ of transactions, are view-equivalent, that is, $s_1 \approx_v s_2$ (both s_1 and s_2 produce the same 'next state' from whatever the given state is, and while doing so always 'see' the same data values).

After these preparations, it is possible to introduce a first correctness criterion for schedules.

Definition 18.5

Let T be a set of transactions, and s be a schedule for T. s is **view-serializable** if there exists a serial schedule s' for T such that $s \approx_v s'$. Let VSR(T) (or simply VSR if T is understood or immaterial) denote the class of all view-serializable schedules (for T).

It follows that, in the example above, s_1 is view-serializable ($s_1 \in$ VSR) since it is view-equivalent to the serial schedule s_2.

A view-serializable schedule can always be transformed into a serial one that has the same effect on any given database state; since the latter is 'correct' by definition, the view-serializable one is also correct.

Thus, a 'merge rule' as requested in Section 18.2 for actions from distinct transactions is now available. The next question that immediately arises is how this condition of serializability or, stated differently, membership in the class VSR (more precisely, in VSR(T) for a given T) can be tested. Clearly, it is crucial to have an efficient test for this condition, since otherwise it would not be applicable for schedulers in practice.

To answer this question, first note that view-equivalence of two given schedules is easy to test. For both schedules, determine their read-from relations as well as their final writes and check whether they are equal. Indeed, it can be shown that it can be decided in polynomial time whether two given schedules are view-equivalent. On the other hand, testing view-serializability is more tricky. For a given set T of n transactions and a given schedule s, one way to test s for membership in VSR(T) is to generate all serial schedules for T and test whether (at least) one of them is view-equivalent to s. Unfortunately, this approach is not feasible since, as mentioned above, there are $n!$ serial schedules for n transactions. Using results from complexity theory and in particular from the theory of NP-completeness, it can further be shown that probably no better way exists, since testing view-serializability is NP-complete (see the Bibliographic Notes). One way out of this dilemma is to come up with at least a *sufficient* condition for membership in VSR or a restricted notion of serializability, which will be described next. Note that as long as a scheduler is able to generate schedules all of which satisfy the restricted condition, it is guaranteed that these are view-serializable, an issue that will be discussed in the next section.

Definition 18.6

Let T be a set of transactions, and let s and s' be schedules for T.

(i) Two steps a and b from distinct transactions in s are in **conflict**

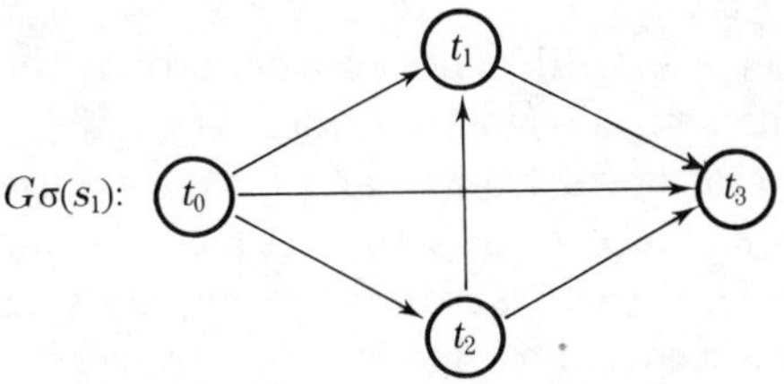

Figure 18.4 The conflict graph of s_1.

if they operate on the same database object and at least one of them is a write, that is, $a = r_i(x)$ and $b = w_j(x)$, or $a = w_i(x)$ and $b = r_j(x)$, or $a = w_i(x)$ and $b = w_j(x)$, $i \neq j$.

(ii) s and s' are **conflict-equivalent**, denoted $s \approx_c s'$, if all pairs of conflicting steps occur in the same order in both s and s', that is, if a and b are in conflict in s and a appears before b in s, then the same holds in s' and vice versa.

(iii) s is **conflict-serializable** if there exists a serial schedule s'' for T such that $s \approx_c s''$. Let CSR(T) (or simply CSR) denote the class of all conflict-serializable schedules (for T).

As for view-equivalence, it is obviously easy to test whether two given schedules for the same set of transactions are conflict-equivalent. For both schedules determine their 'conflict relations' and check whether they are equal. In addition, it is now easy to test for membership in the class CSR, as shown next.

Definition 18.7

Let $T = \{t_0, \ldots, t_n\}$ and s be a schedule for T. The **conflict** (or serialization) **graph** $G(s)$ of s is defined as follows: $G(s) = (T, E)$, where $(t_i, t_j) \in E$ if some step from t_i is in conflict with a subsequent step from t_j.

As an example, Figure 18.4 shows the conflict graph $G(s_1) = (T, E)$ for the schedule s_1 from above; for example, $(t_0, t_1) \in E$ since $w_0(x)$ is before the conflicting $r_1(x)$ in s_1, $(t_2, t_1) \in E$ since $r_2(x)$ is before the conflicting $w_1(x)$ in s_1, and so on.

Theorem 18.1

For every schedule s the following holds:

$$s \in \text{CSR} \iff G(s) \text{ is acyclic}$$

Proof. (only if) Let $s \in$ CSR. Then, by definition, there exists a serial schedule s' such that $s \approx_c s'$. Now consider $G(s)$. If (t_i, t_j) is an edge in $G(s)$, s contains operations a from t_i and b from t_j in conflict such that a comes before b in s. Since s and s' have the same conflict relation, the same holds in s'. Now, since s' is serial, this implies that all of t_i appears before all of t_j in s'. Hence, an edge in $G(s)$ 'triggers' an ordering of its endpoints in s', and via induction this observation can be extended from edges to paths in $G(s)$. Now suppose $G(s)$ contains a cycle of the form $(t_{i_1}, t_{i_2}, t_{i_3}, \ldots, t_{i_1})$. This implies that t_{i_1} appears in s' before itself, which is impossible. The assertion follows.

(if) Let $G(s)$ be acyclic. Then $G(s)$ can be sorted topologically (see below), which yields a serial order of the transactions involved. Let s' denote that order, and let a from t_i and b from t_j be in conflict in s such that a comes before b. Then (t_i, t_j) is an edge in the acyclic $G(s)$, which means that all of t_i is before all of t_j in the topological order s'. Hence the conflict relations of s and s' are equal, which means $s \approx_c s'$. $\square$

As a result, conflict-serializability of a given schedule s can be polynomially decided by constructing $G(s)$ and testing this graph for acyclicity.

As was mentioned above, conflict-serializability is a more restricted correctness criterion for schedules than view-serializability. For example, consider

$$s = r_1(y) r_3(w) r_2(y) w_1(y) w_1(x) w_2(x) w_2(z) w_3(x)$$

Clearly, $s \notin$ CSR since edges (t_2, t_1) and (t_1, t_2) are in $G(s)$. On the other hand, $s \in$ VSR since it is easily verified that $s \approx_v t_1 t_2 t_3$. The relationship between CSR and VSR is established in the following theorem.

Theorem 18.2

Every conflict-serializable schedule is view-serializable, but not necessarily vice versa, that is,

$$\text{CSR} \subset \text{VSR}$$

As another example, consider the three transactions $t_0 = r_0(x) w_0(x)$, $t_1 = w_1(x)$ and $t_2 = w_2(x)$ and the schedule $s = r_0(x) w_1(x) w_0(x) w_2(x)$ for $T = \{t_0, t_1, t_2\}$; Figure 18.5 shows the conflict graph of s. Clearly, $G(s)$ is cyclic. However, it is easily verified that s is view-equivalent to the serial schedule $s' = t_0 t_1 t_2$. In both cases, the reads-from relation is empty, and $w_2(x)$ is final in both schedules. This example shows that the edges in a conflict graph are sometimes too restrictive with respect to pairs of write operations. In fact, the edge from t_1 to t_0 in $G(s)$ from Figure 18.5 is redundant since the x values written by t_0 and t_1 are not used by t_2; t_2 writes a new x value independent of the other two transactions. The

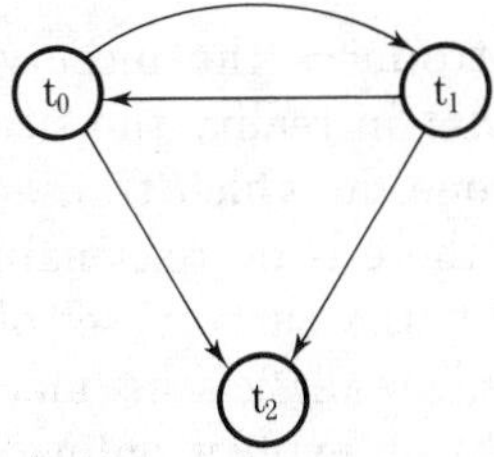

Figure 18.5 Example showing that the inclusion in Theorem 18.2 is strict.

general problem behind this observation is that in the general read-write model of transactions it is allowed that a transaction writes an object *without* having read the object before (a transaction is allowed to contain 'blind writes'). If the model is restricted to exclude such transactions ('no blind writes'), that is, whenever an action of the form $w_i(x)$ appears in t_i, then an action of the form $r_i(x)$ is also in t_i preceding $w_i(x)$, then a schedule is view-serializable iff it is conflict-serializable. In this case, which excludes transactions that are also termed 'dead' or 'useless', an efficient test for view-serializability is available. For a given schedule s construct $G(s)$ and test it for acyclicity. If $G(s)$ has n vertices, the latter test can be performed in linear time $O(n)$ (if the graph is stored in an appropriate data structure). Moreover, if the test ends positive, that is, the graph is a direct acyclic graph (DAG), an equivalent serial schedule can be explicitly constructed by topological sorting as a 'by-product'. If $G(s)$ is a DAG, it has (at least) one vertex without incoming edges (a so-called *input*). The transaction corresponding to this vertex is placed in the serial schedule as the first one; the vertex itself is removed from the graph (together with all its incident edges). As a result, a subgraph is obtained which is still a DAG, and the procedure can be iterated (until the remaining graph is empty).

An interesting observation about conflict-serializability is that its characterization in Theorem 18.1 straightforwardly implies a dynamic scheduling method, known as **serialization graph testing** (SGT). The scheduler needs to maintain a conflict graph in which all active and already committed transactions are represented as nodes, and in which for each newly arriving operation it is checked whether this operation adds new edges and, if so, a cycle is closed. If the latter is the case, the operation is rejected and the transaction aborted; otherwise it can be executed. Committed transactions remain in the graph until they cannot be involved in a cycle any more, which is the case iff the corresponding node has no more incoming edges. For practical implementations, this approach has a number of shortcomings (including its space consumption, see the references), which is why it has not been used up to now in commercial systems.

The next section introduces the most widely applied 'protocol', which takes into account that in reality the situation a scheduler is confronted with is a *dynamic* one, in which transactions come and go in an asynchronous fashion, and there is no reasonable point in time at which a scheduler could talk about 'the current' set of transactions being completely at its disposal. Thus, a realistic scheduler needs 'merge procedures' which on the one hand make an explicit online test for CSR membership obsolete, but which on the other can be proved to produce correct outputs by means introduced in this section.

18.4 Two-phase locking (2PL)

The observations and subsequent requirements from Section 18.2 can now be made more precise by requesting that a scheduler has to produce schedules which are conflict-serializable. According to Theorem 18.1, acyclicity of the corresponding conflict graph is a necessary and sufficient condition for CSR membership, so that it can now be employed to prove the correctness ('safety') of a scheduler.

A scheduler uses a certain 'merge' or 'concurrency control' procedure to produce conflict-serializable schedules. In this section a prominent type of scheduler will be described, the *two-phase locking protocol*, which is frequently used in database management systems.

Notice the use of the word 'protocol' here, which indicates that a scheduler, unlike a program that produces an output for some arbitrary, but fixed (finite) input, is basically a 'procedure' consisting of an infinite loop. Thus, both input and output are *infinite* in general; this section will indicate how the notion of a history or schedule introduced earlier can still be used in correctness proofs for schedulers.

The basic idea underlying any locking approach is to require that the access to database objects by distinct transactions is executed in a mutually exclusive way; in particular, a transaction cannot modify (write) an object as long as another transaction is still operating on it (reading or writing it). The central paradigm to implement this idea is the use of two new actions which can be 'injected' into a transaction by the scheduler.

Through the action 'lock(x)' a **lock** is put on object x; as a result, x is now at the exclusive disposal of the transaction which imposed the lock, and as long as the lock is held no other transaction can read or write x. Through the 'inverse' action 'unlock(x)' object x is **unlock**ed, that is, a previously set lock is released.

As an example, consider the lost update problem (see Section 18.1) once more, where the effect achievable by the use of locks becomes immediately obvious. The 'loss' of an update can be avoided if the two transactions are, for instance, scheduled as follows:

$$\text{BOT}(t_1)\ \text{BOT}(t_2)\ \text{lock}_1(x)\ r_1(x)\ u_1(x)\ w_1(x)\ \text{unlock}_1(x)$$
$$\text{lock}_2(x)\ r_2(x)\ \text{EOT}(t_1)\ u_2(x)\ w_2(x)\ \text{unlock}_2(x)\ \text{EOT}(t_2)$$

Now t_2 has to wait for t_1 to release the lock t_1 holds on x. Clearly, the result is basically serial in this case.

It is obvious that the introduction of exclusively locking actions only is unnecessarily restrictive. Since the point is to lock an object, before it is written, so that other transactions get the impression that the object was not in the database, a more liberal policy is apt for read accesses. If an object is locked only because a certain transaction wants to read it, it is possible to grant read access to other transactions as well.

Therefore, the action 'lock(.)' introduced above is replaced by two new actions 'rlock(.)' and 'wlock(.)' as follows. If a transaction t has locked an object x in **lock mode** 'rlock(x)', t can at most read x afterwards, but not write x. This type of lock is therefore called a **read lock**; after an action 'rlock(x)' object x is also said to be locked in **shared mode**. Next, if t has locked x by an action 'wlock(x)', t can afterwards access x with both read and write steps; x is then locked in **exclusive mode**, and t holds a **write lock** on x. A transaction has to rlock an object before it reads the object, and to wlock it before it writes the object. If this rule is employed, it is necessary to introduce the concept of **lock conversion** for cases in which a transaction first rlocks an object and *later* wlocks it for writing (or vice versa). It is assumed here that a wlock is set in the first place if both reading and writing of an object is intended (although it remains open at this point — and subject to implementation — where a scheduler can obtain this information from). As a consequence, no particular distinction is needed between a 'read-unlock' and a 'write-unlock' operation; the unlock used here is intended to remove whatever lock currently exists on the respective object.

The use and in particular the obtaining of locks is further bound to the following rules:

(1) If a transaction t_i contains an action of the form $r_i(x)$ ($w_i(x)$), then object x has to be locked via rlock$_i(x)$ (wlock$_i(x)$) before this operation is executed. The corresponding lock has to be held for at least the duration of the execution of this action (for example, 'rlock(x) unlock(x) $r(x)$' is not allowed). If t_i both reads and writes x, t_i locks x in exclusive mode.

(2) If x is locked by t_i by rlock$_i$ or wlock$_i$, this lock will be released at some later time by unlock$_i(x)$.

(3) Locks of the same kind (mode) are set at most once within the same transaction; all unlock actions refer to objects that have previously been locked (that is, no redundant lock or unlock operations occur).

Next consider two transactions which can set write and read locks (on the same set of objects); then a *conflict* arises between the two if both lock the same object and (at least) one of the locks is an exclusive one (wlock). In this case, only one of the lock requests can be granted since the requests are *incompatible*; the following table summarizes the compatibility between rlock and wlock with respect to *one* database object (where '1' means 'compatible' and '0' means the contrary):

	rlock	wlock
rlock	1	0
wlock	0	0

Hence, a second transaction can only be granted a (simultaneous) read lock if the object in question is locked by every other transaction in shared mode only (if at all).

After these preparations, the following notions can now be introduced.

Definition 18.8

(i) A scheduler operates according to a **locking protocol** if in every schedule generated by it for a set $T = \{t_0, \ldots, t_n\}$ of transactions, the following conditions are satisfied:

(a) each transaction $t_i, 0 \leq i \leq n$, satisfies the rules (1) – (3) stated above;

(b) if x is locked by t_i and t_j, these locks are compatible.

(ii) A locking protocol is **two-phase** (it is a *two-phase locking protocol*, abbreviated **2PL**) if the following holds for each $t_i \in T$. After the first unlock action no further rlock or wlock actions follow ('no new lock is acquired after the first one has been released').

Notice that a distinction between the *lock* that is set on an object and the *operation* which sets a lock is mostly neglected here. In an implementation, the scheduler will have to communicate lock requests to the data manager before they can actually be set. The data manager keeps track of the various lock 'flags' associated with the objects it manages, while the scheduler will keep track of which transaction has locked what object (and which transaction is waiting for a lock to be released). If the scheduler receives an operation, say, $w_i(x)$, it first requests a wlock on x from the data manager. If the latter reports that x is not wlocked yet and the scheduler finds that this wlock does not conflict with a lock already set on this object (which in this case means that no other transaction has locked x at the moment), the scheduler outputs wlock$_i(x)$, thereby asking the data manager to wlock object x. At later points in time, the scheduler

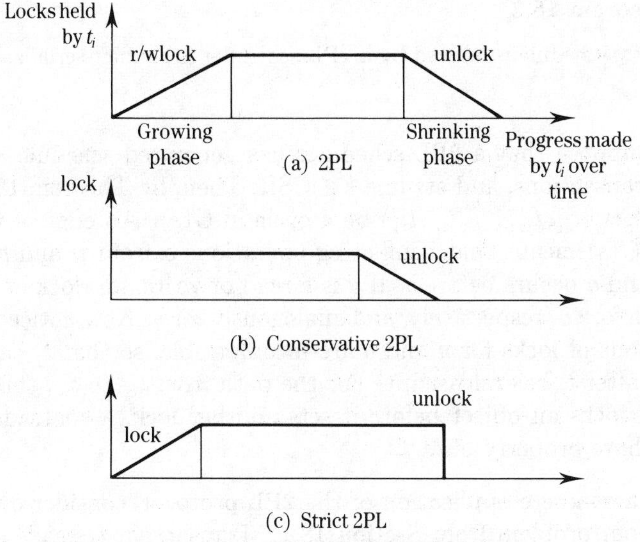

Figure 18.6 Two-phase locking and its variants.

will then output $w_i(x)$ as well as unlock$_i(x)$ (in that order).

Condition (ii) of Definition 18.8 intuitively says that the setting and releasing of locks takes place in *two phases* for each transaction; during the **growing phase**, a transaction sets all the locks it needs, without releasing any of them. If the first lock is released, the transaction enters its **shrinking phase**, during which locks can only be released; no further locks can be set.

Figure 18.6(a) illustrates this lapse over time. Figure 18.6(b) shows a variant of this protocol in which all locks needed are set (at once) at the beginning of a transaction ('locking from BOT on', known as **conservative** or **static 2PL**). Figure 18.6(c) shows another variant frequently used in concrete implementations in which all locks are held until the transaction ends ('locking until EOT', known as **strict** or **dynamic 2PL**). A straightforward motivation for the use of strict 2PL is the fact the a scheduler has little knowledge on the transactions it is processing in general; in particular, a point at which it can definitely be sure that a transaction will not request any further locks is the *end* of the transaction.

The 'verification' of the two-phase locking protocol, or the guarantee that this protocol is *safe* in the sense that all schedules produced by it are 'correct' (in the sense of Definition 18.6), is provided by the following theorem.

Theorem 18.3

Every schedule produced by a 2PL scheduler is conflict-serializable.

Proof. Suppose that a 2PL scheduler has generated schedule s for the set T of transactions, and assume $s \notin$ CSR. Then, by Theorem 18.1, $G(s)$ is cyclic. Let $(t_{i_1}, t_{i_2}, \ldots, t_{i_n}, t_{i_1})$ be a cycle in $G(s)$. An edge of the form (t_i, t_j) in $G(s)$ means that conflicting operations a from t_i and b from t_j are in s, and a occurs before b. If a is a read or write, an rlock or wlock is required before a, respectively, and analogously for b. Now notice that any combinations of locks for a and b are incompatible, so that t_j can set its lock only after t_i has released it. For the path from t_{i_1} to t_{i_1}, this implies that t_{i_1} unlocks an object before it sets another lock, a contradiction to the two-phase property of t_i. □

As a concrete application of the 2PL protocol, consider once more the phantom problem from Section 18.1. Transaction t_1 reads x, y and z without writing, so that rlock actions are sufficient. Transaction t_2 modifies x and z and hence needs corresponding wlock actions. Since rlock and wlock (with respect to x or z) are incompatible, either t_1 has to wait until t_2 has released the corresponding locks or vice versa. The schedule shown in Figure 18.7 is therefore correct in the sense of the 2PL protocol.

An important point should be considered here which has been mentioned earlier. Since a scheduler actually operates in a *dynamic* environment, in which at no point in time does there exist a 'current' set of transactions, and in which the output is in fact *infinite*, the question arises of how the results obtained and tools provided so far, which were developed for a *static* situation, carry over to this more realistic situation. The solution, in particular regarding the verification of a scheduling protocol, is to 'reduce' the dynamic situation to the static one, informally, as follows.

Given a schedule (an 'execution sequence') s, consider *projections* of prefixes p of s obtained by omitting from p all actions which belong to transactions that are not yet committed. If every such projection is conflict-serializable, then s is called conflict-serializable. Since it can be shown that the class CSR is closed under projections (see Exercise 8), this justifies the use of 2PL in the dynamic case as well.

Due to condition (b) in Definition 18.8 (i), the following situation may arise in a 2PL schedule. Two transactions t_1 and t_2 set rlocks on objects x and y, respectively, in order to be able to read these objects. At some later time, both try to set a wlock on the respective other object as well, that is, t_1 tries to wlock y, while t_2 tries to wlock x. Now the following 'conflict' occurs:

t_1	*Time*	t_2
BOT(t_1)	1	
	2	BOT(t_2)
$sum := 0$	3	
rlock(y)	4	
$r(y)$	5	
$sum := sum + y$	6	
	7	wlock(x)
	8	wlock(z)
	9	$r(x)$
	10	$r(z)$
	11	$z := z - 10$
	12	$x := x + 10$
	13	$w(z)$
	14	unlock(z)
rlock(z)	15	
$r(z)$	16	
$sum := sum + z$	17	
	18	$w(x)$
	19	unlock(x)
rlock(x)	20	
$r(x)$	21	
$sum := sum + x$	22	
unlock(x)	23	
unlock(y)	24	
unlock(z)	25	
	26	EOT(t_2)
EOT(t_1)	27	

Figure 18.7 A solution to the phantom problem using 2PL.

t_1	t_2
rlock$_1$(x)	
	rlock$_2$(y)
⋮	⋮
wlock$_1$(y)	
	wlock$_2$(x)

Since the new locks are incompatible with the ones already set, both transactions have to wait for each other to release the lock in question. Since each wlock, however, has to be set *before* a transaction can unlock, t_1 and t_2 are in a **deadlock** situation.

Thus, the two-phase locking protocol has the potential of running into deadlocks and hence requires additional provisions to detect and to resolve them. One possibility for detecting deadlocks is to maintain a **wait-for graph** (WFG) whose vertices represent the currently active transactions, and whose edges capture the fact that one transaction waits for an unlock action of another. A deadlock occurs if the wait-for graph contains a cycle. Hence, if the graph is properly maintained, it can be checked for (freedom from) cycles on a regular basis; if a cycle is detected, at least one of the transactions involved has to be aborted (in order to break the cycle, thereby resolving the deadlock) and restarted at some later time.

Checking a WFG for cycles 'on a regular basis' can obviously be implemented in various ways. One approach is to use a *timer* which runs for a predefined duration; a cycle test is performed every time the timer times out. As a result, a cycle could remain undetected for a 'long' period, so that little or no progress would be made in the meantime. At the other extreme, a WFG could be checked for cycles each time a new edge is added, which may introduce an unnecessary overhead. A 'good' strategy would probably be an intermediate one which borrows ideas from both approaches; final decisions on what to emphasize remain subject to performance evaluation and (eventually) application-oriented tuning.

Finally, notice that it is not sufficient for a scheduler to determine whether the (current) WFG has a cycle, but it needs to *detect all cycles*. After that, a *victim* (which breaks all cycles) needs to be chosen for abort. The appropriate choice of the victim may also have an impact on the overall performance. For example, a victim may be chosen which has the least recovery costs among all candidate victims. In another approach, a victim may be chosen which removes as many edges as possible from the WFG, where techniques from graph theory (such as the search for articulation points or for strongly connected components) may be employed. Again, a combination of both approaches might result in the 'best' performance.

Another aspect in choosing a victim (a transaction that is aborted and restarted from scratch later) is that the same transaction might be involved in a WFG cycle in consecutive attempts to schedule it, and that it might each time be chosen as the victim. Thus, the transaction would be delayed forever, a phenomenon called **starvation**. Clearly, starvation of transactions should also be avoided (by an appropriate implementation of the determination of the victim).

The obvious question arises of whether the additional overhead of maintaining a wait-for graph when scheduling can be avoided. The locking protocol described next guarantees conflict-serializable schedules, but at the same time is deadlock-free. This **tree-locking protocol**, abbreviated TL, does without the two-phase property of the transactions under consideration; this property is 'replaced' by additional information regarding the sequencing in which a transaction may access the objects in a database.

For the remainder of this section, it is assumed that the underlying database d consists of n objects, that is, $d = \{x_1, \dots, x_n\}$, which are

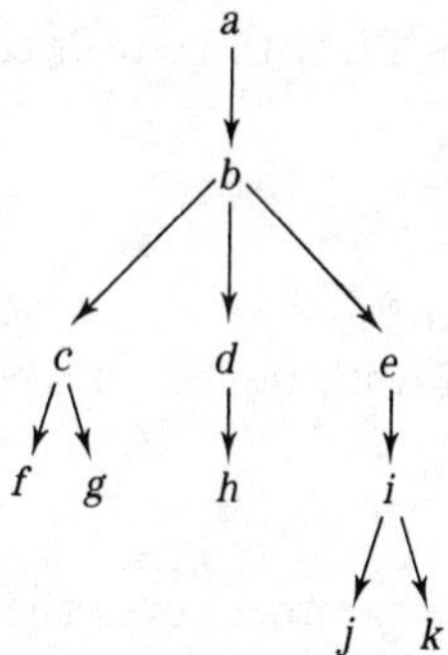

Figure 18.8 A database tree with 10 objects.

partially ordered (this ordering may result, for example, from the physical organization of the database). Then d can be represented by a database graph; to simplify the exposition, only graphs which are rooted trees are considered here. Figure 18.8 shows such a *database tree* with 10 objects.

Each transaction operating on a tree-structured database is now required to access object x_i *before* object x_j if it accesses both objects, and x_i precedes x_j in the ordering. In addition, it is assumed that only a lock action is available for setting a lock, that is, only exclusive locks are considered.

Definition 18.9

Let d be a database tree, and let t be a transaction (operating on d) containing lock and unlock actions. t satisfies the **tree locking protocol** (or 't is TL with respect to d') if the following holds:

(i) If lock(x) is the *first* lock action occurring in t then x may be an arbitrary database object.
(ii) For every other action of the form lock(x), the following applies. If y is the father of x, then the action 'lock(x)' is *preceded* by 'lock(y)' in t, and *followed* by 'unlock(y)' in t.
(iii) Locks can be released at any time.
(iv) At most one lock can be set on any object, that is, no 'lock(x)' may (again) follow some 'unlock(x)' (in one transaction).

It is also assumed, as for 2PL, that an object is locked before it is read or written, and that every lock set on an object is eventually released; thus, a **TL scheduler** in particular operates according to a locking protocol in the sense of Definition 18.8 (i). As an example, consider the following transaction:

$$t = \text{lock}(b), \text{lock}(d), r(d), \text{lock}(e), \text{unlock}(b), \text{lock}(i), w(i), \text{unlock}(i), \text{unlock}(e), \text{lock}(h), r(h), w(d), \text{unlock}(d), \text{unlock}(h)$$

It is easily verified that t is TL with respect to the database state d shown in Figure 18.8.

Theorem 18.4

Let s be a schedule produced by a TL scheduler, that is, all transactions occurring in s are TL with respect to the same database tree. Then s is conflict-serializable.

An advantage of this protocol over the two-phase locking approach is that it avoids deadlocks, so that it is never necessary to abort a transaction and restart it because of a 'congestion'. Since unlock actions may now occur *before* lock actions in a transaction, the waiting time between transactions may be shorter so that a higher degree of parallelism is eventually achieved. A disadvantage is that, because of condition (ii) in Definition 18.9, it may happen that more objects have to be locked than are actually needed by the transaction in question.

18.5 Additional scheduling methods

In general, concurrency control methods can be divided into two major classes:

(1) **Pessimistic protocols**: These include the locking protocols 2PL and TL described in the previous section, which are based on the assumption that conflicts between concurrent transactions occur frequently or with a high probability. This assumption has the practical consequence that provisions need to be taken to handle such conflicts. They also include *timestamping*, discussed below, and the SGT protocol described at the end of Section 18.3.

(2) **Optimistic protocols**: These include various *validation methods* (see below) and are based on the assumption that conflicts are rare.

In the remainder of this section some other members of both classes will be briefly described; finally, some refinements are discussed with which the 2PL protocol, for example, is frequently equipped in practical applications.

One alternative to locking protocols (in the 'pessimistic' class) is the **timestamping** approach. While in a locking protocol the ordering of two transactions t_i and t_j is determined at execution time as soon as t_i and t_j request conflicting locks on an object, this 'serializability ordering' is determined prior to execution time in a timestamping approach. In particular, each transaction t_i (that enters the input pool of the transaction manager) is assigned a (globally unique) *timestamp* $Z(t_i)$, which may, for instance, be the current value of the system clock. Next, if t_j reaches the input pool *after* t_i, then $Z(t_i) < Z(t_j)$ holds. These timestamps finally determine the execution sequence of the transactions; if $Z(t_i) < Z(t_j)$ holds, the scheduler has to guarantee that the schedule generated is equivalent to a serial one in which t_i *precedes* t_j.

An **optimistic method** is based on the assumption that conflicts between individual concurrent transactions are rare events. As a consequence, it is possible to produce *any* schedule and execute it. Only *after* the execution of a transaction, but before it enters the state 'committed', it is checked whether a conflict with another transaction has occurred (or some consistency condition has been violated); if this is the case, the transaction is aborted and (later) restarted.

It is obvious that an optimistic approach is preferable over a pessimistic one where 'almost all' transactions are of type 'read-only'. Thus, the decision in favour of or against the use of an optimistic method could at least in part be based on knowledge (of the 'dynamic' requirements profile) obtained during the design phase of the underlying database. An optimistic method can be realized as follows (using the **validation** approach). The entire execution time of a transaction is (logically) devided into *three* phases. During the *read phase* the execution proper takes place; all database objects needed are read and stored in local variables in a buffer. Updates and/or write actions are performed on these variables only and hence do not affect the database yet. Next, during the *validation phase*, it is checked whether the updates made by this transaction on these database objects can be 'committed', that is, written (back) into the database, without violating the serializability property of the corresponding schedule. If the result of this test is positive, the transaction finally enters its *write phase*, during which all write actions of the transaction are executed with respect to the database (and no longer with respect to the buffer); otherwise, the transaction is aborted.

To perform a validation, one possibility is to use timestamps which are issued at the beginning of this phase; if $Z(t)$ denotes the timestamp associated with the beginning of the validation phase of a transaction t and $Z(t_i) < Z(t_j)$ holds in a particular situation, the schedule generated has to be equivalent to a serial one in which t_i precedes t_j. Further details can again be found in the references cited in the Bibliographic Notes.

So far it has been assumed in this chapter that an individual database object is the 'unit' of synchronization, without specifying what an object actually is. In reality, a database is often structured hierarchically at the physical level (see Figure 18.9), and it might be advantageous to make use of this structuring in the scheduling process. This idea will be explained in more detail next, where two-phase locking is again used as the concurrency control method. Recall that in the previous section only rlock and

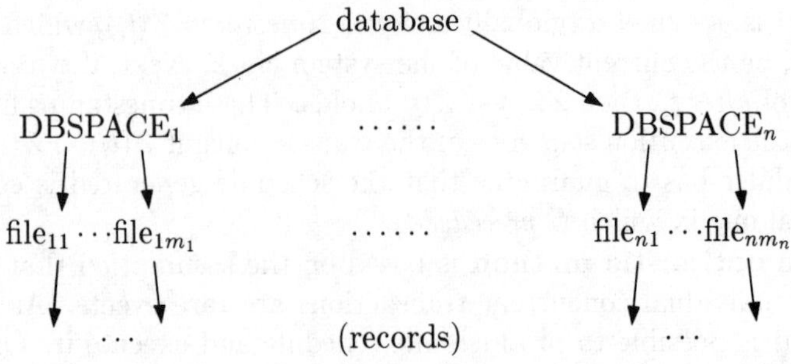

Figure 18.9 A multiple-granularity database.

wlock actions were allowed on 'objects'. In reality, an object could be a dbspace, a file or a record, for instance, which has been neglected up to now.

Now consider the case that all database objects accessed by transactions are of type 'record', and assume that a particular transaction accesses the *entire* database. Then all records in the database have to be locked one after the other, until this transaction has exclusive access. Clearly, the 'implemented version' of a scheduler needs to keep track of all these locks (in a *lock table*), so that it would be desirable in this case — to reduce the effort of managing locks — to lock the entire database in *one* operation. On the other hand, it could also happen that the only object that can be locked is of type 'database', even if a transaction accesses a particular file from that database only.

In order to remedy this situation, it seems reasonable to introduce (lock) objects of different 'sizes', and to establish a hierarchy in which 'large' objects are located at a higher level than 'small' ones (see Figure 18.9); thus, multiple **levels of granularity** are introduced. In the presence of such a hierarchy, so-called **implicit** locks can be employed by a locking protocol. For example, if a dbspace is locked in Figure 18.9, then all other objects in the hierarchy which are located in the subtree starting at this dbspace's node, that is, all 'lower' files and records, are also locked *implicitly*.

In the situation depicted in Figure 18.9, it may now happen that a transaction t_i has locked some file F_{kl} through an rlock action, and that another transaction t_j wants to lock the dbspace D_k, which is a distinct object to which F_{kl} belongs, through a wlock action; afterwards, file F_{kl} would be locked by t_j implicitly with a wlock which conflicts with the rlock already held by t_i on this file. This observation serves to introduce additional **lock modes** or lock actions in the presence of a hierarchy of lock objects.

The locks of type 'read' (shared) and 'write' (exclusive) were introduced in the previous section; in what follows, they will be denoted by SL and XL, respectively. Even in the presence of a hierarchy of lock objects, SL and XL clearly remain incompatible; only SL pairs can implicitly or explicitly occur simultaneously.

If a node in a given hierarchy is locked by some transaction t_i, the conflict described above is avoidable if all corresponding 'higher' objects (which occur on a path from the given node to the root of the hierarchy) are 'marked' appropriately. To this end, an **intention lock** can be used, which indicates, for instance, at the level of dbspaces that a file or record in a dbspace is locked already; if it is locked by SL or XL, the dbspace is locked ISL or IXL, respectively, where the latter acronyms stands for '*intention shared lock*' and '*intention exclusive lock*'.

Even with these extensions of the locking protocol at hand, the following case may occur. If a transaction reads a subtree and modifies (writes) only certain objects in it, it may either lock the root of the subtree by XL (and hence all other nodes implicitly), or it may lock the root by IXL and the other nodes explicitly by SL or XL as needed. Using the first variant, no concurrent access is possible for another transaction, while the second variant, which intuitively allows for more parallelism, requires more management overhead for the individual locks. This necessitates the introduction of yet another lock mode by which a subhierarchy can be locked implicitly by SL recording at the same time that certain objects in this hierarchy are to be modified. This mode is hence meant to combine the 'properties' of IXL and SL; it is therefore termed SIXL (*shared and intention exclusive lock*). The compatibilities between these five lock modes are as described in the following table, where '1' means 'compatible' and '0' its opposite:

	ISL	IXL	SL	SIXL	XL
ISL	1	1	1	1	0
IXL	1	1	0	0	0
SL	1	0	1	0	0
SIXL	1	0	0	0	0
XL	0	0	0	0	0

An (extended) two-phase locking protocol for generating conflict-serializable schedules, known as **multiple-granularity 2PL** (**MGL**), can now be stated as follows. Each transaction t_i can lock a vertex x of the given hierarchy according to the following rules:

(1) The compatibility table shown above has to be observed.

(2) The root of the hierarchy has to be locked first (in any mode).

(3) If x is locked by t_i with SL or ISL, the father of x is already locked by t_i with IXL or ISL.

(4) If x is locked by t_i with XL, SIXL or IXL, the father of x is already locked with IXL or SIXL.

(5) t_i is two-phase (if t_i sets a lock, it has not yet released any).

(6) If t_i unlocks node x, no son of x is still locked by t_i.

Thus, in this protocol, locks are set in a 'top-down' fashion and released 'bottom-up'. It should be mentioned that this protocol (as the original 2PL) is also not deadlock-free (see Exercise 13).

18.6 Using semantic information in concurrency control

In the previous sections, several approaches to concurrency control in database systems have been described which are based on a simple and purely syntactic model of transactions. As it turned out (and is supported further by the huge amount of existing literature on this topic), this model provides a solution to the concurrency control problem which can be used in many practical applications. However, since the 'ultimate goal' is to achieve as much parallelism as possible, it may be suspected that even more could be done if information on the semantics of transactions to be scheduled was available. This section will indicate that this is indeed the case, and several approaches in this direction will be outlined.

As an example, consider the following set of three transactions and a schedule s for them:

$$
\begin{aligned}
t_1 &= w(x)w(y)w(z)\\
t_2 &= r(x)w(y)\\
t_3 &= r(z)w(y)w(z)
\end{aligned}
$$

$$s = w_1(x)r_2(x)w_1(y)w_2(y)r_3(z)w_1(z)w_3(y)w_3(z)$$

Since the corresponding conflict graph is cyclic, it cannot be concluded immediately that s is not view-serializable. Now consider step $w_1(z)$, which is in conflict with $r_3(z)$ (causing the edge (t_3, t_1) in the graph) and $w_3(z)$ (causing the edge (t_1, t_3), thereby closing a cycle). If it was known that $w_1(z)$ actually does *not* write a *new* value of z, in other words, that transaction t_1 only *copies* the old value of z, this step could in fact be omitted from s. As a result, t_3 is no longer involved in a conflict regarding z, and the (modified) schedule becomes conflict- and hence view-serializable.

As this example indicates, *semantic* information on (the *interpretation* of) a transaction could be used by a scheduler to determine whether conflicts are 'real'. As a second example, consider two (numerical) database objects x and y representing *counters* which can be either incremented or decremented, and let transactions t_1 and t_2 both increment both counters in different order. That is, the two transactions can 'semantically' be written as

$$t_1 = \text{incr}(x)\ \text{incr}(y)$$
$$t_2 = \text{incr}(y)\ \text{incr}(x)$$

Syntactically, however, let an action 'incr(z)' be executed as '$r(z)w(z)$', and consider the following schedule:

$$s = r_1(x)r_2(y)w_1(x)w_2(y)r_1(y)w_1(y)r_2(x)w_2(x)$$

Since the corresponding conflict graph is again cyclic, one might be motivated to look for further evidence that s is not view-serializable. However, reconsider s from from a semantic point of view, from which it represents the sequence

$$\text{incr}_1(x)\ \text{incr}_2(y)\ \text{incr}_1(y)\ \text{incr}_2(x)$$

of actions. Despite the fact that $G(s)$ is cyclic, s seems acceptable, since the increment operations *commute*, or, in other words, they are *compatible.*

In general, it is said that two (consecutive) operations (from distinct transactions) which 'operate' on the same database object *commute* if the order in which they are executed is immaterial, that is, for any given initial state (value) of the object the 'final' states (values) produced by ordering the operations either way are equal. Notice that, in the light of Definition 18.6, two operations in the read-write model of transactions do not commute if they access the same object and at least one of them is a write. This is so because, owing to the 'pseudo-semantics' introduced in Section 18.3, for example the x value read by $r_j(x)$ in a sequence '$\ldots w_i(x)r_j(x)\ldots$' will in general *differ* from the x value read by this operation in '$\ldots r_j(x)w_i(x)\ldots$'. Also, the terms 'commutativity' and 'compatibility' are used interchangeably here, although strictly speaking the former refers to operations, while the latter refers to their associated locks (if locking is used for synchronization).

The observation made above can be generalized in at least two different ways which are outlined below to conclude this chapter.

First, the transaction *model* employed can be extended by introducing new operations which are to be executed atomically (like read and write). For the case just described, a possible extension of the read-write model of transactions would be to allow 'increment' and 'decrement' operations on *numerical* objects (in addition to ordinary reads and writes on arbitrary objects). Thus, a *transaction* is allowed to consist of $r(.)$, $w(.)$, incr(.) and decr(.) actions. Next, the notion of *conflict* is extended correspondingly, as described in the following table (whose entries are to be interpreted as before):

	r	w	incr	decr
r	1	0	0	0
w	0	0	0	0
incr	0	0	1	1
decr	0	0	1	1

It is now straightforward to extend, for example, a 2PL scheduler to take into account these new operations. Associate a corresponding lock operation with each of them, and schedule so that no conflicting locks are held simultaneously (where locks conflict iff the corresponding operations conflict).

This approach is widely used, for example, in the presence of **hot spots**, that is, data objects that are frequently accessed by many transactions in a uniform way. The most prominent example is aggregate data (like the total assets of a bank) being accessed (updated) by 'debit/credit' transactions (for withdrawal or deposit) at a high rate (that is, 50 or more transactions per second). Notice that ordinary 2PL would not be useful in this context, due to the permanent use of write locks. Obviously, this extension is easily made applicable to other situations as well (see the Bibliographic Notes); the common approach is to define new operations, whose *semantic* commutativity (compatibility) when considered as mappings from consistent states to consistent states is recorded in a corresponding table, which is then made available to the scheduler.

Of particular interest in this context is the use of *abstract data types* (ADTs), in which the type declaration of an object comes together (is *encapsulated*) with a set of operations exclusively applicable to objects of this type (see Part VII). ADTs have been used to enrich the transaction concept with additional operations (and to make it usable even beyond the context of database management), and to take information on the *state* of the underlying database into account. The properties of ADTs make them particularly interesting for the area of *object-oriented database systems* which will be discussed in Chapter 22.

Another way of generalizing the observation made above, also suggested by the second example, is to consider operations like 'increment' as *higher-level* operations which are 'implemented' by more elementary ones. In this approach, which can be pursued for more than two levels in general, at any level an individual operation is considered as *atomic*, that is, its execution should be uninterruptible. Thus, a sequence of operations at a lower level, which implements one higher-level operation, constitutes a *subtransaction*, and a sequence of operations (a transaction) at some level i yields a sequence of subtransactions at level $i+1$, each element of which may yield another subtransaction at level $i+2$, and so on. This leads to the subject of **nested transactions** and of **multi-level concurrency control**, in which the notions 'schedule' and 'serializability' as well as the scheduling process need to be re-examined carefully. The use of semantic information on transactions can now be employed at any level; in addition, such information could be *inherited* by a lower level from a higher one. An approach like the one sketched above can then be followed at each level *in isolation*, that is, without regarding the fact that a transaction might be implement differently 'below'. Multi-level concurrency control and nested transactions have also gained great interest recently, in particular in connection with *non-standard* applications of database management (see also Part VII). Some references to relevant literature will be given in the Bibliographic Notes.

Chapter 19
Recovery, Integrity and Security

This chapter introduces **recovery** in database systems, which is necessary in order to provide fault-tolerance. In addition, the issues of **integrity** and **security** are briefly discussed.

19.1 Recovery from failures

19.1.1 Introduction

In Chapter 18, the case of *failure* of a transaction resulting in an 'abort' has been mentioned several times without indicating how it can be handled or how the DBMS, or more precisely its transaction and recovery manager, have to react in this situation. This issue is discussed in a more general setting in this section; in particular, three important 'classes' of failures are introduced next, which cover basically all situations a DBMS allowing for fault tolerance has to cope with, and which go beyond the simple abort of a transaction. These classes are:

(1) **Transaction failure**: This type of failure, which was meant above by 'abort', occurs when a transaction does not terminate normally (reach the state 'committed'), because inconsistencies in the database were detected while it was running, the 'surrounding program' has tried to divide by zero, or the transaction became involved in a deadlock and was chosen as the victim.

(2) **System failure**: This type of failure refers to anything that destroys main memory, termed **volatile storage** in this context. The major sources for this type of failure are bugs in the DBMS code or in the operating system, hardware failures in the CPU, or power failures which corrupt semiconductor memory.

(3) **Media failures**: This type of failure occurs when parts of secondary memory, called **stable storage** in this context, are lost, for example, because of a headcrash on a disk or a bug in an operating-system routine that writes to a disk.

In the discussion that follows, emphasis will be put on failures of the second type, system failures, for several reasons. First, these failures must be expected frequently, so that provisions for tolerating them must always be taken. Secondly, transaction failures, as will be seen shortly, are somewhat simpler in nature so that they can be dealt with at the same time. Finally, the techniques sketched here for coping with system failures can, with appropriate but straightforward modifications, be applied to cope with media failures as well.

The basic scenario after a system failure, which is illustrated in Figure 19.1, is that the contents of (primary) memory can be considered lost, and that the transactions which already wrote into this memory can be put in two classes: those which committed before the crash (of type t_1, t_2 or t_3 in Figure 19.1) and those that were still active at the time the failure occurred (of type t_4 or t_5 in Figure 19.1). For the former type, the

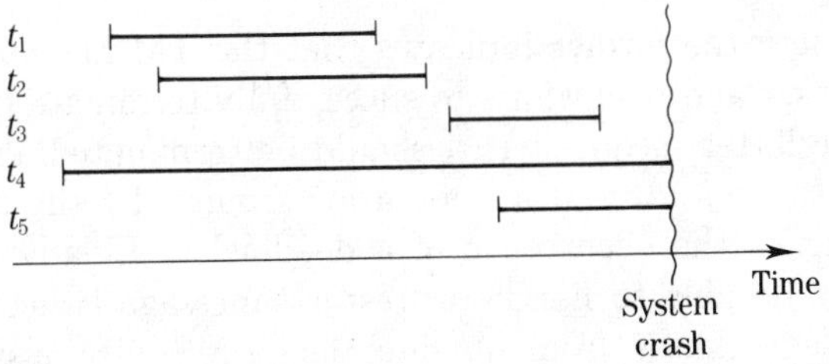

Figure 19.1 Basic scenario for a system failure.

appropriate action is to **redo** them if the updates they produced had not yet been written to the database, so that subsequent transactions will find the database in the state it 'was' in after only these transactions had run; notice that this reaction to a crash of redoing committed transactions is 'implied' by the requirement that a transaction is *persistent* (see Chapter 18). For the latter type, however, the appropriate reaction is to **undo** ('rollback') them (and repeat them at a later time), in particular if some or all of the updates they produced have been written into the database already, since, because of the *atomicity* requirement, there is no way to complete this transaction from the crash point on.

As should not be surprising to anyone familiar with computer systems, the basic paradigm for handling failures in database systems, or to allow for *fault tolerance*, is to introduce some kind of **redundancy**. In particular, it seems reasonable (for coping with system and also with media failures) to generate ('dump') *backup copies* (on disk or even on tape) of the entire database or of parts of it at least from time to time so that a consistent state can be restored after an error has been detected. (It is assumed here that the errors considered are successfully detected, by mechanisms such as error-detecting codes provided by the operating system.) Since some kind of memory is affected by a failure, it seems appropriate now to take a closer look at the internal organization of the *data manager* or, more generally, the *database storage subsystem* which, according to the discussion in Chapters 3 and 18, is responsible for handling memory.

19.1.2 The recovery manager

In order to be able to correctly handle transaction aborts as well as redos and undos after a system failure, every DBMS which allows for a multi-user mode of operation comprises a **recovery manager** (RM), which can be considered as a 'device' that takes three kinds of input. First, it receives the various reads and writes from transactions as output by the scheduler. Secondly, it receives 'signals' of the form 'commit(t_i)' and 'abort(t_i)', where the former indicates that the TM has encountered an 'EOT(t_i)' marker and now wants to successfully terminate transaction t_i, and where the latter means that t_i should be terminated abnormally (as the result of the *rejection* of an operation from t_i by the scheduler, for instance owing to the occurrence of a deadlock). Finally, the recovery manager must be able to handle a 'restart' message issued, say, by the operating system (that is, from 'outside' the DBMS) after a system failure; it may also receive an *acknowledgement* from 'below' for an operation just completed, which may include a *return value* if the operation was a read.

The RM communicates with the 'data manager' of the DBMS, which is the actual 'device' for managing storage. To facilitate the following discussion, it seems reasonable to extend (and slightly rearrange) the 'model' of DBMS internals presented earlier so that the various kinds of storage are incorporated. To this end, consider Figure 19.2 which shows another 'magnification' of an excerpt from Figure 3.1. The communication between the database and the various DBMS components that act on it takes place via a **database buffer** which is a distinct part of main memory reserved for DBMS operations. The buffer is assumed to be organized into *pages* (more precisely, into page *frames*) of fixed length, each of which can be read from or written into secondary memory in one (atomic) step; for simplicity it is further assumed that a page (both in the buffer and in secondary memory) is large enough to hold one database object, and that every object is small enough to fit into a page. The buffer itself is under the control of a **buffer manager** whose primary responsibilities include *address translation* (mapping logical to physical addresses) and execution of the *paging algorithm* employed; the latter in particular comprises a *page-replacement strategy*, which is applied whenever a new page needs to be written into a full buffer. Notice that a point is reached here where the DBMS may rely heavily on what the operating system at hand generally provides.

As an aside it should be mentioned that database buffers originally (that is, 15 to 20 years ago) were quite 'small' fractions of main memory, because of the limited overall capacity of this type of memory. In present-day (mainframe) computers, however, this is rarely true; a buffer may actually be realized as a separate *cache*, or the size of main memory may even be large enough to hold the *entire* database ('main-memory databases'). These issues will be neglected here.

Basically, the RM outputs the reads and writes it receives directly to the buffer when it is guaranteed that the object in question is already available there. Otherwise, it may first have to ask the buffer manager to make it available, that is, fetch it from secondary memory ('db-read'); finally, it may issue a 'db-write' in order to tell the buffer manager to 'save' a new result in the database. If the RM reads from the buffer, it receives a return-value back; if it has issued a 'db-read' or a 'db-write', it

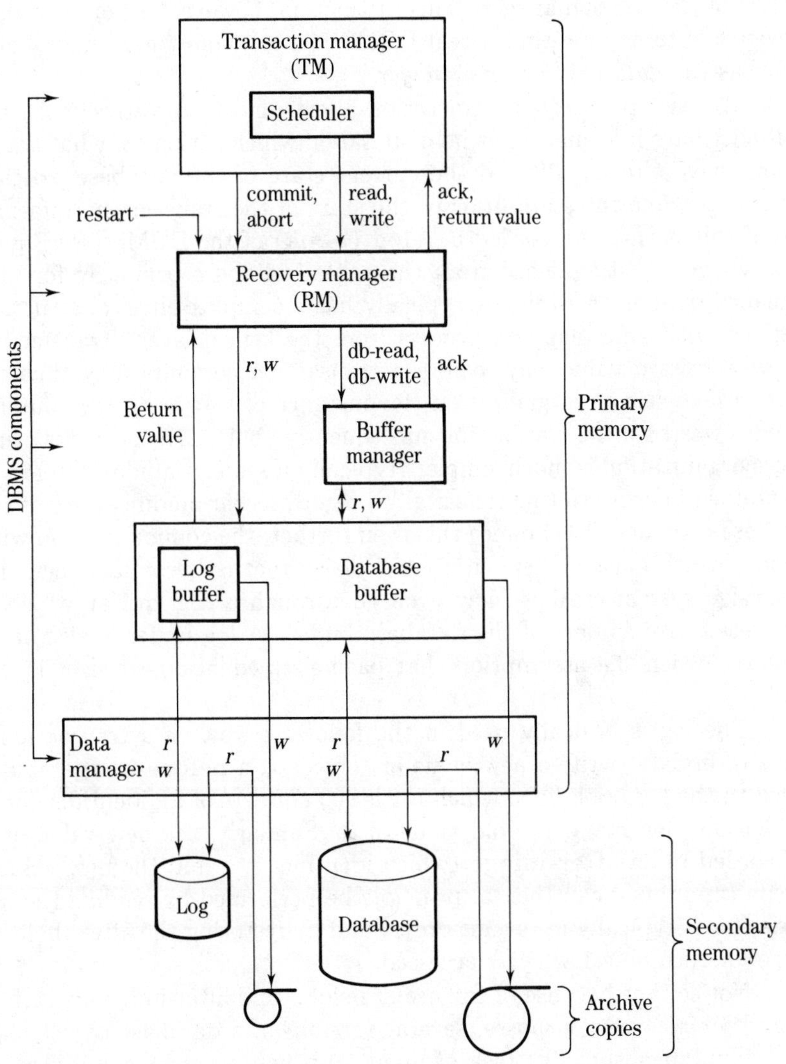

Figure 19.2 Organization of the primary/secondary memory interface around a recovery manager.

receives an acknowledgement when the operation is completed.

According to the terminology used so far, it is still assumed here that the actual transfer of pages back and forth between the buffer and secondary memory is done by the *data manager*, which operates under the control of the buffer manager. This distinction, however, is not crucial; it is even safe to assume that a real DBMS has *one* component here which serves as the *data and buffer manager*.

To react properly to transaction aborts and to restart signals, the RM must have information at its disposal on which actions of what transactions have already affected the current state of the database, so that it can determine the state prior to the start of the transaction. Information of this nature is recorded in a **log (book)** of the DBMS (see Figure 3.1), which is distinguished from the actual database primarily for performance reasons. A database typically has a complex physical structure that requires some mapping process from the logical level. Transferring a newly written value, say, before a transaction commits may then require an expensive reorganization (for instance of a B-tree), the time for which is wasted if the transaction subsequently aborts. Hence, a structure whose organization is much simpler (typically a sequential file), the log, is maintained in order to ('incrementally') record recent modifications of the database contents. To enhance this even further, the communication with the log, which must be kept in a 'safe' place, that is, secondary memory, to survive system crashes, may even go through a **log buffer** which is considered here as part of the database buffer. A log buffer is also often employed when the assumption that page sizes equal object sizes is not valid.

The log is basically used in the following way. If a transaction t wants to update (write a new value of) object x, a **before-image** of x is added to the log book first, which (at least) consists of an identifier for t, an identifier for x and the old value of x. Similarly, the new value of x is recorded in an **after-image** (which identifies t, x and the new value). A redo (undo) of t can then in principle be performed by reading the log entries for t (typically in reverse order) and by restoring the after (before) image for each object which t accessed.

Notice that because of the use of before- and after-images, which is natural for recovery purposes, several *versions* of a database object may exist simultaneously. The task of managing these versions could also be added to the responsibility of the scheduler, which leads to the subject of *multiversion concurrency control* not discussed here (see the Bibliographic Notes for references on this topic).

Notice also that transfers between the log buffer and the log proper have to be realized differently from transfers between database buffer and database; in particular, these transfers have to be 'safer' so that the log can meet its purpose. (Notice that the contents of a buffer will always be lost after a system crash, since it is part of main memory. Therefore, the log buffer must always be copied (completely or in part) into the log in an atomic (non-interruptible) action if its contents have changed.)

Finally, in a real DBMS environment there may also exist **archive copies** of log and database (on tape), in a similar way to that in which system *safety* (as opposed to *security*, see below) is accomplished in general; these copies can be activated after a media failure. The various read and write operations a data manager then has to perform with respect to secondary storage are also shown in Figure 19.2.

From the discussion above, two *classification criteria* for recovery algorithms can immediately be derived. First, different methods can be employed for structuring and maintaining the information pertaining to the log (like whether before- or after-images are kept or both, or when these are written). Secondly, various strategies can be thought of for determining *when* to 'propagate' newly written pages from the buffer into the database. To this end, notice that, with the organization shown in Figure 19.2, a *read* operation issued by some transaction can be 'implemented' by first transferring the object in question from secondary memory into the buffer (if it is not there already), which eventually also involves the allocation of a new buffer frame if the buffer is full. A *write* operation writes a new value of an object into the appropriate buffer page; this page could then be propagated right away or at some later time, and its determination may be completely at the buffer manager's discretion (in any case, write operations force new entries to be written into the log). Clearly, if the recovery manager executes the writes of a transaction by just writing into the buffer and keeps the updates in the buffer beyond the commit of this transaction, redo will be required if a crash occurs before the necessary propagation could be executed. Conversely, if updates made by a transaction are propagated to the database before the transaction commits, undo will be required if the transaction aborts.

Thus, four classes of recovery algorithms can basically be distinguished, based on whether:

(1) redo *and* undo are required (during the execution of the restart procedure after a system failure),

(2) *no* redo, but undo is required,

(3) redo, but *no* undo is required,

(4) *neither* redo *nor* undo is required.

Before examples for the first three approaches to recovery can be sketched, it should be understood that *every* recovery algorithm has to observe (at least) the following two *rules*:

(1) **Commit rule**: In order to ensure that any committed transaction survives a subsequent crash (that is, it can be redone if necessary), the after-images produced by a transaction must be written to secondary memory (database or log) *before* that transaction commits.

(2) **Write-ahead-log protocol**: In order to guarantee that an active transaction can be properly undone after a crash (if necessary), the before-image of an object must be written into the log *before* the after-image of this object is transferred into the database, in case the latter takes place before the transaction commits.

It follows that a recovery algorithm which does not require redo must make sure that *all* after-images produced by a transaction must be written into the *database* before (or when) the transaction commits, so that the commit rule is trivially satisfied. Similarly, a recovery algorithm which does not require undo must make sure that *no* after-image produced by a transaction is written into the database (but only into the log) before the transaction commits.

Two conclusions can be derived from these observations regarding (1) the basic logic behind each of the four approaches to recovery and (2) what to write into a log. These issues will be discussed next, together with some fundamental ideas for the implementation of the former.

As was mentioned earlier, an RM must support (at least) the five operations read, write, commit, abort (each on behalf of a transaction) and restart, and it may ask the buffer manager to 'propagate' a buffer page to secondary memory. As will be seen shortly, various degrees of freedom for the latter are possible for the buffer manager.

19.1.3 A recovery strategy requiring undo and redo

In the most liberal approach, the RM does not control the writing of buffer pages to the database at all. Hence, the only reason for the buffer manager to execute such a propagation is when the buffer is full and a new page needs to be read in. Thus, a *write* operation is executed by reading the object in question into the buffer if it is not there already, writing a corresponding entry into the log, and finally overwriting the old value of the object in the buffer.

If this page p is afterwards replaced (and hence written into the database since it contains a new value) and the transaction t which wrote p aborts, an undo of t becomes necessary. On the other hand, if t commits and a crash destroys p before it has been replaced, it will be necessary to redo t.

A strategy of this kind is used in IBM's relational prototype DBMS System/R, the forerunner of SQL/DS. Some details of its realization will be discussed next, which also introduce several implementation aspects. Consider the following scenario. Suppose a database d consists of four integer objects x, y, z and u with current values 10, 20, 30, 40, respectively. Four transactions currently operate on d as follows (where '$w_i(x, n)$' means that transaction t_i updates x to n):

$$w_1(x, 20)w_2(y, 30)w_2(z, 40)w_1(u, 50)w_3(z, 45)w_4(y, 25)$$

Next assume that a crash occurs after this sequence of steps has been executed, and that at the time of the crash t_2 and t_3 are already committed, while t_1 and t_4 are still active. To see how System/R's RM handles this situation, two important new concepts need to be introduced, *shadowing* and *checkpoints*, which can also be found in other implementations.

So far it has been assumed that the database in secondary memory contains exactly one copy (version) of each object (but several versions — before- and after-images — may exist elsewhere). As a result, this copy is 'lost' when a new value for the object is written into the database. This scheme is known as **in-place updating**. Another approach, employed in System/R, is to keep *two* versions of each object around, where 'old' ones are referred to as **shadow copies** (clearly, this approach can be generalized to more than two versions, which will not be discussed here). To manage 'shadow' and 'current' copies of objects, two directories D_S and D_C are used, respectively, where D_C describes the current database state in primary and secondary memory, and where D_S describes a shadow copy of the database in secondary memory.

Shadow copies are produced whenever a **checkpoint** is set. In general, to reduce the amount of work to be done by a restart procedure (which can be very time consuming, and which prevents the DBMS from continuing to process transactions), some of this work may be done earlier, during normal processing; any activity of this kind is called a *checkpoint.* Thus, generating a checkpoint means collecting information in a safe place (to limit the amount of recovery). Checkpoint generation involves the three steps of:

(1) writing a 'begin checkpoint' record to the log,

(2) writing all 'checkpoint pages' to the log and/or to the database,

(3) writing an 'end checkpoint' record to the log.

Notice that the begin/end markers are needed to indicate whether the generation of some checkpoint could be completed or has been interrupted by a crash. Also, the address of the checkpoint entry in the log should be entered into a 'restart file'. Any such checkpoint entry also contains a list of transactions active at the time the checkpoint is set. After a system crash, the recovery manager can read the 'most recent' record from the restart file, locate the corresponding checkpoint entry within the log, and search the log from that point on for redo or undo candidates.

Returning to the System/R approach to recovery, the example above can now be continued as follows. Initially, D_C contains a pointer to each object in the database in secondary memory (since no part of it is in the buffer and in updated form yet), and D_S is empty. The sequence of steps shown above, into which a checkpoint as well as two commits are now injected, is then processed as follows:

(1) $w_1(x, 20)$ produces $x' = 20$ in the buffer and a corresponding update of D_C.

(2) $w_2(y, 30)$ writes $y' = 30$ into the buffer; D_C is updated again.

(3) A checkpoint is set; as a result, (a) $x' = 20$ and $y' = 30$ are written into the database, and their new locations are recorded in D_C; (b) D_C is copied to D_S and (c) undo information of the form 'undo(t_1 : $x = 10$), undo(t_2 : $y = 20$)' is written into the log.

(4) $w_2(z, 40)$ produces $z' = 40$ in the buffer (with an update of D_C); assume the buffer is now full.

(5) $w_1(u, 50)$ forces some page to be replaced; since y' has been propagated already, let its page be overwritten with $u' = 50$; D_C is updated accordingly.

(6) $w_3(z, 45)$ overwrites $z' = 40$ in the buffer to produce z'', which is recorded in D_C.

(7) $w_4(y, 25)$ needs a page frame for y; let z'' be replaced. Then z'', whose value is not yet in the database, becomes a shadow copy of z in the database, and D_C is updated to point to its new location in secondary memory. $y'' = 25$ is written into the buffer; D_C is updated again. (Notice that D_C and D_S from now on refer to different 'versions' of d.)

(8) Let t_2 and t_3 commit (prior to the crash); since their updates are not necessarily in the database yet, log information of the form

$$\text{redo}(t_2 : y' = 30, z' = 40), \text{redo}(t_3 : z'' = 45)$$

will be written.

The situation immediately prior to the crash is illustrated in Figure 19.3. When the crash occurs, the contents of buffer, D_C and D_S are lost. Using the log information, however, it is straightforward to (1) restore a

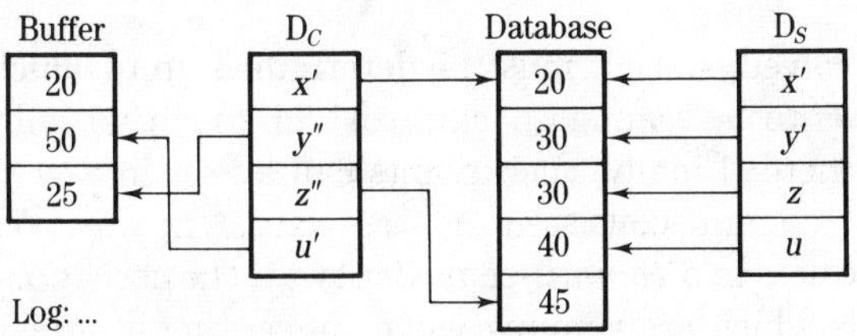

Log: undo($t_1 : x = 10$), undo($t_2 : y = 20$), redo($t_2 : y' = 30, z' = 40$), redo($t_3 : z'' = 45$)

Figure 19.3 State of buffer and database before a crash (System/R example).

'consistent' database state which reflects the changes made by t_2 and t_3 to the initial state, and (2) reinitialize D_S (and then D_C).

The following distinction can be made according to what type of information gets written into a log. A *physical* log contains physical values of database objects (in the form of pages holding before- or after-images); thus, its information says exactly *what* was done to a database state. Opposed to this, a *logical* log (as used in System/R) contains information on *how* certain modifications were achieved. For example, if a new value is inserted into a database which is organized as a B-tree and, as a result, a reorganization is of this tree is performed, a physical log would contain *every* node/page of the tree that was modified, whereas a logical log could only contain a description of the operation ('insert into tree') performed. Thus, a logical log might be easier to store, at the expense of more work to be done during restart. A physical log, on the other hand, generally requires more space, and may hence need a *garbage collection* applied to it from time to time, in order to remove entries which are no longer needed and to make the space they occupied available for reuse. In general, the organization of a log is a non-trivial problem, because of the variety of information that must be distinguished; for example, the log must also contain information on which transactions are or have been active at a particular point in time. Hence, for each currently 'existing' transaction t a log-book entry must be written at 'time' BOT(t) as well as at time EOT(t). (After a crash it is then possible to determine candidates for a redo by searching the log book for BOT-EOT pairs of the same transaction; if EOT is missing for some BOT marker, the corresponding transaction will undergo an undo.)

A restart procedure, in particular in the 'presence' of undo and redo information, can be thought of as a two-step process, which searches the log backwards, beginning from the end, for undo entries and after that proceeds in forward direction for the redo entries.

In the presence of checkpoints, the execution of restart might actually be more involved, since it must be determined up to which checkpoint entry the log has to be scanned backwards, an issue that will not be considered further here. Finally, checkpoints can be set in a variety of ways, for example in a commit-consistent or step-consistent way. When a checkpoint procedure acts in a *commit-consistent* way, the checkpoint is set after the transactions which are running when the setting of a new checkpoint is initiated have committed; in the meantime, no new transactions will be processed, which may introduce considerable delays. When checkpoints are set in a *step-consistent* fashion, the 'checkpoint generator' waits only for the steps currently being executed (reads, writes, etc.) to complete, which in general results in a better performance than the former approach with respect to transaction delays.

19.1.4 Recovery strategies requiring either undo or redo

A recovery manager can do without redo if it makes sure that all updates made by a transaction appear in the database before, or when, that transaction commits, which actually means that the execution of a 'commit(t_i)' operation by the RM includes a propagation of t_i's updates into the database.

A strategy of this type can be found in UDS as well as in IMS. In both systems, updates are made in place (no shadowing), and checkpoints are set in a commit-consistent way. As an illustration, consider the database $d = \{x, y, z, u\}$ used in the previous subsection, and the following sequence of steps:

$$w_1(x, 20)w_2(y, 30)w_2(z, 40)w_1(u, 50)$$

Furthermore, assume that a checkpoint is set after the first two steps have been executed, that a crash occurs after this sequence has been processed, and that t_2 has committed after its second step. If the buffer has three frames, it will contain $x' = 20$ and $y' = 30$ when the checkpoint is set, so that the new values of x and y are written into the database. Next, $z' = 40$ is written into the buffer, and finally the frame of x is overwritten by $w_1(u, 50)$ to produce $u' = 50$, which forces an undo entry of the form

$$\text{undo}(t_1 : x = 10)$$

to be written into the log; when t_2 commits, z' appears in the database, so that the latter contains x', y', z' and u at the time of the crash. Processing the log during restart then results in $d = \{x, y', z', u\}$, which is the correct state reflecting t_2's changes only.

In order to avoid an undo after a crash, it is clear that no updates from transactions which are still in progress may be written into the database, which can be accomplished by not writing them into the buffer (since a subsequent page replacement would propagate them), but only into the log. When a transaction commits, the corresponding log entries are 'applied' to the buffer.

As an example, the strategy employed in IBM's *Fast Path* version of IMS, which was designed for high transaction rates, is considered. Assume that the four transactions considered in the previous subsection are given, but that updates are again made in place, and no checkpoint has been set yet. When the crash occurs at the same time as before, the database will still be $d = \{x, y, z, u\}$, with its original values, if no replacement has been performed yet (which may be the case for a large buffer required for high transaction rates). Since the buffer is updated only when a transaction commits, the updates performed by t_2 and t_3, which caused the log entries redo($t_2 : y' = 30, z' = 40$) and redo($t_3 : z'' = 45$) to be written, are also in the buffer. Processing these entries during a restart then ensures that a consistent database state is restored, without performing any undos.

Finally, it follows from the exposition above that a recovery manager can do without redo and undo completely if all updates made by a transaction are written into the database exactly at commit-time in a single atomic operation; however, in general this is difficult to implement.

19.2 Integrity control

In this section an issue is briefly discussed which has been mentioned several times already, and which is of central importance to various aspects of database processing, namely the control of the integrity of a stored database. Recall the *integrity constraints* introduced in Chapter 7 for the relational model of data as a way to capture certain semantic information about a given application. It turned out that such constraints can serve at least two different purposes. The obvious one is of course that they form a 'control instance' for updates; every update made to a given consistent database state (satisfying the integrity constraints) should result in a state which is again consistent. As a result, transactions were introduced in Chapter 18 as *consistency-preserving* units. Another purpose is database design as discussed, for example, in Chapter 12, where integrity constraints can help to 'structure' the schema of a database appropriately (for example, so that normal forms are observed).

Clearly, the question arises of *how* a DBMS actually performs integrity control, and *which* constraints are actually supported. To this end, a brief look at *Ingres* is taken next, which supports the following two kinds of constraints:

(1) data type constraints (along the lines of SQL/DS as just mentioned),

(2) single-variable constraints which are *predicates* involving exactly one variable any database state has to satisfy.

As an example, the constraint '*Salary* > 0' imposed on an employee relation or the 'NOT NULL' option available in the CREATE TABLE command fall into the latter category. Integrity constraints of the second kind can be declared explicitly using the following statement:

DEFINE INTEGRITY ON base-table IS predicate

The 'base-table' has to be the only 'range-variable' (in INGRES terminology) which is referenced in the predicate part. Notice that integrity constraints in INGRES need not be declared at database design time; if a constraint is added at run-time, the system will reject it if the predicate is not satisfied by the current state, and will enforce it from that point on otherwise.

'Enforcing' a constraint is done by the important technique of **query modification** described next. Suppose a relation *PROPA* has three attributes, *Project*, *Part* and *No*, specifying how many parts are needed for certain projects. A reasonable integrity constraint would be the following:

```
DEFINE INTEGRITY ON PROPA IS PROPA.NO > 0
```

Next assume a user issues the update command

```
REPLACE PROPA ( NO = PROPA.NO – 10 )
      WHERE PROJECT = 'SHUTTLE'
```

which reduces the number of parts used in a shuttle by 10. This command would then be modified automatically by the system to

```
REPLACE PROPA ( NO = PROPA.NO – 10 )
      WHERE PROJECT = 'SHUTTLE' AND PROPA.NO – 10 > 0
```

thus making sure that the resulting number of parts is still positive.

A second important method for enforcing integrity constraints is the use of **event-trigger** mechanisms, in which some *event* such as the recognition or execution of an update command or the arrival at some particular database state *triggers* some *action* to be invoked and subsequently executed. In the example above, the actual checking of whether the number of parts for a project is still greater than zero could be realized as a triggered action, which is activated as a final step in the processing of the 'update transaction' that replaces an old value with a new one and which results in a commit (abort) of this transaction if the predicate is satisfied (violated).

19.3 Database security

A final important issue that will be briefly discussed is the *security* of data stored in a database and managed by a DBMS. A primary reason for security is the necessity for privacy arising in an enterprise, which must in particular restrict access to data that is confidential. It is straightforward that any database that can be accessed by many users simultaneously needs some *authorization mechanism* by which this access can be controlled. However, this alone is usually not sufficient for guaranteeing a secure operation, and a *physical protection* on stored data is needed as well.

Notice that several 'mechanisms' for supporting (logical) security have been discussed already. In Section 8.5, the concept of *views* was investigated, which can be employed to *hide* data from unauthorized users. For example, a user who is not allowed to query the salary column of an employee relation could be provided with a (projection) view over this relation in which the salary column is missing. In Chapter 16 (and also 14) various language constructs were described for granting permission to access certain data to individual users. In the case of SQL/DS, the basic commands to that end are GRANT and REVOKE, the former of which creates corresponding dictionary entries which are read before a command issued by a user is executed, in order to make sure that this user is allowed to issue the command.

These two mechanisms represent important approaches for supporting security; additional measures will be discussed next.

(1) **Authentication at log-on time**: As was the case for some issues in the context of recovery discussed above, this issue relies on features provided by the underlying operating system, in particular the support of *passwords.* Just as an operating system may use passwords to protect files, a DBMS can borrow this mechanism from the operating system to protect its database(s). Passwords can be used to distinguish various types of access (full, read-only, etc.) and need to be kept in an *encrypted* file. Other approaches to authentication which rely, for example, on hardware keys or on a person's fingerprints are not common in the database field at present.

(2) **Authorization**: As should have become clear from Chapter 16, authorization serves to protect database objects. Crucial issues to be considered are:
(a) the *schema level* (internal, conceptual, external) to be protected,
(b) the *granularity* of protection,
(c) the *method* of protection, like protection through views or through query modification (as introduced in the last section for integrity

control), where 'view-defining' constructs are 'injected' into a user-supplied query or update command.

Physical protection is typically based on some *encryption* method which replaces *plain* data by *cipher* data; in order to read encrypted data, a *decryption* method has to be applied for restoring the original. A primary goal here is to make both encryption and decryption efficient and at the same to ensure that the cipher used is difficult to break. Further information on this topic can be found in the references.

Completely different and much more complicated security issues arise in *statistical* databases, which can contain sensitive information about individuals or companies, and where the objective is to provide access to statistics about *groups* without rendering the identification or recognition of *individuals* possible. A discussion of inference and access control methods and of ways to cope with attacks goes beyond the scope of this text; the reader is therefore referred to the references cited in the Bibliographic Notes.

Bibliographic Notes

A detailed and application-oriented exposition of the theory of algorithms for concurrency control and recovery in centralized (as well as in distributed) databases can be found in Bernstein et al. (1987). An excellent presentation of both fields which emphasizes their theoretical aspects is given by Papadimitriou (1986). The latter reference introduces a third notion of correctness, also well known in the literature, namely **final-state serializability**, in which attention is restricted to 'live' transactions occurring in a schedule (and how they affect the 'next' state). The notion of conflict-serializability goes back to Eswaran et al. (1976) who also introduced the 2PL protocol (for transaction synchronization in System/R). Papadimitriou (1979) shows that testing membership in the class VSR is NP-complete. This result is obtained by showing (1) that the problem of testing a given schedule for view-serializability can be reduced (without an increase in complexity) to the problem of testing a 'polygraph' for 'acyclicity' and (2) that the latter is NP-complete. See also Sethi (1982) or Korth and Silberschatz (1986) in this context. Generalized notions of serializability are proposed and investigated, for example, by Vidyasankar (1987).

An in-depth discussion of two-phase locking, of its variants and of other, non-locking schedulers (like timestamping or SGT) can also be found in the books by Bernstein et al. (1987) and Papadimitriou (1986). The tree protocol was originally proposed by Silberschatz and Kedem (1980); an improved 'dynamic' variant is presented in Croker and Maier (1986). Protocols using timestamps are described, for instance, by Bernstein and Goodman (1980b) and Reed (1983); for optimistic methods the reader is referred, for example, to Härder (1982), Kung and Robinson (1981) or Schlageter (1981). Granularity of lock objects was first investigated by Gray et al. (1975).

Additional surveys of the area of concurrency control can be found, for instance, in Date (1983), Gray (1978, 1980), Schlageter (1978), Casanova (1981) and Casanova and Bernstein (1980). For the most popular approach, locking, see also Devor and Carlson (1982) or Korth (1983).

For investigating important questions like the safety of a system of locked transactions or its freedom from deadlocks and the power of locking in general (that is, the question of whether locking is capable of generating the entire class of conflict-serializable schedules, not only a subset of it), a geometrical interpretation for (locked) transactions is introduced by Papadimitriou (1982, 1983). Here, a *locked* transaction consists of ordinary read and write steps together with corresponding, non-redundant lock and unlock steps (along the lines of Definition 18.8 (i)), where the distinction between rlock and wlock is neglected for the moment.

For a given set T of transactions, let $\overline{T}$ denote a (not uniquely determined) set of locked transactions such that each $\overline{t_i} \in \overline{T}$ corresponds to $t_i \in T$. $\overline{T}$ is *safe* if every $\overline{T}$-legal schedule s for T is conflict-serializable, where s is $\overline{T}$-legal if it equals the reduction (lock and unlock steps removed) of a schedule $\overline{s}$ for $\overline{T}$ in which an unlock(x) occurs between any pair of lock(x) steps. The interest in algorithms that efficiently decide on the safety of some $\overline{T}$ can be motivated as follows. Suppose T is delivered to a scheduler, and the scheduler generates some $\overline{T}$ out of it. If $\overline{T}$ was safe, the scheduler could basically output *any* schedule that obeys the simple syntactic condition stated above, so that scheduling would become very efficient. The test for safety is based on concepts and results from *computational geometry.*

For the case of two transactions, the geometric interpretation is roughly as follows. For each transaction, its *sequence* of steps is represented as a sequence of equidistant integer points on one of the axes spanning the Euclidian plane. Thus, the two transactions define a rectangular *grid* in the plane. Grid points representing a pair of conflicting steps from the two transactions are *conflict points*, which fall into a *forbidden region* of the plane (when locking is used for synchronization) that is defined by the corresponding lock and unlock steps (points). Next, a *schedule* becomes a monotone *curve* through the grid starting at point (0,0). *Legal* schedules then are the ones that avoid forbidden regions, since any point within such a region represents a state in which the two transactions hold conflicting locks on the same object (which is not allowed). However, legal schedules may not be (conflict-) serializable. It can be shown that (1) a (legal) schedule is serializable iff its curve does not separate two forbidden regions, and that (2) a locking for the two transactions is *safe* iff the 'closure' of the forbidden regions is connected. This interpretation can also be extended to more than two transactions; see Papadimitriou (1982, 1983, 1986).

The issue of safety in locked transaction systems as well as the power of locking as a concurrency control paradigm is also investigated by Yannakakis (1982, 1984). Lausen et al. (1986) use the geometric approach for proposing *pre-analysis locking* as a safe and deadlock-free locking policy. Ehrig and Kreowski (1980) apply the theory of graph grammars to problems of synchronizing concurrent database operations. Performance investigations for concurrency control methods are reported, for example, by Carey and Stonebraker (1984), Pirahesh and Cardenas (1986), or Ryu and Thomasian (1985).

Another important branch of concurrency control is concerned with the issue of synchronizing access to multiple versions of database objects, which arise when updates are no longer made 'in place' (write operations no longer overwrite) but create a new version of an object, or which occur in the context of recovery as before- and after-images of objects. Information on this topic is provided by Bernstein and Goodman (1983), Hadzilacos and Papadimitriou (1986), Lausen (1983), and Papadimitriou and Kanellakis (1984).

The use of semantic information in transaction processing is also introduced in Papadimitriou (1986) and Bernstein et al. (1987). The example of increment and decrement operations is from Bernstein et al. (1983b). A survey of approaches to cope with 'hot spots' in databases is given by Härder (1988); Gawlick (1985) describes the particular method employed by IBM's Fast Path version of IMS. The general approach of 'encoding' semantic information in a compatibility table which is made available to a scheduler is pursued, for example, by Garcia-Molina (1983) or, in the context of abstract data types, by Schwarz and Spector (1984). Roesler and Burkhard (1987) investigate how such a table can be modified dynamically, depending on the knowledge on the states of objects acquired at execution time (where the objects considered are instances of abstract data types); for this approach, see also Roesler (1988) or Roesler and Burkhard (1988).

Several proposals have been made to improve concurrency control based on the particular data structures used for storing the underlying database, including Biliris (1987), Lausen (1984), Sagiv (1985) and Shasha and Goodman (1988). The theory of nested transactions was founded by Moss (1985); for surveys of the theory of multilevel concurrency control, the reader is referred to Beeri et al. (1983, 1988, 1989), Lynch and Merritt (1988) and Weikum (1987). Vianu and Vossen (1988) describe a different approach for using semantic information, which considers transactions as they arise at the *conceptual* level of a *relational* database; their model of transactions is the one proposed by Abiteboul and Vianu (1988a) (see also Section 8.4). Vianu and Vossen (1989) describe an alternative correctness criterion for schedules in this model, which turns out not to be comparable to serializability.

The basics of database and transaction recovery are also covered by Bernstein et al. (1987), Date (1983) and Korth and Silberschatz (1986). A formal treatement of 'reliability' of schedules is presented by Papadimitriou and Yannakakis (1987) and Hadzilacos (1988). The latter reference shows that (view- or conflict-) serializability alone is not sufficient as a correctness criterion for schedules, and remedies this situation by introducing formal properties of *commit-serializability* as well as of *recoverability* of schedules, which cannot be compared with each other, and argues that 'correct' schedules should have both properties. Classifications of recovery algorithms are given by Bernstein et al. (1983a) or Härder and Reuter (1983). Performance investigations for a number of recovery techniques are reported by Reuter (1984).

A detailed discussion of database security and integrity is given by Fernandez et al. (1981). The query modification approach to integrity control is due to Stonebraker (1975). Another method for maintaining semantic integrity is proposed by Bernstein et al. (1980). A recent approach to extending relational systems with new capabilities to support integrity constraints is described by Stonebraker et al. (1988). Fagin (1978) discusses authorization in databases. Hsiao et al. (1978) consider issues of privacy and security in general; physical security, in particular cryptographic methods, are discussed by Denning (1982).

Exercises

(1) Prove Theorem 18.2.

(2) Consider the following transactions t_1 and t_2 (in 'program form'):

BOT(t_1)	BOT(t_2)
$r_1(x)$	$r_2(x)$
$y := x$	$x := x + 30$
$x := x - 50$	$w_2(x)$
$w_1(x)$	EOT(t_2)
$w_1(y)$	
EOT(t_1)	

Next, consider the following schedules:

$$s_1 = r_2(x)r_1(x)w_1(x)w_1(y)w_2(x)$$
$$s_2 = r_1(x)r_2(x)w_1(x)w_1(y)w_2(x)$$
$$s_3 = r_1(x)w_1(x)r_2(x)w_1(y)w_2(x)$$
$$s_4 = r_1(x)w_1(x)w_1(y)r_2(x)w_2(x)$$
$$s_5 = r_2(x)r_1(x)w_2(x)w_1(x)w_1(y)$$
$$s_6 = r_1(x)w_1(x)r_2(x)w_2(x)w_1(y)$$

(a) Determine the serial schedules.

(b) Determine the view- as well as the conflict-serializable ones.

(3) Consider the following schedules:

$$s_1 = r_1(x)r_2(x)w_2(z)w_1(z)r_3(z)w_2(y)r_1(y)w_3(z)w_1(y)$$

$$s_2 = r_1(z)r_2(x)w_3(x)w_1(z)r_3(z)r_2(z)r_3(y)w_2(z)w_3(y)r_2(y)$$

(a) For $i = 1, 2$ draw $G(s_i)$ and decide whether or not s_i is conflict-serializable.

(b) For each conflict-serializable schedule found in (a) give an equivalent serial one.

(4) Prove that the classes CSR and VSR coincide in the absence of blind writes.

(5) Consider the following transactions:

t_1 :	t_2 :
$r_1(a)$	$r_2(b)$
$r_1(b)$	$r_2(a)$
if $a = 0$ then $b := b + 1$	if $b = 0$ then $a := a + 1$
$w_1(b)$	$w_2(a)$

For the 'database' $d = \{a, b\}$ let '$a = 0 \vee b = 0$' be the only integrity constraint; let a and b be initialized to 0.

(a) Describe a schedule (in which t_1 and t_2 are interleaved) which is conflict-serializable; describe a second one which is not.

(b) Extend t_1 and t_2 by rlock, wlock and unlock actions in such a way that both transactions conform to the two-phase protocol. Can the non-serializable schedule from (a) be avoided? Can a deadlock occur and, if so, how?

(c) Show that every serial schedule for t_1 and t_2 preserves the consistency of the database.

(6) Consider the following transactions:

$$t_0 = w_0(x)w_0(z)r_0(y)$$
$$t_1 = r_1(z)w_1(x)w_1(y)$$
$$t_2 = r_2(z)r_2(y)w_2(y)$$

(a) For $T = \{t_0, t_1, t_2\}$, find a conflict-serializable as well as a non-serializable schedule and prove your answers.

(b) For the serializable schedule from (a), give a (non-serial) schedule that could have been produced by a 2PL scheduler.

(7) Exhibit a schedule whose conflict graph is acyclic, but which cannot have been produced by a 2PL scheduler.

(8) Show that CSR is closed under projection, that is, if $s \in$ CSR is a schedule for a set T of transactions and $T' \subseteq T$, then the result of removing all steps of $T - T'$ from s also belongs to CSR.

(9) Prove Theorem 18.4.

(10) Describe a polynomial-time algorithm for deciding whether two schedules are view-equivalent.

(11) Generalize the TL protocol into a DAG locking protocol, for which the underlying database d is assumed to have a DAG structure.

(12) Show that the TL protocol is deadlock-free.

(13) Show that the MGL protocol is safe, but not deadlock-free.

Part VII

Towards Database Management for New Areas of Application

Chapter 20
Applications of Database Management

This chapter reviews domains in which database management systems have successfully been used over the years. It contrasts them with various new domains that have recently begun to demand support from 'database technology'.

20.1 Traditional applications

As was explained in Part I, database management systems evolved from file management systems and are today characterized, among other things, by the use of a *logical* data model for describing *physical* structures, by a 'high' degree of data independence and by the availability of 'powerful' languages. They generally support a transaction concept and hence data sharing as well as methods to achieve persistence, to perform recovery and to achieve integrity and security. On the other hand, *semantic* aspects of an application are often captured at a very basic level only (which was the reason, for example, for the consideration of 'semantic' data models in Chapter 11). In particular, powerful integrity constraints are seldom supported yet, and if they are this is often achieved by paying a price in terms of efficiency and/or performance. As was indicated in Chapter 8, the 'power' of current query languages can also be considered as 'limited', which is today overcome only by embedding the language at hand into a high-level programming language (at the price of a loss in terms of abstraction).

Database systems of the kind described so far, which are based on a 'syntactic' data model (see Chapter 11), are now successfully used in so-called 'commercial' administrative applications, among which are airline seat reservations, management of materials in economic enterprises, library administration, applications in insurance companies, banks (automated teller machines, account management), government agencies (motor vehicle registration, population counts, revenue service) and information services, production planning and supervision, employee administration, and paperless file management in offices. These 'traditional' areas of application have a lot of characteristics in common, which include the following:

(1) *Simply structured data objects* which in particular can be cast into a *fixed format* and hence be logically described by 'record-oriented' data models. For this reason, database systems based on one of the three network, hierarchical or relational models have become very popular.

(2) *Simple data types*, that is, domains for attributes or fields are primarily of type 'number' or 'character string' and hence resemble the 'primitive' types available in high-level programming languages.

(3) *Short transactions* which realize queries or updates arising in an online production environment; in particular, because of the atomicity requirement 'inherent' in the transaction concept, there is no way for a user to manipulate or modify the execution of a transaction while it is running (for example, in a dialogue that is based on intermediate results).

(4) A *high transaction rate* is typically required by the commercial orientation of the underlying application; for example, in banking environments, transaction rates are typically far beyond 100 transactions per second. Today dialogue users of a database system generally expect a response within 'real time', that is, without 'visible' delay.

(5) *Frequent in-place updates*: When the stored values of a record are modified, the old ones are most often no longer needed, since the update reflects a change in the underlying 'real world'; hence, old values can be discarded.

In addition, these areas of application are often characterized by a large number of 'classes' of queries and updates whose members are frequently repeated; as a result, it makes sense to introduce menu interfaces or to provide special 'transaction codes' especially for the casual user, through which use of the dialogue language of the system or the writing of specific application programs can be circumvented.

It should no longer come as a surprise that these characteristics are well supported by current DBMS, which in particular:

(1) support a *three-level architecture* for databases along the lines of the ANSI proposal (Chapter 2), thereby providing *logical and physical data independence*, through a data model supporting structures and operations on these structures;

(2) distinguish *data description* from *data manipulation*, which on the one hand eases database *design* and *administration* and on the other results in *high-level languages* and *user interfaces*;

(3) provide efficient *sharing* of data, using efficiently manageable structures for storing, retrieving and updating large amounts of data which avoid redundancies;

(4) support *security* and *integrity* of stored data through a concept of persistent and stable memory.

As will be discussed next, even areas other than the traditional ones need to use such features for their data-intensive applications.

20.2 New (non-standard) applications

20.2.1 Introduction

As follows from the discussion above, it is justified to state nowadays that database systems have been successfully integrated into the field of commercial and administrative data processing. However, application areas other than the ones mentioned above have been relying on computers for quite some time. Aspects like data independence or the provision of an *integrated* information resource for a *variety* of users are also of importance in technical and scientific fields like electrical engineering or other engineering sciences, in biology, chemistry, or even in linguistics and the arts. It is therefore not surprising that a number of such areas are now increasingly asking for 'database support', since this 'technology' has apparently proved useful in the many 'standard' applications. These new or **non-standard** areas of application are typically non-commercial in nature and more specifically include the following:

(1) Statistical data gathering

(2) Text processing ('texual databases')

(3) Image processing, in particular image analysis and evaluation

(4) Office information systems

(5) (Natural) language processing, in particular language recognition and language synthesis from text

(6) Geographical information systems

(7) Supervision and control systems for technical processes

(8) Collection, management and evaluation of data arising from scientific experiments

(9) Data-intensive artificial intelligence applications, knowledge representation and processing, in particular in connection with expert systems

(10) Computer-integrated manufacturing (CIM) and more specifically computer-aided design (CAD), for instance in the areas of electrical engineering, architecture, structural engineering, mechanical engineering, and the automobile industry, for which the collective term 'engineering database system' is becoming common

(11) Computer-aided software engineering (CASE), software production environments

(12) Robotics

(13) Computer-aided music composition and reproduction

What most of these new areas have in common is that the problems arising with respect to storing and manipulating data have so far often been solved in an *ad hoc* manner based on a file management system. There have also been a number of attempts to use traditional database systems to that end, but what can easily be learned from these attempts is that the integration of a 'traditional' DBMS into any of these areas is subject to a number of restrictions, for instance regarding the modelling of 'real-world objects'. The reasons for this stem partially from the fundamental differences between the new and the old application areas for which these systems were originally designed. As a result, it becomes necessary to search for new solutions to old problems, which is a major topic in research on and development of non-standard DBMS (NDBMS).

The differences between traditional and new applications can be found in almost any of the criteria discussed in the last section; in particular, they include the following.

(1) The *data model* used serves the purpose of describing a certain application from a logical or conceptual point of view in some formalism and provides operators or operations on the resulting constructs. As was discussed in Chapter 11, a real-world object frequently has an inner structure that is difficult to capture within a 'flat', record-oriented model, unless a large body of side-information (like integrity constraints) is added. As a first example, consider a design object from mechanical engineering like some building block which is composed of a number of subparts that in turn can be building blocks of their own. An example of a completely different nature is a piece of text whose length is not fixed *a priori* and for which a structure is difficult or unnatural to impose.

(2) The *data types* provided by a 'standard' DBMS are, as could be seen in Part V, presently limited to such simple types as 'integer' or 'string'. Clearly, this is inappropriate as soon as types like 'image' or 'picture' are needed. Next, while it is 'easy' for a DBMS to check whether a newly entered value conforms to the domain-specification of an attribute if the latter is a string or an integer, *type-checking* will be much more involved for the case of, say, an image-type.

(3) If a new data model as well as new data types are available, it follows that new types of *operations* are needed as well; for example, images of the same spot taken by a satellite at different times might have to be 'subtracted' in order to see what has changed. In addition, a user might want to manipulate the available types and structures, and might need an appropriate declarative *query language* to specify *what* to do, not *how*.

(4) As was described above, commercially available DBMS up to now provide only limited possibilities for (defining and) maintaining *consistency* of data. This notion, however, is much more complex in most of the new areas than the simple notion of a key in the relational model, for instance, so that it needs considerably more attention. Besides the quality of consistency constraints, their quantity is also important. Particular

problems that require attention are *dynamic* constraints describing 'state transitions' and toleration of consistency *violations* in a controlled manner over some time.

(5) The *recovery* manager of a DBMS, as was discussed in Chapter 19, has the primary task of making a database robust against failures. Opposed and in addition to this, applications like the control of a production line have new requirements with respect to failure tolerance; in particular, a redo of transactions may no longer be an option in a real-time environment.

(6) A *multi-user mode of operation*, which in particular renders it possible for several users to access shared data, receives new characteristics, for instance, in a design environment. If several design engineers work on the same project, locally autonomous work is often performed for some time, during which casual access to shared data occurs. Thus parallel work on the same object happens less frequently, but at the same time the duration of work increases considerably (since design is an 'evolutionary process'). As a result, the *transaction concept* as introduced in Chapter 18 has to be questioned. In particular, the atomicity requirement to a transaction, the 'all-or-nothing-principle', collides with long durations, which eventually need an interaction with the user while they are in process, and which may need to tolerate temporary inconsistencies.

(7) The term *data integration* has been used so far to mean the collection of large, but uniformly structurable and formattable set of data into a centrally controlled database that is mostly free of redundancy. This integration may now refer, for example, to data objects that are no longer uniformly structured, and each of which comes with its own consistency constraints and even manipulation operations. This aspect is particularly striking in a multi-media database which tries to integrate ordinary data, text, graphics, images and other types of 'objects'.

(8) As was briefly mentioned in Part IV, the *data structures* presently used to physically store data are commonly oriented on 'point objects'. In new applications, however, it is more frequently necessary to store 'space objects' which have a complex inner structure. As a result, new techniques for storing and for efficiently searching and manipulating such objects (*access methods*) are needed.

This list could be extended further with respect to several other aspects that generally arise in new application areas. However, each of these areas comes with a number of *specific* requirements to database management, which makes it reasonable to analyse some of them individually in more detail; this will be the subject of the following subsections. It will become apparent that, unlike in traditional applications, it can no longer be expected that there will be some kind of 'universal' NDBMS which serves all purposes equally well. However, it *is* possible to establish a *kernel architecture* as some kind of 'common intersection' (see Chapter 23); a genuine NDBMS will typically go beyond this architecture and (at least) provide measures for an application-dependent 'configuration'. (Database systems of the kind used so far are not always completely unsuited for a non-standard application area; in particular, 'minor' extensions such as the provision of new data types (like 'long fields' for texts) often enhance the applicability of a system considerably. See the Bibliographic Notes.)

20.2.2 Computer-aided design (CAD)

The first non-standard area for database application considered here is the area of **computer-aided design** (CAD). Since the CAD domain can be considered as a subdomain of the broader area of **computer-integrated manufacturing** (CIM), a brief look at the latter is taken first. *Manufacturing*, generally speaking, denotes the production activities of an enterprise from the initial design of an artefact up to its availability and production as a final product. Computers have always played an important role in supporting this process, where the emphasis so far has been primarily on providing independent tools for such specific tasks as computation (finite element analysis, etc.), simulation of mechanisms, planning and control of production, gathering and analysis of test data and production statistics, job scheduling, control of material handling, and numerical control. However, more recently attention has shifted to producing an *integrated* environment in which these tools may be invoked or invoke each other in a 'consistent' way and may easily exchange data.

A (simplified) scenario for manufacturing some assembly from its initial design stage to the final production relying on a database could be described as follows. The engineer enters a textual specification of the assembly to be designed into the database, then starts working on the design using, say, an interactive tool based on a constructive solid geometry data structure to define the part. The resulting data is also stored in the database; the graphics package may use a boundary representation which is also added to the data collection. Once the design is completed, computations might be required to determine certain characteristics of the part, where the corresponding programs operate on data generated previously. The engineer can now start working on a higher level assembly to determine which and how many elementary parts are needed and what their relative positions in the assembly should be. Suppose next that a production of n of these assemblies is intended. Then orders are entered into the database, which together with the parts information on the assembly can be used to generate a bill of material. This bill can be compared with the list of parts which are in stock, which can also be found in the database. Parts not in stock are ordered from suppliers (stored in the database) if possible, and it is determined which parts can be ordered and which have to be manufactured in house. The requirements for machine tools can be added to the database, as can scheduling information on the different machines used for production. Finally, operations can be scheduled and executed. Start and completion times are recorded (and checked against the scheduling times). Finished assemblies are stocked, and documentation for them can be completed.

In CIM, the various types of data arising in the course of this process (formatted and unformatted information, highly structured data) are used together, so that it is desirable that they are managed by a system which provides an integrated view of the database, which serves as the central data repository during all stages of the process, and which provides a single, homogeneous user interface and integrity among data of the same or different type.

A more detailed look at the *design phase* of the process outlined above is taken next. Design engineers are typically familiar with the use of computers and of CAD packages which have done without DBMS support so far. The 'design objects' in the CAD domain could be VLSI chips, automobiles or airplanes; to manage them in a database, the following requirements arise.

(1) In most design applications, *complex objects* with a rich structure have to be modelled. Typically, each individual object is *hierarchically* structured, that is, it is (recursively) composed from (eventually also complex) subobjects which may be used to compose a number of different objects.

As a first example, consider a computer system, whose hierarchical structure can be depicted as in Figure 20.1. As a second example, which will be used several times in this part, consider a single chip which might be used in the ALU of a computer. Figure 20.2 shows the hierarchical structure of a 4-bit parallel adder which is capable of adding two 4-bit binary numbers with a carry bit. Figure 20.3 shows this adder with its $2 \times 4 = 8$ inputs (coming from two 4-bit binary numbers $x = (x_3x_2x_1x_0)_2$ and $y = (y_3y_2y_1y_0)_2$) and its 5 outputs ($z = (z_4z_3z_2z_1z_0)_2$) in chip notation. In detail, the adder consists of four *full adders*, each of which in turn consists of two *half adders* and one *or gate*; the former is shown in Figure 20.4, while the latter is shown in Figure 20.5. Finally, each half adder consists of one *xor* (exclusive or) and one *and gate*, as shown in Figure 20.6. For the sake of completeness, Table 20.1 gives the definition of the Boolean functions *and*, *or* and *xor* used in these figures.

(2) A single design object typically has *several different descriptions* for which it should be possible to represent (and store) them individually; these descriptions can even be correlated in such a way that none of them gives a complete description of the object in question alone, but that they supplement each other to provide a complete description. In the case of the adder (or of VLSI chips in general), the following description methods or *representations* could be used: informal description in the form

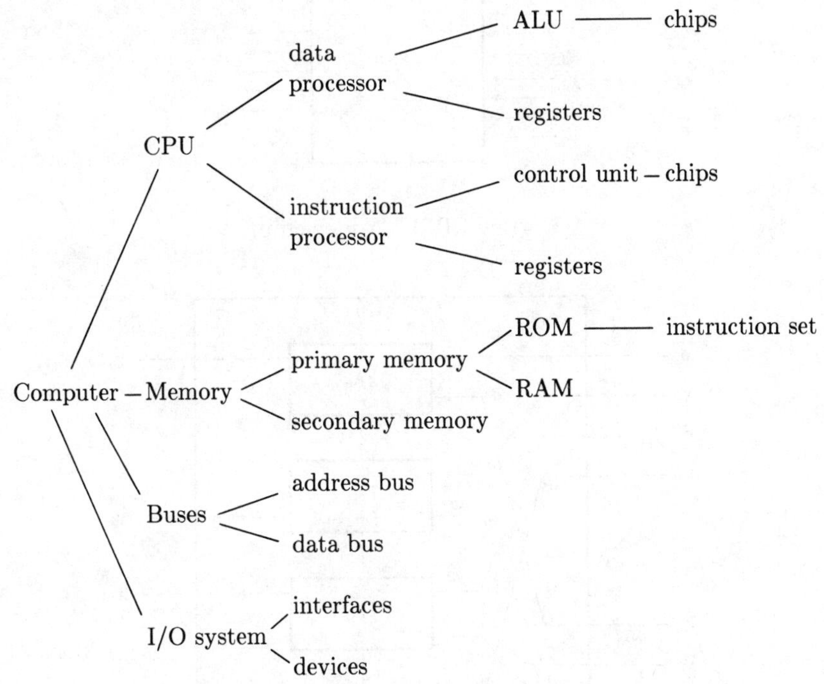

Figure 20.1 Logical organization of a computer system.

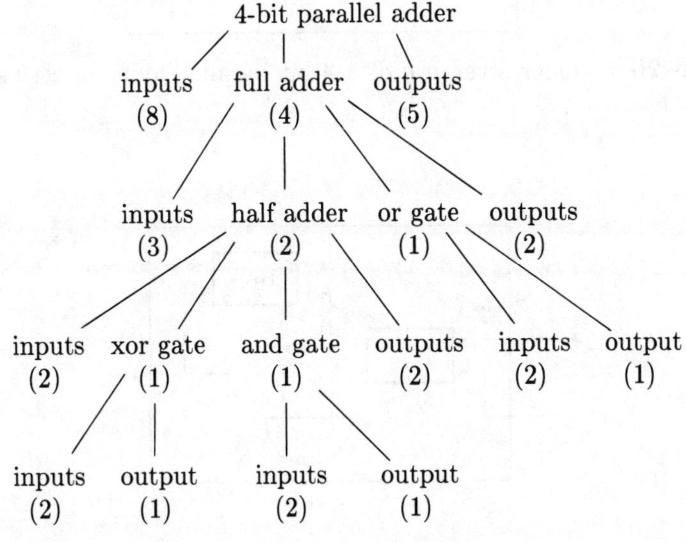

Figure 20.2 Logical decomposition of a 4-bit parallel adder.

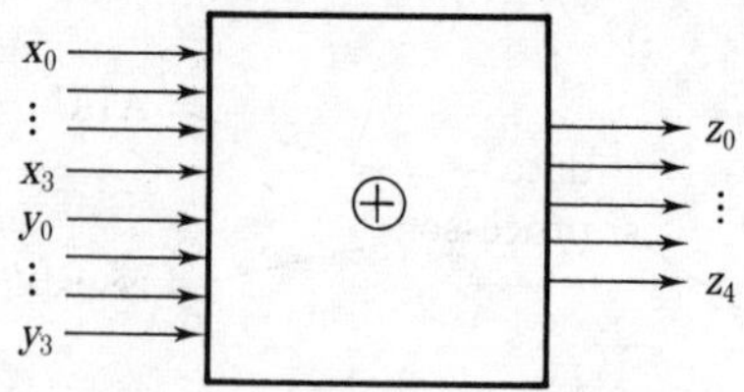

Figure 20.3 Adder chip.

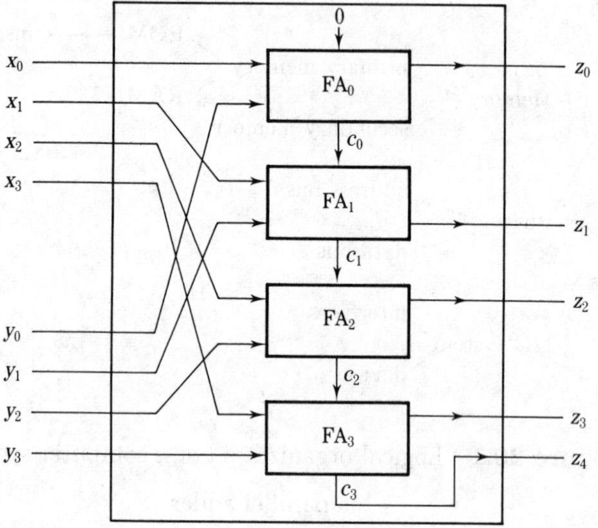

Figure 20.4 Inner structure of a 4-bit parallel adder in terms of full adders.

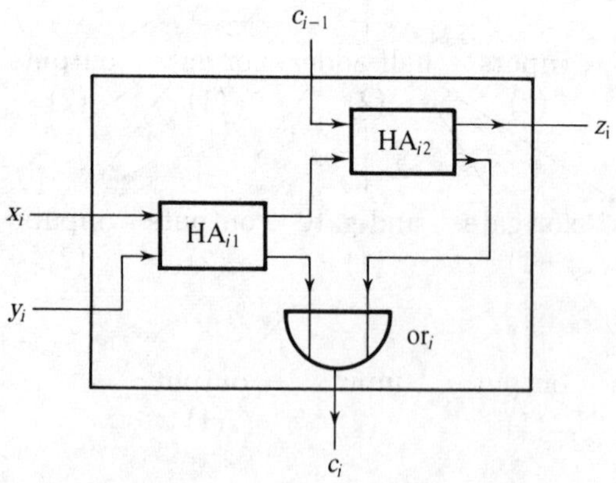

Figure 20.5 Full adder FA_i.

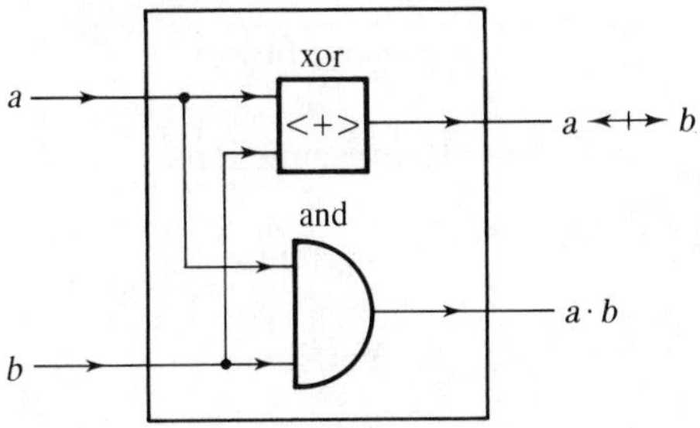

Figure 20.6 Half adder HA.

of text, functional description (by way of a switching function), description in the form of a component list and their connections, description in a hardware description language, geometric description as a VLSI layout diagram, description through a circuit diagram (as in Figures 20.4 to 20.6). Furthermore, each individual representation can come in distinct *variants*; for example, in Figure 20.4 the uppermost full adder could be replaced by a half adder, or an XOR gate could be further decomposed into *and*, *or* and *not* gates. Variants in turn can have different *versions*; versions can finally be combined into distinct *configurations* of the same design object.

This classification, which is collectively shown in Figure 20.7, reflects the fact that the development of some 'assembly' is an *evolutionary* process, in the course of which modifications may become desirable or necessary or the 'return' to some previous version might become appropriate; at the same time, it is a cooperative effort by many people.

(3) As a result of (1) and (2) above, *large volumes of data* have to be managed even for single objects. In addition, both 'base' data and its descriptions are dynamic, that is, may change over time.

(4) With respect to the *consistency constraints* which can be established in a design environment, not only static constraints are apt. For example, CAD constructions have to be performed according to predefined plans and procedures, which among other things define 'control points' that can be crossed only if certain (consistent) states have been

Table 20.1 Logical *and*, *or* and *xor*.

x	y	and(x, y)	or(x, y)	xor(x, y)
0	0	0	0	0
0	1	0	1	1
1	0	0	1	1
1	1	1	1	0

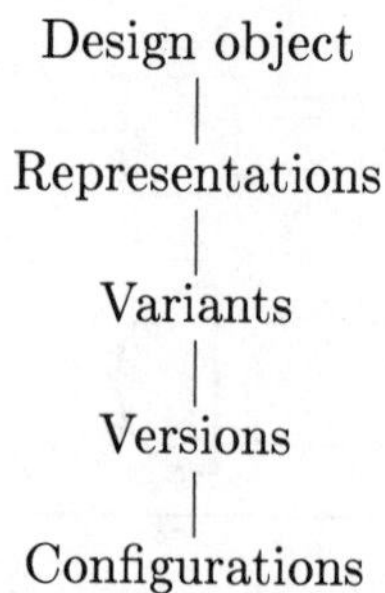

Figure 20.7 Different 'views' of a design object.

reached and that may be crossed in reverse direction only under special conditions. In addition, the various descriptions and representations of an object must be free of contradictions; during 'state transitions', implied changes (on subobjects) need to be taken into account which might require the support of a *communication* process between designers, and specifications and standards have to be observed.

(5) *Design transactions* (that is, user-defined transitions from one 'consistent' state to another) can last weeks or even months; the common term here is *long transactions.* While such a transaction is running, an intermediate dialogue with the user (designer) may become necessary in which the system asks for decisions, further information, details or deviations from the original plan. Clearly, most such transactions will never occur more than once in the same form, and the notion of *atomicity* of a transaction no longer makes sense. As a consequence, a new transaction concept is needed which in particular accounts for the various 'instantiations' of a design object shown in Figure 20.7. In particular the capability of managing *versions* is a crucial requirement in most CAD applications since alternate designs might be tried within one or different transactions.

(6) *Accesses* typically refer to a certain 'current' design object, where queries are used to retrieve details of some superobject (which is located at a higher level in the overall hierarchy). For storing design objects and for supporting access to them, multidimensional and dynamic data structures are needed which support spatial queries to geometric objects, similarity searches, and so on. On the other hand, corresponding language concepts are needed which support these types of accesses at a high, abstract level. Finally, the fact that accesses are often 'local' in nature has to be reflected; an engineer's work is often independent of the work of others for some time; an integration takes place towards the end, and in the meantime there will be only casual communication.

Finally notice that a database system in this domain must coexist with many other tools (like the ones mentioned above), and it must be genuinely *integrated* into a design (or even manufacturing) environment by supporting various types of activities arising in the process (like data flow and timing specification, algorithm synthesis, partitioning, floor planning, data path and control synthesis, test generation, module selection, placement and routing, validation, verification and documentation in the special CAD area of VLSI design).

20.2.3 Computer-aided software engineering (CASE)

The next application area considered is **computer-aided software engineering** (CASE), which has several similarities to the previous domain, but also a number of special requirements for DBMS support. A CASE environment consists of integrated tools to assist programmers (editors, compilers, assemblers, debuggers, etc.), to manage multi-component product configurations (like versions control as in CAD or automated regression testers), and to plan and track large projects (like schedulers). Such tools must store source and object versions of programs and the modules or procedures, utility libraries, internal forms of programs (like flow graphs), documents, test data, and project management information. Specific requirements to DBMS resulting from this 'big picture' include the following.

(1) Tools for a CASE environment need a large number of atomic and composite *data types* which software developers can use. Examples are ordinary (non-recursive) record types, arrays, nested structures, 'procedural' types (allowing calculations) and directed graphs (for parse trees, flow graphs, etc.). For any such type, corresponding *operations* must be provided.

(2) The *integrity* of objects in the database should be checked relative to the corresponding type definition. However, integrity constraints for database objects might be more complex than can be expressed using the type definition language (think, for example, of a style checker that determines whether a program conforms to a company's standards). To this end, a *trigger mechanism* could be provided which activates actions relative to the occurrence of certain events (like an update).

(3) A DBMS for CASE must be able to store *large* variable-length *objects* (like documents or programs), where restructuring (such as storing the procedures of a program as separate objects) should be possible.

(4) As in CAD, different *versions* of documents, programs or other objects need to be stored, and versions may be correlated to time. The sequence of versions of an object may be thought of as the history of this object, and it may be desirable to retrieve versions based on the time they were created.

(5) Data may also come in different *representations*, where these differences may now be caused by a machine architecture (word length, data representation, addressing modes, instruction set, etc.), a programming language or the tools employed. Translations from one representation

into another must be supported.

(6) *Content-based retrieval* is a desirable feature for CASE (think of an assembler searching for all programs modifying a given variable), which asks for data structures supporting associative access.

(7) A CASE environment is often configured (like a CAD environment) as a fileserver-workstation topology, in which a fileserver manages central resources, designers read data from it into the local memory of their workstation and operate on it by way of transactions for a long time. If the system fails during that period, it is unacceptable for all work to be lost. Also, the sharing of data by several programmers with intermediate communication with the fileserver (passing data back and forth) may result in an 'execution sequence' which is not 'serializable', although it is acceptable.

20.2.4 Conclusions

In conclusion, although the various new areas of application have significant differences and many unique features, several general requirements can be stated which database systems for non-standard applications are faced with, and which distinguish them considerably from their 'traditional' counterparts:

(1) *Modelling of complex objects*; of particular interest are data models which allow the capture of both structure and semantics in a uniform way.

(2) *New data types* which support an appropriate distinction of data objects, together with corresponding sophisticated *type checking mechanisms* and the ability to treat new types as specializations of existing types, sharing the semantics of existing types as appropriate.

(3) *Data manipulation languages* which allow for a high level of abstraction, but at the same time provide powerful operators for manipulating complex objects, in particular the ability to treat structured data both as an aggregate or in terms of its components, the ability to reuse code from one type of data on other types of data with similar structure, and the possibility for users to add new operators or operations of interest.

(4) Support of *long transactions* and *version management*; transactions may have arbitrary durations and are not necessarily atomic; appropriate concurrency control and recovery mechanisms are needed, which allow for a partial rollback, and updates are generally not made 'in place' but create new versions of existing objects.

(5) *Multi-dimensional, dynamic storage structures* for large objects and for multiple versions of them, which provide efficient and associative access.

The subject of the remaining chapters will be to (1) discuss extensions of the relational model which at least account for increased modelling capabilities, (2) introduce *object-orientation* as a promising paradigm for coping with the requirements of non-standard areas of database application, and object-oriented *systems* as the first (commercially available) approaches in this direction, and (3) discuss other approaches as well as a kernel architecture for future database management systems.

Chapter 21
Extensions and Generalizations of the Relational Model

In order to cope with the requirements from non-standard applications, it is necessary to enhance the capabilities of existing systems; an approach in this direction will be discussed in this chapter. After that, a generalization of the relational model is presented, which abandons the requirement that all relation schemas are in first normal form. As will be seen, it then becomes possible to model hierarchical structures. A general, simplifying assumption made in this chapter is that the complex objects to be modelled have a non-recursive structure.

21.1 The Postgres data model

In this section, an extension of the relational model is described which can be found in the Postgres system, a successor of the Ingres database management system, under development at the University of California, Berkeley. Postgres ('Post Ingres') is an 'extensible' DBMS (see Chapter 23) whose design goals are the support of complex objects, the provision of user extendibility for data types, operators and access methods, and the provision of inference mechanisms among others. The data model employed is based on the relational model.

As for ordinary relational systems, a Postgres database is a collection of relations. To each relation corresponds a schema consisting of attributes of fixed type as well as a (primary) key, where the latter (as usual) consists of attributes from that schema. A first important feature of the Postgres data model is that attribute types ('domains') can be either *atomic* or *structured*, where the latter are entirely user-defined and the former are either user-defined or predefined. The *predefined* **atomic types** include 'int2', 'int4', 'float4', 'float8', 'bool', 'char' and 'date' (where, for example, 'int2' denotes integers whose binary representation has a length of 2 bytes). These types are defined as *abstract data types* (ADTs, see also Chapter 22), which generally consist of a structure definition as well as a definition of operators that are *exclusively* applicable to this type. In Postgres, a structure definition consists of:

(1) a type name,

(2) the length of the (internal) representation in bytes,

(3) procedures for converting a value from an external to an internal representation and vice versa,

(4) a default value.

For example, the type 'int4' is internally defined as follows:

```
define type int4 is
    (InternalLength = 4,
    InputProc = CharToInt4,
    OutputProc = Int4ToChar,
    Default = '0')
```

Here, the input and output procedures are coded in a high-level programming language (typically C) and made known to the system via a special 'define procedure' command.

Operators on ADTs are defined by specifying:

(1) the number and type of operands,

(2) the return type,

(3) the precedence and associativity of the operator,

(4) the procedure that implements it.

For example, the '+' operator on type 'int4' is defined as follows:

```
define operator '+'(int4, int4)
    returns int4
    is (Proc = Plus,
       Precedence = 5
       Associativity = 'left')
```

Here, the precedence is specified by a number (the higher this number, the higher the precedence), and 'Plus' denotes the corresponding procedure which implements '+'.

Users can add *new* atomic types to the predefined ones, using the approach outlined above. For example, suppose a user wants a type 'box' (for use as pictures), where a box is represented by its upper-left and lower-right corners, given as two pairs of integer coordinates in the plane comprising a character string like '(2,5:1,7)'. A definition of this type could look as follows:

```
define type box is
    (InternalLength = 16,
    InputProc = CharToBox,
    OutputProc = BoxToChar,
    Default = '')
```

To determine whether two boxes have an equal area, a corresponding operator ('AE') is needed:

```
define operator AE(box, box)
    returns bool
    is (Proc = BoxAE,
       Precedence = 3,
       Associativity = 'left',
       Sort = BoxArea)
```

Here, the additional 'Sort' property of the operator specifies a procedure to be employed for sorting the relation containing values of type 'box' (according to area values) when necessary during query processing.

Finally, **structured types** for representing complex objects can be defined using type constructors for arrays and procedures. A variable- or fixed-sized *array* is defined using the *array constructor*. For example,

char[25]

defines an array of characters of fixed length 25. If the upper bound is omitted, an array of variable size results. The *procedure type-constructor* allows values of type 'procedure' to be stored in an attribute, where a procedure is a sequence of commands written in Postquel, the query language of Postgres. The corresponding type is called the 'postquel' data type and will be explained in more detail below.

A relation schema in Postgres is declared using the following command:

> **create** table-name
>   (column-name-1 = type-1,
>   column-name-2 = type-2, ...)
> [**key** (list of column-names)]
> [**inherits** (list of column-names)]

As a first example, consider the following revised version of the university database from Section 16.1 (where attention is restricted to professors and students only). First, a relation is defined which represents people:

```
CREATE PERSON ( NAME = CHAR[25],
    CITY = CHAR[20],
    BIRTHDATE = DATE )
KEY ( NAME, BIRTHDATE )
```

Notice that the array type constructor has already been used twice. Next, university people can be either professors or students (ignoring the staff for the moment). Both groups have common attributes (collected in *PERSON*) and also distinctive features; in the language of Chapter 4, the following can be stated:

> *PROFESSOR* IS-A *PERSON*
> *STUDENT* IS-A *PERSON*

Unlike the approach described in Chapter 7, where inclusion dependencies were used to capture IS-A relationships, Postgres provides data **inheritance**, through which a 'child relation' (specialization) can inherit all attributes from a 'father relation' (generalization). Thus, a *PROFESSOR* and a *STUDENT* relation schema can be defined as follows:

```
CREATE PROFESSOR ( DEPT = CHAR[20],
    FIELD = CHAR[50],
    TENURE = BOOL )
INHERITS ( PERSON )

CREATE STUDENT ( STUDID = CHAR[12],
    COLLEGE = CHAR[10],
```

```
        MAJOR = CHAR[10],
        LEVEL = CHAR[20] )
    INHERITS ( PERSON )
```

In each case the 'inherits' clause specifies that the new relation (schema) inherits all attributes (and the key) from *PERSON*. Thus, a student, for example, has seven attributes in total, three of which are stored in *PERSON*. A query that asks for the name of every student majoring in computer science can then be written as:

```
SELECT NAME FROM STUDENT WHERE MAJOR = 'CS'
```

(For pedagogical reasons, this and the other examples of the section are written in SQL, which has been emphasized throughout this text, although, as mentioned earlier, the actual language of Postgres is Postquel.)

As a second example, consider the 'box' data type defined above. The following command defines a relation (schema) with a key attribute of type box that uses the 'area equals' operator (AE, see above) to determine key value equality:

```
CREATE PICTURE ( TITLE = CHAR[30],
    ITEM = BOX )
KEY ( ITEM USING AE )
```

As a final example, a possible definition of relation schemas for representing complex objects like the adder from Section 20.2.2 is given. To this end, it is assumed that three relations named *CHIP*, *MODULE* and *SUBMOD*, respectively, are needed, where *CHIP* describes chips like the adder at a high level just through an identifier, a name and some kind of reference to its inner structure, *MODULE* describes the second highest level of abstraction (see Figure 20.2), that is, full adders, by an identifier, a name and a reference, and *SUBMOD* describes the level of half adders analogously. In addition, let us assume that an adder with id 125 is composed of the four full adders with ids 201 to 204, that full adder 201 has components 301 to 303, 202 has 304 to 306 and so on. A schema declaration for Postgres can then be stated as follows:

```
CREATE CHIP ( CHIPID = INT4,
    CHIPNAME = CHAR[30],
    MODULES = POSTQUEL )
KEY ( CHIPID )

CREATE MODULE ( MODID = INT4,
    MODNAME = CHAR[20],
    SUBMODULES = POSTQUEL )
KEY ( MODID )
```

```
CREATE SUBMOD ( SID = INT4,
    SNAME = CHAR[4] )
KEY ( SID )
```

The important feature here is the use of the 'postquel' data type, which allows (sequences of) Postquel statements to be entered as values for attributes. Thus, a corresponding database could look as shown in Figure 21.1.

With respect to querying these relations, the following is now important. First, a query like

```
SELECT MODULES FROM CHIP WHERE CHIPID = 125
```

would return the string which contains the (stored) Postquel command(s). Second, it is possible to execute a stored query, and to get as a return value the result rather than the definition. The command

```
SELECT CHIPID, MODULES.MODID FROM CHIP
    WHERE CHIPID = 125
```

implicitly executes the query stored as *MODULES* value for the *CHIP* tuple whose *CHIPID* value is 125, and returns a relation whose *MODULES* values are again tuples from which only the *MODID* component will be shown. Hence, the result will look as follows:

CHIPID	*MODULES.MODID*
125	201
125	202
125	203
125	204

Similarly, a more complex command could be used to retrieve the entire description of the adder. A different way to execute a stored query is to use the *execute* command. The above result can alternatively be obtained by saying

```
EXECUTE CHIP.MODULES FROM CHIP WHERE CHIPID = 125
```

This concludes the introductory description of Postgres. More information on the many other new features of this system (like the transitive closure operator available in Postquel, the maintenance of historical data or the use of 'rules' for supporting integrity constraints) can be found in the references listed below.

21.2 The nested relational model

In this and the following section, generalizations of the relational model will be described which are intended to cope with the representation or

CHIP	CHIPID	CHIPNAME	MODULES
	125	ADDER	select * from MODULE where MODID ≥ 201 and MODID ≤ 204
	⋮		

MODULE	MODID	MODNAME	SUBMODULES
	201	FA1	select * from SUBMOD where SID ≥ 301 and SID ≤ 303
	202	FA2	select * from SUBMOD where SID ≥ 304 and SID ≤ 306
	203	FA3	select * from SUBMOD where SID ≥ 307 and SID ≤ 309
	204	FA4	select * from SUBMOD where SID ≥ 310 and SID ≤ 312

SUBMOD	SID	SNAME
	301	HA11
	302	HA12
	303	OR1
	304	HA21
	305	HA22
	306	OR2
	307	HA31
	308	HA32
	309	OR3
	310	HA41
	311	HA42
	312	OR4

Figure 21.1 Partial Postgres description of the adder from Figure 20.2.

R:	A	B	E	
			C	D
	1	1	{(1	1)}
	1	2	{(2	2)}
	2	2	{(2	2),
			(1	1)}

Figure 21.2 A relation not in 1NF.

representability and in addition the manipulation of (non-recursive) complex objects. Remember the general requirement stated in Section 7.2 that relation schemas considered in this text have to be in 1NF, that is, the domain of each attribute occurring in a relation schema consists of elementary values only. Thus, a value for an attribute is not allowed to be a set or a relation or any other structured item, but is 'atomic'. If this prerequisite is dropped, structured objects can easily be represented in tables, which will be shown below.

As a first intuitive example, Figure 21.2 shows a relation whose 'format' R consists of three attributes A, B and E, where A and B are 'ordinary' attributes, and where E consists of attributes C and D. (If no confusion can arise, braces for delimiting tuples will be omitted from now on.) The format of the relation shown in Figure 21.2 has the hierarchical structure shown in Figure 21.3.

Relation schemas with such a format are called unnormalized; corresponding relations are generally termed **nested** relations (sometimes also called 'NF^2 relations', which is a shorthand for *N*on *F*irst *N*ormal *F*orm).

To illustrate the idea of how to define an extended relational model formally, some definitions are presented next which generalize the relational model as introduced in Chapter 7; additionally, some basics of an *algebra* for nested relations are introduced in this section, in order to direct the reader's attention to some of the problems that may be encountered when dealing with data models for complex objects.

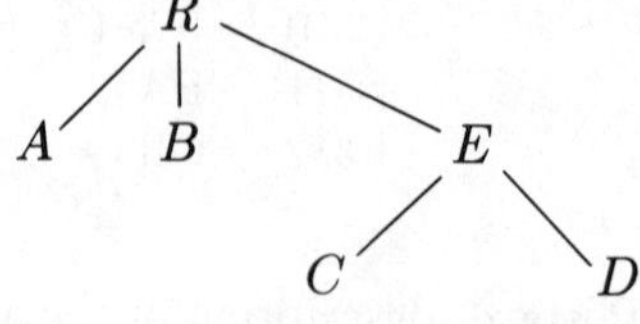

Figure 21.3 Structure of the format from Figure 21.2.

21.2.1 Nested formats

Let U be a (finite) set of (uniquely named) *attributes*; to each $A \in U$ corresponds a (non-empty, finite) domain dom(A) of (atomic) values in the usual sense. The first goal is to generalize the notion of a (relation) *format* so that complex objects (with a non-recursive, tree-like structure) can be described; the term 'format' will be used throughout this section since integrity constraints (which supplement formats yielding a *schema* according to Chapter 7) are mostly neglected here.

Definition 21.1

A **(nested) format** over U is recursively defined as follows:

(i) If $A_1, \ldots, A_n$ are distinct attributes from U, then

$$R = (A_1, \ldots, A_n)$$

is a (flat) format over U with name R.

(ii) If $A_1, \ldots, A_n$ are distinct attributes from U and $R_1, \ldots, R_m$ are distinct names of formats such that $\{A_1, \ldots, A_n\}$ and the sets of attributes associated with R_i, $1 \leq i \leq m$ (denoted attr(R_i) when needed) are pairwise disjoint, then

$$R = (A_1, \ldots, A_n, R_1, \ldots, R_m)$$

is a (nested) format with name R (and subformats $R_1, \ldots, R_m$).

Although a format is for simplicity written as a sequence in this section, the order in which names appear in a format is not important (see examples below).

As a first example, let an employee have an id, a name, an address, a set of children and a set of skills. The latter two can be described by the (flat) formats:

CHILDREN = (*CNAME, BIRTHDATE, SEX*)
SKILLS = (*TYPE, EXAMDATE*)

which can then be *nested* into the format:

EMP = (*ID, NAME, ADDR, CHILDREN, SKILLS*)

the latter could also be written in 'expanded' form as

EMP = (*ID, NAME, ADDR,* (*CNAME, BIRTHDATE, SEX*),
(*TYPE, EXAMDATE*))

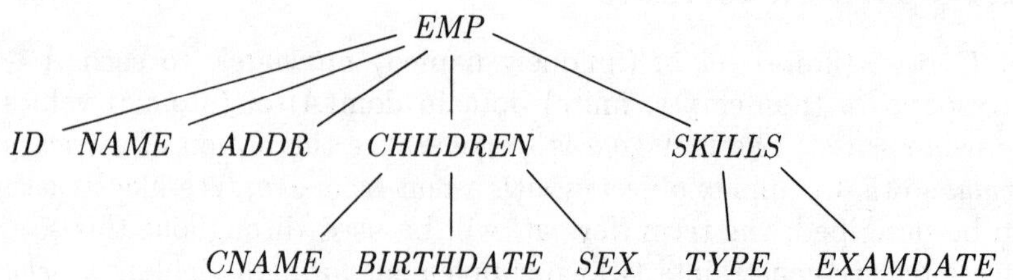

Figure 21.4 Structure tree for the *EMP* format.

Thus, *EMP* exhibits one level of (two) nesting(s). Notice that attr(*CHILDREN*), attr(*SKILLS*) and attr(*EMP*) = { *ID, NAME, ADDR* } are pairwise disjoint.

Notice that the following 'problem' arises at this point. If a relation format is given a *name* in a database declaration, a generally agreed implication is that this name can subsequently be used to reference that format (for example in queries). Following this interpretation, the above example suggests that *CHILDREN*, *SKILLS* and *EMP* are 'valid' names for queries, that is, the user is allowed to query the *EMP* relation as a whole, or just the *CHILDREN* relation nested into it without even referencing an employee as the father. The latter does not make sense, however, so that, strictly speaking, a distinction seems appropriate between 'external' names which are 'visible' to the user (as names for formats) and 'internal' ones which can just be used in the same way as attributes. Such a distinction is implicitly made in what follows and in particular underlies the definitions of the operations in the next section.

With a nested format R, a **structure tree** T_R can be associated as follows. All attributes and (sub)format names occurring in R (including the name R itself) form the nodes of T_R, and R is the root; in addition, T_R contains an edge (V, W) from V to W if $V = (\ldots, W, \ldots)$ is nested into R.

Continuing the last example, the structure tree T_{EMP} for the format *EMP* defined above is the one shown in Figure 21.4.

Notice that a structure tree is a tree whose leaves are labelled with attributes, and whose other nodes are labelled with names for formats. It is obviously easy to derive a flat (1NF) format from a given structure tree by retaining its leaves (attributes) only, and also to derive a nested one.

The latter is illustrated by a second example. Consider the adder once more, for which a possible structure tree is shown in Figure 21.5. The corresponding format is as follows:

CHIP = (*CHIPID, CHIPNAME, MODULE*)
= (*CHIPID, CHIPNAME,* (*MODID, MODNAME, SUBMOD*))

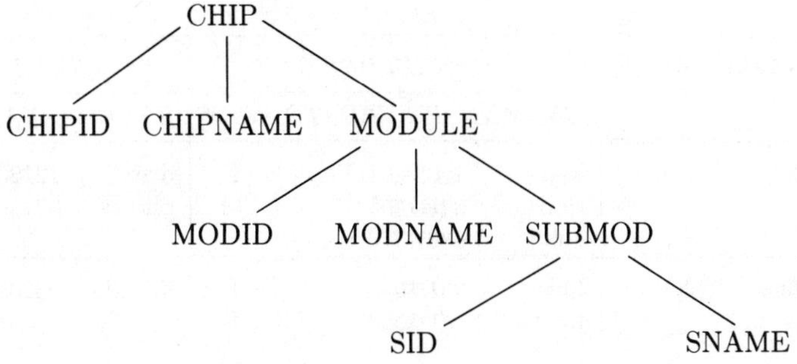

Figure 21.5 Structure tree for the adder.

= (*CHIPID, CHIPNAME,* (*MODID, MODNAME,*
(*SID, SNAME*)))

Notice that this format exhibits two levels of nesting.

21.2.2 Nested relations

The subject of defining *instances* over a format is studied next. Informally, a nested relation (over a nested format) is a relation whose tuple components are either atomic values or repeating group instances. More formally, a nested relation can be defined via the notion of a 'domain' of a format (along the lines of the development in Chapter 7) as follows.

Definition 21.2

Let R denote a format over a set U of attributes. The **domain** of R, denoted dom(R), is recursively defined as follows:

(i) If $R = (A_1, \ldots, A_n)$, where $A_i \in U$, $1 \leq i \leq n$, then

$$\text{dom}(R) = \text{dom}(A_1) \times \ldots \times \text{dom}(A_n)$$

(ii) if $R = (A_1, \ldots, A_n, R_1, \ldots, R_m)$, then

$$\text{dom}(R) = \text{dom}(A_1) \times \ldots \times \text{dom}(A_n) \times 2^{\text{dom}(R_1)} \times \ldots \times 2^{\text{dom}(R_m)}$$

where 2^P denotes the power set of the set P.

Finally, instances over (nested) formats can be defined in a similar way to the way tuples and relations were defined over flat formats in Chapter 7.

EMP							
ID	*NAME*	*ADDR*	*CHILDREN*			*SKILLS*	
			CNAME	*BIRTHDATE*	*SEX*	*TYPE*	*EXAMDATE*
100	Joe	LA	Mary Peter John	120261 041465 082270	F M M	driv_lic phd_cs	121255 021565
200	Theo	NY	Mary Laura	051578 051578	F F	driv_lic	082686

Figure 21.6 A nested relation over the *EMP* format.

Definition 21.3

Let R be a format over U as above.

(i) A **(nested) tuple** over R is an element of dom(R). Let Tup(R) denote the set of all tuples over R.

(ii) A **(nested) relation** over R is a (finite) subset of Tup(R).

Notice that the ordinary relational model follows from the above definitions as a special case. Clearly, the format ('schema') is just a sequence (or set) of attributes, whose domain is given by the Cartesian product of its elements (or a mapping into their union if the set-representation is chosen). A tuple is an element in that domain, and a relation is a subset of it.

Complex objects which can be represented as a (structure) tree can now alternatively be modelled by nested relations or a nested format. As a first example of a nested relation, consider the instance of the *EMP* format defined above shown in Figure 21.6. Employee Joe has three children and two different skills, whereas Theo has two children and just a driving licence. Notice that nested relations with null values, which might be reasonable in practical applications ('John has no children'), are not considered here to simplify the exposition.

As a second example, consider the representation of the 4-bit adder from Section 20.2.2 as a nested relation as shown in Figure 21.7. Notice that *one tuple* is now sufficient to capture the information that was spread over three 1NF relations in Figure 21.1. This tuple can alternatively be written as follows:

(125, ADDER,
{ (201, FA1, {(301, HA11), (302, HA12), (303, OR1)}),
(202, FA2, {(304, HA21), (305, HA22), (306, OR2)}),

CHIP					
CHIPID	*CHIPNAME*	*MODULE*			
		MODID	*MODNAME*	*SUBMOD*	
				SID	*SNAME*
125	ADDER	201	FA1	301	HA11
				302	HA12
				303	OR1
		202	FA2	304	HA21
				305	HA22
				306	OR2
		203	FA3	307	HA31
				308	HA32
				309	OR3
		204	FA4	310	HA41
				311	HA42
				312	OR4
⋮		⋮		⋮	

Figure 21.7 A nested-relation representation of the adder.

(203, FA3, {(307, HA31), (308, HA32), (309, OR3)}),
(204, FA4, {(310, HA41), (311, HA42), (312, OR4)})})

21.2.3 Operations on nested relations

Some basic operations on nested relations, which are extensions of those known from relational algebra (see Chapter 8), and which together with two new operations can be used to define the semantics of a *nested relational algebra*, are discussed next. Attention is restricted here to four unary operations and one binary operation, which on the one hand do not yet form a 'complete' set of operations, but which on the other exhibit a variety of 'complications' that arise in this model as opposed to the traditional one.

The approach described here attempts to treat components of tuples in a nested relation as indivisible units, analogous to atomic values in a normalized relation; this avoids the necessity of defining the new operations recursively.

Projection and selection

Unary operations for restricting a given relation either horizontally or vertically are considered first.

Definition 21.4

Let $R = (A_1, \ldots, A_n, R_1, \ldots, R_m)$ be a format, and let names(R) denote the set of all (attribute or format) names of R (without R itself), that is, names$(R) = \{A_1, \ldots, R_m\}$; also, let $Y \subseteq$ names(R), and let $r \subseteq$ Tup(R) be a (nested) relation over R.

$$\pi_Y(r) := \{\mu[Y] \mid \mu \in r\}$$

is called the **projection** of r onto Y, where $\mu[Y]$ denotes the restriction of tuple μ onto Y.

Although the *restriction* of a tuple onto some subset of the names of its format has not been defined formally, it should be clear what is meant by this term. As an example of projection, consider the following relation r_1 over format $R_1 = (A, B, E) = (A, (C, D), E)$:

r_1	A	B		E
		C	D	
	1	1	3	3
		1	4	
	1	1	4	4
	2	2	3	3
	2	2	3	4

Here, names$(R_1) = \{A, B, E\}$. Now let $Y = \{A, B\}$; then the projection $\pi_Y(r_1)$ of r_1 onto Y is the following relation:

r'_1	A	B	
		C	D
	1	1	3
		1	4
	1	1	4
	2	2	3

Notice that duplicate elements in the result are removed as was the case for ordinary projection defined in Chapter 8.

The next unary operation considered is *selection*; to this end, the notion of a (selection) *condition* needs to be introduced first.

Definition 21.5

Let $R = (A_1, \ldots, A_n, R_1, \ldots, R_m)$ be a format. A (simple) **condition** (over R) can have one of the following forms:

(i) $A \Theta a$, where $A \in \{A_1, \ldots, A_n\}$, $a \in \text{dom}(A)$, and $\Theta \in \{<, \leq, >, \geq, =, \neq\}$;

(ii) $R' \Delta r'$, where $R' \in \{R_1, \ldots, R_m\}$, r' is a relation over R', and $\Delta \in \{\subset, \subseteq, \supset, \supseteq, =, \neq\}$.

The selection operation defined next is introduced for simple conditions only, although a variety of more complex conditions can be used in a selection on nested relations.

Definition 21.6

Let R be as above, let C be a simple condition over R, and let r be a relation over R.

$$\sigma_C(r) := \{\mu \in r \mid \mu \text{ satisfies } C\}$$

is called **selection** of r with respect to C (where it should be intuitively clear what is meant by *satisfaction* of a condition by a tuple).

As an example, consider the relation r_1 above. The selections

$$\sigma_{A=1}(r_1) \text{ and } \sigma_{B \subset \{(1,4),(2,3)\}}(r_1)$$

yield the following relations s_1 and s_2, respectively:

s_1	A	B		E
		C	D	
	1	1	3	3
		1	4	
	1	1	4	4

s_2	A	B		E
		C	D	
	1	1	4	4
	2	2	3	3
	2	2	3	4

The operations on nested relations, like their non-nested counterparts, yield relations whose format will in general be different from that of the operand (so that *views* over nested relations can be defined without regard for the current contents). Hence, the above definitions (as well as the following ones) could be extended to state how the format of the result is obtained, an aspect that is also neglected here.

Nest and unnest

The next two (unary) operations are new for (nested) relations; they are particularly useful in reorganizing the data stored in a nested relation, and are called *nest* and *unnest*.

Informally, a nest operation takes a (nested or flat) relation and aggregates over equal data values in some subset of the names occurring in the corresponding format. Formally, this operation is defined as follows.

Definition 21.7

Let $R = (A_1, \ldots, A_n, R_1, \ldots, R_m)$ be a format, and let names(R) denote the set of names of R as above. Furthermore, let N_1 and N_2 be a (disjoint) partition of names(R) (that is, $N_1 \cap N_2 = \emptyset$ and $N_1 \cup N_2 =$ names(R)) such that $N_1 = \{B_1, \ldots, B_k\}$ and either the structure tree T_R of R contains a node R' whose set of (direct) sons equals N_1, or neither does T_R contain such a node R' nor does N_1 equal the set of (direct) sons of another node. Finally, let r be a relation over R. Then

$$\begin{aligned} n_{R'=(B_1,\ldots,B_k)}(r) := \{\mu \mid (\exists\, \nu \in r)\ \mu[N_2] = \nu[N_2] \wedge \\ \mu[R'] = \{\rho[N_1] \mid \rho \in r\ \wedge\ \rho[N_2] = \mu[N_2]\}\} \end{aligned}$$

is called the **nest** of r with respect to R'.

(Here and in the following, the symbols 'n' and 'u' are used for the nest and unnest operations, respectively. The use of 'ν' and 'μ' is more common in the literature; however, the latter symbols are used throughout this text to denote tuples.)

To construct the nest of a relation r over $R = (A_1, \ldots, A_n, R_1, \ldots, R_m)$ with respect to $R' = (B_1, \ldots, B_k)$, one can proceed as follows. For each tuple $\mu \in \pi_{N_2}(r)$, the result contains a tuple composed of μ and $s = \{\rho[N_1] \mid \rho \in r\ \wedge\ \rho[N_2] = \mu\}$.

As an example, consider the following relation r over the flat format $R = (A, C, D, E)$:

r	A	C	D	E
	1	1	3	3
	1	1	4	3
	1	1	4	4
	2	2	3	3
	2	2	3	4

Here, names$(R) = \{A, C, D, E\}$, and let $N_1 = \{C, D\}$, $N_2 = \{A, E\}$; note that no node of T_R has exactly the elements of N_1 as sons. Then the result of $n_{B=(C,D)}(r)$ is the relation r_1 shown above during the illustration of the projection operation. For example, tuple $\mu = (1, \{(1,3), (1,4)\}, 3)$ is in $n_{B=(C,D)}(r)$ since

(1) for $\nu = (1,1,3,3) \in r$ it is true that $\nu[AE] = \mu[AE]$, and

(2) $\mu[B] = \{\rho[CD] \mid \rho \in r \land \rho[AE] = \mu[AE]\}$
$= \{(1,1,3,3)[CD], (1,1,4,3)[CD]\}$

Stated differently, $\pi_{AE}(r) = \{(1,3),\ (1,4),\ (2,3),\ (2,4)\}$; hence $n_{B=(C,D)}(r)$ contains the four tuples $(1, s_1, 3)$, $(1, s_2, 4)$, $(2,\ s_3,\ 3)$ and $(2,\ s_4,\ 4)$, where s_1, s_2, s_3 and s_4 are over $B = (C, D)$ and

$$s_1 = \{(1,3), (1,4)\} \qquad s_2 = \{(1,4)\} \qquad s_3 = s_4 = \{(2,3)\}$$

Next, the result r_1 obtained from the first nest operation is nested further according to $F = (E)$. The result r_2 of computing $n_{F=(E)}(r_1)$ is the following relation:

r_2	A	B		F
		C	D	E
	1	1	3	3
		1	4	
	1	1	4	4
	2	2	3	3
				4

To see this, first notice that $R_1 = (A, B, E) = (A, (C, D), E)$ is the format of r_1 (see above). Hence, names$(R_1) = \{A, B, E\}$; now let $N_1 = (E)$ and $N_2 = (A, B)$. r_1 is partitioned according to equal (A, B) values and nested along this partition.

An important fact which can easily be seen from this example is that a sequence of nest operations may yield different results depending on the order in which the operations are executed. Consider relation r above once more; then $r_3 = n_{F=(E)}(r)$ is the following relation:

r_3	A	C	D	F
				E
	1	1	3	3
	1	1	4	3
				4
	2	2	3	3
				4

Finally, $n_{B=(C,D)}(r_3) = r_3 \neq r_2$ and hence

$$n_{F=(E)}(n_{B=(C,D)}(r)) \neq n_{B=(C,D)}(n_{F=(E)}(r))$$

An 'inverse' operation to nest is unnest, which informally takes a relation that is nested on some set of attributes and disaggregates it to make it 'flatter'. This operation can be defined formally as follows.

Definition 21.8

Let $R = (A_1, \ldots, A_n, R_1, \ldots, R_m)$ be a format, and for some $i \in \{1, \ldots, m\}$ let R_i be a node of the structure tree T_R of R whose set N_1 of (direct) sons equals $\{B_1, \ldots, B_k\}$; let names$(R) - \{R_i\} = N_2$ and r be a relation over R. Then

$$u_{R_i}(r) := \{\mu \mid (\exists\, \nu \in r)\ \mu[N_2] = \nu[N_2]\ \wedge\ \mu[N_1] \in \nu[R_i]\}$$

is called the **unnest** of r with respect to R_i.

To construct the unnest of a relation r over format R (as in the last definition) with respect to R_i, one can proceed as follows. For each tuple $\nu = (a_1, \ldots, a_n, r_1, \ldots, r_m) \in r$ and every tuple $(b_1, \ldots, b_k) \in \nu[R_i]$, $u_{R_i}(r)$ contains a tuple of the form

$$\mu = (a_1, \ldots, a_n, r_1, \ldots, r_{i-1}, b_1, \ldots, b_k, r_{i+1}, \ldots, r_m)$$

where $\mu[N_2] = \nu[N_2]$ and $\mu[B_1 \ldots B_k] \in \nu[R_i]$. As a result, a nested relation can be transformed into a 1NF relation by a sequence of unnests (see Exercise 4).

As an illustration of unnest, the following is easily verified for the example relations above:

(1) $r = u_B(r_1)$, and hence

(2) $r = u_B(n_{B=(C,D)}(r))$

As this example demonstrates, a nest operation can be 'reversed' by a subsequent unnest operation. Indeed, it can be shown that this property holds in general. For each nest operation there exists an unnest operation which makes the result of the former undone. More precisely, the following holds.

Theorem 21.1

Under the assumptions of Definition 21.7,

$$u_{R'}(n_{R'=(B_1,\ldots,B_k)}(r)) = r$$

for every relation r (over R).

Proof. By Definition 21.7,

$$n_{R'=(B_1,\ldots,B_k)}(r) \;=\; \{\mu \mid (\exists\, \nu \in r)\ \mu[N_2] = \nu[N_2] \wedge \mu[R'] = \{\rho[B_1 \ldots B_k] \mid \rho \in r\ \wedge\ \rho[N_2] = \mu[N_2]\}\}$$

Next, by Definition 21.8,

$$\begin{aligned}
\mu \in \quad & u_{R'}(n_{R'=(B_1,\ldots,B_k)}(r)) \\
\iff & (\exists\, \nu \in n_{R'=(B_1,\ldots,B_k)}(r))\ \mu[N_2] = \nu[N_2] \ \wedge\ \mu[N_1] \in \nu[R'] \\
\iff & (\exists\, \delta \in r)\ \mu[N_2] = \delta[N_2] \\
& \wedge\ \mu[N_1] \in \{\rho[N_1] \mid \rho \in r \ \wedge\ \rho[N_2] = \mu[N_2]\} \\
\iff & (\exists\, \delta \in r)(\exists\, \rho \in r)\ \mu[N_2] = \delta[N_2] \ \wedge\ \mu[N_2] = \rho[N_2] \\
& \wedge\ \mu[N_1] = \rho[N_1] \\
\iff & (\exists\, \rho \in r)\ \mu[N_2] = \rho[N_2] \ \wedge\ \mu[N_1] = \rho[N_1] \\
\iff & (\exists\, \rho \in r)\ \rho = \mu \\
\iff & \mu \in r
\end{aligned}$$

(δ and ρ may be chosen as equal). □

However, the 'converse' of Theorem 21.1, that is,

$$n_{R'=(B_1,\ldots,B_k)}(u_{R'}(r)) = r$$

does not hold in general. To see this, consider the following relation r over format $R = (A, B) = (A, (C))$:

r	A	B
		C
	0	0
		1
	0	1
		2

Then $u_B(r)$ yields the following relation r_1:

r_1	A	C
	0	0
	0	1
	0	2

Finally, $n_{B=(C)}(r_1)$ yields the following relation r_2:

r_2	A	B
		C
	0	0
		1
		2

Obviously, $r_2 = n_{B=(C)}(u_B(r)) \neq r$.

It can even be shown that relation r above cannot be derived from *any* 1NF relation using the operations n and u only. Thus, relation r can, in a sense, be considered as exhibiting an anomaly. A reasonable question to ask, then, is how such anomalies can be excluded or, stated differently, how the model can be re tricted to relations for which some nest operation always 'renests' a relation that has been unnested. One approach in this direction is sketched next; the idea is to impose a 'structural' constraint using dependencies.

Definition 21.9

Let R be as in Definition 21.7, and let X and Y be two disjoint subsets of names(R). An **extended functional dependency** (EFD) $X \hookrightarrow Y$ denotes the following semantic constraint. Let r be a relation over R:

$$(X \hookrightarrow Y)(r) := \begin{cases} 1 & \text{if } (\forall \mu, \nu \in r)\ (\mu[X] = \nu[X] \Longrightarrow \mu[Y] = \nu[Y]) \\ 0 & \text{otherwise} \end{cases}$$

where equality means equality of the tuple components as sets if X or Y denote (sub)formats.

The following can now be proved.

Theorem 21.2

Under the assumptions of Definition 21.8,

$$n_{R_i=(B_1,\ldots,B_k)}(u_{R_i}(r)) = r \iff (N_2 \hookrightarrow R_i)(r) = 1$$

In the light of this result, the anomalous behaviour of relation r above is due to the fact that the EFD $A \hookrightarrow B$ is violated.

The next observation exhibits another difference between nest and unnest, namely that the order in which a sequence of unnest operations is applied to a given relation is immaterial. More precisely, the following holds.

Theorem 21.3

Let $R = (A_1, \ldots, A_n, R_1, \ldots, R_m)$, and let r be a relation over R. Then

$$u_{R_i}(u_{R_j}(r)) = u_{R_j}(u_{R_i}(r))$$

for every $R_i, R_j \in \{R_1, \ldots, R_m\}$, $R_i \neq R_j$.

The next theorems state several properties of the operations introduced so far which are easily verified.

Theorem 21.4

Under the assumptions of Definition 21.7, let C be a (simple) condition not involving names R' or $B_1, \ldots, B_k$. Then the following holds for every relation r over R:

(1) $n_{R'=(B_1,\ldots,B_k)}(\sigma_C(r)) = \sigma_C(n_{R'=(B_1,\ldots,B_k)}(r))$

(2) $u_{R'}(\sigma_C(r)) = \sigma_C(u_{R'}(r))$

(3) $\sigma_C(r) = u_{R'}(\sigma_C(n_{R'=(B_1,\ldots,B_k)}(r)))$

Theorem 21.5

Let $R = (A_1, \ldots, A_n, R_1, \ldots, R_m)$, r be a relation over R, $X \subseteq \text{names}(R)$ and $R_i = (B_1, \ldots, B_k)$. Then

$$u_{R_i}(\pi_{XR_i}(r)) = \pi_{XB_1\ldots B_k}(u_{R_i}(r))$$

However, a corresponding statement for nest does not hold in general, that is

$$n_{R'=(B_1,\ldots,B_k)}(\pi_{XB_1\ldots B_k}(r)) \neq \pi_{XR'}(n_{R'=(B_1,\ldots,B_k)}(r))$$

Indeed, consider the following relation r:

r	A	B	C
	0	0	1
	0	1	1
	0	1	2

Then $n_{D=(B)}(\pi_{AB}(r))$ is the following relation r_1:

r_1	A	D
		B
	0	0
		1

On the other hand, $\pi_{AD}(n_{D=(B)}(r))$ is the following relation r_2:

r_2	A	D
		B
	0	0
		1
	0	1

Obviously, $r_1 \neq r_2$.

Natural join

Finally, one binary operation on nested relations is introduced which extends the natural join as defined in Chapter 8. The new definition is stated for two operands only.

Definition 21.10

Let R and S be two formats, let r and s be relations over R and S, respectively, and let Z = names(R) ∩ names(S), X = names(R)−Z, Y = names(S)−Z:

$$\begin{aligned} r \bowtie s := \{\mu \mid\ & \mu \text{ is a tuple over format } P \\ & \text{with names}(P) = \text{names}(R) \cup \text{names}(S) \\ & \wedge (\exists\, \nu \in r)(\exists\, \rho \in s)\ \mu[X] = \nu[X] \\ & \wedge\ \mu[Y] = \rho[Y]\ \wedge\ \mu[Z] = \nu[Z] = \rho[Z]\} \end{aligned}$$

is called the **natural join** of r and s.

Speaking in terms of the structure trees T_R and T_S of the formats associated with the two join operands r and s, the above definition requires equality of tuples participating in the join on those common (attribute or format) names which are direct sons of the root. In this way, difficulties arising from different depths of nesting of attributes or subformats are avoided.

As an example for a natural join involving nested relations, consider the following relations r and s:

r	A	B	F	
			C	D
	1	1	1	1
			2	2
			1	3
	2	1	3	1
			2	2
			1	1
	2	2	1	2
			3	2
	4	2	3	2

s	E	B	F	
			C	D
	1	1	1	1
			1	3
			2	2
	3	2	3	2
	4	1	3	1
			4	2

Then $r \bowtie s$ is the following relation:

$r \bowtie s$	A	E	B	F	
				C	D
	1	1	1	1	1
				1	3
				2	2
	4	3	2	3	2

Clearly, several reasonable ways exist for defining a join operation for nested relations (see Exercise 11), which may differ with respect to their properties.

As a conclusion of this section, it should have become clear that the relational model as introduced earlier in this text can indeed be generalized for coping with complex objects. On the other hand, in order to make the resulting nested relational model the basis of a DBMS, (among other things) a language is needed for querying (and updating) databases in this model. To this end, the discussion above should have exposed some of the problems that may arise and need to be addressed. In particular, some of the 'nice' rules that hold for ordinary relational algebra (see Chapter 8) and which, for instance, are applied in query optimization, might be lost. Thus, restrictions (along the lines of the condition stated in Theorem 21.2) seem to be desirable in this context; these and other issues are still subject to research in the area.

21.3 A generalization

This section outlines another approach to model complex objects, which will easily be seen to subsume both the flat and the nested relational model. It makes use of **type constructors** found in high-level programming languages like Pascal, adapted to the database context. The description of this model also serves as a preparation for the discussion of *object-oriented* concepts in the following chapter; as will also become apparent, the approach is easily extendable further.

To introduce the discussion in this section, first reconsider the basic way in which 'structures' are formed in the relational model and its generalization discussed in the previous section. In an ordinary relation, an attribute value may only be atomic, whereas in a nested relation, an attribute value may be either atomic or a relation. Speaking in terms of (data types in) programming languages (or of structured types in Postgres), two constructors are applied in both cases, the **set constructor** and the **tuple constructor**, to derive complex types from primitive (atomic) ones. For ordinary relations, the tuple constructor is used first to obtain the format (structure) of a relation from attributes; then the set constructor is applied to obtain a relation 'schema' as a time-invariant description of relations as sets of tuples. In the nested relational model, both constructors are used as well, but now in a (strictly) alternating fashion: A nested relation is a set of tuples, in which components may again be sets of tuples, and so on.

The model described in this section gives up this restriction of alternate application of the two constructors; specifically, a complex object is obtained from atomic values by using the set and tuple constructors in any order. As a result, one may have a tuple in which one of the components is a tuple, a set of 'atoms', a set of sets, and so on.

As before, the model is defined in two steps: as a generalization of (nested) formats, *complex object types* are defined first, which are basically derived from atomic (domain) types by applying the constructors. Following the same construction process, *complex objects* are defined next, which are objects of a given (complex object) type.

Definition 21.11

Complex object types are (recursively) defined as follows:

(i) Let D be a name for a domain, then D is a (domain) type.

(ii) If $T_1, \ldots, T_n$ are (names of) types and $A_1, \ldots, A_n$ are distinct attributes, then

$$T = [A_1 : T_1, \ldots, A_n : T_n]$$

is a (tuple) type, where $T \neq T_i$ for $1 \leq i \leq n$.
(Note that the distinction between a *type* and a *type name* is neglected here. Strictly speaking, *types* are formed over a set of *type names* by applying (eventually 'trivial') *constructors.*)

(iii) If T is a type, then $T' = \{T\}$ is a (set) type, where $T' \neq T$.

(iv) Recursion is not allowed in the definition of a type. (More formally, the declaration of a type denoted by T is *non-recursive* if T does not occur in the set of all type names used in the declaration of T.)

The requirement that recursion is forbidden excludes type definitions like '$T = [A : T]$' (where recursion occurs at the 'same level' of nesting) or

Books = { *Book* }
Book = [*Author*: ..., *Title*: ..., *References: Books*]

(where recursion occurs at different levels of nesting). Thus, the 'generalization' presented in this section basically consists of giving up the strict alternation in the use of the set and tuple constructors and of allowing 'arbitrary' domains.

Although recursion in type definitions (with respect to names) is excluded here, it *is* allowed to repeat already defined types in the definition of a new one (see example below). For the examples that follow, it is assumed that the following names for domains are available:

integer, *string* and *date*.

Then the following are examples of types:

CHILD = [*CNAME* : *string*, *BIRTHDATE* : *date*, *SEX* : *string*]
Children = { *CHILD* }

is a tuple type, as is

SKILL = [*SKTYPE* : *string*, *EXAMDATE* : *date*]
Skills = { *SKILL* }

These types are next used to declare another tuple type in which two set types occur:

EMP = [*ID* : *integer*, *NAME* : *string*, *ADDR* : *string*,
CHILDREN : *Children*, *SKILLS* : *Skills*]

Finally, a type *EMPLOYEES* = { *EMP* } defines a set type whose 'data elements' will be of type *EMP* (a set of employees).

While the previous example showed that a nested format can be represented as a (complex) type, the next example makes use of the fact that set and tuple constructors no longer need to alternate: a type *PERSON* as was used in Chapter 11 can be defined as follows:

PERSON = [*PNAME* : *string*,
HOME_ADDR : *ADDR*,
SPEAKS : *LANGUAGES*,
WORKS_FOR : *COMPANY*]

ADDR = [*STREET* : *string*, *CITY* : *string*,
ZIP : *integer*]

LANGUAGES = { *string* }

COMPANY = [*CNAME* : *string*, *LOCATION* : *ADDR*]

Definition 21.12

Complex objects are recursively defined as follows:

(i) If D is a domain type and dom(D) is a set of distinct values associated with D, then every $o \in \text{dom}(D)$ is an (atomic) object of type D.

(ii) If $T = [A_1 : T_1, \ldots, A_n : T_n]$ is a tuple type and o_i is an object of type T_i, $1 \leq i \leq n$, then

$$[A_1 : o_1, A_2 : o_2, \ldots, A_n : o_n]$$

is a (tuple) object (of type T).

(iii) If $T' = \{T\}$ is a set type and $o_1, o_2, \ldots, o_n$ are objects of type T, then

$$\{o_1, o_2, \ldots, o_n\}$$

is a (set) object (of type T').

Continuing the employee example from above, the following is an object of type *EMP* (see Figure 21.6):

$$\begin{aligned} e_1 = [\ & ID: 100,\ NAME: \text{Joe},\ ADDR: \text{LA}, \\ & CHILDREN: \{[\ CNAME: \text{Mary},\ BIRTHDATE: 120261, \\ & \qquad SEX: \text{F}\ ], \\ & \quad [\ CNAME: \text{Peter},\ BIRTHDATE: 041465,\ SEX: \text{M}\ ], \\ & \quad [\ CNAME: \text{John},\ BIRTHDATE: 082270,\ SEX: \text{M}\ ]\}, \\ & SKILLS: \{[\ TYPE: \text{driv\_lic},\ EXAMDATE: 121255\ ], \\ & \quad [\ TYPE: \text{phd\_cs},\ EXAMDATE: 021565\ ]\}] \end{aligned}$$

As the reader can easily see, a relational tuple, a nested tuple, a flat relation and a nested relation are all examples of complex objects. Even a relational database can be described in this model as a single complex object (which is a set of relations that in turn are sets of tuples).

It should also be straightforward to extend the model described above, for example by introducing a **list** type (for ordered multisets). These ideas will be used in the next chapter when attention is shifted from value-based models to object-oriented ones. For more information on the model for complex objects defined above and related ones, as well as on query languages for such models, the reader is referred to the references cited in the Bibliographic Notes.

Chapter 22
Object-Oriented Database Management

In this chapter a branch of research and development is considered which has gained considerable interest in recent years in the area of database management, and which is generally subsumed under the term **object-orientation**. This paradigm has been studied in programming languages for some time already, but its use and application in the context of databases is new. First a survey is given of the central principles of object-orientation and the main reasons behind them. A variety of issues are currently still under investigation, but a preliminary stage has already been reached and is manifested in the release of commercially available systems. One such system, **GemStone**, is described in some detail.

22.1 Principles of object-orientation

As has (hopefully) been communicated by the preceding chapters, the database field is concerned with the management of large amounts of persistent, reliable and shared data. As was explained in Chapter 20, there is an increasing interest now in transferring this approach to non-standard areas of application, but a number of problems have to be solved in order to achieve satisfactory results. While Chapter 21 concentrated on extending the relational model, which seems reasonable because this data model is now very well understood even from a theoretical point of view, a more general perspective is pursued here; it can be motivated as follows.

Assume that a database for VLSI circuits (like the adder discussed in the preceding chapters) has been built up using the relational model. Now suppose that a chip designer (or some tool used in the design process) needs data on a microprocessor in its entirety. A first approach for the designer could be to read through Chapter 8 of this text on relational algebra, and then to start writing the (probably complex) query expression(s) that plug together the various relations or pieces thereof over which the data on the microprocessor is spread, and finally retrieve the data desired. If the database designer has managed to set up the database so that some building blocks of the microprocessor (like registers) may recursively appear in various components (like ALU and control store), the chip designer might even end up finding out that relational algebra alone does not help (because of its 'limited' computational power, see Section 8.3). As a result, the designer decides to incorporate a host language; however, it is now necessary to define data structures in that language into whose instances (variables) the data retrieved from the database can be 'loaded' for further processing. If the language at hand is, say, Pascal, the designer will probably use record types as well as variables of these types as 'cursors' through relations. The problem with this approach is that the abstraction available in the database language (namely that query operands *and* results are of type 'relation') is lost during the transition to the programming language, a phenomenon that is generally termed the *impedance mismatch* between a database language and a general-purpose programming language.

The impedance mismatch as illustrated by the above example has led people in the database field to take into consideration 'technologies' that have been developed elsewhere, in particular in the field of programming languages, and to combine them with new database concepts (like complex objects) as well as traditional ones (like persistence, reliability and data sharing). Two approaches in this direction are the *logic-oriented* and the *object-oriented* approaches; while the former was merely briefly touched upon in Chapter 8, the latter will be discussed in more detail in what follows.

Independent research in the area of programming languages has a long tradition too. In particular, it was discovered a long time ago that conventional procedural or *imperative* languages are strongly tied to the specific model of a computer known as the *von Neumann machine.* Opposed to this (and motivated, among other things, by the so-called von Neumann *bottleneck*), there is an increased interest today in *descriptive* languages, which for example has led to logic programming as well as object-oriented programming. Especially in the latter field, some people are working on adding database functionality to those languages or language environments, so that *object-oriented database systems* can be considered as the merging of efforts in two previously distinct fields.

Given this historical development, it should no longer come as a surprise that many concepts and issues now discussed in the context of object-oriented database management already have a tradition in various programming languages. To the reader familiar with modern programming languages, this will become evident in the remainder of this section, where the main characteristics of an object-oriented system will be described; in brief, these are:

(1) objects, messages and methods,

(2) data abstraction and encapsulation, types and classes,

(3) object identity,

(4) inheritance,

(5) overloading and late binding.

Hence, a *database system* can be considered *object-oriented* if it shares these characteristics and in addition provides general DBMS functionality as mentioned above. The following description of these characteristics is somewhat directed towards Section 22.2, so that alternative descriptions found in the literature might vary slightly in the use of terms and notions.

22.1.1 Objects, messages and methods

The central notion in any object-oriented database system is that of an **object** and this will be discussed first. Basically, everything in an object-oriented database system is considered an object; examples include numbers, character strings, sets of numbers, sequences of tuples, type declarations, database schemas, and even a data dictionary. Common to all objects are two basic characteristics: an object has a **private memory** and a **public interface**. The private memory stores the state of the object, whereas the public interface is a 'protocol' consisting of a set of

messages the object responds to. Objects communicate with other objects (and users communicate with objects) by passing such messages, which are requests for the receiver to change its state, return a result or both. The means by which an object responds to a message is a **method**, which is a procedure that is invoked when an object receives a message.

22.1.2 Types, classes and encapsulation

A **type** describes a set of objects with the same characteristics. From a programming language point of view, the arrival of the notion of type has been a major step in devising languages that are capable of supporting *structured programming*, in which programs are developed by decomposing the problem at hand based on the recognition of certain abstractions. The data abstraction useful for this purpose should classify objects according to their static complexity and structure *and* according to their (expected or intended) dynamic behaviour. Such behaviour can be expressed in terms of the *operations* that are applicable to the object (the messages it responds to), which form the only means for creating, modifying and accessing it.

Many programming languages (including SIMULA, CLU, Modula-2, Ada and Smalltalk) allow the programmer to define an **abstract data type** (ADT) by providing special language constructs for the **encapsulation** of structure and operations (see also the description of the Postgres data model in Section 21.1). Thus, encapsulation is the principle that data *and* operations should be modelled at the same time. As a result, an object gets the 'structure' described above; its private memory contains the current state of the object and together with the methods, which are implementations of the operations, forms its *implementation part.* The public interface provides the methods (in the form of messages) and hence is a specification of the set of operations which can be performed on the object.

The important point is that the operations included in the definition of an ADT are exclusively applicable to objects of this type only. Thus, if T and T' denote distinct ADTs for which operations o^T and $o^{T'}$ have been defined, and x $[x']$ is an object of type T $[T']$, respectively, then

$$o^T(x) \text{ and } o^{T'}(x')$$

are legal applications of operations, whereas

$$o^T(x') \text{ and } o^{T'}(x)$$

are not. For a concrete example, if x and y are objects of type *integer* whose ADT definition includes an operation '+' for addition, then '$+(x, y)$' is defined; however, if u and v were (other) objects of type *real* and '+'

```
class complex (x,y); real x,y;
begin real angle, radius;
   radius := sqrt(x**2 + y**2);
   if abs(x) < epsilon
      then
         begin
            if abs(y) < epsilon
               then error
               else
                  begin
                     if y > epsilon
                        then angle := pi/2;
                        else angle := 3*pi/2
                  end
         end
      else angle := arctan(y/x)
end complex;
```

Figure 22.1 SIMULA class declaration for complex numbers.

was not included in the corresponding ADT definition, '$+(u, v)$' would be undefined, since '+' has so far been defined for integers only.

ADT facilities come under various names in the world of programming languages (like 'class' in SIMULA or 'cluster' in CLU). As an example, consider the declaration of a SIMULA class for complex numbers in polar form shown in Figure 22.1, where parameters x and y denote the components of the complex number in Cartesian form, the local variables `angle` and `radius` denote them in polar form, functions `sqrt` and `arctan` are built-in, and `error` is a procedure accessible from the class; `epsilon` and `pi` are global variables denoting a positive real value that approximates 0 and the value of π, respectively.

In SIMULA, a class declaration defines a *template* for some set of objects; each *instance* (concrete object) can be referred to only via a pointer. For example, the following first declares c to be a pointer to a 'complex' and then makes it point to a newly created complex number:

```
ref (complex) c;
c :- new complex (1.0,1.0)
```

The second statement sends the class 'complex' the message 'new', thereby asking it to create a new instance with parameters $x = 1.0$ and $y = 1.0$. Notice that the declaration of 'complex' shown in Figure 22.1 does not yet include procedures for implementing the operations on the class objects. For example, for being able to add complex numbers a procedure with the following heading must be included:

```
procedure add (operand); ref (complex) operand;
        ⋮
```

In the context of object-oriented database systems, the notion of a class can be distinguished from that of a type (although the two terms are often used interchangeably) in the following sense. While a *type* can be considered as a *compile-time* notion used for checking correctness, a *class* is, in a sense, a *run-time* notion used for the creation (performing the operation `new` on the class) and manipulation of objects. Speaking in terms of the relational model, a 'type' corresponds to a schema, while a 'class' corresponds to an instance (a *set* of objects).

Finally, the structural portion of an ADT as used in object-oriented database systems consists of **instance variables**, which are comparable to the attributes of a relation schema; a concrete object (of a given type) consists of *values* for these instance variables, which may (and often will) be references to other objects. ADTs can hence straightforwardly be used to define *complex* objects (see Definition 22.1).

22.1.3 Object identity

The next important characteristic of an object-oriented system is that every object in the system has an existence which is *independent* of its value; in other words, **identity** is the property of an object which distinguishes it from every other object. If identity is supported, it becomes possible to distinguish whether two given objects are *equal* (that is, have the same value) from whether they are *identical* (that is, are the same object).

To illustrate the concept of identity, consider a relational database containing the following relation:

Emp	*Name*	*Child*
	Peter	John
	Joe	Mary
	Susan	Bill

If a second employee named Peter, who also has a child named John, was hired, this would not be representable in the above database, since a relation is a *set*, and a set is not allowed to contain duplicate elements. Hence, although there exist two distinct 'employee objects' valued '(Peter, John)', as soon as the second was entered into the above relation one of them would disappear, since there already exists another, equal object. Also, if there was another tuple valued '(Mary, John)', it would have to remain open whether or not Peter and Mary are parents of the same child John. It follows that the relational model is basically unable to support object identity.

A solution to this problem commonly used in applications of relational systems is to introduce an (often artificial) *identifier key*. For example, if the relation shown above had a third attribute *Emp#*, the problem of distinguishing two employees named Peter with a child named John could immediately be solved as follows:

Emp	*Emp#*	*Name*	*Child*
	1	Peter	John
	2	Joe	Mary
	3	Susan	Bill
	4	Peter	John

(Clearly, what would still cause difficulties in this latter approach is, for example, the case that Peter (with *EMP#* = 1) has more than one child; to capture the identity of every employee as well as that of each of his or her children, additional provisions would be needed which go beyond the modelling capabilities of the relational approach.)

Several problems arise with the identifier key as a concept for supporting object identity, which result from the fact that the concepts of data *value* and *identity* actually are mixed. One such problem is that key values can now no longer be allowed to change, although they are user-defined descriptive data. For example, if the name of a department was used as a key in a relation and the company undergoes a reorganization during which these names change, the strict implication would be that the department with the old name no longer exists, which is not the case. Another problem is that the choice of attributes used for an identifier key may need to change over time. For example, one company may use employee numbers of their own to identify employees, while another uses social security numbers for that purpose; if the two companies merge, one is required to change its employee identifiers, which would again cause a discontinuity in identity for their employees.

In contrast to relational systems, object identity *is* supported in network (and hierarchical) systems. Recall from Chapter 5 that each record stored in a network database is equipped by the system with a *database-key value*, which is globally unique and even survives a deletion of the record from the database (since it is a physical address). As a result, record objects can be represented and manipulated independent of their values, which is why network systems can be considered closer to object-orientation than relational ones.

What the above discussion implies is that the identifier of an object has to be considered as being distinct from values for its instance variables. Speaking in terms of formal models of data, as in Section 21.3, this could, for example, lead to the following preliminary definition of objects.

Definition 22.1

Let X be a set of attributes, I be a set of identifiers, and Dom be a set of domain types ('base' or 'atomic' types). An *object* is a triple

$$o = (identifier,\ constructor,\ value),$$

where

(i) *identifier* $\in I$,

(ii) *constructor* $\in$ { *atom*, *set*, *tuple* },

(iii) if *constructor* $\equiv$ *atom*, then *value* $\in \text{dom}(D)$, where $D \in \text{Dom}$; if *constructor* $\equiv$ *set*, then *value* $= \{i_1, \ldots, i_n\}$, where $i_j \in I$, $1 \leq j \leq n$, and $i_j \neq i_k$ for $j \neq k$; if *constructor* $\equiv$ *tuple*, then *value* $= [A_1 : i_1, \ldots, A_n : i_n]$, where $A_i \in X$, $1 \leq i \leq n$, $A_i \neq A_j$ for $i \neq j$ and $i_j \in I$, $1 \leq j \leq n$,

(iv) recursion is not allowed.

Notice that this definition can be considered as an extension of Definition 21.12 by object identity and allows for objects of arbitrary nesting (and graphical structure). For example, the employee object e_1 from Section 21.3, which had the form

$$\begin{aligned} e_1 = [\ & ID : 100,\ NAME : \text{Joe},\ ADDR : \text{LA}, \\ & CHILDREN : \{[\ CNAME : \text{Mary},\ BIRTHDATE : 120261, \\ & \qquad SEX : \text{F}\ ], \\ & \quad [\ CNAME : \text{Peter},\ BIRTHDATE : 041465,\ SEX : \text{M}\ ], \\ & \quad [\ CNAME : \text{John},\ BIRTHDATE : 082270,\ SEX : \text{M}\ ]\}, \\ & SKILLS : \{[\ TYPE : \text{driv\_lic},\ EXAMDATE : 121255\ ], \\ & \quad [\ TYPE : \text{phd\_cs},\ EXAMDATE : 021565\ ]\}], \end{aligned}$$

now gets the following form (where *atom* is used as a synonym for *integer*, *string* or *date* as needed):

$$e_1 = (i,\ tuple,\ v_1)$$

where

$$\begin{aligned} v_1 = [\ & ID : i_1,\ NAME : i_2,\ ADDR : i_3,\ CHILDREN : i_4, \\ & SKILLS : i_5\ ] \end{aligned}$$

Next, i_1 identifies the following object:

$$o_1 = (i_1,\ atom,\ 100)$$

(Similarly for i_2 and i_3.) Notice that the *ID* instance variable is not really needed any more. i_4 identifies the following set-type object:

$o_2 = (i_4,\ set,\ v_2)$

where

$v_2 = \{i_6, i_7, i_8\}$

and each identifier denotes a 'child object', the first of which is as follows:

$o_3 = (i_6,\ tuple,\ v_3)$
$v_3 = [\ CNAME : i_9,\ BIRTHDATE : i_{10},\ SEX : i_{11}\ ]$
$o_4 = (i_9,\ atom,\ \text{Mary}),$
$o_5 = (i_{10},\ atom,\ 120261),$
$o_6 = (i_{11},\ atom,\ \text{F})$

This example indicates at least two important aspects. First, identity is well supported in this model. For example, two employee objects $e_1 = (i_1,\ tuple,\ v_1)$ and $e_2 = (i_2,\ tuple,\ v_2)$ would be considered identical (equal) if $i_1 = i_2$ ($v_1 = v_2$), respectively (assuming that all objects occurring in the database have distinct identities).

Secondly, a consequent support of object identity implies that every character string or every number occurring in a database has an identity of its own, which poses an enormous burden on the system in terms of managing identifiers. Since this may have a serious (negative) impact on performance, efficient implementation schemes are needed for supporting identity; it may help not to consider 'atoms' (numbers, strings) as objects in the strict sense. Indeed, the GemStone system described in the next section chooses a 'direct' representation (not via identifiers) for atomic objects.

The support of object identity has two important implications. (Sub)objects can now be *shared* by (higher order) objects; as a consequence, *updating* an object which is shared by other objects is done only once, but the result simultaneously goes into effect for all the sharers. For example, two flights may share the same plane in an airline application; if the plane is exchanged for a bigger one, both flights get new planes at one stroke.

22.1.4 Inheritance

Recall from Section 21.1 that for IS-A related 'types' (like *STUDENT* and *PERSON*) it seems appropriate to let the subtype *inherit* properties (attributes) from its associated supertype, in order to avoid a (redundant) repetition of those properties. In an object-oriented system, where types are ADTs comprising structure *and* behaviour, this concept is extended to capture operations as well. Hence, **inheritance** is the concept that allows objects of even different structure to share operations related to their common part.

As an example, consider an airline application (see Chapter 4) with types *EMPLOYEE* and *PILOT*, where every pilot IS-A employee. If both types were defined as ADTs, the operations on *EMPLOYEE* could include *hire*, *fire*, *raise_pay* and *transfer* (from one department to another); similarly, the operations on *PILOT* could include *promote* (for example, from copilot to captain) and *overtime* (for computing the number of hours a pilot has been flying too long). If *PILOT* is then declared as a subtype of *EMPLOYEE*, the former would inherit all the (instance variables and) operations from the latter, so that pilots could be hired, fired, transferred or get a pay raise *without* the corresponding procedures being written again.

As a result, the database designer has provided the user with a concise and precise description of the application; also, this approach facilitates the reusability of code, since every 'program' is 'installed' at the level at which the largest number of objects can share it.

Consider, on the other hand, a system not supporting inheritance, like a standard relational DBMS. In this case, application programs would have to be written for hiring, firing and transferring employees, for raising their salary *and* for hiring, firing, transferring and promoting pilots as well as for raising their salary and for computing their overtime. Clearly, the effort is highly redundant and also contains more sources for mistakes.

As will also be seen in Section 22.2, many object-oriented systems have a generic type 'object' as the most general type (forming the root of a *type* or *class hierarchy*), so that every other type is 'by default' a subtype of type 'object'. Consequently, all subtypes inherit the operations declared on 'object', that is, all objects of any subtype respond to the messages that an object of type 'object' responds to (like the message 'new' for instantiating a new object of some type).

22.1.5 Overriding and late binding

While inheritance supports the idea of reusing the *same operation* on *distinct subtypes* of some type that are related, there are cases in which one wants to reuse the *same name* for *different operations*. As an example, consider an operation named `display`; let its purpose be to display an object on a screen. Depending on the object, different kinds of display operations are intended. If the object is a picture, a bitmap should appear on the screen; if the object is a person, a mask showing relevant information on this person should be displayed; if the object is the adjacency matrix of a graph, its graphical representation should be shown.

In a conventional system, a specific `display` operation would be implemented for each type to which it should apply, and these operations would probably go under different names. If they did not, the system would have to check at compile-time whether the display operation specified conformed to the type of the object to which it was to be applied.

In an object-oriented system, however, it would be sufficient to specify one `display` operation at the level of the type 'object' (which commonly is the most general type available, as was mentioned above), so that this operation has a single name and can be used on any object of type 'object' or one of its subtypes (like pictures, persons or graphs). In addition, the body of the procedure implementing the `display` operation is *redefined* for each of these subtypes according to their specific properties, which is called **overriding** (of a previously stated specification). As a result, a single name ('`display`') is used for a variety of procedures; in other words, the name is **overloaded**. If the `display` operation is then applied to a specific object, the system has to determine the type of this object and choose the appropriate version of `display`; thus, the system can no longer bind operation names to procedures at compile-time, but only at run-time, which is called **late binding**.

This concludes the introduction to the principles of object-orientation. The above description covers only features that are considered mandatory for object-oriented systems; clearly, in order to make such a system an object-oriented *database* system, it additionally needs to support central database features, including high-level languages, especially for *ad hoc* queries, data sharing and persistence, transaction support or secondary memory management. Several other features are at present considered optional for object-oriented systems; these include multiple inheritance and type checking and inferencing (see the Bibliographic Notes).

22.2 The GemStone system (Servio Logic)

22.2.1 System overview

In this section, the **GemStone** object-oriented database management system is described, which has been developed and is now marketed by Servio Logic Development Corporation. It combines the concepts of an object-oriented language, in this case Smalltalk, with the functionality of a DBMS. Specifically, its main characteristics are as follows:

(1) It supports large collections of large objects; an individual object may be simple or complex and, as a byte string, may occupy up to a gigabyte of storage; a database may contain up to 2 billion objects.

(2) It supports object-oriented concepts like user-defined types and behaviour, object identity, and inheritance; methods can even be created and modified dynamically.

(3) It has a uniform language for data definition and manipulation, **OPAL**, which can be considered as a descendant of Smalltalk-80; programs written in OPAL are themselves objects in the system,

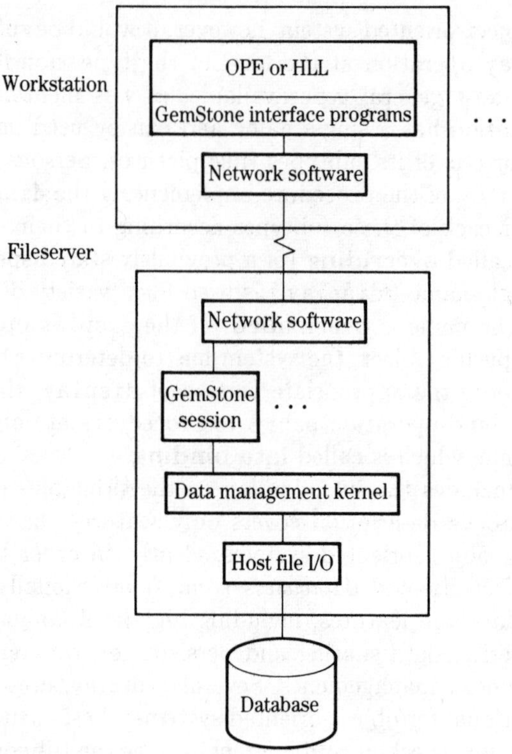

Figure 22.2 The GemStone architecture.

and the OPAL compiler and interpreter both call on the data management kernel of the system for accessing objects.

(4) A variety of high-level languages (HLLs), including Smalltalk, C, C++, FORTRAN, Pascal and Ada, can additionally be used for writing application programs, and GemStone can interface to SQL databases.

(5) It provides a multi-user environment with security and authorization facilities, indexing and clustering for storing objects, and it supports data integrity and even the replication of data (up to six copies can be kept of each object).

The global architecture of GemStone is shown in Figure 22.2. Basically, the system has a *client-server* architecture, where the latter acts as a host for the *data management kernel* of GemStone and typically is a minicomputer like a DEC VAX. The kernel ('Stone') is responsible for managing secondary storage, concurrency control, recovery and authorization, and supports associative access; it also manages workspaces for active sessions. The kernel uses unique surrogates, called *object-oriented pointers* (OOPs), for referring to objects, and it uses an *object table* to map an OOP to a physical location; the object table can have up to 2^{31} entries, which results in the above mentioned maximal number of 2 billion objects in a database ($2^{31} \approx 2 \cdot 10^9$). Finally, the kernel is built upon the file system of the underlying operating system (typically VMS), and only provides operators for structural update and access. An object may be stored separately from its subobjects, but the OOPs for the values of its instance variables are always grouped together.

The kernel communicates through interprocess channels with some number of instances of a virtual machine incorporating a compiler or an interpreter for OPAL. The data management kernel and the communicating virtual machine processes, which are also called *Gem processes* or *GemStone sessions*, together constitute the server. Technically, each such process may involve the compilation of OPAL methods into bytecode as well as the execution of that code, and this 'layer' of the system also provides authentication and session control.

Each virtual machine process communicates with a host- or workstation-resident *GemStone interface program* that performs terminal I/O and other user interface functions. When this interface program runs directly on the host, user I/O is done on an ordinary terminal attached to that host; when it runs on a workstation, I/O, screen management and user interface functions are all executed by this workstation. Workstation ('client') programs can communicate with host-resident GemStone software via Ethernet or RS-232 links; workstations currently supported by the system include Tektronix 440x, Sun 3/4, Apple Mac-II and IBM PCs.

The GemStone interface programs call on libraries of functions or methods for the high-level language used; for example, the *GemStone C Interface* (GCI) comprises a library of C functions. These functions can be called from an application program to compose and execute OPAL code in response to user requests, to send messages to GemStone objects, or to access the data management kernel directly. More specifically, the interface functions can be used:

(1) to build data objects as data structures in an HLL program and transmit them to GemStone; for example, an object may be an OPAL query which is sent to GemStone for execution;

(2) to import GemStone data objects into the 'memory' of an interface program for manipulation as HLL data structure (for example, to format the result of an OPAL query for display);

(3) to perform system functions like committing a transaction, or beginning and ending a GemStone session.

Thus, the communication links between the server and the interface programs are needed for transmitting objects, including OPAL code and results, as byte streams, since OPAL itself has no direct terminal or disk I/O facilities. In addition, the interface program 'layer' provides 'structural access' calls which perform the following functions:

(1) determination of the size, class or implementation of an object,

(2) inspection of a class-defining object (see below),

(3) object creation,

(4) fetching/storing bytes or pointers from/in an object.

To aid the user in building, executing and debugging OPAL database programs, GemStone includes a set of special-purpose interface programs called the *OPAL Programming Environment* (OPE), which provides program editing and database browsing tools, and support for the creation of OPAL classes and methods as well as for bulk loading and dumping GemStone databases.

The following subsections introduce the OPAL language. In general, OPAL has the scope and power of a general-purpose programming language; in addition to the ability to read and write stored objects, OPAL provides multiple flow-of-control constructs, a maths package, error handlers and system calls, so that many applications can be written entirely in this language. Clearly, the following subsections cover only basic features of this language as they pertain to DDL and DML capabilities; for more information, the reader is advised to consult the original OPAL documents referenced in the Bibliographic Notes.

22.2.2 Introduction to the OPAL language

This subsection is concerned with the basic OPAL capabilities. First recall from Section 22.1 that *objects* in an object-oriented system have a private memory and a public interface, and that communication between objects takes place by exchanging *messages* which are requests to execute *methods*; objects which have the same internal structure and behaviour are grouped together in a class. In OPAL, the methods and structure common to all instances of a class are kept in a **class-defining object** (CDO) (that is, the definition of a new class is itself considered an object); all instances contain a reference to 'their' CDO. In addition, every object in GemStone is an instance of exactly one class, a feature not agreed upon by every other object model and system.

Most objects are internally divided into *instance variables*, each of which can hold a value. As a first example, consider the *Employee* object shown in Figure 22.3; the following conventions are used for identifiers: (1)

```
Employee
  empName
    PersonName
      first
        String
          Ray
      last
        String
          Ross
  ssNo
    SmallInteger
      111223333
  address
    StreetAddress
      stNumber
        SmallInteger
          1055
      street
        String
          Alameda
      city
        String
          Gresham
  salary
    SmallInteger
      45578
```

Figure 22.3 Employee object with four instance variables.

The names of *private* OPAL variables like instance variables begin with lower-case letters; (2) the names of *shared* objects like classes, class or pool variables (see below) begin with upper-case letters.

The object shown in Figure 22.3 has the four instance variables *empName, ssNo, address* and *salary. empName* holds an object which is an instance of the class *PersonName*; similarly, *address* holds an object of the class *StreetAddress.* An object of class *PersonName* in turn has the two instance variables *first* and *last*; an object of class *StreetAddress* has the three instance variables *stNumber, street* and *city.* Hence, values of instance variables need not be simple data values, but can be (references to) other objects of arbitrary complexity.

Not all objects are internally divided into instance variables. Specifically, certain basic types like *SmallInteger* or *Character* are not decomposed further. These basic types internally have a direct representation (without separate identifier).

An OPAL **message expression** has the following basic form:

receiver list-of-selectors [list-of-arguments]

The first component of a message is an identifier (or an expression) denoting an object to receive and interpret the message. The specification of the **receiver** is followed by one or more identifiers called **selectors** that specify the message to be sent. Finally, a number of messages has a third part consisting of one or more **arguments** that pass information with the message; the arguments are analogous to procedure or function arguments in conventional languages, and may in turn be written as message expressions. Every message returns a result to its sender; a result is also an object.

As a simple example, in the message expression

```
2 + 8
```

object 2 is the receiver, + is the selector and 8 is the argument. When object 2 sees the selector, it looks for the corresponding method in its private memory and finds instructions to add the argument to itself and return the result; thus, object 2 returns another numeric object 10 in this case.

The selectors an object understands, that is, the selectors for which instructions are stored in the **method dictionary** of an object, are determined by the class the object belongs to. It will be described below how classes and their selectors are created (see Sections 22.2.3 and 22.2.4, respectively).

OPAL knows three types of messages, which are classified according to the kinds and numbers of their selectors and arguments:

(1) **Unary messages** have no arguments, and have selectors that are a single identifier. For example,

```
7 negated
```

tells number 7 to return its negated value. For the employee example above, let *emp* denote a variable holding an *Employee* object. If there exists a unary message `firstName` to retrieve the employee's first name, then

```
emp firstName
```

returns a string object representing the first name of *emp*.

(2) **Binary message expressions** have a receiver, a single argument and a single message selector consisting of one or two non-alphanumeric characters. For example,

```
8 * 4
```

tells 8 to multiply itself by 4, which returns 32. Moreover, binary messages are used for comparisons. For example,

```
4 < 5
```

would simply return 'true'. Similarly,

```
myObject = yourObject
```

returns 'true' if both objects have the same value(s), whereas

```
myObject == yourObject
```

returns 'true' if both objects are identical (have the same OOP). For a more complex example, consider

```
(emp1 salary) <= (emp2 salary)
```

in which receiver and argument of the '<=' binary message are both results of unary message expressions.

(3) **Keyword messages** contain a receiver and up to 15 keyword-argument pairs, where each keyword (each selector) is an identifier ending in a colon. For example, the keyword message

```
7 rem:  3
```

will return the remainder from the division of 7 by 3. The following keyword message expression has two keyword-argument pairs:

```
arrayOfStrings at:  (2+1) put:  'Curly'
```

It puts the string 'Curly' at index position 3 in the receiver.

As some of the above examples have shown, message expressions, whose complete syntax is described in Section 22.2.4, can be nested within each other, where parentheses may be useful for determining the order of evaluation. For example,

```
2 + 2 negated
```

returns 0, while

```
(2 + 2) negated
```

returns −4.

In addition, series of messages can be sent to the same object without repeating the name of the receiver for each message. A *cascaded* message expression consists of the name of the receiver, a message, a semicolon and an arbitrary number of subsequent messages separated by semicolons. For example,

```
arrayOfComposers add:  'Mozart'; add:  'Beethoven'.
```

has the same effect as

```
arrayOfComposers add:  'Mozart'.
arrayOfComposers add:  'Beethoven'.
```

22.2.3 Structure definition in OPAL

In this subsection, the basics of defining the structural portion of a database 'schema' using OPAL are introduced. As was mentioned before, every GemStone object belongs to some class, which is a 'template' for a data structure together with a set of methods for updating and reading concrete instances of the structure. While objects themselves can hold data in many kinds of abstract structures, there are four basic 'storage formats' from which all others are built:

(1) *Atomic*: Objects such as integers or characters have no internal structure.

(2) *Named instance variables* are 'storage slots' of an object which can be referred to by *name* (see Figure 22.3), just like the attributes of a relation schema.

(3) *Indexable instance variables* are storage slots referred to by *number*; examples are *Array* objects, whose 'fields' are numbered (see `arrayOfStrings` above).

(4) *Anonymous instance variables* are variables of an object that are accessed neither by name nor by number, but by *value* (that is, associatively); variables of this type appear, for example, as *Set* objects.

The important point for defining classes in OPAL is that the language provides a large number of predefined or **kernel classes** which are organized in a **class hierarchy**, and each of which establishes some specialized structure and behaviour for storing and manipulating commonly used kinds of data. The hierarchy of kernel classes is shown in Figure 22.4. Each class in this hierarchy inherits both instance variables and methods from its *superclass* (that is, its 'parent class' in the hierarchy). Thus, to introduce a new class, the user has to determine the 'most appropriate' kernel class provided in OPAL, and to make the new class a *subclass* of this class; if no class fits the user's intention, the new class is defined to be a subclass of the class *Object*, which is the root of the class hierarchy and

```
Object
    Association
        SymbolAssociation
    Behaviour
        Class
        Metaclass
    Boolean
    Collection
        SequenceableCollection
            Array
                InvariantArray
                Repository
            String
                InvariantString
                    Symbol
        Bag
            Set
                Dictionary
                    SymbolDictionary
                        LanguageDictionary
                SymbolSet
                UserProfileSet
    CompiledMethod
    Magnitude
        Character
        DateTime
        Number
            Float
            Fraction
            Integer
                LargeNegativeInteger
                LargePositiveInteger
                SmallInteger
    MethodContext
        Block
            SelectionBlock
    Segment
    Stream
        PositionableStream
            ReadStream
            WriteStream
    System
    UndefinedObject
    UserProfile
```

Figure 22.4 OPAL kernel class hierarchy.

hence the most general class available. Some of the (other) kernel classes will briefly be described in the sequel.

Creating a new subclass of an already existing (kernel or user-defined) class is done by sending that class the message '`subclass`', which causes the receiver to create a subclass of itself, and which is understood by most kernel classes. The subclass creation message is a keyword message that has the following general form:

receiver subclass: '*subclass-name*'
instVarNames: ...
classVars: ...
poolDictionaries: ...
inDictionary: ...
constraints: ...
isInvariant: ... .

This message is sent to the specified *receiver* and asks it to create a new subclass named *subclass-name* with the characteristics as specified. In particular, 'instVarNames:' can take as argument a sequence of (up to 255) strings in the form

#('string1' 'string2' ...)

each of which is the name of an instance variable. The second keyword, 'classVars:', can have as argument one or more named *class variables* which are different from instance variables in that their values can be read or altered for all instances of a class simultaneously. For example, if an employee class has an instance variable *profession* and a class variable *PilotCount*, a method can be written to keep the latter number up-to-date for all instances, without accessing each instance individually (whereas updating *profession* requires an individual treatement of each instance).

The keyword 'poolDictionaries:' can have as argument a list of *pool variables*, which are special-purpose storage structures enabling any number of classes and their instances to share information. The 'inDictionary:' keyword is used to install the newly defined class in a particular dictionary. For example,

```
inDictionary: UserGlobals
```

would make the class in question available for future use. (The examples which follow will utilize only this dictionary.)

The instance variables of a class can be *constrained* to store certain kinds of objects only. To this end, the keyword 'constraints:' in a class creation message takes an argument which specifies the kinds of objects to which some or all instance variables may refer at run-time. For example, let an *Employee* class have an instance variable *name*, then

```
constraints:  #[ #[ #name, String ]]
```

would constrain names to be strings. Hence, the 'constraints:' keyword, among other things, resembles domain definitions in other types of database systems.

Finally, it can be specified in a class definition whether or not the instances of this class should be *invariant*, that is, unable to be modified; the argument to the corresponding 'isInvariant:' keyword is either 'true' or 'false'.

As a first example for using the DDL facilities of OPAL, consider a conventional relation describing *employees*, where each employee has a *name*, works in some *department* and receives a *salary*. In OPAL, a corresponding structure must be defined in two steps as follows:

(1) In the first step, a class for *tuple objects* must be defined, whose instances are individual tuples with the above attributes as (named) instance variables.

(2) In the second step, a *set object* is defined, whose elements are the tuple objects already defined.

Since the kernel class hierarchy has no 'tuple' class, the first step is accomplished by defining the following subclass of *Object*:

```
Object subclass:  'Employee'
             instVarNames:  #('name' 'department'
                                'salary')
                classVars:  #()
        poolDictionaries:  #()
             inDictionary:  UserGlobals
              constraints:  #[ #[ #name, String ],
                                #[ #department, String ],
                                #[ #salary,
                                   SmallInteger ] ]
              isInvariant:  false.
```

Next, a subclass of the class *Set* is created for sets of employee tuples (relations) as follows:

```
Set subclass:  'Employees'
          instVarNames:  #()
             classVars:  #()
     poolDictionaries:  #()
          inDictionary:  UserGlobals
           constraints:  Employee
           isInvariant:  false.
```

Here, the 'constraints:' keyword takes a single class name as its argument, meaning that every member of a set of employees is an object of type

Employee.

A more detailed example for defining a database structure in OPAL is presented next. The example is the library example from earlier chapters, structurally enhanced with several features for a more appropriate representation of its semantics. The new description of the library is shown in Figure 22.5, which shows an ERD that has been extended with set (*) and tuple (×) constructors as can be found in the IFO model discussed in Chapter 11. A list of (sub)class declarations corresponding to this ERD is given next, where it is again sufficient (though probably not the most sophisticated solution) to use the *Object* and *Set* superclasses only:

```
Object subclass:  'Publ'
          instVarNames:  #('name' 'city' 'state')
             classVars:  #()
      poolDictionaries:  #()
          inDictionary:  UserGlobals
           constraints:  #[ #[ #name, String ],
                              #[ #city, String ],
                              #[ #state, String ] ]
           isInvariant:  false.
```

```
Object subclass:  'Author'
          instVarNames:  #( 'name' 'initials' )
             classVars:  #()
      poolDictionaries:  #()
          inDictionary:  UserGlobals
           constraints:  #[ #[ #name, String ] ,
                              #[ #initials,
                                 String ] ]
           isInvariant:  false.
```

```
Set subclass:  'TheAuthors'
          instVarNames:  #()
             classVars:  #()
      poolDictionaries:  #()
          inDictionary:  UserGlobals
           constraints:  Author
           isInvariant:  false.
```

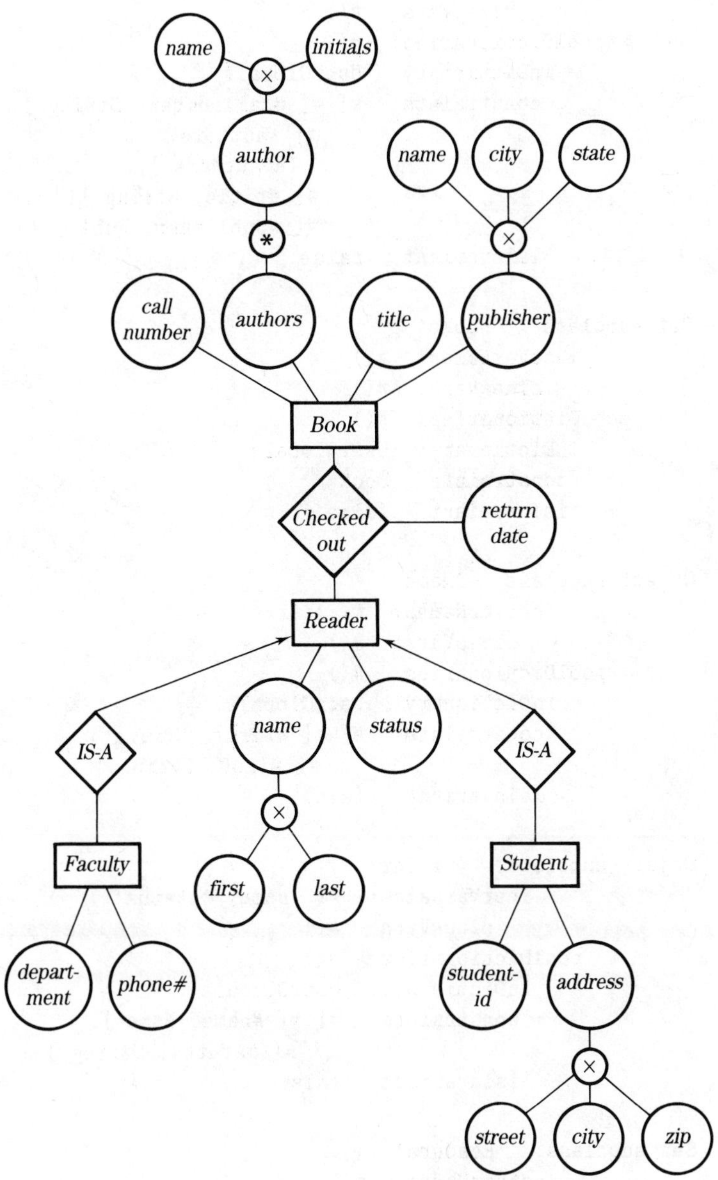

Figure 22.5 The library application revisited.

```
Object subclass:  'Book'
          instVarNames:  #( 'callnumber' 'authors' 'title'
                              'publisher' )
             classVars:  #()
      poolDictionaries:  #()
          inDictionary:  UserGlobals
           constraints:  #[ #[ #callnumber, String ],
                              #[ #authors,
                                TheAuthors ],
                              #[ #title, String ],
                              #[ #publisher, Publ ] ]
           isInvariant:  false.

Set subclass:  'Books'
          instVarNames:  #()
             classVars:  #()
      poolDictionaries:  #()
          inDictionary:  UserGlobals
           constraints:  Book
           isInvariant:  false.

Object subclass:  'Name'
          instVarNames:  #( 'first' 'last' )
             classVars:  #()
      poolDictionaries:  #()
          inDictionary:  UserGlobals
           constraints:  #[ #[ #first, String ],
                              #[ #last, String ] ]
           isInvariant:  false.

Object subclass:  'Reader'
          instVarNames:  #( 'name' 'status' )
             classVars:  #()
      poolDictionaries:  #()
          inDictionary:  UserGlobals
           constraints:  #[ #[ #name, Name ],
                              #[ #status, String ] ]
           isInvariant:  false.

Set subclass:  'Readers'
          instVarNames:  #()
             classVars:  #()
      poolDictionaries:  #()
          inDictionary:  UserGlobals
           constraints:  Reader
           isInvariant:  false.
```

```
Object subclass:  'Addr'
         instVarNames:  #( 'street' 'city' 'zip' )
            classVars:  #()
     poolDictionaries:  #()
         inDictionary:  UserGlobals
          constraints:  #[ #[ #street, String ],
                             #[ #city, String ],
                             #[ #zip, SmallInteger ] ]
          isInvariant:  false.

Reader subclass:  'Student'
         instVarNames:  #( 'studentId' 'address' )
            classVars:  #()
     poolDictionaries:  #()
         inDictionary:  UserGlobals
          constraints:  #[ #[ #studentId, String ],
                             #[ #address,
                               Addr ] ]
          isInvariant:  false.

Reader subclass:  'Faculty'
         instVarNames:  #('department' 'phoneNumber')
            classVars:  #()
     poolDictionaries:  #()
         inDictionary:  UserGlobals
          constraints:  #[ #[ #department, String ],
                             #[ #phoneNumber,
                               SmallInteger ] ]
          isInvariant:  false.

Readers subclass:  'Students'
         instVarNames:  #()
            classVars:  #()
     poolDictionaries:  #()
         inDictionary:  UserGlobals
          constraints:  Student
          isInvariant:  false.

Readers subclass:  'Professors'
         instVarNames:  #()
            classVars:  #()
     poolDictionaries:  #()
         inDictionary:  UserGlobals
          constraints:  Faculty
          isInvariant:  false.
```

```
Object
   Publ
   Author
   Name
   Addr
   Collection
      Bag
         Set
            TheAuthors
            Books
            Readers
               Students
               Professors
            CheckedOut
   Book
   Reader
      Student
      Faculty
```

Figure 22.6 Partial class hierarchy after library application has been declared.

```
Set subclass:  'CheckedOut'
             instVarNames:  #( 'reader' 'book'
                               'returnDate' )
                classVars:  #()
       poolDictionaries:  #()
            inDictionary:  UserGlobals
             constraints:  #[ #[ #reader, Reader ],
                              #[ #book, Book ],
                              #[ #returnDate,
                                DateTime ] ]
             isInvariant:  false.
```

As a result of the above declarations, the kernel class hierarchy has been extended by user-defined classes, which is shown in Figure 22.6 (where only the relevant kernel classes are included and underlined).

It is important to keep in mind that a subclass inherits instance variables *and* methods from its superclass. Hence, in the above example everything the subclasses inherit comes from *Object* or *Set*, or from subclasses thereof. In general, every object in a GemStone database is an instance of class *Object* or of some subclass of *Object*. Both the *Object* and the *Set* class are classes without named instance variables of their own, so that their subclasses do not inherit structure. On the other hand, since *Student* is a subclass of class *Reader*, every student (instance) has a reader number, a name and a status; in addition, a student has a student identification as well as an address.

As an example of a class with predefined named instance variables, the class *Association*, whose instances are pairs of associated objects, has two such variables named *key* and *value*. Similarly, every object belonging to the class *Fraction* has the two instance variables *numerator* and *denominator* (a fraction is a number represented as the ratio of two integers).

Some other kernel classes notable in this context are the following. Class *Magnitude* defines methods for kinds of objects that can be linearly ordered, including numbers, dates and characters. Correspondingly, magnitudes can be *compared* (by $<, <=, >, >=, =, \tilde{}=$), where characters are ordered according to their ASCII representation; in addition, characters can be *converted* (they understand messages like '`asInteger`', '`asLowercase`' or '`asUppercase`').

Class *Boolean* defines the behaviour of 'true' and 'false', which are the only instances of this class; hence, a user is not allowed to create new *Booleans* or subclasses of class *Boolean*. Boolean objects understand messages which perform the logical functions And, Or, Xor and Not. Class *UndefinedObject* has even less instances, namely just the constant 'nil', which is used as a placeholder ('null value') in OPAL programming.

22.2.4 Method creation in OPAL

Once the definition of a new database *structure* has been specified, the next step is to add a description of its intended *behaviour*, that is, to define *methods* through which the classes and their instances can be created, initialized and finally used. Unlike a relational system such as SQL/DS, GemStone does not create an 'empty' instance automatically for a newly defined class, once its structural description has been completed. Instead, methods are needed which can be 'activated' through corresponding messages; therefore, the creation of methods is considered next.

The first important issue with respect to methods is the distinction between **class methods** and **instance methods**. As these names suggest, the former are understood by classes, while the latter are understood by the instances of a class, but not by the class itself. Specifically, most classes understand the message `new`, which causes the receiving class to execute a method that creates a new instance of it. For example,

```
Book new
```

would create a new instance of the class *Book*.

Before additional examples are considered, some general remarks about methods are appropriate. Basically, a method is the code that an object executes in response to a message. The definition of a method always includes a *message pattern* (which can subsequently be used for activating the method), naming of the selector of the method (which may consist of several keywords) and optionally some formal parameters. Selector and parameters occur in the *body* of the method, which may additionally contain:

(1) the declaration of one or more temporary variables which reserve 'local' storage for use by the method,

(2) OPAL statements,

(3) a return statement by which a value is returned upon execution to the expression that invoked the method.

The syntax for OPAL methods in Backus-Naur form (BNF) is shown below, where the notational conventions used are those that have been applied earlier in this text (see Chapters 14 or 16); an underlined symbol in this listing is always some token of the language which could otherwise be confused with elements of the BNF description.

```
Method           ::= MessagePattern MethodBody

MessagePattern   ::= UnaryPattern | BinaryPattern | KeywordPattern
UnaryPattern     ::= Identifier
BinaryPattern    ::= BinarySelector VariableName
BinarySelector   ::= SelChar[SelChar] | ˜ SelChar
SelChar          ::= + | \ | * | ˜ | < | > | = | | | / | &
VariableName     ::= Identifier
KeywordPattern   ::= Keyword VariableName
                     [ Keyword VariableName ... ]
Keyword          ::= Identifier :

MethodBody       ::= [ Temporaries ] [ Statements ]
Temporaries      ::= | VariableName [ VariableName ... ] |
Statements       ::= Statement . [ Statement . ... ]
                     [[ ˆ ] Statement [ . ] ]
Statement        ::= Assignment | Expression
Assignment       ::= VariableName := Statement


Expression       ::= Primary [ Message [ ; CascadeMessage ... ] ]
Primary          ::= ArrayBuilder | Literal | Path | Block
                     | SelectionBlock | ParenStatement
ArrayBuilder     ::= #[ [ Expression [ , Expression ... ]] ]
Literal          ::= Number | NegNumber | StringLiteral
                     | CharacterLiteral | SymbolLiteral | ArrayLiteral
                     | SpecialLiteral
```

```
Path              ::= Identifier.Identifier[.Identifier ... ]
Block             ::= [ [ BlockParams ] Statements ]
BlockParams       ::= Parameter [ Parameter ... ] |
Parameter         ::= :VariableName
SelectionBlock    ::= { [ BlockParams ] Predicate }
Predicate         ::= { AnyTerm | ParenTerm } [ & Term ... ]
AnyTerm           ::= Operand [ Operator Operand ]
Operand           ::= Path | Literal | Identifier
Operator          ::= = | == | < | > | <= | >= | ~= | ~~
ParenTerm         ::= ( AnyTerm )
Term              ::= ParenTerm | Operand
ParenStatement    ::= ( Statement )

Message           ::= [ UnaryMessages ][ BinaryMessages ]
                      [ KeywordMessage ]
UnaryMessages     ::= UnaryMessage [ UnaryMessage ... ]
UnaryMessage      ::= Identifier
BinaryMessages    ::= BinaryMessage [ BinaryMessage ... ]
BinaryMessage     ::= BinarySelector Primary [ UnaryMessages ]
KeywordMessage    ::= KeywordPart [ KeywordPart ... ]
KeywordPart       ::= Keyword Primary [ UnaryMessages ]
                      [ BinaryMessages ]
CascadeMessage    ::= UnaryMessage | BinaryMessage
                      | KeywordMessage

StringLiteral     ::= '[ { Character | ' ' } ... ]'
CharacterLiteral  ::= $Character
SymbolLiteral     ::= # { Identifier | BinarySelector
                      | Keyword [ Keyword ... ] }
ArrayLiteral      ::= #( [ Literal [ Literal ... ]] )
SpecialLiteral    ::= True | False | Nil
```

This listing will aid the reader in understanding the various examples for methods presented in the remainder of this chapter. It should be mentioned that *primitive* methods are missing in the above listing; these exist for arithmetic, comparisons and other functions. Primitives correspond to built-in operators or assembly language routines and directly call on machine code rather than OPAL code.

Recall from above that '`new`' is a (class) message for creating a new instance of a class. All variables of the resulting object are set to 'nil' when the instance is created. So, in order to create a new instance of a class in which the instance variables are set appropriately, a corresponding class method has to be defined, which can then be sent to that class in a message. The following example shows such a method for *Publ*:

```
classmethod: Publ
```

```
makePubl
     ^ (self new) name:  'Addison-Wesley';
        city:  'Reading'; state:  MA
%
```

The first and the last line are commands for *TOPAZ*, the version of the OPAL Programming Environment running on a VAX/VMS host of the object server (see Section 22.2.1), and included here for completeness; the first line tells TOPAZ to treat the indicated text as a method to be compiled and installed in a class (in this case *Publ*); the last line contains the TOPAZ command terminator. The second line is the message pattern, which can subsequently be used for actually instantiating a class through the message

```
Publ makePubl.
```

The third line starts with a 'hat' (^), which denotes the return value of the method; the return value is specified in whatever follows the hat. In the example above, the message expression `(self new)` is next. `self` is a special variable to which all methods have access, and which represents the receiver. Hence, `(self new)` sends the receiver, in this case the class *Publ*, the message `new`, through which a new instance of *Publ* is created. The remaining parts of the above piece of code are keyword-argument pairs sending the given values to the corresponding instance variables. Thus, the value returned by this method (the value resulting from an invocation of this method) is a new instance of *Publ* which has the values as specified. If the following message was then sent to *Publ*

```
(Publ makePubl) name
```

this would cause a new instance of *Publ* to be created as indicated, from which the value 'Addison-Wesley' for the instance variable *name* is returned, provided the following *instance method* has been defined on (instances of) *Publ*, which 'projects' onto *name* (comments are written in double quotes):

```
method:  Publ
name                          "message pattern"
        ^ name                "return statement"
%
```

Notice that in the class method shown above the three messages '`name:`', '`city:`' and '`state:`' are sent, instead of simply *assigning* values to these instance variables. The reason for this is that instance variables are only known within instance methods; a class method can never assign a value to such a variable, but must send it a corresponding message.

The way described above for initializing objects is cumbersome, however, since there are no 'formal parameters' yet which make the method reusable for various publishers. This problem is solved by providing an instance creation method whose arguments specify the values to which the instance variables are to be set; this method is obtained by referring to the class method `new` from the corresponding superclass (*Object* in this case) and use this in the method body as follows:

```
classmethod: Publ
newName: aName newCity: aCity newState: aState
| tempPubl |
tempPubl := super new.
tempPubl name: aName; city: aCity; state: aState;
^ tempPubl
%
```

This method provides a (keyword) instance creation message whose arguments specify instance variable values for the newly created object. The object is created as follows. First a temporary (local) variable `tempPubl` is defined (in Line 3), which is instantiated by activating the method '`new`' inherited from the superclass; the resulting object is then sent a keyword message containing the values, and is finally returned. To enter a new publisher as above, the following would now suffice:

```
Publ newName: 'Addison-Wesley' newCity: 'Reading'
        newState: 'MA'
```

Methods can be assigned to *categories*, which are user-defined 'directories' for organizing methods. To establish a category, the TOPAZ command

```
category: aName
```

is available; subsequent method definitions will then be assigned to the named category. For example, the previous example could be extended by

```
category: 'Instance Creation'
classmethod: Publ
          ⋮
```

22.2.5 Data manipulation methods

Once the structure of a database as well as methods for 'loading' data have been declared, methods are needed for manipulating class instances. To illustrate this aspect, the following is a list of instance methods applicable to objects of type *Employee(s)*; it is assumed that such objects already exist (see Exercise 14):

```
category: 'Accessing'
method: Employee
name
    ^ name                  "returns the receiver's name"
%

method: Employee
department
    ^ department             "returns the receiver's
                             department"
%

method: Employee
salary
    ^ salary                 "returns the receiver's salary"
%

category: 'Modifying'
method: Employee
department: aString            "message pattern"
department := aString          "sets the receiver's
                               department to a new value"
%

method: Employee
salary: aSmallInt
salary := aSmallInt            "sets the receiver's salary
                               to a new value"
%
```

The 'Accessing' category here contains almost trivial messages so far, however, these are needed to access the value in one of the instance variables of an *Employee* object. They will be used below for writing several queries.

Methods in category 'Modifying' can be used for at least two purposes. First, they are needed for things like transferring an employee from one department to another or for raising his or her salary, that is, for value updates in the ordinary sense. Furthermore, they provide an alternative for assigning values to a newly created instance. For example, suppose the (class) method for creating a new instance of class *Employee* was defined as follows:

```
classmethod: Employee
newName: aName
| tempEmp |
tempEmp := super new.
```

```
tempEmp name:  aName
^ tempEmp
%
```

Then the (instance) methods **department** and **salary** above could be used to change the values of instance variables *department* and *salary*, respectively, from 'nil' to something meaningful.

To complete the description of the standard update operations (insert, delete and modify), the *deletion* of objects is considered next. The approach taken by GemStone is as unusual as its approach to insertion (instance creation); specifically, it destroys the 'reachability' of an object that should be deleted, so that the system can reclaim the storage space that was occupied by this object during its next garbage collection for reuse. This is in some ways similar to network systems, where a record is reachable (via its database key) independent of the values for its attributes, and a deletion candidate can either be disconnected from a set-occurrence or erased from the database (see Chapter 5). Similarly, GemStone objects can be 'disconnected' by setting all relevant variable values (some of which may occur in dictionaries) to 'nil'; they can be 'erased' by either setting the appropiate dictionary entry to 'nil' or using the **remove** method avavilable in many (but not all) class protocols.

For example, if an object is an instance of class *Set*, this class inherits a **remove** method from its superclass *Bag*; hence, to delete a particular employee referred to by **victim** from an instance of the *Employees* set subclass defined earlier, the following message would suffice:

```
Employees remove:  victim
```

Clearly, the victim can be selected in a variety of ways, which make use of the possibilities to formulate query expressions sketched below.

The next two methods again refer to employees and encode simple queries about individual employees or sets of them:

```
category:  'Formatting'
method:  Employee
asString
| tempString |
^ tempString := (self name) + '    ' +
                (self department) + '    ' +
                (self salary asString)
%
```

In this method, the return value is assigned a string which is obtained by concatenating (+) three strings representing values, interrupted by two strings of blanks for better readability. The value strings are taken from the instance variables of the receiver, where the value for salary has to be converted temporarily from *SmallInteger* to *String*.

The intention of the next method is to print (return) a set of employees in table form, that is, to show the information on each employee on a separate line:

```
method: Employees
asTable
| aString |
aString := String new.
self do: [ :n | aString := aString + n asString.
               aString := aString add: Character lf ].
^ aString
%
```

First, a new instance of class *String* is created and assigned to the temporary variable *aString*. Next, the receiver (that is, an instance of the *Set* subclass *Employees*) is instructed to execute a `do:` method, whose argument is a 'Block' (see OPAL BNF in Section 22.2.4) delimited by brackets. The do method loops through the elements of its receiver and evaluates this block for each of them. In the above case, variable `n` is used to process each employee in the receiving set of employees in turn. During the first iteration, *aString* is assigned a new value obtained by concatenating (+) its old value (nil) and the first object assigned to `n`, where the latter is first represented as a string by invoking the `asString` method shown above; to the result of this concatenation a linefeed character is finally attached. During the second iteration, the string generated so far is concatenated with another employee string (followed by a linefeed character), and this process is repeated until the set of employees in question is exhausted. The resulting string is then returned.

The next issue to be considered is querying a Gemstone database. As before, messages have to be sent to instances of classes to do so, for which a series of examples is now presented. Once again, these examples refer to the *Employee* and *Employees* classes; writing analogous methods for the library example is left to the reader (see Exercises 14 and 15). The reader should note the use of methods already declared in these examples, which are for simplicity no longer written as complete methods in TOPAZ format, but only as sequences of OPAL statements (as which they will probably occur in more complex queries), most of which do not even produce a return value yet.

The following piece of OPAL code *selects* all employees who work in the research department, where it is assumed that an instance of *Employees* named *CurrEmps* has been created already:

```
| resEmps |
resEmps := CurrEmps select: [ :anEmp
```

```
                    | anEmp.department = 'research' ].
resEmps asTable.
```

The `select:` method used here is a method inherited from superclass *Collection*. It evaluates a block (as does the `do:` method) with each of the receiver's elements as the argument; the values for which the block evaluates to 'true' are stored in a collection of the same class as the receiver, which is finally returned. Thus, in the example above `select:` loops through *CurrEmps* and returns its research members by accessing the value of the department instance variable in a *path*. The result is a table obtained by invoking the `asTable` method created earlier.

The same result could be obtained if the *block* argument to `select:`, which is delimited by brackets, was replaced by a *selection block* argument, which is delimited by braces, that is, if

```
... select: { :anEmp | anEmp.department = 'research' }.
```

was used. The difference between the two is that a selection block can be evaluated faster by the system.

The next example shows how to retrieve all research employees who make more than 50K:

```
| resOver50KEmps |
resOver50KEmps := CurrEmps select: { :anEmp |
                       (anEmp.department = 'research')
                       & (anEmp.salary > 50000) }.
resOver50KEmps asTable.
```

(Here, '&' stands for logical 'and'; '|' would be used for 'or' and '~' for 'not'.) If it is desired to retrieve all objects for which a given selection block evaluates to 'false', the `reject:` method can be used as a replacement for `select:`. The following query returns all employees *not* working in the research department:

```
| nonResEmps |
nonResEmps := CurrEmps reject: { :anEmp
                    | anEmp.department = 'research' }.
nonResEmps asTable.
```

The `detect:` method is available (for constraint *Collections*) to retrieve a *single* element of the receiver for which a given selection block evaluates to 'true'. For example, the following expression would (attempt to) return an employee named Smith:

```
CurrEmps detect: { :anEmp | anEmp.name = 'Smith' } .
```

If no employee named Smith was currently employed, an error message would be returned and the interpreter would halt; both of these can be avoided if an *exception block* is included, as in

```
CurrEmps detect:  { :anEmp | anEmp.name = 'Smith' }
                  ifNone:  [ nil ].
```

In order to (further) improve the efficiency of query processing, OPAL can create and maintain *indexes* which use the values of instance variables as keys; indexes can be used on instances of (constrained) *Collection* subclasses and come in two flavours: **identity indexes** facilitate identity queries, while **equality indexes** facilitate equality queries.

For example, the following message to *CurrEmps* creates an identity index on instance variable *name*:

```
CurrEmps createIdentityIndexOn:  'name'
```

It should be mentioned that the system also creates and maintains various indexes automatically for speeding up query processing.

Finally, class *Bag* contains methods which use parts of the associative access mechanisms of the system to *sort* (*Collection*) elements without message passing. For example, in the following piece of code the sorting method takes an *Array* of paths as its argument; the first path is taken as the primary sort key, and the second is taken as subordinate key:

```
| returnArray tempString |
tempString := String new.
returnArray := CurrEmps sortAscending:
                  #( 'name' 'department' ).
returnArray do:  [ :n | tempString add:  (n name);
         add:  '  '; add:  (n department);
         add:  Character lf ].
  tempString.
```

Here, employees are first sorted by *name*; employees with the same name are additionally sorted by *department*. Then a printable list of the sorted objects is built.

If it is desired to sort names in ascending order, but departments in descending order, the third line above has to be replaced by

```
returnArray := CurrEmps sortWith:
                         #( 'name' 'Ascending'
                         'department' 'Descending').
```

22.2.6 User profiles and segments

To conclude our introductory survey of GemStone, some other kernel classes primarily used by the system are finally explained.

When users start a new session, GemStone collects information about them from an object belonging to the class *UserProfile*, describing the objects the users are allowed to work with, and the messages they may send as well as other relevant facts. The system uses this information together with data gathered in the course of a session to deliver error messages, to monitor the (possibly concurrent) access to objects, to store newly created objects in default logical categories and physical locations or to translate new names for objects into system-wide references. A user's own profile can be inspected by sending a message to the class *System* as in the following example, in which the current user's identification is asked for:

```
| myProfile |
myProfile := System myUserProfile.
myProfile userId.
```

A user's profile stores a reference to a *segment* (an instance of class *Segment*) serving as the default segment. A segment groups objects together and stores information about their 'owner' and who can read or write them. All objects in a segment have the same kind of protection, and each segment is owned by a single user. A user's default segment is the one in which GemStone stores the objects newly created by this user. *UserProfile* understands the message `defaultSegment` which returns a default segment as in

```
| mySegment |
mySegment := System myUserProfile defaultSegment.
```

To find out what the owner is authorized to do with objects in the default segment, the message `ownerAuthorization` can be used, as in

```
System myUserProfile defaultSegment ownerAuthorization.
```

which returns one of 'write', 'read' or 'none'. OPAL represents the entire disk space used by GemStone as a single instance of class *Repository* which is composed of 4096 segments.

A more detailed description of what can be done with segments is beyond the scope of this chapter and can be found in various papers listed in the Bibliography.

Chapter 23
Open Database Systems

In this chapter, the outlook on how database management may evolve in the future is concluded by taking a brief look at another important research direction, which is based on the notion of **extensibility**, and which considerably departs from the idea that a DBMS is a 'closed' monolithic software package. An **open** database system is a collection of software modules, each of which has a well-defined functionality as well as a corresponding interface, which can be 'plugged' or configured to yield some customized DBMS; alternatively, an open system may contain **generators** and other tools for the (partially) automatic construction of DBMS software. The key paradigm to (re)configurability or customizability is extensibility (both at the logical *and* at the physical level).

23.1 The extensibility paradigm

In brief, an **extensible DBMS** (EDBMS) is a database management system which allows the 'outside world' (which includes *ad hoc* and sophisticated users, application programmers, system managers and database administrators) to add new features to already existing database software, in order to customize the overall system for a specific class of applications. Clearly, such 'features' may pertain to a variety of issues, ranging from new data types at the conceptual level to new storage structures at the internal one. Therefore, a distinction is made in this section between extensibility at the *logical* level and extensibility at the *physical* level, which are discussed in turn.

Notice that the idea of employing extensibility, in particular in the context of non-standard applications, is an immediate consequence of the requirements that were collected in Chapter 20, where it became clear that there is little hope for one DBMS to fit all needs in the future. In particular, the motivation for exploring and providing extensibility is basically the same as for exploiting object-orientation, namely that standard data types and operations are unsuited for non-standard applications, and that an impedance mismatch arises when a standard database language is embedded into a high-level programming language.

23.1.1 Logical extensibility

A system which provides extensibility at the *logical* level allows us to:

(1) introduce new data types as well as new operations on these types,

(2) support new abstraction concepts (like versions or configurations of data objects as discussed in Section 20.2.2),

(3) express and process recursive queries and rules (see Section 8.3).

As a result, a user who makes use of this feature is required to supply code for the operations on the new types and for their corresponding access methods. This code is then incorporated into the already existing DBMS code and hence dynamically impacts its language processor and query optimizer. On the other hand, a basic set of services (pertaining to issues like concurrency control, recovery or buffer and storage management) is already provided by the EDBMS, as is a language interface and hence a user interface.

Notice that two examples of logically extensible systems have already been discussed in this text: clearly, the abstract data type facility of Postgres lets this system falls into the EDBMS category. By the same token, the object-oriented system GemStone is an extensible system, and the same is true for most object-oriented database systems currently under development. (However, truly object-oriented systems are characterized, as was discussed in the previous chapter, by several other requirements not necessarily shared by extensible ones.) Several other (experimental) systems in this class are mentioned in the Bibliographic Notes.

23.1.2 Physical extensibility

While extensibility at the logical level is certainly desirable in the context of non-standard database applications, a truly extensible system has to go beyond it and provide extensibility at the *physical* level as well. To this end, it should be possible to:

(1) introduce new data structures for storing data objects at the physical level,

(2) add new (or exchange existing) algorithms for concurrency control and recovery,

(3) extend the capabilities of query optimization and access path selection.

As a result, physical extensibility poses considerably more challenges to DBMS developers than does logical extensibility alone, since even the 'core components' of a database system may now be (and in general are) affected. Thus, it seems reasonable to first decompose a database system (and in particular an extensible one) into *layers*, and to fix (1) a functionality which should be provided by each layer, (2) the interface through which each layer communicates with its neighbours, and (3) how (and by whom) the individual components of each layer should be realized.

23.2 Architectural and functional layers

The ideas and concepts described in the previous section considerably impact the *architecture* of a database management system, which is why a brief look at the *layers* that are or should be present in such a system is taken next. The decomposition of a complex enterprise like a database system into various, hierarchically organized layers is a common approach that can be found in many computer-related areas. As a first example, in a *computer system* a layer-based decomposition can be stated as shown in Figure 23.1. As a second example, consider the functional and organizational decomposition of a *computer network* as described in the *ISO-OSI Reference Model*, in which layers are distinguished as shown in Figure 23.2. In both cases, there exists a hierarchy of layers which are distinct with respect to function and service; from bottom to top the level of abstraction

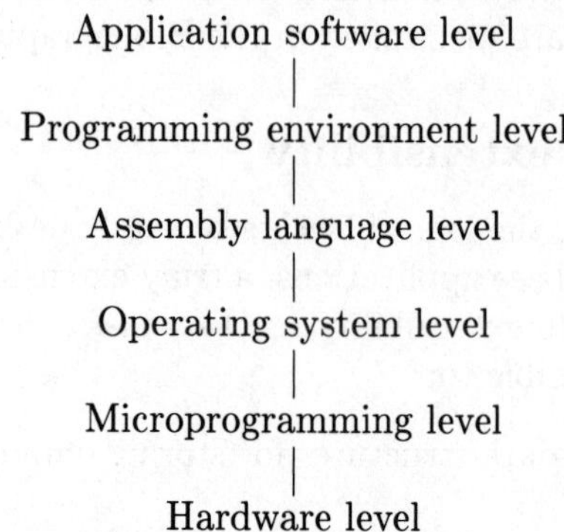

Figure 23.1 Layers in a computer system.

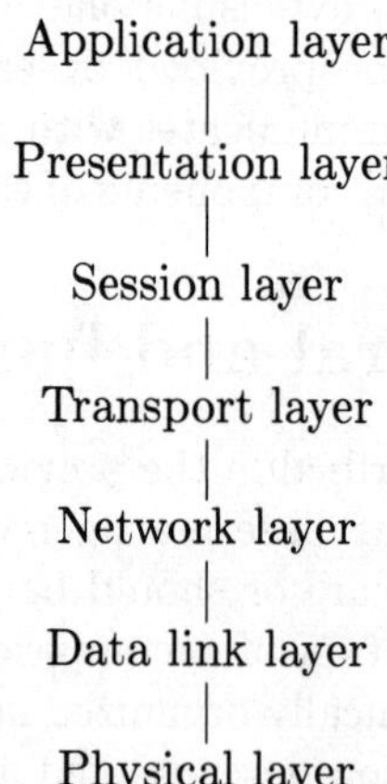

Figure 23.2 Network layers in the ISO-OSI Reference Model.

increases, and each layer *provides* services to the next higher one, and *expects* functions from the next lower one.

The same idea turns out to be useful in the context of database management. Recall from Chapter 2 that a *database* can be considered at (at least) three different levels of abstraction, which together form the basis of the ANSI/SPARC model. However, it seems unreasonable to expect this model to be general enough to underlie all future developments. Several committees involved in database system standardization are already in the process of discussing the proposal for a *four-level system architecture* (in extension and replacement of the three-level database architecture introduced in Chapter 2) which is roughly organized as follows.

At the lowest ('internal') level, in the **basic service layer**, the primary goal is to realize the storage mapping structures; in addition, this layer provides a buffer as well as a storage manager. At the next higher level, called the **database service layer**, common database functions like query and update processing, integrity checking, authorization control, or transaction and recovery management are provided. At the third level, the **tool service layer**, new database services are offered, which can include, for example, text, graphics or image processing, or the management of complex objects. Finally, the **user request layer** represents the system's interface to the outside world, and hence should provide powerful functions for using the 'tools' available at lower levels in both dialogues and application programs.

However, the scenario sketched above is not necessarily 'open' yet in the sense required by extensible systems. Therefore, refinements of this general approach are needed to provide customized systems. One approach in this direction is the **kernel architecture** for database management systems, whose basic organization is shown in Figure 23.3. The idea here is to provide optimal support of a specific application by implementing a *user interface* that is configurable with respect to the given application class. Depending on that class, the second highest layer provides a *model mapping* from the class to the (complex) objects of some (semantic) data model. Finally, a vastly application-independent *storage server* is used internally, which — as a 'system kernel' — avoids the independent and possibly redundant coexistence of the individual systems.

Thus, a clear distinction is made in the kernel approach between application-dependent and application-independent functions and layers. Returning to the discussion of Chapter 3, the various components of a DBMS can broadly be divided into the five layers shown in Figure 23.4. Above the highest layer sits the specific application class, and underneath the lowest layer is the database. While the level of abstraction again increases bottom-up, the same holds for the degree of dependence on the application class considered. As a result, an EDBMS can be completely application-*independent* at the level of storage management, application-

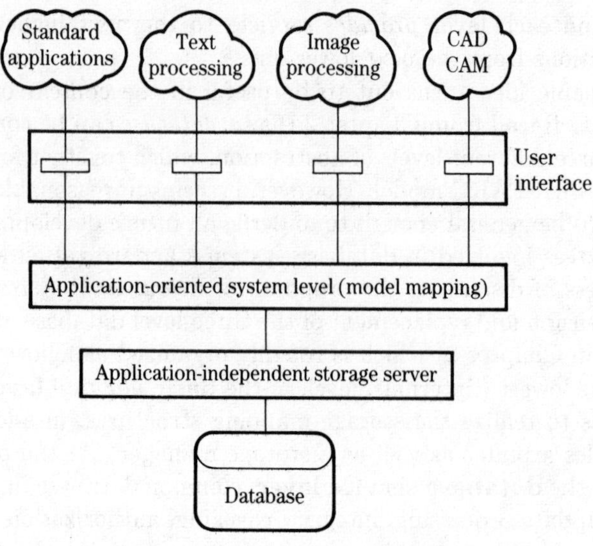

Figure 23.3 The kernel architecture for EDBMS.

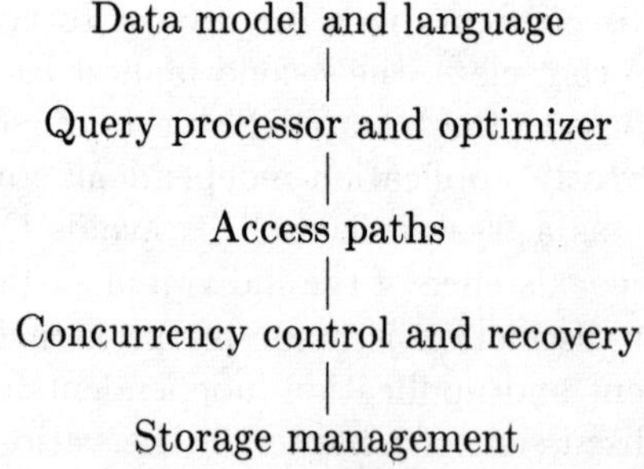

Figure 23.4 General layers in a DBMS.

dependent at the data model layer, and *partially* application-*dependent* at the intermediate layers. For example, certain rules and techniques governing query optimization may be fixed, while a versioning mechanism could be embodied into the transaction manager upon request. Hence, each layer can be composed of both *fixed* and *variable* components, and a configurator can select a particular set of components to obtain a specific DBMS. In addition, some components may have to be written from scratch for each new application class, while others are generatable by the system based on specific input. The next section presents an approach in this direction.

23.3 The Exodus database system generator

In this section, the introduction to open database systems is concluded by surveying the architecture of **Exodus**, a database-system generator under development at the University of Wisconsin, Madison. Exodus is a (logically and physically) extensible system whose goal is to facilitate the rapid development of high-performance and application-specific database systems. It provides certain kernel facilities as well as an architectural framework for building customized systems, tools to partially automate the generation of such systems and libraries of software components that will probably be used in more than one application class. Hence, and unlike Postgres or GemStone, Exodus is intended more as an easily adaptable 'toolbox' than as a complete system with provisions for user-added (logical) extensions. To achieve this goal, *generic* solutions that are (or should be) applicable to any application-specific DBMS are provided where feasible; as an example, the lowest architectural layer consists of a 'Storage Object Manager' which supports concurrent and recoverable operations on storage objects of arbitrary size. In addition, *generators* as well as *libraries* are provided where generic solutions appear inappropriate, which aid the Exodus user in generating what is needed; for example, the system has an *optimizer generator* capable of producing a query optimizer for some given algebraic language.

As a consequence, an Exodus environment includes a new type of 'user', besides the ordinary user and the database administrator, namely the **database implementor** (DBI), whose primary task is the customization of the system towards a given application class. This task is aided by the following tools and components, which are summarized in Figure 23.5:

(1) the Storage Object Manager,

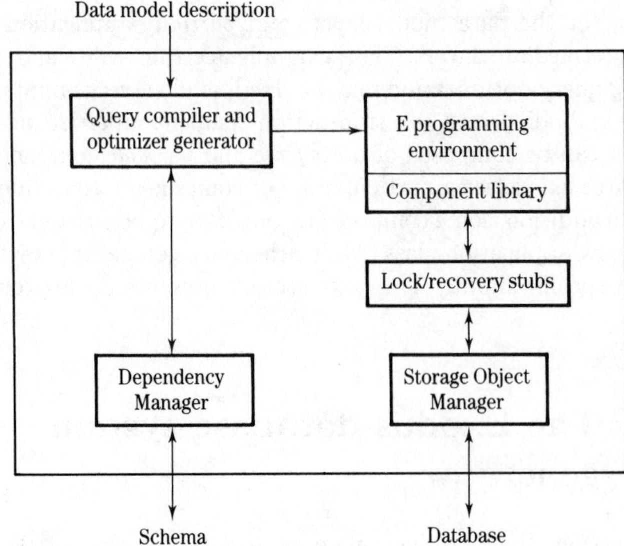

Figure 23.5 The architecture of Exodus.

(2) the Dependency Manager (initially called 'Type Manager') for defining and maintaining system and 'schema' information,

(3) the E programming language and its compiler for writing DBMS-internal system software,

(4) a query optimizer and compiler generator,

(5) a component library including (type-independent) access methods,

(6) a lock manager 'stub' and a recovery protocol 'stub' to simplify the writing of new access methods and other database operators.

In addition, tools for constructing user front-ends are expected to be added in the future. It should be mentioned that the first two are not actually tools but the 'fixed' components which interface with whatever is generated by Exodus or provided by the DBI additionally. The tools and components shown in Figure 23.5 are described in more detail next.

The *Storage Object Manager* forms the 'bottom level' of the system and provides capabilities for reading, writing and updating untyped, uninterpreted, variable-length byte sequences of arbitrary size ('storage objects'). Storage objects can be logically and physically grouped together in a file (resulting in a *file object*), for example in order to ease the sequential scanning of related objects, or for placing them in colocated pages on disk. In addition, this system component provides a buffer manager and basic concurrency control and recovery mechanisms for operations on shared storage objects. Finally, a versioning mechanism is supported which can be used to implement an application-dependent versioning scheme. The operations on storage objects include reading a byte range from within an object (where the specified bytes are buffered in a buffer pool), writing a byte range, appending bytes to the end of an object, inserting a byte sequence at a specified point, and deleting a specified range of bytes. The interface to the Storage Object Manager also provides procedures for creating and destroying file objects or storage objects within a file, or to open and close file objects for file scans.

The second fixed component of Exodus is the *Dependency Manager*, which maintains information about the modules which make up the DBMS generated using Exodus in the form of a dependency graph (whose nodes are the modules); for example, dependencies exist between modules containing type definitions and modules using these definitions. In addition, the Dependency Manager represents a persistent repository for information about query components and thereby provides 'schema' support for a variety of application-specific systems. Its data modelling facilities basically include a generalized class hierarchy with multiple inheritance, where class definitions are based on base types (like *integer, real, character* and *object ID*) and type constructors. In addition, it provides facilities for the creation of new base types and operations on these using an abstract data type mechanism; ADT definitions are first processed by the E compiler. The Dependency Manager maintains two categories of schema information, the *class hierarchy* and the *file catalogue*, where the latter contains information on the class of each file as well as file statistics for use during query optimization.

A database system generated through Exodus consists of three kinds of components, those that are fixed, those implemented by the DBI using the E programming environment, and those generated by an Exodus tool from a DBI-supplied specification. As was mentioned above, the Storage Object Manager and the Dependency Manager are *fixed* and hence are always present in a resulting DBMS. The components that are *implemented* by the DBI are the access methods and the operator methods as well as the operations associated with newly defined ADTs. For example, a DBI implementing a relational DBMS has to write code for access methods like B-trees, for operator methods like nested-loop or sort-merge join, and eventually for new data types like *date* or *time.* As a result, an Exodus-produced DBMS as shown in Figure 23.6 has an *access methods layer*, located above the Storage Object Manager, which ultimately provides access to storage objects (and also supports version control if needed), and an *operator methods layer*, which contains both DBI-supplied and Exodus-supplied code, namely a collection of methods that can be combined with each other in order to operate on (typed) storage objects. More specifically, this layer contains the E procedures used to implement the operators

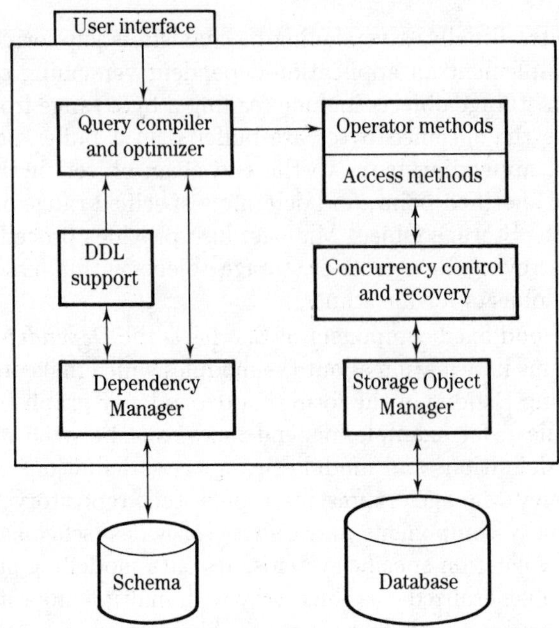

Figure 23.6 Architecture of a DBMS produced by Exodus.

provided to the user of the system, where one or more procedures may exist for each operator.

The implementation of both layers can take advantage of a library of methods; new methods are written in the E language. E is the implementation language for all system components for which the DBI must provide code, and is basically an extension of C++ with a typed file facility, a construct ('dbclass') for defining nested and/or large ADTs, generator classes for dealing with missing type information, and generalized iterators for writing operator methods for use in scans and query processing. (New) access methods can then be implemented using the 'type parameters' available in E, through which existing access methods can be used in conjunction with DBI-defined abstract data types without modification. It should be mentioned that a DBMS generated by Exodus is fully compiled, that is, the system code is written in E, user schemas are compiled into E types and user queries are compiled into E procedures.

The third kind of components present in a DBMS produced by Exodus are those *generated* from DBI specifications. One of them is the query optimizer and compiler (see also Figure 23.6) which is produced from a (data) *model description file* by the *Optimizer Generator.* The generated optimizer takes an algebraic query tree and repeatedly applies algebraic transformations yielding a tree that represents an access plan;

the query compiler then translates this plan into an E program, which is finally compiled and executed. The optimizer generator expects four kinds of input, namely the operators and their methods, the rules which specify legal transformations of query trees (reorderings of operators), and the relevant implementation rules. In addition to this declarative description of the specific data model, the optimizer generator requires the DBI to supply a collection of C procedures. For each method, a *cost function* must be supplied that calculates the cost of this method based on the characteristics of its input. In addition, a *property function* is needed for each operator and each method, where the former determines logical properties of intermediate results (like cardinalities or record widths), and the latter determine physical properties (like sort orders).

A more detailed description of the Exodus architecture, the E programming environment and the optimizer generator can be found in the references given in the Bibliographic Notes. While the system is not based on a specific data model and query language, the Extra (EXtensible Types for Relations and Attributes) data model and the associated Excess (EXtensible Calculus with Entity and Set Support) language are currently available for demonstrating the capabilities of the system; further information on this model and language can also be found in the references given in the Bibliographic Notes.

Bibliographic Notes

An introduction to the area of non-standard database applications and systems together with a presentation of recent research activities is provided by Dittrich and Dayal (1986). Introductions to specific areas mentioned in Chapter 20 can be found in the following papers: Shoshani (1982) for statistical databases, Kellogg (1986) and Zaniolo et al. (1986) for knowledge processing, Abbott (1985) for computer music. Our discussion of CIM mostly follows Lorie and Bever (1987), that of CASE Bernstein and Lomet (1987). Multimedia databases are investigated by Woelk et al. (1986) or Christodoulakis et al. (1984). For the CAD domain, see also Gray (1984), Katz (1984, 1985), Katz and Weiss (1984) or Katz et al. (1986). The adder example used in Chapter 20 is due to Batory and Kim (1985); the details of the circuit elements used follow Oberschelp and Vossen (1989). Data models for complex objects in particular in the CAD domain are proposed by Batory and Buchmann (1984), Bancilhon et al. (1985), Buchmann and de Celis (1985), Afsarmanesh et al. (1985) and Hardwick (1984).

The description of the Postgres data model in Section 21.1 closely follows Rowe and Stonebraker (1987). The abstract data type facility of Postgres is described in detail by Stonebraker (1986a, b) or Stonebraker et al. (1984, 1987a, b). Its rule system for the enforcement of integrity constraints is explained by Stonebraker et al. (1987c, 1988). Finally, a description of the system as a whole can be found in Stonebraker (1987), Stonebraker and Rowe (1986) and Stonebraker et al. (1990).

The idea of giving up the first normal form requirement on relations in a relational database goes back to Makinouchi (1977), although not much attention was devoted to this idea until Jäschke and Schek (1982) started investigating it further; see also Schek and Scholl (1986). The exposition of the model in Section 21.2 follows Thomas and Fischer (1986) and partially also Roth et al. (1988). The former paper in particular presents a (complete) extended relational algebra for nested relations (among other things with more than 'simple' selection conditions); also, the proof of Theorem 21.1 is from there, and the paper contains proofs of Theorems 21.2 through 21.5 as well as solutions to Exercises 5–11. The question of whether a restriction on the structure of schemes (formats) or a different approach to extending the relational operators is appropriate is addressed by Abiteboul and Bidoit (1986), Bidoit (1987) and Hull (1987), who introduce *V-relations*, the data model underlying the VERSO database machine (see Abiteboul et al. (1986)). The same question is considered by Roth et al. (1988), who define a (nested) relational algebra as well as a calculus which are of equivalent computational power if relations are in *partitioned normal form* (PNF). A strictly more general normal form, *nested normal form* (NNF), is introduced and investigated by Özsoyoglu and Yuan (1987). Hull (1987) relates nested relational structures to the IFO data model (see Chapter 11). Other relevant work in this area, in which various issues and aspects of this model not covered in this text are discussed (like dependencies in nested relations, SQL extensions, expressive power of languages for nested relations, design into NNF), includes Fischer et al. (1985), Gyssens and van Gucht (1988a, b), Hull (1987), Özsoyoglu et al. (1987), Roth and Kirkpatrick (1988), Roth and Korth (1987), and Roth et al. (1987). A recent collection of relevant papers is Abiteboul et al. (1989).

The model for complex objects sketched in Sections 21.3 follows Beeri (1988); see also Bancilhon and Khoshafian (1989), Bancilhon et al. (1987) or Valduriez et al. (1986). The latter reference investigates storage structures for complex objects, which are also investigated by Hafez and Özsoyoglu (1988). If a list type constructor is added to the model, the model underlying the AIM-P experimental system results, on which further information can be found in Dadam et al. (1986), Dadam (1988) and Linnemann et al. (1988). The issue of allowing recursion in type declarations (which was excluded in Definitions 21.11 and 22.1) is also discussed in several of these papers; for this, see also Lecluse et al. (1988) or Vossen and Witt (1989).

An introduction to the general principles behind object-orientation and their application to the database context can be found in Ullman (1987, 1988), Zaniolo et al. (1986), Dittrich and Dayal (1986), Bancilhon (1988), Stein and Maier (1988) and Beeri (1988); Ullman (1988) as well as Stein and Maier (1988) also survey GemStone and the OPAL language. Zdonik and Maier (1990) is a collection of relevant papers on the subject. The 'manifesto' by Atkinson et al. (1989) describes mandatory, optional and open features of an object-oriented database system and surveys the state of the art, which is characterized by a lot of implementation activities (see below), but also by the lack of formal foundations or a common data model. The latter issue is addressed by Beeri (1989); see also Maier (1989). Our description of ADTs as they appear in SIMULA follows Ghezzi and Jazayeri (1987). An introduction to object identity is given by Khoshafian and Copeland (1986); Definition 22.1 is from there. Abiteboul and Kanellakis (1989) propose a logic-oriented query language based on object identity; other proposals to combine logic- and object-orientation include Kifer and Lausen (1989) and Abiteboul (1989). For more information on the design of object-oriented database (programming) languages, the reader is referred to Bloom and Zdonik (1987), Khoshafian and Valduriez (1990) or Atkinson and Buneman (1987).

The GemStone system is described in more detail by Maier et al. (1985, 1986b), Maier and Stein (1986), Stein and Maier (1988), Penney and Stein (1987) and Purdy et al. (1987). For a brief introduction to OPAL, see also Ullman (1988). Our description of OPAL follows Servio Logic (1988a), which in particular introduces the kernel classes as well as to programming in this language; the OPAL Programming Environment (for VAX/VMS) is described in Servio Logic (1988b), while the GemStone C Interface is described in Servio Logic (1988c).

For a survey of other developments in the area of object-oriented database systems, the reader should consult Dittrich (1988) or Kim and Lochovsky (1989).

Notable systems currently in various stages of development include Vbase (now called Ontos), see Andrews and Harris (1987), Cactis, see Hudson and King (1987), ENCORE/Observer, see Hornick and Zdonik (1987), HiPAC, see Dayal (1988) or Dayal et al. (1988), Iris, see Fishman et al. (1987) and Wilkinson et al. (1990), O_2, see Bancilhon et al. (1988), Bancilhon (1989), Lecluse et al. (1988), Lecluse and Richard (1989), Velez et al. (1989) and Deux (1990), Orion, see Banerjee et al. (1987a, b, 1988) or Kim et al. (1987, 1990), and Zeitgeist, see Ford et al. (1988).

An introduction to the principles of DBMS extensibility can be found in Batory (1987) or Wilms et al. (1988). Other EDBMS, besides Postgres and GemStone, include object-oriented systems like Orion and HiPAC mentioned above, AIM-P (see the references above) or IBM's Starburst project, see Schwarz et al. (1986), Lindsay et al. (1987), McPherson and Pirahesh (1987) and Haas et al. (1988, 1990). For more information on the architectural and functional layers of a DBMS in the context of non-standard applications, the reader should consult the work on the DASDBS system by Schek and Weikum (1986), Schek (1987), Paul et al. (1987) and Schek et al. (1990).

The architecture of Exodus is described in greater detail by Carey et al. (1986) as well as Carey and DeWitt (1987). For the E programming environment, see Richardson and Carey (1987); Graefe and DeWitt (1987) describe the optimizer generator of Exodus, and Carey et al. (1988) present the Extra data model as well as the Excess query language. Other, significantly different approaches to DBMS software generation include the Data Model Compiler, see Maryanski et al. (1986), and the Genesis project, see Batory (1986) and Batory et al. (1988a,b).

Exercises

(1) State the definition of a *teaching assistant* (TA) relation schema in the DDL of Postgres, where a TA has attributes *QUARTER* and *COURSE* and in addition inherits all attributes from *STUDENT* (as defined in Section 21.1). Next, write a Postquel command (in SQL) for the query 'show the name and the level of each TA who majors in computer science and was hired for the spring 89 quarter'.

(2) Define a nested format for the courses offered by a university department, which are informally described as follows: each course offered by the department has a name, a day, an hour, a room, a set of books associated with it, and a set of students enrolled in it, where each student is characterized by an id and a set of grades for that course. Give a (nested) relation over the resulting format.

(3) For the nested relation shown in Figure 21.6, compute the result of each of the following (sequence of) operations:

(a) $\pi_{NAME,SKILLS}(EMP)$

(b) $\pi_{NAME}(\sigma_{CNAME=\text{'}Mary\text{'}}(u_{CHILDREN}(EMP)))$

(c) $\pi_{ID}(\sigma_{TYPE=\text{'}driv\_lic\text{'}}(u_{SKILLS}(EMP)))$

(4) Compute the following (flat) relation from the (nested) one shown in Figure 21.7:

$$u_{SUBMOD}(u_{MODULE}(CHIP))$$

(5) Prove Theorem 21.2.

(6) Prove that, under the assumptions of Definition 21.7,

$$\text{if } r' := n_{R'=(B_1,\ldots,B_k)}(r), \text{ then } (N_2 \hookrightarrow R')(r') = 1 .$$

(7) Prove Theorem 21.4.

(8) Show that the properties stated in Theorem 21.4 are not necessarily meaningful if condition C involves names R' or $\{B_1, \ldots, B_k\}$.

(9) Let r and s be (nested) relations over the same format R. The **set operations** union, intersection and difference can then be defined as follows:

$$r \cup s := \{\mu \mid \mu \in r \ \vee \ \mu \in s\}$$
$$r \cap s := \{\mu \mid \mu \in r \ \wedge \ \mu \in s\}$$
$$r - s := \{\mu \in r \mid \mu \notin s\}$$

Prove that, under the assumptions of Definition 21.8,

$$u_{R_i}(r \cup s) = u_{R_i}(r) \cup u_{R_i}(s)$$

(10) Give counterexamples which show that in general:

(a) a statement of the form given in Exercise 9 does not hold if operation 'u' is replaced by 'n' (according to Definition 21.7),

(b) a statement of the form given in Exercise 9 holds neither for u nor for n if '$\cup$' is replaced by '$\cap$', '$-$' or '$\bowtie$'.

(11) Let R, S be formats, r, s relations over R, S, respectively, Z = names(R) $\cap$ names(S), $Z_1 \subseteq Z$ be the set of format names in Z, $Z_2 \subseteq Z$ be the set of attribute names in Z, X = names(R)$-Z$, and Y = names(S)$-Z$. The **intersection join** of r and s is defined as follows:

$$\begin{aligned} r \otimes s \ := \ & \{\mu \mid \mu \text{ is a tuple over format } P \\ & \quad \text{with names}(P) = \text{names}(R) \cup \text{names}(S) \\ & \quad \wedge (\exists\, \nu \in r)(\exists\, \rho \in s)\ \mu[X] = \nu[X] \\ & \quad \wedge \mu[Y] = \rho[Y] \ \wedge \ \mu[Z_2] = \nu[Z_2] = \rho[Z_2] \\ & \quad \wedge \mu[Z_1] = \nu[Z_1] \cap \rho[Z_1] \neq \emptyset\} \end{aligned}$$

Give counterexamples showing that n and u do not distribute over $\otimes$ (that is, the property from Exercise 9 holds neither for n nor for u when '$\cup$' is replaced by '$\otimes$').

(12) Try to represent the *PERSON* type as defined in Section 21.3 as an (unnormalized) relation format and give a corresponding relation.

(13) Write a complete set of OPAL subclass creation messages for the airline application described in Figure 4.3.

(14) Write OPAL class methods for creating instances of the library application from Section 22.2.3. Do the same for the *Employee(s)* classes defined in that section.

(15) Write OPAL instance methods which implement the following informally stated queries:

(a) Show all authors of some (given) book.

(b) Show the return date for each book currently checked out.

(c) Show the address of every student.

(d) Show the last name of each reader.

(e) Select the call number for a book with a given title.

(f) Select all titles written by some (given) author.

(g) Select the title of each book currently checked out.

(h) Select all publishers located in NY.

(i) Select the name of every student from LA.

(j) Select the phone number of every professor from the computer science department.

(k) Select the return date of a book with a given call number.

Bibliography

Abbott C., ed. (1985). Special issue on computer music. *ACM Computing Surveys*, **17**(2)

Abiteboul S. (1988). Updates, a new frontier. In *Proc. 2nd International Conference on Database Theory (ICDT)*, LNCS 326, pp. 1–18. Berlin: Springer-Verlag

Abiteboul S. (1989). Towards a deductive object-oriented database language. In *Proc. 1st International Conference on Deductive and Object-Oriented Databases*, pp. 419–38

Abiteboul S. and Bidoit N. (1986). Non first normal form relations: an algebra allowing data restructuring. *Journal of Computer and System Sciences*, **33**, pp. 361–93

Abiteboul S. and Hull R. (1985). Update propagation in the IFO database model. In *Proc. International Conference on Foundations of Data Organization*, Kyoto, pp. 243–51

Abiteboul S. and Hull R. (1987). IFO: a formal semantic database model. *ACM Transactions on Database Systems*, **12**, pp. 525–65

Abiteboul S. and Kanellakis P.C. (1989). Object identity as a query language primitive. In *Proc. ACM SIGMOD International Conference on Management of Data*, pp. 159–73. New York: ACM

Abiteboul S. and Vianu V. (1985). Transactions and integrity constraints. In *Proc. 4th ACM SIGACT-SIGMOD Symposium on Principles of Database Systems*, pp. 193–204. New York: ACM

Abiteboul S. and Vianu V. (1986). Deciding properties of transactional schemas. In *Proc. 5th ACM SIGACT-SIGMOD Symposium on Principles of Database Systems*, pp. 235–9. New York: ACM

Abiteboul S. and Vianu V. (1988a). Equivalence and optimization of relational transactions. *Journal of the ACM*, **35**, pp. 70–120

Abiteboul S. and Vianu V. (1988b). Procedural and declarative database update languages. In *Proc. 7th ACM SIGACT-SIGMOD-SIGART Symposium on Principles of Database Systems*, pp. 240–50. New York: ACM

Abiteboul S., Bancilhon F., Bidoit N. et al. (1986). *VERSO: A Database Machine Based on Non 1NF Relations.* Rapport de Recherche No. 523, INRIA Centre de Rocquencourt, France

Abiteboul S., Fischer P.C. and Schek H.J., eds. (1989). *Nested Relations and Complex Objects in Databases.* Springer LNCS 361

Afsarmanesh H., Knapp D., McLeod D. and Parker A. (1985). An extensible object-oriented approach to databases for VLSI/CAD. In *Proc. 11th International Conference on Very Large Data Bases*, pp. 13–24

Aho A.V. and Ullman J.D. (1979). Universality of data retrieval languages. In *Proc. 6th ACM Symposium on Principles of Programming Languages*, pp. 110–20. New York: ACM

Aho A.V., Beeri C. and Ullman J.D. (1979). The theory of joins in relational databases. *ACM Transactions on Database Systems*, **4**, pp. 297–314

Aho A.V., Hopcroft J.E. and Ullman J.D. (1983). *Data Structures and Algorithms.* Reading, MA: Addison-Wesley

Andrews T. and Harris C. (1987). Combining language and database advances in an object-oriented development environment. In *OOPSLA '87 Proceedings*, pp. 430–40

ANSI (1975). X3/SPARC Study Group on Data Base Management Systems. Interim Report. *FDT* (*ACM SIGMOD Record*), **7**(2)

ANSI (1984). *Draft Proposed Network Database Language NDL.* Document X3H2-84-100. New York: ANSI

ANSI (1985). *Draft Proposed American Standard Database Language SQL.* Draft ISO/TC 97/SC 21/WG 5–15/N 90. New York: ANSI

Apt K.R. and van Emden M.H. (1982). Contributions to the theory of logic programming. *Journal of the ACM*, **29**, 841–62

Apt K.R. and Pugin J.M. (1987). Maintenance of stratified databases viewed as a belief revision system. In *Proc. 6th ACM SIGACT-SIGMOD-SIGART Symposium on Principles of Database Systems*, pp. 136–45. New York: ACM

Apt K.R., Blair H. and Walker A. (1988). Towards a theory of declarative knowledge. In Minker (1988), pp. 89–148

Armstrong W.W. (1974). Dependency structures of data base relationships. In *Proc. IFIP Congress*, pp. 580–3

Arnow D.M. and Tenenbaum A.M. (1984). An empirical comparison of B-trees, compact B-trees and multiway trees. In *Proc. ACM SIGMOD International Conference on Management of Data*, pp. 33–46. New York: ACM

Astrahan M.M., Blasgen M.W., Chamberlin D.D. et al. (1976). System/R: a relational approach to data base management. *ACM Transactions on Database Systems*, **1**, pp. 97–137

Atkinson M.P. and Buneman P. (1987). Types and persistence in database programming languages. *ACM Computing Surveys*, **19**, pp. 105–90

Atkinson M., Bancilhon F., DeWitt D., Dittrich K., Maier D. and Zdonik S. (1989). The object-oriented database system manifesto. In *Proc. 1st In-*

ternational Conference on Deductive and Object-Oriented Databases, pp. 40–57

Atzeni P. and Chen P.P.-S. (1983). Completeness of query languages for the entity-relationship model. In *Entity-Relationship Approach to Information Modeling and Analysis* (Chen P.P.-S., ed.). pp. 109–22. Amsterdam: North-Holland

Atzeni P., Batini C., Lenzerini M. and Villanelli F. (1983). INCOD: a system for conceptual design of data and transactions in the entity-relationship model. In *Entity-Relationship Approach to Information Modeling and Analysis* (Chen P.P.-S., ed.). pp. 375–410. Amsterdam: North-Holland

Bachman C.W. (1973). The programmer as navigator. *Communications of the ACM*, **16**, pp. 653–8

Bancilhon F. (1988). Object-oriented database systems. In *Proc. 7th ACM SIGACT-SIGMOD-SIGART Symposium on Principles of Database Systems*, pp. 152–62. New York: ACM

Bancilhon F. (1989). Query languages for object-oriented database systems: analysis and a proposal. In *Proc. 3rd GI/SI Conference on 'Datenbank-Systeme für Büro, Technik und Wissenschaft'*. Informatik-Fachbericht No. 204, pp. 1–18. Berlin: Springer-Verlag

Bancilhon, F. and Khoshafian S. (1989). A calculus for complex objects. *Journal of Computer and System Sciences*, **38**, pp. 326–40

Bancilhon F. and Ramakrishnan R. (1986). An amateur's introduction to recursive query processing strategies. In *Proc. ACM SIGMOD International Conference on Management of Data*, pp. 16–52. New York: ACM

Bancilhon F. and Spyratos N. (1981). Update semantics of relational views. *ACM Transactions on Database Systems*, **6**, pp. 557–75

Bancilhon F., Kim W. and Korth H.F. (1985). A model of CAD transactions. In *Proc. 11th International Conference on Very Large Data Bases*, pp. 25–33

Bancilhon F., Briggs T., Khoshafian S. and Valduriez P. (1987). FAD, a powerful and simple database language. In *Proc. 13th International Conference on Very Large Data Bases*, pp. 97–105

Bancilhon F., Barbedette G., Benzaken V. et al. (1988). The design and implementation of O_2, an object-oriented database system. In Dittrich (1988), pp. 1–22

Banerjee J., Chou H.T., Garza J.F., Kim W., Woelck D. and Ballou N. (1987a). Data model issues for object-oriented applications. *ACM Transactions on Office Information Systems*, **5**, pp. 3–26

Banerjee J., Kim W., Kim H.J. and Korth H.F. (1987b). Semantics and implementation of schema evolution in object-oriented databases. In *Proc. ACM SIGMOD International Conference on Management of Data*, pp. 311–22. New York: ACM

Banerjee J., Kim W. and Kim K.C. (1988). Queries in object-oriented databases. In *Proc. 4th IEEE International Conference on Data Engineering*, pp. 31–8. Los Alamitos, CA: IEEE Computer Society Press

Barzilai G. and Barzilai H. (1985). *Functional Testing of a Relational Data Base.* IBM Research Report RC 11351, Yorktown Heights, NY: IBM

Batini C. and Lenzerini M. (1984). A methodology for data schema integration in the entity relationship model. *IEEE Transactions on Software Engineering*, **SE-10**, pp. 650–64

Batini C. and Santucci G. (1980). Top-down design in the entity-relationship model. In *Entity-Relationship Approach to Systems Analysis and Design* (Chen P.P.-S., ed.). pp. 323–38. Amsterdam: North-Holland

Batini C., Furlani L. and Nardelli E. (1985). What is a good diagram? A pragmatic approach. In *Proc. 4th International Conference on Entity-Relationship Approach*, Chicago, IL, pp. 312–19

Batory D.S. (1986). GENESIS: a project to develop an extensible database management system. In Dittrich and Dayal (1986), pp. 207–8

Batory D.S. (1987). Principles of database management system extensibility. *Bulletin of the IEEE Computer Society Technical Committee on Database Engineering*, **10**(2), pp. 40–6

Batory D.S. and Buchmann A.P. (1984). Molecular objects, abstract data types, and data models: a framework. In *Proc. 10th International Conference on Very Large Data Bases*, pp. 172–84

Batory D.S. and Kim W. (1985). Modeling concepts for VLSI CAD objects. *ACM Transactions on Database Systems*, **10**, pp. 322–46

Batory D.S., Barnett J.R., Garza J.F. et al. (1988a). GENESIS: an extensible database management system. *IEEE Transactions on Software Engineering*, **SE-14**, pp. 1711–29

Batory D.S., Leung T.Y. and Wise T.E. (1988b). Implementation concepts for an extensible data model and data language. *ACM Transactions on Database Systems*, **13**, pp. 231–62

Bayer R. and McCreight E. (1972). Organization and maintenance of large ordered indexes. *Acta Informatica*, **1**, pp. 173–89

Bayer R. and Schkolnick M. (1977). Concurrency of operations on B-trees. *Acta Informatica*, **9**, pp. 1–21

Beeri C. (1980). On the membership problem for functional and multivalued dependencies in relational databases. *ACM Transactions on Database Systems*, **5**, pp. 241–59

Beeri C. (1988). Data models and languages for databases. In *Proc. 2nd International Conference on Database Theory*, LNCS 326, pp. 19–40. Berlin: Springer-Verlag

Beeri C. (1989). Formal models for object oriented databases. In *Proc. 1st International Conference on Deductive and Object-Oriented Databases*, pp. 370–95

Beeri C. and Bernstein P.A. (1979). Computational problems related to the design of normal form relational schemas. *ACM Transactions on Database Systems*, **4**, pp. 30–59

Beeri C. and Kifer M. (1986). An integrated approach to logical design of relational database schemes. *ACM Transactions on Database Systems*, **11**, pp. 134–58

Beeri C., Fagin R. and Howard J.H. (1977). A complete axiomatization for functional and multivalued dependencies. In *Proc. ACM SIGMOD International Conference on Management of Data*, pp. 47–61. New York: ACM

Beeri C., Bernstein P.A. and Goodman N. (1978). A sophisticate's introduction to database normalization theory. In *Proc. 4th International Conference on Very Large Data Bases*, pp. 113–24

Beeri C., Bernstein P.A., Goodman N., Lai M.Y. and Shasha D.E. (1983). A concurrency control theory for nested transactions. In *Proc. 2nd Annual ACM Symposium on Principles of Distributed Computing*, pp. 45–62. New York: ACM

Beeri C., Dowd M., Fagin R. and Stratman R. (1984). On the structure of Armstrong relations for functional dependencies. *Journal of the ACM*, **31**, pp. 30–46

Beeri C., Schek H.J. and Weikum G. (1988). Multi-level transaction management, theoretical art or practical need? In *Proc. 1st International Conference on Extending Database Technology (EDBT)*, LNCS 303, pp. 134–54. New York: Springer-Verlag

Beeri C., Bernstein P.A. and Goodman N. (1989). A model for concurrency in nested transaction systems. *Journal of the ACM*, **36**, pp. 230–69

Bentley J.L. (1975). Multidimensional binary search trees used for associative searching. *Communications of the ACM*, **18**, pp. 509–17

Bentley J.L. (1979). Multidimensional binary search trees in database applications. *IEEE Transactions on Software Engineering*, **SE-5**, pp. 333–40

Berge C. (1976). *Graphs and Hypergraphs*. Amsterdam: North-Holland

Bernstein P.A. (1976). Synthesizing third normal form relations from functional dependencies. *ACM Transactions on Database Systems*, **1**, pp. 272–98

Bernstein P.A. and Goodman N. (1980a). What does Boyce-Codd normal form do?. In *Proc. 6th International Conference on Very Large Data Bases*, pp. 245–59

Bernstein P.A. and Goodman N. (1980b). Timestamp-based algorithms for concurrency control in distributed database systems. In *Proc. 6th International Conference on Very Large Data Bases*, pp. 285–300

Bernstein P.A. and Goodman N. (1983). Multiversion concurrency control — theory and algorithms. *ACM Transactions on Database Systems*, **8**, pp. 465–83

Bernstein P.A. and Lomet D.B. (1987). CASE requirements for extensible database systems. *Bulletin of the IEEE Computer Society Technical Committee on Database Engineering*, **10**(2), pp. 2–9

Bernstein P.A., Blaustein B.T. and Clarke E.M. (1980). Fast maintenance of semantic integrity assertions using redundant aggregate data. In *Proc. 6th International Conference on Very Large Data Bases*, pp. 126–36

Bernstein P.A., Goodman N. and Hadzilacos V. (1983a). Recovery algorithms for database systems. In *Information Processing 83* (Proc. IFIP Congress) (Mason, R.E.A., ed.). pp. 799–807. Amsterdam: North-Holland

Bernstein P.A., Goodman N. and Lai M.Y. (1983b). Analyzing concurrency control algorithms when user and system operations differ. *IEEE Transactions on Software Engineering*, **SE-9**, pp. 233–9

Bernstein P.A., Hadzilacos V. and Goodman N. (1987). *Concurrency Control and Recovery in Database Systems.* Reading, MA: Addison-Wesley

Bic L. and Gilbert J.P. (1986). Learning from AI: new trends in database technology. *IEEE Computer*, **19**(3), pp. 44–54

Bidoit N. (1987). The Verso algebra or how to answer queries with fewer joins. *Journal of Computer and System Sciences*, **35**, pp. 321–64

Biliris A. (1987). Operation specific locking in B-trees. In *Proc. 6th ACM SIGACT-SIGMOD-SIGART Symposium on Principles of Database Systems*, pp. 159–69. New York : ACM

Biskup J. (1978). On the complementation rule for multivalued dependencies in database relations. *Acta Informatica*, **10**, pp. 297–305

Biskup J. (1980). Inferences of multivalued dependencies in fixed and undetermined universes. *Theoretical Computer Science*, **10**, pp. 93–105

Biskup J. (1981). A formal approach to null values in database relations. In *Advances in Database Theory*, Vol. 1. (Gallaire H., Minker J. and Nicolas J.M., eds.), pp. 299–341. New York: Plenum Press

Biskup J. (1983). A foundation of Codd's relational maybe-operations. *ACM Transactions on Database Systems*, **8**, pp. 608–36

Biskup J. and Brüggemann H.H. (1983). Universal relation views: a pragmatic approach. In *Proc. 9th International Conference on Very Large Data Bases*, pp. 172–85

Biskup J. and Convent B. (1986). A formal view integration method. In *Proc. ACM SIGMOD International Conference on Management of Data*, pp. 398–407. New York : ACM

Biskup J. and Meyer R. (1987). Design of relational database schemes by deleting attributes in the canonical decomposition. *Journal of Computer and System Sciences*, **35**, pp. 1–22

Biskup J., Dayal U. and Bernstein P.A. (1979). Synthesizing independent database schemas. In *Proc. ACM SIGMOD International Conference on Management of Data*, pp. 143–51. New York : ACM

Biskup J., Brüggemann H.H., Kramer M. and Schnetgöke L. (1986). One-flavor assumption and γ-acyclicity for universal relation views. In *Proc. 5th ACM SIGACT-SIGMOD Symposium on Principles of Database Systems*, pp. 148–59. New York: ACM

Bitton D., DeWitt D.J. and Turbyfill C. (1983). Benchmarking database systems — a systematic approach. In *Proc. 9th International Conference on Very Large Data Bases*, pp. 8–19

Blasgen M.W., Astrahan M.M., Chamberlin D.D. et al. (1981). System R: an architectural overview. *IBM Systems Journal*, **20**, pp. 41–61

Bloom T. and Zdonik S.B. (1987). Issues in the design of object-oriented database programming languages. In *OOPSLA '87 Proceedings*, pp. 441–51

Bolour A. (1979). Optimal properties of multiple-key hashing functions. *Journal of the ACM*, **26**, pp. 196–210

Boral H. and DeWitt D.J. (1984). A methodology for database system performance evaluation. In *Proc. ACM SIGMOD International Conference on Management of Data*, pp. 176–85. New York: ACM

Brägger R.P., Dudler A.M., Rebsamen J. and Zehnder C.A. (1985). Gambit: an interactice database design tool for data structures, integrity constraints, and transactions. *IEEE Transactions on Software Engineering*, **SE-11**, pp. 574–83

Brodie M.L. (1984). On the development of data models. In *On Conceptual Modeling (Perspectives from Artificial Intelligence, Databases, and Programming Languages)* (Brodie M.L., Mylopoulos J. and Schmidt J.W., eds.). pp. 19–47. Berlin: Springer-Verlag

Brodie M.L. and Ridjanovic D. (1984). On the design and specification of database transactions. In: *On Conceptual Modeling (Perspectives from Artificial Intelligence, Databases, and Programming Languages)* (Brodie M.L., Mylopoulos J. and Schmidt J.W., eds.). pp. 277–312. Berlin: Springer-Verlag

Brosda V. (1984). *Design and Implementation of a Universal Relation User Interface for a Relational Database System.* Master's Thesis (in German), Lehrstuhl für angewandte Mathematik, insbesondere Informatik, RWTH Aachen, FRG

Brosda V. and Vossen G. (1988). Update and retrieval in a relational database through a universal schema interface. *ACM Transactions on Database Systems*, **13**, pp. 449–85

Brüggemann H.H. (1986). *Semantik von Universalrelation-Sichten und ihre Datenbankschemas.* Ph.D. Dissertation (Forschungsbericht Nr. 214), Abteilung Informatik, Universität Dortmund, FRG

Bryce D. and Hull R. (1986). SNAP: a graphics-based schema manager. In *Proc. 2nd IEEE International Conference on Data Engineering*, pp. 151–64. Los Alamitos, CA: IEEE Computer Society Press

Buchmann A.P. and de Celis C.P. (1985). An architecture and data model for CAD databases. In *Proc. 11th International Conference on Very Large Data Bases*, pp. 105–14

Burkhard W.A. (1976). Hashing and trie algorithms for partial match retrieval. *ACM Transactions on Database Systems*, **1**, pp. 175–87

Burkhard W.A. (1979). Partial-match hash coding: benefits of redundancy. *ACM Transactions on Database Systems*, **4**, pp. 228–39

Burkhard W.A. (1983). Interpolation-based index maintenance. In *Proc. 2nd ACM SIGACT-SIGMOD Symposium on Principles of Database Systems*, pp. 76–89. New York: ACM

Campbell P.M., Czejdo B. and Embley D.W. (1985). A relationally complete query language for an entity-relationship model. In *Proc. 4th International Conference on the Entity-Relationship Approach*, Chicago, IL, pp. 90–97

Cardenas A.F. (1985). *Data Base Management Systems* 2nd edn. Boston, MA: Allyn and Bacon

Carey M.J. and DeWitt D.J. (1987). An overview of the EXODUS project. *Bulletin of the IEEE Computer Society Technical Committee on Database Engineering*, **10**(2), pp. 47–54

Carey M.J. and Stonebraker M.R. (1984). The performance of concurrency control algorithms for database management systems. In *Proc. 10th International Conference on Very Large Data Bases*, pp. 107–18

Carey M.J., DeWitt D.J., Frank D., Graefe G., Muralikrishna M. and Richardson J.E. (1986). The architecture of the EXODUS extensible DBMS. In Dittrich and Dayal (1986), pp. 52–65

Carey M.J., DeWitt D.J. and Vandenberg S.L. (1988). A data model and query language for EXODUS. In *Proc. ACM SIGMOD International Conference on Management of Data*, pp. 413–23. New York: ACM

Casanova M.A. (1981). *The Concurrency Control Problem for Database Systems.* LNCS 116. Berlin: Springer-Verlag

Casanova M.A. and Bernstein P.A. (1980). General purpose schedulers for database systems. *Acta Informatica*, **14**, pp. 195–220

Casanova M.A. and de Sa J.E.A. (1983). Designing entity-relationship schemes for conventional information systems. In *Entity-Relationship Approach to Software Engineering* (Davis C.G. et al., eds.), pp. 265–77. Amsterdam: North-Holland

Casanova M.A. and Vidal V.M.P. (1983). Towards a sound view integration methodology. In *Proc. 2nd ACM SIGACT-SIGMOD Symposium on Principles of Database Systems*, pp. 36–47. New York: ACM

Casanova M.A., Fagin R. and Papadimitriou C.H. (1984). Inclusion dependencies and their interaction with functional dependencies. *Journal of Computer and System Sciences*, **28**, pp. 29–59

Casanova M.A., Tucherman L., Furtado A.L. and Braga A.P. (1989). Optimization of relational schemas containing inclusion dependencies. In *Proc. 15th International Conference on Very Large Data Bases*, pp. 317–25

Ceri S. (1983). *Methodology and Tools for Database Design.* Amsterdam: North-Holland

Ceri S. and Gottlob G. (1985). Translating SQL into relational algebra: optimization, semantics, and equivalence of SQL queries. *IEEE Transactions of Software Engineering*, **SE-11**, pp. 324–45

Ceri S., Gottlob G. and Lavazza L. (1986). Translation and optimization of logic queries: the algebraic approach. In *Proc. 12th International Conference on Very Large Data Bases*, pp. 395–402

Ceri S., Gottlob G. and Tanca L. (1989). What you always wanted to know about Datalog (and never dared to ask). *IEEE Transactions on Knowledge and Data Engineering*, **1**, pp. 146–66

Ceri S., Gottlob G. and Tanca L. (1990). *Logic Programming and Databases.* Berlin: Springer-Verlag

Chamberlin D.D., Gilbert A.M. and Yost R.A. (1981). A history of System R and SQL/Data System. In *Proc. 7th International Conference on Very Large Data Bases*, pp. 456–64

Chan E.P.F. and Lochovsky F.H. (1980). A graphical data base design aid using the entity-relationship model. In *Entity-Relationship Approach to Systems Analysis and Design* (Chen P.P.-S., ed.), pp. 295–310. Amsterdam: North-Holland

Chandra A.K. (1988). Theory of database queries. In *Proc. 7th ACM SIGACT-SIGMOD-SIGART Symposium on Principles of Database Systems*, pp. 1–9. New York: ACM

Chandra A.K. and Harel D. (1980). Computable queries for relational data bases. *Journal of Computer and System Sciences*, **21**, pp. 156–78

Chandra A.K. and Harel D. (1982). Structure and complexity of relational queries. *Journal of Computer and System Sciences*, **25**, pp. 99–128

Chandra A.K. and Harel D. (1985). Horn clause queries and generalizations. *Journal of Logic Programming*, **1**, pp. 1–15

Chang J.M. and Fu K.S. (1981). Extended K-d tree database organization: a dynamic multiattribute clustering method. *IEEE Transactions on Software Engineering*, **SE-7**, pp. 284–90

Chen P.P.-S. (1976). The entity-relationship model — toward a unified view of data. *ACM Transactions on Database Systems*, **1**, pp. 9–36

Chen P.P.-S. (1980). Recent literature of the entity-relationship approach. In *Entity-Relationship Approach to Systems Analysis and Design* (Chen P.P.-S., ed.), pp. 3–12. Amsterdam: North-Holland

Chen P.P.-S. (1983). A preliminary framework for entity-relationship models. In *Entity-Relationship Approach to Information Modeling and Analysis*

(Chen P.P.-S., ed.), pp. 19–28. Amsterdam: North-Holland,

Chen P.P.-S. (1985). Database design based on entity and relationship. In Yao (1985), pp. 174–210

Chimenti D., Gamboa R., Krishnamurthy R., Naqvi S., Tsur S. and Zaniolo C. (1990). The LDL System Prototype. *IEEE Transactions on Knowledge and Data Engineering*, **2**, pp. 76–90

Christodoulakis S., Vanderbroek J., Li J. et al. (1984). Development of a Multimedia Information System for an Office Environment. In *Proc. 10th International Conference on Very Large Data Bases*, pp. 261–71

Clemons E. (1985). Data models and the ANSI/SPARC architecture. In Yao (1985), pp. 66–114

Cobb R.E., Fry J.P. and Teorey T.J. (1984). *The Database Designer's Workbench.* Technical Report CRL-TR-18-84, Computing Research Laboratory, University of Michigan at Ann Arbor

CODASYL (1971). *Data Base Task Group April 71 Report.* New York: ACM

CODASYL (1978). Report of the Data Description Language Committee. *Information Systems*, **3**, pp. 247–320

Codd E.F. (1970). A relational model of data for large shared data banks. *Communications of the ACM*, **13**, pp. 377–87

Codd E.F. (1971). Further normalization of the data base relational model. In *Data Base Systems* (Rustin R., ed.), pp. 33–64. Englewood Cliffs, NJ: Prentice-Hall

Codd E.F. (1975). Understanding Relations. *FDT (ACM SIGMOD Bulletin)* **7**(3–4), pp. 23–8

Codd E.F. (1979). Extending the database relational model to capture more meaning. *ACM Transactions on Database Systems*, **4**, pp. 397–434

Codd E.F. (1982). Relational databases: a practical foundation for productivity. *Communications of the ACM*, **25**, pp. 109–117

Codd E.F. (1986). An evaluation scheme for database management systems that are claimed to be relational. In *Proc. 2nd IEEE International Conference on Data Engineering*, pp. 720–729. Los Alamitos, CA: IEEE Computer Society Press

Convent B. (1986). Unsolvable problems related to the view integration approach. In *Proc. 1st International Conference on Database Theory*, LNCS 243, pp. 141–56. Berlin: Springer-Verlag

Cosmadakis S.S. and Papadimitriou C.H. (1984). Updates of relational views. *Journal of the ACM*, **31**, pp. 742–60

Croker A. and Maier D. (1986). A dynamic tree-locking protocol. In *Proc. 2nd IEEE International Conference on Data Engineering*, pp. 49–56. Los Alamitos, CA: IEEE Computer Society Press

Dadam P. (1988). Advanced Information Management (AIM): research in extended nested relations. *Bulletin of the IEEE Computer Society Technical*

Committee on Database Engineering, **11**(3), pp. 4–14

Dadam P., Küspert K., Anderson F. et al. (1986). A DBMS prototype to support extended NF^2 relations: an integrated view on flat tables and hierarchies. In *Proc. ACM SIGMOD International Conference on Management of Data*, pp. 356–67. New York: ACM

Date C.J. (1981). *An Introduction to Database Systems* Vol. 1, 3rd edn. Reading, MA: Addison-Wesley

Date C.J. (1983). *An Introduction to Database Systems* Vol. 2. Reading, MA: Addison-Wesley

Date C.J. (1986). *An Introduction to Database Systems* Vol. 1, 4th edn. Reading, MA: Addison-Wesley

Date C.J. (1987). *A Guide to INGRES*. Reading, MA: Addison-Wesley

Date C.J. (1989). *A Guide to the SQL Standard*, 2nd edn. Reading, MA: Addison-Wesley

Date C.J. and White C.J. (1989a). *A Guide to SQL/DS*. Reading, MA: Addison-Wesley

Date C.J. and White C.J. (1989b). *A Guide to DB2*, 3rd edn. Reading, MA: Addison-Wesley

Dayal U. (1988). Active database management systems. In *Proc. 3rd International Conference on Data and Knowledge Bases: Improving Usability and Responsiveness*, Jerusalem, Israel, pp. 150–69. San Mateo, CA: Morgan Kaufmann Publishers

Dayal U. and Bernstein P.A. (1982). On the correct translation of update operations on relational views. *ACM Transactions on Database Systems*, **7**, pp. 381–416

Dayal U., Buchmann A.P. and McCarthy D.R. (1988). Rules are objects too: a knowledge model for an active, object-oriented database system. In Dittrich (1988), pp. 129–43

De Antonellis, V. and Di Leva A. (1985a). DATAID-1: A database design methodology. *Information Systems*, **10**, pp. 181–95

De Antonellis, V. and Di Leva A. (1985b). A case study of database design using the DATAID approach. *Information Systems*, **10**, pp. 339–59

de Bra P. (1985). *Functional Dependency Implications, Inducing Horizontal Decompositions*. Technical Report 85–30, Department of Mathematics, University of Antwerp

Delobel C. (1978). Normalization and hierarchical dependencies in the relational data model. *ACM Transactions on Database Systems*, **3**, pp. 201–22

Delobel C. and Casey R.G. (1973). Decomposition of a data base and the theory of Boolean switching functions. *IBM Journal of Research and Development*, **17**, pp. 374–86

Denning D.E.R. (1982). *Cryptography and Data Security*. Reading, MA: Addison-Wesley

Deux O. et al. (1990). The story of O_2. *IEEE Transactions on Knowledge and Data Engineering*, **2**, pp. 91–108

Devor C. and Carlson C.R. (1982). Structural locking mechanisms and their effect on database management system performance. *Information Systems*, **7**, pp. 345–58

Dittrich K.R. (ed.) (1988). *Advances in Object-Oriented Database Systems* (Proc. 2nd International Workshop on Object-Oriented Database Systems). LNCS 334. Berlin: Springer-Verlag

Dittrich K.R. and Dayal U., eds. (1986). *Proceedings 1986 International Workshop on Object-Oriented Database Systems.* Washington, DC: IEEE Computer Society Press

Dogac A. and Chen P.P.-S. (1983). Entity-Relationship Model in the ANSI SPARC Framework. In *Entity-Relationship Approach to Information Modeling and Analysis* (Chen P.P.-S., ed.), pp. 357–74. Amsterdam: North-Holland

Dubois E., Hagelstein J., Lahou E., Rifaut A. and Williams F. (1986). A data model for requirements analysis. In *Proc. 2nd IEEE International Conference on Data Engineering*, pp. 646–53. Los Alamitos, CA: IEEE Computer Society Press

Ehrig H. and Kreowski H.-J. (1980). Applications of graph grammar theory to consistency, synchronization and scheduling in data base systems. *Information Systems*, **5**, pp. 225–38

Elmasri R.A. and Larson L.A. (1985). A graphical query facility for ER databases. In *Proc. 4th International Conference on Entity-Relationship Approach*, Chicago, IL, pp. 236–45

Elmasri R.A. and Navathe S.B. (1989). *Fundamentals of Database Systems.* Redwood, CA: Benjamin/Cummings

Eswaran K.P., Gray J.N., Lorie R.A. and Traiger I.L. (1976). The notions of consistency and predicate locks in a database system. *Communications of the ACM*, **19**, pp. 624–33

Fagin R. (1977a). The decomposition versus the synthetic approach to relational database design. In *Proc. 3rd International Conference on Very Large Data Bases*, pp. 441–6

Fagin R. (1977b). Multivalued dependencies and a new normal form for relational databases. *ACM Transactions on Database Systems*, **2**, pp. 262–78

Fagin R. (1977c). Functional dependencies in a relational database and propositional logic. *IBM Journal of Research and Development*, **21**, pp. 534–44

Fagin R. (1978). On an authorization mechanism. *ACM Transactions on Database Systems*, **3**, pp. 310–19

Fagin R. (1979). Normal forms and relational database operators. In *Proc. ACM SIGMOD International Conference on Management of Data*, pp. 153–60. New York: ACM

Fagin R. (1981). A normal form for relational databases that is based on domains and keys. *ACM Transactions on Database Systems*, **6**, pp. 387–415

Fagin R. (1982). Horn clauses and database dependencies. *Journal of the ACM*, **29**, pp. 952–85

Fagin R. (1983). Degrees of acyclicity for hypergraphs and relational database schemes. *Journal of the ACM*, **30**, pp. 514–50

Fagin R. and Vardi M.Y. (1984). The theory of data dependencies — an overview. In *Proc. 11th International Colloquium on Automata, Languages, and Programming (ICALP)*, LNCS 172, pp. 1–22. Berlin: Springer-Verlag

Fagin R., Nievergelt J., Pippenger N. and Strong H.R. (1979). Extendible hashing — a fast access method for dynamic files. *ACM Transactions on Database Systems*, **4**, pp. 315–44

Fernandez E.B., Summers R.C. and Wood C. (1981). *Database Security and Integrity*. Reading, MA: Addison-Wesley

Finkelstein S., Schkolnick M. and Tiberio P. (1986). *Physical Database Design for Relational Databases*. IBM Research Report RJ 5034, Almaden Research Center, San Jose, CA

Fischer P.C. and van Gucht D. (1984). *Structure of Relations Satisfying Certain Families of Dependencies*. manuscript, Vanderbilt University

Fischer P.C., Saxton L.V., Thomas S.J. and van Gucht D. (1985). Interactions between dependencies and nested relational structures. *Journal of Computer and System Sciences*, **31**, pp. 343–54

Fishman D.H., Beech D., Cate H.P. et al. (1987). Iris: an object-oriented database management system. *ACM Transactions on Office Information Systems*, **5**, pp. 48–69

Flajolet P. and Puech C. (1983). Tree structures for partial match retrieval. In *Proc. 24th IEEE Symposium on Foundations of Computer Science*, pp. 282–88. Los Alamitos, CA: IEEE Computer Society Press

Ford S., Joseph J., Langworthy D.E. et al. (1988). ZEITGEIST: database support for object-oriented programming. In Dittrich (1988), pp. 23–42

Freeston M. (1987). The BANG file: a new kind of grid file. In *Proc. ACM SIGMOD International Conference on Management of Data*, pp. 260–9. New York: ACM

Furtado A.L. and Casanova M.A. (1985). Updating relational views. In *Query Processing in Database Systems* (Kim W., Reiner D.S. and Batory D.S., eds.), pp. 127–42. Berlin: Springer-Verlag

Furtado A.L., Sevcik K.C. and dos Santos C.S. (1979). Permitting updates through views of data bases. *Information Systems*, **4**, pp. 269–83

Galil Z. (1982). An almost linear-time algorithm for computing a dependency basis in a relational database. *Journal of the ACM*, **29**, pp. 96–102

Garcia-Molina H. (1983). Using semantic knowledge for transaction processing in a distributed database. *ACM Transactions on Database Systems*, **8**, pp. 186–213

Garey M. and Johnson D.S. (1979). *Computers and Intractability — A Guide to the Theory of NP-Completeness.* San Francisco: W.H. Freeman

Gawlick D. (1985). Processing 'hot spots' in high performance systems. In *Proc. 13th IEEE COMPCON Spring Conference*, pp. 249–51. Los Alamitos, CA: IEEE Computer Society Press

Ghezzi C. and Jazayeri M. (1987). *Programming Language Concepts*, 2nd edn. New York: Wiley

Goodman N. and Tay Y.C. (1983). *Synthesizing Fourth Normal Form Relations from Multivalued Dependencies.* Technical Report TR-17-83, Aiken Computation Laboratory, Harvard University

Goodman N., Shmueli O. and Tay Y.C. (1984). GYO reductions, canonical connections, tree and cyclic schemas, and tree projections. *Journal of Computer and System Sciences*, **29**, pp. 338–58

Graefe G. and DeWitt D.J. (1987). The EXODUS optimizer generator. In *Proc. ACM SIGMOD International Conference on Management of Data*, pp. 160–72. New York: ACM

Graham M.H. (1979). *On the Universal Relation.* Technical Report, University of Toronto

Grant J. (1987). *Logical Introduction to Databases.* San Diego, CA: Harcourt Brace Jovanovich

Gray J. (1978). Notes on data base operating systems. In *Operating Systems — An Advanced Course* (Bayer R., Graham M.R. and Seegmüller G., eds.). LNCS 60, pp. 393–481. Berlin: Springer Verlag

Gray J.N. (1980). *A Transaction Model.* IBM Research Report RJ 2895, San Jose, CA

Gray J.N., Lorie R.A. and Putzolu G.R. (1975). Granularity of locks and degrees of consistency in a shared data base. In *Proc. 1st International Conference on Very Large Data Bases*, pp. 428–51

Gray M. (1984). Databases for computer-aided design. In *New Applications of Data Bases* (Gardarin G. and Gelenbe E., eds.), pp. 247–58. London: Academic Press

Gurevich Y. (1988). Logic and the challenge of computer science. In *Trends in Theoretical Computer Science* (Börger E., ed.), pp. 1–57. Rockville, MD: Computer Science Press

Güting H. and Kriegel H.P. (1980). Multidimensional B-tree: an efficient dynamic file structure for exact match queries. In *Proc. 10th Annual GI Conference*, IFB 33, pp. 375–88. Berlin: Springer-Verlag

Guttman A. (1984). R-trees: a dynamic index structure for spatial searching. In *Proc. ACM SIGMOD International Conference on Management of Data*, pp. 47–57. New York: ACM

Gyssens M. and van Gucht D. (1988a). The expressiveness of query languages for nested relations. *Bulletin of the IEEE Computer Society Technical Committee on Database Engineering*, **11**(3), pp. 48–55

Gyssens M. and van Gucht D. (1988b). The powerset algebra as a result of adding programming constructs to the nested relational algebra. In *Proc. ACM SIGMOD International Conference on Management of Data*, pp. 225–32. New York: ACM

Haas L.M., Cody W.F., Freytag J.C. et al. (1988). *An Extensible Processor for an Extended Relational Query Language.* IBM Research Report RJ 6182, San Jose, CA

Haas L.M., Chang W., Lohman G.M. et al. (1990): Starburst mid-flight: as the dust clears. *IEEE Transactions on Knowledge and Data Engineering*, **2**, pp. 143–60

Hadzilacos T. and Papadimitriou C.H. (1986). Algorithmic aspects of multiversion concurrency control. *Journal of Computer and System Sciences*, **33**, pp. 297–310

Hadzilacos V. (1988). A theory of reliability in database systems. *Journal of the ACM*, **35**, pp. 121–45

Hafez A. and Özsoyoglu G. (1988). Storage structures for nested relations. *Bulletin of the IEEE Computer Society Technical Committee on Database Engineering*, **11**(3), pp. 31–8

Hammer M. and McLeod D. (1981). Database description with SDM: a semantic database model. *ACM Transactions on Database Systems*, **6**, pp. 351–86

Hanatani Y. and Fagin R. (1985). *A Simple Characterization of Database Dependency Implication.* IBM Research Report RJ 4777, San Jose, CA

Härder T. (1982). *Observations on Optimistic Concurrency Control Schemes.* IBM Research Report RJ 3645, San Jose, CA

Härder T. (1988). Handling hot spot data in DB-sharing systems. *Information Systems*, **13**, pp. 155–66

Härder T. and Reuter A. (1983). Principles of transaction-oriented database recovery. *ACM Computing Surveys*, **15**, pp. 287–317

Hardwick M. (1984). Extending the relational database data model for design applications. In *Proc. 21st IEEE Design Automation Conference*, pp. 110–16. Los Alamitos, CA: IEEE Computer Society Press

Heath I.J. (1971). Unacceptable file operations in a relational database. In *Proc. ACM-SIGFIDET Workshop on Data Description, Access, and Control*, pp. 19–33. New York: ACM

Held G. and Stonebraker M. (1978). B-trees re-examined. *Communications of the ACM*, **21**, pp. 139–43

Hevner A.R. and Yao S.B. (1985). Network database design methods. In Yao (1985), pp. 294–324

Hinrichs K.H. (1985). *The Grid File System: Implementation and Case Studies of Applications.* Ph.D. Dissertation, ETH Zürich, Switzerland

Honeyman P. (1980). *Functional Dependencies and the Universal Instance Property in the Relational Model of Database Systems.* Ph.D. Dissertation, Princeton University

Honeyman P. (1982). Testing satisfaction of functional dependencies. *Journal of the ACM*, **29**, pp. 668–77

Hornick M.F. and Zdonik S. (1987). A shared, segmented memory system for an object-oriented database. *ACM Transactions on Office Information Systems*, **5**, pp. 70–95

Horowitz E. and Sahni S. (1976). *Fundamentals of Data Structures.* Rockville, MD: Computer Science Press

Hsiao D.K., Kerr D.S. and Madnick S.E. (1978). Privacy and security of data communications and data bases. In *Proc. 4th International Conference on Very Large Data Bases*, pp. 55–67

Hubbard G.U. (1985). Computer-assisted hierarchical database design. In Yao (1985), pp. 255–93

Hudson S.E. and King R. (1987). Object-oriented support for software environments. In *Proc. ACM SIGMOD International Conference on Management of Data*, pp. 491–503. New York: ACM

Hull R. (1987). A survey of theoretical research on typed complex database objects. In *Databases* (Paredaens J., ed.), pp. 193–256. London: Academic Press

Hull R. and King R. (1987). Semantic database modeling: survey, applications, and research issues. *ACM Computing Surveys*, **19**, pp. 201–60

Hutflesz A., Six H.W. and Widmayer P. (1988a). Globally order preserving multidimensional linear hashing. In *Proc. 4th IEEE International Conference on Data Engineering*, pp. 572–9. Los Alamitos, CA: IEEE Computer Society Press

Hutflesz A., Six H.W. and Widmayer P. (1988b). Twin grid files: space optimizing access schemes. In *Proc. ACM SIGMOD International Conference on Management of Data*, pp. 183–90. New York: ACM

IBM (1983a). *SQL/Data System Terminal User's Reference Summary*, 2nd edn. Publ. No. SX24-5121-1. Endicott, NY: IBM

IBM (1983b). *SQL/Data System Terminal User's Guide — VM/SP*, Release 2. Publ. No. SH24-5045-0. Endicott, NY: IBM

IBM (1983c). *SQL/Data System Terminal User's Reference*, Release 2. Publ. No. SH24-5017-2. Endicott, NY: IBM

IBM (1987). *SQL/DS Version 2 Release 1 Usage Guide.* IBM International Technical Support Center, Boeblingen, West Germany, Publ. No. GG24-3191

Immermann N. (1986). Relational queries computable in polynomial time. *Information and Control*, **68**, pp. 86–104

Jarke M. and Vassiliou Y. (1985). A framework for choosing a database query language. *ACM Computing Surveys*, **17**, pp. 313–40

Jäschke G. and Schek H.J. (1982). Remarks on the algebra of non first normal form relations. In *Proc. 1st ACM SIGACT-SIGMOD Symposium on Principles of Database Systems*, pp. 124–38. New York: ACM

Jou J.H. and Fischer P.C. (1980). *A New View of Functional Dependency Structures and Normal Forms.* Technical Report CS-80-6, Department of Computer Science, Pennsylvania State University

Jou J.H. and Fischer P.C. (1982). The complexity of recognizing 3NF relation schemes. *Information Processing Letters*, **14**, pp. 187–90

Kahn B.K. (1985). Requirements specification techniques. In Yao (1985), pp. 1–65

Kambayashi Y. (1981). *Database: A Bibliography.* Rockville, MD: Computer Science Press

Kanellakis P.C. (1988). *Elements of Relational Database Theory.* Techn. Report, Brown University, Providence, RI (In *Handbook of Theoretical Computer Science*, Amsterdam: North-Holland, to appear)

Karabeg D. and Vianu V. (1988). *Axiomatization, Simplification Rules and Parallelization for Relational Transactions.* Techn. Report CS88-118, CSE Department, University of California, San Diego

Katz R.H. (1984). Transaction management in the design environment. In *New Applications of Data Bases* (Gardarin G. and Gelenbe E., eds.), pp. 259–73. London: Academic Press

Katz R.H. (1985). *Information Management for Engineering Design.* Berlin: Springer-Verlag

Katz R.H. and Weiss S. (1984). Design transaction management. In *Proc. 21st IEEE Design Automation Conference*, pp. 692–6. Los Alamitos, CA: IEEE Computer Society Press

Katz R.H., Chang E. and Bhateja R. (1986). Version modeling concepts for computer-aided design databases. In *Proc. ACM SIGMOD International Conference on Management of Data*, pp. 379–86. New York: ACM

Keller A.M. (1985). *Updating Relational Databases Through Views.* Ph.D. Dissertation, Stanford University (Techn. Report No. STAN-CS-85-1040)

Kelley K.L. and Rusinkiewicz M. (1986). Implementation of multikey extendible hashing as an access method for a relational DBMS. In *Proc. 2nd IEEE International Conference on Data Engineering*, pp. 124–31. Los Alamitos, CA: IEEE Computer Society Press

Kellogg C. (1986). From data management to knowledge management. *IEEE Computer*, **19**(1), pp. 75–84

Kent W. (1979). Limitations of record-based information models. *ACM Transactions on Database Systems*, **4**, pp. 107–31

Kent W. (1983). A simple guide to five normal forms in relational database theory. *Communications of the ACM*, **26**, pp. 120–5

Khoshafian S.N. and Copeland G.P. (1986). Object identity. In *OOPSLA '86 Proceedings*, pp. 406–16

Khoshafian, S.N. and Valduriez P. (1990). Sharing, persistence, and object orientation. a database perspective. In *Advances in Database Programming Languages* (Bancilhon F. and Buneman P., eds.), pp. 221–40. Reading, MA: Addison-Wesley

Kifer M. and Lausen G. (1989). F-logic: a higher-order language for reasoning about objects, inheritance, and scheme. In *Proc. ACM SIGMOD International Conference on Management of Data*, pp. 134–46. New York: ACM

Kim W. and Lochovsky F.H., eds. (1989). *Object-Oriented Concepts, Databases, and Applications*. Reading, MA: Addison-Wesley

Kim W., Banerjee J., Chou H.T., Garza J.F. and Woelck D. (1987). Composite object support in an object-oriented database system. In *OOPSLA '87 Proceedings*, pp. 118–25

Kim W., Garza J.F., Ballou N. and Woelck D. (1990). Architecture of the ORION next-generation database system. *IEEE Transactions on Knowledge and Data Engineering*, **2**, pp. 109–24

King R. and McLeod D. (1984). A unified model and methodology for conceptual database design. In *On Conceptual Modeling (Perspectives from Artificial Intelligence, Databases, and Programming Languages)* (Brodie M.L., Mylopoulos J. and Schmidt J.W., eds.), pp. 313–31. Berlin: Springer-Verlag

King R. and McLeod D. (1985). Semantic data models. In Yao (1985), pp. 115–50

Knuth D.E. (1973). *The Art of Computer Programming* Vol. III: *Sorting and Searching.* Reading, MA: Addison-Wesley

Kolaitis P.G. and Papadimitriou C.H. (1988). Why not negation by fixpoint? In *Proc. 7th ACM SIGACT-SIGMOD-SIGART Symposium on Principles of Database Systems*, pp. 231–9. New York: ACM

Korth H.F. (1983). Locking primitives in a database system. *Journal of the ACM*, **30**, pp. 55–79

Korth H.F. and Silberschatz A. (1986). *Database System Concepts.* New York: McGraw-Hill

Korth H.F., Kuper G.M., Feigenbaum J., van Gelder A. and Ullman J.D. (1984). System/U: a database system based on the universal relation assumption. *ACM Transactions on Database Systems*, **9**, pp. 331–47

Kriegel H.P. (1982). Variants of multidimensional B-trees as dynamic index structures for associative retrieval in database systems. In *Proc. 8th Work-*

shop on Graphtheoretic Concepts in Computer Science, pp. 109–28. Munich: Carl Hanser Verlag

Kriegel H.P. (1984). Performance comparison of index structures for multi-key retrieval. In *Proc. ACM SIGMOD International Conference on Management of Data*, pp. 186–96. New York: ACM

Kriegel H.P. and Seeger B. (1986). Multidimensional order preserving linear hashing with partial expansions. In *Proc. 1st International Conference on Database Theory*, LNCS 243, pp. 203–20. Berlin: Springer-Verlag

Kriegel H.P. and Seeger B. (1988). PLOP-hashing: a grid file without directory. In *Proc. 4th IEEE International Conference on Data Engineering*, pp. 369–76. Los Alamitos, CA: IEEE Computer Society Press

Kroenke D. (1983). *Database Processing: Fundamentals, Design, Implementation*, 2nd edn. Chicago: SRA

Kuchen H. (1984). *Implementation of Relational Algebra on Multidimensional Dynamic Data Structures*. Master's Thesis (in German), Lehrstuhl für angewandte Mathematik, insbesondere Informatik, RWTH Aachen, FRG

Kung H.T. and Robinson J.T. (1981). On optimistic methods for concurrency control. *ACM Transactions on Database Systems*, **6**, pp. 213–26

Larson B.L. (1988). *The Database Expert's Guide to Database 2*. New York: McGraw-Hill

Larson P.A. (1978). Dynamic hashing. *BIT*, **18**, pp. 184–201

Larson P.A. (1980). Linear hashing with partial expansions. In *Proc. 6th International Conference on Very Large Data Bases*, pp. 224–32

Lausen G. (1983). Formal aspects of optimistic concurrency control in a multiple version database system. *Information Systems*, **8**, pp. 291–301

Lausen G. (1984). Integrated concurrency control in shared B-trees. *Computing*, **33**, pp. 13–26

Lausen G., Soisalon-Soininen E. and Widmayer P. (1986). Pre-analysis locking. *Information and Control*, **70**, pp. 193–215

Laver K. (1985). *Semantic and Syntactic Properties of Universal Relation Scheme Data Bases*. Ph.D. Thesis, University of Toronto, CSRI-163

Lecluse C. and Richard P. (1989). The O_2 database programming language. In *Proc. 15th International Conference on Very Large Data Bases*, pp. 411–22

Lecluse C., Richard P. and Velez F. (1988). O_2, an object-oriented data model. In *Proc. ACM SIGMOD International Conference on Management of Data*, pp. 424–33. New York: ACM and *Proc. 1st International Conference on Extending Database Technology (EDBT)*, LNCS 303, pp. 556–62. Berlin: Springer-Verlag

LeDoux C.H. and Parker D.S. (1982). Reflections on Boyce-Codd normal form. In *Proc. 8th International Conference on Very Large Data Bases*, pp. 131–41

Lien Y.E. (1985). Relational database design. In Yao (1985), pp. 211–54

Lindsay B., McPherson J. and Pirahesh H. (1987). A data management extension architecture. In *Proc. ACM SIGMOD International Conference on Management of Data*, pp. 220–6. New York: ACM

Ling T.W., Tompa F.W. and Kameda T. (1981). An improved third normal form for relational databases. *ACM Transactions on Database Systems*, **6**, pp. 329–46

Linnemann V., Küspert K., Dadam P. et al. (1988). Design and implementation of an extensible database management system supporting user defined data types and functions. In *Proc. 14th International Conference on Very Large Data Bases*, pp. 294–305

Lipski W. (1977). Two NP-complete problems related to information retrieval. In *Fundamentals of Computation Theory (Proc. of the FCT-Conference)* (Karpinski M., ed.). LNCS 56, pp. 452–8. Berlin: Springer-Verlag

Lipski W. (1981). On databases with incomplete information. *Journal of the ACM*, **28**, pp. 41–7

Litwin W. (1978). Virtual hashing: a dynamically changing hashing. In *Proc. 4th International Conference on Very Large Data Bases*, pp. 517–23

Litwin W. (1980). Linear hashing: a new algorithm for files and table addressing. In *Proc. BCS International Conference on Data Bases*, Aberdeen, pp. 260–76

Lloyd J.W. (1984). *Foundations of Logic Programming*. Berlin: Springer-Verlag

Lochovsky F., ed. (1985). Special issue on object-oriented systems. *IEEE Computer Society Bulletin on Database Engineering*, **8**(4)

Lohman G.M. (1986). Do semantically equivalent SQL queries perform differently? In *Proc. 2nd IEEE International Conference on Data Engineering*, pp. 225–6. Los Alamitos, CA: IEEE Computer Society Press

Lorie R.A. and Bever M. (1987). *Database Support for Computer Integrated Manufacturing*. IBM Research Report RJ 5538, San Jose, CA

Lucchesi C.L. and Osborn S.L. (1978). Candidate keys for relations. *Journal of Computer and System Sciences*, **17**, pp. 270–9

Lusk E.L. and Overbeek R.A. (1980). A DML for entity-relationship models. In *Entity-Relationship Approach to Systems Analysis and Design* (Chen P.P.-S., ed.), pp. 445–61. Amsterdam: North-Holland

Lynch N. and Merritt M. (1988). Introduction to the theory of nested transactions. *Theoretical Computer Science*, **62**, pp. 123–85

Lyngbaek P. and Vianu V. (1987). Mapping a semantic database model to the relational model. In *Proc. ACM SIGMOD International Conference on Management of Data*, pp. 132–42. New York: ACM

Maier D. (1980). Minimum covers in the relational database model. *Journal of the ACM*, **27**, pp. 664–74

Maier D. (1983). *The Theory of Relational Databases.* Rockville, MD: Computer Science Press

Maier D. (1989). Why isn't there an object-oriented data model? In *Information Processing 89* (Ritter G.X., ed.), pp. 793–8. Amsterdam: Elsevier

Maier D. and Stein J. (1986). Indexing in an object-oriented DBMS. In Dittrich and Dayal (1986), pp. 171–82

Maier D. and Ullman J.D. (1984). Connections in acyclic hypergraphs. *Theoretical Computer Science*, **32**, pp. 185–99

Maier D. and Warren D.S. (1988). *Computing with Logic — Logic Programming with Prolog.* Menlo Park, CA: Benjamin/Cummings

Maier D., Rozenshtein D., Salveter S.C., Stein J. and Warren D.S. (1982). Toward logical data independence: a relational query language without relations. In *Proc. ACM SIGMOD International Conference on Management of Data*, pp. 51–60. New York: ACM

Maier D., Ullman J.D. and Vardi M.Y. (1984). On the foundations of the universal relation model. *ACM Transactions on Database Systems*, **9**, pp. 283–308

Maier D., Otis A. and Purdy A. (1985). Object-oriented database development at Servio Logic. *Bulletin of the IEEE Computer Society Technical Committee on Database Engineering*, **8**(4), pp. 58–65

Maier D., Rozenshtein D. and Warren D.S. (1986a). Window functions. In *Advances in Computing Research* Vol. 3: *The Theory of Databases* (Kanellakis P.C. and Preparata F.P., eds.), pp. 213–46. Greenwich, CT: JAI Press

Maier D., Stein J., Otis A. and Purdy A. (1986b). Development of an object-oriented DBMS. In *OOPSLA '86 Proceedings*, pp. 472–82

Makinouchi A. (1977). A consideration on normal form of not-necessarily-normalized relation in the relational data model. In *Proc. 3rd International Conference on Very Large Data Bases*, pp. 447–53

Malhotra A., Tsalalikhin Y., Markowitz H.M., Pazel D.P. and Burns L.M. (1986). *Implementing an Entity-Relationship Language on a Relational Data Base.* IBM Research Report RC 12134, Yorktown Heights, NY

Mannila H. and Räihä K.J. (1983). On the relationship of minimum and optimum covers for a set of functional dependencies. *Acta Informatica*, **20**, pp. 143–58

Mannila H. and Räihä K.J. (1986a). Inclusion dependencies in database design. In *Proc. 2nd IEEE International Conference on Data Engineering*, pp. 713–18. Los Alamitos, CA: IEEE Computer Society Press

Mannila H. and Räihä K.J. (1986b). Design by Example: an application of Armstrong relations. *Journal of Computer and System Sciences*, **33**, pp. 126–41

Markowitz V.M. and Raz Y. (1983). ERROL — an entity relationship role oriented query language. In *Entity-Relationship Approach to Software Engineering* (Davis C.G. et al., eds.), pp. 329–45. Amsterdam: North-Holland

Maryanski F., Bedell J., Hoelscher S. et al. (1986). The Data Model Compiler: a tool for generating object-oriented database systems. In Dittrich and Dayal (1986), pp. 73–84

Masunaga Y. (1984). A relational database view update translation mechanism. In *Proc. 10th International Conference on Very Large Data Bases*, pp. 309–20

McFadden F.R. and Hoffer J.A. (1988). *Data Base Management*, 2nd edn. Menlo Park, CA: Benjamin/Cummings

McGee W.C. (1977). The information management system IMS/VS. Part I: General structure and operation. Part II: Data base facilities. *IBM Systems Journal*, **16**, pp. 84–122

McPherson J. and Pirahesh H. (1987). An overview of extensibility in Starburst. *Bulletin of the IEEE Computer Society Technical Committee on Database Engineering*, **10**(2), pp. 32–9

Medeiros C.B. and Tompa F.W. (1985). Understanding the implications of view update policies. In *Proc. 11th International Conference on Very Large Data Bases*, pp. 316–23

Mehlhorn K. (1984). *Sorting and Searching (Data Structures and Algorithms 1)*. EATCS Monographs on Theoretical Computer Science, Vol. 1. Berlin: Springer-Verlag

Mendelson H. (1982). Analysis of extendible hashing. *IEEE Transactions on Software Engineering*, **SE-8**, pp. 611–19

Mendelzon A.O. (1979). On axiomatizing multivalued dependencies in relational databases. *Journal of the ACM*, **26**, pp. 37–44

Minker J., ed. (1988). *Foundations of Deductive Databases and Logic Programming*. Los Altos, CA: Morgan Kaufmann Publishers

Mitchell J.C. (1983). Inference rules for functional and inclusion dependencies. *Proc. 2nd ACM SIGACT-SIGMOD Symposium on Principles of Database Systems*, pp. 58–69. New York: ACM

Moss J.E.B. (1985). *Nested Transactions: An Approach to Reliable Distributed Computing*. Cambridge, MA: MIT Press

Mullin J.K. (1981). Tightly controlled linear hashing without separate overflow storage. *BIT*, **21**, pp. 390–400

Mylopoulos J., Bernstein P.A. and Wong H.K.T. (1980). A language facility for designing database-intensive applications. *ACM Transactions on Database Systems*, **5**, pp. 185–207

Naqvi S. and Tsur S. (1989). *A Logical Language for Data and Knowledge Bases*. New York: Computer Science Press

Navathe S.B., Sashidhar T. and Elmasri R. (1984). Relationship merging in schema integration. In *Proc. 10th International Conference on Very Large Data Bases*, pp. 78–90

Ng P.A. and Paul J.F. (1980). A formal definition of entity-relationship models. In *Entity-Relationship Approach to Systems Analysis and Design* (Chen P.P.-S., ed.), pp. 211–30. Amsterdam: North-Holland

Nievergelt J., Hinterberger H. and Sevcik K.C. (1984). The grid file: an adaptable, symmetric multikey file structure. *ACM Transactions on Database Systems*, **9**, pp. 38–71

Oberschelp W. and Vossen G. (1989). *Computer Organization and Computer Structures*, 3rd edn. Munich: R. Oldenbourg Verlag (in German)

Otoo E. (1985). A multidimensional digital hashing scheme for files with composite keys. In *Proc. ACM SIGMOD International Conference on Management of Data*, pp. 214–29. New York: ACM

Otoo E. (1988). Linearizing the directory growth in order preserving extendible hashing. In *Proc. 4th IEEE International Conference on Data Engineering*, pp. 580–8. Los Alamitos, CA: IEEE Computer Society Press

Ouksel M. (1985). The interpolation-based grid file. In *Proc. 4th ACM SIGACT-SIGMOD Symposium on Principles of Database Systems*, pp. 20–7. New York: ACM

Ouksel M. and Scheuermann P. (1981). Multidimensional B-trees: analysis of dynamic behaviour. *BIT*, **21**, pp. 401–18

Özsoyoglu Z.M. and Yuan L.Y. (1985). *Reduced MVD's and Minimum Covers*. manuscript, Computer Engineering and Science Department, Case Western Reserve University, Cleveland, OH

Özsoyoglu Z.M. and Yuan L.Y. (1987). A new normal form for nested relations. *ACM Transactions on Database Systems*, **12**, pp. 111–36

Özsoyoglu G., Özsoyoglu Z.M. and Matos V. (1987). Extending relational algebra and relational calculus with set-valued attributes and aggregate functions. *ACM Transactions on Database Systems*, **12**, pp. 566–92

Papadimitriou C.H. (1979). The serializability of concurrent database updates. *Journal of the ACM*, **26**, pp. 631–53

Papadimitriou C.H. (1982). A theorem in database concurrency control. *Journal of the ACM*, **29**, pp. 998–1006

Papadimitriou C.H. (1983). Concurrency control by locking. *SIAM Journal on Computing*, **12**, pp. 215–26

Papadimitriou C.H. (1986). *The Theory of Database Concurrency Control*. Rockville, MD: Computer Science Press

Papadimitriou C.H. and Kanellakis P.C. (1984). On concurrency control by multiple versions. *ACM Transactions on Database Systems*, **9**, pp. 89–99

Papadimitriou C.H. and Yannakakis M. (1987). The complexity of reliable concurrency control. *SIAM Journal on Computing*, **16**, pp. 538–53

Paredaens, J., De Bra P., Gyssens M. and van Gucht D. (1989). *The Structure of the Relational Database Model.* EATCS Monographs on Theoretical Computer Science No. 17. Berlin: Springer-Verlag

Parker D.S. and Delobel C. (1979). Algorithmic applications for a new result on multivalued dependencies. In *Proc. 5th International Conference on Very Large Data Bases*, pp. 67–74

Paul H.B., Schek H.J., Scholl M.H., Weikum G. and Deppisch U. (1987). Architecture and implementation of the Darmstadt database kernel system. In *Proc. ACM SIGMOD International Conference on Management of Data*, pp. 196–207. New York: ACM

Peckham J. and Maryanski F. (1988). Semantic data models. *ACM Computing Surveys*, **20**, pp. 153–89

Penney D.J. and Stein J. (1987). Class modification in the GemStone object-oriented DBMS. In *OOPSLA '87 Proceedings*, pp. 111–17

Pirahesh H. and Cardenas A. (1986). *Performance Analysis of Locking Based Database Concurrency Control in Centralized and Distributed Systems.* IBM Research Report RJ 5052, Almaden Research Center, San Jose, CA

Purdy A., Schuchardt B. and Maier D. (1987). Integrating an object server with other worlds. *ACM Transactions on Office Informations Systems*, **5**, pp. 27–47

Ramamohanarao K. and Lloyd J.W. (1982). Dynamic hashing schemes. *The Computer Journal*, **25**, pp. 478–85

Raz Y. (1987a). *Supporting Structured English Interfaces for Relational Databases Using RRA — A Reshaped Relational Algebra.* Technical Report CS-093, EECS Department, University of California, San Diego

Raz Y.(1987b). The ERROL System, Version 2.0 — an Overview. Manuscript, CSE Department, University of California, San Diego

Reed D. (1983). Implementing atomic actions on decentralized data. *ACM Transactions on Computer Systems*, **1**, pp. 3–23

Reiner D., ed. (1984). Special issue on database design aids, methods, and environments. *IEEE Computer Society Bulletin on Database Engineering*, **7**(4)

Reisner P. (1984). *Measurement of SQL: Problems and Progress.* IBM Research Report RJ 4510, San Jose, CA

Reuter A. (1984). *Performance Analysis of Recovery Techniques.* IBM Research Report RJ 4300, San Jose, CA

Richardson J.E. and Carey M.J. (1987). Programming constructs for database system implementation in EXODUS. In *Proc. ACM SIGMOD International Conference on Management of Data*, pp. 208–19. New York: ACM

Rissanen J. (1977). Independent Components of Relations. *ACM Transactions on Database Systems*, **2**, pp. 317–25

Rissanen J. (1978). Theory of relations for databases — a tutorial survey. In *Proc. 7th Symposium on Mathematical Foundations of Computer Science*,

LNCS 64, pp. 537–51. Berlin: Springer-Verlag

Robinson J.T. (1981). The K-D-B-tree: a search structure for large multidimensional indexes. In *Proc. ACM SIGMOD International Conference on Management of Data*, pp. 10–18. New York: ACM

Roesler M. (1988). *Sharing Objects in Distributed Systems.* Ph. D. Dissertation, University of California, San Diego

Roesler M. and Burkhard W.A. (1987). Concurrency control scheme for shared objects: a peephole approach based on semantics. In *Proc. 7th International Conference on Distributed Computing Systems*, pp. 224–31. Los Alamitos, CA: IEEE Computer Society Press

Roesler M. and Burkhard W.A. (1988). Deadlock resolution and semantic lock models in object-oriented distributed systems. In *Proc. ACM SIGMOD International Conference on Management of Data*, pp. 361–70. New York: ACM

Roesner W. (1985). DESPATH: an ER manipulation language. In *Proc. 4th International Conference on Entity-Relationship Approach*, Chicago, IL, pp. 72–81

Roth M.A. and Kirkpatrick J.E. (1988). Algebras for nested relations. *Bulletin of the IEEE Computer Society Technical Committee on Database Engineering*, **11**(3), pp. 39–47

Roth M.A. and Korth H.F. (1987). The design of ¬1NF relational databases into nested normal form. In *Proc. ACM SIGMOD International Conference on Management of Data*, pp. 143–59. New York: ACM

Roth M.A., Korth H.F. and Batory D.S. (1987). SQL/NF: a query language for ¬1NF relational databases. *Information Systems*, **12**, pp. 99–114

Roth M.A., Korth H.F. and Silberschatz A. (1988). Extended algebra and calculus for nested relational databases. *ACM Transactions on Database Systems*, **13**, pp. 389–417

Rowe L.A. and Stonebraker M. (1987). The POSTGRES data model. In *Proc. 13th International Conference on Very Large Data Bases*, pp. 83–96

Ryu I.K. and Thomasian A. (1985). *Performance Analysis of Centralized Databases with Optimistic Concurrency Control.* IBM Research Report RC 11420, Yorktown Heights, NY

Sagiv Y. (1980). An algorithm for inferring multivalued dependencies with an application to propositional logic. *Journal of the ACM*, **27**, pp. 250–62

Sagiv Y. (1981). Can we use the universal instance assumption without using nulls? In *Proc. ACM SIGMOD International Conference on Management of Data*, pp. 108–20. New York: ACM

Sagiv Y. (1983). A characterization of globally consistent databases and their correct access paths. *ACM Transactions on Database Systems*, **8**, pp. 266–86

Sagiv Y. (1985). Concurrent operations on B-trees with overtaking. In *Proc.*

4th ACM SIGACT-SIGMOD Symposium on Principles of Database Systems, pp. 28–37. New York: ACM

Sagiv Y. (1988). Optimizing Datalog programs. In Minker (1988), pp. 659–98

Sagiv Y., Delobel C., Parker D.S. and Fagin R. (1981). An equivalence between relational database dependencies and a fragment of propositional logic. *Journal of the ACM*, **28**, pp. 435–53

Schek H.J. (1987). DASDBS: a kernel DBMS and application-specific layers. *Bulletin of the IEEE Computer Society Technical Committee on Database Engineering*, **10**(2), pp. 62–4

Schek H.J. and Scholl M.H. (1986). The relational model with relation-valued attributes. *Information Systems*, **11**, pp. 137–47

Schek H.J. and Weikum G. (1986). *DASDBS: Concepts and Architecture of a Database System for Advanced Applications.* Technical Report DVSI-1986-T1, Fachbereich Informatik, TH Darmstadt, FRG

Schek H.J., Paul H.B., Scholl M.H. and Weikum G. (1990). The DASDBS project: objectives, experiences, and future prospects. *IEEE Transactions on Knowledge and Data Engineering*, **2**, pp. 25–43

Scheuermann P. and Ouksel M. (1982). Multidimensional B-trees for associative searching in database systems. *Information Systems*, **7**, pp. 123–37

Schkolnick M. (1982). Physical database design techniques. In *Data Base Design Techniques II* (Yao S.B. and Kunii T.L., eds.). LNCS 133, pp. 229–52. Berlin: Springer-Verlag

Schlageter G. (1978). Process synchronization in database systems. *ACM Transactions on Database Systems*, **3**, pp. 248–71

Schlageter G. (1981). Optimistic methods for concurrency control in distributed database systems. In *Proc. 7th International Conference on Very Large Data Bases*, pp. 125–30

Schlatter-Ellis C. (1985). Concurrency and linear hashing. In *Proc. 4th ACM SIGACT-SIGMOD Symposium on Principles of Database Systems*, pp. 1–7. New York: ACM

Schmidt J.W. and Brodie M.L. (1983). *Relational Database Systems — Analysis and Comparison.* Berlin: Springer-Verlag

Scholl M. (1981). New file organizations based on dynamic hashing. *ACM Transactions on Database Systems*, **6**, pp. 194–211

Schwarz P., Chang W., Freytag J.C. et al. (1986). Extensibility in the Starbust database system. In Dittrich and Dayal (1986), pp. 85–92

Schwarz, P.M. and Spector A.Z. (1984). Synchronizing shared abstract types. *ACM Transactions on Computer Systems*, **2**, pp. 223–50

Sciore E. (1983). Inclusion dependencies and the universal instance. In *Proc. 2nd ACM SIGACT-SIGMOD Symposium on Principles of Database Systems*, pp. 48–57. New York: ACM

Sellis T., Roussopoulos N. and Faloutsos C. (1987). The R^+-tree: a dynamic index for multi-dimensional objects. In *Proc. 13th International Conference on Very Large Data Bases*, pp. 507–18

Servio Logic Development Corp. (1988a). *Programming in OPAL (Version 1.4)*. Beaverton, OR: Servio Logic

Servio Logic Development Corp. (1988b). *OPAL Programming Environment Manual (Version 1.4, for VAX/VMS)*. Beaverton, OR: Servio Logic

Servio Logic Development Corp. (1988c). *GemStone C Interface Manual (Version 1.4)*. Beaverton, OR: Servio Logic

Sethi R. (1982). Useless actions make a difference: strict serializability of database updates. *Journal of the ACM*, **29**, pp. 394–403

Shasha D. and Goodman N. (1988). Concurrent search structure algorithms. *ACM Transactions on Database Systems*, **13**, pp. 53–90

Shipman D. (1981). The functional data model and the data language DAPLEX. *ACM Transactions on Database Systems*, **6**, pp. 140–73

Shmueli O. and Itai A. (1984). Maintenance of views. In *Proc. ACM SIGMOD International Conference on Management of Data*, pp. 240–55. New York: ACM

Shoshani A. (1982). Statistical databases: characteristics, problems, and some solutions. In *Proc. 8th International Conference on Very Large Data Bases*, pp. 208–22

Siemens (1982a). *UDS Version 3.2 (BS2000) Design and Definition (User's Guide)*. Order No. U929-J-Z55-1-7600 (Revision Version 5.0B, Order No. U929-J1-Z55-2-7600, 1987), Munich: Siemens AG

Siemens (1982b). *UDS Version 3.2 (BS2000) Applications Programming (User's Guide)*. Order No. U930-J-Z55-1-7600 (Revision Version 5.0B, Order No. U930-J2-Z55-4-7600, 1987), Munich: Siemens AG

Siemens (1982c). *UDS Version 3.2 (BS2000) Creation and Restructuring (User's Guide)*. Order No. U931-J-Z55-1-7600 (Revision Version 5.0A, Order No. U931-J4-Z55-5-7600, 1986), Munich: Siemens AG

Siemens (1982d). *UDS Version 3.2 (BS2000) Administration and Operation (User's Guide)*. Order No. U932-J-Z55-1-7600 (Revision Version 5.0B, Order No. U932-J2-Z55-6-7600, 1987), Munich: Siemens AG

Siemens (1984). *UDS Version 4.0 (BS2000) Messages*. Order No. U1811-J-Z55-1-7600 (Revision Version 5.0B, Order No. U1811-J2-Z55-4-7600, 1987), Munich: Siemens AG

Siemens (1985). *UDS (BS2000) IQS Interactive Query System Version 3.1C (User's Guide)*. Order No. U327-J-Z55-5-7600, Munich: Siemens AG

Siemens (1986). *UDS (BS2000) System Reference Guide Version 5.0A*. Order No. U934-J-Z55-5-7600 (Revision Version 5.0B, Order No. U934-J1-Z55-6-7600, 1987), Munich: Siemens AG

Silberschatz A. and Kedem Z. (1980). Consistency in hierarchical database systems. *Journal of the ACM*, **27**, pp. 72–80

Smith J.M. and Smith D.C.P. (1977a). Database abstractions: aggregation. *Communications of the ACM*, **20**, pp. 405–13

Smith J.M. and Smith D.C.P. (1977b). Database abstractions: aggregation and generalization. *ACM Transactions on Database Systems*, **2**, pp. 105–33

Solomon M.K. and Bickel R.W. (1986). Self-assessment procedure XV: A self-assessment procedure dealing with file processing. *Communications of the ACM*, **29**, pp. 745–50

Stein J. and Maier D. (1988). Concepts in object-oriented data management. *Database Programming and Design*, **1**(4), pp. 58–67

Stonebraker M. (1975). Implementation of integrity constraints and views by query modification. In *ACM SIGMOD International Conference on Management of Data*, pp. 65–78. New York: ACM

Stonebraker M. (1986a). Inclusion of new types in relational database systems. In *Proc. 2nd IEEE International Conference on Data Engineering*, pp. 262–9. Los Alamitos, CA: IEEE Computer Society Press

Stonebraker M. (1986b). Object management in POSTGRES using procedures. In Dittrich and Dayal (1986), pp. 66–72

Stonebraker M., ed. (1986c). *The INGRES Papers: Anatomy of a Relational Database System.* Reading, MA: Addison-Wesley

Stonebraker M. (1987). The design of the POSTGRES storage system. In *Proc. 13th International Conference on Very Large Data Bases*, pp. 289–300

Stonebraker M. and Rowe L.A. (1986). The design of POSTGRES. In *Proc. ACM SIGMOD International Conference on Management of Data*, pp. 340–55. New York: ACM

Stonebraker M., Anderson E., Hanson E.N. and Rubenstein B. (1984). QUEL as a data type. In *Proc. ACM SIGMOD International Conference on Management of Data*, pp. 208–14. New York: ACM

Stonebraker M., Anton J. and Hanson E.N. (1987a). Extending a database system with procedures. *ACM Transactions on Database Systems*, **12**, pp. 350–76

Stonebraker M., Anton J. and Hirohama M. (1987b). Extendability in POSTGRES. *Bulletin of the IEEE Computer Society Technical Committee on Database Engineering*, **10**(2), pp. 16–23

Stonebraker M., Hanson E.N. and Hong C.H. (1987c). The design of the POSTGRES rules system. In *Proc. 3rd IEEE International Conference on Data Engineering*, pp. 365–74. Los Alamitos, CA: IEEE Computer Society Press

Stonebraker M., Hanson E.N. and Potamianos S. (1988). The POSTGRES rule manager. *IEEE Transactions on Software Engineering*, **SE-14**, pp. 897–907

Stonebraker M., Rowe L.A. and Hirohama M. (1990). The implementation of

POSTGRES. *IEEE Transactions on Knowledge and Data Engineering*, **2**, pp. 125–42

Tamassia R., Batini C. and Talamo M. (1983). An algorithm for automatic layout of entity relationship diagrams. In *Entity-Relationship Approach to Software Engineering* (Davis C.G. et al., eds.). pp. 421–39. Amsterdam: North-Holland

Tamminen M. (1982). Extendible hashing with overflow. *Information Processing Letters*, **15**, pp. 227–32

Taylor R.W. and Frank R.L. (1976). CODASYL data-base management systems. *ACM Computing Surveys*, **8**, pp. 67–103

Teorey T.J. and Fry J.P. (1982). *Design of Database Structures.* Englewood Cliffs, NJ: Prentice-Hall

Teorey T.J., Yang D. and Fry J.P. (1986). A logical design methodology for relational databases using the extended entity-relationship model. *ACM Computing Surveys*, **18**, pp. 197–222

Thalheim B. (1986). *A Review of Research on Dependency Theory in Relational Databases.* Technical Report, University of Dresden, GDR

Thomas S.J. and Fischer P.C. (1986). Nested relational structures. In *Advances in Computing Research* Vol. 3: *The Theory of Databases* (Kanellakis P.C. and Preparata F.P., eds.), pp. 269–307. Greenwich, CT: JAI Press

Tsichritzis D. and Klug A. (1978). The ANSI/X3/SPARC DBMS framework report of the Study Group on Database Management Systems. *Information Systems*, **3**, pp. 173–91

Tsichritzis D.C. and Lochovsky F.H. (1976). Hierarchical data base management: a survey. *ACM Computing Surveys*, **8**, pp. 67–103

Tsichritzis D.C. and Lochovsky F.H. (1982). *Data Models.* Englewood Cliffs, NJ: Prentice-Hall

Ullman J.D. (1983). Universal relation interfaces for database systems. In *Information Processing 83 (Proc. IFIP Congress)* (Mason R.E.A., ed.), pp. 243–52. Amsterdam: North-Holland

Ullman J.D. (1987). Database theory: past and future. In *Proc. 6th ACM SIGACT-SIGMOD-SIGART Symposium on Principles of Database Systems*, pp. 1–10. New York: ACM

Ullman J.D. (1988). *Principles of Database and Knowledge-Base Systems* Vol. I. Rockville, MD: Computer Science Press

Ullman J.D. (1989). *Principles of Database and Knowledge-Base Systems* Vol. II. Rockville, MD: Computer Science Press

Urban S.D. and Delcambre L.M.L. (1986). An analysis of the structural, dynamic, and temporal aspects of semantic data models. In *Proc. 2nd IEEE International Conference on Data Engineering*, pp. 382–9. Los Alamitos, CA: IEEE Computer Society Press

Valduriez P. and Gardarin G. (1989). *Analysis and Comparison of Relational Database Systems*. Reading, MA: Addison-Wesley

Valduriez P., Khoshafian S. and Copeland G. (1986). Implementation techniques for complex objects. In *Proc. 12th International Conference on Very Large Data Bases*, pp. 101–10

van Emden M.H. and Kowalski R.A. (1976). The semantics of predicate logic as a programming language. *Journal of the ACM*, **23**, pp. 733–42

Vardi M.Y. (1982). The complexity of relational query languages. In *Proc. 14th ACM Symposium on Theory of Computing*, pp. 137–46. New York: ACM

Vardi M.Y. (1987). *The Universal Relation Data Model.* IBM Research Report RJ 5849, San Jose, CA

Vardi M.Y. (1988). Fundamentals of dependency theory. In *Trends in Theoretical Computer Science* (Börger E., ed.), pp. 171–224. Rockville, MD: Computer Science Press

Vassiliou Y. (1980). Functional dependencies and incomplete information. In *Proc. 6th International Conference on Very Large Data Bases*, pp. 260–9

Velez F., Bernard G. and Darnis V. (1989). The O_2 object manager: an overview. In *Proc. 15th International Conference on Very Large Data Bases*, pp. 357–66

Vianu V. and Vossen G. (1988). Conceptual level concurrency control for relational update transactions (extended abstract). In *Proc. 2nd International Conference on Database Theory (ICDT)*, LNCS 326, pp. 353–67. Berlin: Springer-Verlag (full version to appear in *Theoretical Computer Science*)

Vianu V. and Vossen G. (1989). Goal-oriented concurrency control (extended abstract). In *Proc. 2nd Symposium on Mathematical Fundamentals of Database Systems (MFDBS)*, LNCS 364, pp. 398–414. Berlin: Springer-Verlag

Vidyasankar K. (1987). Generalized theory of serializability. *Acta Informatica*, **24**, pp. 105–19

Vossen G. (1986). *Design and Manipulation of Databases under the Universal Relation Data Model.* Ph.D. Dissertation (in German), RWTH Aachen, FRG. English abstract in *Bulletin of the EATCS*, **30**, 1986, pp. 291–3

Vossen G. (1988). A new characterization of FD implication with an application to update anomalies. *Information Processing Letters*, **29**, pp. 131–5

Vossen G. and Brosda V. (1985a). A high-level user interface for update and retrieval in relational databases — language aspects. In *Proc. ACM SIGMOD International Conference on Management of Data*, pp. 343–53. New York: ACM

Vossen G. and Brosda V. (1985b). The single-relation user interface of the MEMODAX database system. *Angewandte Informatik*, **27**, pp. 534–40 (in German)

Vossen G. and Witt K.U. (1988). *The SQL/DS Handbook*. Bonn: Addison-Wesley (in German)

Vossen G. and Witt K.U. (1989). *SUXESS: Towards a Sound Unification of Extensions of the Relational Data Model.* Computer Science Report No. 89-16, RWTH Aachen (to appear in *Journal of Data and Knowledge Engineering*)

Vossen G. and Witt K.U. (1990). *The DB2 Handbook*. Bonn: Addison-Wesley (in German)

Vossen G. and Yacabucci J. (1988). An extension of the database language SQL to capture more relational concepts. *ACM SIGMOD Record*, **17**(4), pp. 70–8

Weikum G. (1987). Enhancing concurrency in layered systems. In *Proc. 2nd International Workshop on High Performance Transaction Systems*, LNCS 359, pp. 200–18. Berlin: Springer-Verlag

Whang K.Y. and Krishnamurthy R. (1985). *Multilevel Grid Files.* IBM Research Report RC 11516, Yorktown Heights, NY

Wiederhold G. (1987). *File Organization for Database Design.* New York: McGraw-Hill

Wilkinson K., Lyngbaek P. and Hasan W. (1990). The Iris architecture and implementation. *IEEE Transactions on Knowledge and Data Engineering*, **2**, pp. 63–75

Wilms P.F., Schwarz P.M., Schek H.J. and Haas L.M. (1988). Incorporating data types in an extensible database architecture. In *Proc. 3rd International Conference on Data and Knowledge Bases: Improving Usability and Responsiveness*, Jerusalem, Israel, pp. 180–92. San Mateo, CA: Morgan Kaufmann Publishers

Woelk D., Kim W. and Luther W. (1986). An object-oriented approach to multimedia databases. In *Proc. ACM SIGMOD International Conference on Management of Data*, pp. 311–25. New York: ACM

Yang C.C. (1986). *Relational Databases.* Englewood Cliffs, NJ: Prentice-Hall

Yang D., Teorey T. and Fry J. (1985). *On the Automatic Transformation of Extended ER Diagrams into the Relational Model.* Technical Report CRL-TR-6-85, Computing Research Laboratory, University of Michigan at Ann Arbor

Yannakakis M. (1981). Algorithms for acyclic database schemes. In *Proc. 7th International Conference on Very Large Data Bases*, pp. 82–94

Yannakakis M. (1982). A theory of safe locking policies in database systems. *Journal of the ACM*, **29**, pp. 718–40

Yannakakis M. (1984). Serializability by locking. *Journal of the ACM*, **31**, pp. 227–44

Yannakakis M. and Papadimitriou C.H. (1982). Algebraic dependencies. *Journal of Computer and System Sciences*, **25**, pp. 2–41

Yao S.B., ed. (1985). *Principles of Database Design* Vol. 1: *Logical Organizations.* Englewood Cliffs, NJ: Prentice-Hall

Yao S.B., Navathe S.B. and Weldon J.-L. (1982). An integrated approach to database design. In *Data Base Design Techniques I* (Yao S.B. et al., eds.). LNCS 132, pp. 1–30. Berlin: Springer-Verlag

Yost R.A. and Haas L.M. (1985). *R*: A Distributed Data Sharing System.* IBM Research Report RJ 4676, San Jose, CA

Yu C.T. and Özsoyoglu Z.M. (1979). An algorithm for tree-query membership of a distributed query. In *Proc. 3rd IEEE International Computer Software and Applications Conference (COMPSAC)*, pp. 306–12

Yuen T.S. and Du H.C. (1986). Dynamic file organizations for partial match retrieval based on linear hashing. In *Proc. 2nd IEEE International Conference on Data Engineering*, pp. 116–23. Los Alamitos, CA: IEEE Computer Society Press

Zaniolo C. (1976). *Analysis and Design of Relational Schemata for Database Systems.* Ph.D. Dissertation, University of California, Los Angeles

Zaniolo C. (1982). A new normal form for the design of relational database schemata. *ACM Transactions on Database Systems*, **7**, pp. 489–99

Zaniolo C., Ait-Kaci H., Beech D., Cammarata S., Kerschberg L. and Maier D. (1986). Object oriented database systems and knowledge systems. In *Expert Database Systems* (Proc. 1st International Workshop on Expert Database Systems, Kerschberg L., ed.), pp. 49–65. Menlo Park, CA: Benjamin/Cummings

Zdonik S.B. and Maier D., eds. (1990). *Readings in Object-Oriented Database Systems.* San Mateo, CA: Morgan Kaufmann Publishers

Index